TEACHER GUID

Ready® | 7

Mathematics
PRACTICE AND
PROBLEM SOLVING
Teacher Guide

Program Authors

Mark Ellis, Ph.D.
Department Chair and Professor, Education, CSU Fullerton
Board of Directors, Executive Committee, NCTM
National Board Certified Teacher

Gladis Kersaint, Ph.D.
Professor, Mathematics Education, USF
Board of Directors, Executive Committee, NCTM
Board of Directors, Association of Mathematics Teacher Educators

Acknowledgments

Vice President–Product Development: Adam Berkin
Editorial Director: Cynthia Tripp
Executive Editor: Kathy Kellman
Editors: Stacie Cartwright, Pamela Halloran, Lauren Van Wart
Project Manager: Grace Izzi
Cover Design: Matt Pollock
Book Designer: Scott Hoffman

ISBN 978-1-4957-0487-1

North Billerica, MA 01862

15 14

BTS19

Table of Contents

Getting Started with *Ready Practice and Problem Solving*

Mathematics Lessons

Unit 1 **The Number System**

Student Book includes a Family Letter for every lesson and Unit Vocabulary for every unit.

Mathematics Lessons *continued*

Unit 1 *continued*

Unit 2 Ratios and Proportional Relationships

Student Book includes a Family Letter for every lesson and Unit Vocabulary for every unit.

Mathematics Lessons *continued*

Student Book includes a Family Letter for every lesson and Unit Vocabulary for every unit.

Mathematics Lessons *continued*

Student Book includes a Family Letter for every lesson and Unit Vocabulary for every unit.

Mathematics Lessons *continued*

Teacher Resource Blackline Masters

Teacher Resource blackline masters are provided for use with the collaborative practice games in *Ready Practice and Problem Solving*. Full instructions for use of these teacher resources can be found in the Step by Step for each unit game.

Student Book includes a Family Letter for every lesson and Unit Vocabulary for every unit.

Ready® Program Overview

Ready Mathematics prepares students for mastery of rigorous national and state standards through a balance of conceptual understanding, procedural skills, fluency, and application. Use *Ready's* clear, thoughtful pedagogy to support rich classroom instruction in which meaningful reasoning, mathematical discourse, and a range of mathematical practices thrive.

Built for the new standards. Not just aligned.

For Students

Ready Instruction provides whole class and small group instruction and independent practice of concepts and skills for every standard. Interim assessments give frequent opportunities for standards mastery monitoring.

Ready Practice and Problem Solving complements ***Ready Instruction*** through rich practice, games, and performance tasks that develop understanding of and fluency with key skills and concepts.

Ready Assessments provides three full-length benchmark assessments that match the latest consortia guidance.

For Teachers

The ***Ready Teacher Resource Book*** and ***Ready Practice and Problem Solving Teacher Guide*** support teachers with point-of-use strategies and tips, step-by-step guidance, and best practices for implementing rigorous standards.

Ready Teacher Toolbox provides online access to prerequisite lessons from previous grades, student-led center activities differentiated for three levels, and teacher-led activities for students requiring additional instruction on prerequisite or on-level skills.

Ready Program Features

 Built with **all-new content** written specifically for rigorous national and state standards

 Uses a research-based, **gradual release** instructional model

 Requires **higher-order thinking** and complex reasoning to solve problems

 Integrates **Standards for Mathematical Practice** throughout every lesson

 Embeds thoughtful **teacher support**

 Encourages students to develop **deeper understanding** of concepts and to understand and use a variety of mathematical strategies and models

 Promotes **fluency** and connects hands-on learning with clearly articulated models throughout

What's in *Ready®* *Practice and Problem Solving*

Building on ***Ready Instruction, Ready Practice and Problem Solving*** encourages students to reason, use strategies, solve extended problems, and engage in collaborative work to extend classroom learning. Designed for flexibility, ***Ready Practice and Problem Solving*** can be used for homework, independent classroom practice, and in after-school settings.

Lesson Features

Practice specific to each part of every *Ready Instruction* lesson gives students multiple opportunities to reinforce procedural fluency and synthesize concepts and skills learned in the classroom. Lesson practice pages can be used at the end of a lesson or after completing each part of a lesson.

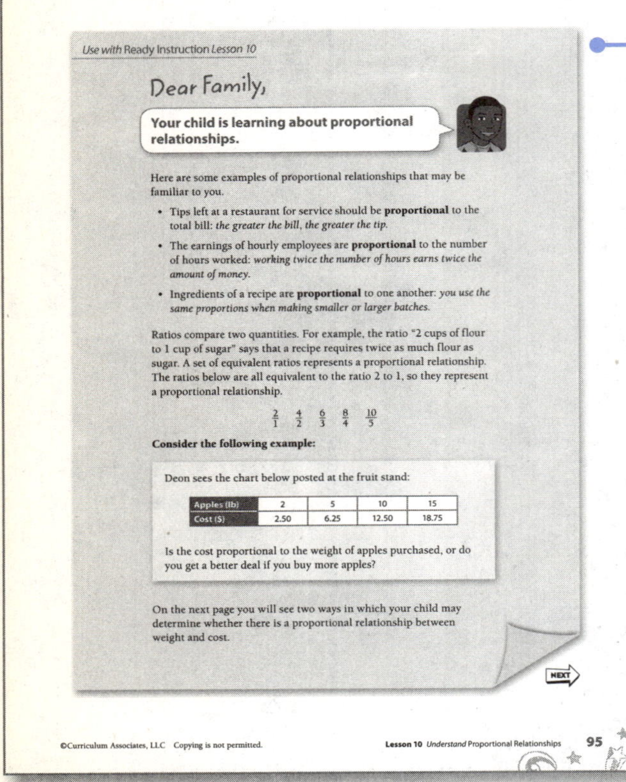

Use with Ready Instruction Lesson 10

Dear Family,

Your child is learning about proportional relationships.

Here are some examples of proportional relationships that may be familiar to you.

- Tips left at a restaurant for service should be **proportional** to the total bill: *the greater the bill, the greater the tip.*
- The earnings of hourly employees are **proportional** to the number of hours worked: *working twice the number of hours earns twice the amount of money.*
- Ingredients of a recipe are **proportional** to one another: *you use the same proportions when making smaller or larger batches.*

Ratios compare two quantities. For example, the ratio "2 cups of flour to 1 cup of sugar" says that a recipe requires twice as much flour as sugar. A set of equivalent ratios represents a proportional relationship. The ratios below are all equivalent to the ratio 2 to 1, so they represent a proportional relationship.

$\frac{2}{1}$ $\frac{4}{2}$ $\frac{6}{3}$ $\frac{8}{4}$ $\frac{10}{5}$

Consider the following example:

Deon sees the chart below posted at the fruit stand:

Apples (lb)	2	5	10	15
Cost ($)	2.50	6.25	12.50	18.75

Is the cost proportional to the weight of apples purchased, or do you get a better deal if you buy more apples?

On the next page you will see two ways in which your child may determine whether there is a proportional relationship between weight and cost.

NEXT

©Curriculum Associates, LLC Copying is not permitted. Lesson 10 *Understand* Proportional Relationships 95

Family Letters

- Family Letters can be sent home separately before each lesson, or as part of a family communication package.
- Letters include a summary statement, vocabulary definitions, and models that help family members support their child's mathematical learning.
- A Spanish version of each Family Letter is available on the Teacher Toolbox.

Prerequisite Skill Practice

- Students apply lesson prerequisite concepts or skills as they work with models that support those in the *Ready Instruction* lesson Introduction.
- This serves as a review of previous understanding and prepares students for the next section of the *Ready Instruction* lesson.

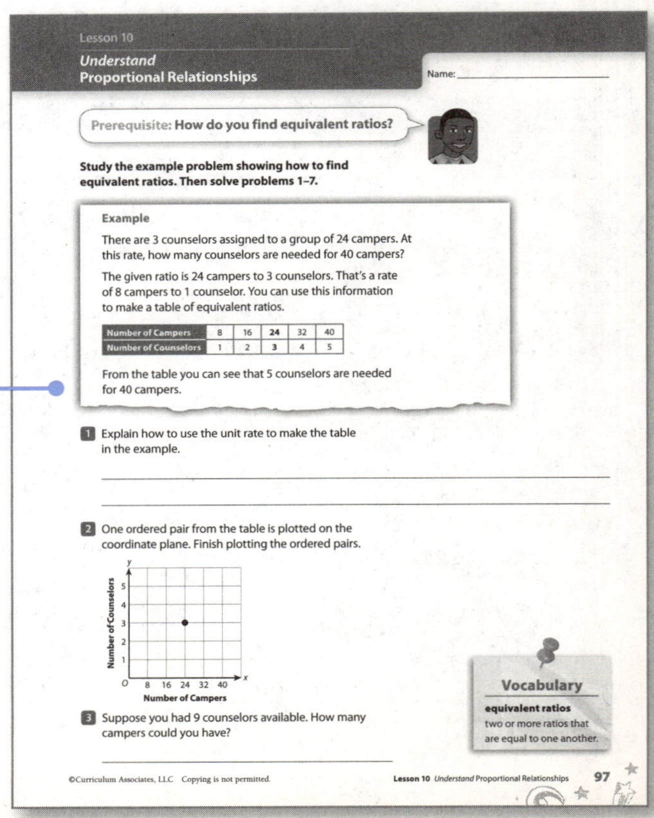

Lesson 10

Understand
Proportional Relationships

Name: ______

Prerequisite: How do you find equivalent ratios?

Study the example problem showing how to find equivalent ratios. Then solve problems 1–7.

Example

There are 3 counselors assigned to a group of 24 campers. At this rate, how many counselors are needed for 40 campers?

The given ratio is 24 campers to 3 counselors. That's a rate of 8 campers to 1 counselor. You can use this information to make a table of equivalent ratios.

Number of Campers	8	16	**24**	32	40
Number of Counselors	1	2	**3**	4	5

From the table you can see that 5 counselors are needed for 40 campers.

1 Explain how to use the unit rate to make the table in the example.

2 One ordered pair from the table is plotted on the coordinate plane. Finish plotting the ordered pairs.

3 Suppose you had 9 counselors available. How many campers could you have?

Vocabulary

equivalent ratios two or more ratios that are equal to one another.

©Curriculum Associates, LLC Copying is not permitted. Lesson 10 *Understand* Proportional Relationships 97

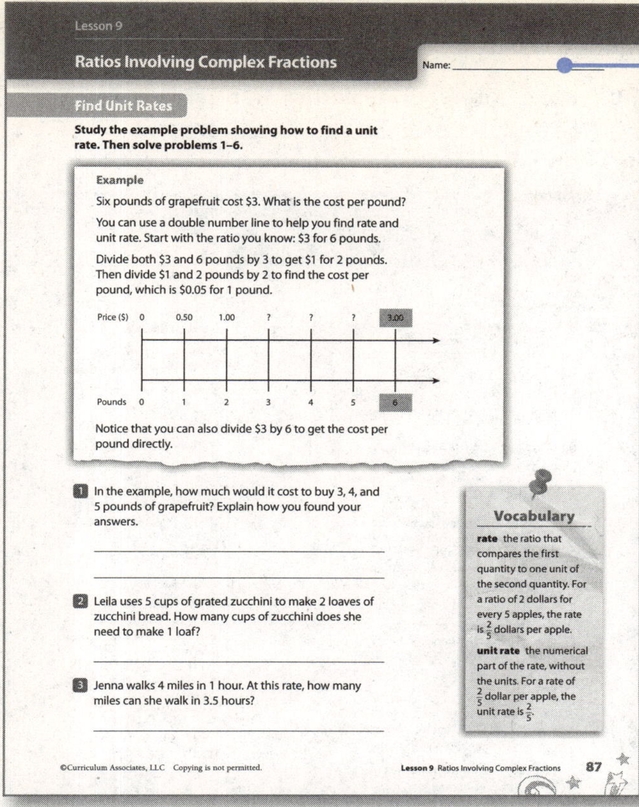

Lesson 9

Ratios Involving Complex Fractions

Name: ____________

Find Unit Rates

Study the example problem showing how to find a unit rate. Then solve problems 1–6.

Example

Six pounds of grapefruit cost $3. What is the cost per pound?

You can use a double number line to help you find rate and unit rate. Start with the ratio you know: $3 for 6 pounds.

Divide both $3 and 6 pounds by 3 to get $1 for 2 pounds. Then divide $1 and 2 pounds by 2 to find the cost per pound, which is $0.05 for 1 pound.

Notice that you can also divide $3 by 6 to get the cost per pound directly.

1 In the example, how much would it cost to buy 3, 4, and 5 pounds of grapefruit? Explain how you found your answers.

2 Leila uses 5 cups of grated zucchini to make 2 loaves of zucchini bread. How many cups of zucchini does she need to make 1 loaf?

3 Jenna walks 4 miles in 1 hour. At this rate, how many miles can she walk in 3.5 hours?

Vocabulary

rate the ratio that compares the first quantity to one unit of the second quantity. For a ratio of 2 dollars for every 5 apples, the rate is $\frac{2}{5}$ dollars per apple.

unit rate the numerical part of the rate, without the units. For a rate of $\frac{2}{5}$ dollar per apple, the unit rate is $\frac{2}{5}$.

©Curriculum Associates, LLC Copying is not permitted. **Lesson 9** Ratios Involving Complex Fractions 87

Solve.

4 It takes 30 cups of milk to make 4 sticks of butter. Use this ratio to complete the double number line. Describe the unit rate.

Cups of Milk 0 ☐ ☐ ☐ 30 ☐ ☐

Sticks of Butter 0 ☐ ☐ ☐ 4 ☐ ☐

5 Rashid is paid by the hour. He earned $50 for a 4-hour workday. How much does he earn for a $5\frac{1}{2}$-hour workday?

Show your work.

Solution: ____________

6 Ace Bike Rentals rents bikes for $28 per day. Renters can keep the bike for 8 hours. Bart's Bikes rents bikes for $30 per day. Renters can keep the bike for 10 hours. Which company charges a lower hourly rate? How much lower?

Show your work.

Solution: ____________

88 **Lesson 9** Ratios Involving Complex Fractions ©Curriculum Associates, LLC Copying is not permitted.

Skills and Concepts Practice

- **Two pages of skills and concept practice** are provided after each Modeled and Guided Instruction section and each Guided Practice section of a *Ready Instruction* lesson. These can be used in class, after school, or at home.
- **Worked-out examples** support and reinforce students' classroom learning. They also provide family members assisting at home helpful explanations of the lesson content.
- Problems are **differentiated** to provide maximum flexibility when assigning practice as independent classwork or homework. The differentiation is marked in the Teacher Guide as basic B, medium M, or challenging C.
- **Vocabulary** is defined at helpful points in the lesson.
- Students are encouraged to show their work and **use models and strategies** they learned in the *Ready Instruction* lesson.
- Lessons conclude with **mixed practice** problems that vary in type, including multiple choice, yes-no, true-false formats, and open-ended questions.

Unit Features

Unit materials cover multiple skills and concepts, helping students make connections across standards. Use Unit Games, Unit Practice, Unit Performance Tasks, and Unit Vocabulary after completing each unit to apply and integrate skills and to consolidate learning.

Unit Game

- Unit Games are engaging, collaborative experiences designed to encourage students to use **strategic thinking** as they play with a partner.
- Students record the mathematics of each game to **promote fluency** and reinforce learning. The recording sheet also serves as an opportunity for informal assessment for teachers to monitor students' work.
- These partner games can be used at classroom centers and/or sent home for play with a family member.

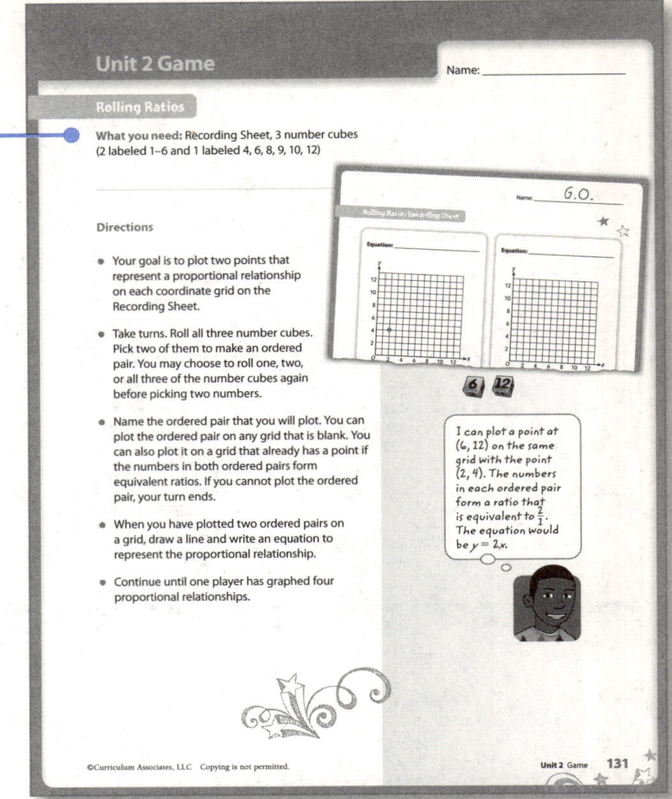

Unit 2 Game

Name: ____________

Rolling Ratios

What you need: Recording Sheet, 3 number cubes (2 labeled 1–6 and 1 labeled 4, 6, 8, 9, 10, 12)

Directions

- Your goal is to plot two points that represent a proportional relationship on each coordinate grid on the Recording Sheet.
- Take turns. Roll all three number cubes. Pick two of them to make an ordered pair. You may choose to roll one, two, or all three of the number cubes again before picking two numbers.
- Name the ordered pair that you will plot. You can plot the ordered pair on any grid that is blank. You can also plot it on a grid that already has a point if the numbers in both ordered pairs form equivalent ratios. If you cannot plot the ordered pair, your turn ends.
- When you have plotted two ordered pairs on a grid, draw a line and write an equation to represent the proportional relationship.
- Continue until one player has graphed four proportional relationships.

Unit Practice

- The Unit Practice provides **mixed practice** of lesson skills and concepts.
- The first page references the Self-Check chart in the *Ready Instruction* Unit Opener. This helps students quickly identify the lesson(s) to revisit for additional support.
- Unit Practice problems **integrate multiple skills**.
- These pages present problems with a **variety of formats**, including multiple choice and constructed response, to help students become familiar with items they will encounter on their state tests.
- The unit practice pages can be assigned as homework, used as independent or small group practice, or for whole class discussion.

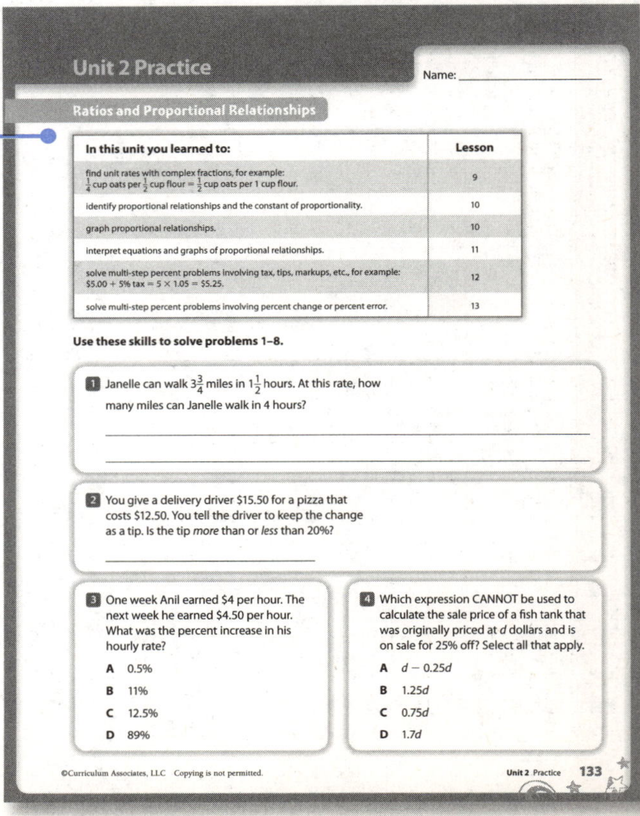

Unit 2 Practice

Name: ____________

Ratios and Proportional Relationships

In this unit you learned to:	Lesson
find unit rates with complex fractions, for example: $\frac{1}{4}$ cup oats per $\frac{1}{2}$ cup flour = $\frac{1}{2}$ cup oats per 1 cup flour.	9
identify proportional relationships and the constant of proportionality.	10
graph proportional relationships.	10
interpret equations and graphs of proportional relationships.	11
solve multi-step percent problems involving tax, tips, markups, etc., for example: \$5.00 + 5% tax = 5 × 1.05 = \$5.25.	12
solve multi-step percent problems involving percent change or percent error.	13

Use these skills to solve problems 1–8.

1 Janelle can walk $3\frac{3}{4}$ miles in $1\frac{1}{2}$ hours. At this rate, how many miles can Janelle walk in 4 hours?

2 You give a delivery driver \$15.50 for a pizza that costs \$12.50. You tell the driver to keep the change as a tip. Is the tip *more* than or *less* than 20%?

3 One week Anil earned \$4 per hour. The next week he earned \$4.50 per hour. What was the percent increase in his hourly rate?

A 0.5%

B 11%

C 12.5%

D 89%

4 Which expression CANNOT be used to calculate the sale price of a fish tank that was originally priced at *d* dollars and is on sale for 25% off? Select all that apply.

A $d - 0.25d$

B $1.25d$

C $0.75d$

D $1.7d$

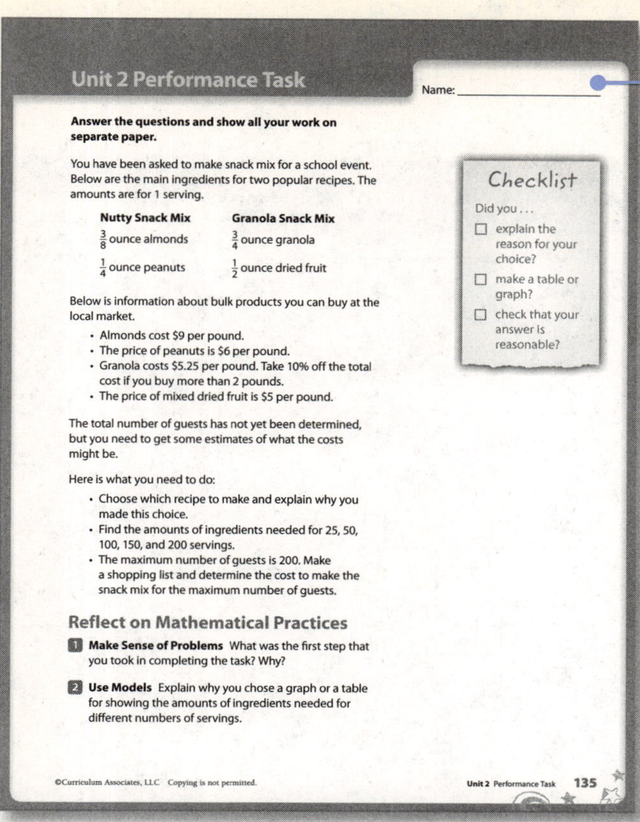

Unit 2 Performance Task

Name: ____________________

Answer the questions and show all your work on separate paper.

You have been asked to make snack mix for a school event. Below are the main ingredients for two popular recipes. The amounts are for 1 serving.

Nutty Snack Mix	Granola Snack Mix
$\frac{3}{8}$ ounce almonds	$\frac{3}{4}$ ounce granola
$\frac{1}{4}$ ounce peanuts	$\frac{1}{2}$ ounce dried fruit

Below is information about bulk products you can buy at the local market.

- Almonds cost $9 per pound.
- The price of peanuts is $6 per pound.
- Granola costs $5.25 per pound. Take 10% off the total cost if you buy more than 2 pounds.
- The price of mixed dried fruit is $5 per pound.

The total number of guests has not yet been determined, but you need to get some estimates of what the costs might be.

Here is what you need to do:

- Choose which recipe to make and explain why you made this choice.
- Find the amounts of ingredients needed for 25, 50, 100, 150, and 200 servings.
- The maximum number of guests is 200. Make a shopping list and determine the cost to make the snack mix for the maximum number of guests.

Checklist

Did you . . .

- ☐ explain the reason for your choice?
- ☐ make a table or graph?
- ☐ check that your answer is reasonable?

Reflect on Mathematical Practices

1. **Make Sense of Problems** What was the first step that you took in completing the task? Why?
2. **Use Models** Explain why you chose a graph or a table for showing the amounts of ingredients needed for different numbers of servings.

©Curriculum Associates, LLC Copying is not permitted. Unit 2 Performance Task 135

Unit Performance Task

- Real-world Unit Performance Tasks require students to **integrate skills and concepts**, apply higher-order thinking, and explain their reasoning.
- Engaging real-world tasks encourage students to become active participants in their learning by requiring them to organize and manage mathematical content and processes.
- **Performance Task Tips** help students organize their thinking.
- Students are asked to reflect on **Mathematical Practices** after they have completed the Performance Task.

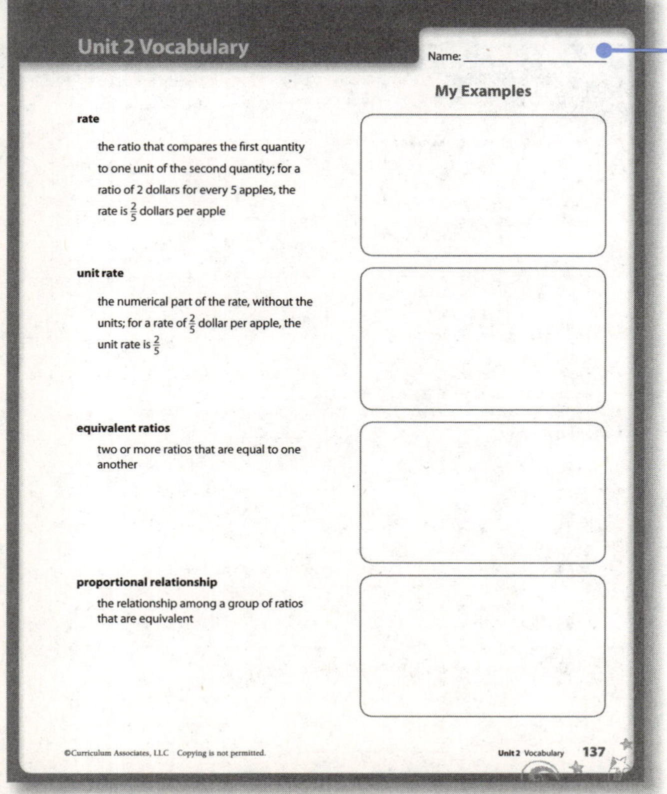

Unit 2 Vocabulary

Name: ____________________

My Examples

rate

the ratio that compares the first quantity to one unit of the second quantity; for a ratio of 2 dollars for every 5 apples, the rate is $\frac{2}{5}$ dollars per apple

unit rate

the numerical part of the rate, without the units; for a rate of $\frac{2}{5}$ dollar per apple, the unit rate is $\frac{2}{5}$

equivalent ratios

two or more ratios that are equal to one another

proportional relationship

the relationship among a group of ratios that are equivalent

©Curriculum Associates, LLC Copying is not permitted. Unit 2 Vocabulary 137

Unit Vocabulary

- The Unit Vocabulary is a way for students to integrate vocabulary into their learning. Vocabulary pages provide a **student-friendly definition** for each new and review vocabulary term in the unit.
- Students are given space to write **examples** for each term to help them connect the term to their own understanding.
- After students have completed these pages, they can use them as a reference.
- Students are also given opportunities to further personalize their acquisition of mathematics vocabulary by selecting terms they want to define.

Fluency Practice

Throughout instruction, use Fluency Skills and Fluency Repeated Reasoning worksheets to reinforce procedural fluency.

Skills Practice

- Fluency practice worksheets in multiple formats provide flexibility and promote the **use of grade-appropriate strategies and algorithms**.
- These worksheets address grade-level facts and operations and can be used any time after the skill has been taught.

Addition and Subtraction with Rational Numbers—Skills Practice

Name: ____________

Add and subtract rational numbers.

Form B

1. $5\frac{5}{8} - \left(-3\frac{3}{8}\right) =$ ______
2. $-14.5 - 8 =$ ______
3. $9.75 - 16.25 =$ ______
4. $\frac{1}{6} - \left(-\frac{5}{6}\right) =$ ______
5. $-6\frac{1}{4} - (-2) =$ ______
6. $-14.3 - (-17.1) =$ ______
7. $9.2 - (-8.6) =$ ______
8. $4\frac{2}{5} - 7\frac{1}{5} =$ ______
9. $4.7 - (-9.3) =$ ______
10. $9.84 - 8.5 =$ ______
11. $3\frac{5}{6} - 2\frac{1}{3} + 6\frac{1}{6} =$ ______
12. $6.7 - 19.2 + 3.3 =$ ______
13. $-13.4 + 3.9 - (-3.4) =$ ______
14. $-6\frac{1}{2} - 7\frac{1}{2} + 16\frac{1}{2} =$ ______
15. $-4.5 + 13 - (-4.5) =$ ______
16. $-4.1 - 8 - (-4.1) + 18 =$ ______
17. $\frac{2}{5} - 1\frac{3}{5} + 3\frac{3}{5} - \left(-3\frac{3}{5}\right) =$ ______
18. $\frac{1}{3} - (-8) + 2 - \left(-\frac{2}{3}\right) =$ ______
19. $9\frac{3}{8} - \frac{5}{8} + \left(-\frac{5}{8}\right) - \left(-1\frac{1}{4}\right) =$ ______
20. $4.25 - 16.75 - (-0.75) + (-3.25) =$ ______

Repeated Reasoning

- Repeated Reasoning worksheets encourage students to **make use of structure and look for regularity** as part of their development of grade-level fluency.
- In this type of fluency practice, students identify and describe patterns in the relationship between the answers and the problems. This develops their **abstract reasoning** and mental math skills.

Addition and Subtraction with Rational Numbers—Repeated Reasoning

Name: ____________

Find patterns in adding integers.

Set A

1. $-6 + (-48) + 6 =$ ______
2. $-6 + (-148) + 6 =$ ______
3. $-16 + (-48) + 16 =$ ______
4. $-16 + (-148) + 16 =$ ______
5. $-26 + (-48) + 26 =$ ______
6. $-26 + (-148) + 26 =$ ______
7. $-36 + (-48) + 36 =$ ______
8. $-36 + (-148) + 36 =$ ______

Set B

1. $-6 + (-48) + 16 =$ ____
2. $-16 + (-48) + 26 =$ ____
3. $-26 + (-48) + 36 =$ ____
4. $-6 + (-148) + 16 =$ ____
5. $-16 + (-148) + 26 =$ ____
6. $-26 + (-148) + 36 =$ ____
7. $-16 + (-48) + 6 =$ ____
8. $-26 + (-48) + 16 =$ ____
9. $-36 + (-48) + 26 =$ ____
10. $-16 + (-148) + 6 =$ ____
11. $-26 + (-148) + 16 =$ ____
12. $-36 + (-148) + 26 =$ ____

Describe a pattern you see in one of the sets of problems above.

Correlation Charts

Common Core Standards in *Ready*® *Practice and Problem Solving*

The tables below show the standards addressed in ***Ready Practice and Problem Solving***, all of which correspond to ***Ready Instruction***. Use this information to plan and focus meaningful practice.

Common Core State Standards for Grade 7 — Mathematics Standards			Content Emphasis	*Ready*® *Practice and Problem Solving* Lesson(s)
Ratios and Proportional Relationships				
Analyze proportional relationships and use them to solve real-world and mathematical problems.				
7.RP.A.1	Compute unit rates associated with ratios of fractions, including ratios of lengths, areas and other quantities measured in like or different units. *For example, if a person walks $\frac{1}{2}$ mile in each $\frac{1}{4}$ hour, compute the unit rate as the complex fraction $\frac{\frac{1}{2}}{\frac{1}{4}}$ miles per hour, equivalently 2 miles per hour.*		Major	9, 22
7.RP.A.2	Recognize and represent proportional relationships between quantities.		Major	10, 11
	7.RP.A.2a	Decide whether two quantities are in a proportional relationship, e.g., by testing for equivalent ratios in a table or graphing on a coordinate plane and observing whether the graph is a straight line through the origin.	Major	10
	7.RP.A.2b	Identify the constant of proportionality (unit rate) in tables, graphs, equations, diagrams, and verbal descriptions of proportional relationships.	Major	10
	7.RP.A.2c	Represent proportional relationships by equations. *For example, if total cost t is proportional to the number n of items purchased at a constant price p, the relationship between the total cost and the number of items can be expressed as $t = pn$.*	Major	11
	7.RP.A.2d	Explain what a point (x, y) on the graph of a proportional relationship means in terms of the situation, with special attention to the points $(0, 0)$ and $(1, r)$ where r is the unit rate.	Major	11
7.RP.A.3	Use proportional relationships to solve multistep ratio and percent problems. *Examples: simple interest, tax, markups and markdowns, gratuities and commissions, fees, percent increase and decrease, percent error.*		Major	12, 13
The Number System				
Apply and extend previous understandings of operations with fractions to add, subtract, multiply, and divide rational numbers.				
7.NS.A.1	Apply and extend previous understandings of addition and subtraction to add and subtract rational numbers; represent addition and subtraction on a horizontal or vertical number line diagram.		Major	1, 2, 3, 7
	7.NS.A.1a	Describe situations in which opposite quantities combine to make 0. *For example, a hydrogen atom has 0 charge because its two constituents are oppositely charged.*	Major	1, 7
	7.NS.A.1b	Understand $p + q$ as the number located a distance $\lvert q \rvert$ from p, in the positive or negative direction depending on whether q is positive or negative. Show that a number and its opposite have a sum of 0 (are additive inverses). Interpret sums of rational numbers by describing real-world contexts.	Major	1, 7
	7.NS.A.1c	Understand subtraction of rational numbers as adding the additive inverse, $p - q = p + (-q)$. Show that the distance between two rational numbers on the number line is the absolute value of their difference, and apply this principle in real-world contexts.	Major	2, 7
	7.NS.A.1d	Apply properties ofoperations as strategies to add and subtract rational numbers.	Major	3, 7

The Standards for Mathematical Practice are integrated throughout the lessons, unit practices, performance tasks, and unit games.

Common Core State Standards for Grade 7 — Mathematics Standards			Content Emphasis	*Ready®* *Practice and Problem Solving* Lesson(s)
The Number System ***(continued)***				
Apply and extend previous understandings of operations with fractions. ***(continued)***				
7.NS.A.2	Apply and extend previous understandings of multiplication and division and of fractions to multiply and divide rational numbers.		Major	4, 5, 6
	7.NS.A.2a	Understand that multiplication is extended from fractions to rational numbers by requiring that operations continue to satisfy the properties of operations, particularly the distributive property, leading to products such as $(-1)(-1) = 1$ and the rules for multiplying signed numbers. Interpret products of rational numbers by describing real-world contexts.	Major	4, 6
	7.NS.A.2b	Understand that integers can be divided, provided that the divisor is not zero, and every quotient of integers (with non-zero divisor) is a rational number. If p and q are integers, then $-\left(\frac{p}{q}\right) = \frac{(-p)}{q} = \frac{p}{(-q)}$. Interpret quotients of rational numbers by describing real-world contexts.	Major	4, 6
	7.NS.A.2c	Apply properties of operations as strategies to multiply and divide rational numbers.	Major	4, 6
	7.NS.A.2d	Convert a rational number to a decimal using long division; know that the decimal form of a rational number terminates in 0s or eventually repeats.	Major	5
7.NS.A.3	Solve real-world and mathematical problems involving the four operations with rational numbers.		Major	8
Expressions and Equations				
Use properties of operations to generate equivalent expressions.				
7.EE.A.1	Apply properties of operations as strategies to add, subtract, factor, and expand linear expressions with rational coefficients.		Major	14
7.EE.A.2	Understand that rewriting an expression in different forms in a problem context can shed light on the problem and how the quantities in it are related. *For example,* $a + 0.05a = 1.05a$ *means that "increase by 5%" is the same as "multiply by 1.05."*		Major	15
Solve real-life and mathematical problems using numerical and algebraic expressions and equations.				
7.EE.B.3	Solve multi-step real-life and mathematical problems posed with positive and negative rational numbers in any form (whole numbers, fractions, and decimals), using tools strategically. Apply properties of operations to calculate with numbers in any form; convert between forms as appropriate; and assess the reasonableness of answers using mental computation and estimation strategies. *For example: If a woman making $25 an hour gets a 10% raise, she will make an additional* $\frac{1}{10}$ *of her salary an hour, or $2.50, for a new salary of $27.50. If you want to place a towel bar* $9\frac{3}{4}$ *inches long in the center of a door that is* $27\frac{1}{2}$ *inches wide, you will need to place the bar about 9 inches from each edge; this estimate can be used as a check on the exact computation.*		Major	8, 16, 17
7.EE.B.4	Use variables to represent quantities in a real-world or mathematical problem, and construct simple equations and inequalities to solve problems by reasoning about the quantities.		Major	16, 17
	7.EE.B.4a	Solve word problems leading to equations of the form $px + q = r$ and $p(x + q) = r$, where p, q, and r are specific rational numbers. Solve equations of these forms fluently. Compare an algebraic solution to an arithmetic solution, identifying the sequence of the operations used in each approach. *For example, the perimeter of a rectangle is 54 cm. Its length is 6 cm. What is its width?*	Major	16
	7.EE.B.4b	Solve word problems leading to inequalities of the form $px + q > r$ or $px + q < r$, where p, q, and r are specific rational numbers. Graph the solution set of the inequality and interpret it in the context of the problem. *For example: As a salesperson, you are paid $50 per week plus $3 per sale. This week you want your pay to be at least $100. Write an inequality for the number of sales you need to make, and describe the solutions.*	Major	17

Common Core State Standards for Grade 7 — Mathematics Standards		Content Emphasis	*Ready® Practice and Problem Solving* Lesson(s)
Geometry			
Draw, construct, and describe geometrical figures and describe the relationships between them.			
7.G.A.1	Solve problems involving scale drawings of geometric figures, such as computing actual lengths and areas from a scale drawing and reproducing a scale drawing at a different scale.	Supporting/ Additional	22
7.G.A.2	Draw (freehand, with ruler and protractor, and with technology) geometric shapes with given conditions. Focus on constructing triangles from three measures of angles or sides, noticing when the conditions determine a unique triangle, more than one triangle, or no triangle.	Supporting/ Additional	19
7.G.A.3	Describe the two-dimensional figures that result from slicing three-dimensional figures, as in plane sections of right rectangular prisms and right rectangular pyramids.	Supporting/ Additional	25
Solve real-life and mathematical problems involving angle measure, area, surface area, and volume.			
7.G.B.4	Know the formulas for the area and circumference of a circle and use them to solve problems; give an informal derivation of the relationship between the circumference and area of a circle.	Supporting/ Additional	21
7.G.B.5	Use facts about supplementary, complementary, vertical, and adjacent angles in a multi-step problem to write and solve simple equations for an unknown angle in a figure.	Supporting/ Additional	18
7.G.B.6	Solve real-world and mathematical problems involving area, volume and surface area of two- and three-dimensional objects composed of triangles, quadrilaterals, polygons, cubes, and right prisms.	Supporting/ Additional	20, 23, 24
Statistics and Probability			
Use random sampling to draw inferences about a population.			
7.SP.A.1	Understand that statistics can be used to gain information about a population by examining a sample of the population; generalizations about a population from a sample are valid only if the sample is representative of that population. Understand that random sampling tends to produce representative samples and support valid inferences.	Supporting/ Additional	26
7.SP.A.2	Use data from a random sample to draw inferences about a population with an unknown characteristic of interest. Generate multiple samples (or simulated samples) of the same size to gauge the variation in estimates or predictions. *For example, estimate the mean word length in a book by randomly sampling words from the book; predict the winner of a school election based on randomly sampled survey data. Gauge how far off the estimate or prediction might be.*	Supporting/ Additional	27
Draw informal comparative inferences about a population.			
7.SP.B.3	Informally assess the degree of visual overlap of two numerical data distributions with similar variabilities, measuring the difference between the centers by expressing it as a multiple of a measure of variability. *For example, the mean height of players on the basketball team is 10 cm greater than the mean height of players on the soccer team, about twice the variability (mean absolute deviation) on either team; on a dot plot, the separation between the two distributions of heights is noticeable.*	Supporting/ Additional	28
7.SP.B.4	Use measures of center and measures of variability for numerical data from random samples to draw informal comparative inferences about two populations. *For example, decide whether the words in a chapter of a seventh-grade science book are generally longer than the words in a chapter of a fourth-grade science book.*	Supporting/ Additional	29
Investigate chance processes and develop, use, and evaluate probability models.			
7.SP.C.5	Understand that the probability of a chance event is a number between 0 and 1 that expresses the likelihood of the event occurring. Larger numbers indicate greater likelihood. A probability near 0 indicates an unlikely event, a probability around $\frac{1}{2}$ indicates an event that is neither unlikely nor likely, and a probability near 1 indicates a likely event.	Supporting/ Additional	30
7.SP.C.6	Approximate the probability of a chance event by collecting data on the chance process that produces it and observing its long-run relative frequency, and predict the approximate relative frequency given the probability. *For example, when rolling a number cube 600 times, predict that a 3 or 6 would be rolled roughly 200 times, but probably not exactly 200 times.*	Supporting/ Additional	31

Common Core State Standards for Grade 7 — Mathematics Standards		Content Emphasis	*Ready*® *Practice and Problem Solving* Lesson(s)
Statistics and Probability *(continued)*			
Investigate chance processes and develop, use, and evaluate probability models. *(continued)*			
7.SP.C.7	Develop a probability model and use it to find probabilities of events. Compare probabilities from a model to observed frequencies; if the agreement is not good, explain possible sources of the discrepancy.	Supporting/ Additional	32
	7.SP.C.7a Develop a uniform probability model by assigning equal probability to all outcomes, and use the model to determine probabilities of events. *For example, if a student is selected at random from a class, find the probability that Jane will be selected and the probability that a girl will be selected.*	Supporting/ Additional	32
	7.SP.C.7b Develop a probability model (which may not be uniform) by observing frequencies in data generated from a chance process. *For example, find the approximate probability that a spinning penny will land heads up or that a tossed paper cup will land open-end down. Do the outcomes for the spinning penny appear to be equally likely based on the observed frequencies?*	Supporting/ Additional	32
7.SP.C.8	Find probabilities of compound events using organized lists, tables, tree diagrams, and simulation.	Supporting/ Additional	33
	7.SP.C.8a Understand that, just as with simple events, the probability of a compound event is the fraction of outcomes in the sample space for which the compound event occurs.	Supporting/ Additional	33
	7.SP.C.8b Represent sample spaces for compound events using methods such as organized lists, tables and tree diagrams. For an event described in everyday language (e.g., "rolling double sixes"), identify the outcomes in the sample space which compose the event.	Supporting/ Additional	33
	7.SP.C.8c Design and use a simulation to generate frequencies for compound events. *For example, use random digits as a simulation tool to approximate the answer to the question: If 40% of donors have type A blood, what is the probability that it will take at least 4 donors to find one with type A blood?*	Supporting/ Additional	33

Unit Correlations in *Ready Practice and Problem Solving*

Unit Correlations	
Unit	**Common Core State Standards**
Unit 1	
Game: Operation: Integers	7.NS.A.1c, 7.NS.A.1d
Unit Practice	7.NS.A.1a, 7.NS.A.1b, 7.NS.A.1c, 7.NS.A.1d, 7.NS.A.2a, 7.NS.A.2b, 7.NS.A.2c, 7.NS.A.2d, 7.NS.A.3
Performance Task	7.NS.A.1b, 7.NS.A.1c, 7.NS.A.1d, 7.NS.A.2c
Unit 2	
Game: Rolling Ratios	7.RP.A.2a
Unit Practice	7.RP.A.1, 7.RP.A.2a, 7.RP.A.2b, 7.RP.A.2c, 7.RP.A.3
Performance Task	7.RP.A.1, 7.RP.A.2a, 7.RP.A.3
Unit 3	
Game: The Inequality Solution	7.EE.B.4b
Practice	7.EE.A.1, 7.EE.A.2, 7.EE.B.3, 7.EE.B.4a, 7.EE.B.4b
Performance Task	7.EE.A.2, 7.EE.B.3, 7.EE.B.4a
Unit 4	
Game: Shape Up	7.G.B.4, 7.G.B.6
Practice	7.G.A.1, 7.G.A.2, 7.G.A.3, 7.G.B.4, 7.G.B.5, 7.G.B.6
Performance Task	7.G.A.1, 7.G.B.4, 7.G.B.6, 7.RP.A.1
Unit 5	
Game: It's Probable	7.SP.C.5, 7.SP.C.7a
Practice	7.SP.A.1, 7.SP.A.2, 7.SP.B.3, 7.SP.B.4, 7.SP.C.5, 7.SP.C.6, 7.SP.C.7a, 7.SP.C.8a, 7.SP.C.8c
Performance Task	7.SP.C.6, 7.SP.C.7a, 7.SP.C.7b

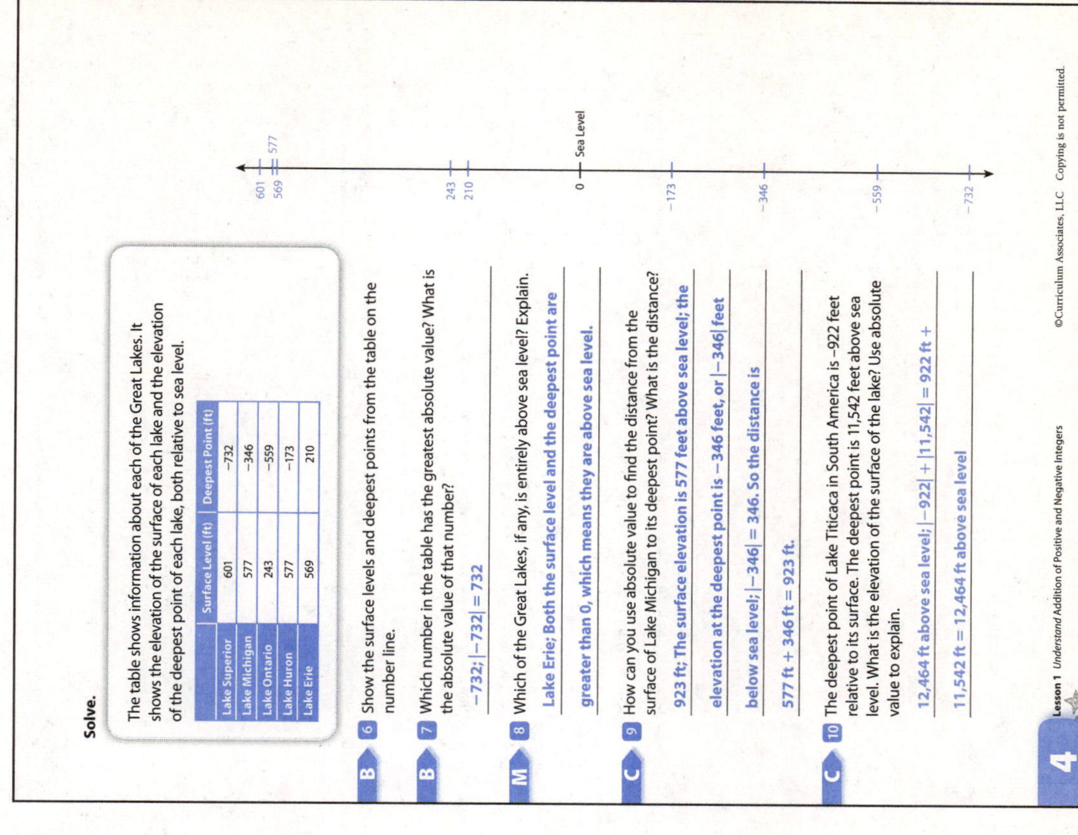

Solve.

The table shows information about each of the Great Lakes. It shows the elevation of the surface of each lake and the elevation of the deepest point of each lake, both relative to sea level.

	Surface Level (ft)	Deepest Point (ft)
Lake Superior	601	–732
Lake Michigan	577	–346
Lake Ontario	243	–559
Lake Huron	577	–173
Lake Erie	569	210

B 6 Show the surface levels and deepest points from the table on the number line.

B 7 Which number in the table has the greatest absolute value? What is the absolute value of that number?

−732; |−732| = 732

M 8 Which of the Great Lakes, if any, is entirely above sea level? Explain.

Lake Erie; Both the surface level and the deepest point are greater than 0, which means they are above sea level.

C 9 How can you use absolute value to find the distance from the surface of Lake Michigan to its deepest point? What is the distance?

923 ft; The surface elevation is 577 feet above sea level; the elevation at the deepest point is −346 feet, or |−346| feet below sea level; |−346| = 346. So the distance is 577 ft + 346 ft = 923 ft.

C 10 The deepest point of Lake Titicaca in South America is –922 feet relative to its surface. The deepest point is 11,542 feet above sea level. What is the elevation of the surface of the lake? Use absolute value to explain.

12,464 ft above sea level; |−922| + |11,542| = 922 ft + 11,542 ft = 12,464 ft above sea level

4 Lesson 1 *Understand* Addition of Positive and Negative Integers ©Curriculum Associates, LLC Copying is not permitted.

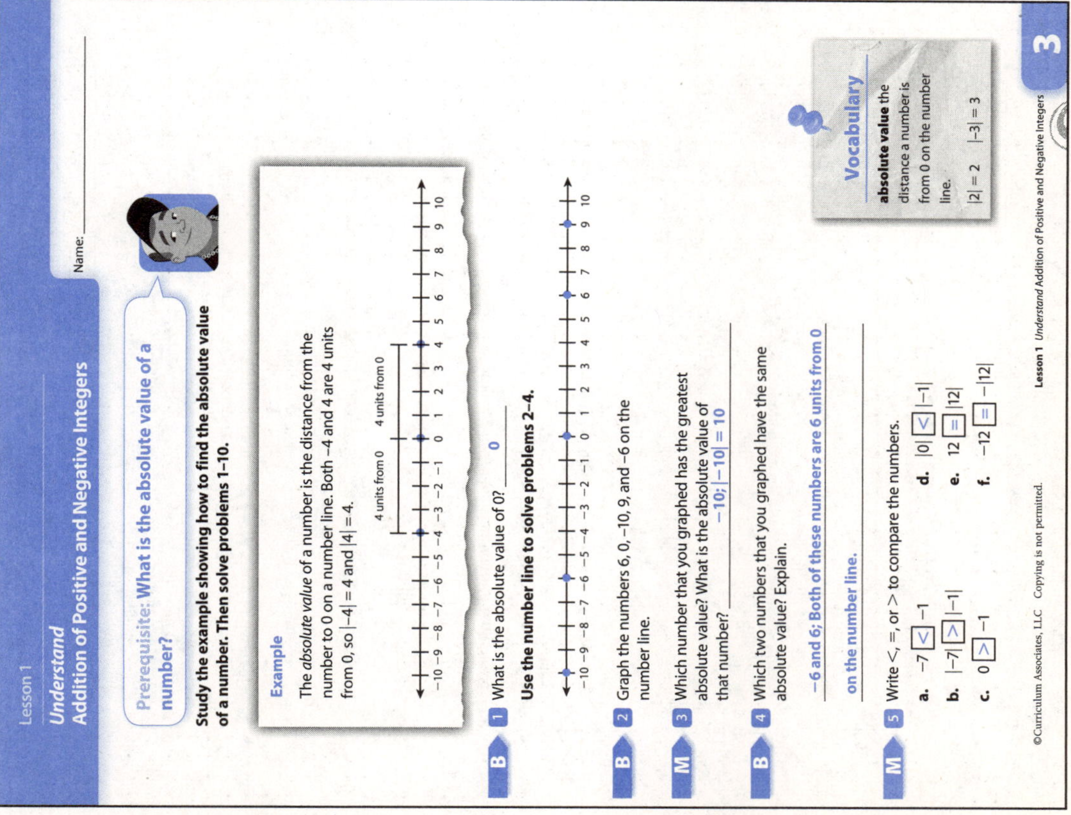

Lesson 1

Understand
Addition of Positive and Negative Integers

Name: ____________

Prerequisite: What is the absolute value of a number?

Study the example showing how to find the absolute value of a number. Then solve problems 1–10.

Example

The *absolute value* of a number is the distance from the number to 0 on a number line. Both –4 and 4 are 4 units from 0, so |–4| = 4 and |4| = 4.

B 1 What is the absolute value of 0? **0**

Use the number line to solve problems 2–4.

B 2 Graph the numbers 6, 0, –10, 9, and –6 on the number line.

M 3 Which number that you graphed has the greatest absolute value? What is the absolute value of that number? **−10; |−10| = 10**

B 4 Which two numbers that you graphed have the same absolute value? Explain.

−6 and 6; Both of these numbers are 6 units from 0 on the number line.

M 5 Write <, =, or > to compare the numbers.

a. –7 [<] –1
b. |–7| [>] |–1|
c. 0 [>] –1
d. |0| [<] |–1|
e. 12 [=] |12|
f. –12 [=] –|12|

Vocabulary

absolute value the distance a number is from 0 on the number line.

|2| = 2 |–3| = 3

©Curriculum Associates, LLC Copying is not permitted. Lesson 1 *Understand* Addition of Positive and Negative Integers 3

Key

B Basic **M** Medium **C** Challenge

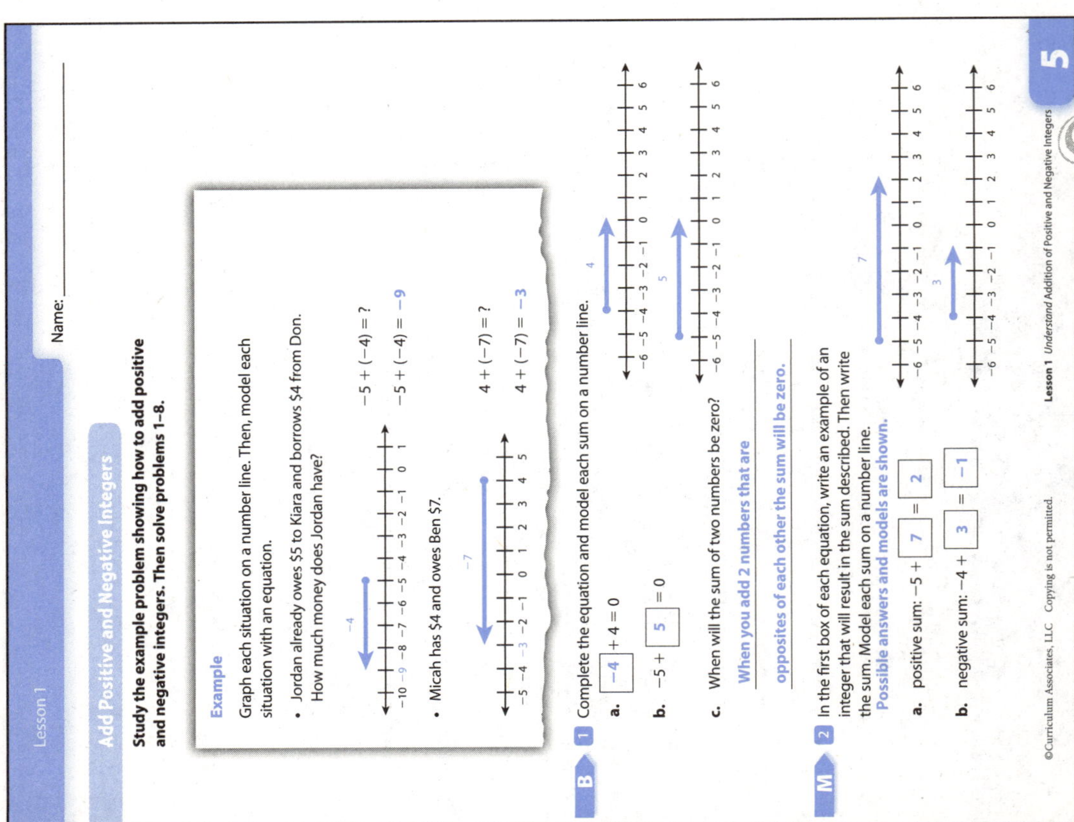

Lesson 1

Name: ____________

Add Positive and Negative Integers

Study the example problem showing how to add positive and negative integers. Then solve problems 1–8.

Example

Graph each situation on a number line. Then, model each situation with an equation.

- Jordan already owes $5 to Kiara and borrows $4 from Don. How much money does Jordan have?

$-5 + (-4) = ?$

$-5 + (-4) = -9$

- Micah has $4 and owes Ben $7.

$4 + (-7) = ?$

$4 + (-7) = -3$

B **1** Complete the equation and model each sum on a number line.

a. $\boxed{-4} + 4 = 0$

b. $-5 + \boxed{5} = 0$

c. When will the sum of two numbers be zero?

When you add 2 numbers that are opposites of each other the sum will be zero.

M **2** In the first box of each equation, write an example of an integer that will result in the sum described. Then write the sum. Model each sum on a number line.
Possible answers and models are shown.

a. positive sum: $-5 + \boxed{7} = \boxed{2}$

b. negative sum: $-4 + \boxed{3} = \boxed{-1}$

©Curriculum Associates, LLC Copying is not permitted. Lesson 1 *Understand* Addition of Positive and Negative Integers 5

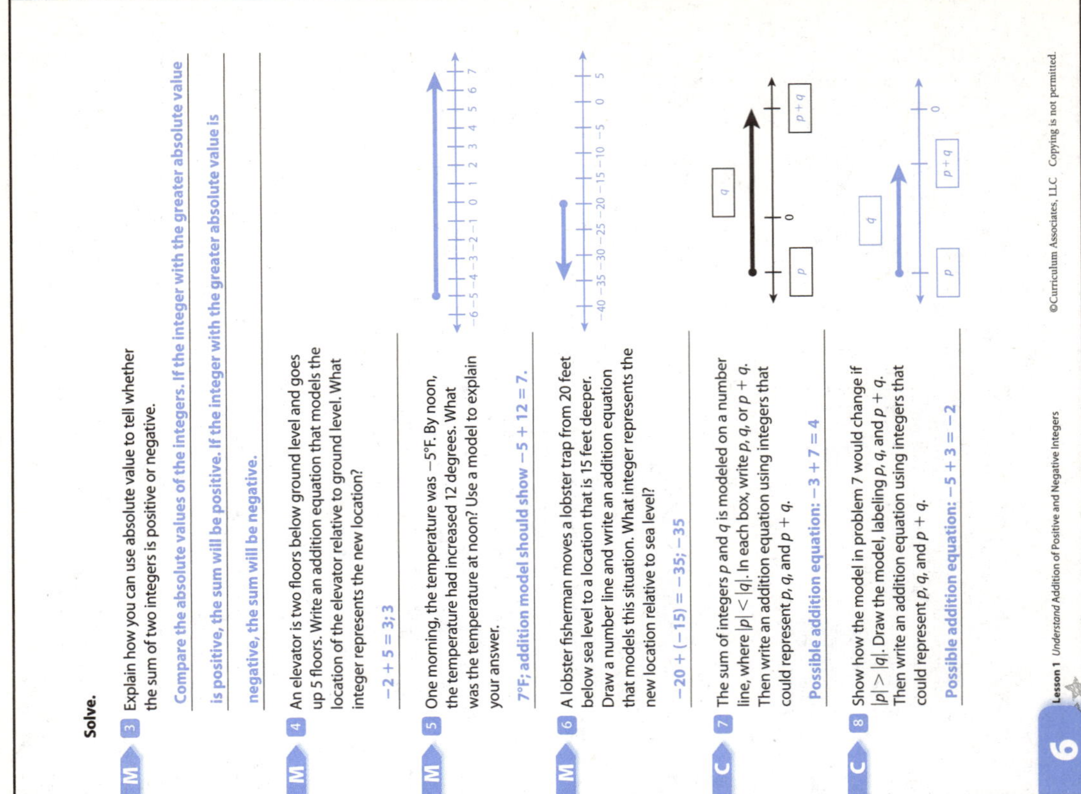

Solve.

M **3** Explain how you can use absolute value to tell whether the sum of two integers is positive or negative.

Compare the absolute values of the integers. If the integer with the greater absolute value is positive, the sum will be positive. If the integer with the greater absolute value is negative, the sum will be negative.

M **4** An elevator is two floors below ground level and goes up 5 floors. Write an addition equation that models the location of the elevator relative to ground level. What integer represents the new location?

$-2 + 5 = 3$; 3

M **5** One morning, the temperature was −5°F. By noon, the temperature had increased 12 degrees. What was the temperature at noon? Use a model to explain your answer.

7°F; addition model should show $-5 + 12 = 7$.

M **6** A lobster fisherman moves a lobster trap from 20 feet below sea level to a location that is 15 feet deeper. Draw a number line and write an addition equation that models this situation. What integer represents the new location relative to sea level?

$-20 + (-15) = -35$; −35

C **7** The sum of integers p and q is modeled on a number line, where $|p| < |q|$. In each box, write p, q, or $p + q$. Then write an addition equation using integers that could represent p, q, and $p + q$.

Possible addition equation: $-3 + 7 = 4$

C **8** Show how the model in problem 7 would change if $|p| > |q|$. Draw the model, labeling p, q, and $p + q$. Then write an addition equation using integers that could represent p, q, and $p + q$.

Possible addition equation: $-5 + 3 = -2$

6 Lesson 1 *Understand* Addition of Positive and Negative Integers ©Curriculum Associates, LLC Copying is not permitted.

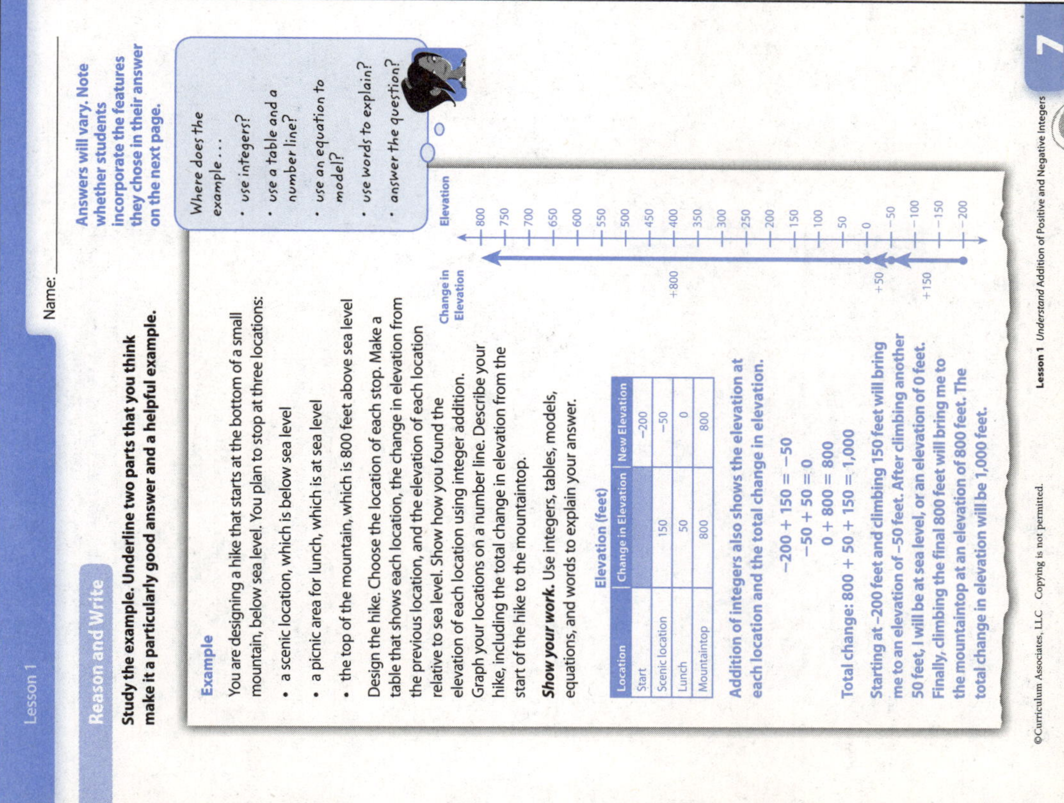

Lesson 1

Name: ____________

Reason and Write

Study the example. Underline two parts that you think make it a particularly good answer and a helpful example.

Answers will vary. Note whether students incorporate the features they chose in their answer on the next page.

Example

You are designing a hike that starts at the bottom of a small mountain, below sea level. You plan to stop at three locations:

- a scenic location, which is below sea level
- a picnic area for lunch, which is at sea level
- the top of the mountain, which is 800 feet above sea level

Design the hike. Choose the location of each stop. Make a table that shows each location, the change in elevation from the previous location, and the elevation of each location relative to sea level. Show how you found the elevation of each location using integer addition. Graph your locations on a number line. Describe your hike, including the total change in elevation from the start of the hike to the mountaintop.

Show your work. Use integers, tables, models, equations, and words to explain your answer.

Elevation (feet)

Location	Change in Elevation	New Elevation
Start		−200
Scenic location	150	−50
Lunch	50	0
Mountaintop	800	800

Addition of integers also shows the elevation at each location and the total change in elevation.

$-200 + 150 = -50$
$-50 + 50 = 0$
$0 + 800 = 800$

Total change: $800 + 50 + 150 = 1{,}000$

Starting at −200 feet and climbing 150 feet will bring me to an elevation of −50 feet. After climbing another 50 feet, I will be at sea level, or an elevation of 0 feet. Finally, climbing the final 800 feet will bring me to the mountaintop at an elevation of 800 feet. The total change in elevation will be 1,000 feet.

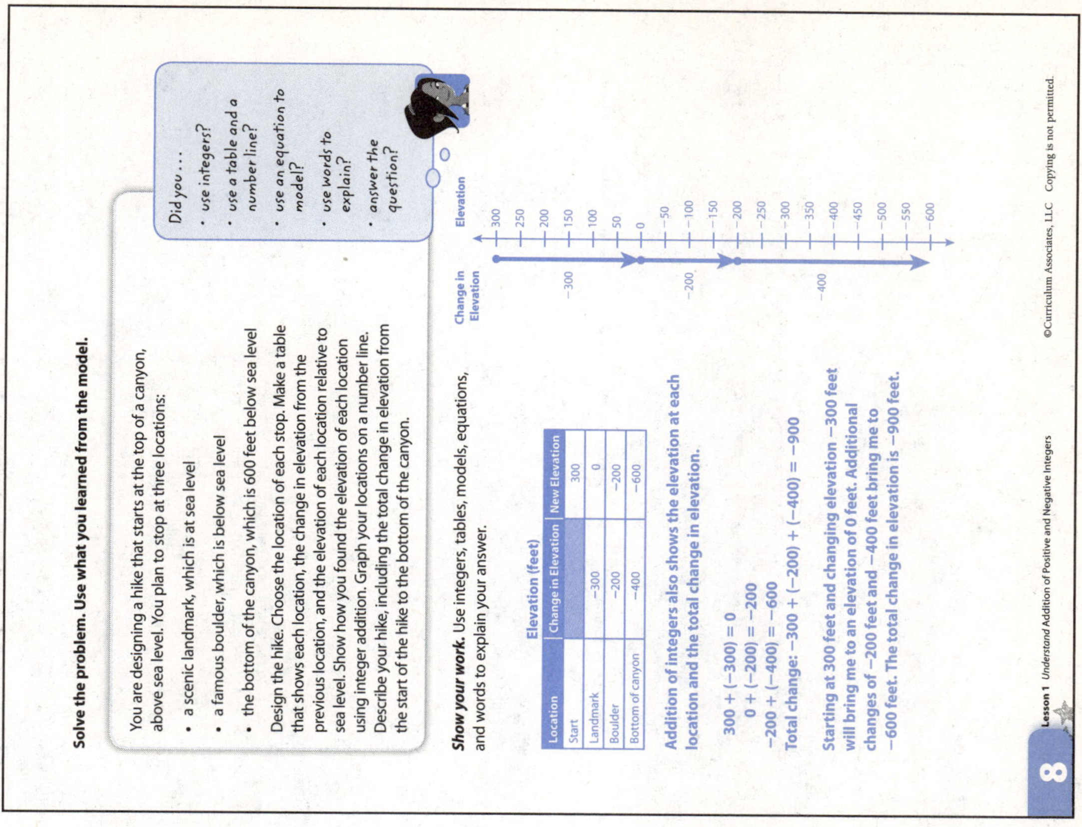

Solve the problem. Use what you learned from the model.

You are designing a hike that starts at the top of a canyon, above sea level. You plan to stop at three locations:

- a scenic landmark, which is at sea level
- a famous boulder, which is below sea level
- the bottom of the canyon, which is 600 feet below sea level

Design the hike. Choose the location of each stop. Make a table that shows each location, the change in elevation from the previous location, and the elevation of each location relative to sea level. Show how you found the elevation of each location using integer addition. Graph your locations on a number line. Describe your hike, including the total change in elevation from the start of the hike to the bottom of the canyon.

Show your work. Use integers, tables, models, equations, and words to explain your answer.

Elevation (feet)

Location	Change in Elevation	New Elevation
Start		300
Landmark	−300	0
Boulder	−200	−200
Bottom of canyon	−400	−600

Addition of integers also shows the elevation at each location and the total change in elevation.

$300 + (-300) = 0$
$0 + (-200) = -200$
$-200 + (-400) = -600$

Total change: $-300 + (-200) + (-400) = -900$

Starting at 300 feet and changing elevation −300 feet will bring me to an elevation of 0 feet. Additional changes of −200 feet and −400 feet bring me to −600 feet. The total change in elevation is −900 feet.

Lesson 2

Understand
Subtraction of Positive and Negative Integers

Name: ______________________

Prerequisite: How do you add integers using a number line?

Study the example problem showing how to add positive and negative integers. Then solve problems 1–7.

Example

When Leo woke up he saw that the temperature was −8°F. By noon the temperature had increased 5°F. What was the temperature at noon?

You can use a number line to add −8 + 5.

−8 + 5 = −3, so the temperature at noon was −3°F.

B **1** By 3:00 PM, the temperature had increased by another 5°F. Was the temperature at 3:00 PM positive or negative? How do you know? What was the temperature at 3:00 PM?

positive; Possible explanation: The temperature only had to increase by 3°F to reach 0°F, but it increased by another 2°F. So the temperature was positive, 2°F, at 3:00 PM.

B **2** By 11:00 PM, the temperature had dropped 8°F. Was the temperature at 11:00 PM positive or negative? Explain.

negative; Possible explanation: The temperature only had to decrease by 2°F to reach 0°F, but it decreased by another 6°F. So the temperature was negative, −6°F, at 11:00 PM.

M **3** A swimmer dives 10 feet below the surface of a lake. How far must she swim before she reaches the surface? Use an addition equation to explain, and tell what each part of the equation means.

10 feet; −10 + 10 = 0. −10 is the starting position of the swimmer, 10 is the number of feet she has to swim to reach the surface, and 0 is the location of the surface.

©Curriculum Associates, LLC Copying is not permitted. Lesson 2 *Understand* Subtraction of Positive and Negative Integers 11

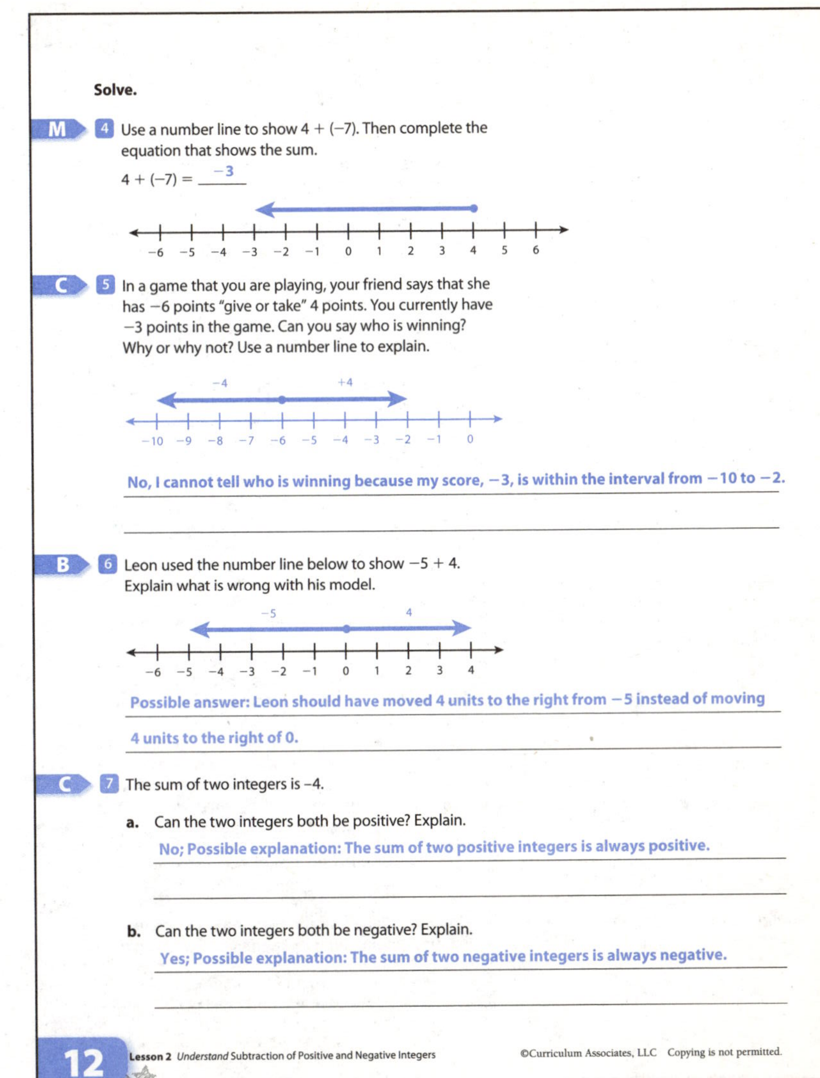
Solve.

M **4** Use a number line to show 4 + (−7). Then complete the equation that shows the sum.

4 + (−7) = **−3**

C **5** In a game that you are playing, your friend says that she has −6 points "give or take" 4 points. You currently have −3 points in the game. Can you say who is winning? Why or why not? Use a number line to explain.

No, I cannot tell who is winning because my score, −3, is within the interval from −10 to −2.

B **6** Leon used the number line below to show −5 + 4. Explain what is wrong with his model.

Possible answer: Leon should have moved 4 units to the right from −5 instead of moving 4 units to the right of 0.

C **7** The sum of two integers is −4.

a. Can the two integers both be positive? Explain.

No; Possible explanation: The sum of two positive integers is always positive.

b. Can the two integers both be negative? Explain.

Yes; Possible explanation: The sum of two negative integers is always negative.

12 Lesson 2 *Understand* Subtraction of Positive and Negative Integers ©Curriculum Associates, LLC Copying is not permitted.

Key

B Basic **M** Medium **C** Challenge

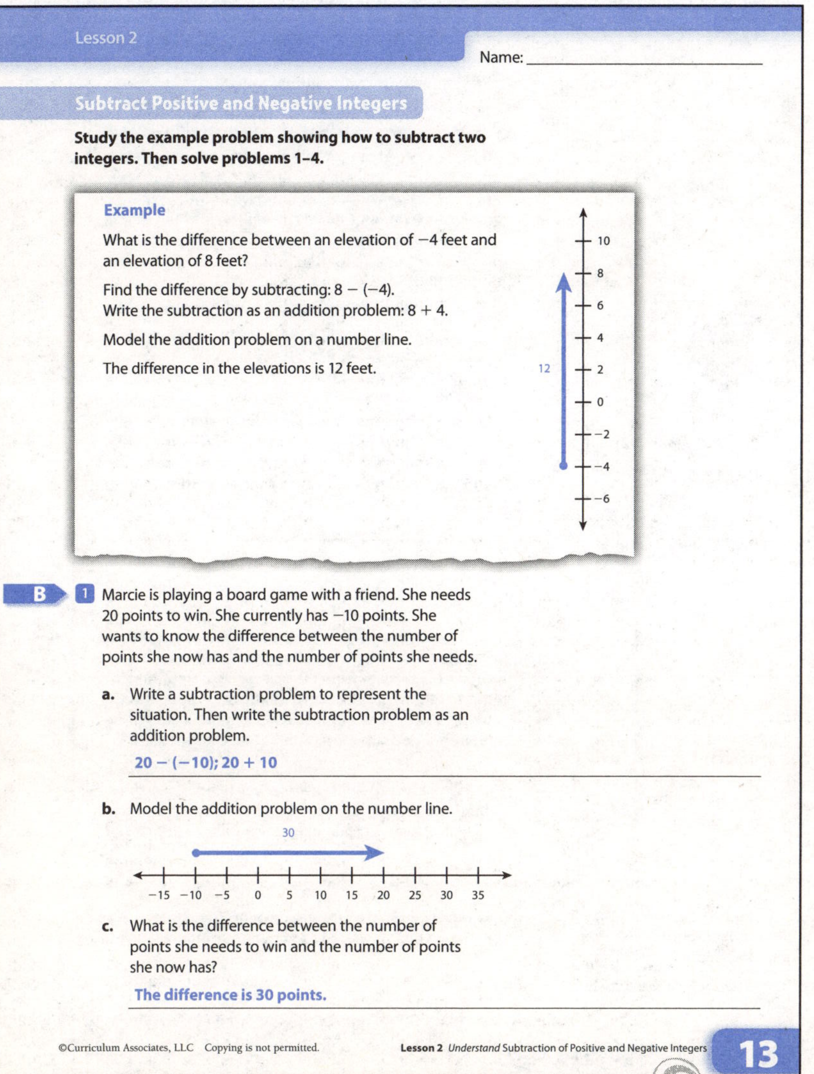

Lesson 2

Name: ____________

Subtract Positive and Negative Integers

Study the example problem showing how to subtract two integers. Then solve problems 1–4.

Example

What is the difference between an elevation of −4 feet and an elevation of 8 feet?

Find the difference by subtracting: 8 − (−4).
Write the subtraction as an addition problem: 8 + 4.

Model the addition problem on a number line.

The difference in the elevations is 12 feet.

B **1** Marcie is playing a board game with a friend. She needs 20 points to win. She currently has −10 points. She wants to know the difference between the number of points she now has and the number of points she needs.

a. Write a subtraction problem to represent the situation. Then write the subtraction problem as an addition problem.

20 − (−10); 20 + 10

b. Model the addition problem on the number line.

c. What is the difference between the number of points she needs to win and the number of points she now has?

The difference is 30 points.

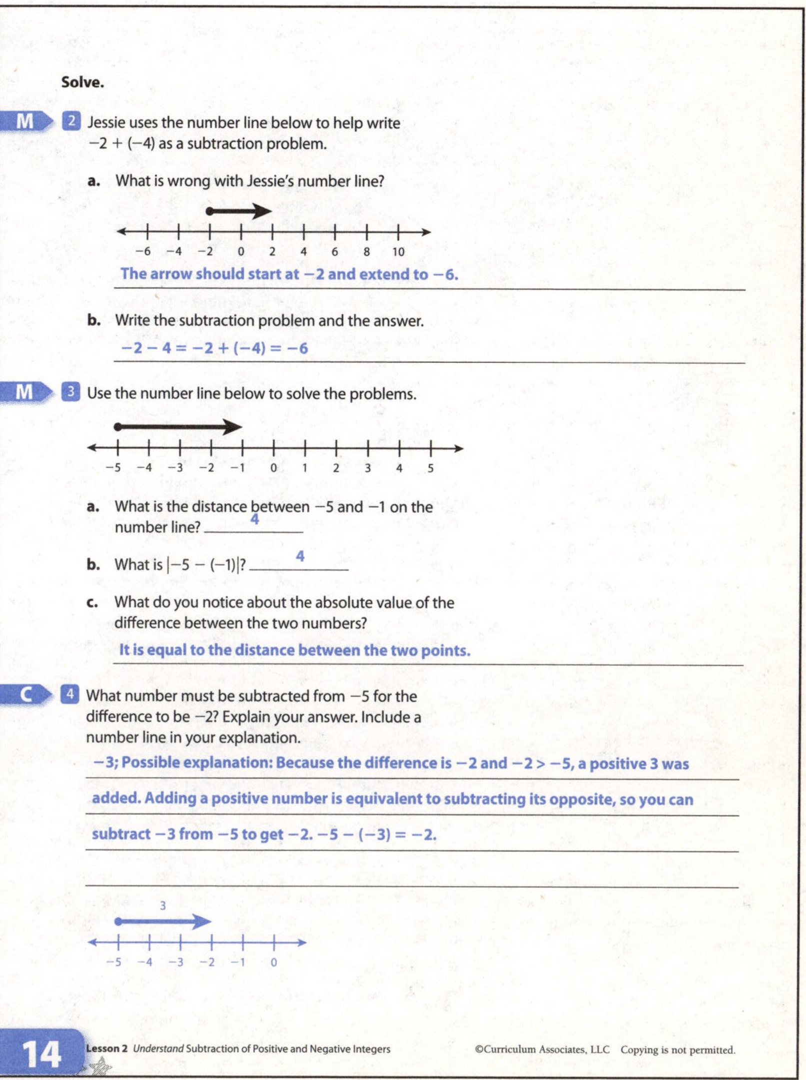

Solve.

M **2** Jessie uses the number line below to help write −2 + (−4) as a subtraction problem.

a. What is wrong with Jessie's number line?

The arrow should start at −2 and extend to −6.

b. Write the subtraction problem and the answer.

−2 − 4 = −2 + (−4) = −6

M **3** Use the number line below to solve the problems.

a. What is the distance between −5 and −1 on the number line? 4

b. What is |−5 − (−1)|? 4

c. What do you notice about the absolute value of the difference between the two numbers?

It is equal to the distance between the two points.

C **4** What number must be subtracted from −5 for the difference to be −2? Explain your answer. Include a number line in your explanation.

−3; Possible explanation: Because the difference is −2 and −2 > −5, a positive 3 was added. Adding a positive number is equivalent to subtracting its opposite, so you can subtract −3 from −5 to get −2. −5 − (−3) = −2.

Lesson 2

Name: ____________________

Reason and Write

Study the example. Underline two parts that you think make it a particularly good answer and a helpful example.

Answers will vary. Note whether students incorporate the features they chose in their answer on the next page.

Example

You and your friends Aaron, Beth, and Craig all live on the same street that the school is on. Aaron lives farthest from the school. You and Aaron live the same distance from Beth's house. Craig lives closest to the school.

Place points *A* for Aaron's house, *B* for Beth's house, *C* for Craig's house, and *S* for the school on a number line. Let your house *X* be at 0. Describe each person's location and use absolute value to find the distance that each person has to walk to and from school. Then, list the locations in order from farthest from the school to closest to the school.

Show your work. Use the number line, words, absolute value, and equations to explain your answer.

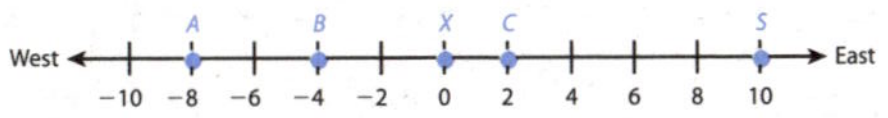

Aaron's house is located at −8 on my number line, and the school is at 10. So his distance from school is:
$|10 - (-8)| = |18| = 18$ units. He has to walk
$2(18) = 36$ units to and from school each day.

Beth's house is located at −4 on my number line, and the school is at 10. So her distance from school is:
$|10 - (-4)| = |14| = 14$ units. She has to walk
$2(14) = 28$ units to and from school each day.

My house is located at 0 on my number line, and the school is at 10. So my distance from school is:
$|10 - 0| = |10| = 10$ units. I have to walk
$2(10) = 20$ units to and from school each day.

Craig's house is located at 2 on my number line, and the school is at 10. So his distance from school is:
$|10 - 2| = |8| = 8$ units. He has to walk
$2(8) = 16$ units to and from school each day.

In order from farthest to closest, the locations are Aaron's house, Beth's house, my house, Craig's house.

Where does the example . . .
- use the number line?
- use words?
- use absolute value?
- use equations?
- answer each part of the problem?

Solve the problem. Use what you learned from the model.

You and your friends Ari, Ben, and Carla all live on the same street that some tennis courts are on. Ari and Carla live the same distance from the tennis courts. Ben lives farthest from the courts. You live the same distance from Ben's house and the tennis courts.

Place points *A* for Ari's house, *B* for Ben's house, *C* for Carla's house, and *T* for the tennis courts on a number line. Let your house *X* be at 0. Describe each person's location and use absolute value to find the distance that each person has to walk to and back home from the tennis courts. Then, list the locations in order from farthest from the courts to closest to the courts.

Show your work. Use the number line, words, absolute value, and equations to explain your answer.

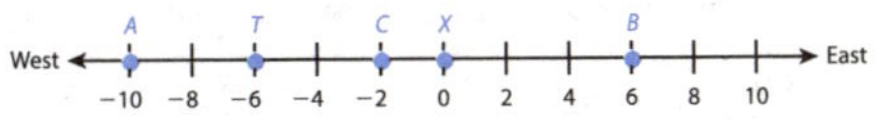

Ari's house is located at −10 on my number line, and the tennis courts are at −6. So his distance from the courts is:
$|-6 - (-10)| = |4| = 4$ units. He has to walk
$2(4) = 8$ units to get to and home from the courts.

Carla's house is located at −2 on my number line. Because she lives the same distance from the courts as Ari, she will also have to walk 8 units to get to and home from the courts.

My house is located at 0 on my number line, and the tennis courts are at −6. So my distance from the courts is:
$|-6 - 0| = |-6| = 6$ units. I have to walk
$2(6) = 12$ units to get to and home from the courts.

Ben's house is located at 6 on my number line, and the tennis courts are at −6. So his distance from the courts is:
$|-6 - 6| = |-12| = 12$ units. He has to walk
$2(12) = 24$ units to get to and home from the courts.

In order from farthest to closest, the locations are Ben's house, my house, and then Ari's and Carla's houses.

Did you . . .
- use the number line?
- use words?
- use absolute value?
- use equations?
- answer each part of the problem?

Lesson 3

Add and Subtract Positive and Negative Integers

Name: ______________

Prerequisite: Connect Addition and Subtraction

Study the example showing how to connect addition and subtraction. Then solve problems 1–9.

Example

Solve the subtraction problem: 7 − 4 = □.

To solve, you can represent 7 − 4 = □ using a number line. Start at 7 and move 4 units to the left to represent subtracting 4 from 7. You end at 3, so 7 − 4 = 3.

4

1 2 3 4 5 6 7 8

Because addition and subtraction are inverse operations, you can also rewrite the subtraction problem as an addition problem. Think: "What number do I add to 4 to get 7?" Because 4 + 3 = 7, you know 7 − 4 = 3.

B 1 Draw a number line that represents 7 + (−4).

−4

1 2 3 4 5 6 7 8

B 2 How does the number line you drew in problem 1 compare to the number line in the example?

Possible answer: They are the same, but one shows 7 − 4 and one shows 7 + (−4).

B 3 Use your answers to the last two problems to complete this equation.

7 − 4 = 7 + __(−4)__

M 4 Complete each equation.

a. −1 + (−4) = __−5__

b. −1 − __4__ = −5

c. −1 + (−4) = −1 − __4__

d. 1 − (−4) = 1 + 4 = __5__

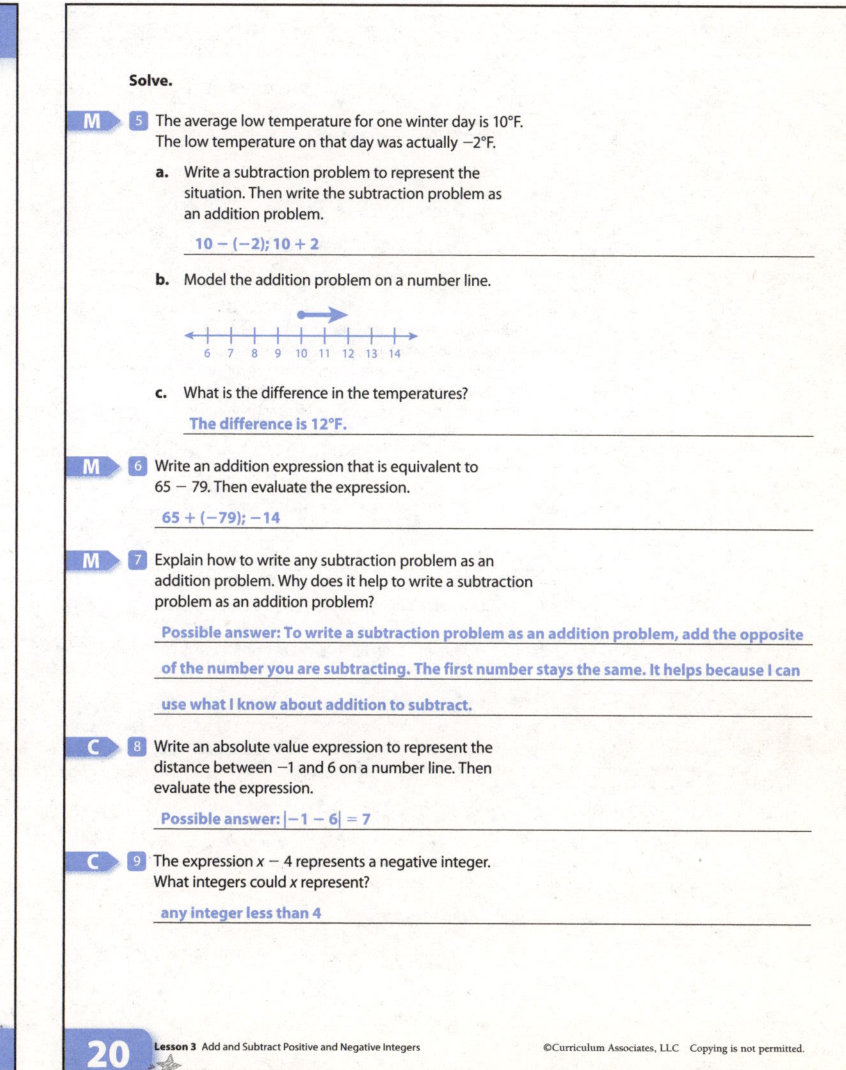

Solve.

M 5 The average low temperature for one winter day is 10°F. The low temperature on that day was actually −2°F.

a. Write a subtraction problem to represent the situation. Then write the subtraction problem as an addition problem.

10 − (−2); 10 + 2

b. Model the addition problem on a number line.

6 7 8 9 10 11 12 13 14

c. What is the difference in the temperatures?

The difference is 12°F.

M 6 Write an addition expression that is equivalent to 65 − 79. Then evaluate the expression.

65 + (−79); −14

M 7 Explain how to write any subtraction problem as an addition problem. Why does it help to write a subtraction problem as an addition problem?

Possible answer: To write a subtraction problem as an addition problem, add the opposite of the number you are subtracting. The first number stays the same. It helps because I can use what I know about addition to subtract.

C 8 Write an absolute value expression to represent the distance between −1 and 6 on a number line. Then evaluate the expression.

Possible answer: |−1 − 6| = 7

C 9 The expression $x - 4$ represents a negative integer. What integers could x represent?

any integer less than 4

Key

B Basic **M** Medium **C** Challenge

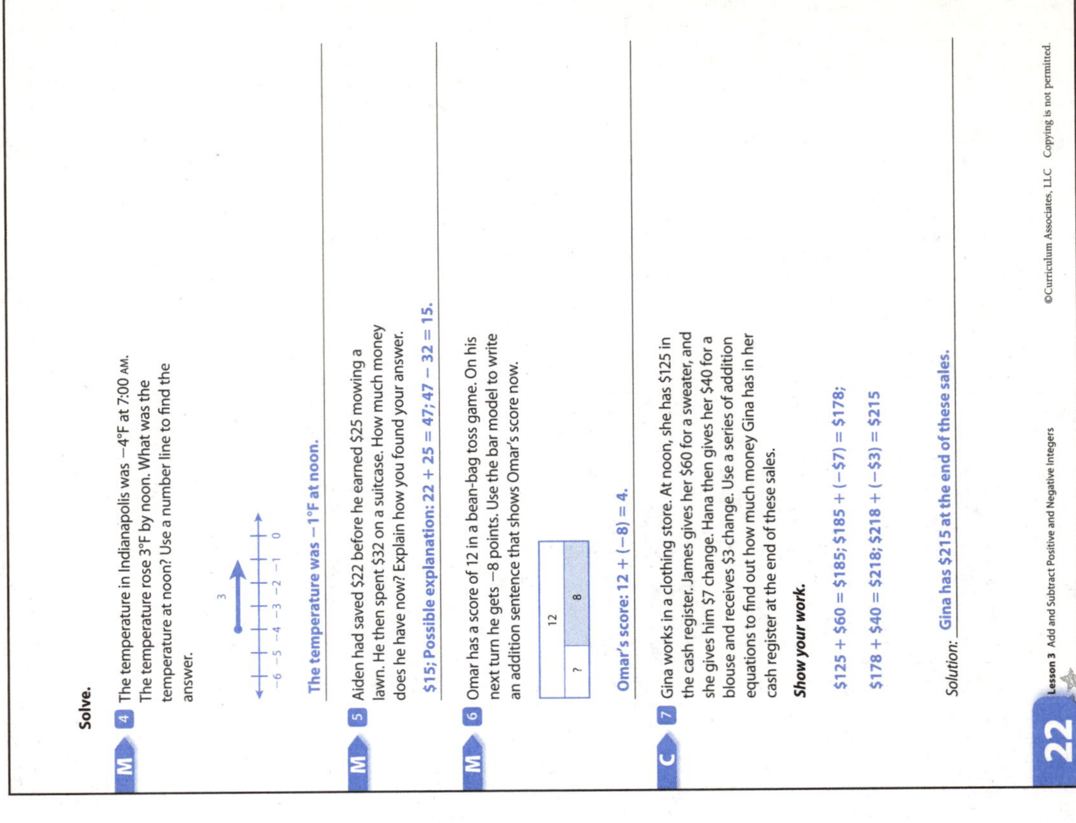

Solve.

M 4 The temperature in Indianapolis was −4°F at 7:00 AM. The temperature rose 3°F by noon. What was the temperature at noon? Use a number line to find the answer.

The temperature was −1°F at noon.

M 5 Aiden had saved $22 before he earned $25 mowing a lawn. He then spent $32 on a suitcase. How much money does he have now? Explain how you found your answer.

$15; Possible explanation: 22 + 25 = 47; 47 − 32 = 15.

M 6 Omar has a score of 12 in a bean-bag toss game. On his next turn he gets −8 points. Use the bar model to write an addition sentence that shows Omar's score now.

Omar's score: 12 + (−8) = 4.

C 7 Gina works in a clothing store. At noon, she has $125 in the cash register. James gives her $60 for a sweater, and she gives him $7 change. Hana then gives her $40 for a blouse and receives $3 change. Use a series of addition equations to find out how much money Gina has in her cash register at the end of these sales.

Show your work.

$125 + $60 = $185; $185 + (−$7) = $178;

$178 + $40 = $218; $218 + (−$3) = $215

Solution: **Gina has $215 at the end of these sales.**

22 Lesson 3 Add and Subtract Positive and Negative Integers ©Curriculum Associates, LLC Copying is not permitted.

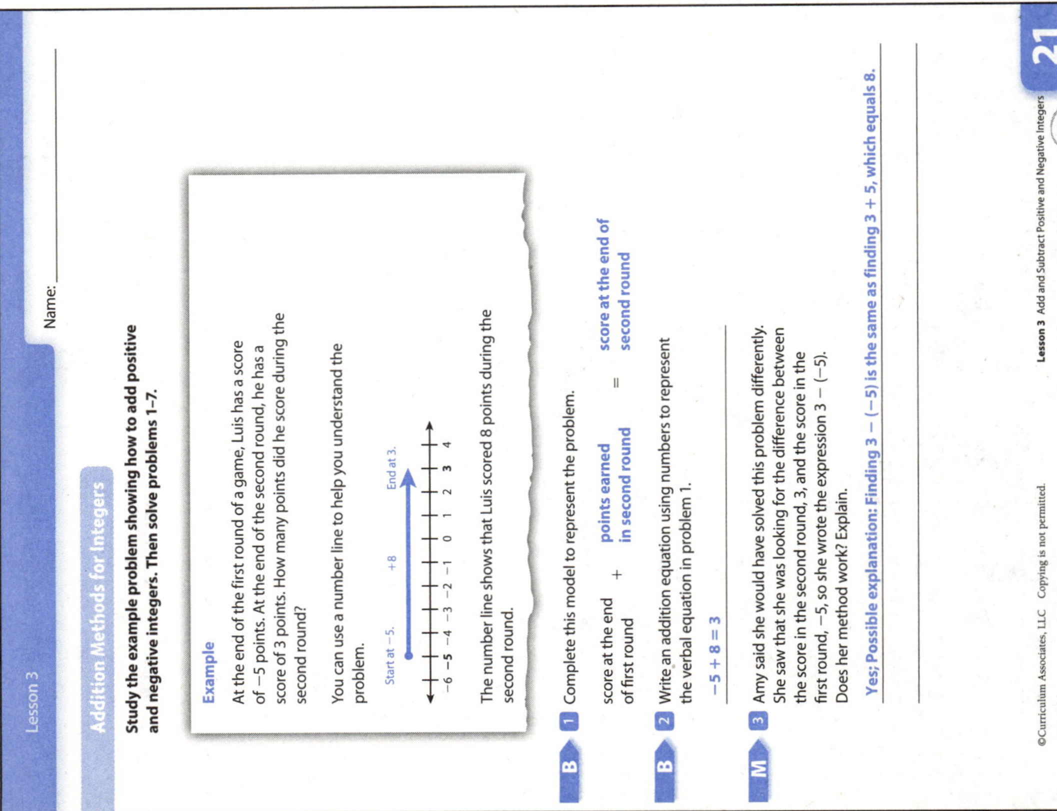

Lesson 3

Name: ____________

Addition Methods for Integers

Study the example problem showing how to add positive and negative integers. Then solve problems 1–7.

Example

At the end of the first round of a game, Luis has a score of −5 points. At the end of the second round, he has a score of 3 points. How many points did he score during the second round?

You can use a number line to help you understand the problem.

The number line shows that Luis scored 8 points during the second round.

B 1 Complete this model to represent the problem.

score at the end of first round + **points earned in second round** = **score at the end of second round**

B 2 Write an addition equation using numbers to represent the verbal equation in problem 1.

−5 + 8 = 3

M 3 Amy said she would have solved this problem differently. She saw that she was looking for the difference between the score in the second round, 3, and the score in the first round, −5, so she wrote the expression 3 − (−5). Does her method work? Explain.

Yes; Possible explanation: Finding 3 − (−5) is the same as finding 3 + 5, which equals 8.

©Curriculum Associates, LLC Copying is not permitted. Lesson 3 Add and Subtract Positive and Negative Integers 21

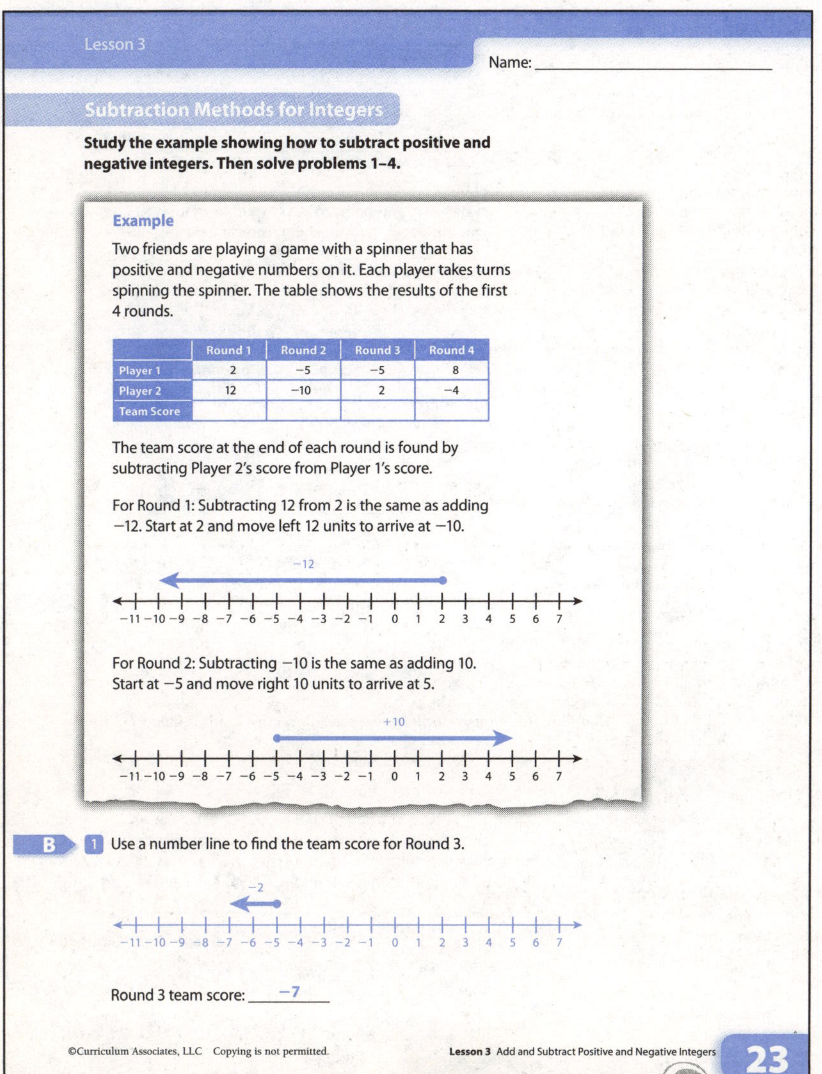

Lesson 3

Name: ____________

Subtraction Methods for Integers

Study the example showing how to subtract positive and negative integers. Then solve problems 1–4.

Example

Two friends are playing a game with a spinner that has positive and negative numbers on it. Each player takes turns spinning the spinner. The table shows the results of the first 4 rounds.

	Round 1	Round 2	Round 3	Round 4
Player 1	2	−5	−5	8
Player 2	12	−10	2	−4
Team Score				

The team score at the end of each round is found by subtracting Player 2's score from Player 1's score.

For Round 1: Subtracting 12 from 2 is the same as adding −12. Start at 2 and move left 12 units to arrive at −10.

For Round 2: Subtracting −10 is the same as adding 10. Start at −5 and move right 10 units to arrive at 5.

B 1 Use a number line to find the team score for Round 3.

Round 3 team score: −7

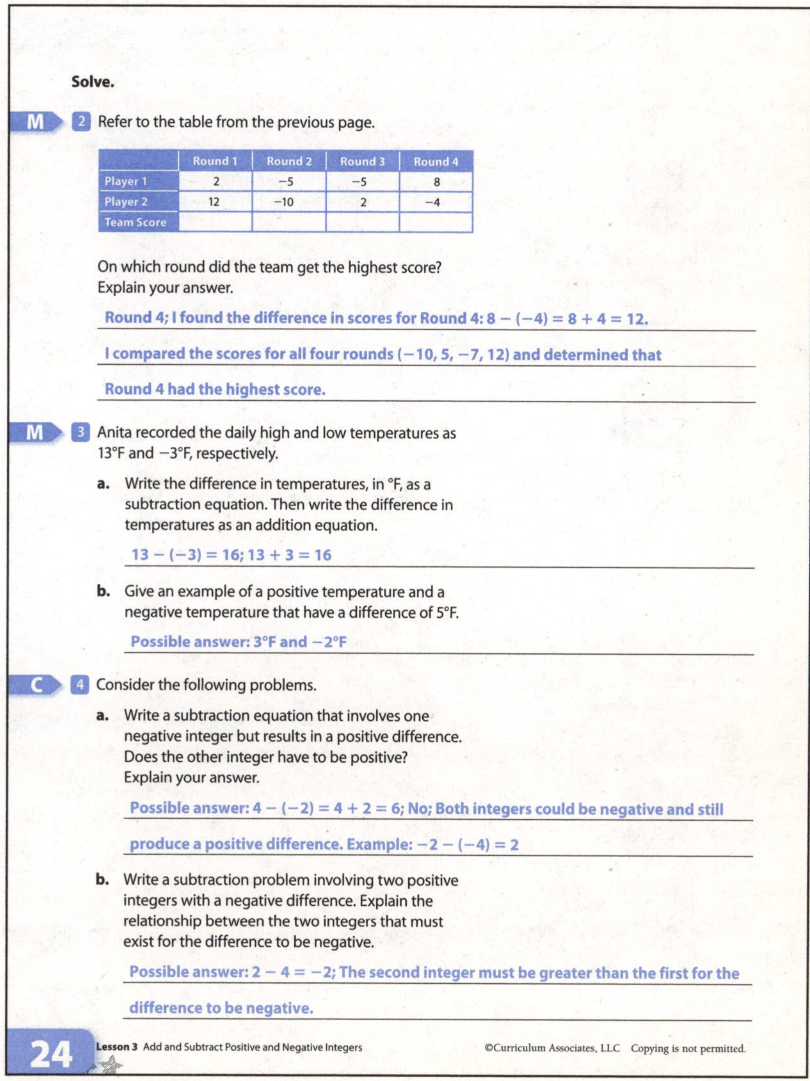

Solve.

M 2 Refer to the table from the previous page.

	Round 1	Round 2	Round 3	Round 4
Player 1	2	−5	−5	8
Player 2	12	−10	2	−4
Team Score				

On which round did the team get the highest score? Explain your answer.

Round 4; I found the difference in scores for Round 4: 8 − (−4) = 8 + 4 = 12. I compared the scores for all four rounds (−10, 5, −7, 12) and determined that Round 4 had the highest score.

M 3 Anita recorded the daily high and low temperatures as 13°F and −3°F, respectively.

a. Write the difference in temperatures, in °F, as a subtraction equation. Then write the difference in temperatures as an addition equation.

13 − (−3) = 16; 13 + 3 = 16

b. Give an example of a positive temperature and a negative temperature that have a difference of 5°F.

Possible answer: 3°F and −2°F

C 4 Consider the following problems.

a. Write a subtraction equation that involves one negative integer but results in a positive difference. Does the other integer have to be positive? Explain your answer.

Possible answer: 4 − (−2) = 4 + 2 = 6; No; Both integers could be negative and still produce a positive difference. Example: −2 − (−4) = 2

b. Write a subtraction problem involving two positive integers with a negative difference. Explain the relationship between the two integers that must exist for the difference to be negative.

Possible answer: 2 − 4 = −2; The second integer must be greater than the first for the difference to be negative.

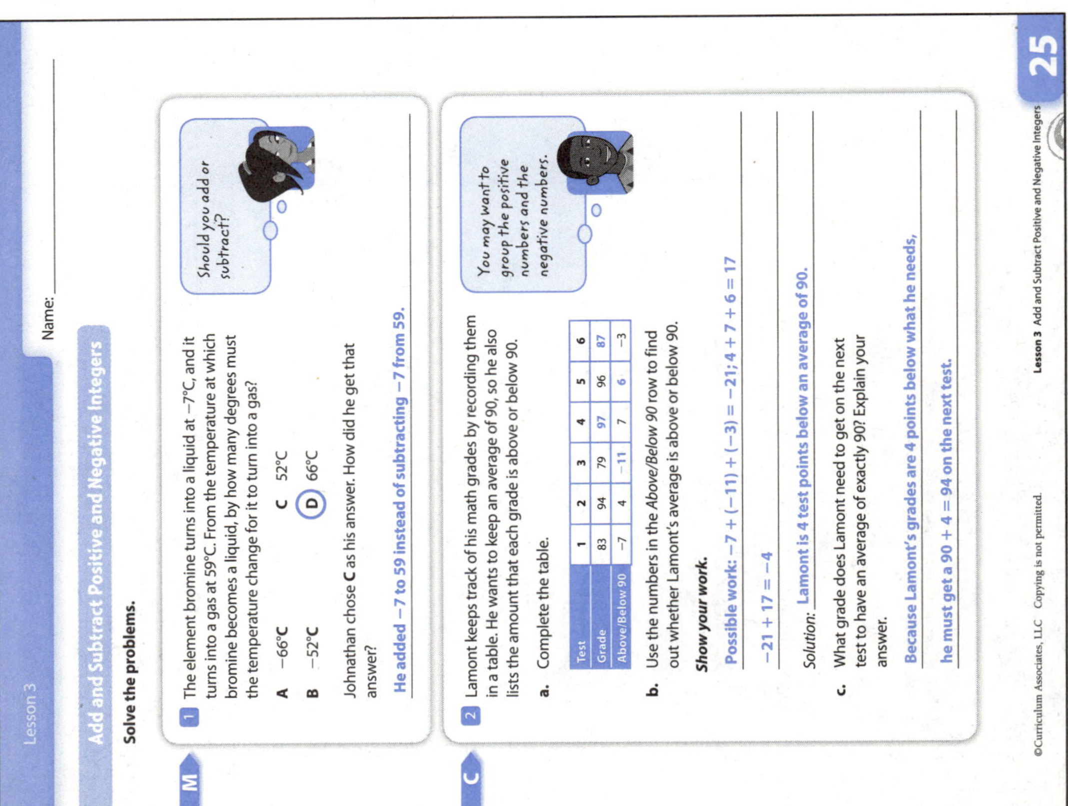

Lesson 3

Name: ____________________

Add and Subtract Positive and Negative Integers

Solve the problems.

M

1 The element bromine turns into a liquid at −7°C, and it turns into a gas at 59°C. From the temperature at which bromine becomes a liquid, by how many degrees must the temperature change for it to turn into a gas?

A −66°C

B −52°C

C 52°C

(D) 66°C

Johnathan chose **C** as his answer. How did he get that answer?

He added −7 to 59 instead of subtracting −7 from 59.

C

2 Lamont keeps track of his math grades by recording them in a table. He wants to keep an average of 90, so he also lists the amount that each grade is above or below 90.

a. Complete the table.

Test	1	2	3	4	5	6
Grade	83	94	79	97	96	87
Above/Below 90	−7	4	−11	7	6	−3

b. Use the numbers in the *Above/Below 90* row to find out whether Lamont's average is above or below 90.

Show your work.

Possible work: $-7 + (-11) + (-3) = -21$; $4 + 7 + 6 = 17$

$-21 + 17 = -4$

Solution: **Lamont is 4 test points below an average of 90.**

c. What grade does Lamont need to get on the next test to have an average of exactly 90? Explain your answer.

Because Lamont's grades are 4 points below what he needs, he must get a $90 + 4 = 94$ on the next test.

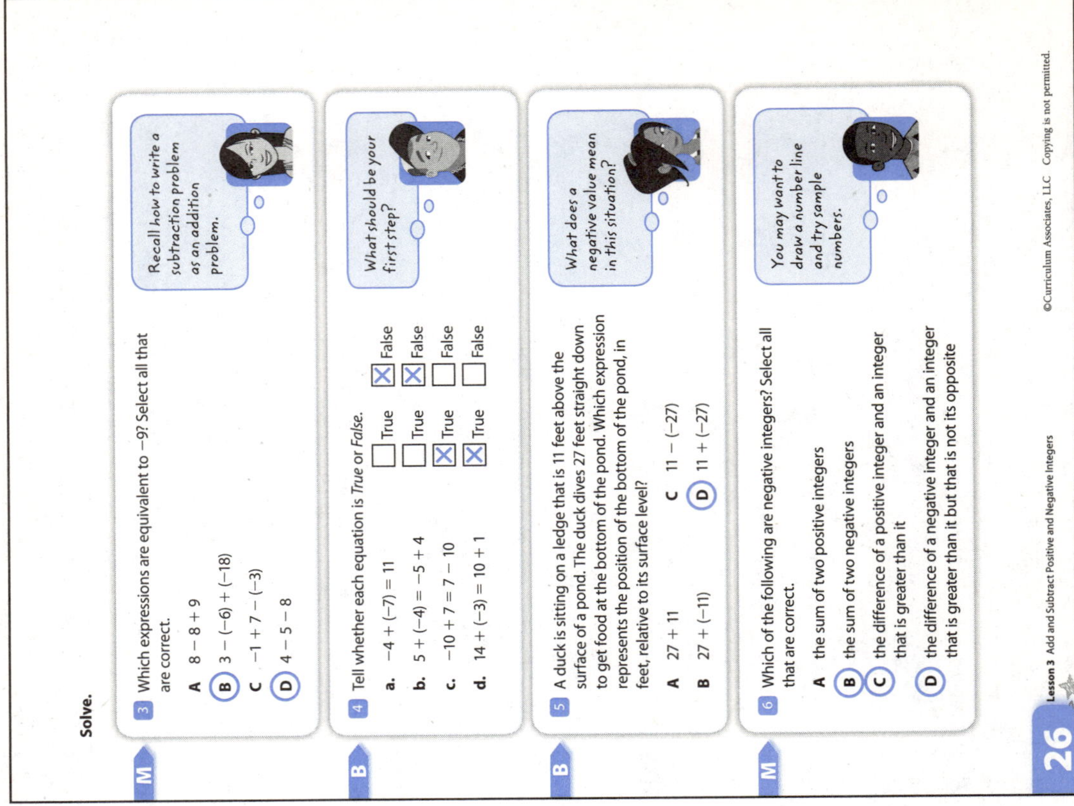

Solve.

M

3 Which expressions are equivalent to −9? Select all that are correct.

A 8 − 8 + 9

(B) 3 − (−6) + (−18)

C −1 + 7 − (−3)

(D) 4 − 5 − 8

B

4 Tell whether each equation is *True* or *False*.

	Equation	True	False
a.	−4 + (−7) = 11	☐	☒
b.	5 + (−4) = −5 + 4	☐	☒
c.	−10 + 7 = 7 − 10	☒	☐
d.	14 + (−3) = 10 + 1	☒	☐

B

5 A duck is sitting on a ledge that is 11 feet above the surface of a pond. The duck dives 27 feet straight down to get food at the bottom of the pond. Which expression represents the position of the bottom of the pond, in feet, relative to its surface level?

A 27 + 11

B 27 + (−11)

C 11 − (−27)

(D) 11 + (−27)

M

6 Which of the following are negative integers? Select all that are correct.

A the sum of two positive integers

(B) the sum of two negative integers

(C) the difference of a positive integer and an integer that is greater than it

(D) the difference of a negative integer and an integer that is greater than it but that is not its opposite

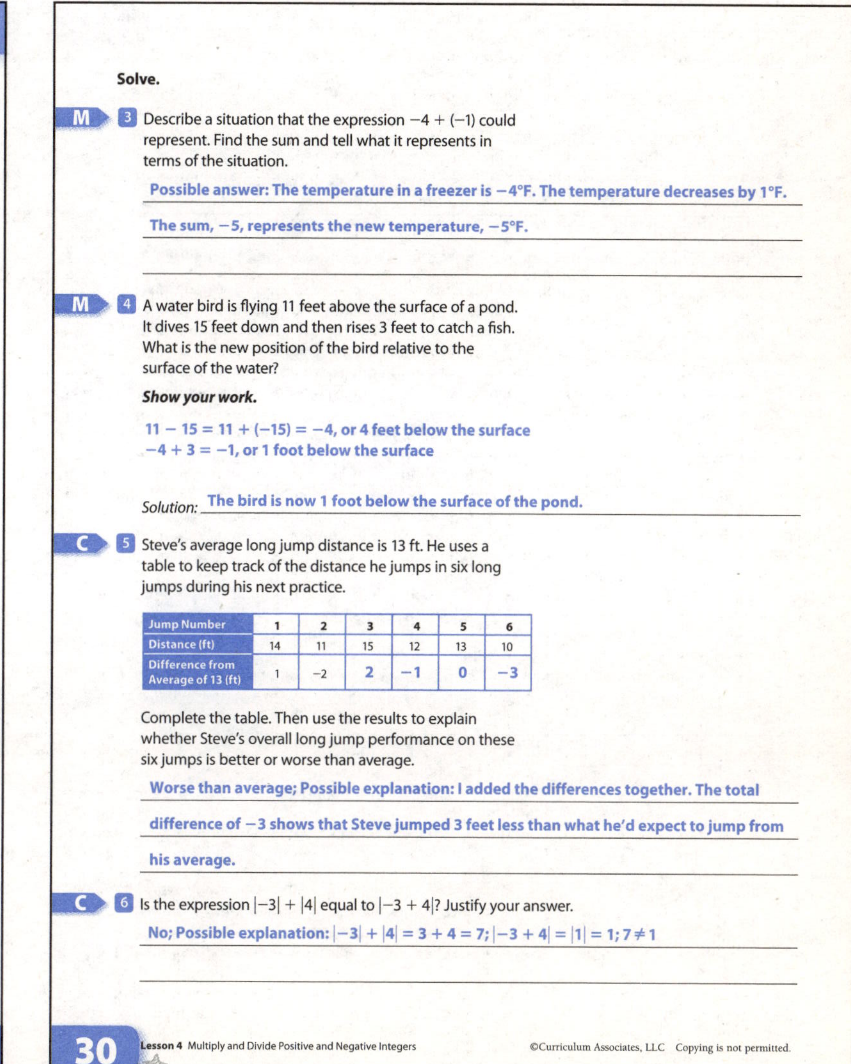

Lesson 4

Multiply and Divide Positive and Negative Integers

Name: ____________

Prerequisite: Add and Subtract Positive and Negative Integers

Study the example showing how to add and subtract positive and negative integers. Then solve problems 1–6.

Example

Geneva and Juan are playing a game that involves a spinner. The table shows how the player's score changes according to the color the spinner lands on.

Color	Red	Yellow	Blue	Green
Number of Points	+2	−4	+3	−1

Juan has 32 points. Then his spin lands on yellow. What is his score now?

Yellow means Juan's score changes by −4 points.

$32 - 4 = 32 + (-4) = 28$. Juan's score is 28 points.

B 1 Geneva has 24 points. Then her spin lands on blue. What is her score now? Explain.

27 points; Landing on blue means she gains 3 points, and $24 + 3 = 27$.

M 2 Geneva and Juan start a new game. Each player has 0 points.

a. Geneva's first two spins are yellow and red. What is her score now? Explain.

-2; $0 - 4 = -4$; $-4 + 2 = -2$

b. Juan's first two spins are red and green. What is his score now? Explain.

1; $0 + 2 = 2$; $2 + (-1) = 1$

c. Which player has a greater score now? Explain.

Juan; $1 > -2$, so Juan's score is greater.

©Curriculum Associates, LLC Copying is not permitted. **Lesson 4** Multiply and Divide Positive and Negative Integers 29

Solve.

M 3 Describe a situation that the expression $-4 + (-1)$ could represent. Find the sum and tell what it represents in terms of the situation.

Possible answer: The temperature in a freezer is −4°F. The temperature decreases by 1°F. The sum, −5, represents the new temperature, −5°F.

M 4 A water bird is flying 11 feet above the surface of a pond. It dives 15 feet down and then rises 3 feet to catch a fish. What is the new position of the bird relative to the surface of the water?

Show your work.

$11 - 15 = 11 + (-15) = -4$, or 4 feet below the surface
$-4 + 3 = -1$, or 1 foot below the surface

Solution: **The bird is now 1 foot below the surface of the pond.**

C 5 Steve's average long jump distance is 13 ft. He uses a table to keep track of the distance he jumps in six long jumps during his next practice.

Jump Number	1	2	3	4	5	6
Distance (ft)	14	11	15	12	13	10
Difference from Average of 13 (ft)	1	−2	**2**	**−1**	**0**	**−3**

Complete the table. Then use the results to explain whether Steve's overall long jump performance on these six jumps is better or worse than average.

Worse than average; Possible explanation: I added the differences together. The total difference of −3 shows that Steve jumped 3 feet less than what he'd expect to jump from his average.

C 6 Is the expression $|-3| + |4|$ equal to $|-3 + 4|$? Justify your answer.

No; Possible explanation: $|-3| + |4| = 3 + 4 = 7$; $|-3 + 4| = |1| = 1$; $7 \neq 1$

30 **Lesson 4** Multiply and Divide Positive and Negative Integers ©Curriculum Associates, LLC Copying is not permitted.

Key

B Basic **M** Medium **C** Challenge

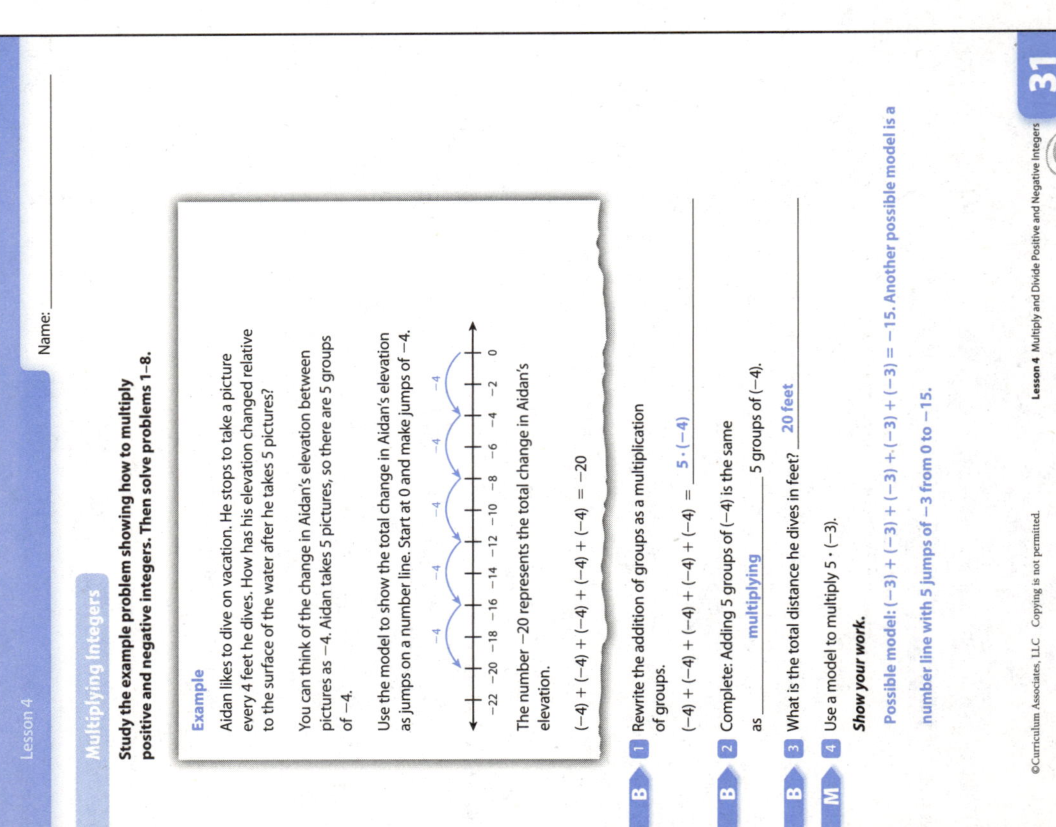

Lesson 4

Name: ______________________

Multiplying Integers

Study the example problem showing how to multiply positive and negative integers. Then solve problems 1–8.

Example

Aidan likes to dive on vacation. He stops to take a picture every 4 feet he dives. How has his elevation changed relative to the surface of the water after he takes 5 pictures?

You can think of the change in Aidan's elevation between pictures as −4. Aidan takes 5 pictures, so there are 5 groups of −4.

Use the model to show the total change in Aidan's elevation as jumps on a number line. Start at 0 and make jumps of −4.

The number −20 represents the total change in Aidan's elevation.

$(-4) + (-4) + (-4) + (-4) + (-4) = -20$

B **1** Rewrite the addition of groups as a multiplication of groups.

$(-4) + (-4) + (-4) + (-4) + (-4) =$ **5 · (−4)**

B **2** Complete: Adding 5 groups of (−4) is the same as **multiplying** 5 groups of (−4).

B **3** What is the total distance he dives in feet? **20 feet**

M **4** Use a model to multiply 5 · (−3).

Show your work.

Possible model: (−3) + (−3) + (−3) + (−3) + (−3) = −15. Another possible model is a number line with 5 jumps of −3 from 0 to −15.

©Curriculum Associates, LLC Copying is not permitted. **Lesson 4** Multiply and Divide Positive and Negative Integers **31**

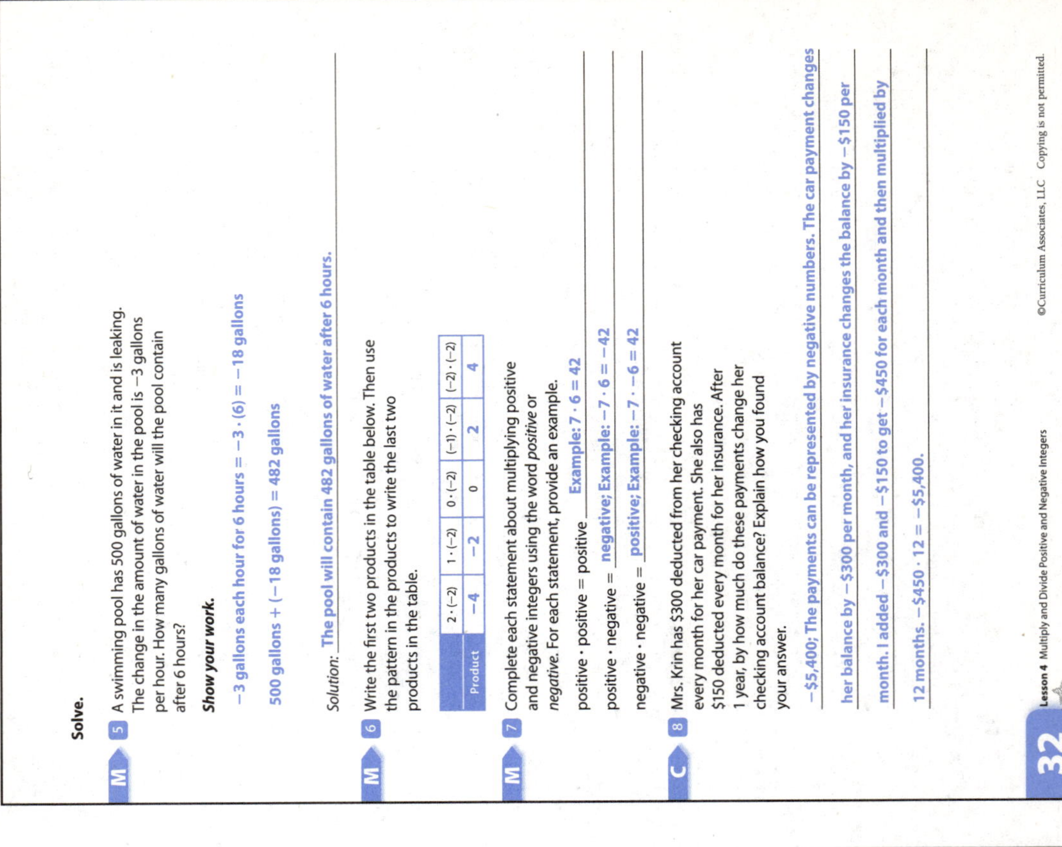

Solve.

M **5** A swimming pool has 500 gallons of water in it and is leaking. The change in the amount of water in the pool is −3 gallons per hour. How many gallons of water will the pool contain after 6 hours?

Show your work.

−3 gallons each hour for 6 hours = −3 · (6) = −18 gallons

500 gallons + (−18 gallons) = 482 gallons

Solution: **The pool will contain 482 gallons of water after 6 hours.**

M **6** Write the first two products in the table below. Then use the pattern in the products to write the last two products in the table.

	2 · (−2)	1 · (−2)	0 · (−2)	(−1) · (−2)	(−2) · (−2)
Product	−4	−2	0	2	4

M **7** Complete each statement about multiplying positive and negative integers using the word *positive* or *negative*. For each statement, provide an example.

positive · positive = positive **Example: 7 · 6 = 42**

positive · negative = **negative; Example: −7 · 6 = −42**

negative · negative = **positive; Example: −7 · −6 = 42**

C **8** Mrs. Krin has $300 deducted from her checking account every month for her car payment. She also has $150 deducted every month for her insurance. After 1 year, by how much do these payments change her checking account balance? Explain how you found your answer.

−$5,400; The payments can be represented by negative numbers. The car payment changes her balance by −$300 per month, and her insurance changes the balance by −$150 per month. I added −$300 and −$150 to get −$450 for each month and then multiplied by 12 months. −$450 · 12 = −$5,400.

32 **Lesson 4** Multiply and Divide Positive and Negative Integers ©Curriculum Associates, LLC Copying is not permitted.

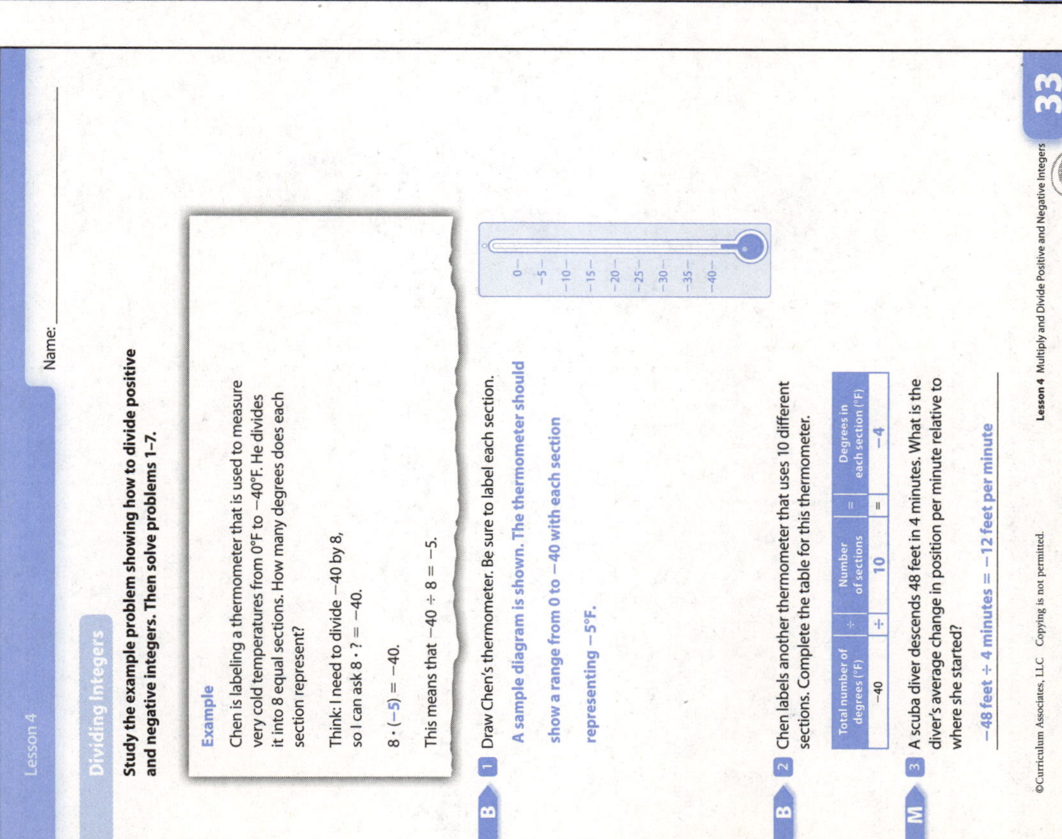
Lesson 4

Name: ______________________

Dividing Integers

Study the example problem showing how to divide positive and negative integers. Then solve problems 1–7.

Example

Chen is labeling a thermometer that is used to measure very cold temperatures from 0°F to −40°F. He divides it into 8 equal sections. How many degrees does each section represent?

Think: I need to divide −40 by 8, so I can ask 8 • ? = −40.

8 • (−5) = −40.

This means that −40 ÷ 8 = −5.

B 1 Draw Chen's thermometer. Be sure to label each section.

A sample diagram is shown. The thermometer should show a range from 0 to −40 with each section representing −5°F.

B 2 Chen labels another thermometer that uses 10 different sections. Complete the table for this thermometer.

Total number of degrees (°F)	÷	Number of sections	=	Degrees in each section (°F)
−40	÷	**10**	=	**−4**

M 3 A scuba diver descends 48 feet in 4 minutes. What is the diver's average change in position per minute relative to where she started?

−48 feet ÷ 4 minutes = −12 feet per minute

©Curriculum Associates, LLC Copying is not permitted. **Lesson 4** Multiply and Divide Positive and Negative Integers 33

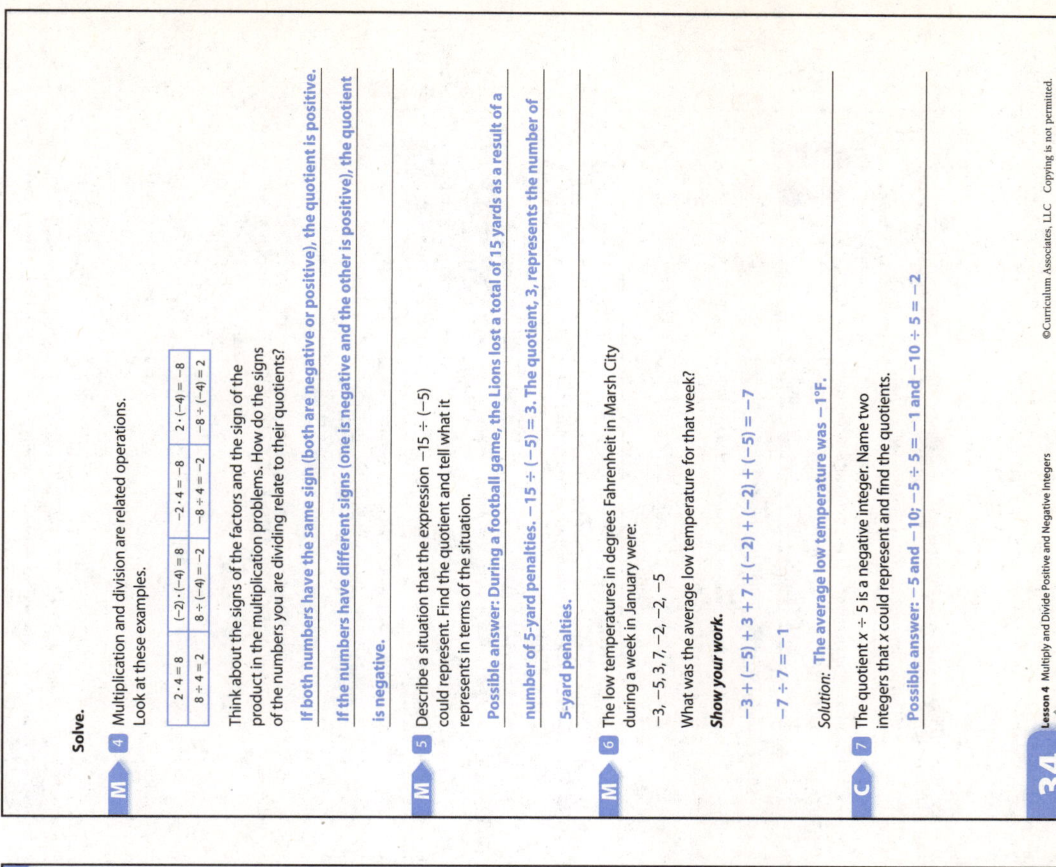
Solve.

M 4 Multiplication and division are related operations. Look at these examples.

2 • 4 = 8	(−2) • (−4) = 8	−2 • 4 = −8	2 • (−4) = −8
8 ÷ 4 = 2	8 ÷ (−4) = −2	−8 ÷ 4 = −2	−8 ÷ (−4) = 2

Think about the signs of the factors and the sign of the product in the multiplication problems. How do the signs of the numbers you are dividing relate to their quotients?

If both numbers have the same sign (both are negative or positive), the quotient is positive.

If the numbers have different signs (one is negative and the other is positive), the quotient is negative.

M 5 Describe a situation that the expression −15 ÷ (−5) could represent. Find the quotient and tell what it represents in terms of the situation.

Possible answer: During a football game, the Lions lost a total of 15 yards as a result of a number of 5-yard penalties. −15 ÷ (−5) = 3. The quotient, 3, represents the number of 5-yard penalties.

M 6 The low temperatures in degrees Fahrenheit in Marsh City during a week in January were:

−3, −5, 3, 7, −2, −2, −5

What was the average low temperature for that week?

Show your work.

−3 + (−5) + 3 + 7 + (−2) + (−2) + (−5) = −7

−7 ÷ 7 = −1

Solution: **The average low temperature was −1°F.**

C 7 The quotient $x \div 5$ is a negative integer. Name two integers that x could represent and find the quotients.

Possible answer: −5 and −10; −5 ÷ 5 = −1 and −10 ÷ 5 = −2

34 **Lesson 4** Multiply and Divide Positive and Negative Integers ©Curriculum Associates, LLC Copying is not permitted.

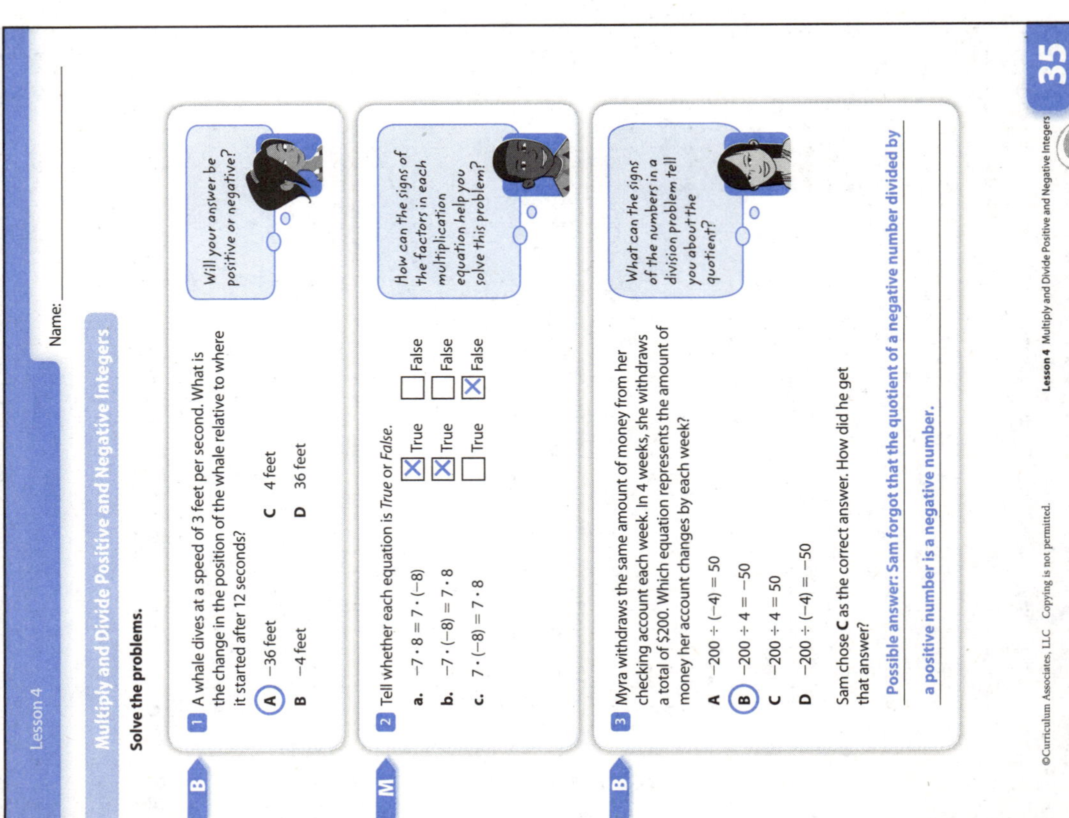

Lesson 4

Name: ______________________

Multiply and Divide Positive and Negative Integers

Solve the problems.

B

1 A whale dives at a speed of 3 feet per second. What is the change in the position of the whale relative to where it started after 12 seconds?

(A) −36 feet C 4 feet
B −4 feet D 36 feet

M

2 Tell whether each equation is *True* or *False*.

	Equation	True	False
a.	$-7 \cdot 8 = 7 \cdot (-8)$	☒ True	☐ False
b.	$-7 \cdot (-8) = 7 \cdot 8$	☒ True	☐ False
c.	$7 \cdot (-8) = 7 \cdot 8$	☐ True	☒ False

B

3 Myra withdraws the same amount of money from her checking account each week. In 4 weeks, she withdraws a total of \$200. Which equation represents the amount of money her account changes by each week?

A $-200 \div (-4) = 50$
(B) $-200 \div 4 = -50$
C $-200 \div 4 = 50$
D $-200 \div (-4) = -50$

Sam chose **C** as the correct answer. How did he get that answer?

Possible answer: Sam forgot that the quotient of a negative number divided by a positive number is a negative number.

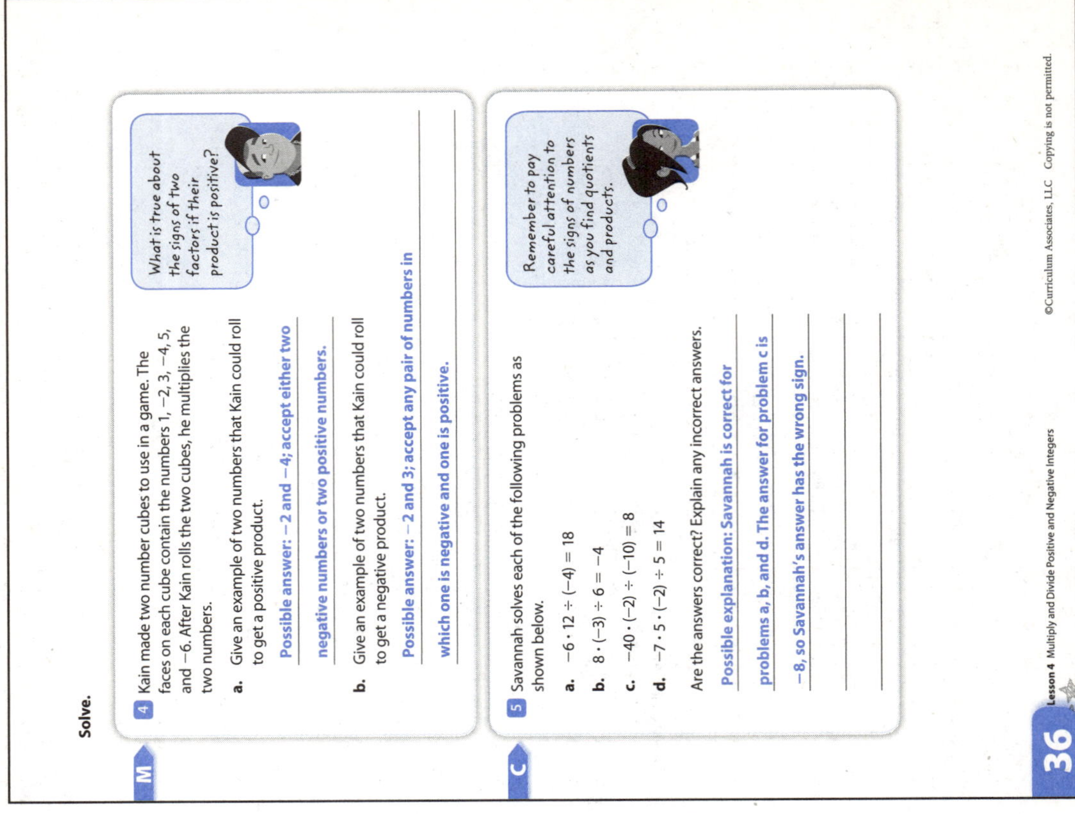

Solve.

M

4 Kain made two number cubes to use in a game. The faces on each cube contain the numbers 1, −2, 3, −4, 5, and −6. After Kain rolls the two cubes, he multiplies the two numbers.

a. Give an example of two numbers that Kain could roll to get a positive product.

Possible answer: −2 and −4; accept either two negative numbers or two positive numbers.

b. Give an example of two numbers that Kain could roll to get a negative product.

Possible answer: −2 and 3; accept any pair of numbers in which one is negative and one is positive.

C

5 Savannah solves each of the following problems as shown below.

a. $-6 \cdot 12 \div (-4) = 18$
b. $8 \cdot (-3) \div 6 = -4$
c. $-40 \cdot (-2) \div (-10) = 8$
d. $-7 \cdot 5 \cdot (-2) \div 5 = 14$

Are the answers correct? Explain any incorrect answers.

Possible explanation: Savannah is correct for problems a, b, and d. The answer for problem c is −8, so Savannah's answer has the wrong sign.

Lesson 5

Terminating and Repeating Decimals

Name: ____________________

Prerequisite: Understand Fractions as Division

Study the example showing fractions as division. Then solve problems 1–5.

Example

A teacher has 3 cups of brown rice to share equally among 4 students in cooking class. How much rice will each student get?

You can model this problem with a picture.

Look at one of the cups. One cup divided among 4 students is $\frac{1}{4}$ cup.

You can think of this as $1 \div 4 = \frac{1}{4}$.

$\frac{1}{4}$ cup $\frac{1}{4}$ cup $\frac{1}{4}$ cup

The teacher has 3 cups, so each student will receive $\frac{3}{4}$ cup of rice.

You can think of this as $\frac{1}{4} \times 3 = \frac{3}{4}$ or $3 \div 4 = \frac{3}{4}$.

B **1** The teacher has 5 cups of broth to share among the 4 students.

a. How much broth will each student get? Draw a model to explain your answer.

$\frac{5}{4}$ cups Possible model shown above.

b. Will each student get more than or less than 1 cup of broth? Explain.

more than 1 cup; Possible explanation: $\frac{5}{4}$ is more than $\frac{4}{4}$, which is 1 whole.

B **2** What if the teacher divides the 5 cups of broth among 6 students? Will each student get more than or less than 1 cup of broth? Explain.

less than 1 cup; Possible explanation: $5 \div 6 = \frac{5}{6}$, which is less than $\frac{6}{6}$, or 1.

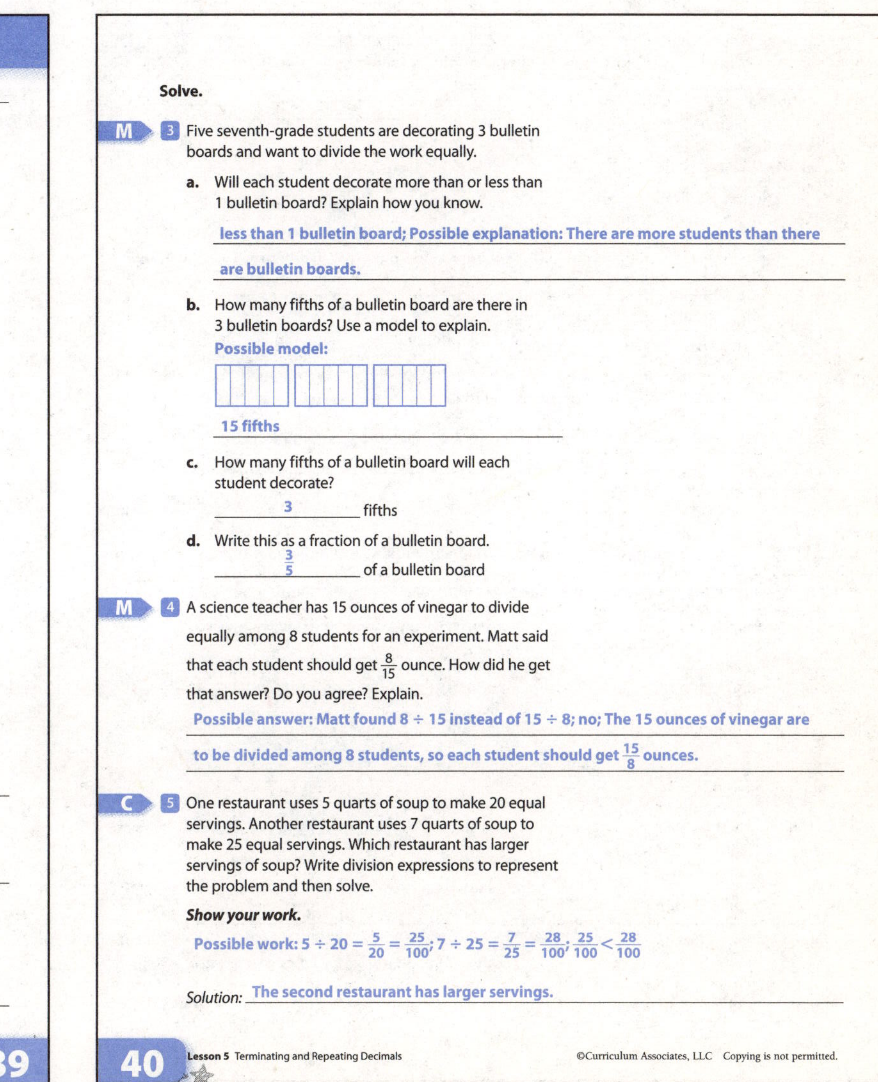

Solve.

M **3** Five seventh-grade students are decorating 3 bulletin boards and want to divide the work equally.

a. Will each student decorate more than or less than 1 bulletin board? Explain how you know.

less than 1 bulletin board; Possible explanation: There are more students than there are bulletin boards.

b. How many fifths of a bulletin board are there in 3 bulletin boards? Use a model to explain.

Possible model:

15 fifths

c. How many fifths of a bulletin board will each student decorate?

3 fifths

d. Write this as a fraction of a bulletin board.

$\frac{3}{5}$ of a bulletin board

M **4** A science teacher has 15 ounces of vinegar to divide equally among 8 students for an experiment. Matt said that each student should get $\frac{8}{15}$ ounce. How did he get that answer? Do you agree? Explain.

Possible answer: Matt found $8 \div 15$ instead of $15 \div 8$; no; The 15 ounces of vinegar are to be divided among 8 students, so each student should get $\frac{15}{8}$ ounces.

C **5** One restaurant uses 5 quarts of soup to make 20 equal servings. Another restaurant uses 7 quarts of soup to make 25 equal servings. Which restaurant has larger servings of soup? Write division expressions to represent the problem and then solve.

Show your work.

Possible work: $5 \div 20 = \frac{5}{20} = \frac{25}{100}$; $7 \div 25 = \frac{7}{25} = \frac{28}{100}$; $\frac{25}{100} < \frac{28}{100}$

Solution: The second restaurant has larger servings.

Key

B Basic **M** Medium **C** Challenge

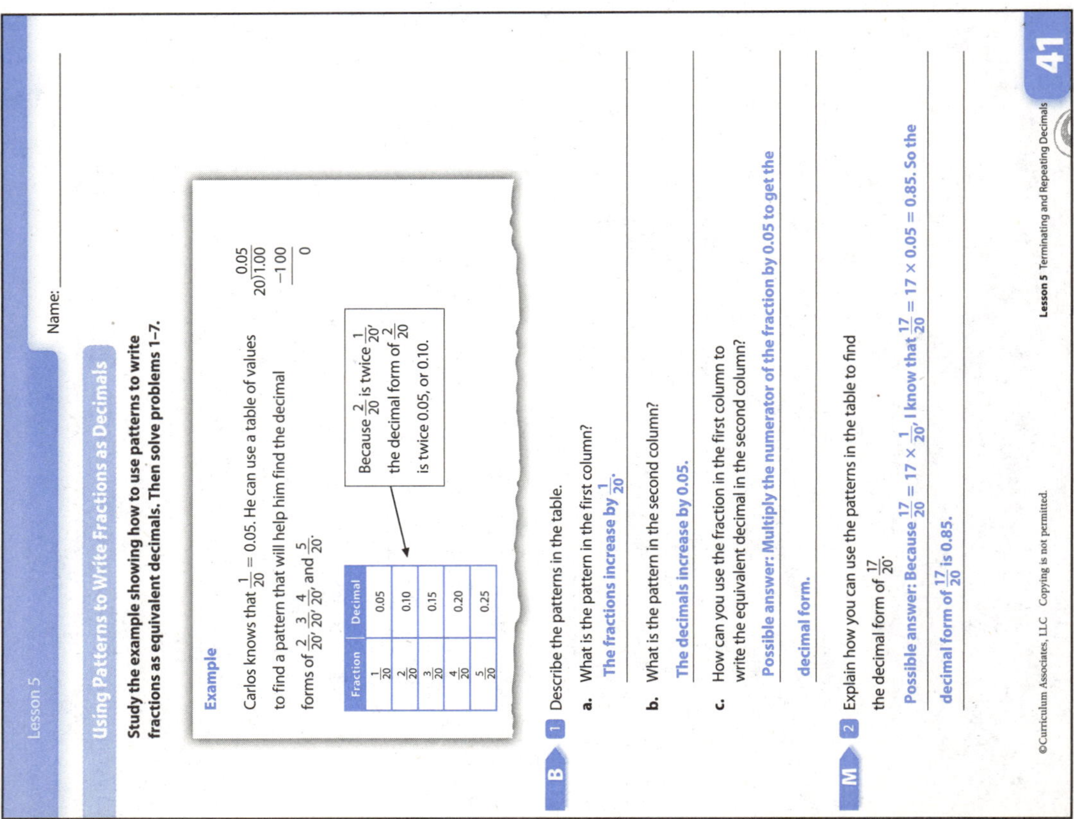

Lesson 5

Name: ____________________

Using Patterns to Write Fractions as Decimals

Study the example showing how to use patterns to write fractions as equivalent decimals. Then solve problems 1–7.

Example

Carlos knows that $\frac{1}{20} = 0.05$. He can use a table of values to find a pattern that will help him find the decimal forms of $\frac{2}{20}$, $\frac{3}{20}$, $\frac{4}{20}$, and $\frac{5}{20}$.

$$\begin{array}{r} 0.05 \\ 20\overline{)1.00} \\ -1\,00 \\ \hline 0 \end{array}$$

Fraction	Decimal
$\frac{1}{20}$	0.05
$\frac{2}{20}$	0.10
$\frac{3}{20}$	0.15
$\frac{4}{20}$	0.20
$\frac{5}{20}$	0.25

Because $\frac{2}{20}$ is twice $\frac{1}{20}$, the decimal form of $\frac{2}{20}$ is twice 0.05, or 0.10.

B 1 Describe the patterns in the table.

a. What is the pattern in the first column?

The fractions increase by $\frac{1}{20}$.

b. What is the pattern in the second column?

The decimals increase by 0.05.

c. How can you use the fraction in the first column to write the equivalent decimal in the second column?

Possible answer: Multiply the numerator of the fraction by 0.05 to get the decimal form.

M 2 Explain how you can use the patterns in the table to find the decimal form of $\frac{17}{20}$.

Possible answer: Because $\frac{17}{20} = 17 \times \frac{1}{20}$, I know that $\frac{17}{20} = 17 \times 0.05 = 0.85$. So the decimal form of $\frac{17}{20}$ is 0.85.

©Curriculum Associates, LLC Copying is not permitted. **Lesson 5** Terminating and Repeating Decimals **41**

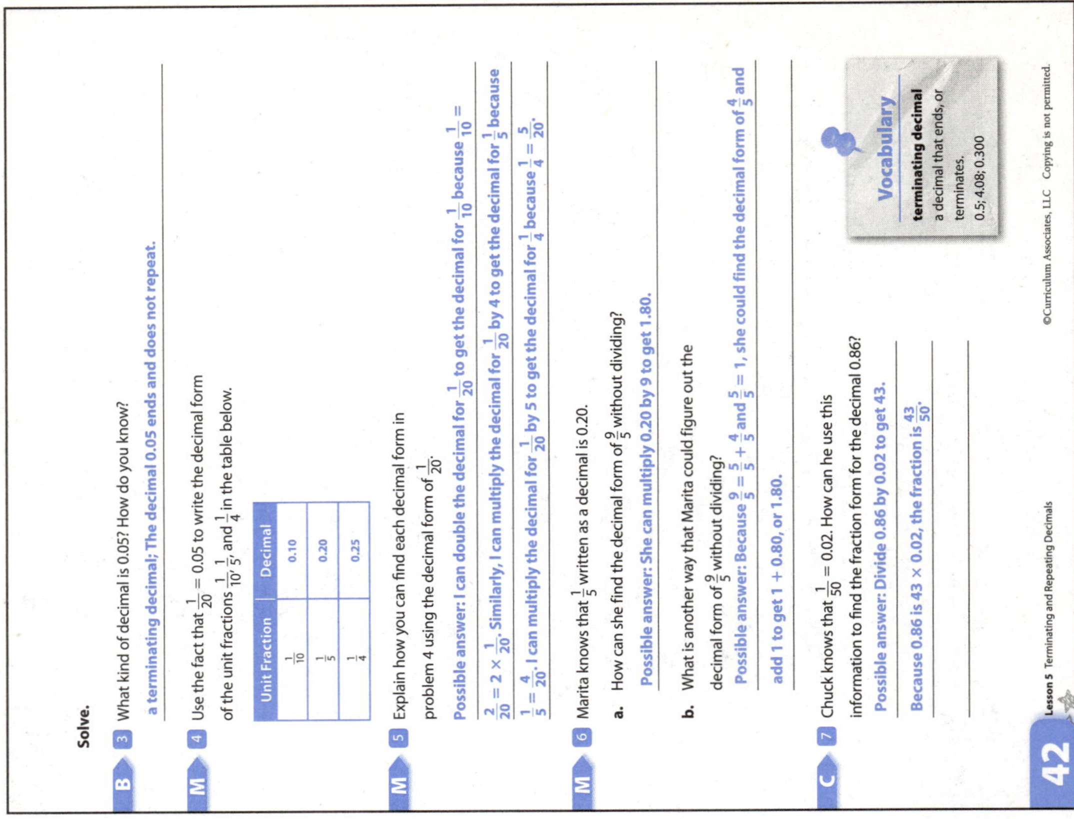

Solve.

B 3 What kind of decimal is 0.05? How do you know?

a terminating decimal; The decimal 0.05 ends and does not repeat.

M 4 Use the fact that $\frac{1}{20} = 0.05$ to write the decimal form of the unit fractions $\frac{1}{10}$, $\frac{1}{5}$, and $\frac{1}{4}$ in the table below.

Unit Fraction	Decimal
$\frac{1}{10}$	**0.10**
$\frac{1}{5}$	**0.20**
$\frac{1}{4}$	**0.25**

M 5 Explain how you can find each decimal form in problem 4 using the decimal form of $\frac{1}{20}$.

Possible answer: I can double the decimal for $\frac{1}{20}$ to get the decimal for $\frac{1}{10}$ because $\frac{1}{10} = \frac{2}{20} = 2 \times \frac{1}{20}$. Similarly, I can multiply the decimal for $\frac{1}{20}$ by 4 to get the decimal for $\frac{1}{5}$ because $\frac{1}{5} = \frac{4}{20}$. I can multiply the decimal for $\frac{1}{20}$ by 5 to get the decimal for $\frac{1}{4}$ because $\frac{1}{4} = \frac{5}{20}$.

M 6 Marita knows that $\frac{1}{5}$ written as a decimal is 0.20.

a. How can she find the decimal form of $\frac{9}{5}$ without dividing?

Possible answer: She can multiply 0.20 by 9 to get 1.80.

b. What is another way that Marita could figure out the decimal form of $\frac{9}{5}$ without dividing?

Possible answer: Because $\frac{9}{5} = \frac{5}{5} + \frac{4}{5}$ and $\frac{5}{5} = 1$, she could find the decimal form of $\frac{4}{5}$ and add 1 to get $1 + 0.80$, or 1.80.

C 7 Chuck knows that $\frac{1}{50} = 0.02$. How can he use this information to find the fraction form for the decimal 0.86?

Possible answer: Divide 0.86 by 0.02 to get 43. Because 0.86 is 43×0.02, the fraction is $\frac{43}{50}$.

Vocabulary

terminating decimal a decimal that ends, or terminates.
0.5; 4.08; 0.300

42 **Lesson 5** Terminating and Repeating Decimals ©Curriculum Associates, LLC Copying is not permitted.

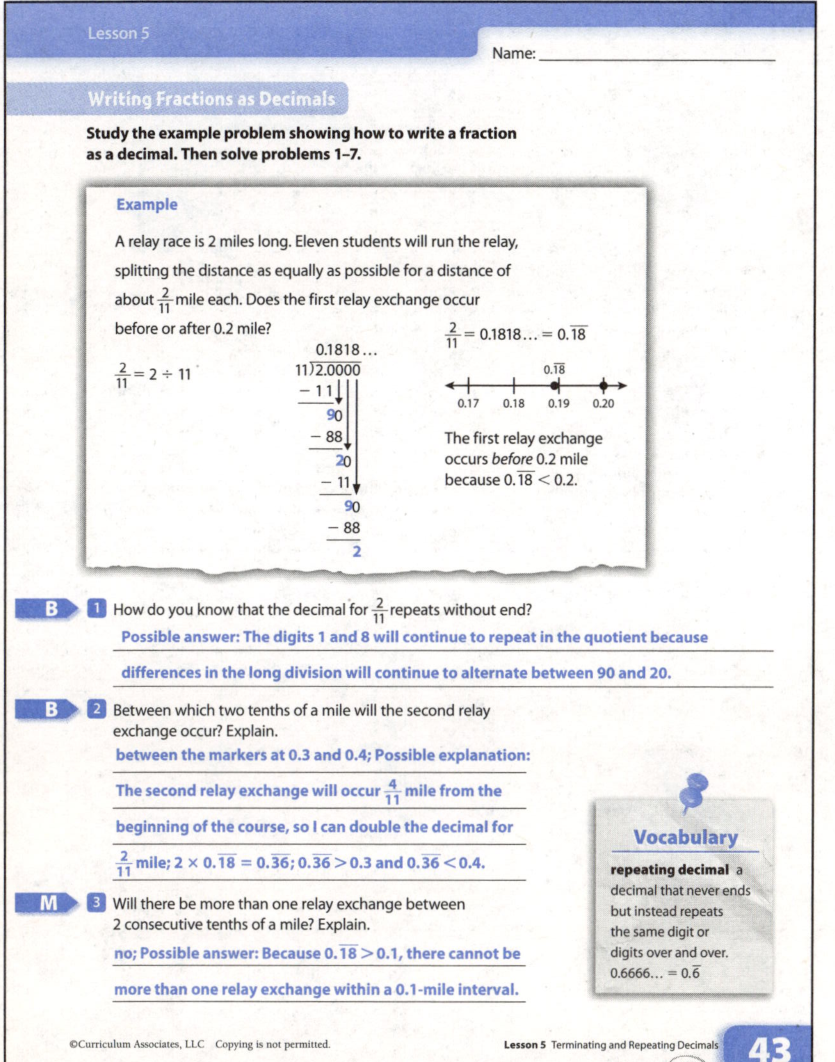

Name: ____________

Writing Fractions as Decimals

Study the example problem showing how to write a fraction as a decimal. Then solve problems 1–7.

Example

A relay race is 2 miles long. Eleven students will run the relay, splitting the distance as equally as possible for a distance of about $\frac{2}{11}$ mile each. Does the first relay exchange occur before or after 0.2 mile?

$\frac{2}{11} = 2 \div 11$

$$\begin{array}{r} 0.1818\ldots \\ 11\overline{)2.0000} \\ -11 \\ \hline 90 \\ -88 \\ \hline 20 \\ -11 \\ \hline 90 \\ -88 \\ \hline 2 \end{array}$$

$\frac{2}{11} = 0.1818\ldots = 0.\overline{18}$

The first relay exchange occurs *before* 0.2 mile because $0.\overline{18} < 0.2$.

B **1** How do you know that the decimal for $\frac{2}{11}$ repeats without end?

Possible answer: The digits 1 and 8 will continue to repeat in the quotient because differences in the long division will continue to alternate between 90 and 20.

B **2** Between which two tenths of a mile will the second relay exchange occur? Explain.

between the markers at 0.3 and 0.4; Possible explanation: The second relay exchange will occur $\frac{4}{11}$ mile from the beginning of the course, so I can double the decimal for $\frac{2}{11}$ mile; $2 \times 0.\overline{18} = 0.\overline{36}$; $0.\overline{36} > 0.3$ and $0.\overline{36} < 0.4$.

M **3** Will there be more than one relay exchange between 2 consecutive tenths of a mile? Explain.

no; Possible answer: Because $0.\overline{18} > 0.1$, there cannot be more than one relay exchange within a 0.1-mile interval.

Vocabulary

repeating decimal a decimal that never ends but instead repeats the same digit or digits over and over.
$0.6666\ldots = 0.\overline{6}$

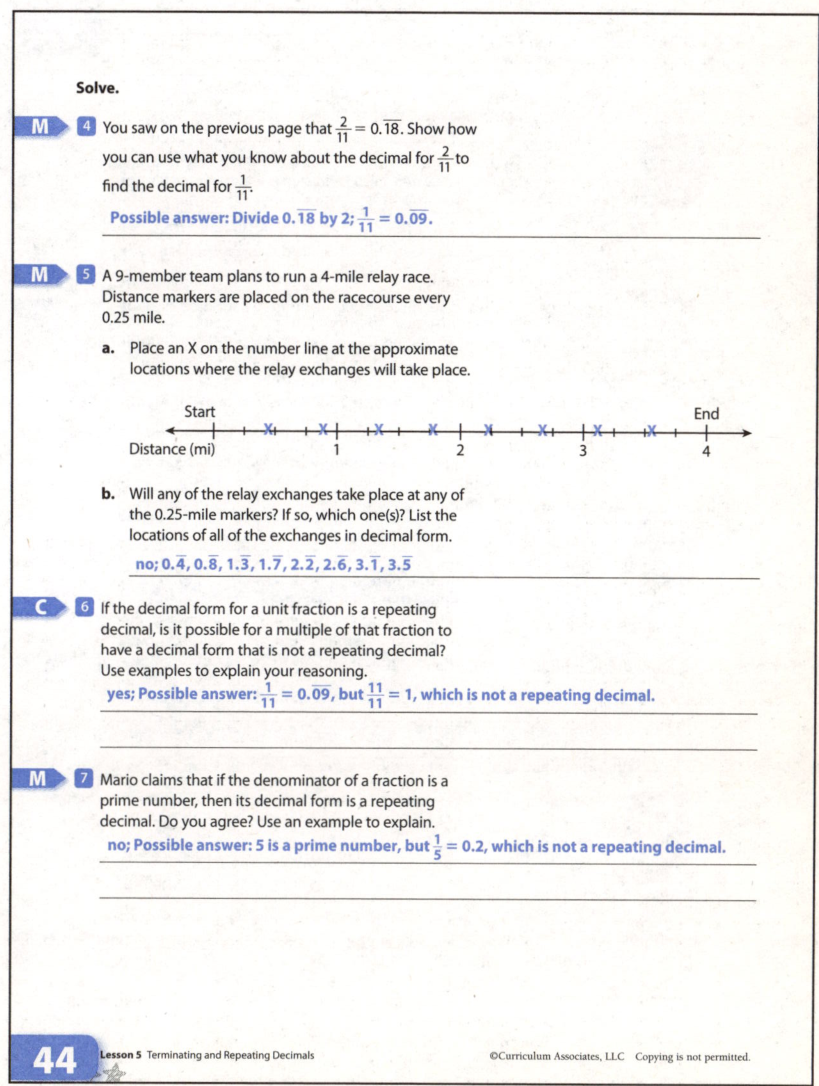

Solve.

M **4** You saw on the previous page that $\frac{2}{11} = 0.\overline{18}$. Show how you can use what you know about the decimal for $\frac{2}{11}$ to find the decimal for $\frac{1}{11}$.

Possible answer: Divide $0.\overline{18}$ by 2; $\frac{1}{11} = 0.\overline{09}$.

M **5** A 9-member team plans to run a 4-mile relay race. Distance markers are placed on the racecourse every 0.25 mile.

a. Place an X on the number line at the approximate locations where the relay exchanges will take place.

b. Will any of the relay exchanges take place at any of the 0.25-mile markers? If so, which one(s)? List the locations of all of the exchanges in decimal form.

no; $0.\overline{4}$, $0.\overline{8}$, $1.\overline{3}$, $1.\overline{7}$, $2.\overline{2}$, $2.\overline{6}$, $3.\overline{1}$, $3.\overline{5}$

C **6** If the decimal form for a unit fraction is a repeating decimal, is it possible for a multiple of that fraction to have a decimal form that is not a repeating decimal? Use examples to explain your reasoning.

yes; Possible answer: $\frac{1}{11} = 0.\overline{09}$, but $\frac{11}{11} = 1$, which is not a repeating decimal.

M **7** Mario claims that if the denominator of a fraction is a prime number, then its decimal form is a repeating decimal. Do you agree? Use an example to explain.

no; Possible answer: 5 is a prime number, but $\frac{1}{5} = 0.2$, which is not a repeating decimal.

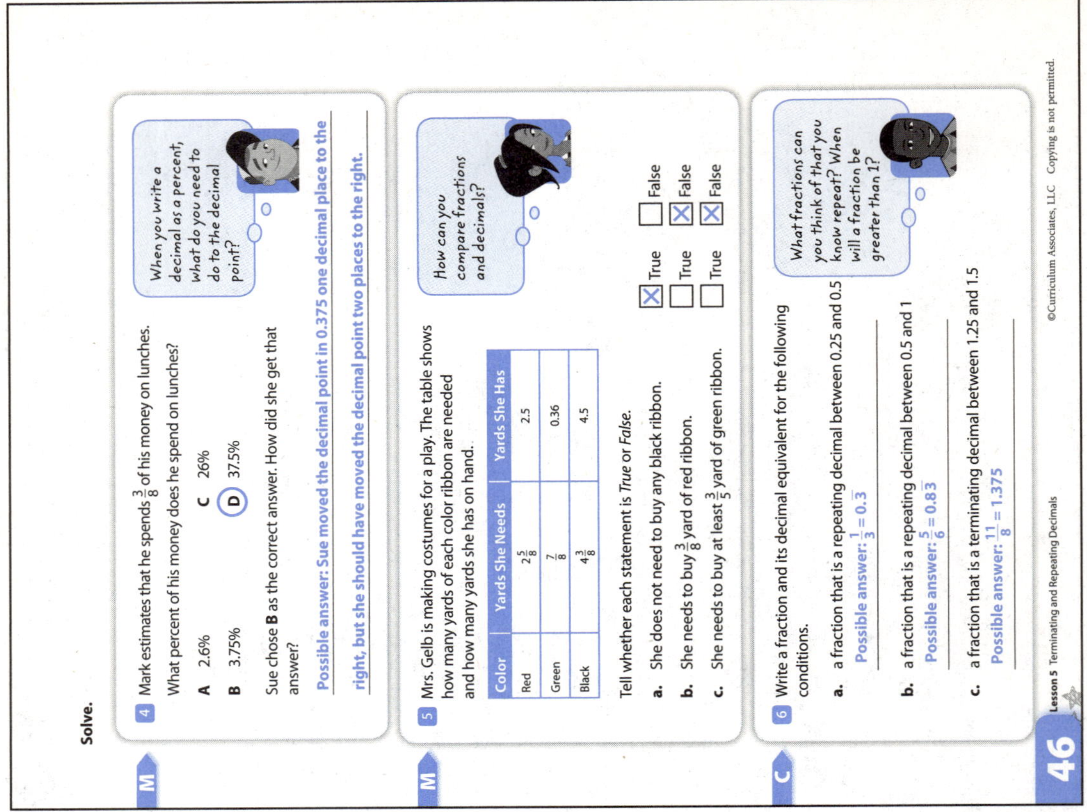
Solve.

M 4 Mark estimates that he spends $\frac{3}{8}$ of his money on lunches. What percent of his money does he spend on lunches?

A 2.6%
B 3.75%
C 26%
(D) 37.5%

Sue chose **B** as the correct answer. How did she get that answer?

Possible answer: Sue moved the decimal point in 0.375 one decimal place to the right, but she should have moved the decimal point two places to the right.

M 5 Mrs. Gelb is making costumes for a play. The table shows how many yards of each color ribbon are needed and how many yards she has on hand.

Color	Yards She Needs	Yards She Has
Red	$2\frac{5}{8}$	2.5
Green	$\frac{7}{8}$	0.36
Black	$4\frac{3}{8}$	4.5

Tell whether each statement is *True* or *False*.

a. She does not need to buy any black ribbon. [X] True [ ] False
b. She needs to buy $\frac{3}{8}$ yard of red ribbon. [ ] True [X] False
c. She needs to buy at least $\frac{3}{5}$ yard of green ribbon. [ ] True [X] False

C 6 Write a fraction and its decimal equivalent for the following conditions.

a. a fraction that is a repeating decimal between 0.25 and 0.5
Possible answer: $\frac{1}{3} = 0.\overline{3}$

b. a fraction that is a repeating decimal between 0.5 and 1
Possible answer: $\frac{5}{6} = 0.8\overline{3}$

c. a fraction that is a terminating decimal between 1.25 and 1.5
Possible answer: $\frac{11}{8} = 1.375$

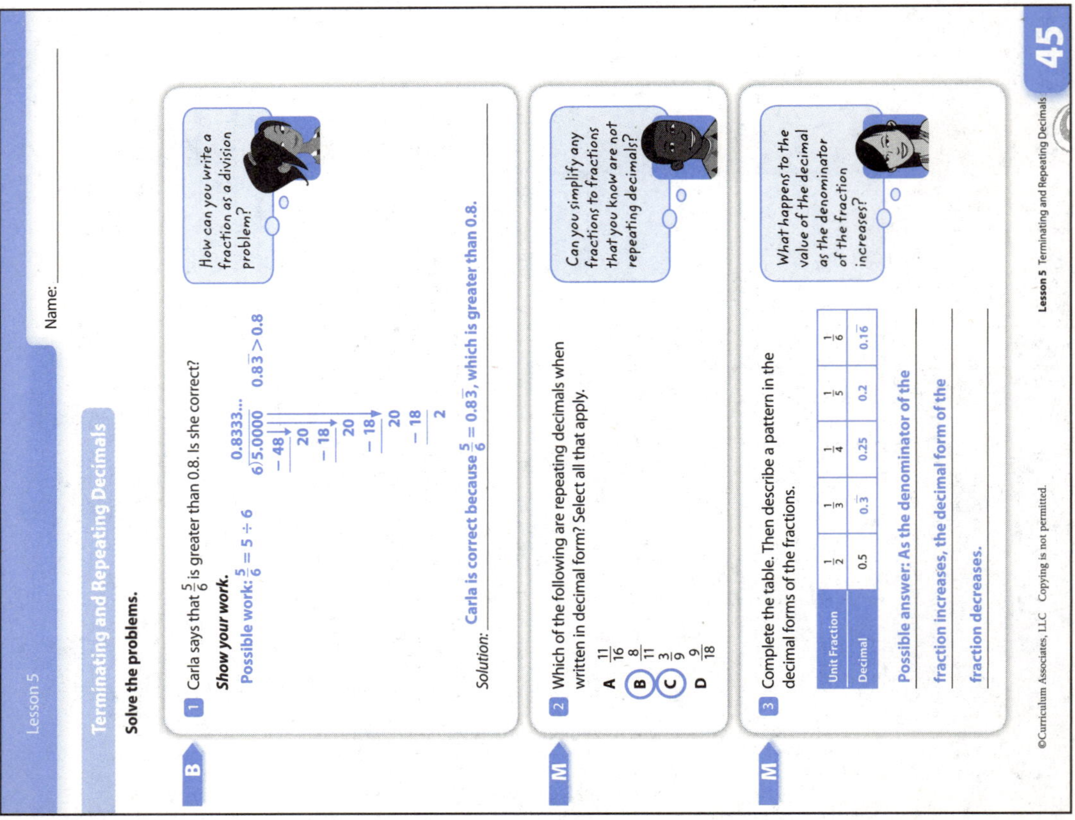
Lesson 5

Name: ____________

Terminating and Repeating Decimals

Solve the problems.

B 1 Carla says that $\frac{5}{6}$ is greater than 0.8. Is she correct?

Show your work.

Possible work: $\frac{5}{6} = 5 \div 6$

$$\begin{array}{r} 0.8333\ldots \\ 6\overline{)5.0000} \\ -48 \\ \hline 20 \\ -18 \\ \hline 20 \\ -18 \\ \hline 20 \\ -18 \\ \hline 2 \end{array}$$

$0.8\overline{3} > 0.8$

Solution: **Carla is correct because $\frac{5}{6} = 0.8\overline{3}$, which is greater than 0.8.**

M 2 Which of the following are repeating decimals when written in decimal form? Select all that apply.

A $\frac{11}{16}$
(B) $\frac{8}{11}$
(C) $\frac{3}{9}$
D $\frac{9}{18}$

M 3 Complete the table. Then describe a pattern in the decimal forms of the fractions.

Unit Fraction	$\frac{1}{2}$	$\frac{1}{3}$	$\frac{1}{4}$	$\frac{1}{5}$	$\frac{1}{6}$
Decimal	0.5	$0.\overline{3}$	0.25	0.2	$0.1\overline{6}$

Possible answer: As the denominator of the fraction increases, the decimal form of the fraction decreases.

Lesson 6

Multiply and Divide Rational Numbers

Name: ____________________

Prerequisite: Multiply Positive and Negative Integers

Study the example problem showing how to use repeated addition to multiply a positive and a negative integer. Then solve problems 1–6.

Example

Dues for the art club are \$2 per week. Noriko pays \$2 each week from her bank account for her art club dues. At the end of 5 weeks, what is the change in the amount of money in Noriko's account?

You can think of this as 5 groups of (–2).

5 groups of (–2) = (–2) + (–2) + (–2) + (–2) + (–2).

You can start at 0 and make 5 jumps of –2.

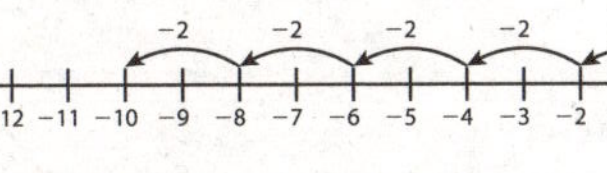

(–2) + (–2) + (–2) + (–2) + (–2) = –10

So, Noriko's account changes by –\$10.

B 1 Complete the table and describe the pattern in the products.

The products increase by 2.

Multiplication	Product
–2 · 3	–6
–2 · 2	–4
–2 · 1	–2
–2 · 0	0
–2 · (–1)	2
–2 · (–2)	4
–2 · (–3)	6

(+2, +2)

B 2 Rewrite the repeated addition expression as a multiplication expression and find the product.

a. (–2) + (–2) + (–2) + (–2) + (–2) = <u>5</u> · (–2) = <u>–10</u>

b. (–3) + (–3) + (–3) + (–3) + (–3) + (–3) = <u>6 · (–3) = –18</u>

c. (–5) + (–5) + (–5) = <u>3 · (–5) = –15</u>

Solve.

M 3 Write and simplify a multiplication expression for each problem. Explain what the product means.

a. The temperature dropped 8 degrees every hour. What was the change in temperature after 4 hours?

4 × (–8) = –32; the temperature is 32 degrees colder.

b. Mae loses 3 points for each wrong answer on a test. How does her score change if she has 7 wrong answers?

7 × (–3) = –21; her test score drops by 21 points.

M 4 Carlo is playing a game with the cards shown. He draws cards at random and multiplies the numbers.

–2	0	–3	–4	8

a. Give an example of two cards Carlo could draw that have a positive product. Find the product.

Possible answer: –2 × (–3) = 6

b. Give an example of two cards Carlo could draw that have a negative product. Find the product.

Possible answer: –2 × 8 = –16

M 5 Each month Marla pays a \$30 cell phone bill from her back account. At the end of one year, what is the change in the amount of money in Marla's account because of her cell phone bill? Write a multiplication equation to represent the problem. Explain what the product represents.

–30 · 12 = –360; Her account balance decreased \$360.

C 6 How many integers must be negative for the product of three integers to be negative? Explain. Find two different groups of three integers whose product is –12.

Show your work.

Possible work:

–2 × (–2) × (–3) = –12

6 × (–2) × 1 = –12

Solution: Possible answer: –2, –2, and –3; 6, –2, and 1; Either 1 or 3 of the integers must be negative for the product to be negative. If all three integers were positive or only two of the integers were negative, the product would be positive.

Key

B Basic **M** Medium **C** Challenge

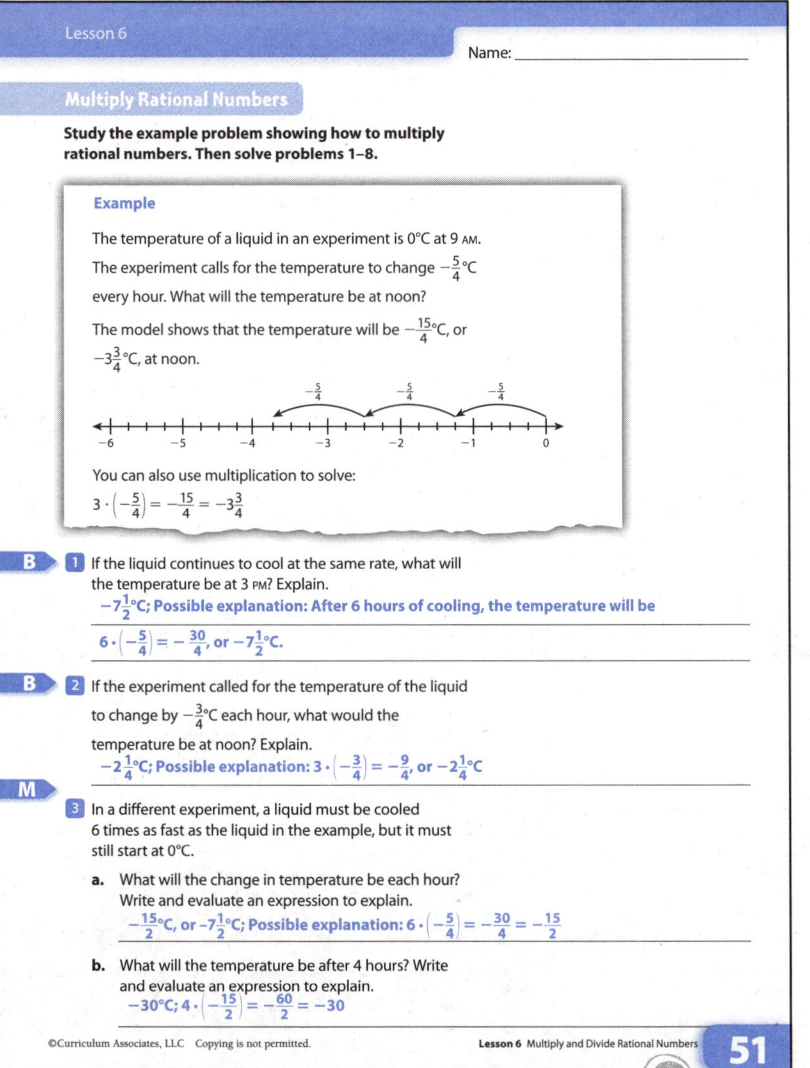

Lesson 6 Name: ______

Multiply Rational Numbers

Study the example problem showing how to multiply rational numbers. Then solve problems 1–8.

Example

The temperature of a liquid in an experiment is 0°C at 9 AM. The experiment calls for the temperature to change $-\frac{5}{4}$°C every hour. What will the temperature be at noon?

The model shows that the temperature will be $-\frac{15}{4}$°C, or $-3\frac{3}{4}$°C, at noon.

You can also use multiplication to solve:

$3 \cdot \left(-\frac{5}{4}\right) = -\frac{15}{4} = -3\frac{3}{4}$

B 1 If the liquid continues to cool at the same rate, what will the temperature be at 3 PM? Explain.

$-7\frac{1}{2}$°C; Possible explanation: After 6 hours of cooling, the temperature will be $6 \cdot \left(-\frac{5}{4}\right) = -\frac{30}{4}$, or $-7\frac{1}{2}$°C.

B 2 If the experiment called for the temperature of the liquid to change by $-\frac{3}{4}$°C each hour, what would the temperature be at noon? Explain.

$-2\frac{1}{4}$°C; Possible explanation: $3 \cdot \left(-\frac{3}{4}\right) = -\frac{9}{4}$, or $-2\frac{1}{4}$°C

M 3 In a different experiment, a liquid must be cooled 6 times as fast as the liquid in the example, but it must still start at 0°C.

a. What will the change in temperature be each hour? Write and evaluate an expression to explain.

$-\frac{15}{2}$°C, or $-7\frac{1}{2}$°C; Possible explanation: $6 \cdot \left(-\frac{5}{4}\right) = -\frac{30}{4} = -\frac{15}{2}$

b. What will the temperature be after 4 hours? Write and evaluate an expression to explain.

−30°C; $4 \cdot \left(-\frac{15}{2}\right) = -\frac{60}{2} = -30$

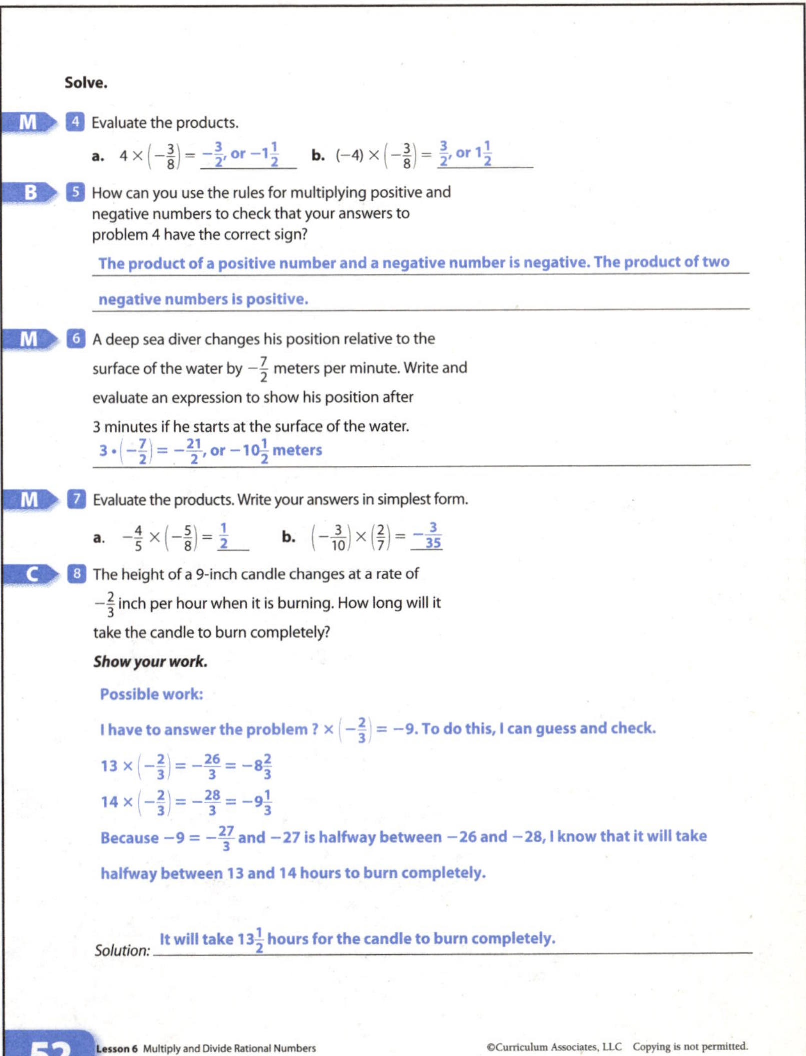

Solve.

M 4 Evaluate the products.

a. $4 \times \left(-\frac{3}{8}\right) =$ **$-\frac{3}{2}$, or $-1\frac{1}{2}$** **b.** $(-4) \times \left(-\frac{3}{8}\right) =$ **$\frac{3}{2}$, or $1\frac{1}{2}$**

B 5 How can you use the rules for multiplying positive and negative numbers to check that your answers to problem 4 have the correct sign?

The product of a positive number and a negative number is negative. The product of two negative numbers is positive.

M 6 A deep sea diver changes his position relative to the surface of the water by $-\frac{7}{2}$ meters per minute. Write and evaluate an expression to show his position after 3 minutes if he starts at the surface of the water.

$3 \cdot \left(-\frac{7}{2}\right) = -\frac{21}{2}$, or $-10\frac{1}{2}$ meters

M 7 Evaluate the products. Write your answers in simplest form.

a. $-\frac{4}{5} \times \left(-\frac{5}{8}\right) =$ **$\frac{1}{2}$** **b.** $\left(-\frac{3}{10}\right) \times \left(\frac{2}{7}\right) =$ **$-\frac{3}{35}$**

C 8 The height of a 9-inch candle changes at a rate of $-\frac{2}{3}$ inch per hour when it is burning. How long will it take the candle to burn completely?

Show your work.

Possible work:

I have to answer the problem ? × $\left(-\frac{2}{3}\right) = -9$. To do this, I can guess and check.

$13 \times \left(-\frac{2}{3}\right) = -\frac{26}{3} = -8\frac{2}{3}$

$14 \times \left(-\frac{2}{3}\right) = -\frac{28}{3} = -9\frac{1}{3}$

Because $-9 = -\frac{27}{3}$ and −27 is halfway between −26 and −28, I know that it will take halfway between 13 and 14 hours to burn completely.

Solution: **It will take $13\frac{1}{2}$ hours for the candle to burn completely.**

Lesson 6

Name: ______________

Divide Rational Numbers

Study the example problem showing how to divide rational numbers. Then solve problems 1–6.

Example

The position of a submersible water vehicle, relative to sea level, changes by −0.5 mile each hour. After how many hours will the vehicle's position have changed by −2.5 miles?

You can use a table to understand the problem.

Time (h)	Position
0	0
1	−0.5
2	−1.0
3	−1.5
4	−2.0
5	−2.5

(each step: −0.5)

You can also use division to understand the problem.

$(-2.5) \div (-0.5) = -25 \div (-5) = 5$

B **1** You can also use repeated addition to evaluate the quotient $(-2.5) \div (-0.5)$. Complete.

$-2.5 = (-0.5) +$ $(-0.5) + (-0.5) + (-0.5) + (-0.5)$

There are __5__ groups of −0.5 in __−2.5__.

It will take __5__ hours for the submersible's position to change by −2.5 miles.

B **2** Mariella's bank statement shows a change of −\$2.50 in her account each week.

a. Complete the table to see how many weeks it will be before the change in Mariella's account is −\$20.

Number of Weeks	1	2	3	4	5	6	7	8
Change in Account (\$)	−2.5	−5.0	−7.5	−10.0	−12.5	−15.0	−17.5	−20.0

b. Why are the amounts in the table negative?

Money is being removed from Mariella's account, not added to it.

c. How many weeks will it take for the the amount deducted to total −\$20? __8 weeks__

Solve.

B **3** A pitcher contains 28 fluid ounces of juice. How many 4-ounce servings can you pour before the pitcher is empty? Complete the repeated subtraction to solve.

$-28 = (-4) +$ $(-4) + (-4) + (-4) + (-4) + (-4) + (-4)$

I can pour __7__ four-ounce glasses of juice.

M **4** A small inflatable pool holds 10 gallons of water. A tiny leak causes the amount of water in the pool to change by −0.05 gallon each hour until the pool is empty.

a. Write the numbers that represent each quantity.

change in amount of water per hour = __−0.05 gallon__

total change in amount of water = __−10 gallons__

b. Will you multiply or divide to find how many hours it will take for the pool to be empty? Will the answer be positive or negative?

divide; positive; The quotient of two negative numbers is positive; also, the number of hours the pool is leaking is a positive number.

c. How many hours will it take for the pool to be empty? __200__ hours

M **5** The temperature at 6 PM was 0°F. At 10 PM the temperature was −11.2°F. Write an expression that you can use to find the average change in temperature per hour during that time. Then evaluate the expression.

$-11.2 \div 4 = -2.8$

C **6** Marlene is solving a number puzzle involving three rational numbers *a*, *b*, and *c*. Here are her clues:

- The quotient of *a* and *c* is 8.
- The product of *a* and *c* is 2.
- The quotient of *a* and *b* is −16.
- The product of *a* and *b* is −1.
- The quotient of *b* and *c* is −0.5.

What are the three numbers in Marlene's puzzle?

$a = -4, b = 0.25, c = -0.5$ or $a = 4, b = -0.25, c = 0.5$

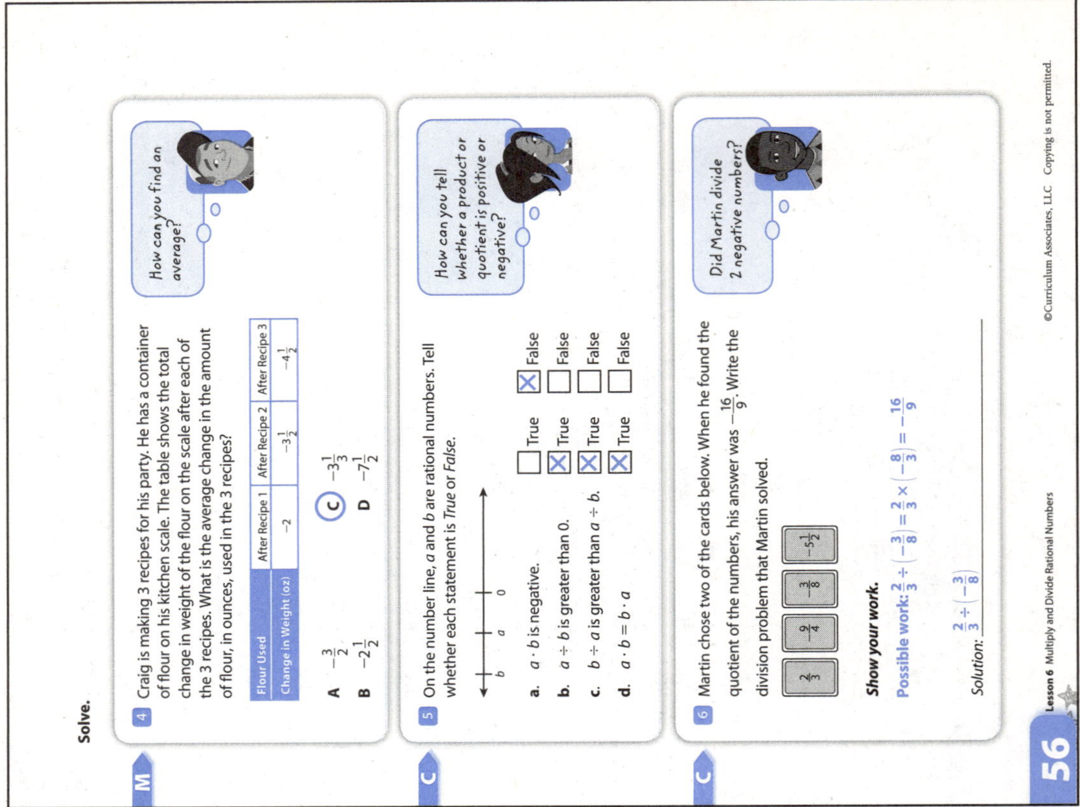

Solve.

M **4** Craig is making 3 recipes for his party. He has a container of flour on his kitchen scale. The table shows the total change in weight of the flour on the scale after each of the 3 recipes. What is the average change in the amount of flour, in ounces, used in the 3 recipes?

Flour Used	After Recipe 1	After Recipe 2	After Recipe 3
Change in Weight (oz)	-2	$-3\frac{1}{2}$	$-4\frac{1}{2}$

A $-\frac{3}{2}$
B $-2\frac{1}{2}$
(C) $-3\frac{1}{3}$
D $-7\frac{1}{2}$

C **5** On the number line, a and b are rational numbers. Tell whether each statement is *True* or *False*.

a. $a \cdot b$ is negative. ☐ True ☒ False
b. $a \div b$ is greater than 0. ☒ True ☐ False
c. $b \div a$ is greater than $a \div b$. ☒ True ☐ False
d. $a \cdot b = b \cdot a$ ☒ True ☐ False

C **6** Martin chose two of the cards below. When he found the quotient of the numbers, his answer was $-\frac{16}{9}$. Write the division problem that Martin solved.

$\frac{2}{3}$ $-\frac{9}{4}$ $-\frac{3}{8}$ $-5\frac{1}{2}$

Show your work.

Possible work: $\frac{2}{3} \div \left(-\frac{3}{8}\right) = \frac{2}{3} \times \left(-\frac{8}{3}\right) = -\frac{16}{9}$

Solution: $\frac{2}{3} \div \left(-\frac{3}{8}\right)$

56 **Lesson 6** Multiply and Divide Rational Numbers ©Curriculum Associates, LLC Copying is not permitted.

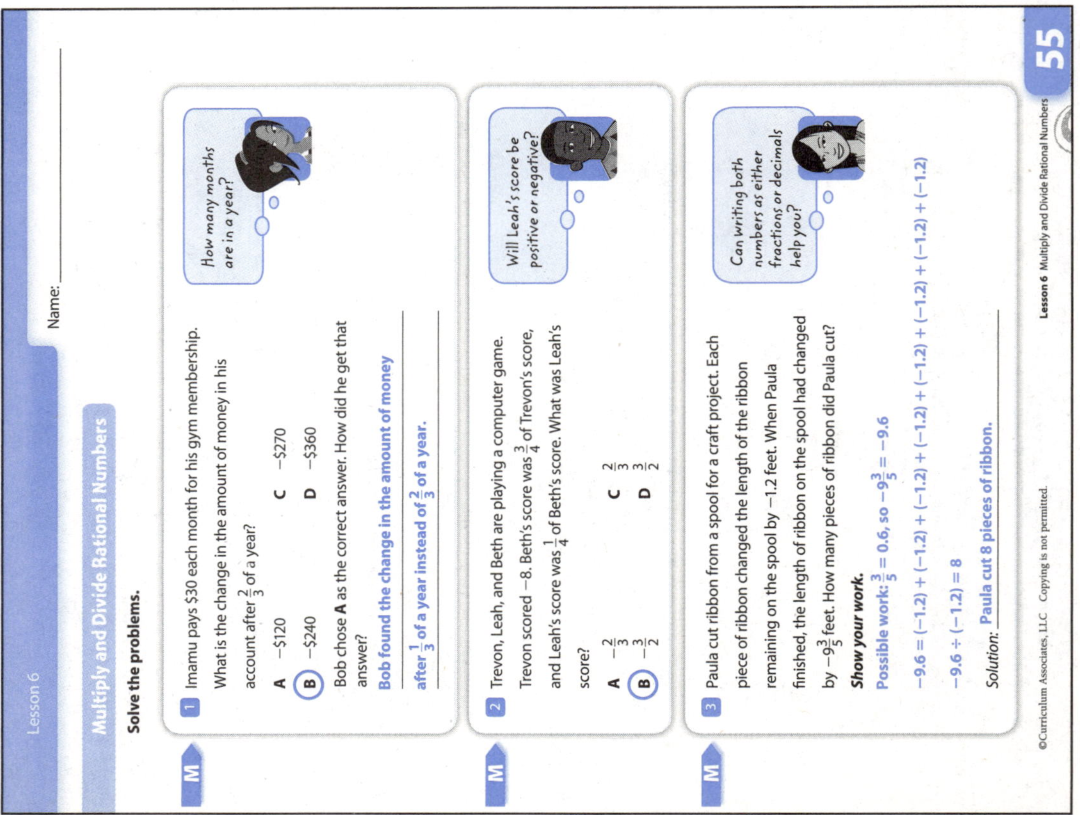

Lesson 6 Name: ____________

Multiply and Divide Rational Numbers

Solve the problems.

M **1** Imamu pays \$30 each month for his gym membership. What is the change in the amount of money in his account after $\frac{2}{3}$ of a year?

A $-\$120$
(B) $-\$240$
C $-\$270$
D $-\$360$

Bob chose **A** as the correct answer. How did he get that answer?

Bob found the change in the amount of money after $\frac{1}{3}$ of a year instead of $\frac{2}{3}$ of a year.

M **2** Trevon, Leah, and Beth are playing a computer game. Trevon scored -8. Beth's score was $\frac{3}{4}$ of Trevon's score, and Leah's score was $\frac{1}{4}$ of Beth's score. What was Leah's score?

A $-\frac{2}{3}$
(B) $-\frac{3}{2}$
C $\frac{2}{3}$
D $\frac{3}{2}$

M **3** Paula cut ribbon from a spool for a craft project. Each piece of ribbon changed the length of the ribbon remaining on the spool by -1.2 feet. When Paula finished, the length of ribbon on the spool had changed by $-9\frac{3}{5}$ feet. How many pieces of ribbon did Paula cut?

Show your work.

Possible work: $\frac{3}{5} = 0.6$, so $-9\frac{3}{5} = -9.6$

$-9.6 = (-1.2) + (-1.2) + (-1.2) + (-1.2) + (-1.2) + (-1.2) + (-1.2) + (-1.2)$

$-9.6 \div (-1.2) = 8$

Solution: Paula cut 8 pieces of ribbon.

©Curriculum Associates, LLC Copying is not permitted. **Lesson 6** Multiply and Divide Rational Numbers 55

Lesson 7

Add and Subtract Rational Numbers

Name: ____________________

Prerequisite: Add and Subtract Integers

Study the example showing how to add positive and negative integers. Then solve problems 1–5.

Example

Guy, Ian, and Bella play a game in which they spin a spinner with both positive and negative numbers on it. They add the values of each spin. The player with the lowest total score wins.

	Guy	Ian	Bella
Score, Spin 1	4	−6	−2
Score, Spin 2	−3	−2	4
Total Score	4 + (−3)	−6 + (−2)	−2 + 4

You can add the numbers on a number line to find each person's total score.

For example, you can find Guy's total score by locating 4 on the number line and moving left 3 units. His final score is 1.

−10 −9 −8 −7 −6 −5 −4 −3 −2 −1 0 1 2 3 4 5 6 7 8 9 10

B **1** Use this number line to find Ian's final score.

−10 −9 −8 −7 −6 −5 −4 −3 −2 −1 0 1 2 3 4 5 6 7 8 9 10

final score: −8

B **2** Use this number line to find Bella's final score.

−10 −9 −8 −7 −6 −5 −4 −3 −2 −1 0 1 2 3 4 5 6 7 8 9 10

final score: 2

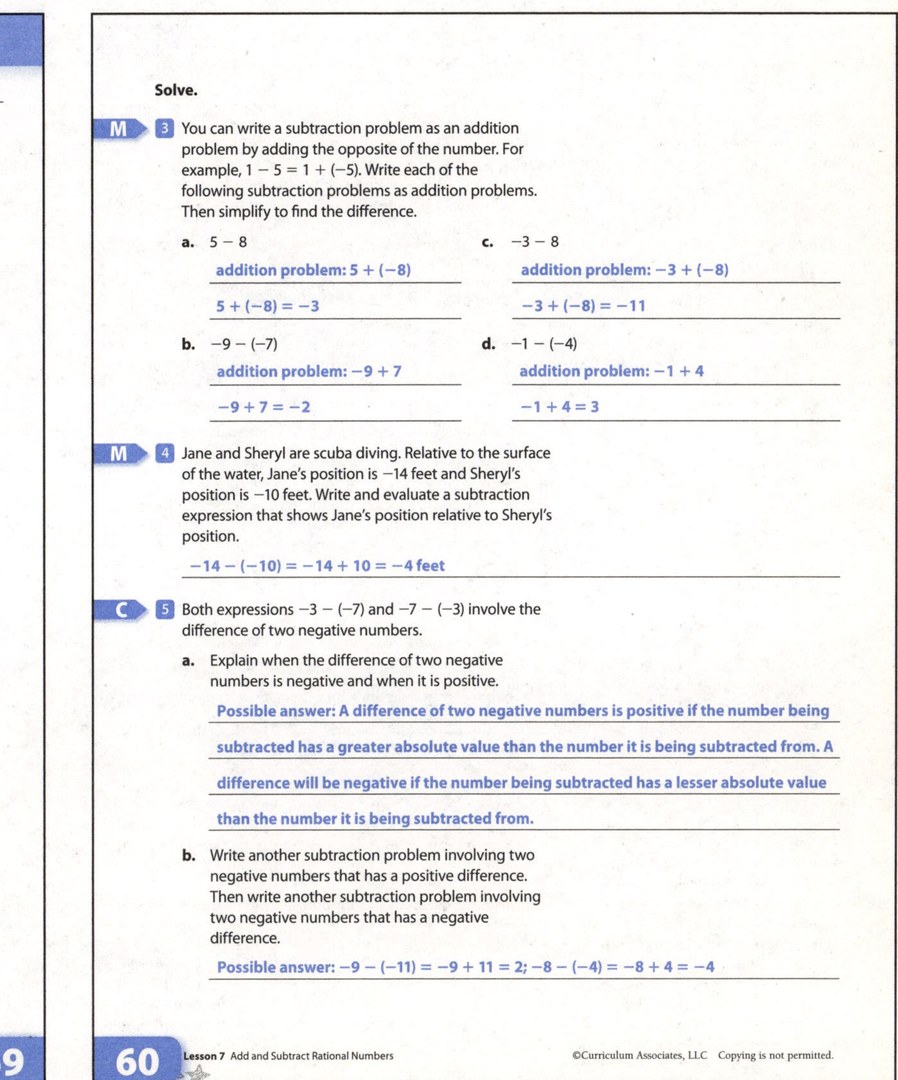

Solve.

M **3** You can write a subtraction problem as an addition problem by adding the opposite of the number. For example, 1 − 5 = 1 + (−5). Write each of the following subtraction problems as addition problems. Then simplify to find the difference.

a. 5 − 8

addition problem: 5 + (−8)

5 + (−8) = −3

b. −9 − (−7)

addition problem: −9 + 7

−9 + 7 = −2

c. −3 − 8

addition problem: −3 + (−8)

−3 + (−8) = −11

d. −1 − (−4)

addition problem: −1 + 4

−1 + 4 = 3

M **4** Jane and Sheryl are scuba diving. Relative to the surface of the water, Jane's position is −14 feet and Sheryl's position is −10 feet. Write and evaluate a subtraction expression that shows Jane's position relative to Sheryl's position.

−14 − (−10) = −14 + 10 = −4 feet

C **5** Both expressions −3 − (−7) and −7 − (−3) involve the difference of two negative numbers.

a. Explain when the difference of two negative numbers is negative and when it is positive.

Possible answer: A difference of two negative numbers is positive if the number being subtracted has a greater absolute value than the number it is being subtracted from. A difference will be negative if the number being subtracted has a lesser absolute value than the number it is being subtracted from.

b. Write another subtraction problem involving two negative numbers that has a positive difference. Then write another subtraction problem involving two negative numbers that has a negative difference.

Possible answer: −9 − (−11) = −9 + 11 = 2; −8 − (−4) = −8 + 4 = −4

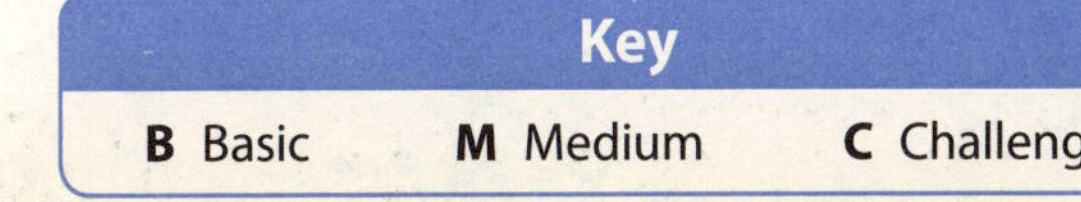

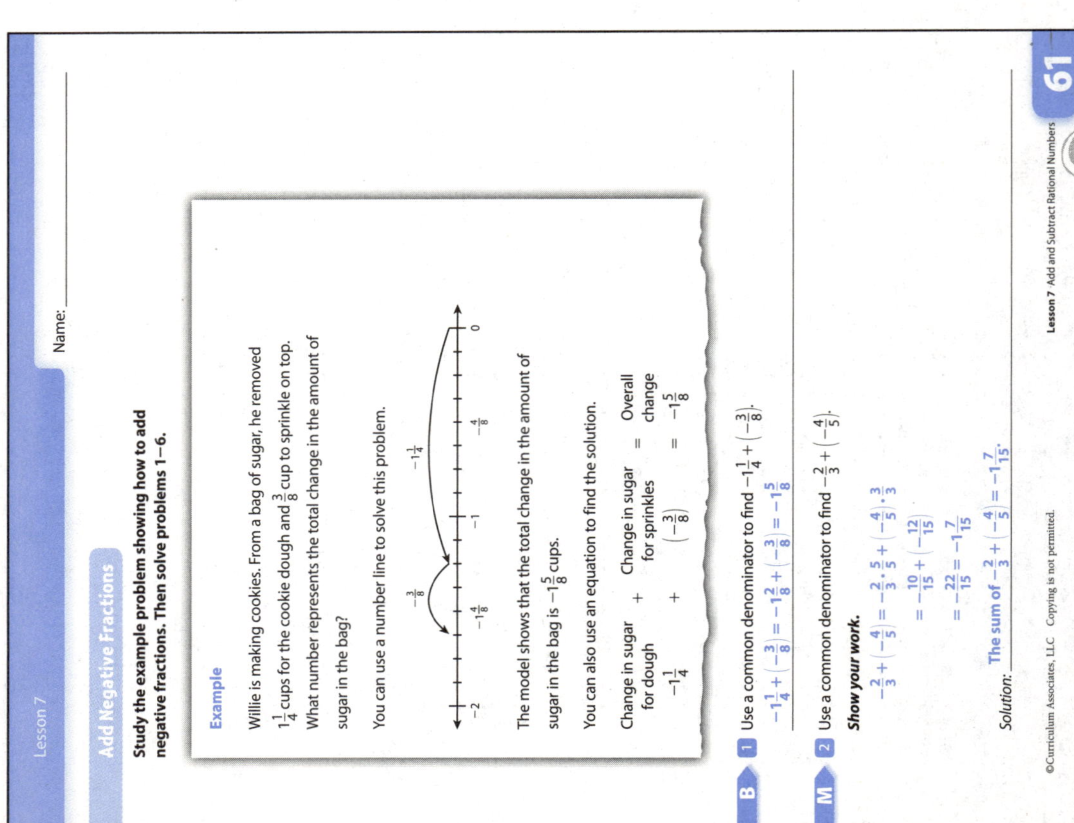

Lesson 7

Name: ______________________

Add Negative Fractions

Study the example problem showing how to add negative fractions. Then solve problems 1–6.

Example

Willie is making cookies. From a bag of sugar, he removed $1\frac{1}{4}$ cups for the cookie dough and $\frac{3}{8}$ cup to sprinkle on top. What number represents the total change in the amount of sugar in the bag?

You can use a number line to solve this problem.

$-\frac{3}{8}$ $-1\frac{1}{4}$

-2 $-1\frac{4}{8}$ -1 $-\frac{4}{8}$ 0

The model shows that the total change in the amount of sugar in the bag is $-1\frac{5}{8}$ cups.

You can also use an equation to find the solution.

Change in sugar for dough	+	Change in sugar for sprinkles	=	Overall change
$-1\frac{1}{4}$	+	$\left(-\frac{3}{8}\right)$	=	$-1\frac{5}{8}$

B **1** Use a common denominator to find $-1\frac{1}{4} + \left(-\frac{3}{8}\right)$.

$-1\frac{1}{4} + \left(-\frac{3}{8}\right) = -1\frac{2}{8} + \left(-\frac{3}{8}\right) = -1\frac{5}{8}$

M **2** Use a common denominator to find $-\frac{2}{3} + \left(-\frac{4}{5}\right)$.

Show your work.

$-\frac{2}{3} + \left(-\frac{4}{5}\right) = -\frac{2}{3}\cdot\frac{5}{5} + \left(-\frac{4}{5}\right)\cdot\frac{3}{3}$

$= -\frac{10}{15} + \left(-\frac{12}{15}\right)$

$= -\frac{22}{15} = -1\frac{7}{15}$

Solution: The sum of $-\frac{2}{3} + \left(-\frac{4}{5}\right) = -1\frac{7}{15}$.

©Curriculum Associates, LLC Copying is not permitted.   **Lesson 7** Add and Subtract Rational Numbers   **61**

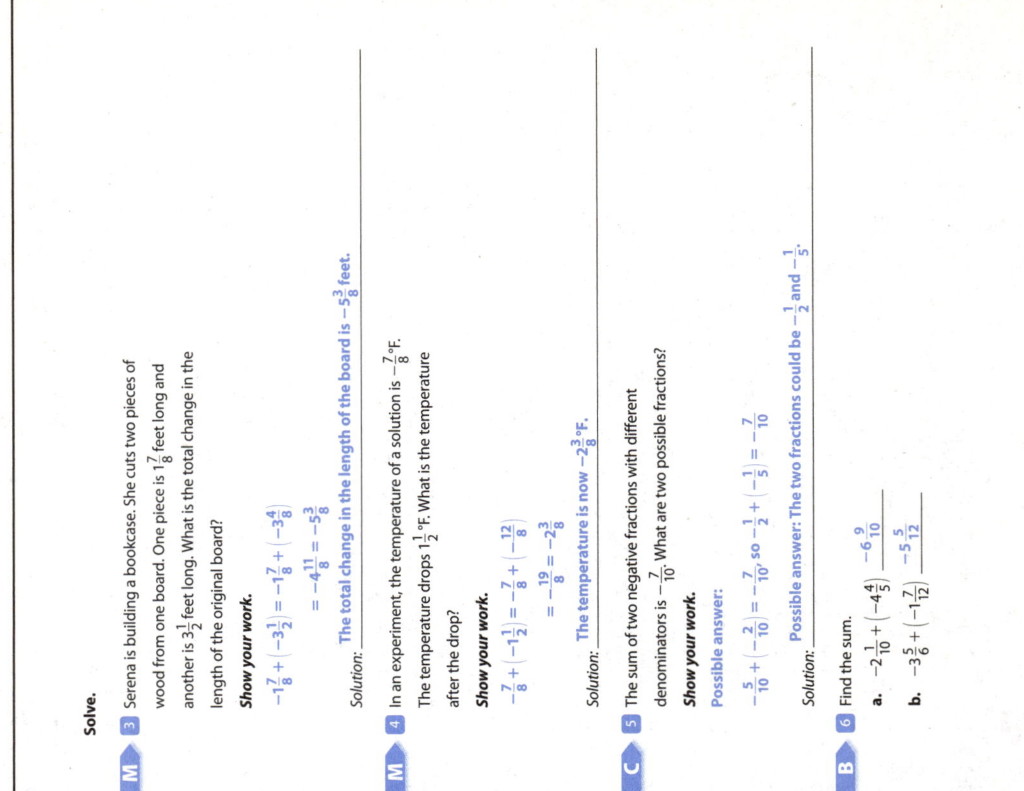

Solve.

M **3** Serena is building a bookcase. She cuts two pieces of wood from one board. One piece is $1\frac{7}{8}$ feet long and another is $3\frac{1}{2}$ feet long. What is the total change in the length of the original board?

Show your work.

$-1\frac{7}{8} + \left(-3\frac{1}{2}\right) = -1\frac{7}{8} + \left(-3\frac{4}{8}\right)$

$= -4\frac{11}{8} = -5\frac{3}{8}$

Solution: The total change in the length of the board is $-5\frac{3}{8}$ feet.

M **4** In an experiment, the temperature of a solution is $-\frac{7}{8}$°F. The temperature drops $1\frac{1}{2}$°F. What is the temperature after the drop?

Show your work.

$-\frac{7}{8} + \left(-1\frac{1}{2}\right) = -\frac{7}{8} + \left(-\frac{12}{8}\right)$

$= -\frac{19}{8} = -2\frac{3}{8}$

Solution: The temperature is now $-2\frac{3}{8}$°F.

C **5** The sum of two negative fractions with different denominators is $-\frac{7}{10}$. What are two possible fractions?

Show your work.

Possible answer:

$-\frac{5}{10} + \left(-\frac{2}{10}\right) = -\frac{7}{10}$, so $-\frac{1}{2} + \left(-\frac{1}{5}\right) = -\frac{7}{10}$

Solution: Possible answer: The two fractions could be $-\frac{1}{2}$ and $-\frac{1}{5}$.

B **6** Find the sum.

a. $-2\frac{1}{10} + \left(-4\frac{4}{5}\right)$ $\underline{-6\frac{9}{10}}$

b. $-3\frac{5}{6} + \left(-1\frac{7}{12}\right)$ $\underline{-5\frac{5}{12}}$

62   **Lesson 7** Add and Subtract Rational Numbers   ©Curriculum Associates, LLC Copying is not permitted.

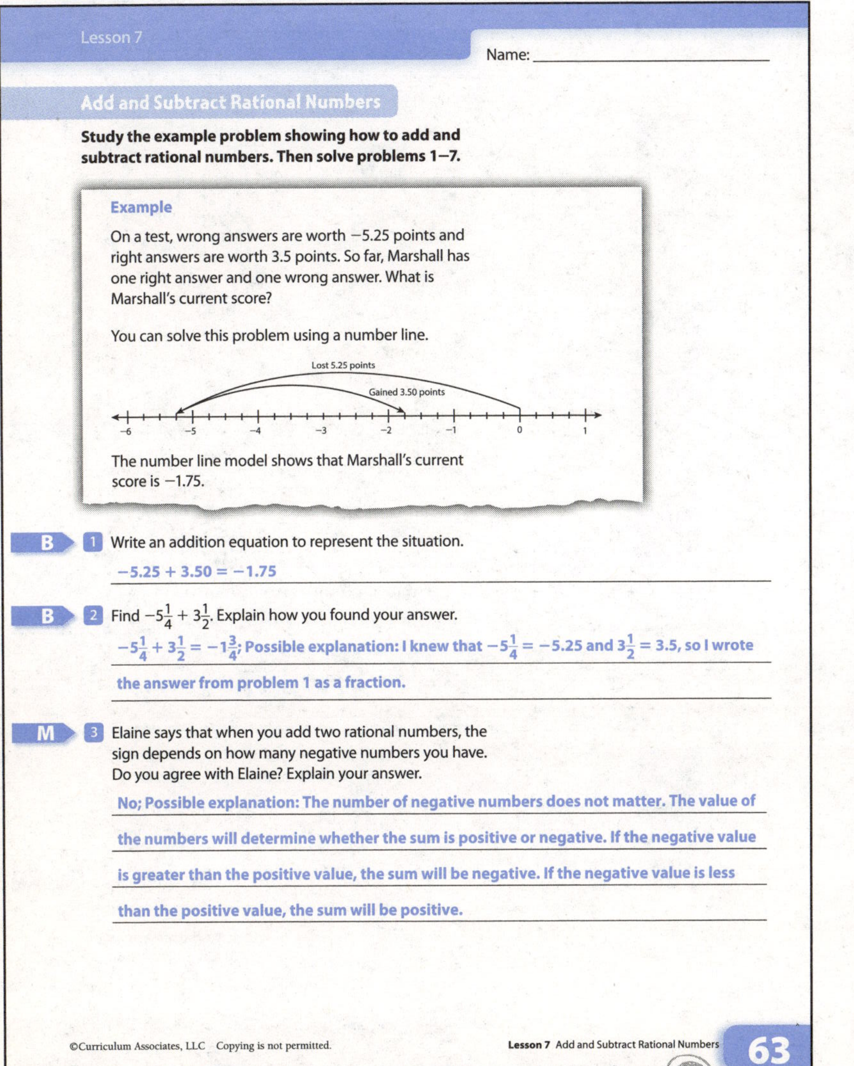

Lesson 7

Name: ____________

Add and Subtract Rational Numbers

Study the example problem showing how to add and subtract rational numbers. Then solve problems 1–7.

Example

On a test, wrong answers are worth −5.25 points and right answers are worth 3.5 points. So far, Marshall has one right answer and one wrong answer. What is Marshall's current score?

You can solve this problem using a number line.

The number line model shows that Marshall's current score is −1.75.

B 1 Write an addition equation to represent the situation.

$-5.25 + 3.50 = -1.75$

B 2 Find $-5\frac{1}{4} + 3\frac{1}{2}$. Explain how you found your answer.

$-5\frac{1}{4} + 3\frac{1}{2} = -1\frac{3}{4}$; Possible explanation: I knew that $-5\frac{1}{4} = -5.25$ and $3\frac{1}{2} = 3.5$, so I wrote the answer from problem 1 as a fraction.

M 3 Elaine says that when you add two rational numbers, the sign depends on how many negative numbers you have. Do you agree with Elaine? Explain your answer.

No; Possible explanation: The number of negative numbers does not matter. The value of the numbers will determine whether the sum is positive or negative. If the negative value is greater than the positive value, the sum will be negative. If the negative value is less than the positive value, the sum will be positive.

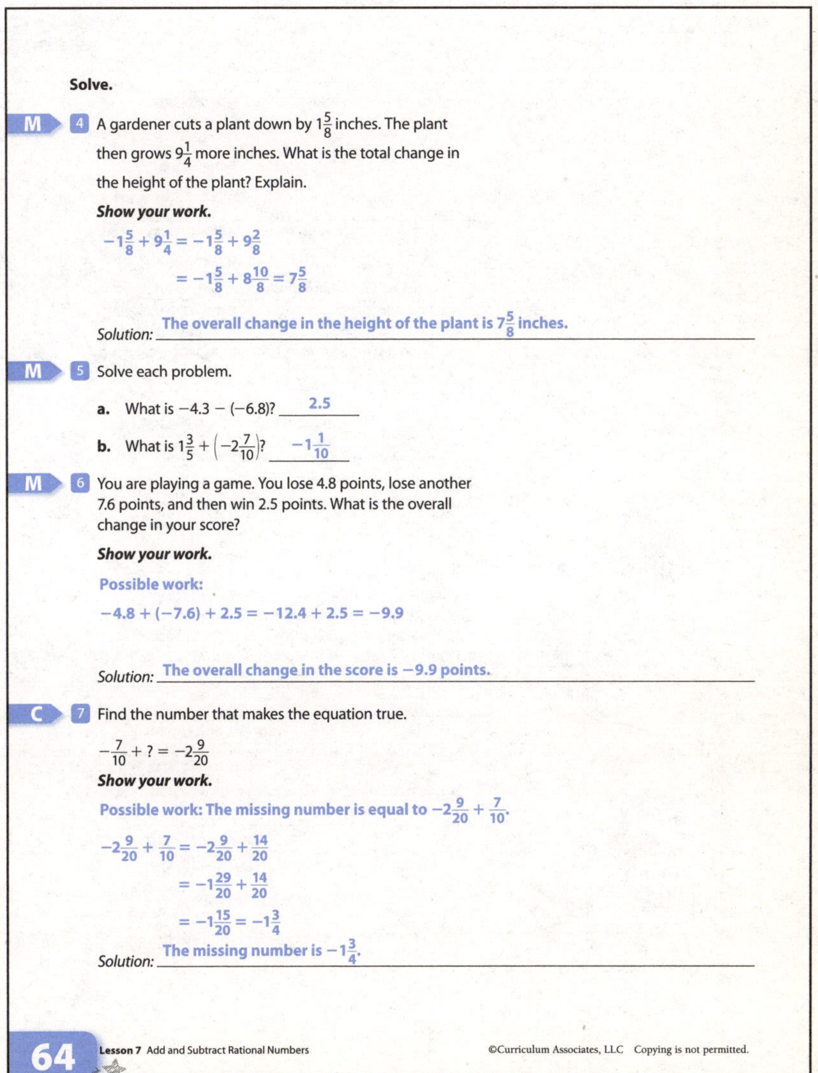

Solve.

M 4 A gardener cuts a plant down by $1\frac{5}{8}$ inches. The plant then grows $9\frac{1}{4}$ more inches. What is the total change in the height of the plant? Explain.

Show your work.

$-1\frac{5}{8} + 9\frac{1}{4} = -1\frac{5}{8} + 9\frac{2}{8}$

$= -1\frac{5}{8} + 8\frac{10}{8} = 7\frac{5}{8}$

Solution: The overall change in the height of the plant is $7\frac{5}{8}$ inches.

M 5 Solve each problem.

a. What is $-4.3 - (-6.8)$? 2.5

b. What is $1\frac{3}{5} + \left(-2\frac{7}{10}\right)$? $-1\frac{1}{10}$

M 6 You are playing a game. You lose 4.8 points, lose another 7.6 points, and then win 2.5 points. What is the overall change in your score?

Show your work.

Possible work:

$-4.8 + (-7.6) + 2.5 = -12.4 + 2.5 = -9.9$

Solution: The overall change in the score is −9.9 points.

C 7 Find the number that makes the equation true.

$-\frac{7}{10} + ? = -2\frac{9}{20}$

Show your work.

Possible work: The missing number is equal to $-2\frac{9}{20} + \frac{7}{10}$.

$-2\frac{9}{20} + \frac{7}{10} = -2\frac{9}{20} + \frac{14}{20}$

$= -1\frac{29}{20} + \frac{14}{20}$

$= -1\frac{15}{20} = -1\frac{3}{4}$

Solution: The missing number is $-1\frac{3}{4}$.

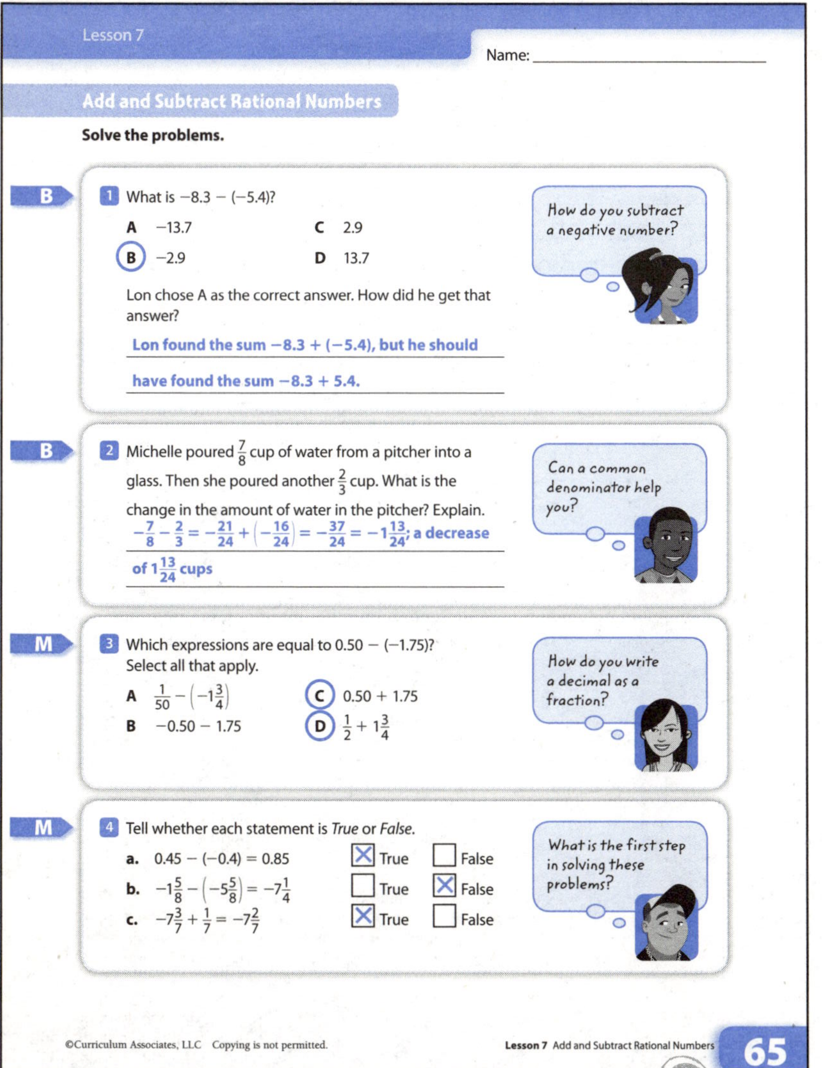

Lesson 7 Name: ____________

Add and Subtract Rational Numbers

Solve the problems.

B

1 What is $-8.3 - (-5.4)$?

A -13.7

(B) -2.9

C 2.9

D 13.7

Lon chose A as the correct answer. How did he get that answer?

Lon found the sum $-8.3 + (-5.4)$, but he should have found the sum $-8.3 + 5.4$.

B

2 Michelle poured $\frac{7}{8}$ cup of water from a pitcher into a glass. Then she poured another $\frac{2}{3}$ cup. What is the change in the amount of water in the pitcher? Explain.

$-\frac{7}{8} - \frac{2}{3} = -\frac{21}{24} + \left(-\frac{16}{24}\right) = -\frac{37}{24} = -1\frac{13}{24}$; a decrease of $1\frac{13}{24}$ cups

M

3 Which expressions are equal to $0.50 - (-1.75)$? Select all that apply.

A $\frac{1}{50} - \left(-1\frac{3}{4}\right)$

B $-0.50 - 1.75$

(C) $0.50 + 1.75$

(D) $\frac{1}{2} + 1\frac{3}{4}$

M

4 Tell whether each statement is *True* or *False*.

		True	False
a.	$0.45 - (-0.4) = 0.85$	☒ True	☐ False
b.	$-1\frac{5}{8} - \left(-5\frac{5}{8}\right) = -7\frac{1}{4}$	☐ True	☒ False
c.	$-7\frac{3}{7} + \frac{1}{7} = -7\frac{2}{7}$	☒ True	☐ False

©Curriculum Associates, LLC Copying is not permitted. **Lesson 7** Add and Subtract Rational Numbers 65

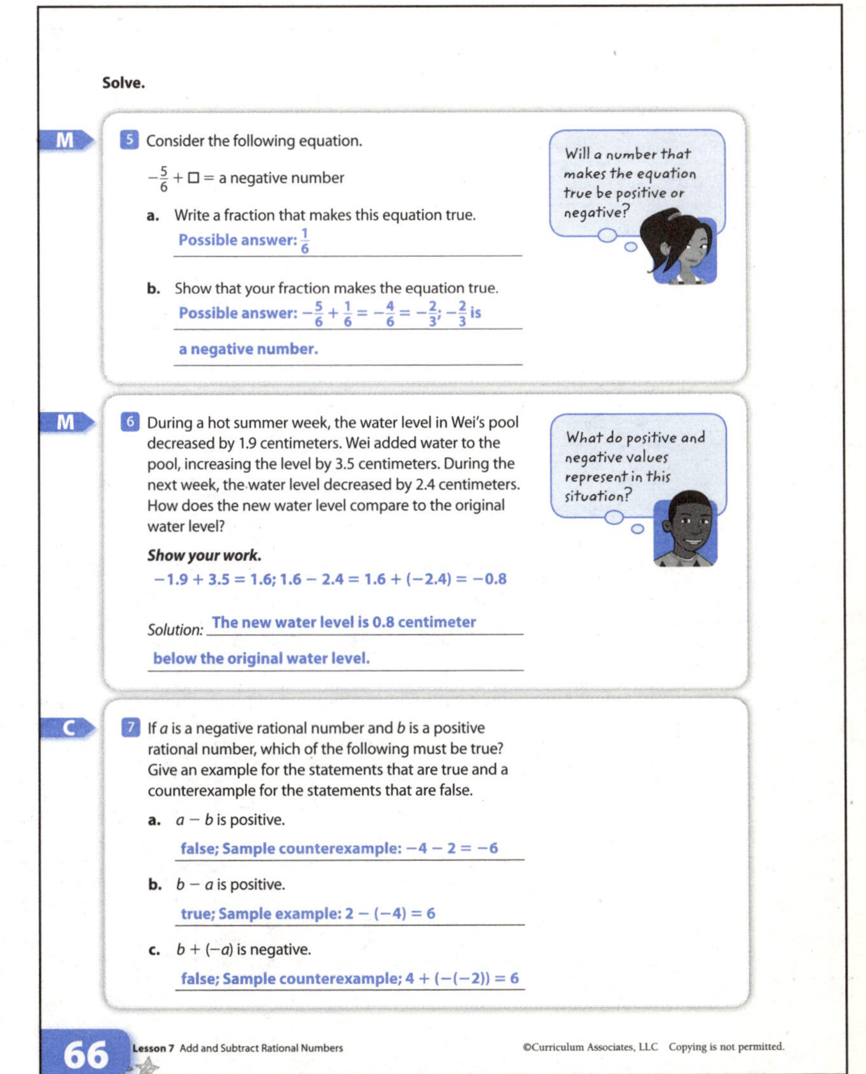

Solve.

M

5 Consider the following equation.

$-\frac{5}{6} + \square =$ a negative number

a. Write a fraction that makes this equation true.

Possible answer: $\frac{1}{6}$

b. Show that your fraction makes the equation true.

Possible answer: $-\frac{5}{6} + \frac{1}{6} = -\frac{4}{6} = -\frac{2}{3}$; $-\frac{2}{3}$ is a negative number.

M

6 During a hot summer week, the water level in Wei's pool decreased by 1.9 centimeters. Wei added water to the pool, increasing the level by 3.5 centimeters. During the next week, the water level decreased by 2.4 centimeters. How does the new water level compare to the original water level?

Show your work.

$-1.9 + 3.5 = 1.6$; $1.6 - 2.4 = 1.6 + (-2.4) = -0.8$

Solution: **The new water level is 0.8 centimeter below the original water level.**

C

7 If *a* is a negative rational number and *b* is a positive rational number, which of the following must be true? Give an example for the statements that are true and a counterexample for the statements that are false.

a. $a - b$ is positive.

false; Sample counterexample: $-4 - 2 = -6$

b. $b - a$ is positive.

true; Sample example: $2 - (-4) = 6$

c. $b + (-a)$ is negative.

false; Sample counterexample; $4 + (-(-2)) = 6$

66 **Lesson 7** Add and Subtract Rational Numbers ©Curriculum Associates, LLC Copying is not permitted.

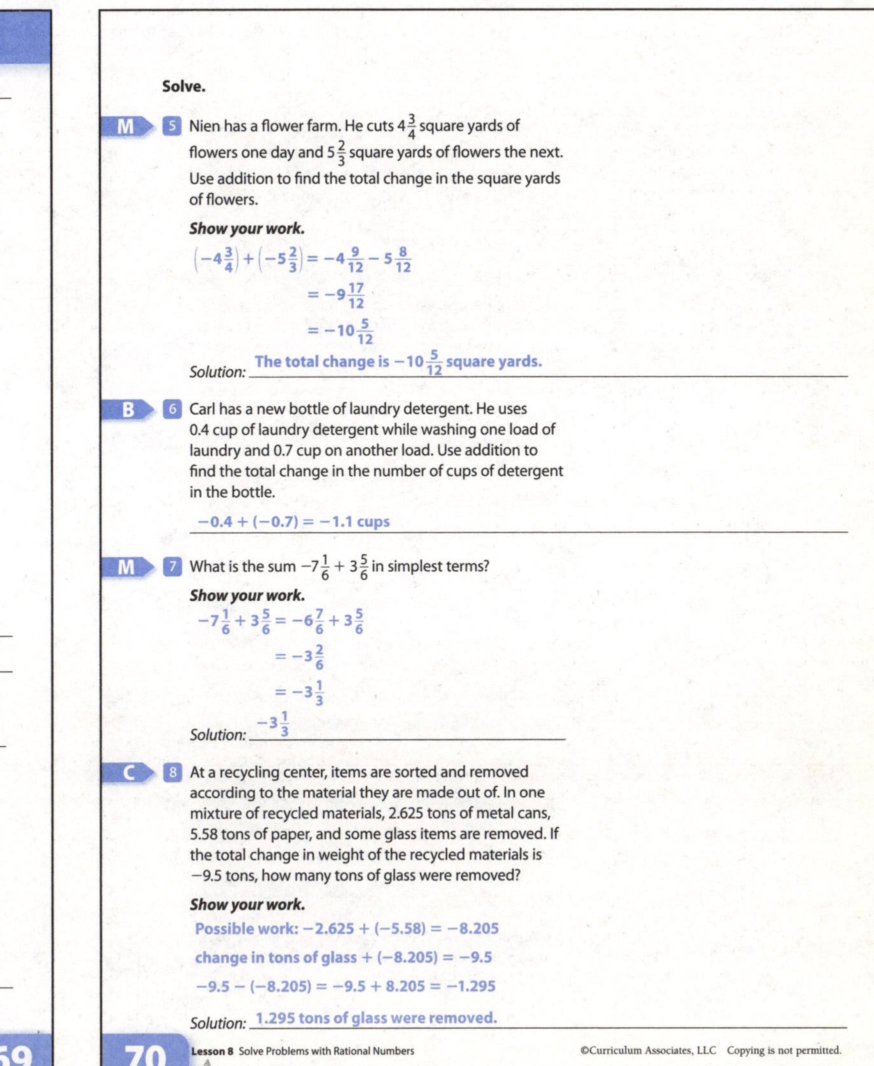

Lesson 8

Solve Problems with Rational Numbers

Name: ____________________

Prerequisite: Add Negative Fractions

Study the example showing how to add negative fractions. Then solve problems 1–8.

Example

Marita has a container of oatmeal. She uses $\frac{1}{4}$ cup of the oatmeal for breakfast and $\frac{3}{8}$ cup for a cookie recipe. What is the total change in the amount of oatmeal she has?

You can use a number line to represent this problem. Keep in mind that $\frac{1}{4}$ is equivalent to $\frac{2}{8}$.

B 1 Why are $\frac{1}{4}$ and $\frac{3}{8}$ represented with negative numbers on the number line in the example?

$\frac{1}{4}$ and $\frac{3}{8}$ are represented with negative numbers on the number line because Marita uses $\frac{1}{4}$ cup and $\frac{3}{8}$ cup of oatmeal, so she is taking these amounts out of the container.

B 2 What do you need to do to $-\frac{1}{4}$ to locate it on a number line that is measured in eighths? **Rewrite $-\frac{1}{4}$ as $-\frac{2}{8}$.**

B 3 You can also use an equation to solve the problem. Complete the addition equation.

Change in oatmeal after breakfast	+	Change in oatmeal after cookie recipe	=	Total change
$\left(-\frac{1}{4}\right)$	+	$\left(-\frac{3}{8}\right)$	=	?

B 4 What is the total change in the number of cups in the oatmeal container? Explain.

$-\frac{5}{8}$; $\left(-\frac{1}{4}\right) + \left(-\frac{3}{8}\right) = -\frac{2}{8} - \frac{3}{8} = -\frac{5}{8}$ cup of oatmeal

©Curriculum Associates, LLC Copying is not permitted. **Lesson 8** Solve Problems with Rational Numbers 69

Solve.

M 5 Nien has a flower farm. He cuts $4\frac{3}{4}$ square yards of flowers one day and $5\frac{2}{3}$ square yards of flowers the next. Use addition to find the total change in the square yards of flowers.

Show your work.

$\left(-4\frac{3}{4}\right) + \left(-5\frac{2}{3}\right) = -4\frac{9}{12} - 5\frac{8}{12}$

$= -9\frac{17}{12}$

$= -10\frac{5}{12}$

Solution: **The total change is $-10\frac{5}{12}$ square yards.**

B 6 Carl has a new bottle of laundry detergent. He uses 0.4 cup of laundry detergent while washing one load of laundry and 0.7 cup on another load. Use addition to find the total change in the number of cups of detergent in the bottle.

$-0.4 + (-0.7) = -1.1$ cups

M 7 What is the sum $-7\frac{1}{6} + 3\frac{5}{6}$ in simplest terms?

Show your work.

$-7\frac{1}{6} + 3\frac{5}{6} = -6\frac{7}{6} + 3\frac{5}{6}$

$= -3\frac{2}{6}$

$= -3\frac{1}{3}$

Solution: **$-3\frac{1}{3}$**

C 8 At a recycling center, items are sorted and removed according to the material they are made out of. In one mixture of recycled materials, 2.625 tons of metal cans, 5.58 tons of paper, and some glass items are removed. If the total change in weight of the recycled materials is −9.5 tons, how many tons of glass were removed?

Show your work.

Possible work: $-2.625 + (-5.58) = -8.205$

change in tons of glass $+ (-8.205) = -9.5$

$-9.5 - (-8.205) = -9.5 + 8.205 = -1.295$

Solution: **1.295 tons of glass were removed.**

70 **Lesson 8** Solve Problems with Rational Numbers ©Curriculum Associates, LLC Copying is not permitted.

Key

B Basic **M** Medium **C** Challenge

Lesson 8

Name: ____________

Estimating with Decimals

Study the example showing how to use estimation when computing with positive and negative decimals. Then solve problems 1–9.

Example

The temperature at noon was 5.6°F. During the afternoon the temperature dropped 2.8°F and then dropped another 2.2°F in the evening. Estimate the new temperature.

You can use a number line to understand the problem by approximating, or *rounding*, each temperature to the nearest degree.

5.6 rounds up to 6.
2.8 rounds up to 3.
2.2 rounds down to 2.

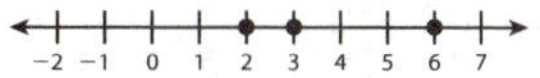

−2 −1 0 1 2 3 4 5 6 7

Now, you can estimate the new temperature by finding 6 − 3 − 2.
So, using estimation, the new temperature will be about 1°F.

B 1 Based on the estimate, do you think the actual new temperature will be above or below 0°F? Explain.

above; The estimate is 1°F, so the actual new temperature should be just a little above 0°F.

B 2 Write and solve an equation to find the new temperature using exact values. What is the exact value of the new temperature?

5.6 − 2.8 − 2.2 = 0.6; 0.6°F

B 3 Peter got an exact new temperature of 11.6°F. Explain how Peter can use the estimate to determine that his answer is wrong. Then find and correct Peter's error.

Peter's answer is much higher than the estimate. It should be pretty close to the estimate.

Peter added 2.8 and 2.2 to 5.6. He should have subtracted 2.8 and 2.2 from 5.6.

M 4 Janet estimated to the nearest half degree before she found her exact answer. Is Janet's estimate more or less accurate than the estimate in the example problem? Explain.

more; In general, the more precise that the estimate of each temperature is, the more accurate the estimate will be.

Solve.

M 5 Kyle and Joan are estimating the total weight of three boxes that each weigh 14.62 pounds. Each student's estimate is shown below.

Kyle	Joan
3(15) = 45 lb	3(14.5) = 43.5 lb

Which estimate is more accurate? Explain how you know. Then find the actual total weight of the boxes.

Joan's estimate should be more accurate because she used a more precise estimate;

3(14.62) = 43.86 lb

M 6 Estimate 55.8 ÷ (−3.1). Then find the exact quotient.

Show your work.

Possible work: estimate: 56 ÷ (−4) = −14

exact: 55.8 ÷ (−3.1) = −18

Solution: **The estimate is −14, and the exact quotient is −18.**

Use the following situation to solve problems 7–9.

Dusan had $49.60 in his checking account. He wrote one check for $24.40 and another check for $25.49.

M 7 Estimate the amount of money in Dusan's account after he wrote the checks.

Possible answers: $50 − $24 − $25 = $1 or $50 − $25 − $25 = $0

M 8 Explain why the estimate might not be enough information to show Dusan whether he has enough money in his checking account to cover the checks.

The estimate shows that Dusan has very little in his account, but it is not accurate enough to say for sure if he has enough in his account to cover the checks.

C 9 Dusan says that because he always rounds to the nearest dollar, he will always have more money in his account than his estimate. Is Dusan correct? Explain.

No; rounding to the nearest dollar does not mean that all numbers will be rounded up.

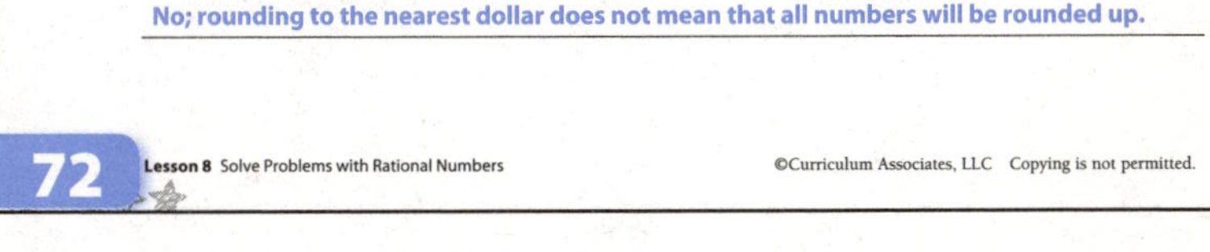

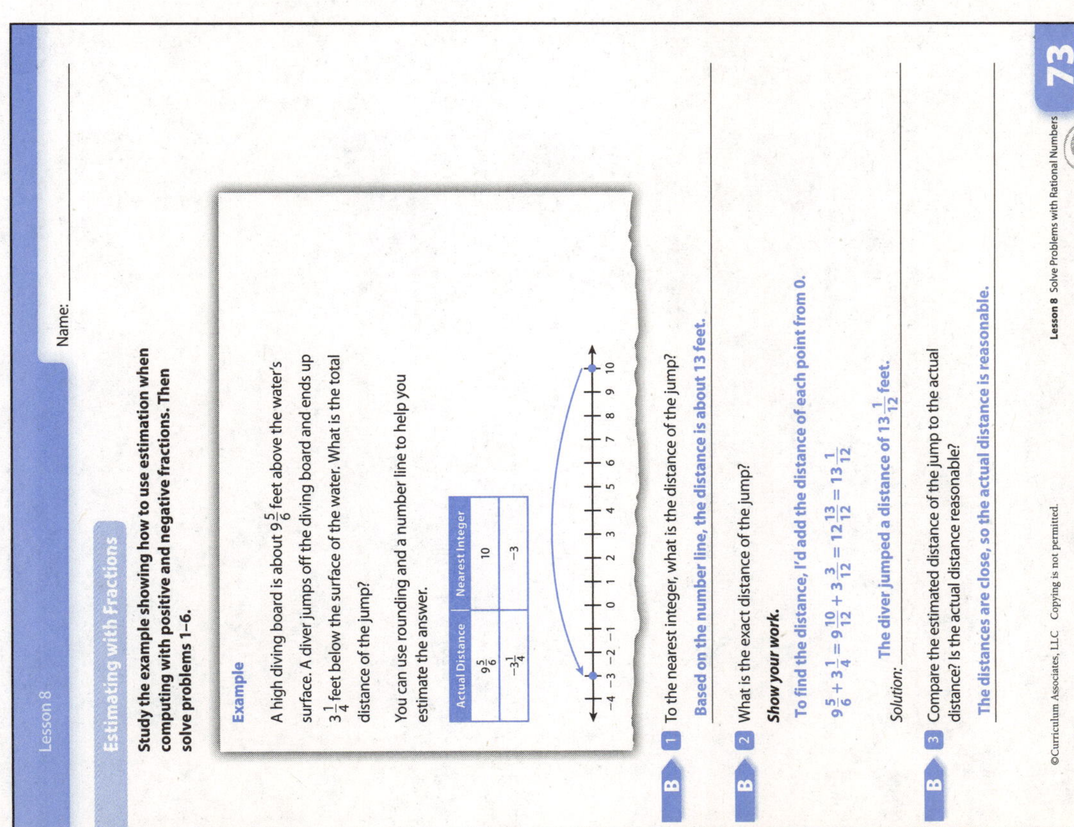

Lesson 8

Name: ____________

Estimating with Fractions

Study the example showing how to use estimation when computing with positive and negative fractions. Then solve problems 1–6.

Example

A high diving board is about $9\frac{5}{6}$ feet above the water's surface. A diver jumps off the diving board and ends up $3\frac{1}{4}$ feet below the surface of the water. What is the total distance of the jump?

You can use rounding and a number line to help you estimate the answer.

Actual Distance	Nearest Integer
$9\frac{5}{6}$	10
$-3\frac{1}{4}$	−3

B **1** To the nearest integer, what is the distance of the jump?

Based on the number line, the distance is about 13 feet.

B **2** What is the exact distance of the jump?

Show your work.

To find the distance, I'd add the distance of each point from 0.

$9\frac{5}{6} + 3\frac{1}{4} = 9\frac{10}{12} + 3\frac{3}{12} = 12\frac{13}{12} = 13\frac{1}{12}$

Solution: The diver jumped a distance of $13\frac{1}{12}$ feet.

B **3** Compare the estimated distance of the jump to the actual distance? Is the actual distance reasonable?

The distances are close, so the actual distance is reasonable.

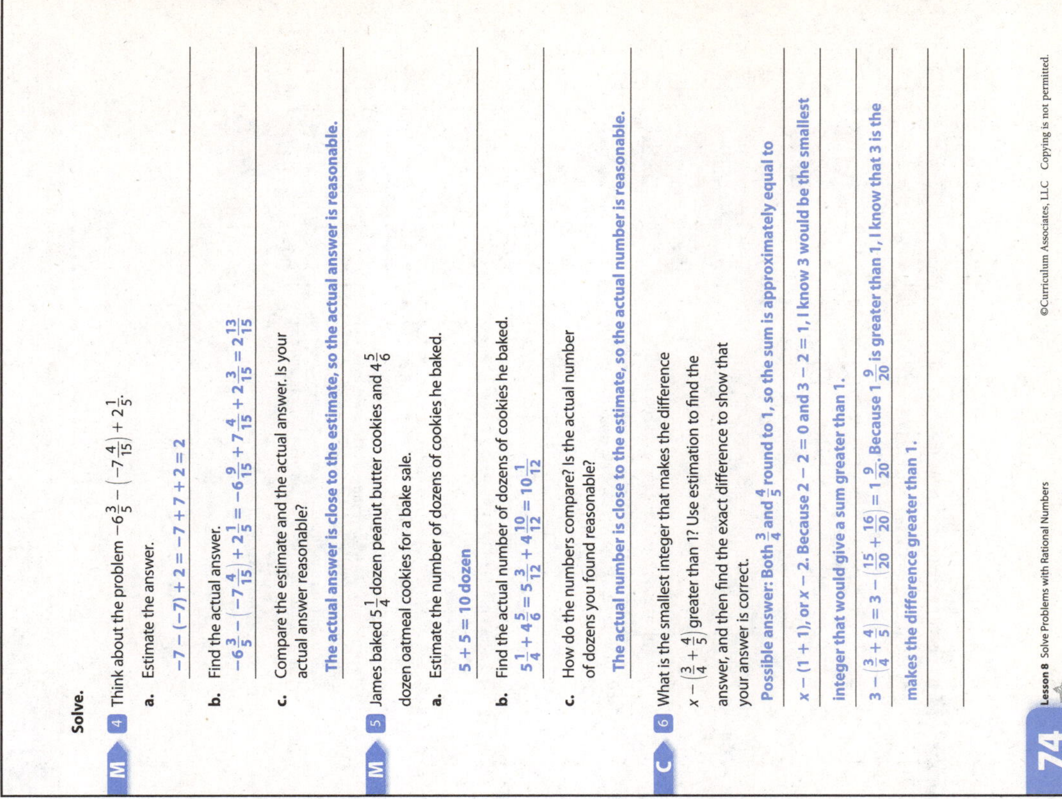

Solve.

M **4** Think about the problem $-6\frac{3}{5} - \left(-7\frac{4}{15}\right) + 2\frac{1}{5}$.

a. Estimate the answer.

$-7 - (-7) + 2 = -7 + 7 + 2 = 2$

b. Find the actual answer.

$-6\frac{3}{5} - \left(-7\frac{4}{15}\right) + 2\frac{1}{5} = -6\frac{9}{15} + 7\frac{4}{15} + 2\frac{3}{15} = 2\frac{13}{15}$

c. Compare the estimate and the actual answer. Is your actual answer reasonable?

The actual answer is close to the estimate, so the actual answer is reasonable.

M **5** James baked $5\frac{1}{4}$ dozen peanut butter cookies and $4\frac{5}{6}$ dozen oatmeal cookies for a bake sale.

a. Estimate the number of dozens of cookies he baked.

$5 + 5 = 10$ dozen

b. Find the actual number of dozens of cookies he baked.

$5\frac{1}{4} + 4\frac{5}{6} = 5\frac{3}{12} + 4\frac{10}{12} = 10\frac{1}{12}$

c. How do the numbers compare? Is the actual number of dozens you found reasonable?

The actual number is close to the estimate, so the actual number is reasonable.

C **6** What is the smallest integer that makes the difference $x - \left(\frac{3}{4} + \frac{4}{5}\right)$ greater than 1? Use estimation to find the answer, and then find the exact difference to show that your answer is correct.

Possible answer: Both $\frac{3}{4}$ and $\frac{4}{5}$ round to 1, so the sum is approximately equal to $x - (1 + 1)$, or $x - 2$. Because $2 - 2 = 0$ and $3 - 2 = 1$, I know 3 would be the smallest integer that would give a sum greater than 1.

$3 - \left(\frac{3}{4} + \frac{4}{5}\right) = 3 - \left(\frac{15}{20} + \frac{16}{20}\right) = 1\frac{9}{20}$. Because $1\frac{9}{20}$ is greater than 1, I know that 3 is the makes the difference greater than 1.

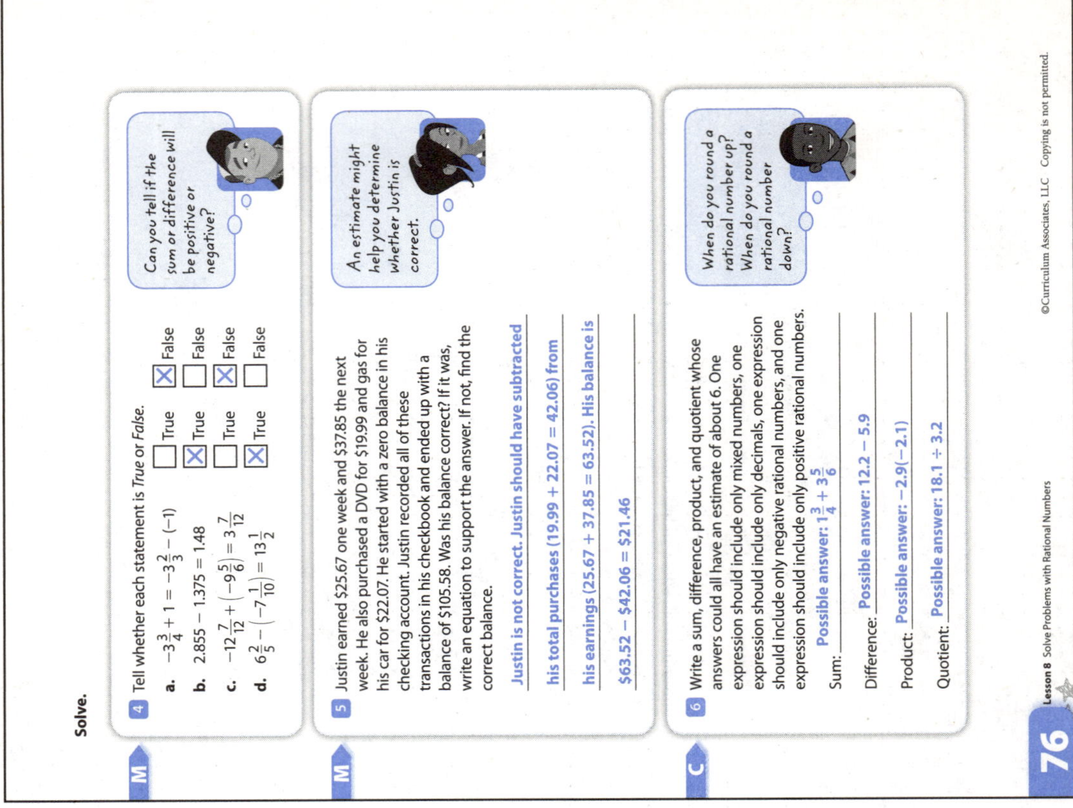

Solve.

M

4 Tell whether each statement is *True* or *False*.

	Statement	True	False
a.	$-3\frac{3}{4} + 1 = -3\frac{2}{3} - (-1)$	☐	☒
b.	$2.855 - 1.375 = 1.48$	☒	☐
c.	$-12\frac{7}{12} + \left(-9\frac{5}{6}\right) = 3\frac{7}{12}$	☐	☒
d.	$6\frac{2}{5} - \left(-7\frac{1}{10}\right) = 13\frac{1}{2}$	☒	☐

M

5 Justin earned $25.67 one week and $37.85 the next week. He also purchased a DVD for $19.99 and gas for his car for $22.07. He started with a zero balance in his checking account. Justin recorded all of these transactions in his checkbook and ended up with a balance of $105.58. Was his balance correct? If it was, write an equation to support the answer. If not, find the correct balance.

Justin is not correct. Justin should have subtracted his total purchases (19.99 + 22.07 = 42.06) from his earnings (25.67 + 37.85 = 63.52). His balance is $63.52 − $42.06 = $21.46

C

6 Write a sum, difference, product, and quotient whose answers could all have an estimate of about 6. One expression should include only mixed numbers, one expression should include only decimals, one expression should include only negative rational numbers, and one expression should include only positive rational numbers.

Sum: **Possible answer: $1\frac{3}{4} + 3\frac{5}{6}$**

Difference: **Possible answer: 12.2 − 5.9**

Product: **Possible answer: −2.9(−2.1)**

Quotient: **Possible answer: 18.1 ÷ 3.2**

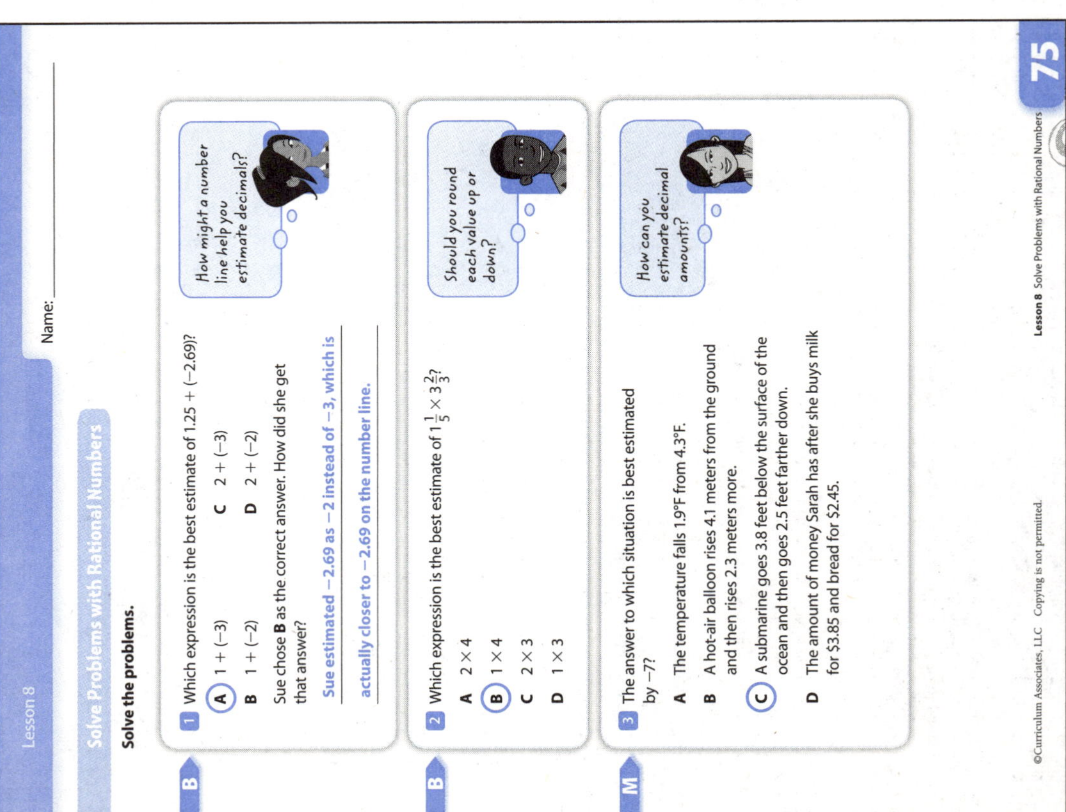

Lesson 8 Name: ____________

Solve Problems with Rational Numbers

Solve the problems.

B

1 Which expression is the best estimate of 1.25 + (−2.69)?

Ⓐ 1 + (−3)

B 1 + (−2)

C 2 + (−3)

D 2 + (−2)

Sue chose **B** as the correct answer. How did she get that answer?

Sue estimated −2.69 as −2 instead of −3, which is actually closer to −2.69 on the number line.

B

2 Which expression is the best estimate of $1\frac{1}{5} \times 3\frac{2}{3}$?

A 2 × 4

Ⓑ 1 × 4

C 2 × 3

D 1 × 3

M

3 The answer to which situation is best estimated by −7?

A The temperature falls 1.9°F from 4.3°F.

B A hot-air balloon rises 4.1 meters from the ground and then rises 2.3 meters more.

Ⓒ A submarine goes 3.8 feet below the surface of the ocean and then goes 2.5 feet farther down.

D The amount of money Sarah has after she buys milk for $3.85 and bread for $2.45.

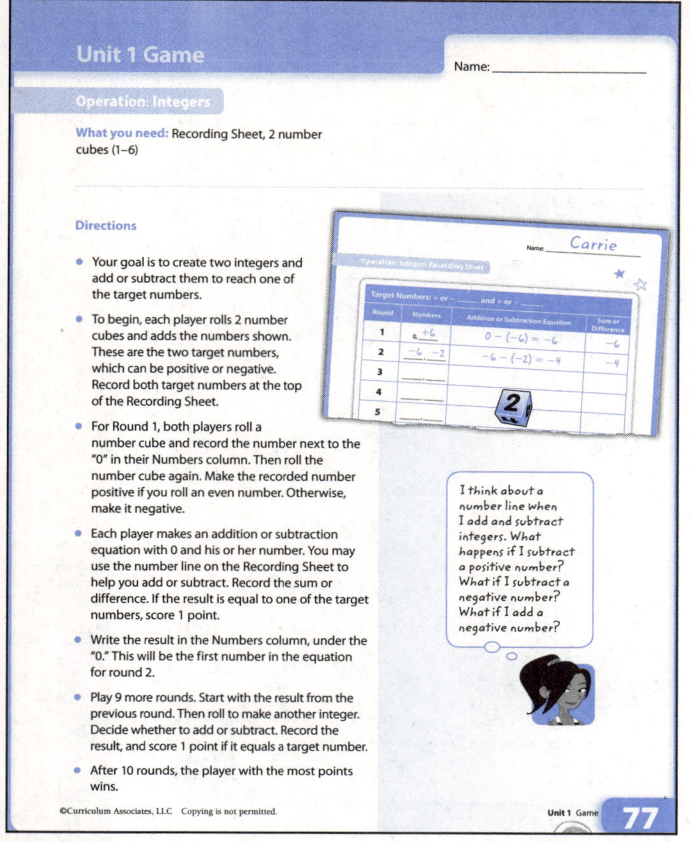

Unit 1 Game

Name: ____________

Operation: Integers

What you need: Recording Sheet, 2 number cubes (1–6)

Directions

- Your goal is to create two integers and add or subtract them to reach one of the target numbers.
- To begin, each player rolls 2 number cubes and adds the numbers shown. These are the two target numbers, which can be positive or negative. Record both target numbers at the top of the Recording Sheet.
- For Round 1, both players roll a number cube and record the number next to the "0" in their Numbers column. Then roll the number cube again. Make the recorded number positive if you roll an even number. Otherwise, make it negative.
- Each player makes an addition or subtraction equation with 0 and his or her number. You may use the number line on the Recording Sheet to help you add or subtract. Record the sum or difference. If the result is equal to one of the target numbers, score 1 point.
- Write the result in the Numbers column, under the "0." This will be the first number in the equation for round 2.
- Play 9 more rounds. Start with the result from the previous round. Then roll to make another integer. Decide whether to add or subtract. Record the result, and score 1 point if it equals a target number.
- After 10 rounds, the player with the most points wins.

Unit 1 Game 77

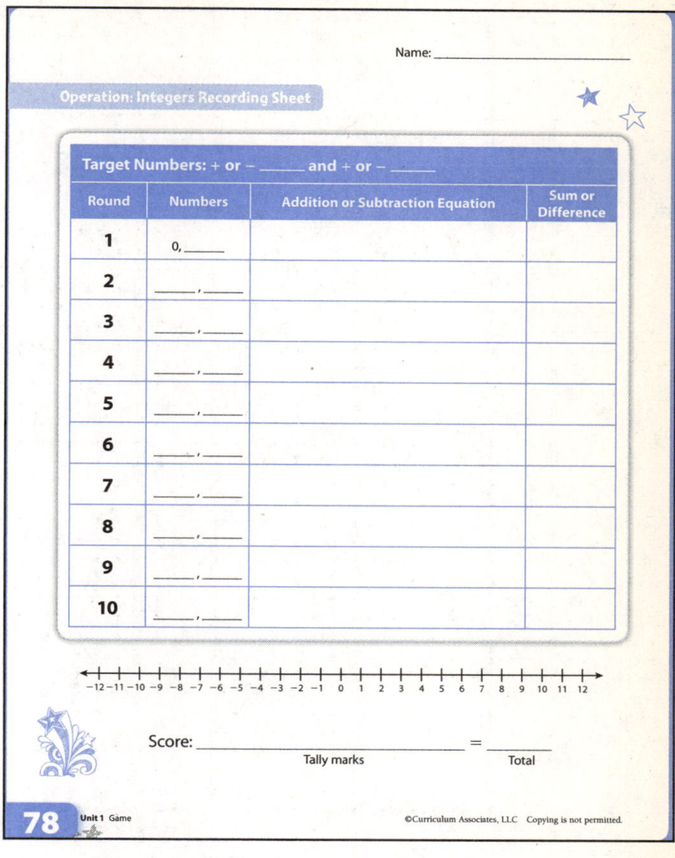

Name: ____________

Operation: Integers Recording Sheet

Target Numbers: + or – ____ and + or – ____			
Round	Numbers	Addition or Subtraction Equation	Sum or Difference
1	0, ____		
2	____, ____		
3	____, ____		
4	____, ____		
5	____, ____		
6	____, ____		
7	____, ____		
8	____, ____		
9	____, ____		
10	____, ____		

Score: ____________ = ______
Tally marks Total

78 Unit 1 Game

STEP BY STEP

CCSS Focus - 7.NS.A.1c, 7.NS.A.1d *Embedded SMPs* - 4, 5, 6, 7

Objective

- Add and subtract integers.

Materials For each pair: Recording Sheets (1 for each player) (TR 1), 2 number cubes (1–6)

- Your goal is to create two integers and add or subtract them to reach one of the target numbers.
- To begin, each player rolls two number cubes and adds the numbers shown. These are the two target numbers, which can be positive or negative. Record both target numbers at the top of the Recording Sheet.
- For Round 1, both players roll a number cube and record the number next to the "0" in their Numbers column. Then roll the number cube again. Make the recorded number positive if you roll an even number. Otherwise, make it negative.
- Each player makes an addition or subtraction equation with 0 and his or her number. You may use the number line on the Recording Sheet to help you add or subtract. Record the sum or difference. If the result is equal to one of the target numbers, score 1 point.
- Write the result in the Numbers column, under the "0." This will be the first number in the equation for round 2.
- Play 9 more rounds. Start with the result from the previous round. Then roll to make another integer. Decide whether to add or subtract. Record the result, and score 1 point if it equals a target number.
- After 10 rounds, the player with the most points wins.
- Model Round 1 for students before they play. Discuss strategies for deciding whether to add or subtract.

Vary the Game Players share a Recording Sheet. Take turns. Player A plays a round. Player B uses Player A's result in his or her equation.

Challenge Play with subtraction only.

Unit 1 Practice

The Number System

Name: ____________

In this unit you learned to:	Lesson
add and subtract positive and negative integers, for example: $-3 + (-4) = -7$.	1, 2, 3
multiply and divide positive and negative integers, for example: $-2 \cdot (-4) = 8$.	4
add and subtract rational numbers, for example: $-2.5 + 3.8 = 1.3$.	7
multiply and divide rational numbers, for example: $-\frac{1}{4} \div \frac{1}{3} = -\frac{3}{4}$.	6
solve word problems with rational numbers.	6, 7, 8

Use these skills to solve problems 1–8.

B **1** Which of the following equations are true? Select all that apply.

A $7 + (-7) = 14$

(B) $-4 + 9 = 5$

C $3 - (-10) = -7$

(D) $-2 - 6 = -8$

B **2** Which expression is equivalent to $5 - 14$? Select all that apply.

(A) $-3 \cdot 3$

(B) $9 \div (-1)$

C $-5 + 14$

D $14 - (-5)$

M **3** A football team loses 3 yards, gains 12 yards, gains 10 yards, and then loses 15 yards. Did the team gain yards or lose yards overall? How many yards?

Show your work.

$(-3) + 12 + 10 + (-15) = 4$

Solution: The team gained 4 yards.

Solve.

M **4** Tell whether each fraction, $\frac{1}{n}$, is written as a terminating decimal or a repeating decimal for the given values of *n*. Write *T* for terminating or *R* for repeating.

n	2	3	4	5	6	8	9	10
Fraction	T	R	T	T	R	T	R	T

C **5** Patrick recorded the daily changes of the value of a stock in dollars: −3.40, −8.09, −2.47, 1.86, and 3.55. What was the average daily change in the stock's value in dollars?

Show your work.

$\frac{-3.40 + (-8.09) + (-2.47) + 1.86 + 3.555}{5}$

$= \frac{-8.55}{5}$

$= -1.71$

Solution: −$1.71

M **6** A fish's position changes by −2.4 feet per second. How long will it take the fish to change its position by −13.2 feet?

A 0.18 seconds

(B) 5.5 seconds

C 10.8 seconds

D 31.68 seconds

M **7** A pelican flies $2\frac{1}{4}$ feet above the surface of the ocean. A dolphin swims $10\frac{1}{2}$ feet below the surface. How far apart are the dolphin and the pelican?

Show your work.

$2\frac{1}{4} - \left(-10\frac{1}{2}\right) = 2\frac{1}{4} + 10\frac{2}{4}$

$= 12\frac{3}{4}$

Solution: The pelican and the dolphin are $12\frac{3}{4}$ feet apart.

C **8** Given the four rational numbers below, find the greatest difference and the greatest product using two of the numbers for each operation.

$2\frac{1}{3}$ 1.5 −1.25 $-3\frac{1}{4}$

Greatest difference: $2\frac{1}{3} - \left(-3\frac{1}{4}\right) = 5\frac{7}{12}$

Greatest product: $-1.25 \cdot \left(-3\frac{1}{4}\right) = 4.0625$, or $4\frac{1}{16}$

Key

B Basic **M** Medium **C** Challenge

TEACHER NOTES

Common Core Standards: 7.NS.A.1b, 7.NS.A.1c, 7.NS.A.1d, 7.NS.A.2c
Standards for Mathematical Practice: 1, 2, 3, 4, 6, 7, 8
DOK: 3
Materials: number cube (1–6) and coin (for Extension).

About the Task

To complete this task, students solve a multi-step problem that involves adding and subtracting positive and negative numbers. The task requires them to reason about the results of integer operations and utilize properties of operations and appropriate models when performing operations with positive and negative numbers.

Getting Started

Read the problem out loud with students. Have them identify the goal. Be sure students understand that the term *balance* means *the amount remaining*. Discuss with students various ways that they might approach the problem. Then go over the checklist with students. Ask them to describe why they might need to try different combinations of numbers [their initial attempts might not provide the desired results]. ***(SMP 1, 3)***

Completing the Task

Students need to translate each game card to a numeric form, identifying the integer specified by the text on the card. To do this, students must correctly interpret the meaning of verbs as positive or negative. If some students find this difficult, support them with concrete models such as play money or two-color counters. ***(SMP 2, 4)***

To add the integers, students may use a number line. They may use properties of operations to group and order numbers for simpler computation. ***(SMP 4, 7, 8)***

Students may need several attempts to have both players ending with a negative balance and Mai's balance being greater. Encourage students to work strategically to modify their choices. ***(SMP 1, 6)***

Have students share how they found solution strategies that worked. ***(SMP 3)***

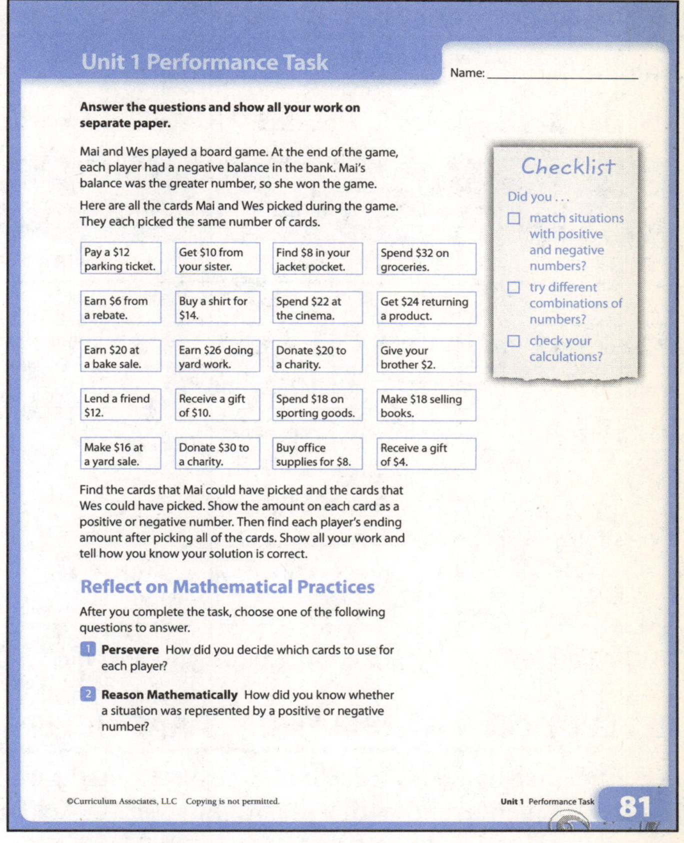

Unit 1 Performance Task

Name: ____________

Answer the questions and show all your work on separate paper.

Mai and Wes played a board game. At the end of the game, each player had a negative balance in the bank. Mai's balance was the greater number, so she won the game.

Here are all the cards Mai and Wes picked during the game. They each picked the same number of cards.

Pay a $12 parking ticket.	Get $10 from your sister.	Find $8 in your jacket pocket.	Spend $32 on groceries.
Earn $6 from a rebate.	Buy a shirt for $14.	Spend $22 at the cinema.	Get $24 returning a product.
Earn $20 at a bake sale.	Earn $26 doing yard work.	Donate $20 to a charity.	Give your brother $2.
Lend a friend $12.	Receive a gift of $10.	Spend $18 on sporting goods.	Make $18 selling books.
Make $16 at a yard sale.	Donate $30 to a charity.	Buy office supplies for $8.	Receive a gift of $4.

Checklist

Did you . . .

- ☐ match situations with positive and negative numbers?
- ☐ try different combinations of numbers?
- ☐ check your calculations?

Find the cards that Mai could have picked and the cards that Wes could have picked. Show the amount on each card as a positive or negative number. Then find each player's ending amount after picking all of the cards. Show all your work and tell how you know your solution is correct.

Reflect on Mathematical Practices

After you complete the task, choose one of the following questions to answer.

1 **Persevere** How did you decide which cards to use for each player?

2 **Reason Mathematically** How did you know whether a situation was represented by a positive or negative number?

Extension

Switch one of Mai's card with one of Wes's cards so that both still have a negative balance, but Wes wins. Tell which cards to trade, and what the final score is. Write equations to show how you found the new scores.

SAMPLE RESPONSE AND RUBRIC

4-Point Solution

Mai and Wes each picked 10 cards. The table shows the cards they could have picked.

Wes's Cards			
Card	**Integer**	**Card**	**Integer**
Pay \$12	−12	Get \$10	+10
Earn \$6	+6	Buy \$14	−14
Donate \$20	−20	Earn \$26	+26
Lend \$12	−12	Receive \$10	+10
Make \$16	+16	Donate \$30	−30
Wes's Total	Add the positive numbers. $6 + 16 + 10 + 26 + 10 = 68$ Add the negative numbers. $-12 + (-20) + (-12) + (-14) + (-30) = -88$ $68 + (-88) = -20$		

Mai's Cards			
Card	**Integer**	**Card**	**Integer**
Find \$8	+8	Spend \$32	−32
Spend \$22	−22	Get \$24	+24
Earn \$20	+20	Give \$2	−2
Spend \$18	−18	Make \$18	+18
Buy \$8	−8	Receive \$4	+4
Mai's Total	Add the positive numbers. $8 + 20 + 24 + 18 + 4 = 74$ Add the negative numbers. $-22 + (-18) + (-8) + (-32) + (-2) = -82$ $74 + (-82) = -8$		

At the end, Wes had −\$20 in the bank and Mai had −\$8 in the bank. Because $-8 > -20$, Mai won.

REFLECT ON MATHEMATICAL PRACTICES

1. Students should address how they distributed cards so that each final result was negative while also ensuring that Mai ended up with a greater number (i.e., closer to zero). ***(SMP 1)***
2. Students should explain how the verbs correlate to positive or negative numbers. ***(SMP 2)***

SCORING RUBRIC

4 points All parts of the problem are complete and correct. Students show which cards Mai had and which cards Wes had and give a correct integer for each card. Students show all work, and their calculations are correct. They tell why the answer meets the criteria.

3 points The student has completed all parts of the problem, with one or two errors. Possible errors might include not using all of the cards, showing the wrong sign for one integer, making an error in the calculation, or not verifying that Mai's balance is greater.

2 points The student has attempted all parts of the problem, with a number of errors. Several integers may have the wrong sign. Not all cards are accounted for. There are calculation errors.

1 point Much of the problem is incomplete, with several errors. Several integers are missing or have the wrong sign. There are several calculation errors. Wes's total may be greater than Mai's total. The student may not have compared the totals or may have compared incorrectly.

SOLUTION TO THE EXTENSION

Possible Solution

I want Mai's balance to go down, and Wes's balance to go up. So, I'll give Mai's "Earn \$20" card to Wes. Now Mai's balance is −28 and Wes has 0. But I need to take a card from Wes, too. I will give Wes's "Earn \$6" card to Mai. Now Mai has −22 and Wes has −6. Mai's new balance is $-8 - 20 + 6 = -22$. Wes's new balance is $-20 + 20 - 6 = -6$. And, $-6 > -22$, so Wes wins.

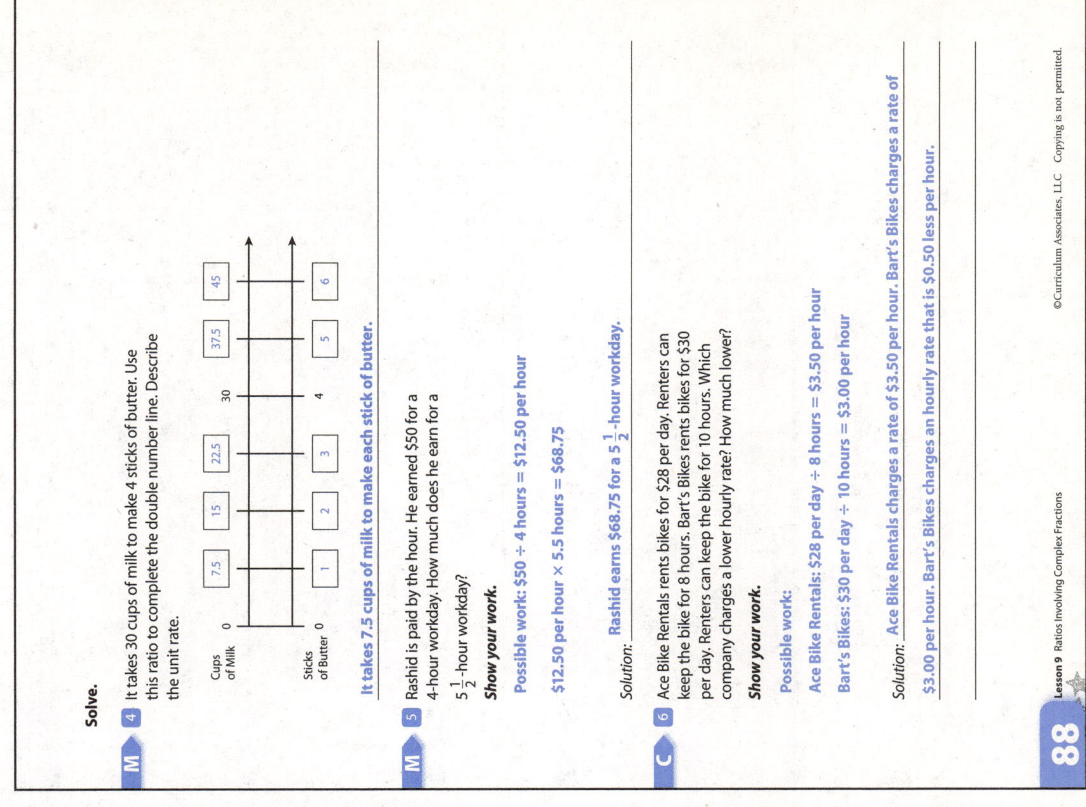

Lesson 9

Ratios Involving Complex Fractions

Name: ____________________

Prerequisite: Find Unit Rates

Study the example problem showing how to find a unit rate. Then solve problems 1–6.

Example

Six pounds of grapefruit cost \$3. What is the cost per pound?

You can use a double number line to help you find rate and unit rate. Start with the ratio you know: \$3 for 6 pounds.

Divide both \$3 and 6 pounds by 3 to get \$1 for 2 pounds. Then divide \$1 and 2 pounds by 2 to find the cost per pound, which is \$0.50 for 1 pound.

Price (\$)	0	0.50	1.00	?	?	?	3.00
Pounds	0	1	2	3	4	5	6

Notice that you can also divide \$3 by 6 to get the cost per pound directly.

Vocabulary

rate the ratio that compares the first quantity to one unit of the second quantity. For a ratio of 2 dollars for every 5 apples, the rate is $\frac{2}{5}$ dollars per apple.

unit rate the numerical part of the rate, without the units. For a rate of $\frac{2}{5}$ dollar per apple, the unit rate is $\frac{2}{5}$.

B 1 In the example, how much would it cost to buy 3, 4, and 5 pounds of grapefruit? Explain how you found your answers.

\$1.50, \$2.00, \$2.50; Possible explanation: I multiplied the cost per pound by 3, 4, and 5 to find each cost.

B 2 Leila uses 5 cups of grated zucchini to make 2 loaves of zucchini bread. How many cups of zucchini does she need to make 1 loaf?

$2\frac{1}{2}$ cups

B 3 Jenna walks 4 miles in 1 hour. At this rate, how many miles can she walk in 3.5 hours?

14 miles

©Curriculum Associates, LLC Copying is not permitted. **Lesson 9** Ratios Involving Complex Fractions **87**

Solve.

M 4 It takes 30 cups of milk to make 4 sticks of butter. Use this ratio to complete the double number line. Describe the unit rate.

Cups of Milk	0	7.5	15	22.5	30	37.5	45
Sticks of Butter	0	1	2	3	4	5	6

It takes 7.5 cups of milk to make each stick of butter.

M 5 Rashid is paid by the hour. He earned \$50 for a 4-hour workday. How much does he earn for a $5\frac{1}{2}$-hour workday?

Show your work.

Possible work: \$50 ÷ 4 hours = \$12.50 per hour

\$12.50 per hour × 5.5 hours = \$68.75

Solution: **Rashid earns \$68.75 for a $5\frac{1}{2}$-hour workday.**

C 6 Ace Bike Rentals rents bikes for \$28 per day. Renters can keep the bike for 8 hours. Bart's Bikes rents bikes for \$30 per day. Renters can keep the bike for 10 hours. Which company charges a lower hourly rate? How much lower?

Show your work.

Possible work:

Ace Bike Rentals: \$28 per day ÷ 8 hours = \$3.50 per hour

Bart's Bikes: \$30 per day ÷ 10 hours = \$3.00 per hour

Solution: **Ace Bike Rentals charges a rate of \$3.50 per hour. Bart's Bikes charges a rate of \$3.00 per hour. Bart's Bikes charges an hourly rate that is \$0.50 less per hour.**

88 **Lesson 9** Ratios Involving Complex Fractions ©Curriculum Associates, LLC Copying is not permitted.

Key

B Basic **M** Medium **C** Challenge

Name: ____________

Find Unit Rates with Fractions

Study the example problem showing how to find a unit rate. Then solve problems 1–8.

Example

Helena uses this recipe to make homemade fabric softener. How much water and vinegar does she use for a half batch? How much water and vinegar does she use for a double batch?

You can use a double number line to help you solve this problem.

You can use the recipe to see that you need 5 cups of water for $2\frac{1}{2}$ cups of vinegar. Label these on the number line. Find half of each quantity for a half batch. Double each quantity for a double batch.

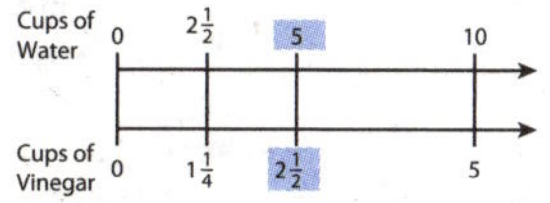

Recipe for Fabric Softener

Ingredients:

5 cups hot water

$2\frac{1}{2}$ cups white vinegar

$1\frac{1}{2}$ cups hair conditioner

Directions:

Mix all ingredients together.

Cups of Water	0	$2\frac{1}{2}$	5	10
Cups of Vinegar	0	$1\frac{1}{4}$	$2\frac{1}{2}$	5

Helena needs $2\frac{1}{2}$ cups water and $1\frac{1}{4}$ cup vinegar for a half batch. She needs 10 cups of water and 5 cups of vinegar for a double batch.

B **1** If Helena uses $1\frac{1}{4}$ cups of water to make fabric softener, how much vinegar does she need?

$\frac{5}{8}$ cup of vinegar

B **2** Use the recipe to find how much hair conditioner Helena needs to make a half batch and a double batch.

$\frac{3}{4}$ cup of conditioner for a half batch and 3 cups for a double batch

M **3** Explain how to find the unit rate of water to vinegar. What does the unit rate mean in this context?

Possible explanation: Use the ratio 10 cups of water to 5 cups of vinegar. The unit rate is $10 \div 5$, or 2. The unit rate means that you need 2 cups of water for each cup of vinegar.

Solve.

Use the following recipe for granola bars to solve problems 4–8.

2 cups of oats	$\frac{1}{4}$ cup of flaxseed
$\frac{1}{2}$ cup of quinoa	$\frac{2}{3}$ cup of soy protein

B **4** Write ratios for the amount of oats to the amount of each of the other grains.

oats to quinoa: $\frac{2}{\frac{1}{2}}$; oats to flaxseed: $\frac{2}{\frac{1}{4}}$; oats to soy protein: $\frac{2}{\frac{2}{3}}$

M **5** Show how to find the unit rate of oats to quinoa. Tell what the unit rate means.

Possible answer: oats to quinoa $= 2 \div \frac{1}{2} = 4$. The unit rate is 4. The recipe uses 4 times the amount of oats compared to quinoa.

M **6** Find unit rates for the other two ratios that you wrote in problem 4.

The unit rate for oats to flaxseed is $2 \div \frac{1}{4}$, or 8. The unit rate for oats to soy protein is $2 \div \frac{2}{3}$, or 3.

C **7** Suppose you are making granola bars with 3 cups of oats. How much quinoa, flaxseed, and soy protein would you need to use? Explain.

Possible answer: The unit rates show how many cups of oats you need per cup of the other ingredients. Divide the amount of oats by each unit rate. Quinoa: 3 cups $\div 4 = \frac{3}{4}$ cup. Flaxseed: 3 cups $\div 8 = \frac{3}{8}$ cup. Soy protein: 3 cups $\div 3 = 1$ cup.

C **8** In addition to the grains listed above, the recipe also includes $1\frac{1}{4}$ cups of dried fruit. Show how to find the amount of dried fruit needed if you use 3 cups of oats.

The ratio of oats to fruit is 2 to $1\frac{1}{4}$, which is a unit rate of $\frac{8}{5}$. For 3 cups of oats: $3 \div \frac{8}{5}$ is $1\frac{7}{8}$. Use $1\frac{7}{8}$ cups of fruit for 3 cups of oats.

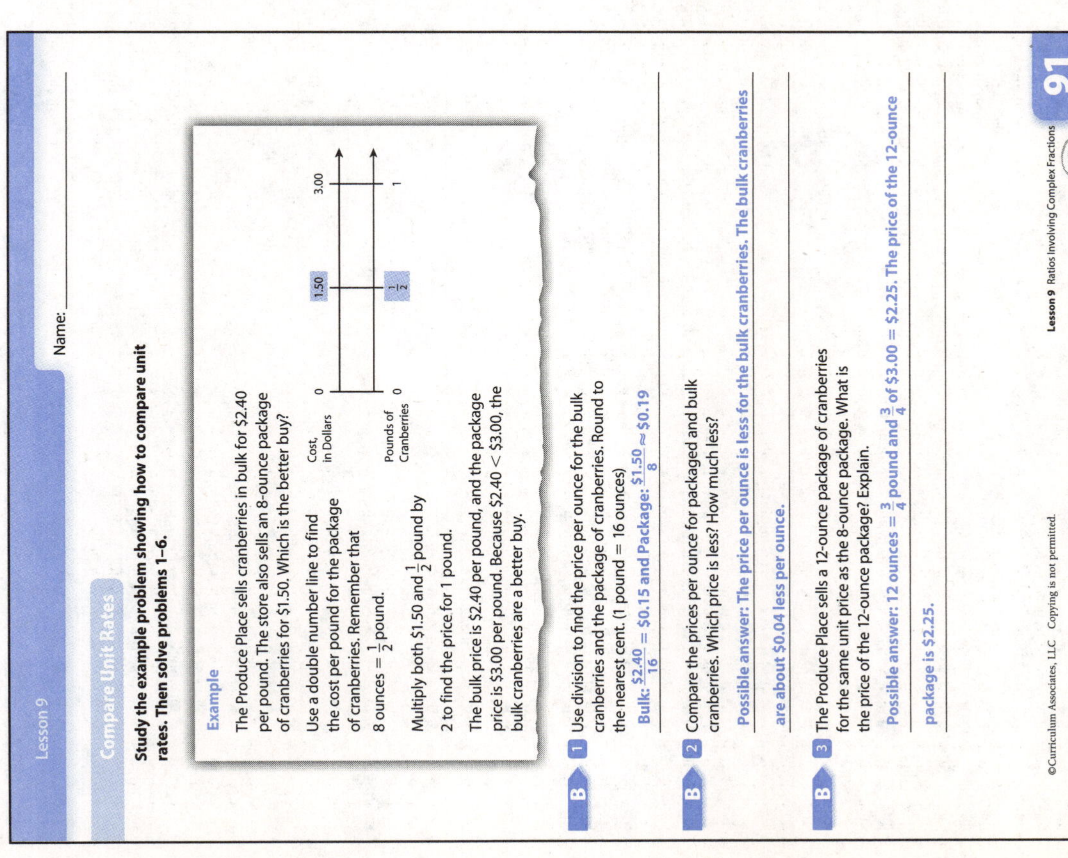

Lesson 9

Name: ____________

Compare Unit Rates

Study the example problem showing how to compare unit rates. Then solve problems 1–6.

Example

The Produce Place sells cranberries in bulk for $2.40 per pound. The store also sells an 8-ounce package of cranberries for $1.50. Which is the better buy?

Use a double number line to find the cost per pound for the package of cranberries. Remember that 8 ounces = $\frac{1}{2}$ pound.

Multiply both $1.50 and $\frac{1}{2}$ pound by 2 to find the price for 1 pound.

The bulk price is $2.40 per pound, and the package price is $3.00 per pound. Because $2.40 < $3.00, the bulk cranberries are a better buy.

B 1 Use division to find the price per ounce for the bulk cranberries and the package of cranberries. Round to the nearest cent. (1 pound = 16 ounces)

Bulk: $\frac{\$2.40}{16}$ = $0.15 and Package: $\frac{\$1.50}{8}$ ≈ $0.19

B 2 Compare the prices per ounce for packaged and bulk cranberries. Which price is less? How much less?

Possible answer: The price per ounce is less for the bulk cranberries. The bulk cranberries are about $0.04 less per ounce.

B 3 The Produce Place sells a 12-ounce package of cranberries for the same unit price as the 8-ounce package. What is the price of the 12-ounce package? Explain.

Possible answer: 12 ounces = $\frac{3}{4}$ pound and $\frac{3}{4}$ of $3.00 = $2.25. The price of the 12-ounce package is $2.25.

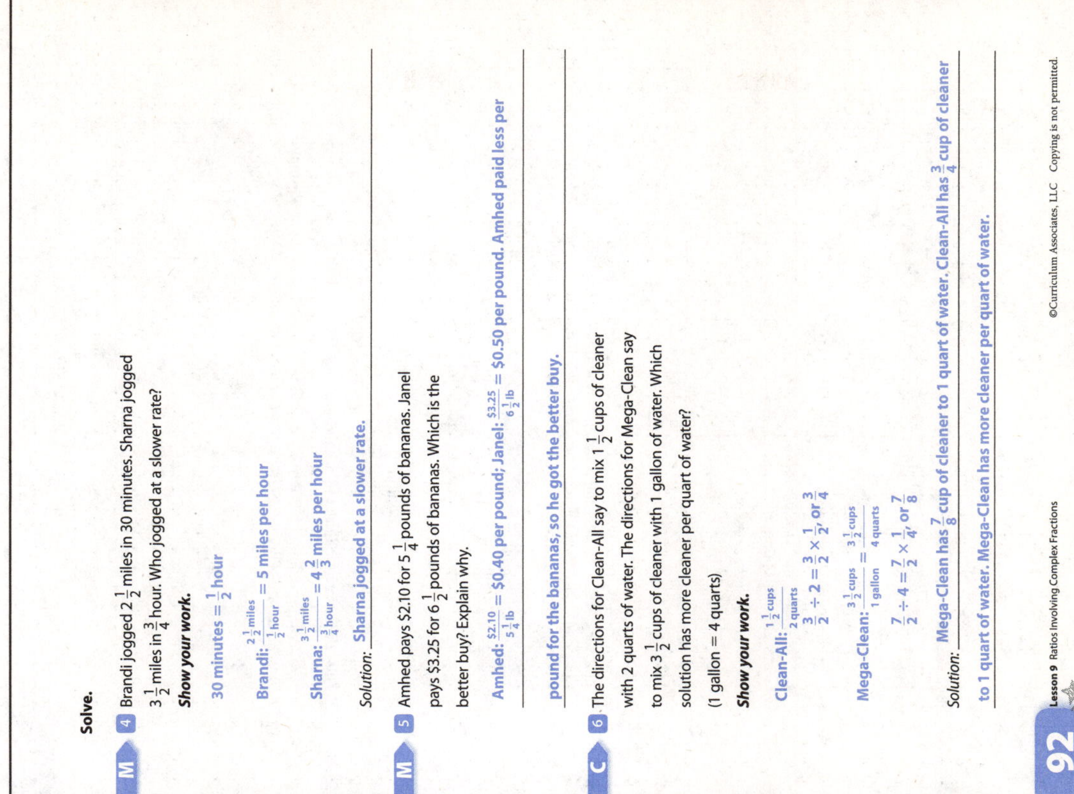

Solve.

M 4 Brandi jogged $2\frac{1}{2}$ miles in 30 minutes. Sharna jogged $3\frac{1}{2}$ miles in $\frac{3}{4}$ hour. Who jogged at a slower rate?

Show your work.

30 minutes = $\frac{1}{2}$ hour

Brandi: $\frac{2\frac{1}{2}\text{ miles}}{\frac{1}{2}\text{ hour}}$ = 5 miles per hour

Sharna: $\frac{3\frac{1}{2}\text{ miles}}{\frac{3}{4}\text{ hour}} = 4\frac{2}{3}$ miles per hour

Solution: **Sharna jogged at a slower rate.**

M 5 Amhed pays $2.10 for $5\frac{1}{4}$ pounds of bananas. Janel pays $3.25 for $6\frac{1}{2}$ pounds of bananas. Which is the better buy? Explain why.

Amhed: $\frac{\$2.10}{5\frac{1}{4}\text{ lb}}$ = $0.40 per pound; Janel: $\frac{\$3.25}{6\frac{1}{2}\text{ lb}}$ = $0.50 per pound. Amhed paid less per pound for the bananas, so he got the better buy.

C 6 The directions for Clean-All say to mix $1\frac{1}{2}$ cups of cleaner with 2 quarts of water. The directions for Mega-Clean say to mix $3\frac{1}{2}$ cups of cleaner with 1 gallon of water. Which solution has more cleaner per quart of water?

(1 gallon = 4 quarts)

Show your work.

Clean-All: $\frac{1\frac{1}{2}\text{ cups}}{2\text{ quarts}}$

$\frac{3}{2} \div 2 = \frac{3}{2} \times \frac{1}{2}$, or $\frac{3}{4}$

Mega-Clean: $\frac{3\frac{1}{2}\text{ cups}}{1\text{ gallon}} = \frac{3\frac{1}{2}\text{ cups}}{4\text{ quarts}}$

$\frac{7}{2} \div 4 = \frac{7}{2} \times \frac{1}{4}$, or $\frac{7}{8}$

Solution: **Mega-Clean has $\frac{7}{8}$ cup of cleaner to 1 quart of water. Clean-All has $\frac{3}{4}$ cup of cleaner to 1 quart of water. Mega-Clean has more cleaner per quart of water.**

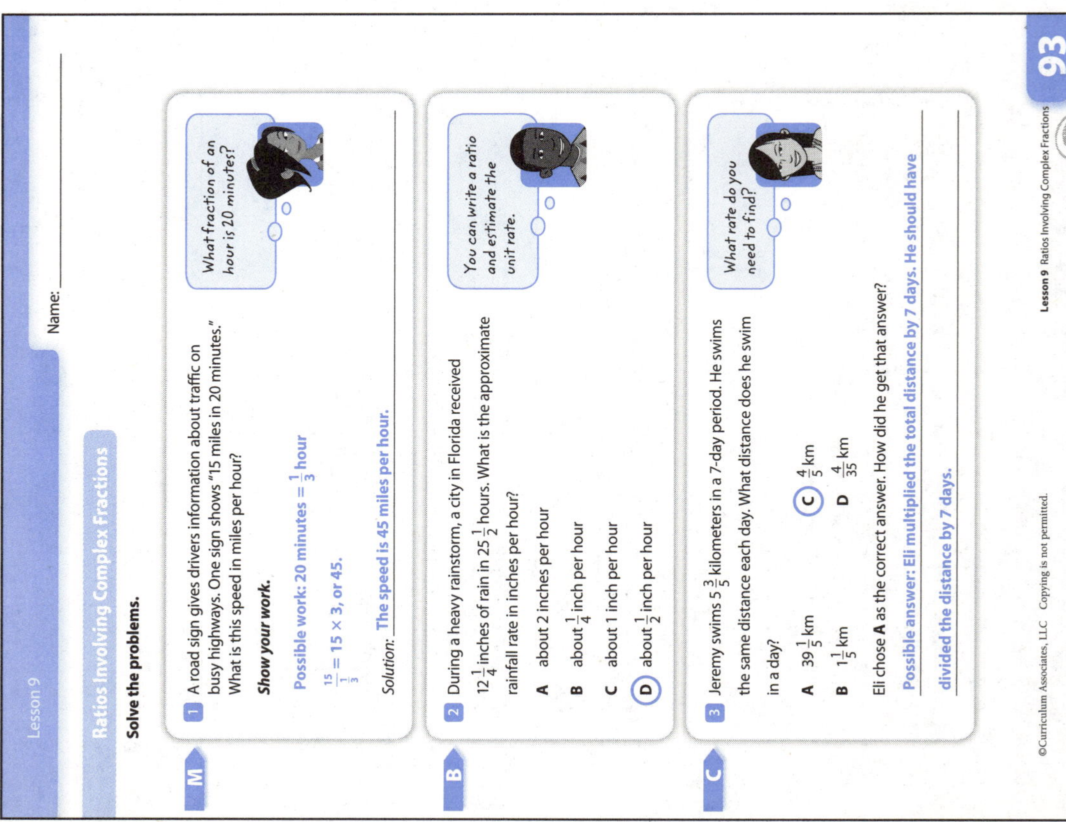

Lesson 9

Name: ____________

Ratios Involving Complex Fractions

Solve the problems.

M

1 A road sign gives drivers information about traffic on busy highways. One sign shows "15 miles in 20 minutes." What is this speed in miles per hour?

Show your work.

Possible work: 20 minutes = $\frac{1}{3}$ hour

$\frac{15}{\frac{1}{3}} = 15 \times 3$, or 45.

Solution: The speed is 45 miles per hour.

B

2 During a heavy rainstorm, a city in Florida received $12\frac{1}{4}$ inches of rain in $25\frac{1}{2}$ hours. What is the approximate rainfall rate in inches per hour?

A about 2 inches per hour

B about $\frac{1}{4}$ inch per hour

C about 1 inch per hour

(D) about $\frac{1}{2}$ inch per hour

C

3 Jeremy swims $5\frac{3}{5}$ kilometers in a 7-day period. He swims the same distance each day. What distance does he swim in a day?

A $39\frac{1}{5}$ km

B $1\frac{1}{5}$ km

(C) $\frac{4}{5}$ km

D $\frac{4}{35}$ km

Eli chose **A** as the correct answer. How did he get that answer?

Possible answer: Eli multiplied the total distance by 7 days. He should have divided the distance by 7 days.

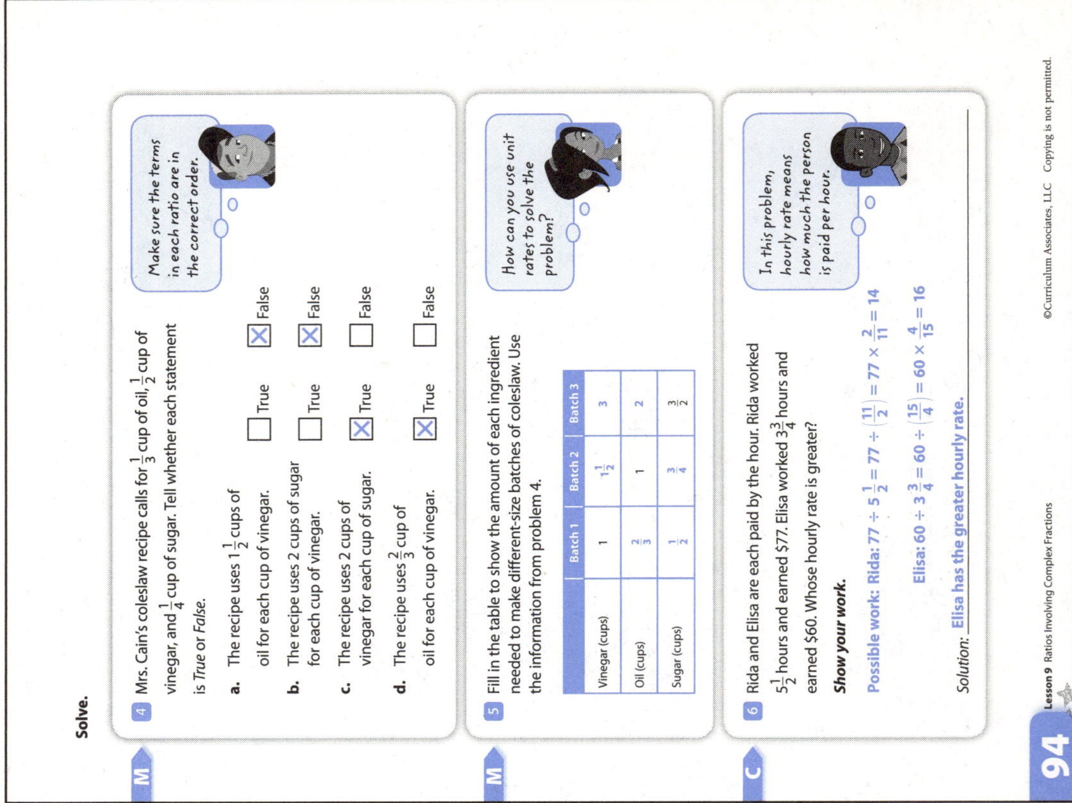

Solve.

M

4 Mrs. Cain's coleslaw recipe calls for $\frac{1}{3}$ cup of oil, $\frac{1}{2}$ cup of vinegar, and $\frac{1}{4}$ cup of sugar. Tell whether each statement is *True* or *False*.

a. The recipe uses $1\frac{1}{2}$ cups of oil for each cup of vinegar. ☐ True ☒ False

b. The recipe uses 2 cups of sugar for each cup of vinegar. ☐ True ☒ False

c. The recipe uses 2 cups of vinegar for each cup of sugar. ☒ True ☐ False

d. The recipe uses $\frac{2}{3}$ cup of oil for each cup of vinegar. ☒ True ☐ False

M

5 Fill in the table to show the amount of each ingredient needed to make different-size batches of coleslaw. Use the information from problem 4.

	Batch 1	Batch 2	Batch 3
Vinegar (cups)	1	$1\frac{1}{2}$	3
Oil (cups)	$\frac{2}{3}$	1	2
Sugar (cups)	$\frac{1}{2}$	$\frac{3}{4}$	$\frac{3}{2}$

C

6 Rida and Elisa are each paid by the hour. Rida worked $5\frac{1}{2}$ hours and earned \$77. Elisa worked $3\frac{3}{4}$ hours and earned \$60. Whose hourly rate is greater?

Show your work.

Possible work: Rida: $77 \div 5\frac{1}{2} = 77 \div \left(\frac{11}{2}\right) = 77 \times \frac{2}{11} = 14$

Elisa: $60 \div 3\frac{3}{4} = 60 \div \left(\frac{15}{4}\right) = 60 \times \frac{4}{15} = 16$

Solution: Elisa has the greater hourly rate.

Lesson 10

Understand Proportional Relationships

Name: ____________________

Prerequisite: How do you find equivalent ratios?

Study the example problem showing how to find equivalent ratios. Then solve problems 1–7.

Example

There are 3 counselors assigned to a group of 24 campers. At this rate, how many counselors are needed for 40 campers?

The given ratio is 24 campers to 3 counselors. That's a rate of 8 campers to 1 counselor. You can use this information to make a table of equivalent ratios.

Number of Campers	8	16	**24**	32	40
Number of Counselors	1	2	**3**	4	5

From the table you can see that 5 counselors are needed for 40 campers.

B **1** Explain how to use the unit rate to make the table in the example.

The unit rate is 8. There are 8 campers for each counselor. I multiply 8 by the number of counselors to complete each column in the table.

B **2** One ordered pair from the table is plotted on the coordinate plane. Finish plotting the ordered pairs.

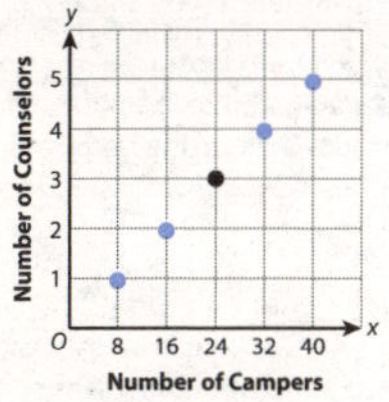

B **3** Suppose you had 9 counselors available. How many campers could you have?

72 campers

Vocabulary

equivalent ratios
two or more ratios that are equal to one another.

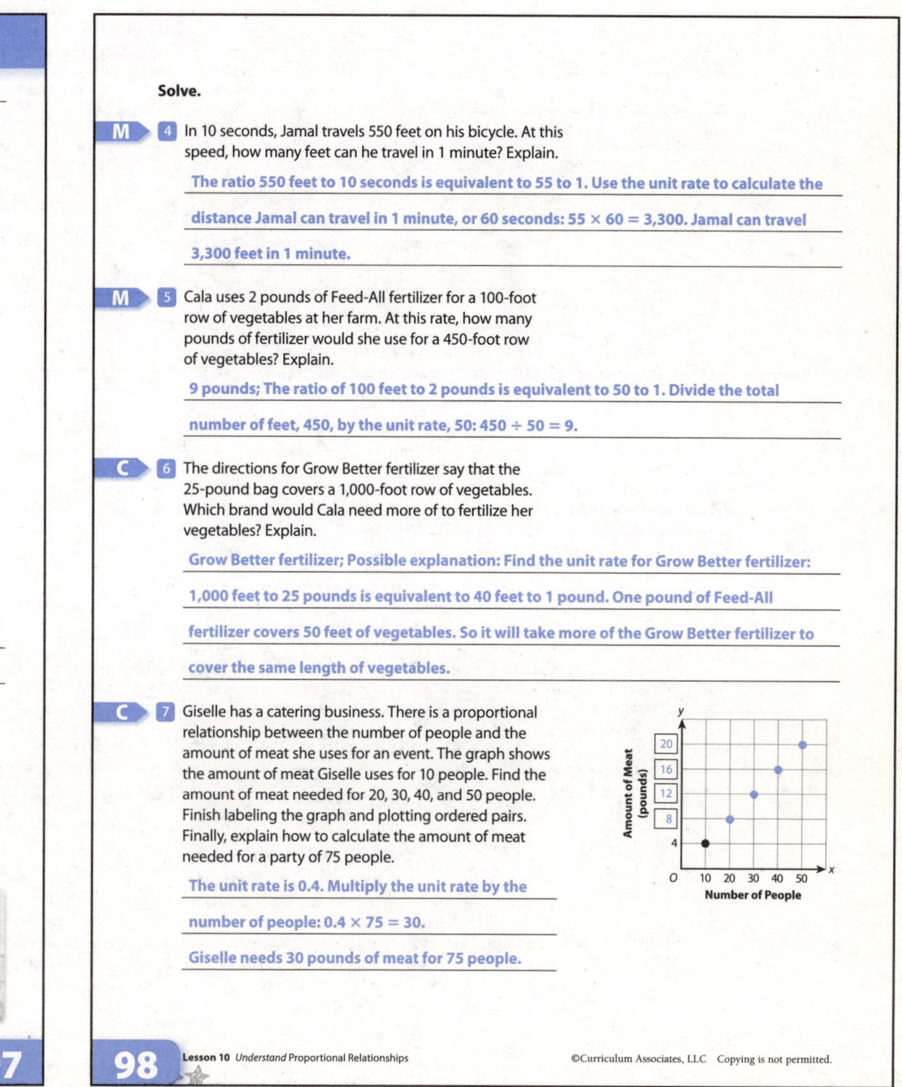

Solve.

M **4** In 10 seconds, Jamal travels 550 feet on his bicycle. At this speed, how many feet can he travel in 1 minute? Explain.

The ratio 550 feet to 10 seconds is equivalent to 55 to 1. Use the unit rate to calculate the distance Jamal can travel in 1 minute, or 60 seconds: 55 × 60 = 3,300. Jamal can travel 3,300 feet in 1 minute.

M **5** Cala uses 2 pounds of Feed-All fertilizer for a 100-foot row of vegetables at her farm. At this rate, how many pounds of fertilizer would she use for a 450-foot row of vegetables? Explain.

9 pounds; The ratio of 100 feet to 2 pounds is equivalent to 50 to 1. Divide the total number of feet, 450, by the unit rate, 50: 450 ÷ 50 = 9.

C **6** The directions for Grow Better fertilizer say that the 25-pound bag covers a 1,000-foot row of vegetables. Which brand would Cala need more of to fertilize her vegetables? Explain.

Grow Better fertilizer; Possible explanation: Find the unit rate for Grow Better fertilizer: 1,000 feet to 25 pounds is equivalent to 40 feet to 1 pound. One pound of Feed-All fertilizer covers 50 feet of vegetables. So it will take more of the Grow Better fertilizer to cover the same length of vegetables.

C **7** Giselle has a catering business. There is a proportional relationship between the number of people and the amount of meat she uses for an event. The graph shows the amount of meat Giselle uses for 10 people. Find the amount of meat needed for 20, 30, 40, and 50 people. Finish labeling the graph and plotting ordered pairs. Finally, explain how to calculate the amount of meat needed for a party of 75 people.

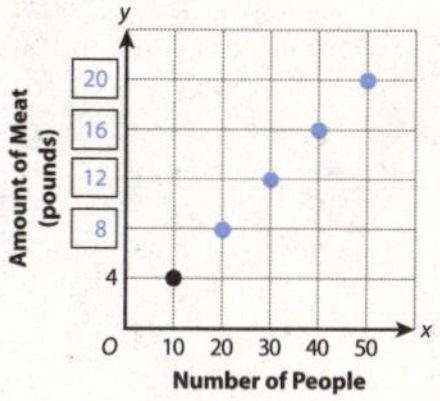

The unit rate is 0.4. Multiply the unit rate by the number of people: 0.4 × 75 = 30.

Giselle needs 30 pounds of meat for 75 people.

Key

B Basic **M** Medium **C** Challenge

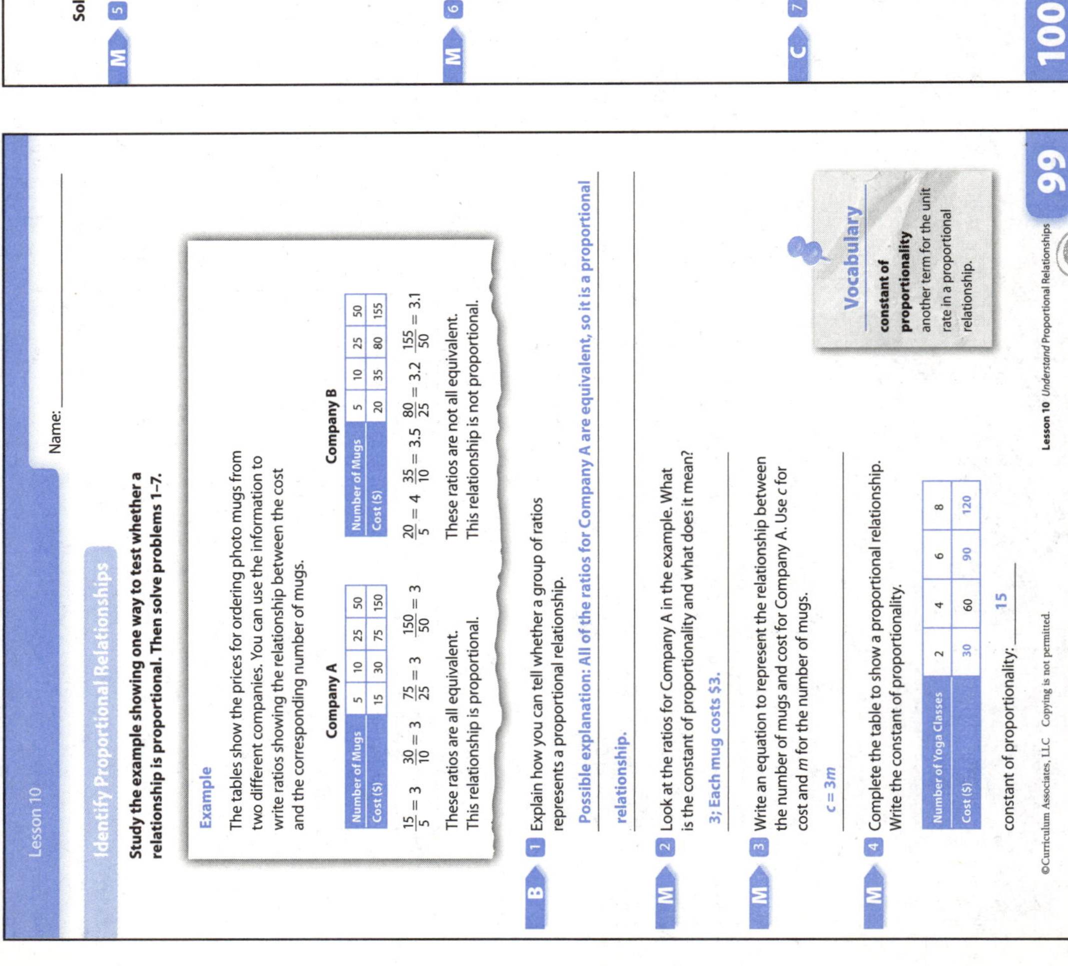

Lesson 10

Name: ____________________

Identify Proportional Relationships

Study the example showing one way to test whether a relationship is proportional. Then solve problems 1–7.

Example

The tables show the prices for ordering photo mugs from two different companies. You can use the information to write ratios showing the relationship between the cost and the corresponding number of mugs.

Company A

Number of Mugs	5	10	25	50
Cost ($)	15	30	75	150

$\frac{15}{5} = 3$ $\frac{30}{10} = 3$ $\frac{75}{25} = 3$ $\frac{150}{50} = 3$

These ratios are all equivalent.
This relationship is proportional.

Company B

Number of Mugs	5	10	25	50
Cost ($)	20	35	80	155

$\frac{20}{5} = 4$ $\frac{35}{10} = 3.5$ $\frac{80}{25} = 3.2$ $\frac{155}{50} = 3.1$

These ratios are not all equivalent.
This relationship is not proportional.

B **1** Explain how you can tell whether a group of ratios represents a proportional relationship.

Possible explanation: All of the ratios for Company A are equivalent, so it is a proportional relationship.

M **2** Look at the ratios for Company A in the example. What is the constant of proportionality and what does it mean?

3; Each mug costs $3.

M **3** Write an equation to represent the relationship between the number of mugs and cost for Company A. Use *c* for cost and *m* for the number of mugs.

$c = 3m$

M **4** Complete the table to show a proportional relationship. Write the constant of proportionality.

Number of Yoga Classes	2	4	6	8
Cost ($)	30	60	90	120

constant of proportionality: 15

Vocabulary

constant of proportionality another term for the unit rate in a proportional relationship.

©Curriculum Associates, LLC Copying is not permitted. Lesson 10 *Understand* Proportional Relationships 99

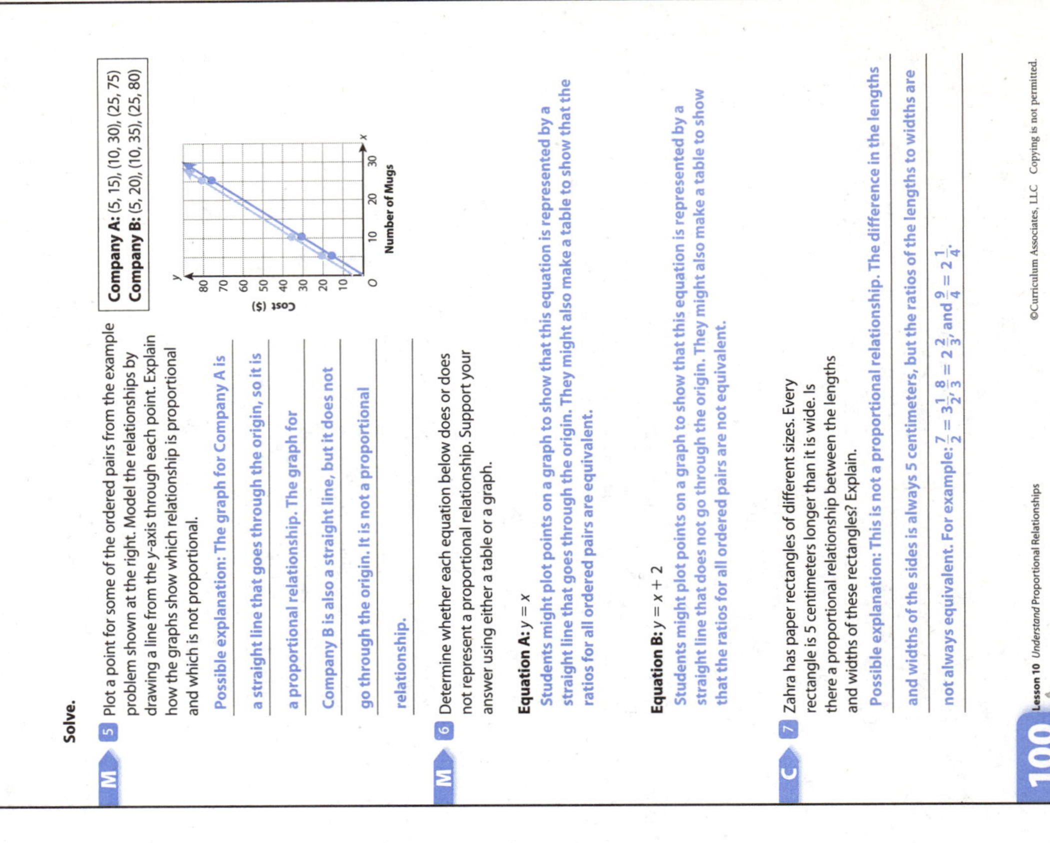

Solve.

M **5** Plot a point for some of the ordered pairs from the example problem shown at the right. Model the relationships by drawing a line from the *y*-axis through each point. Explain how the graphs show which relationship is proportional and which is not proportional.

Company A: (5, 15), (10, 30), (25, 75)
Company B: (5, 20), (10, 35), (25, 80)

Possible explanation: The graph for Company A is a straight line that goes through the origin, so it is a proportional relationship. The graph for Company B is also a straight line, but it does not go through the origin. It is not a proportional relationship.

M **6** Determine whether each equation below does or does not represent a proportional relationship. Support your answer using either a table or a graph.

Equation A: $y = x$

Students might plot points on a graph to show that this equation is represented by a straight line that goes through the origin. They might also make a table to show that the ratios for all ordered pairs are equivalent.

Equation B: $y = x + 2$

Students might plot points on a graph to show that this equation is represented by a straight line that does not go through the origin. They might also make a table to show that the ratios for all ordered pairs are not equivalent.

C **7** Zahra has paper rectangles of different sizes. Every rectangle is 5 centimeters longer than it is wide. Is there a proportional relationship between the lengths and widths of these rectangles? Explain.

Possible explanation: This is not a proportional relationship. The difference in the lengths and widths of the sides is always 5 centimeters, but the ratios of the lengths to widths are not always equivalent. For example: $\frac{7}{2} = 3\frac{1}{2}$, $\frac{8}{3} = 2\frac{2}{3}$, and $\frac{9}{4} = 2\frac{1}{4}$.

100 Lesson 10 *Understand* Proportional Relationships ©Curriculum Associates, LLC Copying is not permitted.

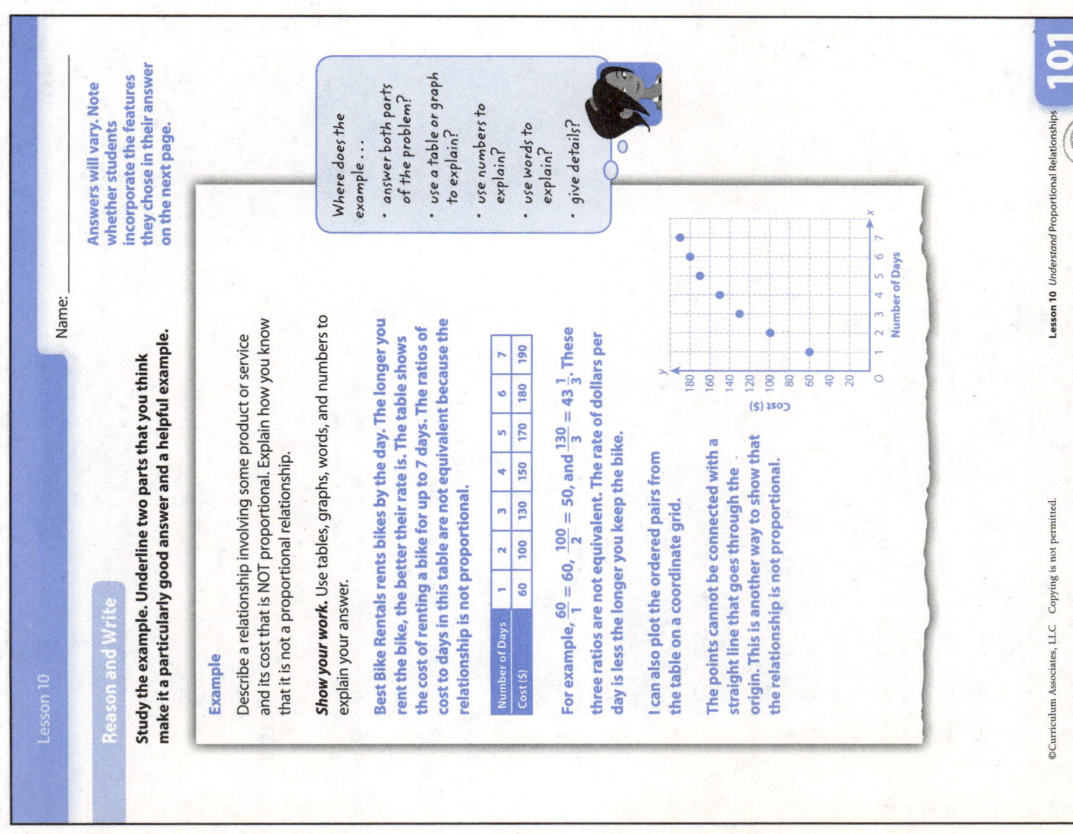

Lesson 10

Name: ____________________

Reason and Write

Study the example. Underline two parts that you think make it a particularly good answer and a helpful example.

Answers will vary. Note whether students incorporate the features they chose in their answer on the next page.

Example

Describe a relationship involving some product or service and its cost that is NOT proportional. Explain how you know that it is not a proportional relationship.

Show your work. Use tables, graphs, words, and numbers to explain your answer.

Best Bike Rentals rents bikes by the day. The longer you rent the bike, the better their rate is. The table shows the cost of renting a bike for up to 7 days. The ratios of cost to days in this table are not equivalent because the relationship is not proportional.

Number of Days	1	2	3	4	5	6	7
Cost ($)	60	100	130	150	170	180	190

For example, $\frac{60}{1} = 60$, $\frac{100}{2} = 50$, and $\frac{130}{3} = 43\frac{1}{3}$. These three ratios are not equivalent. The rate of dollars per day is less the longer you keep the bike.

I can also plot the ordered pairs from the table on a coordinate grid.

The points cannot be connected with a straight line that goes through the origin. This is another way to show that the relationship is not proportional.

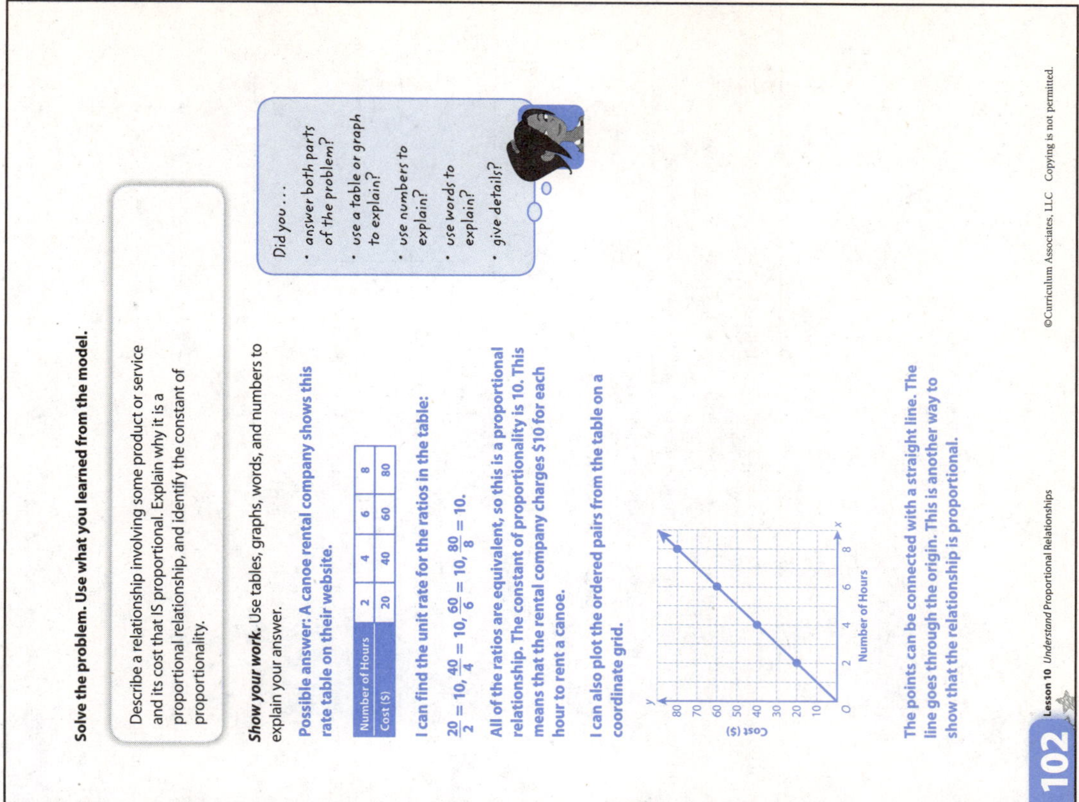

Solve the problem. Use what you learned from the model.

Describe a relationship involving some product or service and its cost that IS proportional. Explain why it is a proportional relationship, and identify the constant of proportionality.

Show your work. Use tables, graphs, words, and numbers to explain your answer.

Possible answer: A canoe rental company shows this rate table on their website.

Number of Hours	2	4	6	8
Cost ($)	20	40	60	80

I can find the unit rate for the ratios in the table:

$\frac{20}{2} = 10$, $\frac{40}{4} = 10$, $\frac{60}{6} = 10$, $\frac{80}{8} = 10$.

All of the ratios are equivalent, so this is a proportional relationship. The constant of proportionality is 10. This means that the rental company charges $10 for each hour to rent a canoe.

I can also plot the ordered pairs from the table on a coordinate grid.

The points can be connected with a straight line. The line goes through the origin. This is another way to show that the relationship is proportional.

Lesson 11

Equations for Proportional Relationships

Name: ____________________

Prerequisite: Understand Proportional Relationships

Study the example showing proportional relationships in a table and a graph. Then solve problems 1–5.

Example

Bottles of water cost $2 each. Is the relationship of the cost to the number of bottles a proportional relationship?

You can use a table or a graph to see whether the relationship is proportional.

Number of Bottles	1	2	3	4
Total Cost ($)	2	4	6	8
$\frac{\text{Total Cost}}{\text{Number of Bottles}}$	$\frac{2}{1}$	$\frac{4}{2}=\frac{2}{1}$	$\frac{6}{3}=\frac{2}{1}$	$\frac{8}{4}=\frac{2}{1}$

Total Cost ($)

Number of Bottles

All of the ratios in the table are equal to $\frac{2}{1}$.

This is the unit rate and means that it costs $2 for one bottle of water. The graph is a straight line through the origin (0, 0).

So this is a proportional relationship.

B 1 What is the cost of 12 bottles? Explain.

$24; $2 \cdot 12 = 24$

B 2 Find the ratio of the cost of 12 bottles to the number of bottles. Is the ratio equivalent to the unit rate?

$\frac{24}{12} = \frac{2}{1}$; yes

M 3 How much will the total cost increase for each additional bottle of water purchased? Compare this value to the constant of proportionality.

The total cost will increase $2 for each additional bottle of water purchased, so it is equal to the constant of proportionality, which is $\frac{2}{1}$, or 2.

Vocabulary

proportional relationship the relationship among a group of ratios that are equivalent.

constant of proportionality the unit rate in a proportional relationship.

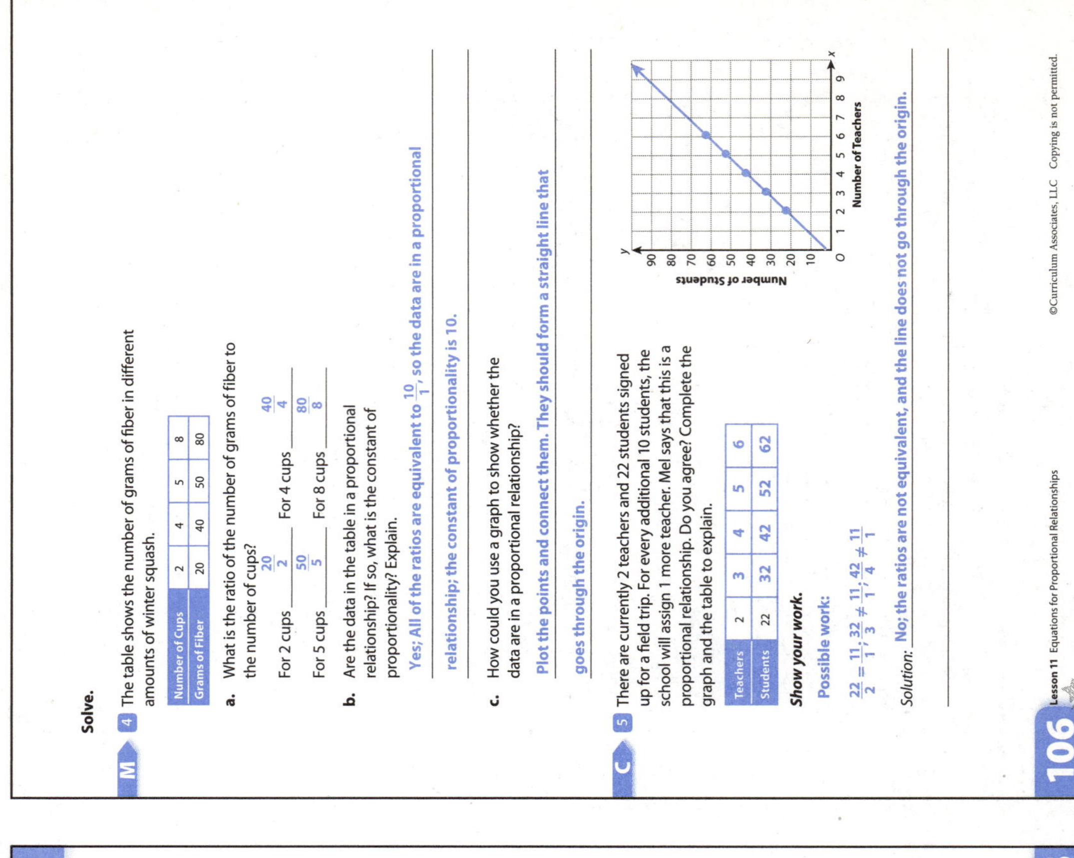

Solve.

M 4 The table shows the number of grams of fiber in different amounts of winter squash.

Number of Cups	2	4	5	8
Grams of Fiber	20	40	50	80

a. What is the ratio of the number of grams of fiber to the number of cups?

For 2 cups $\frac{20}{2}$ For 4 cups $\frac{40}{4}$

For 5 cups $\frac{50}{5}$ For 8 cups $\frac{80}{8}$

b. Are the data in the table in a proportional relationship? If so, what is the constant of proportionality? Explain.

Yes; All of the ratios are equivalent to $\frac{10}{1}$, so the data are in a proportional relationship; the constant of proportionality is 10.

c. How could you use a graph to show whether the data are in a proportional relationship?

Plot the points and connect them. They should form a straight line that goes through the origin.

C 5 There are currently 2 teachers and 22 students signed up for a field trip. For every additional 10 students, the school will assign 1 more teacher. Mel says that this is a proportional relationship. Do you agree? Complete the graph and the table to explain.

Teachers	2	3	4	5	6
Students	22	32	42	52	62

Show your work.

Possible work:

$\frac{22}{2} = \frac{11}{1}, \frac{32}{3} \neq \frac{11}{1}, \frac{42}{4} \neq \frac{11}{1}$

Solution: No; the ratios are not equivalent, and the line does not go through the origin.

Key

B Basic **M** Medium **C** Challenge

Lesson 11

Name: ____________

Write Equations for Proportional Relationships

Study the example showing how to identify a proportional relationship. Then solve problems 1–9.

Example

The table shows the relationship between the money that Leo earns and the number of lawns that he mows. Is the relationship proportional?

Number of Lawns	2	4	5	8
Money Earned ($)	10	20	25	40

The ratios of the money earned to the number of lawns all simplify to $\frac{5}{1}$, or 5, so the relationship is proportional.

B 1 Graph the relationship between the money earned and the number of lawns and connect the points. How does the graph tell you that the relationship is proportional?

The points lie on a straight line through the origin.

B 2 What does the ratio $\frac{5}{1}$ represent in terms of the example?

the unit rate, or the money earned for mowing one lawn

B 3 How can you use the graph to find the constant of proportionality? What is the constant of proportionality?

Possible answer: I can find the value of y when $x = 1$; 5

M 4 Use the constant of proportionality to write an equation that represents the amount of money earned, y, for mowing x lawns. $y = 5x$

M 5 If you know the constant of proportionality, m, for two proportional quantities, x and y, what equation can you write to describe the relationship?

The equation is $y = mx$, where m is the constant of proportionality.

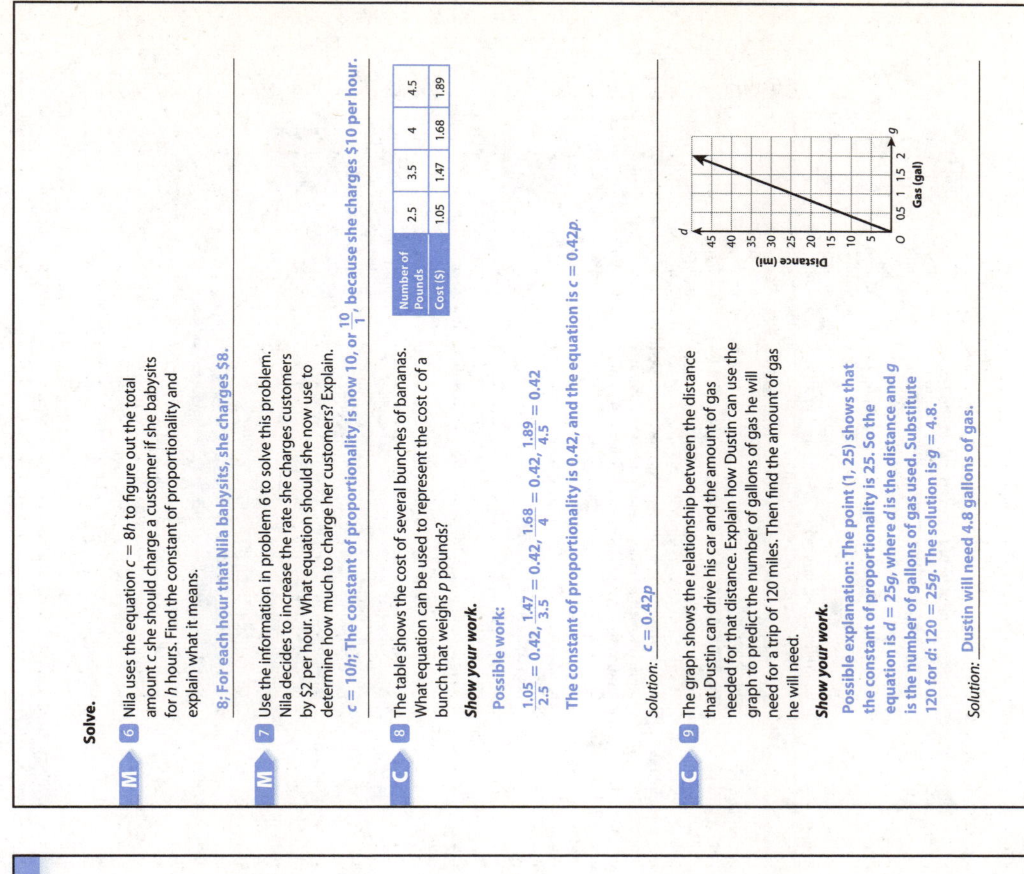

Solve.

M 6 Nila uses the equation $c = 8h$ to figure out the total amount c she should charge a customer if she babysits for h hours. Find the constant of proportionality and explain what it means.

8; For each hour that Nila babysits, she charges $8.

M 7 Use the information in problem 6 to solve this problem. Nila decides to increase the rate she charges customers by $2 per hour. What equation should she now use to determine how much to charge her customers? Explain.

$c = 10h$; The constant of proportionality is now 10, or $\frac{10}{1}$, because she charges $10 per hour.

C 8 The table shows the cost of several bunches of bananas. What equation can be used to represent the cost c of a bunch that weighs p pounds?

Number of Pounds	2.5	3.5	4	4.5
Cost ($)	1.05	1.47	1.68	1.89

Show your work.

Possible work:

$\frac{1.05}{2.5} = 0.42, \frac{1.47}{3.5} = 0.42, \frac{1.68}{4} = 0.42, \frac{1.89}{4.5} = 0.42$

The constant of proportionality is 0.42, and the equation is $c = 0.42p$.

Solution: $c = 0.42p$

C 9 The graph shows the relationship between the distance that Dustin can drive his car and the amount of gas needed for that distance. Explain how Dustin can use the graph to predict the number of gallons of gas he will need for a trip of 120 miles. Then find the amount of gas he will need.

Show your work.

Possible explanation: The point (1, 25) shows that the constant of proportionality is 25. So the equation is $d = 25g$, where d is the distance and g is the number of gallons of gas used. Substitute 120 for d: $120 = 25g$. The solution is $g = 4.8$.

Solution: Dustin will need 4.8 gallons of gas.

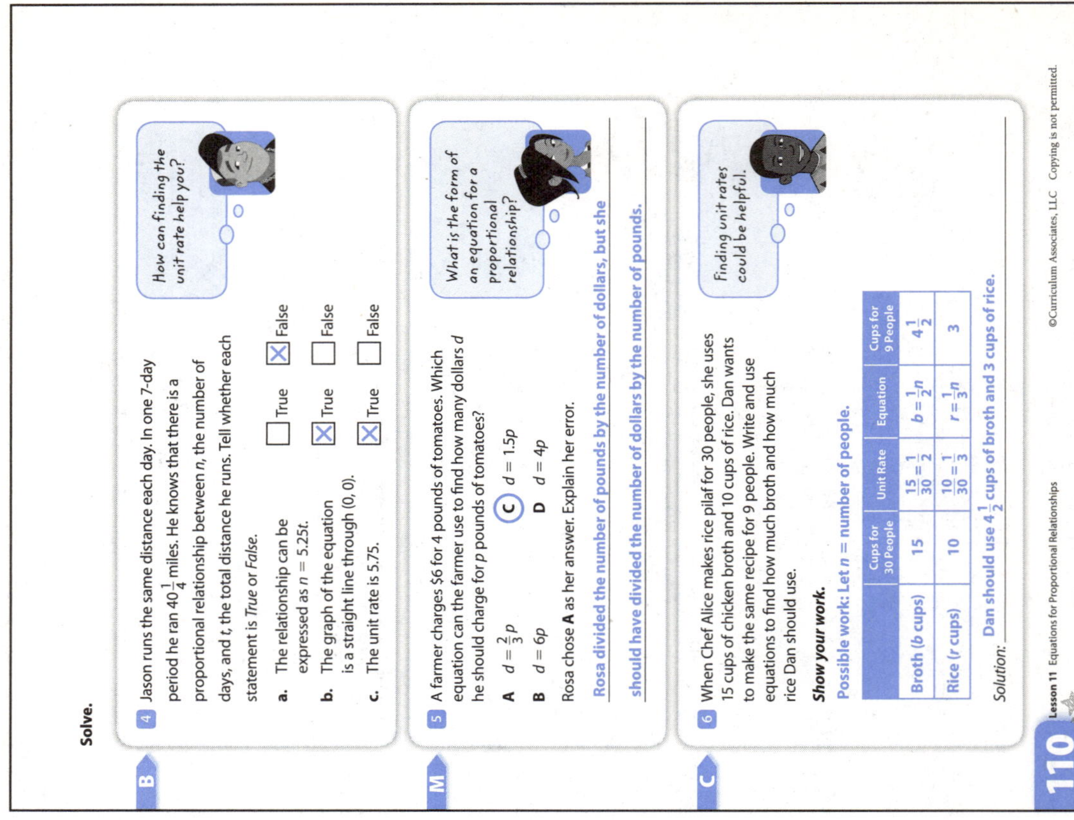

Solve.

B 4 Jason runs the same distance each day. In one 7-day period he ran $40\frac{1}{4}$ miles. He knows that there is a proportional relationship between n, the number of days, and t, the total distance he runs. Tell whether each statement is *True* or *False*.

a. The relationship can be expressed as $n = 5.25t$. ☐ True ☒ False

b. The graph of the equation is a straight line through (0, 0). ☒ True ☐ False

c. The unit rate is 5.75. ☒ True ☐ False

M 5 A farmer charges \$6 for 4 pounds of tomatoes. Which equation can the farmer use to find how many dollars d he should charge for p pounds of tomatoes?

A $d = \frac{2}{3}p$ (C) $d = 1.5p$

B $d = 6p$ D $d = 4p$

Rosa chose **A** as her answer. Explain her error.

Rosa divided the number of pounds by the number of dollars, but she should have divided the number of dollars by the number of pounds.

C 6 When Chef Alice makes rice pilaf for 30 people, she uses 15 cups of chicken broth and 10 cups of rice. Dan wants to make the same recipe for 9 people. Write and use equations to find how much broth and how much rice Dan should use.

Show your work.

Possible work: Let n = number of people.

	Cups for 30 People	Unit Rate	Equation	Cups for 9 People
Broth (b cups)	15	$\frac{15}{30} = \frac{1}{2}$	$b = \frac{1}{2}n$	$4\frac{1}{2}$
Rice (r cups)	10	$\frac{10}{30} = \frac{1}{3}$	$r = \frac{1}{3}n$	3

Solution: Dan should use $4\frac{1}{2}$ cups of broth and 3 cups of rice.

110 **Lesson 11** Equations for Proportional Relationships

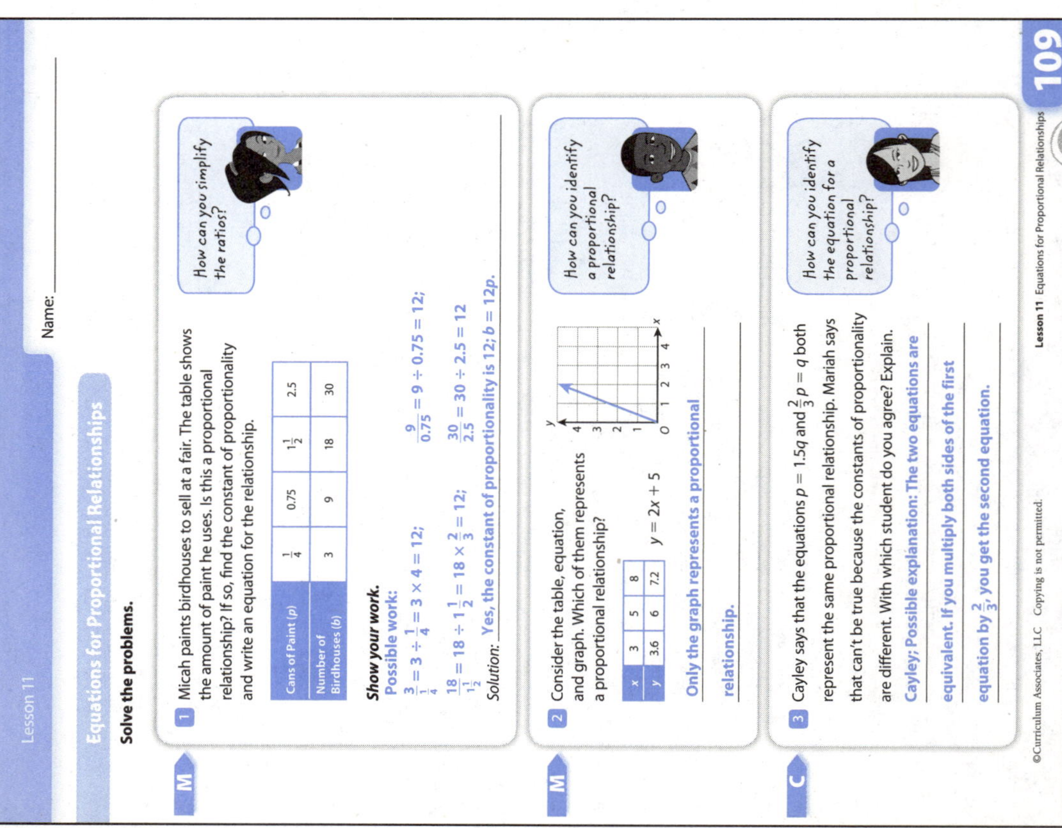

Lesson 11 Name: ______

Equations for Proportional Relationships

Solve the problems.

M 1 Micah paints birdhouses to sell at a fair. The table shows the amount of paint he uses. Is this a proportional relationship? If so, find the constant of proportionality and write an equation for the relationship.

Cans of Paint (p)	$\frac{1}{4}$	0.75	$1\frac{1}{2}$	2.5
Number of Birdhouses (b)	3	9	18	30

Show your work.

Possible work:

$\frac{3}{\frac{1}{4}} = 3 \div \frac{1}{4} = 3 \times 4 = 12$; $\frac{9}{0.75} = 9 \div 0.75 = 12$;

$\frac{18}{1\frac{1}{2}} = 18 \div 1\frac{1}{2} = 18 \times \frac{2}{3} = 12$; $\frac{30}{2.5} = 30 \div 2.5 = 12$

Solution: Yes, the constant of proportionality is 12; $b = 12p$.

M 2 Consider the table, equation, and graph. Which of them represents a proportional relationship?

x	3	5	8
y	3.6	6	7.2

$y = 2x + 5$

Only the graph represents a proportional relationship.

C 3 Cayley says that the equations $p = 1.5q$ and $\frac{2}{3}p = q$ both represent the same proportional relationship. Mariah says that can't be true because the constants of proportionality are different. With which student do you agree? Explain.

Cayley; Possible explanation: The two equations are equivalent. If you multiply both sides of the first equation by $\frac{2}{3}$, you get the second equation.

 Lesson 11 Equations for Proportional Relationships 109

Lesson 12

Problem Solving with Proportional Relationships

Name: ___________________

Prerequisite: Write Equations for Proportional Relationships

Study the example showing how to write an equation for a proportional relationship. Then solve problems 1–6.

Example

Jamie is making bracelets using black and red beads. She uses 6 black beads for every 4 red beads. Represent the number of black beads for any given number of red beads using a table, a graph, and an equation. Identify the constant of proportionality.

The ratio of black beads to red beads will be the same for all quantities.

$\frac{\text{black beads}}{\text{red beads}} = \frac{6}{4} = \frac{3}{2}$

You can use this ratio to make a table.

Red Beads, r	2	4	6
Black Beads, b	3	6	9

You can use the table to make a graph by plotting and connecting the ordered pairs. The constant of proportionality is $\frac{3}{2}$. This situation can be represented by the equation $b = \frac{3}{2}r$.

B 1 If Jaime uses 12 red beads, how many black beads does she use?

18 black beads

M 2 If Jamie wants to maintain the relationship of black beads to red beads, could she make a bracelet with 5 red beads? Explain your answer.

No; Possible explanation: For the relationship to be maintained, she would need $\left(\frac{3}{2}\right)5 = \frac{15}{2}$ black beads for a bracelet with 5 red beads. It is not possible to have half of a bead.

Vocabulary

constant of proportionality the unit rate in a proportional relationship.

©Curriculum Associates, LLC Copying is not permitted. **Lesson 12** Problem Solving with Proportional Relationships **113**

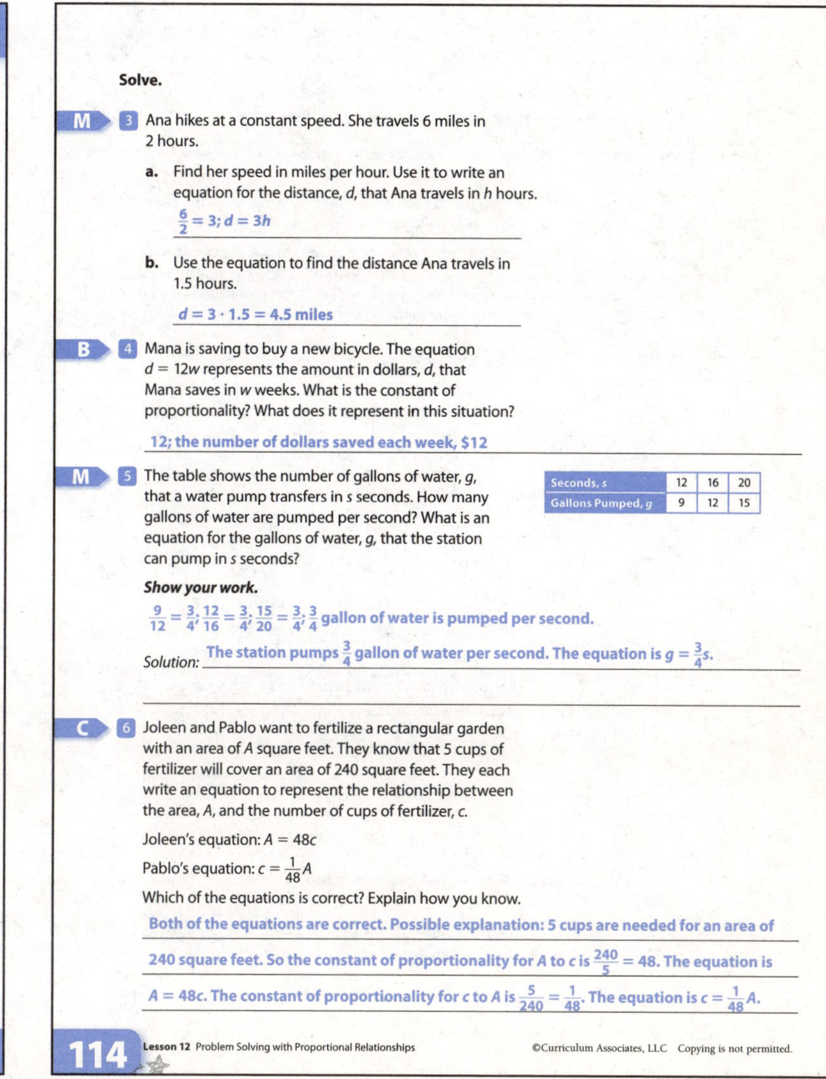

Solve.

M 3 Ana hikes at a constant speed. She travels 6 miles in 2 hours.

a. Find her speed in miles per hour. Use it to write an equation for the distance, d, that Ana travels in h hours.

$\frac{6}{2} = 3;\ d = 3h$

b. Use the equation to find the distance Ana travels in 1.5 hours.

$d = 3 \cdot 1.5 = 4.5$ miles

B 4 Mana is saving to buy a new bicycle. The equation $d = 12w$ represents the amount in dollars, d, that Mana saves in w weeks. What is the constant of proportionality? What does it represent in this situation?

12; the number of dollars saved each week, $12

M 5 The table shows the number of gallons of water, g, that a water pump transfers in s seconds. How many gallons of water are pumped per second? What is an equation for the gallons of water, g, that the station can pump in s seconds?

Seconds, s	12	16	20
Gallons Pumped, g	9	12	15

Show your work.

$\frac{9}{12} = \frac{3}{4}, \frac{12}{16} = \frac{3}{4}, \frac{15}{20} = \frac{3}{4}; \frac{3}{4}$ gallon of water is pumped per second.

Solution: The station pumps $\frac{3}{4}$ gallon of water per second. The equation is $g = \frac{3}{4}s$.

C 6 Joleen and Pablo want to fertilize a rectangular garden with an area of A square feet. They know that 5 cups of fertilizer will cover an area of 240 square feet. They each write an equation to represent the relationship between the area, A, and the number of cups of fertilizer, c.

Joleen's equation: $A = 48c$

Pablo's equation: $c = \frac{1}{48}A$

Which of the equations is correct? Explain how you know.

Both of the equations are correct. Possible explanation: 5 cups are needed for an area of 240 square feet. So the constant of proportionality for A to c is $\frac{240}{5} = 48$. The equation is $A = 48c$. The constant of proportionality for c to A is $\frac{5}{240} = \frac{1}{48}$. The equation is $c = \frac{1}{48}A$.

114 **Lesson 12** Problem Solving with Proportional Relationships ©Curriculum Associates, LLC Copying is not permitted.

Key

B Basic **M** Medium **C** Challenge

Name: ____________________

Proportional Relationships with Simple Interest

Study the example showing how to find simple interest. Then solve problems 1–8.

Example

Nora borrows $500 to buy a computer. She agrees to pay back the total amount of the computer plus 6% simple interest in 1 year. Write an expression for the total amount that Nora will have to pay back.

You can use a bar model to help you write an expression.

Amount Borrowed	Amount of Interest
$500	6% of $500 for 1 year
Total Amount to Pay Back	
t	

Amount Borrowed + Amount of Interest = Total to Pay Back

500 + (0.06 × 500) = t

B **1** What part of the bar model refers to the amount that Nora has to pay back in addition to the $500 that she borrowed?

Amount of Interest: 6% of $500 for 1 year

B **2** What does each number in the expression 0.06 × 500 represent?

0.06 is the interest rate written as a decimal; 500 is the amount borrowed.

B **3** Show how to find the amount of interest and the total amount that Nora will have to pay after 1 year.

0.06 × 500 = $30; 500 + 30 = $530

M **4** Describe how to find the total amount to pay on a 1-year loan when paying simple interest.

Multiply the interest rate by the amount borrowed. Add this to the amount borrowed.

Vocabulary

simple interest a percent of an amount borrowed (or invested) that is paid to the lender (or investor) in addition to the original amount.

Solve.

B **5** Petra borrows $200 for 1 year with a simple interest rate of 4.5%. Complete the equation that represents the total amount that Petra has to pay after 1 year.

Amount Borrowed + Amount of Interest = Total to Pay Back

200 + (0.045 × 200) = t

M **6** Franco borrows $400 and will pay 4% simple interest. Write an equation to answer each question.

a. What will be the amount of interest if Franco pays back the loan in 1 year? 0.04 × 400 = $16

b. What will be the amount of interest if he pays back the loan in 2 years? 2 × 16 = $32

c. If Franco pays off the loan in 2 years, what is the total amount he will pay the lender? 400 + 32 = $432

C **7** Miguel deposits $680 in an account that pays 3.5% simple interest. If he neither adds more money nor withdraws any money, what amount will be in the account after 6 years?

Show your work.

Possible work: t = 680 + (0.035 × 680 × 6)

t = 680 + 142.80 = 822.80

Solution: There will be $822.80 in the account after 6 years.

C **8** Dan borrows money to buy a new trumpet for $400 at a simple interest rate of 5%. He writes the equation t = 400 + (0.5 × 400) to represent the amount of money he will need to pay back after one year.

Is Dan's equation correct? Explain your answer and determine how much money Dan will need to pay back after one year.

No; Possible explanation: Dan wrote the interest rate incorrectly. The equation should be t = 400 + (0.05 × 400). He will need to pay back $420 after one year.

Practice Lesson 12 Problem Solving with Proportional Relationships

Unit 2

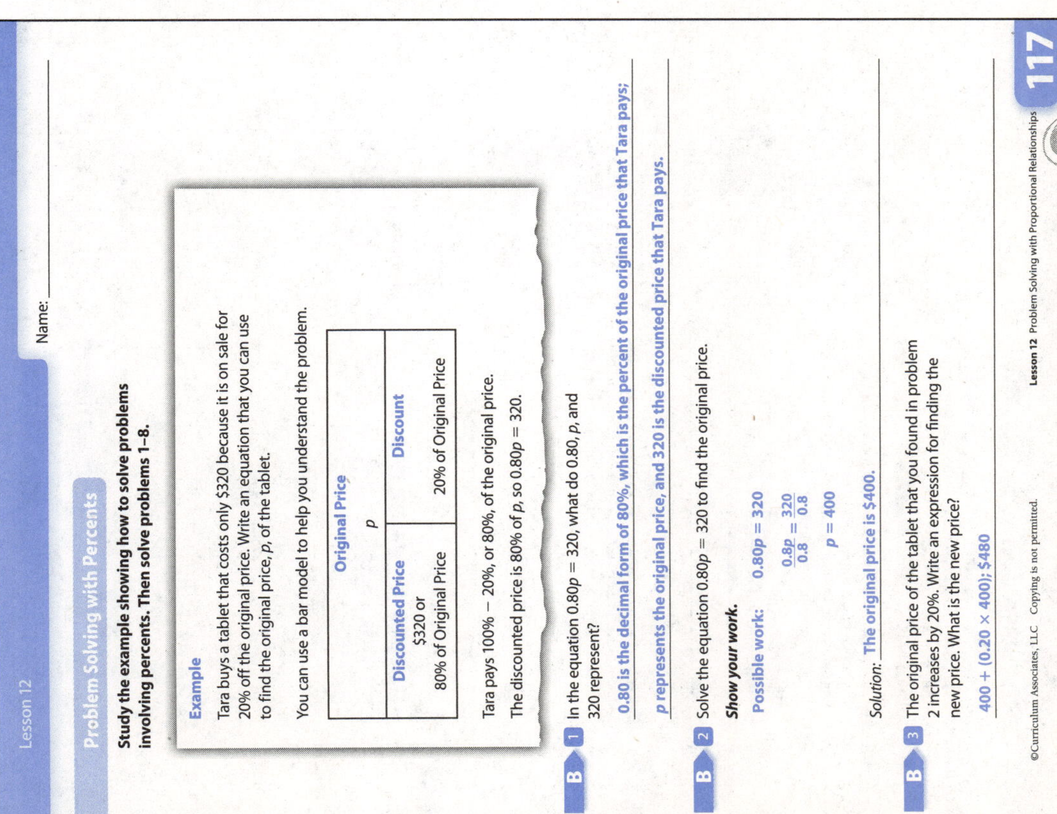

Lesson 12

Name: ____________________

Problem Solving with Percents

Study the example showing how to solve problems involving percents. Then solve problems 1–8.

Example

Tara buys a tablet that costs only $320 because it is on sale for 20% off the original price. Write an equation that you can use to find the original price, p, of the tablet.

You can use a bar model to help you understand the problem.

Original Price	
p	
Discounted Price $320 or 80% of Original Price	**Discount** 20% of Original Price

Tara pays 100% − 20%, or 80%, of the original price.

The discounted price is 80% of p, so $0.80p = 320$.

B 1 In the equation $0.80p = 320$, what do 0.80, p, and 320 represent?

0.80 is the decimal form of 80%, which is the percent of the original price that Tara pays; p represents the original price, and 320 is the discounted price that Tara pays.

B 2 Solve the equation $0.80p = 320$ to find the original price.

Show your work.

Possible work: $0.80p = 320$

$$\frac{0.8p}{0.8} = \frac{320}{0.8}$$

$$p = 400$$

Solution: **The original price is $400.**

B 3 The original price of the tablet that you found in problem 2 increases by 20%. Write an expression for finding the new price. What is the new price?

$400 + (0.20 \times 400)$; $480

©Curriculum Associates, LLC Copying is not permitted. **Lesson 12** Problem Solving with Proportional Relationships **117**

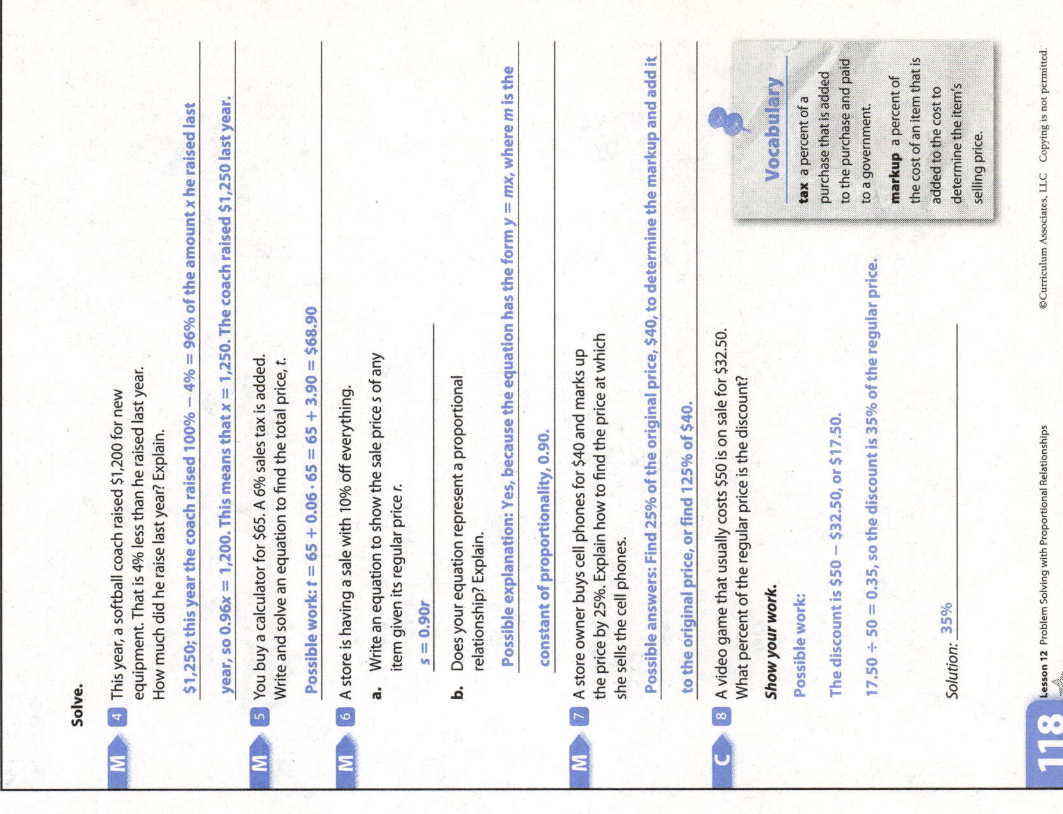

Solve.

M 4 This year, a softball coach raised $1,200 for new equipment. That is 4% less than he raised last year. How much did he raise last year? Explain.

$1,250; this year the coach raised 100% − 4% = 96% of the amount x he raised last year, so $0.96x = 1{,}200$. This means that $x = 1{,}250$. The coach raised $1,250 last year.

M 5 You buy a calculator for $65. A 6% sales tax is added. Write and solve an equation to find the total price, t.

Possible work: $t = 65 + 0.06 \cdot 65 = 65 + 3.90 = \$68.90$

M 6 A store is having a sale with 10% off everything.

a. Write an equation to show the sale price s of any item given its regular price r.

$s = 0.90r$

b. Does your equation represent a proportional relationship? Explain.

Possible explanation: Yes, because the equation has the form $y = mx$, where m is the constant of proportionality, 0.90.

M 7 A store owner buys cell phones for $40 and marks up the price by 25%. Explain how to find the price at which she sells the cell phones.

Possible answers: Find 25% of the original price, $40, to determine the markup and add it to the original price, or find 125% of $40.

C 8 A video game that usually costs $50 is on sale for $32.50. What percent of the regular price is the discount?

Show your work.

Possible work:

The discount is $50 − $32.50, or $17.50.

$17.50 \div 50 = 0.35$, so the discount is 35% of the regular price.

Solution: **35%**

Vocabulary

tax a percent of a purchase that is added to the purchase and paid to a government.

markup a percent of the cost of an item that is added to the cost to determine the item's selling price.

118 **Lesson 12** Problem Solving with Proportional Relationships ©Curriculum Associates, LLC Copying is not permitted.

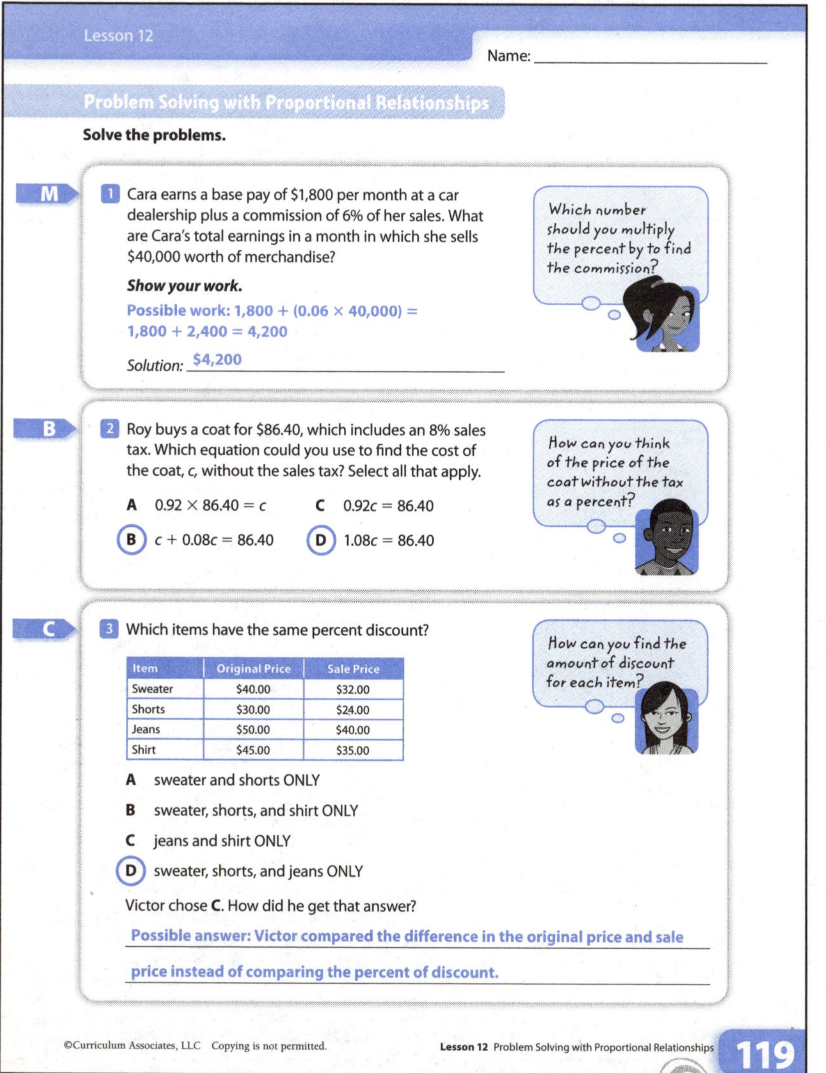

Lesson 12

Name: ____________

Problem Solving with Proportional Relationships

Solve the problems.

M **1** Cara earns a base pay of $1,800 per month at a car dealership plus a commission of 6% of her sales. What are Cara's total earnings in a month in which she sells $40,000 worth of merchandise?

Show your work.

Possible work: $1,800 + (0.06 \times 40,000) = 1,800 + 2,400 = 4,200$

Solution: $4,200

B **2** Roy buys a coat for $86.40, which includes an 8% sales tax. Which equation could you use to find the cost of the coat, *c*, without the sales tax? Select all that apply.

A $0.92 \times 86.40 = c$

(B) $c + 0.08c = 86.40$

C $0.92c = 86.40$

(D) $1.08c = 86.40$

C **3** Which items have the same percent discount?

Item	Original Price	Sale Price
Sweater	$40.00	$32.00
Shorts	$30.00	$24.00
Jeans	$50.00	$40.00
Shirt	$45.00	$35.00

A sweater and shorts ONLY

B sweater, shorts, and shirt ONLY

C jeans and shirt ONLY

(D) sweater, shorts, and jeans ONLY

Victor chose **C**. How did he get that answer?

Possible answer: Victor compared the difference in the original price and sale price instead of comparing the percent of discount.

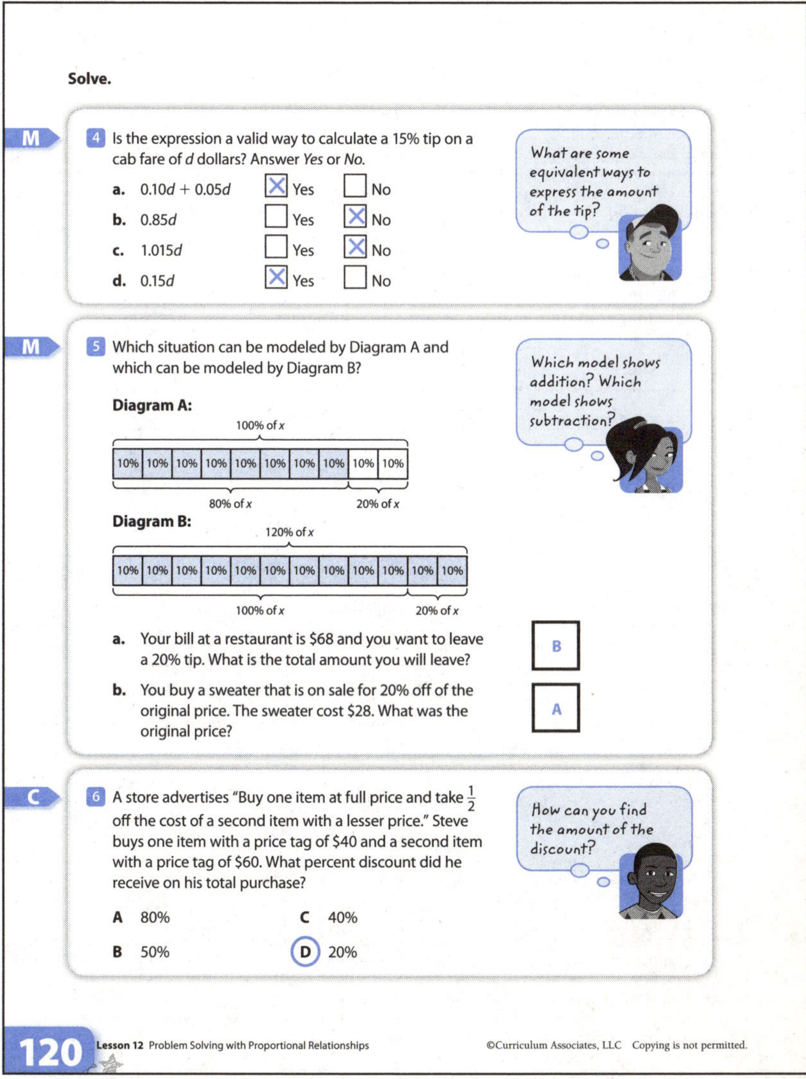

Solve.

M **4** Is the expression a valid way to calculate a 15% tip on a cab fare of *d* dollars? Answer *Yes* or *No.*

a. $0.10d + 0.05d$ ☒ Yes ☐ No

b. $0.85d$ ☐ Yes ☒ No

c. $1.015d$ ☐ Yes ☒ No

d. $0.15d$ ☒ Yes ☐ No

M **5** Which situation can be modeled by Diagram A and which can be modeled by Diagram B?

Diagram A:

Diagram B:

a. Your bill at a restaurant is $68 and you want to leave a 20% tip. What is the total amount you will leave? **B**

b. You buy a sweater that is on sale for 20% off of the original price. The sweater cost $28. What was the original price? **A**

C **6** A store advertises "Buy one item at full price and take $\frac{1}{2}$ off the cost of a second item with a lesser price." Steve buys one item with a price tag of $40 and a second item with a price tag of $60. What percent discount did he receive on his total purchase?

A 80%

B 50%

C 40%

(D) 20%

Lesson 13

Proportional Relationships

Name: ____________

Prerequisite: Solving Problems with Percents

Study the example problem showing how to solve a problem with percents. Then solve problems 1–7.

Example

Chumani has a coupon for 15% off the total bill at a new restaurant. Her original bill is $32.00. After the discount, what amount is her bill?

First, find the amount of the discount.

15% = 0.15 and 0.15 × 32 = $4.80

Subtract the discount from the original amount.

$32.00 − $4.80 = $27.20

So Chumani's bill is $27.20.

B 1 A bar model can also be used to represent the problem. Complete the bar model.

Original Bill	
$32.00	
Discounted Bill	**Amount of Discount**
b	15 % of $ 32

B 2 Write and solve an equation to represent the relationship shown in the bar model.

Possible answer: $b = 32 - (0.15 \times 32) = 32 - 4.80 = \$27.20$

M 3 The percent of the discount in the problem above is 15%. What percent of the original bill is Chumani's bill? How could you solve the problem using this percent?

85%; The amount Chumani paid is 100% − 15%, or 85%, of the original price.

85% of 32 = 0.85 × 32 = $27.20.

Solve.

M 4 Chander earns a base pay of $2,200 per month. He also earns a commission of 4% of his total sales. One month Chander earned $2,400. Explain how to find Chander's total sales for that month. How much were his total sales?

$5,000; Possible answer: Subtract the base pay from the total pay to find the amount of the commission. Then divide the commission amount by 0.04, which is 4% written as a decimal. $200 ÷ 0.04 = 20,000 ÷ 4 = $5,000.

M 5 Marian borrowed money to buy a sound system that costs $450. She is charged 5% simple interest for one year. What is the total amount that she pays for the sound system if she pays the full amount in one year?

Show your work.

Interest: 0.05 × $450 = $22.50; $450 + $22.50 = $472.50

Solution: **Marian pays a total of $472.50 for the sound system.**

M 6 Dan paid $34.30 for a sweater. The price included a 40% markup. Find the cost of the sweater before the markup was added.

Show your work.

Possible work: Let p = the price before the markup.

$(100\% \times p) + (40\% \times p) = 34.30$; $1.40p = 34.30$; $p = \frac{34.30}{1.4} = 24.50$

Solution: **The cost of the sweater before the markup was $24.50.**

C 7 A jacket that originally sold for $60.00 was on sale for 10% off. When it didn't sell after several weeks, the sale price was discounted another 40% off the discounted price. What was the final price of the jacket? Is the total discount equal to 50%? Explain.

$32.40; no; Possible explanation: 1st discount: 0.10 × $60 = $6; 1st sale price: $60 − $6 = $54

2nd discount: 0.40 × $54 = $21.60; Final price: $54 − 21.60 = $32.40

No; 50% of $60.00 = $30, but the actual total discount is $27.60.

Key

B Basic **M** Medium **C** Challenge

Lesson 13

Name: ____________________

Finding Percent Change

Study the example problem showing how to find percent change. Then solve problems 1–7.

Example

The plants that Loma grew for her science project averaged 6 inches in height. Two weeks later, the plants averaged 9 inches in height. What was the percent increase in the average height of the plants?

You can use a bar model to compare the original height to the change in height.

original height
change in height
x%
100%

You can also use the proportion below to compare the change to the original amount.

$\frac{\text{amount of change}}{\text{original amount}}$ = percent change

$\frac{9-6}{6} = \frac{x}{100}$

B **1** Use either the bar model or the proportion to solve for x. What was the percent increase in the average height of the plants?

The percent increase is 50%. Possible work: $\frac{3}{6} = \frac{x}{100}$; $\frac{1}{2} = \frac{50}{100}$; $x = 50$

B **2** Would the percent change be *greater than* or *less than* 50% if the plants had grown to 8 inches instead of 9?

less than 50%

B **3** After 4 weeks, the height of the plants had grown from 6 inches to 12 inches. Write and solve a proportion to find the percent increase in the height of the plants.

$\frac{12-6}{6} = \frac{x}{100}$; $\frac{6}{6} = \frac{x}{100}$; $1 = \frac{100}{100}$; $x = 100$; There was a 100% increase in the height of the plants.

Solve.

M **4** Students donated 2,500 cans of food to the local food pantry last year. They donated 4,000 cans this year. What is the percent increase in the number of cans donated?

Show your work.

$\frac{4{,}000 - 2{,}500}{2{,}500} = \frac{x}{100}$; $\frac{1{,}500}{2{,}500} = \frac{x}{100}$; $\frac{3}{5} = \frac{60}{100}$; $x = 60$

Solution: The percent increase is 60%.

M **5** Mike plays basketball. He attempted 32 free throws in January and 28 free throws in February.

a. Is the percent change a *percent increase* or a *percent decrease?* a percent decrease

b. Write and solve a proportion to find the percent change in the number of free throws.

Show your work.

$\frac{32-28}{32} = \frac{x}{100}$; $\frac{4}{32} = \frac{x}{100}$; $\frac{1}{8} = \frac{x}{100}$; $100 \cdot \frac{1}{8} = 100 \cdot \frac{x}{100}$; $x = 12.5$

Solution: The percent decrease is 12.5%.

C **6** Find the percent of increase or decrease.

a. x to $5x$ 400% increase

b. $2.5y$ to $1.5y$ 40% decrease

c. n to $\frac{4}{5}n$ 20% decrease

d. $3.2t$ to $5.2t$ 62.5% increase

C **7** A store manager pays $40 for a shirt and adds a markup of 20%. During a store sale, the manager marks the cost of the shirt down by 20%. What is the percent of change from the original cost, $40, to the sale price?

The marked-up price is $40 + 0.2 \cdot 40 \Rightarrow \$48$. The sale price is $0.8 \cdot 48 = \$38.40$.

$\frac{40 - 38.40}{40} = \frac{x}{100}$; $\frac{1.6}{40} = \frac{x}{100}$; $0.04 = \frac{x}{100}$; $x = 4$; the percent decrease is 4%.

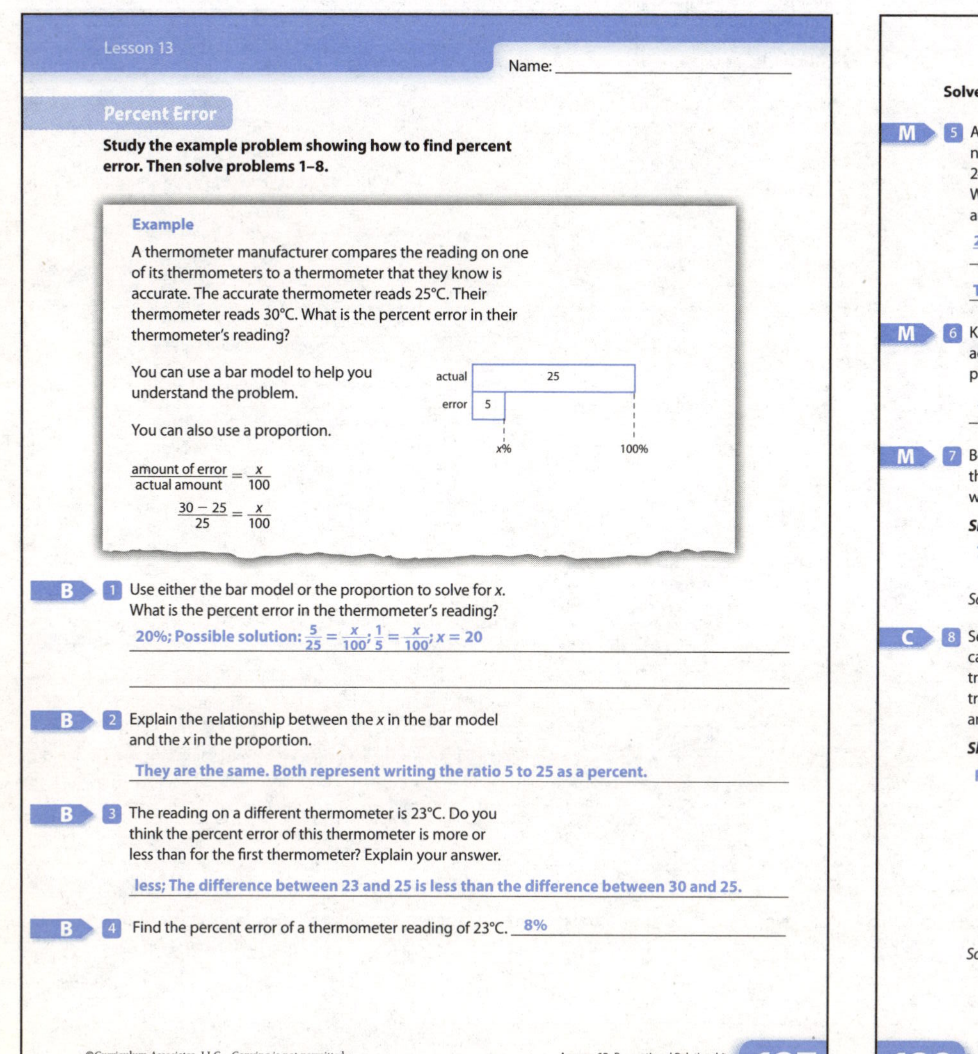

Name: ____________________

Percent Error

Study the example problem showing how to find percent error. Then solve problems 1–8.

Example

A thermometer manufacturer compares the reading on one of its thermometers to a thermometer that they know is accurate. The accurate thermometer reads 25°C. Their thermometer reads 30°C. What is the percent error in their thermometer's reading?

You can use a bar model to help you understand the problem.

You can also use a proportion.

$$\frac{\text{amount of error}}{\text{actual amount}} = \frac{x}{100}$$

$$\frac{30 - 25}{25} = \frac{x}{100}$$

B **1** Use either the bar model or the proportion to solve for x. What is the percent error in the thermometer's reading?

20%; Possible solution: $\frac{5}{25} = \frac{x}{100}$; $\frac{1}{5} = \frac{x}{100}$; $x = 20$

B **2** Explain the relationship between the x in the bar model and the x in the proportion.

They are the same. Both represent writing the ratio 5 to 25 as a percent.

B **3** The reading on a different thermometer is 23°C. Do you think the percent error of this thermometer is more or less than for the first thermometer? Explain your answer.

less; The difference between 23 and 25 is less than the difference between 30 and 25.

B **4** Find the percent error of a thermometer reading of 23°C. 8%

Solve.

M **5** At the school carnival, students are asked to guess the number of marbles in a jar to win a prize. There are 240 marbles in the jar. The closest guess is 280 marbles. What is the percent error of the guess? Explain. Round your answer to the nearest percent.

$\frac{280 - 240}{240} = \frac{x}{100}$; $\frac{40}{240} = \frac{x}{100}$; $\frac{1}{6} = \frac{x}{100}$; $100 \cdot \frac{1}{6} = 100 \cdot \frac{x}{100}$; $x = 16\frac{2}{3}$

To the nearest percent, the percent error is 17%.

M **6** Kai needed to cut 25 inches from a long board. He accidently cut 24 inches from the board. What is his percent error? Explain.

$\frac{25 - 24}{25} = \frac{x}{100}$; $\frac{1}{25} = \frac{4}{100}$; $x = 4$, so the percent error is 4%.

M **7** Bev weighs a bag of apples labeled 5 pounds and finds that the weight is actually 72 ounces. To the nearest percent, what is the percent error in the weight? (1 pound = 16 ounces)

Show your work.

72 ounces = 4.5 pounds; $\frac{5 - 4.5}{4.5} = \frac{x}{100}$; $\frac{0.5}{4.5} = \frac{x}{100}$; $x = 11$

Solution: The percent error is about 11%.

C **8** Semira did a physics activity during which she rolled toy cars down a ramp and measured the distance each car traveled. On one trial, the actual distance that the car traveled was 75 cm. Semira's measurement was too short and had a 12% error. What was her distance measurement?

Show your work.

Possible work:

$$\frac{75 - x}{75} = \frac{12}{100}$$

$$\frac{75 - x}{75} = 0.12$$

$$75 \cdot \frac{75 - x}{75} = 75 \cdot 0.12$$

$$75 - x = 9.0$$

$$x = 66$$

Solution: Semira's measurement was 66 cm.

Practice Lesson 13 Proportional Relationships

Unit 2

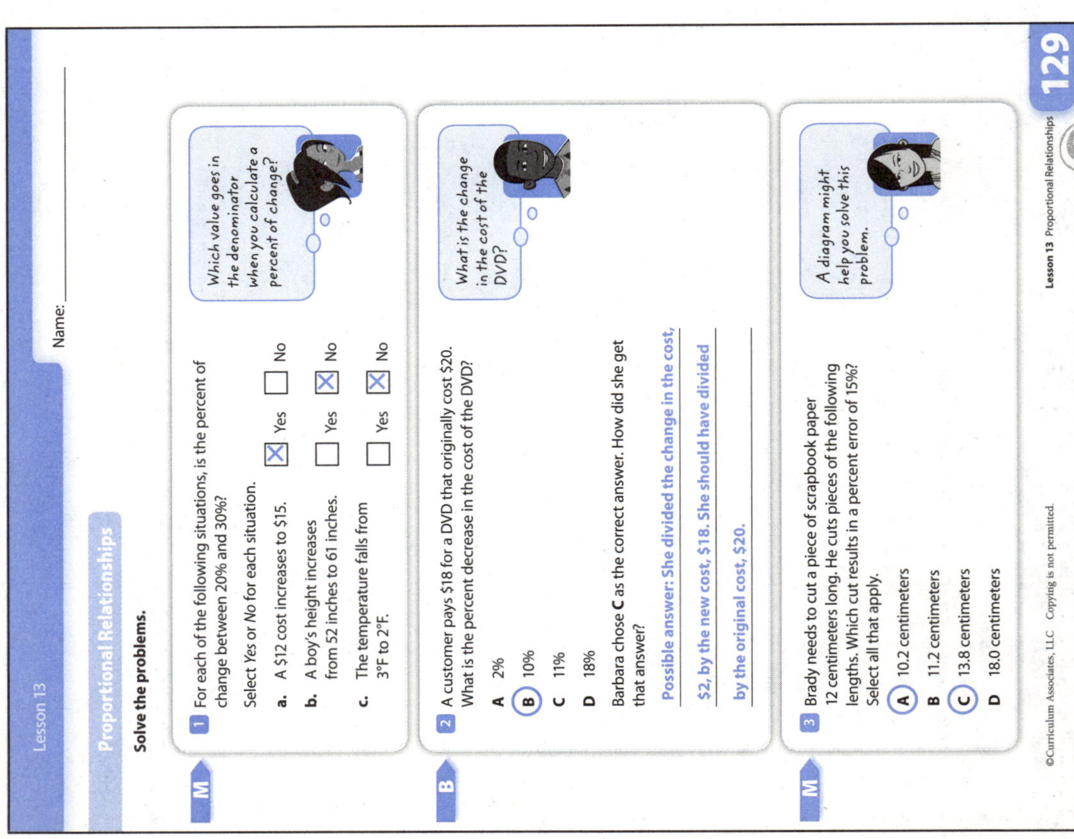

Lesson 13

Name: ____________________

Proportional Relationships

Solve the problems.

M

1 For each of the following situations, is the percent of change between 20% and 30%?

Select *Yes* or *No* for each situation.

a. A $12 cost increases to $15. ☒ Yes ☐ No

b. A boy's height increases from 52 inches to 61 inches. ☐ Yes ☒ No

c. The temperature falls from 3°F to 2°F. ☐ Yes ☒ No

B

2 A customer pays $18 for a DVD that originally cost $20. What is the percent decrease in the cost of the DVD?

A 2%

(B) 10%

C 11%

D 18%

Barbara chose **C** as the correct answer. How did she get that answer?

Possible answer: She divided the change in the cost, $2, by the new cost, $18. She should have divided by the original cost, $20.

M

3 Brady needs to cut a piece of scrapbook paper 12 centimeters long. He cuts pieces of the following lengths. Which cut results in a percent error of 15%? Select all that apply.

(A) 10.2 centimeters

B 11.2 centimeters

(C) 13.8 centimeters

D 18.0 centimeters

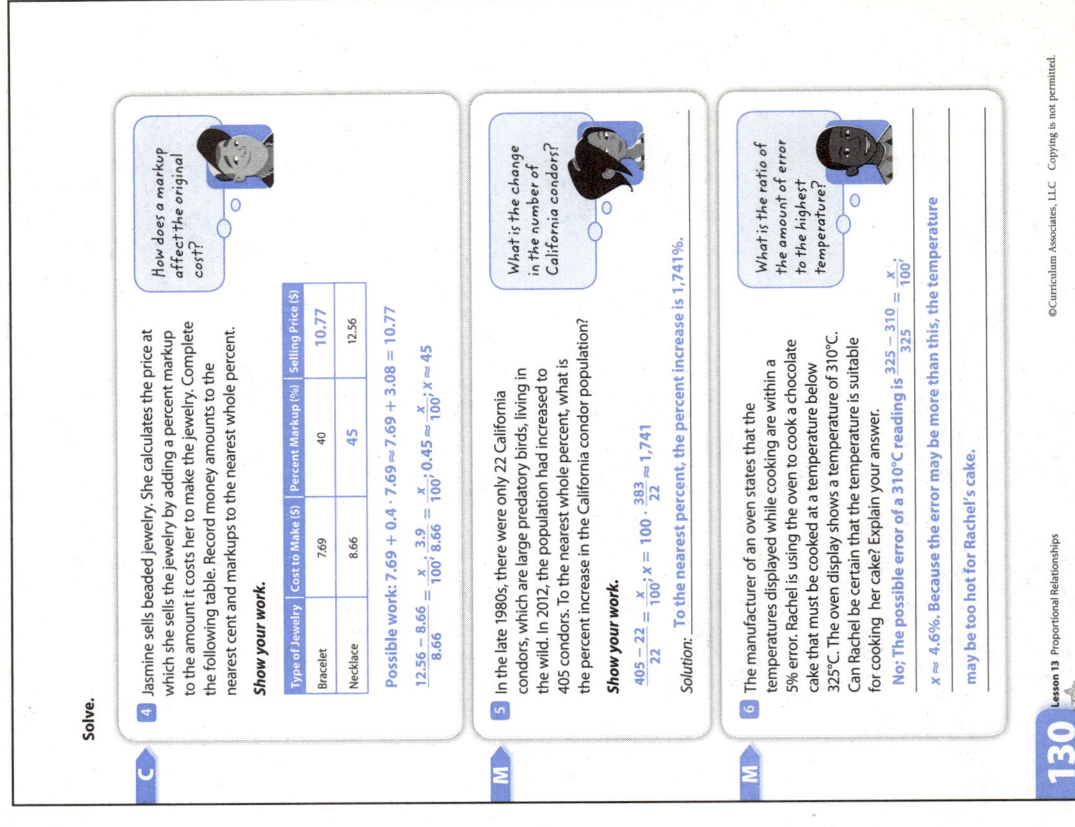

Solve.

C

4 Jasmine sells beaded jewelry. She calculates the price at which she sells the jewelry by adding a percent markup to the amount it costs her to make the jewelry. Complete the following table. Record money amounts to the nearest cent and markups to the nearest whole percent.

Show your work.

Type of Jewelry	Cost to Make ($)	Percent Markup (%)	Selling Price ($)
Bracelet	7.69	40	**10.77**
Necklace	8.66	**45**	12.56

Possible work: $7.69 + 0.4 \cdot 7.69 \approx 7.69 + 3.08 = 10.77$

$\frac{12.56 - 8.66}{8.66} = \frac{x}{100}$; $\frac{3.9}{8.66} = \frac{x}{100}$; $0.45 \approx \frac{x}{100}$; $x \approx 45$

M

5 In the late 1980s, there were only 22 California condors, which are large predatory birds, living in the wild. In 2012, the population had increased to 405 condors. To the nearest whole percent, what is the percent increase in the California condor population?

Show your work.

$\frac{405 - 22}{22} = \frac{x}{100}$; $x = 100 \cdot \frac{383}{22} \approx 1{,}741$

Solution: **To the nearest percent, the percent increase is 1,741%.**

M

6 The manufacturer of an oven states that the temperatures displayed while cooking are within a 5% error. Rachel is using the oven to cook a chocolate cake that must be cooked at a temperature below 325°C. The oven display shows a temperature of 310°C. Can Rachel be certain that the temperature is suitable for cooking her cake? Explain your answer.

No; The possible error of a 310°C reading is $\frac{325 - 310}{325} = \frac{x}{100}$; $x \approx 4.6\%$**. Because the error may be more than this, the temperature may be too hot for Rachel's cake.**

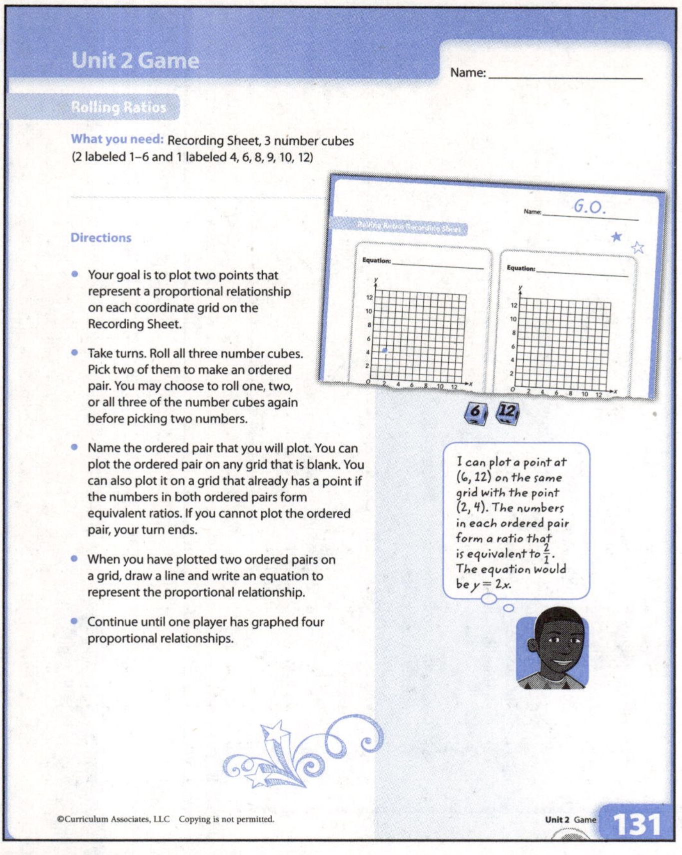

Unit 2 Game

Name: ____________________

Rolling Ratios

What you need: Recording Sheet, 3 number cubes (2 labeled 1–6 and 1 labeled 4, 6, 8, 9, 10, 12)

Directions

- Your goal is to plot two points that represent a proportional relationship on each coordinate grid on the Recording Sheet.
- Take turns. Roll all three number cubes. Pick two of them to make an ordered pair. You may choose to roll one, two, or all three of the number cubes again before picking two numbers.
- Name the ordered pair that you will plot. You can plot the ordered pair on any grid that is blank. You can also plot it on a grid that already has a point if the numbers in both ordered pairs form equivalent ratios. If you cannot plot the ordered pair, your turn ends.
- When you have plotted two ordered pairs on a grid, draw a line and write an equation to represent the proportional relationship.
- Continue until one player has graphed four proportional relationships.

©Curriculum Associates, LLC Copying is not permitted.

Unit 2 Game 131

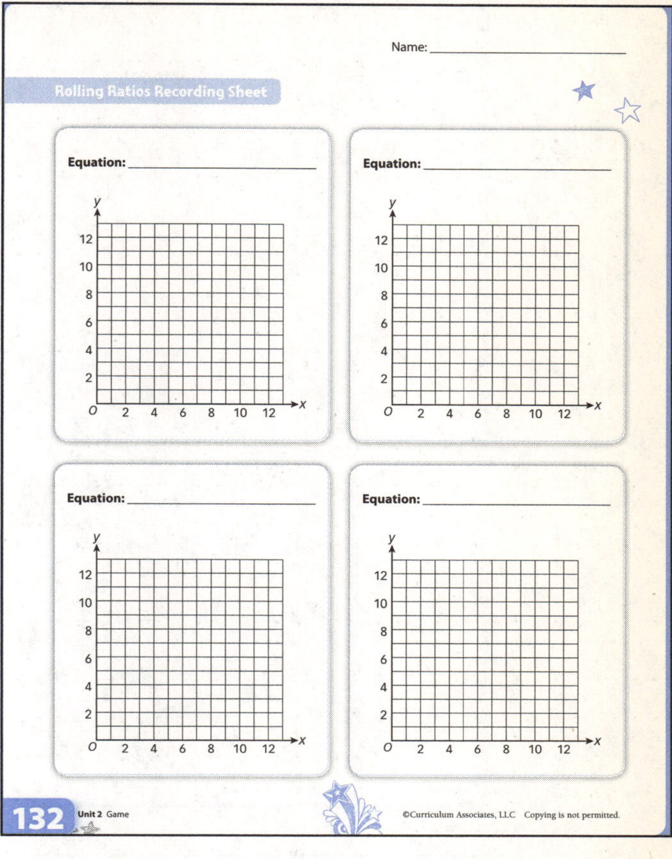

Name: ____________________

Rolling Ratios Recording Sheet

Equation: ____________________

Equation: ____________________

Equation: ____________________

Equation: ____________________

132 Unit 2 Game

©Curriculum Associates, LLC Copying is not permitted.

STEP BY STEP

CCSS Focus - 7.RP.A.2a *Embedded SMPs* - 4, 5, 7 **Objective** • Identify ratios that represent proportional relationships.	**Materials** For each pair: Recording Sheets (1 for each player) (TR 2), 3 number cubes (2 labeled 1–6 and 1 labeled 4, 6, 8, 9, 10, 12)

- Your goal is to plot two points that represent a proportional relationship on each coordinate grid on the Recording Sheet.
- Take turns. Roll all three number cubes. Pick two of them to make an ordered pair. You may choose to roll one, two, or all three of the number cubes again before picking two numbers.
- Name the ordered pair that you will plot. You can plot the ordered pair on any grid that is blank. You can also plot it on a grid that already has a point if the numbers in both ordered pairs form equivalent ratios. If you cannot plot the ordered pair, your turn ends.
- When you have plotted two ordered pairs on a grid, draw a line and write an equation to represent the proportional relationship.
- Continue until one player has graphed four proportional relationships.
- Model Round 1 for students before they play. Discuss strategies for placing points and identifying proportional relationships.

Vary the Game Both players use the same Recording Sheet. The one who plots the second point on a grid wins that grid. The first to win two grids wins the game.

Extra Support Students make a table for each grid. Label one row "x" and the other row "y." When a point is plotted, enter it in the table and generate some other possible points that have an equivalent ratio.

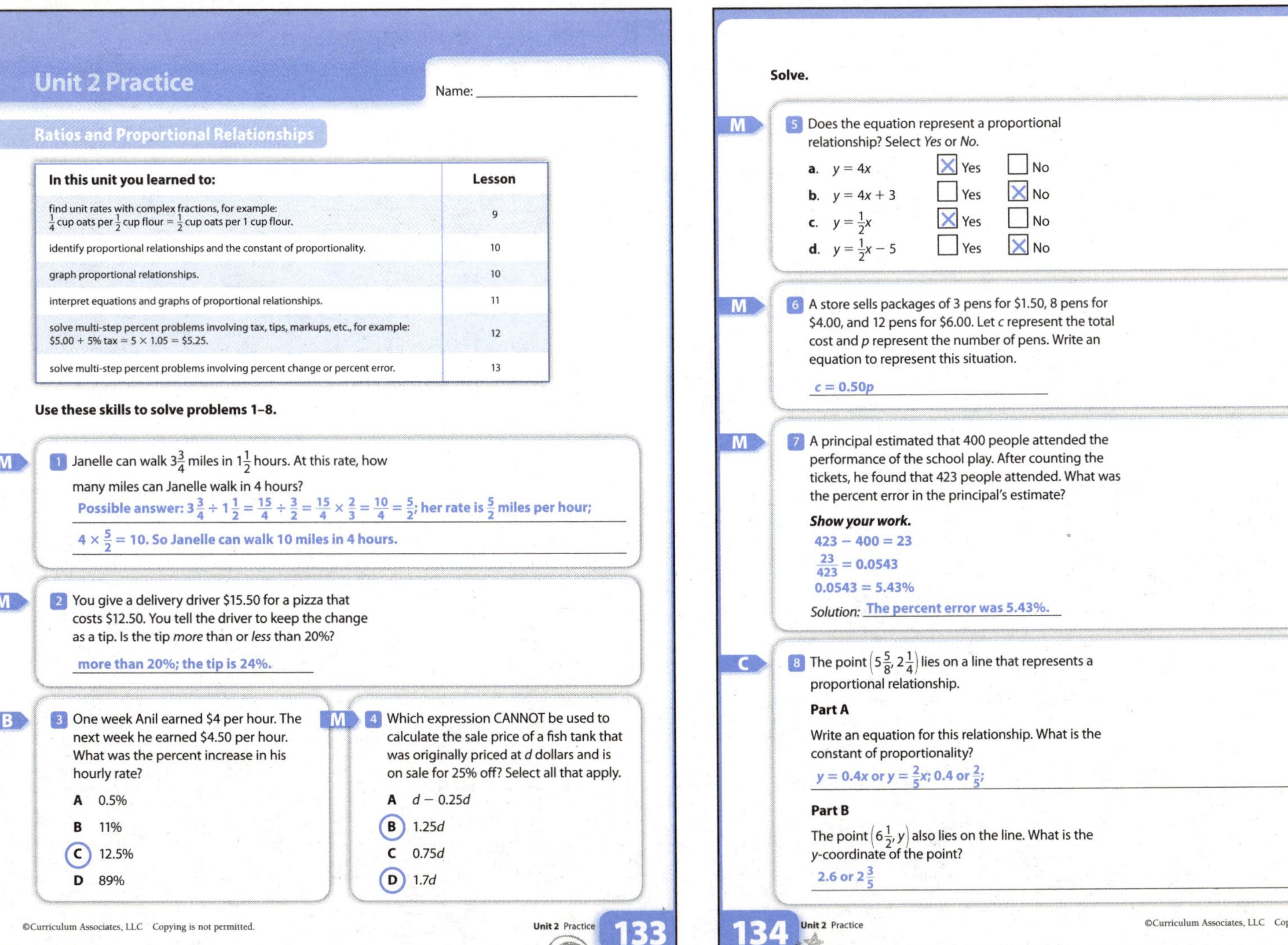

Unit 2 Practice

Name: ____________________

Ratios and Proportional Relationships

In this unit you learned to:	Lesson
find unit rates with complex fractions, for example: $\frac{1}{4}$ cup oats per $\frac{1}{2}$ cup flour = $\frac{1}{2}$ cup oats per 1 cup flour.	9
identify proportional relationships and the constant of proportionality.	10
graph proportional relationships.	10
interpret equations and graphs of proportional relationships.	11
solve multi-step percent problems involving tax, tips, markups, etc., for example: \$5.00 + 5% tax = 5 × 1.05 = \$5.25.	12
solve multi-step percent problems involving percent change or percent error.	13

Use these skills to solve problems 1–8.

M **1** Janelle can walk $3\frac{3}{4}$ miles in $1\frac{1}{2}$ hours. At this rate, how many miles can Janelle walk in 4 hours?

Possible answer: $3\frac{3}{4} \div 1\frac{1}{2} = \frac{15}{4} \div \frac{3}{2} = \frac{15}{4} \times \frac{2}{3} = \frac{10}{4} = \frac{5}{2}$; her rate is $\frac{5}{2}$ miles per hour; $4 \times \frac{5}{2} = 10$. So Janelle can walk 10 miles in 4 hours.

M **2** You give a delivery driver \$15.50 for a pizza that costs \$12.50. You tell the driver to keep the change as a tip. Is the tip *more* than or *less* than 20%?

more than 20%; the tip is 24%.

B **3** One week Anil earned \$4 per hour. The next week he earned \$4.50 per hour. What was the percent increase in his hourly rate?

A 0.5%
B 11%
(C) 12.5%
D 89%

M **4** Which expression CANNOT be used to calculate the sale price of a fish tank that was originally priced at *d* dollars and is on sale for 25% off? Select all that apply.

A $d - 0.25d$
(B) $1.25d$
C $0.75d$
(D) $1.7d$

©Curriculum Associates, LLC Copying is not permitted. Unit 2 Practice 133

Solve.

M **5** Does the equation represent a proportional relationship? Select *Yes* or *No*.

a. $y = 4x$ ☒ Yes ☐ No
b. $y = 4x + 3$ ☐ Yes ☒ No
c. $y = \frac{1}{2}x$ ☒ Yes ☐ No
d. $y = \frac{1}{2}x - 5$ ☐ Yes ☒ No

M **6** A store sells packages of 3 pens for \$1.50, 8 pens for \$4.00, and 12 pens for \$6.00. Let *c* represent the total cost and *p* represent the number of pens. Write an equation to represent this situation.

$c = 0.50p$

M **7** A principal estimated that 400 people attended the performance of the school play. After counting the tickets, he found that 423 people attended. What was the percent error in the principal's estimate?

Show your work.

$423 - 400 = 23$
$\frac{23}{423} = 0.0543$
$0.0543 = 5.43\%$

Solution: **The percent error was 5.43%.**

C **8** The point $\left(5\frac{5}{8}, 2\frac{1}{4}\right)$ lies on a line that represents a proportional relationship.

Part A

Write an equation for this relationship. What is the constant of proportionality?

$y = 0.4x$ or $y = \frac{2}{5}x$; 0.4 or $\frac{2}{5}$;

Part B

The point $\left(6\frac{1}{2}, y\right)$ also lies on the line. What is the *y*-coordinate of the point?

2.6 or $2\frac{3}{5}$

134 Unit 2 Practice ©Curriculum Associates, LLC Copying is not permitted.

Key		
B Basic	**M** Medium	**C** Challenge

TEACHER NOTES

Common Core Standards: 7.RP.A.1, 7.RP.A.2a, 7.RP.A.3
Standards for Mathematical Practice: 1, 2, 3, 4, 5, 6, 7, 8

DOK: 3

Materials: None

About the Task

To complete this task, students solve a multi-step problem that involves ratios of rational numbers. The task requires students to reason about unit rates and use the relationship between pounds and ounces. They will calculate the quantity needed for each ingredient, along with the cost, to make large batches of a snack mix.

Getting Started

Read the problem out loud with students. Have them identify the goal. Have students share different possible rationales for choosing one recipe over the other. Be sure students know that 16 ounces is equivalent to 1 pound, and that they understand that they will need to pay attention to units as they work. Then go over the checklist with students. Ask them to describe how they could use either a graph or a table to organize the information and present a solution. ***(SMP 1, 3, 5, 6)***

Completing the Task

Students need to find the amount of each ingredient to make different sized batches. To do this, students must understand that, for example, a batch that will make 100 servings will require 100 times as much of each ingredient as 1 serving will require. Students may choose to work with either fractions or decimals. They may choose to convert the weights of ingredients to pounds or to convert the prices to dollars per ounce. ***(SMP 4, 5)***

If some students are confused about whether to multiply or divide to convert units, help them make a table based on a ratio of 16 ounces for 1 pound. ***(SMP 2, 4)***

Pair students who made different choices and have them compare their decisions and final costs. ***(SMP 3)***

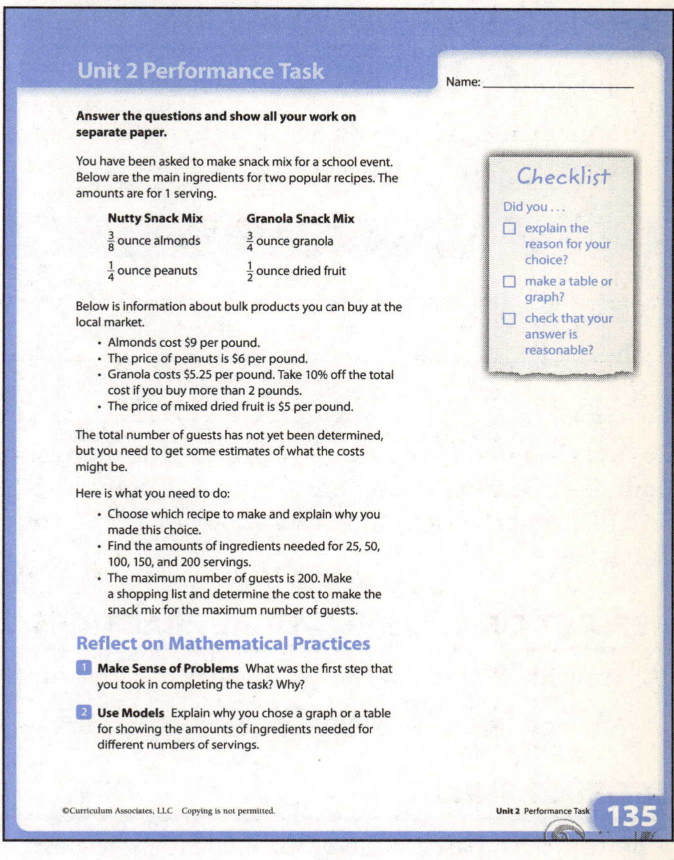

Unit 2 Performance Task

Name: ____________________

Answer the questions and show all your work on separate paper.

You have been asked to make snack mix for a school event. Below are the main ingredients for two popular recipes. The amounts are for 1 serving.

Nutty Snack Mix	Granola Snack Mix
$\frac{3}{8}$ ounce almonds	$\frac{3}{4}$ ounce granola
$\frac{1}{4}$ ounce peanuts	$\frac{1}{2}$ ounce dried fruit

Below is information about bulk products you can buy at the local market.

- Almonds cost $9 per pound.
- The price of peanuts is $6 per pound.
- Granola costs $5.25 per pound. Take 10% off the total cost if you buy more than 2 pounds.
- The price of mixed dried fruit is $5 per pound.

The total number of guests has not yet been determined, but you need to get some estimates of what the costs might be.

Here is what you need to do:

- Choose which recipe to make and explain why you made this choice.
- Find the amounts of ingredients needed for 25, 50, 100, 150, and 200 servings.
- The maximum number of guests is 200. Make a shopping list and determine the cost to make the snack mix for the maximum number of guests.

Checklist

Did you . . .

- ☐ explain the reason for your choice?
- ☐ make a table or graph?
- ☐ check that your answer is reasonable?

Reflect on Mathematical Practices

1. **Make Sense of Problems** What was the first step that you took in completing the task? Why?
2. **Use Models** Explain why you chose a graph or a table for showing the amounts of ingredients needed for different numbers of servings.

©Curriculum Associates, LLC Copying is not permitted. Unit 2 Performance Task 135

Extension

If students have more time to spend on this problem, you can have them solve this extension:

Suppose both recipes are combined. What fraction of a serving is granola? Almonds? A mix of peanuts and fruit?

SAMPLE RESPONSE AND RUBRIC

4-Point Solution

The ingredients for Granola Snack Mix cost less, but 1 serving of that recipe calls for twice as many ounces: $\frac{3}{4} : \frac{3}{8} = 2 : 1$ and $\frac{1}{2} : \frac{1}{4} = 2 : 1$. So I choose the Nutty Snack Mix. I'll write the fractions as decimals.

Nutty Snack Mix						
Servings	1	25	50	100 (50 × 2)	150 (50 × 3)	200 (50 × 4)
Almonds (ounces)	0.375	0.375 × 25 = 9.375	0.375 × 50 = 18.75	18.75 × 2 = 37.5	56.25	75
Peanuts (ounces)	0.25	0.25 × 25 = 6.25	0.25 × 50 = 12.5	12.5 × 2 = 25	37.5	50

To find the number of pounds, I'll divide the number of ounces by 16. For 200 guests I will need to buy 4.6875 pounds (75 ounces) of almonds and 3.125 pounds (50 ounces) of peanuts. Almonds cost: 4.6875 × \$9 = \$42.1875, or \$42.19. Peanuts cost: 3.125 × \$6 = \$18.75. It will cost \$42.19 + \$18.75 = \$60.94 to make the Nutty Snack Mix for 200 people.

REFLECT ON MATHEMATICAL PRACTICES

1. Students should address what considerations were involved in their choosing a recipe. ***(SMP 1)***
2. Students should explain how they felt the table or graph would be more useful to them. ***(SMP 2)***

SCORING RUBRIC

4 points All parts of the problem are complete and correct. Students explain their choice. They find the weights needed for the required quantities and tell the costs for 200 servings.

3 points The student has completed all parts of the problem, with one or two errors in computation. They explain their choice, find the weight needed, and give the costs.

2 points The student has attempted all parts of the problem, with a number of errors. The explanation may be lacking, and several weights are miscalculated. Organization may be lacking.

1 point Much of the problem is incomplete, with several errors. Several weights are incorrect due to using an inappropriate operation. Units may have been chosen incorrectly.

SOLUTION TO THE EXTENSION

Using decimals the total amount is 0.375 + 0.25 + 0.75 + 0.5 = 1.875 ounces.

Granola: 0.75 ÷ 1.875 = 0.4; granola is $\frac{2}{5}$ of the total.

Almonds: 0.375 ÷ 1.875 = 0.2; almonds are $\frac{1}{5}$ of the total.

Fruit and peanuts: 0.75 ÷ 1.875 = 0.4; Fruit and peanuts are also $\frac{2}{5}$ of the total.

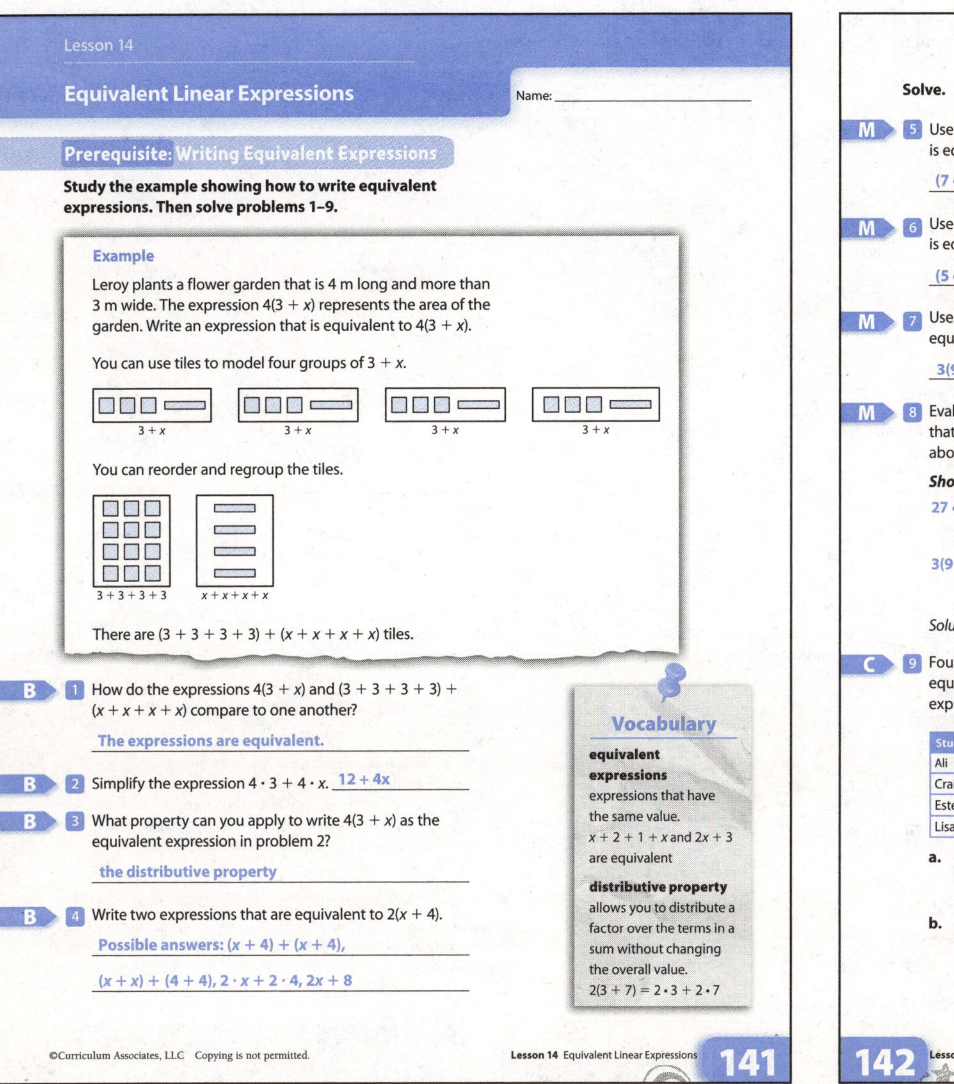

Lesson 14

Equivalent Linear Expressions

Name: ____________________

Prerequisite: Writing Equivalent Expressions

Study the example showing how to write equivalent expressions. Then solve problems 1–9.

Example

Leroy plants a flower garden that is 4 m long and more than 3 m wide. The expression $4(3 + x)$ represents the area of the garden. Write an expression that is equivalent to $4(3 + x)$.

You can use tiles to model four groups of $3 + x$.

You can reorder and regroup the tiles.

There are $(3 + 3 + 3 + 3) + (x + x + x + x)$ tiles.

B 1 How do the expressions $4(3 + x)$ and $(3 + 3 + 3 + 3) + (x + x + x + x)$ compare to one another?

The expressions are equivalent.

B 2 Simplify the expression $4 \cdot 3 + 4 \cdot x$. $12 + 4x$

B 3 What property can you apply to write $4(3 + x)$ as the equivalent expression in problem 2?

the distributive property

B 4 Write two expressions that are equivalent to $2(x + 4)$.

Possible answers: $(x + 4) + (x + 4)$,

$(x + x) + (4 + 4)$, $2 \cdot x + 2 \cdot 4$, $2x + 8$

Vocabulary

equivalent expressions expressions that have the same value.
$x + 2 + 1 + x$ and $2x + 3$ are equivalent

distributive property allows you to distribute a factor over the terms in a sum without changing the overall value.
$2(3 + 7) = 2 \cdot 3 + 2 \cdot 7$

Solve.

M 5 Use the distributive property to write an expression that is equivalent to $7(3x - 4)$.

$(7 \cdot 3x) - (7 \cdot 4)$ or $21x - 28$

M 6 Use the distributive property to write an expression that is equivalent to $10 + 15x$.

$(5 \cdot 2) + (5 \cdot 3x)$ or $5(2 + 3x)$

M 7 Use the distributive property to find an expression that is equivalent to $27x^2 - 42x + 12$.

$3(9x^2 - 14x + 4)$

M 8 Evaluate $27x^2 - 42x + 12$ and the equivalent expression that you wrote in problem 7 for $x = 2$. What do you notice about the value of the two expressions?

Show your work.

$27 \cdot 2^2 - 42 \cdot 2 + 12 = 27 \cdot 4 - 84 + 12$
$= 108 - 84 + 12 = 36$

$3(9 \cdot 2^2 - 14 \cdot 2 + 4) = 3(9 \cdot 4 - 28 + 4)$
$= 3(36 - 28 + 4) = 3(12) = 36$

Solution: The expressions have the same value.

C 9 Four students were asked to write an expression that is equivalent to $8x - 20$. The students' names and the expressions they wrote are shown in the table.

Student	Expression
Ali	$-4(2x + 5)$
Craig	$4(2x - 5)$
Ester	$-2(-4x + 10)$
Lisa	$2(4x - 10)$

a. Which student(s) wrote correct expressions?

Craig, Ester, Lisa

b. For each incorrect expression, explain what the student did to get his or her answer.

Ali factored out -4 instead of 4, resulting in an incorrect sign for $2x$.

Key

B Basic **M** Medium **C** Challenge

Name: ____________

Equivalent Expressions for the Perimeter of a Square

Study the example problem showing how to write equivalent expressions for the perimeter of a square. Then solve problems 1–8.

Example

Tanya plans to make a square deck. She is not sure what size she is going to make the deck, but she knows it needs to be more than 5 feet long. She represents the deck as a square in which each side is $d + 5$ feet long. How can she write an expression for the perimeter of the deck?

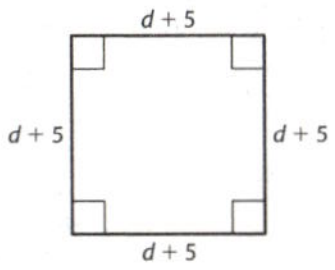

Tanya can add the four equal side lengths to find the perimeter:

Perimeter = $(d + 5) + (d + 5) + (d + 5) + (d + 5)$

B 1 Write $(d + 5) + (d + 5) + (d + 5) + (d + 5)$ as an equivalent expression by grouping the like terms.

$(d + d + d + d) + (5 + 5 + 5 + 5)$

B 2 Write an expression for the perimeter by multiplying the number of sides by the length of a side.

Perimeter = **$4(d + 5)$**

B 3 Simplify each expression for the perimeter of the deck that you wrote in problems 1 and 2. What do you notice?

They are both $4d + 20$.

M 4 The perimeter of an equilateral triangle is given as $15x + 30$. Write two different expressions to represent the perimeter. Use factoring to write one of the expressions.

Possible answers: $3(5x + 10)$;

$(5x + 5x + 5x) + (10 + 10 + 10)$

Vocabulary

like terms terms in an expression that have the same variable raised to the same power. Constants are like terms.

x and $-4x$

1 and 1.5

x^2 and $8x^2$

Solve.

M 5 Write four different expressions for the perimeter of a pentagon whose sides are all $s - 2$ units long.

Possible answers: $(s - 2) + (s - 2) + (s - 2) + (s - 2) + (s - 2)$,

$s + s + s + s + s - 2 - 2 - 2 - 2 - 2$, $5(s - 2)$, $5s - 10$

M 6 Kin made a picture frame for a square picture with sides that are $5f - 4$ inches long. Framing the picture adds 2 inches to the length of each side. Use the distributive property to write two expressions for the perimeter of the framed picture.

Show your work.

Side length of framed picture: $5f - 4 + 2 = 5f - 2$

Solution: **Perimeter of framed picture: $4(5f - 2)$, $20f - 8$**

M 7 The expression $9x + 6$ represents the cost for three friends to go to the movies. Write $9x + 6$ as a product. Then tell how many friends went to the movies and what expression represents the cost of a movie ticket.

$3(3x + 2)$; 3 friends went to the movies; $3x + 2$ represents the cost of a ticket.

C 8 A square playground is surrounded by a sidewalk on all sides. The sidewalk is $2n + 3$ yards long on each side of the park. The sidewalk is 0.5 yard wide. What is the perimeter of the playground? Write two equivalent expressions for the perimeter of the playground.

Show your work.

The side length of the playground is $2n + 3 - 2(0.5) = 2n + 2$.

Solution: **The perimeter of the playground can be represented by the expressions $4(2n + 2)$ and $8n + 4$. (Accept equivalent expressions.)**

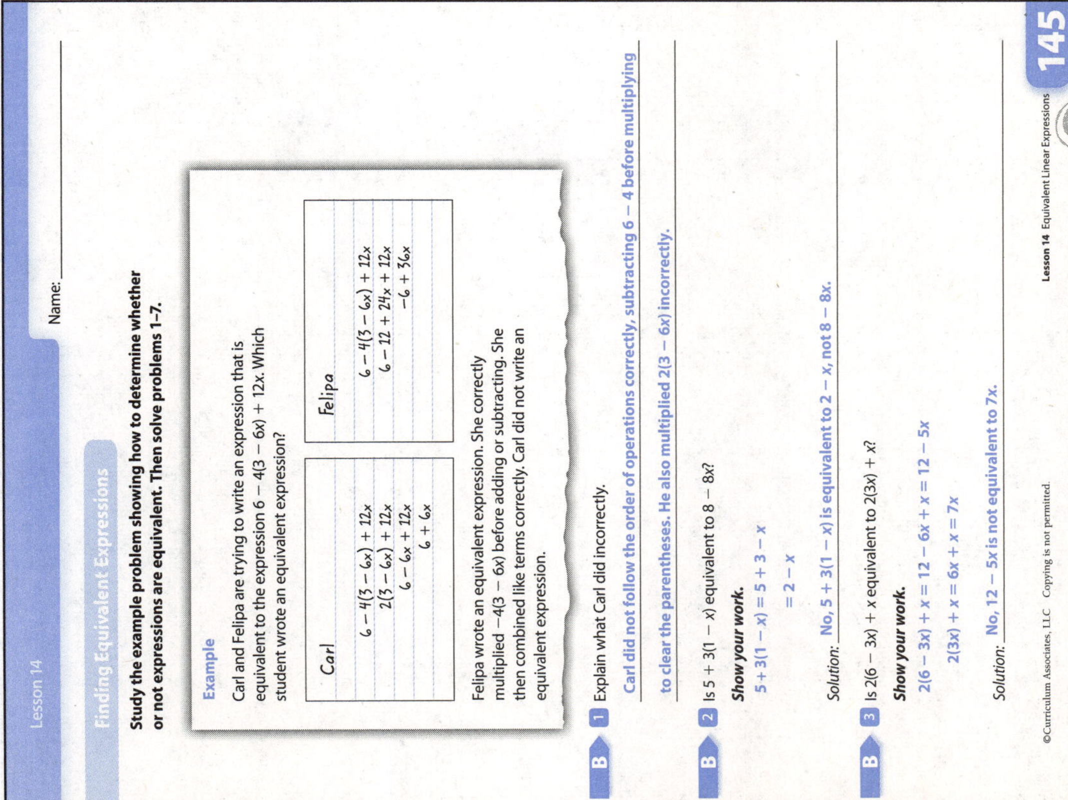

Lesson 14

Name: ____________

Finding Equivalent Expressions

Study the example problem showing how to determine whether or not expressions are equivalent. Then solve problems 1–7.

Example

Carl and Felipa are trying to write an expression that is equivalent to the expression $6 - 4(3 - 6x) + 12x$. Which student wrote an equivalent expression?

Carl	Felipa
$6 - 4(3 - 6x) + 12x$	$6 - 4(3 - 6x) + 12x$
$2(3 - 6x) + 12x$	$6 - 12 + 24x + 12x$
$6 - 6x + 12x$	$-6 + 36x$
$6 + 6x$	

Felipa wrote an equivalent expression. She correctly multiplied $-4(3 - 6x)$ before adding or subtracting. She then combined like terms correctly. Carl did not write an equivalent expression.

B 1 Explain what Carl did incorrectly.

Carl did not follow the order of operations correctly, subtracting $6 - 4$ before multiplying to clear the parentheses. He also multiplied $2(3 - 6x)$ incorrectly.

B 2 Is $5 + 3(1 - x)$ equivalent to $8 - 8x$?

Show your work.

$5 + 3(1 - x) = 5 + 3 - x$

$= 2 - x$

Solution: No, $5 + 3(1 - x)$ is equivalent to $2 - x$, not $8 - 8x$.

B 3 Is $2(6 - 3x) + x$ equivalent to $2(3x) + x$?

Show your work.

$2(6 - 3x) + x = 12 - 6x + x = 12 - 5x$

$2(3x) + x = 6x + x = 7x$

Solution: No, $12 - 5x$ is not equivalent to $7x$.

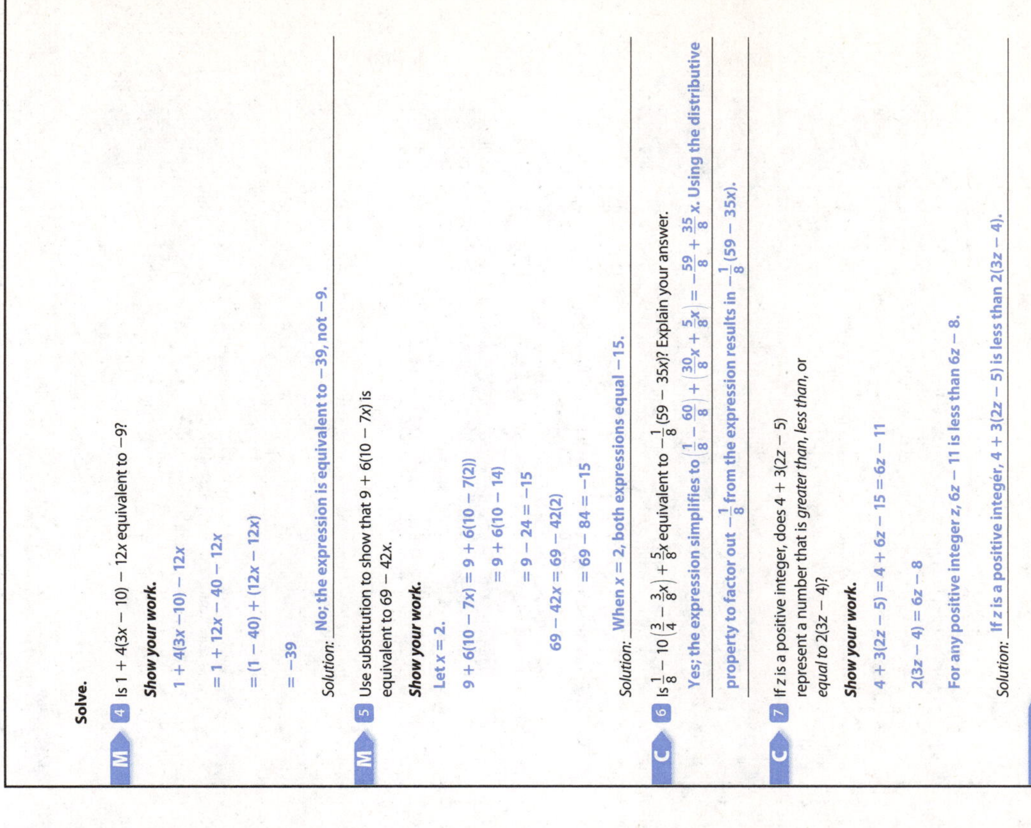

Solve.

M 4 Is $1 + 4(3x - 10) - 12x$ equivalent to -9?

Show your work.

$1 + 4(3x - 10) - 12x$

$= 1 + 12x - 40 - 12x$

$= (1 - 40) + (12x - 12x)$

$= -39$

Solution: No; the expression is equivalent to -39, not -9.

M 5 Use substitution to show that $9 + 6(10 - 7x)$ is equivalent to $69 - 42x$.

Show your work.

Let $x = 2$.

$9 + 6(10 - 7x) = 9 + 6(10 - 7(2))$

$= 9 + 6(10 - 14)$

$= 9 - 24 = -15$

$69 - 42x = 69 - 42(2)$

$= 69 - 84 = -15$

Solution: When $x = 2$, both expressions equal -15.

C 6 Is $\frac{1}{8} - 10\left(\frac{3}{4} - \frac{3}{8}x\right) + \frac{5}{8}x$ equivalent to $-\frac{1}{8}(59 - 35x)$? Explain your answer.

Yes; the expression simplifies to $\left(\frac{1}{8} - \frac{60}{8}\right) + \left(\frac{30}{8}x + \frac{5}{8}x\right) = -\frac{59}{8} + \frac{35}{8}x$. Using the distributive property to factor out $-\frac{1}{8}$ from the expression results in $-\frac{1}{8}(59 - 35x)$.

C 7 If z is a positive integer, does $4 + 3(2z - 5)$ represent a number that is *greater than, less than,* or *equal to* $2(3z - 4)$?

Show your work.

$4 + 3(2z - 5) = 4 + 6z - 15 = 6z - 11$

$2(3z - 4) = 6z - 8$

For any positive integer z, $6z - 11$ is less than $6z - 8$.

Solution: If z is a positive integer, $4 + 3(2z - 5)$ is less than $2(3z - 4)$.

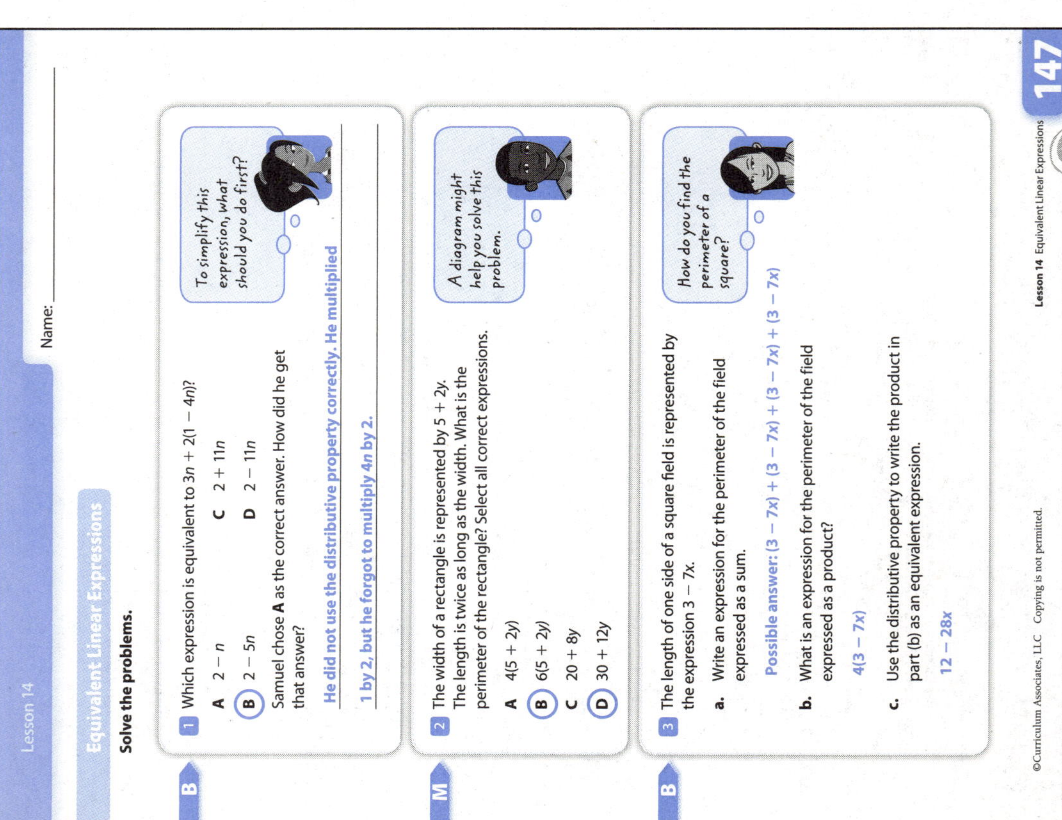

Lesson 14

Name: ______________________

Equivalent Linear Expressions

Solve the problems.

B

1 Which expression is equivalent to $3n + 2(1 - 4n)$?

A $2 - n$ C $2 + 11n$

(B) $2 - 5n$ D $2 - 11n$

Samuel chose **A** as the correct answer. How did he get that answer?

He did not use the distributive property correctly. He multiplied 1 by 2, but he forgot to multiply 4n by 2.

M

2 The width of a rectangle is represented by $5 + 2y$. The length is twice as long as the width. What is the perimeter of the rectangle? Select all correct expressions.

A $4(5 + 2y)$

(B) $6(5 + 2y)$

C $20 + 8y$

(D) $30 + 12y$

B

3 The length of one side of a square field is represented by the expression $3 - 7x$.

a. Write an expression for the perimeter of the field expressed as a sum.

Possible answer: $(3 - 7x) + (3 - 7x) + (3 - 7x) + (3 - 7x)$

b. What is an expression for the perimeter of the field expressed as a product?

$4(3 - 7x)$

c. Use the distributive property to write the product in part (b) as an equivalent expression.

$12 - 28x$

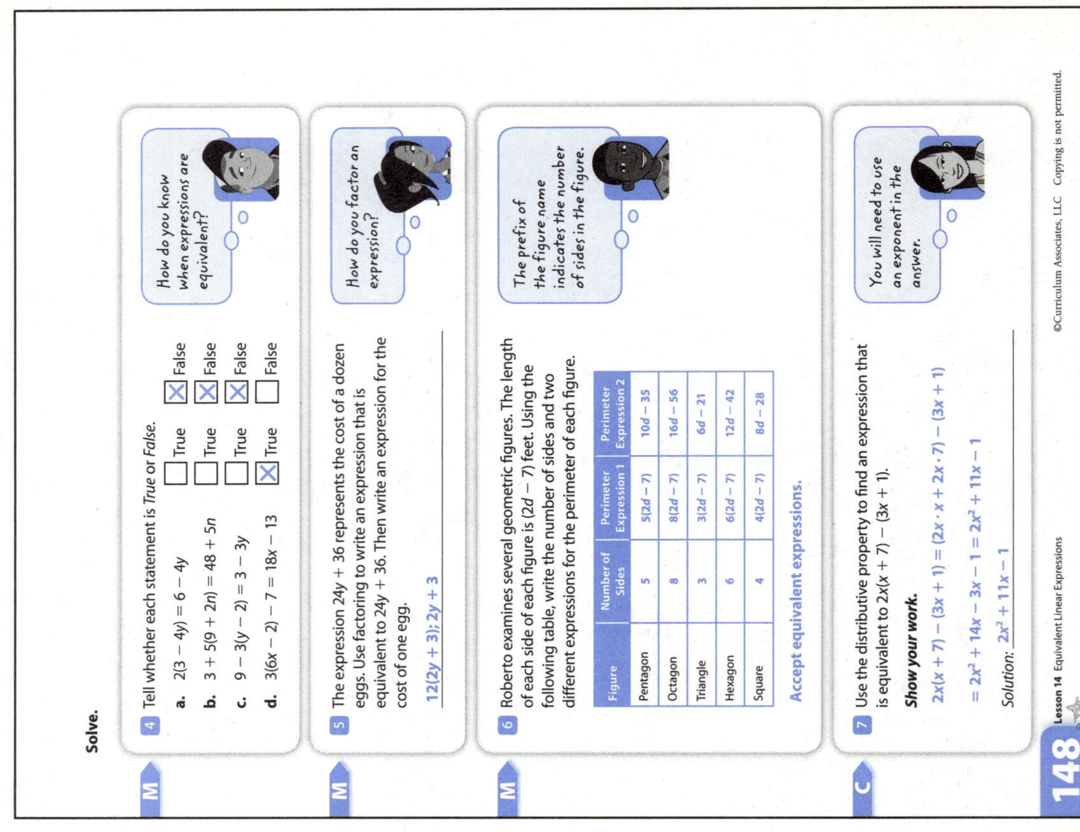

Solve.

M

4 Tell whether each statement is *True* or *False*.

	Statement	True	False
a.	$2(3 - 4y) = 6 - 4y$	☐	☒
b.	$3 + 5(9 + 2n) = 48 + 5n$	☐	☒
c.	$9 - 3(y - 2) = 3 - 3y$	☐	☒
d.	$3(6x - 2) - 7 = 18x - 13$	☒	☐

M

5 The expression $24y + 36$ represents the cost of a dozen eggs. Use factoring to write an expression that is equivalent to $24y + 36$. Then write an expression for the cost of one egg.

$12(2y + 3)$; $2y + 3$

M

6 Roberto examines several geometric figures. The length of each side of each figure is $(2d - 7)$ feet. Using the following table, write the number of sides and two different expressions for the perimeter of each figure.

Figure	Number of Sides	Perimeter Expression 1	Perimeter Expression 2
Pentagon	5	$5(2d - 7)$	$10d - 35$
Octagon	8	$8(2d - 7)$	$16d - 56$
Triangle	3	$3(2d - 7)$	$6d - 21$
Hexagon	6	$6(2d - 7)$	$12d - 42$
Square	4	$4(2d - 7)$	$8d - 28$

Accept equivalent expressions.

C

7 Use the distributive property to find an expression that is equivalent to $2x(x + 7) - (3x + 1)$.

Show your work.

$2x(x + 7) - (3x + 1) = (2x \cdot x + 2x \cdot 7) - (3x + 1)$

$= 2x^2 + 14x - 3x - 1 = 2x^2 + 11x - 1$

Solution: $2x^2 + 11x - 1$

Lesson 15

Writing Linear Expressions

Name: ____________________

Prerequisite: Identify Equivalent Expressions

Study the example problem showing how to write equivalent linear expressions. Then solve problems 1–8.

Example

Mia babysits some children after school. For each child, she charges $x + 2$ dollars per hour. One day she cared for 2 children for 3 hours each. She paid $4 per child for materials for activities. Two students wrote expressions for the amount of money Mia earned. Are their expressions equivalent?

Paolo wrote the expression $3(x + 2) + 3(x + 2) - 8$.
Carla wrote the expression $(3x + 6) - 4 + (3x + 6) - 4$.

Simplify the expressions to see whether they are equivalent.

Paolo's Expression	**Carla's Expression**
$3(x + 2) + 3(x + 2) - 8$	$(3x + 6) - 4 + (3x + 6) - 4$
$= 3x + 6 + 3x + 6 - 8$	$= 3x + 3x + 6 + 6 - 4 - 4$
$= 6x + 4$	$= 6x + 4$

The expressions are equivalent.

B 1 Why did Paolo add $3(x + 2)$ to itself and subtract 8?

The expression $3(x + 2)$ is the amount Mia charged for each child, and $8 is the total amount she spent for materials.

B 2 What is the meaning of each part of Carla's expression?

$(3x + 6)$ is the amount Mia charged for each child, and $4 is the amount she spent on materials for each child.

B 3 How do you know that Paolo's and Carla's expressions are equivalent?

Both expressions are equivalent to $6x + 4$. So the expressions will have the same value for any value of x.

Vocabulary

equivalent expressions expressions that have the same value for every value of the variable.

$2(x + 1)$ and $2 + 2x$ are equivalent expressions.

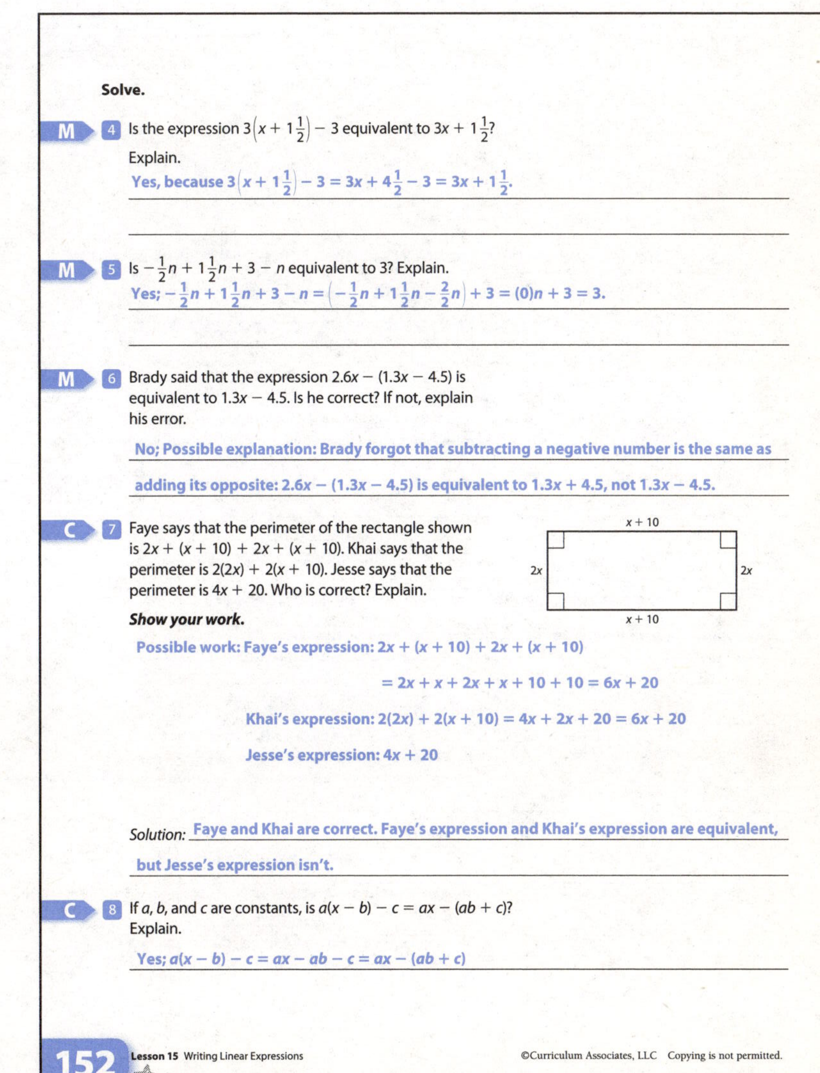

Solve.

M 4 Is the expression $3\left(x + 1\frac{1}{2}\right) - 3$ equivalent to $3x + 1\frac{1}{2}$? Explain.

Yes, because $3\left(x + 1\frac{1}{2}\right) - 3 = 3x + 4\frac{1}{2} - 3 = 3x + 1\frac{1}{2}$.

M 5 Is $-\frac{1}{2}n + 1\frac{1}{2}n + 3 - n$ equivalent to 3? Explain.

Yes; $-\frac{1}{2}n + 1\frac{1}{2}n + 3 - n = \left(-\frac{1}{2}n + 1\frac{1}{2}n - \frac{2}{2}n\right) + 3 = (0)n + 3 = 3$.

M 6 Brady said that the expression $2.6x - (1.3x - 4.5)$ is equivalent to $1.3x - 4.5$. Is he correct? If not, explain his error.

No; Possible explanation: Brady forgot that subtracting a negative number is the same as adding its opposite: $2.6x - (1.3x - 4.5)$ is equivalent to $1.3x + 4.5$, not $1.3x - 4.5$.

C 7 Faye says that the perimeter of the rectangle shown is $2x + (x + 10) + 2x + (x + 10)$. Khai says that the perimeter is $2(2x) + 2(x + 10)$. Jesse says that the perimeter is $4x + 20$. Who is correct? Explain.

Show your work.

Possible work: Faye's expression: $2x + (x + 10) + 2x + (x + 10)$

$= 2x + x + 2x + x + 10 + 10 = 6x + 20$

Khai's expression: $2(2x) + 2(x + 10) = 4x + 2x + 20 = 6x + 20$

Jesse's expression: $4x + 20$

Solution: **Faye and Khai are correct. Faye's expression and Khai's expression are equivalent, but Jesse's expression isn't.**

C 8 If a, b, and c are constants, is $a(x - b) - c = ax - (ab + c)$? Explain.

Yes; $a(x - b) - c = ax - ab - c = ax - (ab + c)$

Key

B Basic **M** Medium **C** Challenge

Name: ____________________

Writing Equivalent Expressions

Study the example showing different ways to write an expression for a problem. Then solve problems 1–7.

Example

The distance from Ari's house, *A*, to Ben's house, *B*, is equal to the distance from Ari's house to Cal's house, *C*. One day the boys all met at Ari's house, and then they went to Ben's house and from there to Cal's house. Then Ari and Ben went home. Ari and Cal each wrote expressions for the distance they walked.

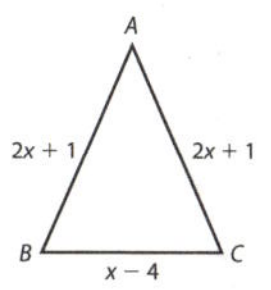

A, B, C; $2x + 1$, $2x + 1$, $x - 4$

Ari's travel distance $= (2x + 1) + (x - 4) + (2x + 1)$

Cal's travel distance $= 2(2x + 1) + (x - 4)$

B **1** Did Ari and Cal walk the same distance? Explain.

Yes; An expression for the distance Ari walked is $(2x + 1) + (x - 4) + (2x + 1) = 5x - 2$. An expression for the distance Cal walked is $2(2x + 1) + (x - 4) = 4x + 2 + x - 4 = 5x - 2$. Because the expressions are equivalent, Ari and Cal walked the same distance.

B **2** In the expression for Cal's distance, why is $(2x + 1)$ multiplied by 2?

Cal walked a distance of $(2x + 1)$ to Ari's house and the same distance to Ben's house.

B **3** Cindy wrote the expression $2x + 2x + x + 1 + 1 - 4$ to represent Ari's distance. Is her expression correct? Explain.

Yes; Cindy's expression simplifies to $5x - 2$, which is equivalent to Ari's distance.

B **4** Did Ben walk the same distance as the other two boys? Use an expression to explain your answer.

No; Ben walked $(2x + 1)$ to Ari's house and $(2x + 1)$ back to his house, then he walked $(x - 4)$ to Cal's house and $(x - 4)$ back to his own house. His distance was $2(2x + 1) + 2(x - 4) = 4x + 2 + 2x - 8 = 6x - 6$. This expression is not equivalent to $5x - 2$.

Solve.

M **5** The perimeter of a square is given as $8x + 20$. Write two different expressions for the perimeter. Use factoring to write one of the expressions.

Factoring: $8x + 20 = 4(2x + 5)$; another way: $(2x + 5) + (2x + 5) + (2x + 5) + (2x + 5)$

(Accept equivalent expressions.)

M **6** The length of a rectangle is 4 times its width. Write three different expressions to describe its perimeter. Explain how you wrote each expression.

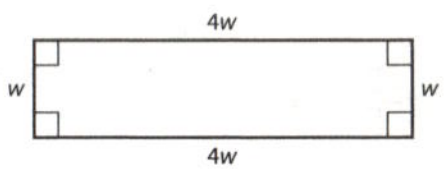

4w, w, w, 4w

(1) $w + 4w + w + 4w$; I added the lengths of all four sides.

(2) $2w + 2(4w)$; I multiplied both the length and the width by 2 and added the products.

(3) $2(w + 4w)$; I added the length and the width and multiplied the sum by 2.

(Students may also write $10w$, simplifying one of the above expressions.)

C **7** Each of the two congruent sides of an isosceles triangle has length $2x - 1.5$, and the third side has length $x + 3$. Label the sides of the triangle. Then write two equivalent expressions for its perimeter.

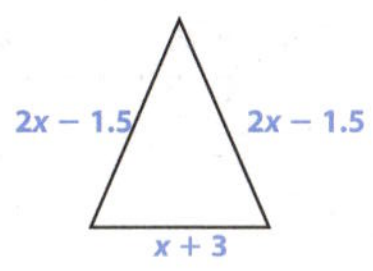

Show your work.

$2x - 1.5$, $2x - 1.5$, $x + 3$

Possible work:

(1) Perimeter $= 2(2x - 1.5) + (x + 3) = 4x - 3 + x + 3 = 5x$

(2) Perimeter $= (2x - 1.5) + (2x - 1.5) + (x + 3) = 2x + 2x + x - 1.5 - 1.5 + 3 = 5x + 0 = 5x$

Both expressions are equivalent to $5x$, so they are equivalent to each other.

Solution: **Possible answers: $2(2x - 1.5) + (x + 3)$ and $(2x - 1.5) + (2x - 1.5) + (x + 3)$**

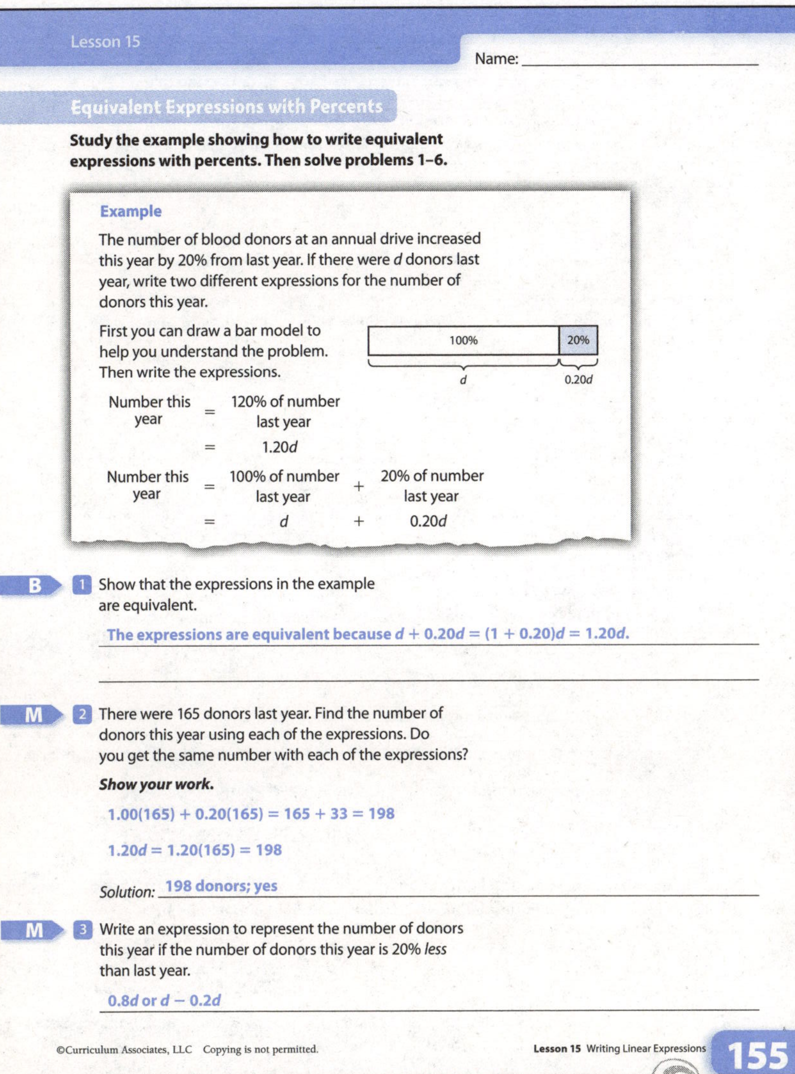

Name: ____________

Equivalent Expressions with Percents

Study the example showing how to write equivalent expressions with percents. Then solve problems 1–6.

Example

The number of blood donors at an annual drive increased this year by 20% from last year. If there were d donors last year, write two different expressions for the number of donors this year.

First you can draw a bar model to help you understand the problem. Then write the expressions.

Number this year = 120% of number last year
= $1.20d$

Number this year = 100% of number last year + 20% of number last year
= d + $0.20d$

B **1** Show that the expressions in the example are equivalent.

The expressions are equivalent because $d + 0.20d = (1 + 0.20)d = 1.20d$.

M **2** There were 165 donors last year. Find the number of donors this year using each of the expressions. Do you get the same number with each of the expressions?

Show your work.

$1.00(165) + 0.20(165) = 165 + 33 = 198$

$1.20d = 1.20(165) = 198$

Solution: 198 donors; yes

M **3** Write an expression to represent the number of donors this year if the number of donors this year is 20% *less* than last year.

$0.8d$ or $d - 0.2d$

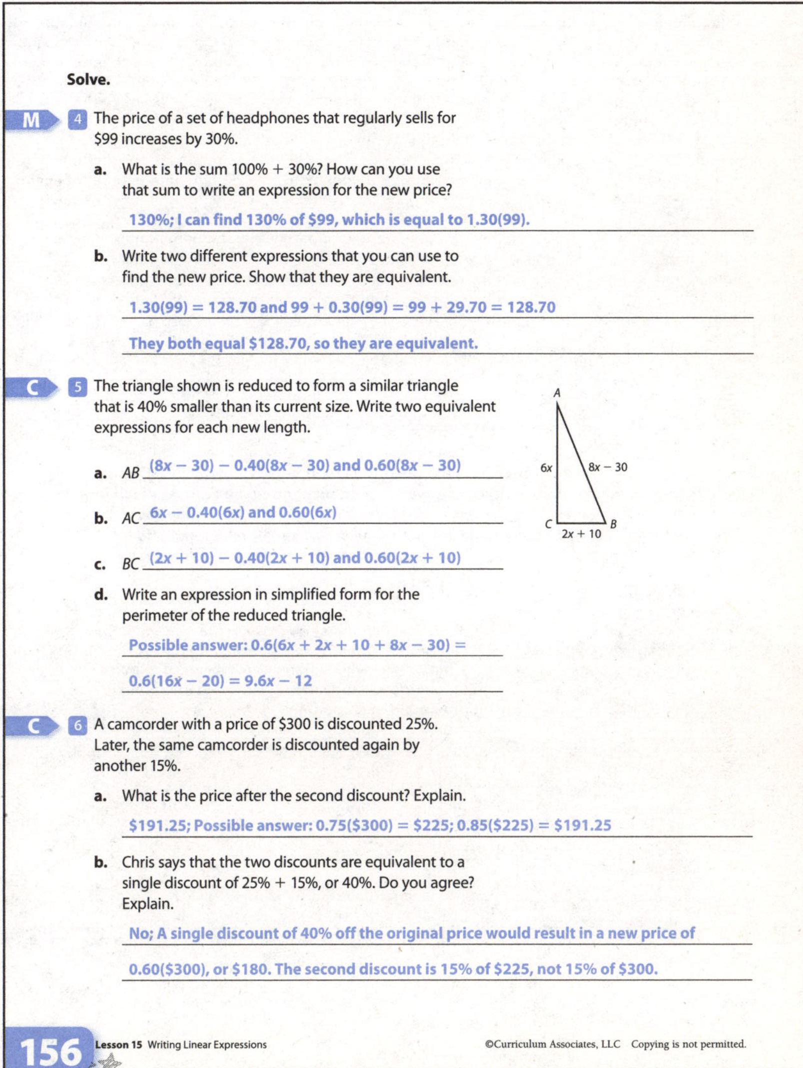

Solve.

M **4** The price of a set of headphones that regularly sells for $99 increases by 30%.

a. What is the sum 100% + 30%? How can you use that sum to write an expression for the new price?

130%; I can find 130% of $99, which is equal to 1.30(99).

b. Write two different expressions that you can use to find the new price. Show that they are equivalent.

$1.30(99) = 128.70$ and $99 + 0.30(99) = 99 + 29.70 = 128.70$

They both equal $128.70, so they are equivalent.

C **5** The triangle shown is reduced to form a similar triangle that is 40% smaller than its current size. Write two equivalent expressions for each new length.

a. AB $(8x - 30) - 0.40(8x - 30)$ and $0.60(8x - 30)$

b. AC $6x - 0.40(6x)$ and $0.60(6x)$

c. BC $(2x + 10) - 0.40(2x + 10)$ and $0.60(2x + 10)$

d. Write an expression in simplified form for the perimeter of the reduced triangle.

Possible answer: $0.6(6x + 2x + 10 + 8x - 30) =$
$0.6(16x - 20) = 9.6x - 12$

C **6** A camcorder with a price of $300 is discounted 25%. Later, the same camcorder is discounted again by another 15%.

a. What is the price after the second discount? Explain.

$191.25; Possible answer: 0.75($300) = $225; 0.85($225) = $191.25

b. Chris says that the two discounts are equivalent to a single discount of 25% + 15%, or 40%. Do you agree? Explain.

No; A single discount of 40% off the original price would result in a new price of 0.60($300), or $180. The second discount is 15% of $225, not 15% of $300.

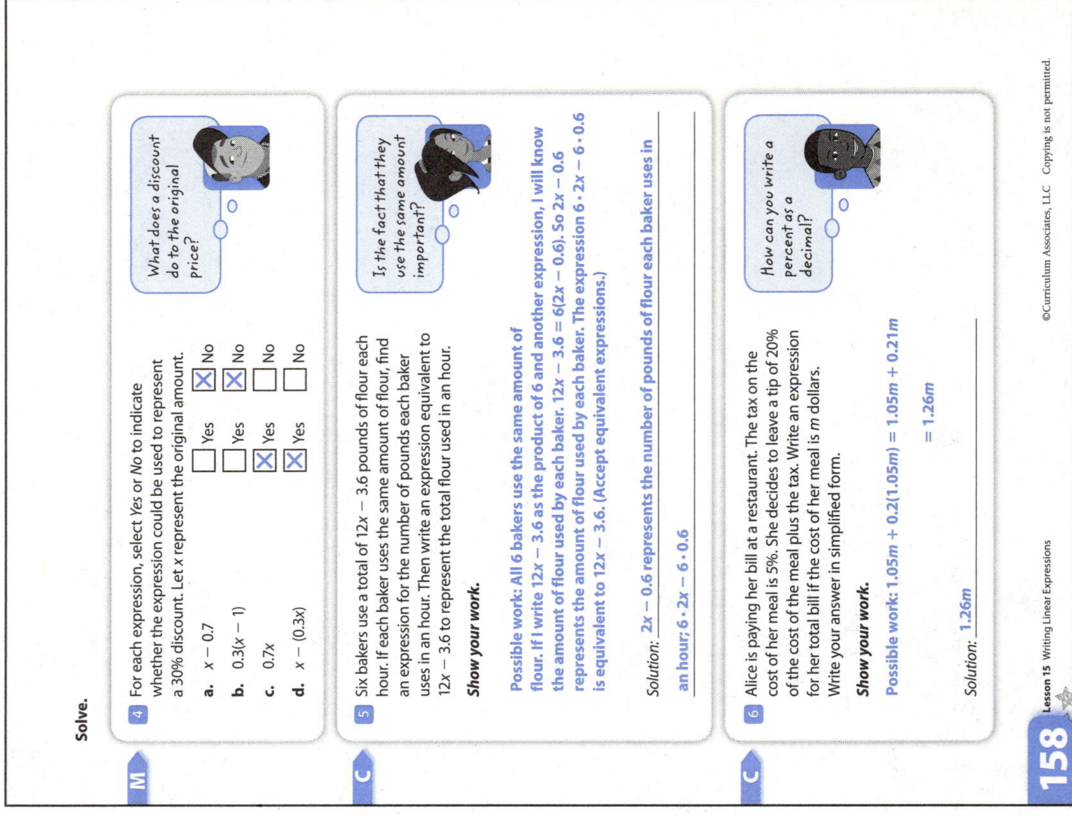

Solve.

M

4 For each expression, select *Yes* or *No* to indicate whether the expression could be used to represent a 30% discount. Let x represent the original amount.

		Yes	No
a.	$x - 0.7$	☐	☒
b.	$0.3(x - 1)$	☐	☒
c.	$0.7x$	☒	☐
d.	$x - (0.3x)$	☒	☐

C

5 Six bakers use a total of $12x - 3.6$ pounds of flour each hour. If each baker uses the same amount of flour, find an expression for the number of pounds each baker uses in an hour. Then write an expression equivalent to $12x - 3.6$ to represent the total flour used in an hour.

Show your work.

Possible work: All 6 bakers use the same amount of flour. If I write $12x - 3.6$ as the product of 6 and another expression, I will know the amount of flour used by each baker. $12x - 3.6 = 6(2x - 0.6)$. So $2x - 0.6$ represents the amount of flour used by each baker. The expression $6 \cdot 2x - 6 \cdot 0.6$ is equivalent to $12x - 3.6$. (Accept equivalent expressions.)

Solution: **$2x - 0.6$ represents the number of pounds of flour each baker uses in an hour; $6 \cdot 2x - 6 \cdot 0.6$**

C

6 Alice is paying her bill at a restaurant. The tax on the cost of her meal is 5%. She decides to leave a tip of 20% of the cost of the meal plus the tax. Write an expression for her total bill if the cost of her meal is m dollars. Write your answer in simplified form.

Show your work.

Possible work: $1.05m + 0.2(1.05m) = 1.05m + 0.21m$

$= 1.26m$

Solution: **$1.26m$**

158 Lesson 15 Writing Linear Expressions ©Curriculum Associates, LLC Copying is not permitted.

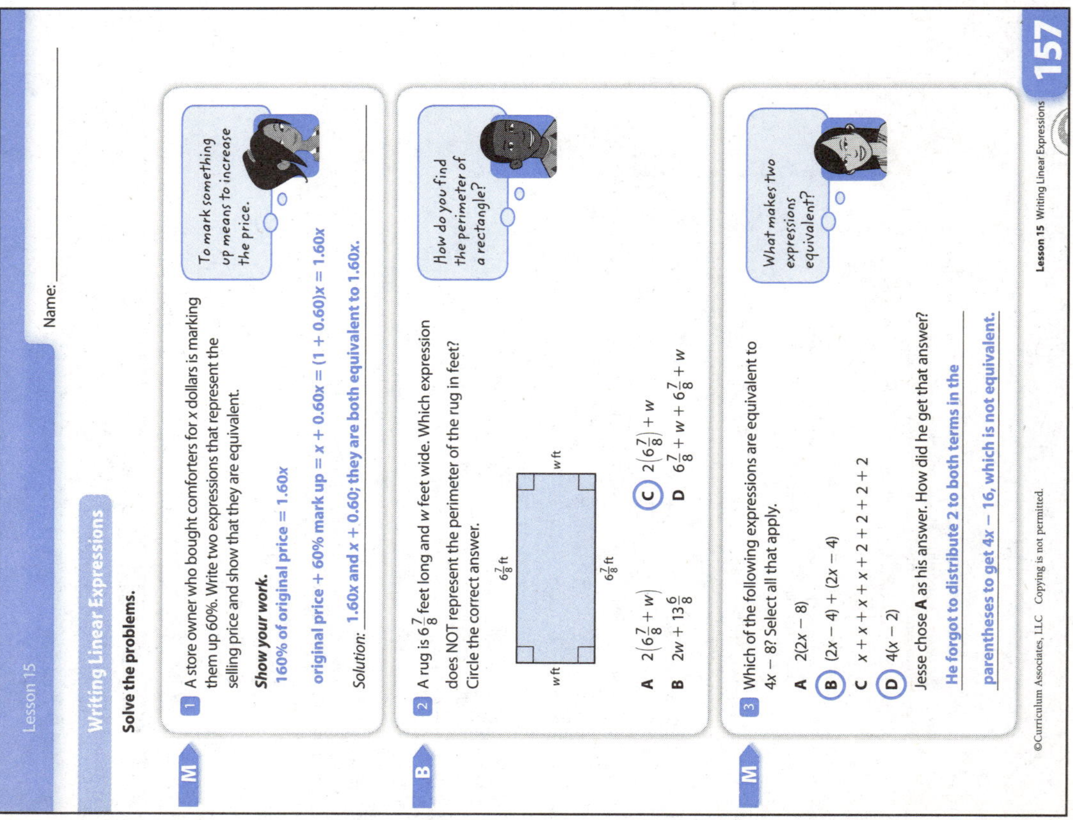

Lesson 15 Name: ____________

Writing Linear Expressions

Solve the problems.

M

1 A store owner who bought comforters for x dollars is marking them up 60%. Write two expressions that represent the selling price and show that they are equivalent.

Show your work.

160% of original price = $1.60x$

original price + 60% mark up = $x + 0.60x = (1 + 0.60)x = 1.60x$

Solution: **$1.60x$ and $x + 0.60$; they are both equivalent to $1.60x$.**

B

2 A rug is $6\frac{7}{8}$ feet long and w feet wide. Which expression does NOT represent the perimeter of the rug in feet? Circle the correct answer.

A $2\left(6\frac{7}{8} + w\right)$

B $2w + 13\frac{6}{8}$

(C) $2\left(6\frac{7}{8}\right) + w$

D $6\frac{7}{8} + w + 6\frac{7}{8} + w$

M

3 Which of the following expressions are equivalent to $4x - 8$? Select all that apply.

A $2(2x - 8)$

(B) $(2x - 4) + (2x - 4)$

C $x + x + x + x + 2 + 2 + 2 + 2$

(D) $4(x - 2)$

Jesse chose **A** as his answer. How did he get that answer?

He forgot to distribute 2 to both terms in the parentheses to get $4x - 16$, which is not equivalent.

©Curriculum Associates, LLC Copying is not permitted. Lesson 15 Writing Linear Expressions 157

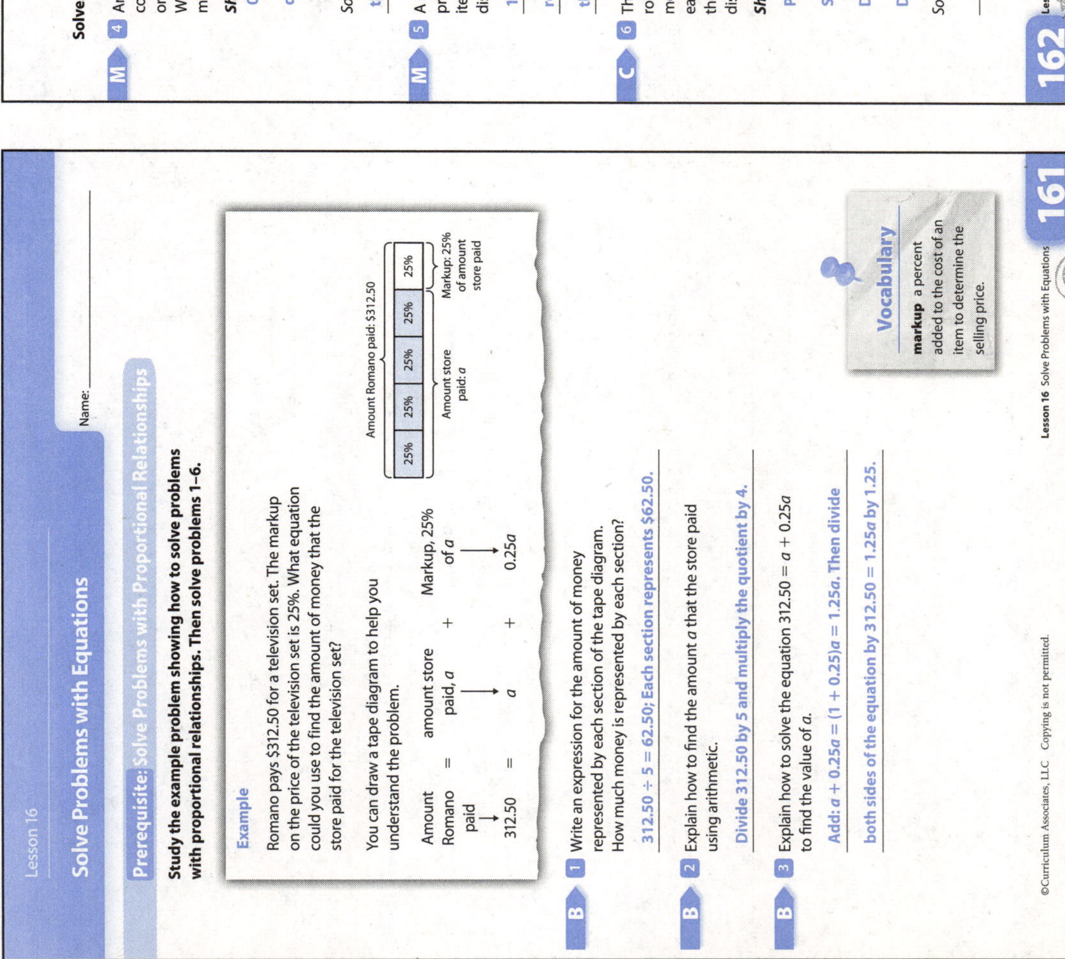

Lesson 16

Solve Problems with Equations

Name: ______________________

Prerequisite: Solve Problems with Proportional Relationships

Study the example problem showing how to solve problems with proportional relationships. Then solve problems 1–6.

Example

Romano pays $312.50 for a television set. The markup on the price of the television set is 25%. What equation could you use to find the amount of money that the store paid for the television set?

You can draw a tape diagram to help you understand the problem.

Amount Romano paid = amount store paid, a + Markup, 25% of a

$312.50 = a + 0.25a$

B **1** Write an expression for the amount of money represented by each section of the tape diagram. How much money is represented by each section?

$312.50 \div 5 = 62.50$; Each section represents $62.50.

B **2** Explain how to find the amount a that the store paid using arithmetic.

Divide 312.50 by 5 and multiply the quotient by 4.

B **3** Explain how to solve the equation $312.50 = a + 0.25a$ to find the value of a.

Add: $a + 0.25a = (1 + 0.25)a = 1.25a$. Then divide both sides of the equation by $312.50 = 1.25a$ by 1.25.

Vocabulary

markup a percent added to the cost of an item to determine the selling price.

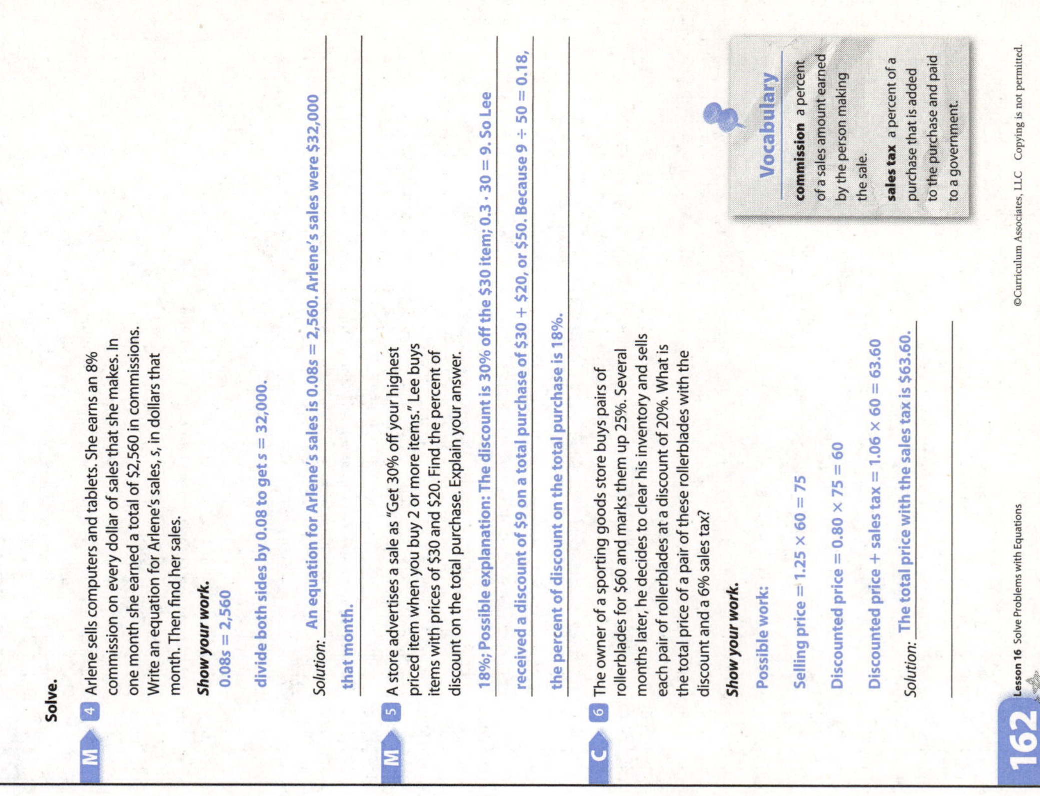

Solve.

M **4** Arlene sells computers and tablets. She earns an 8% commission on every dollar of sales that she makes. In one month she earned a total of $2,560 in commissions. Write an equation for Arlene's sales, s, in dollars that month. Then find her sales.

Show your work.

$0.08s = 2,560$

divide both sides by 0.08 to get $s = 32,000$.

Solution: An equation for Arlene's sales is $0.08s = 2,560$. Arlene's sales were $32,000 that month.

M **5** A store advertises a sale as "Get 30% off your highest priced item when you buy 2 or more items." Lee buys items with prices of $30 and $20. Find the percent of discount on the total purchase. Explain your answer.

18%; Possible explanation: The discount is 30% off the $30 item; $0.3 \cdot 30 = 9$. So Lee received a discount of $9 on a total purchase of $30 + $20, or $50. Because $9 \div 50 = 0.18$, the percent of discount on the total purchase is 18%.

C **6** The owner of a sporting goods store buys pairs of rollerblades for $60 and marks them up 25%. Several months later, he decides to clear his inventory and sells each pair of rollerblades at a discount of 20%. What is the total price of a pair of these rollerblades with the discount and a 6% sales tax?

Show your work.

Possible work:

Selling price $= 1.25 \times 60 = 75$

Discounted price $= 0.80 \times 75 = 60$

Discounted price + sales tax $= 1.06 \times 60 = 63.60$

Solution: The total price with the sales tax is $63.60.

Vocabulary

commission a percent of a sales amount earned by the person making the sale.

sales tax a percent of a purchase that is added to the purchase and paid to a government.

Key

B Basic **M** Medium **C** Challenge

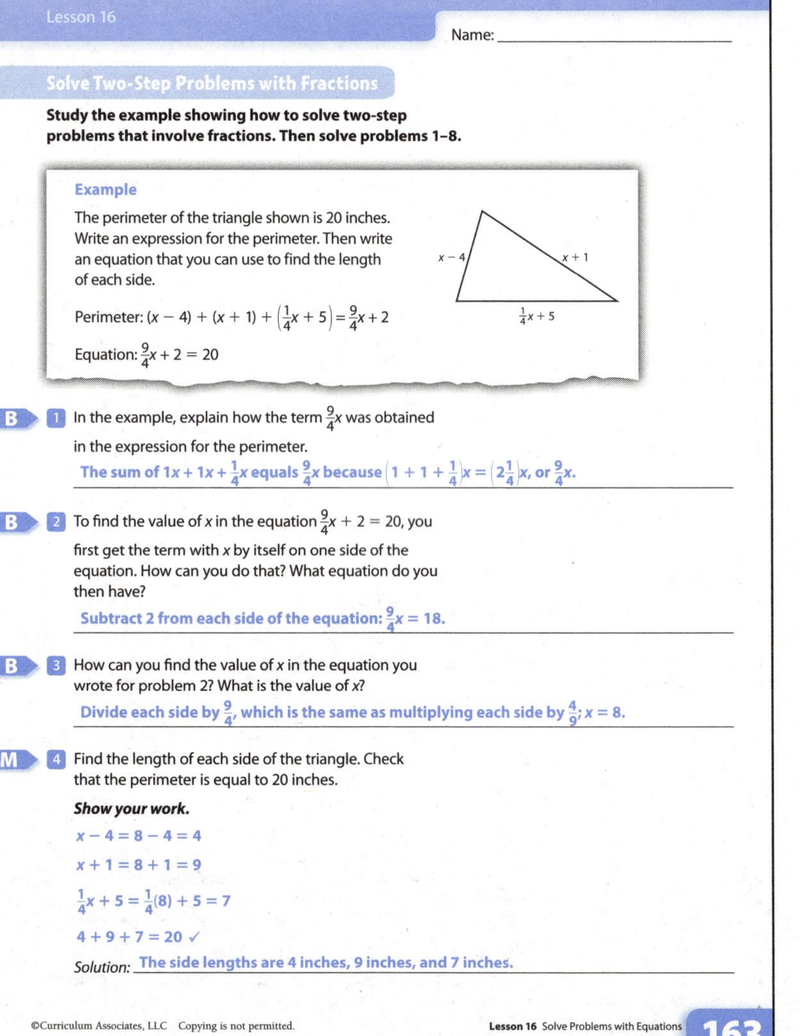

Lesson 16 — Name: ______

Solve Two-Step Problems with Fractions

Study the example showing how to solve two-step problems that involve fractions. Then solve problems 1–8.

Example

The perimeter of the triangle shown is 20 inches. Write an expression for the perimeter. Then write an equation that you can use to find the length of each side.

Perimeter: $(x - 4) + (x + 1) + \left(\frac{1}{4}x + 5\right) = \frac{9}{4}x + 2$

Equation: $\frac{9}{4}x + 2 = 20$

B 1 In the example, explain how the term $\frac{9}{4}x$ was obtained in the expression for the perimeter.

The sum of $1x + 1x + \frac{1}{4}x$ equals $\frac{9}{4}x$ because $\left(1 + 1 + \frac{1}{4}\right)x = \left(2\frac{1}{4}\right)x$, or $\frac{9}{4}x$.

B 2 To find the value of x in the equation $\frac{9}{4}x + 2 = 20$, you first get the term with x by itself on one side of the equation. How can you do that? What equation do you then have?

Subtract 2 from each side of the equation: $\frac{9}{4}x = 18$.

B 3 How can you find the value of x in the equation you wrote for problem 2? What is the value of x?

Divide each side by $\frac{9}{4}$, which is the same as multiplying each side by $\frac{4}{9}$; $x = 8$.

M 4 Find the length of each side of the triangle. Check that the perimeter is equal to 20 inches.

Show your work.

$x - 4 = 8 - 4 = 4$

$x + 1 = 8 + 1 = 9$

$\frac{1}{4}x + 5 = \frac{1}{4}(8) + 5 = 7$

$4 + 9 + 7 = 20$ ✓

Solution: The side lengths are 4 inches, 9 inches, and 7 inches.

©Curriculum Associates, LLC Copying is not permitted. **Lesson 16** Solve Problems with Equations 163

Solve.

M 5 Solve the equation $\frac{2}{5}x - 1 = 9$. Complete each step of the solution and check your solution.

$$\frac{2}{5}x - 1 = 9$$

$$\frac{2}{5}x - 1 \;\underline{\;+1\;} = 9 \;\underline{\;+1\;}$$

$$\frac{2}{5}x = \underline{\;10\;}$$

$$\frac{2}{5}x \;\underline{\;\cdot \frac{5}{2}\;} = \underline{\;10 \cdot \frac{5}{2}\;}$$

$$x = \underline{\;25\;}$$

Check: $\frac{2}{5} \cdot 25 - 1 = 10 - 1 = 9$

M 6 Paco says that the solution to $\frac{2}{5}x - 1 = 9$ is $x = 4$.

Do you agree? Explain.

No; In the last step, Paco multiplied 10 by $\frac{2}{5}$ instead of by $\frac{5}{2}$.

M 7 The width of a rectangle is two-thirds of the length. The perimeter of the rectangle is 15 centimeters. What is the length, ℓ, of the rectangle? Explain.

$4\frac{1}{2}$ cm; Possible explanation: $\ell + \frac{2}{3}\ell + \ell + \frac{2}{3}\ell = 15$; $\frac{10}{3}\ell = 15$;

$\frac{10}{3}\ell \cdot \frac{3}{10} = 15 \cdot \frac{3}{10}$; $\ell = \frac{45}{10} = 4\frac{1}{2}$

C 8 You buy $1\frac{1}{4}$ yards of fabric and an $8 clothing pattern. Your total cost with a 6% sales tax added is $18.55. What is the cost per yard of the fabric?

Show your work.

Possible work: Let p be the cost before the sales tax was added.

$1.06p = 18.55$

$p = 17.50.$

Let y be the cost per yard of the fabric. $\frac{5}{4}y + 8 = 17.50$

$\frac{5}{4}y = 9.50$

$\frac{5}{4}y \cdot \frac{4}{5} = 9.50 \cdot \frac{4}{5}$

$y = 7.60.$

Solution: The cost per yard of the fabric is $7.60.

164 **Lesson 16** Solve Problems with Equations

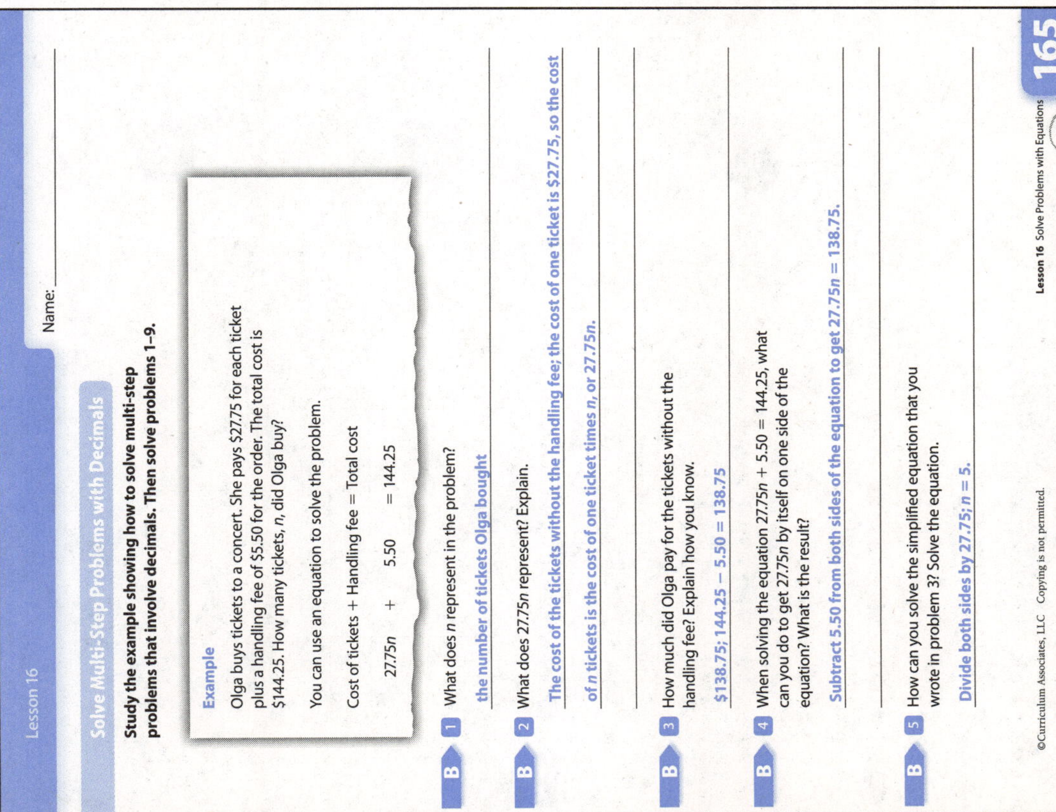

Lesson 16 Name: ______

Solve Multi-Step Problems with Decimals

Study the example showing how to solve multi-step problems that involve decimals. Then solve problems 1–9.

Example

Olga buys tickets to a concert. She pays \$27.75 for each ticket plus a handling fee of \$5.50 for the order. The total cost is \$144.25. How many tickets, n, did Olga buy?

You can use an equation to solve the problem.

Cost of tickets + Handling fee = Total cost

$27.75n \quad + \quad 5.50 \quad = 144.25$

B 1 What does n represent in the problem?

the number of tickets Olga bought

B 2 What does $27.75n$ represent? Explain.

The cost of the tickets without the handling fee; the cost of one ticket is \$27.75, so the cost of n tickets is the cost of one ticket times n, or $27.75n$.

B 3 How much did Olga pay for the tickets without the handling fee? Explain how you know.

\$138.75; $144.25 - 5.50 = 138.75$

B 4 When solving the equation $27.75n + 5.50 = 144.25$, what can you do to get $27.75n$ by itself on one side of the equation? What is the result?

Subtract 5.50 from both sides of the equation to get $27.75n = 138.75$.

B 5 How can you solve the simplified equation that you wrote in problem 3? Solve the equation.

Divide both sides by 27.75; $n = 5$.

©Curriculum Associates, LLC Copying is not permitted. Lesson 16 Solve Problems with Equations 165

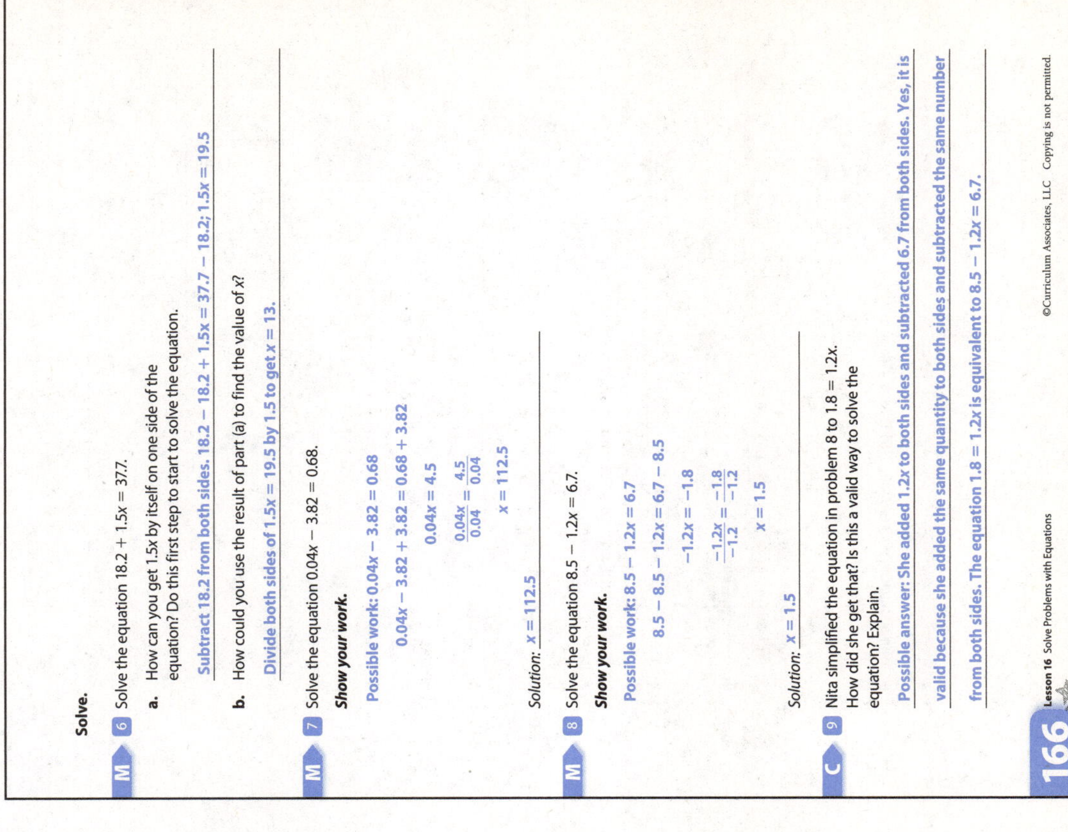

Solve.

M 6 Solve the equation $18.2 + 1.5x = 37.7$.

a. How can you get $1.5x$ by itself on one side of the equation? Do this first step to start to solve the equation.

Subtract 18.2 from both sides. $18.2 - 18.2 + 1.5x = 37.7 - 18.2$; $1.5x = 19.5$

b. How could you use the result of part (a) to find the value of x?

Divide both sides of $1.5x = 19.5$ by 1.5 to get $x = 13$.

M 7 Solve the equation $0.04x - 3.82 = 0.68$.

Show your work.

Possible work: $0.04x - 3.82 = 0.68$

$$0.04x - 3.82 + 3.82 = 0.68 + 3.82$$
$$0.04x = 4.5$$
$$\frac{0.04x}{0.04} = \frac{4.5}{0.04}$$
$$x = 112.5$$

Solution: $x = 112.5$

M 8 Solve the equation $8.5 - 1.2x = 6.7$.

Show your work.

Possible work: $8.5 - 1.2x = 6.7$

$$8.5 - 8.5 - 1.2x = 6.7 - 8.5$$
$$-1.2x = -1.8$$
$$\frac{-1.2x}{-1.2} = \frac{-1.8}{-1.2}$$
$$x = 1.5$$

Solution: $x = 1.5$

C 9 Nita simplified the equation in problem 8 to $1.8 = 1.2x$. How did she get that? Is this a valid way to solve the equation? Explain.

Possible answer: She added $1.2x$ to both sides and subtracted 6.7 from both sides. Yes, it is valid because she added the same quantity to both sides and subtracted the same number from both sides. The equation $1.8 = 1.2x$ is equivalent to $8.5 - 1.2x = 6.7$.

166 Lesson 16 Solve Problems with Equations ©Curriculum Associates, LLC Copying is not permitted.

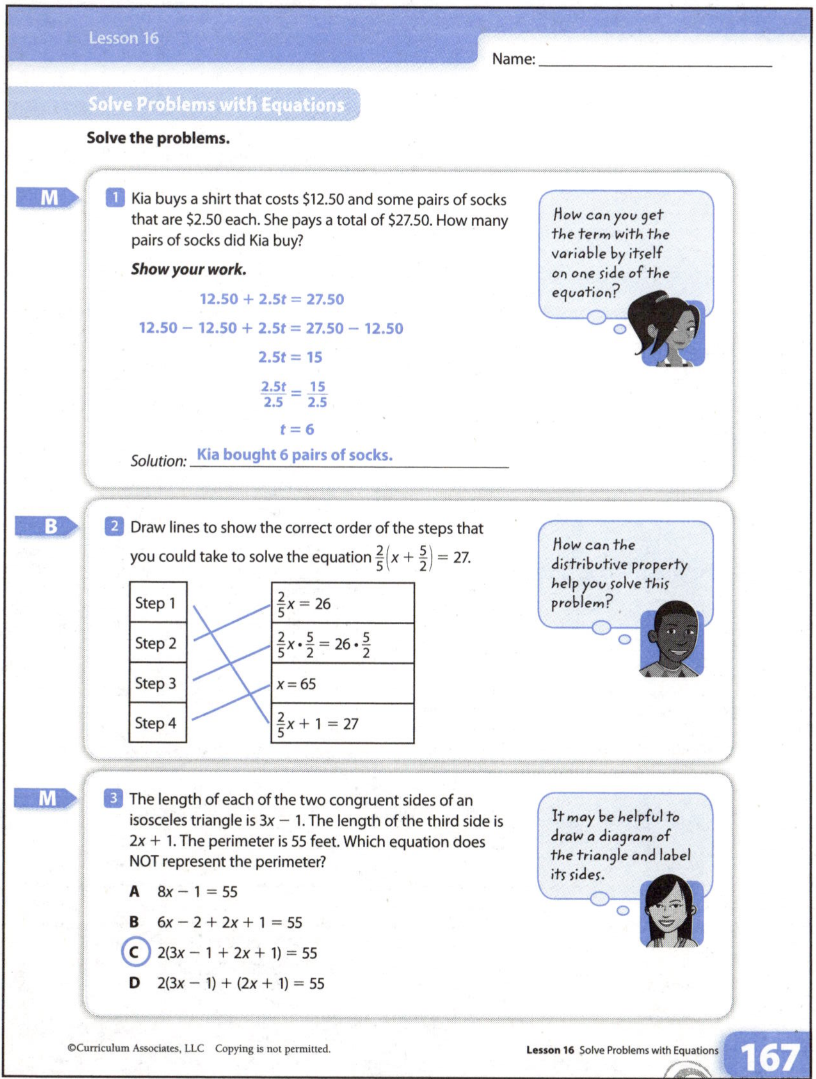

Lesson 16

Solve Problems with Equations

Name: ____________________

Solve the problems.

M 1 Kia buys a shirt that costs $12.50 and some pairs of socks that are $2.50 each. She pays a total of $27.50. How many pairs of socks did Kia buy?

Show your work.

$12.50 + 2.5t = 27.50$

$12.50 - 12.50 + 2.5t = 27.50 - 12.50$

$2.5t = 15$

$\frac{2.5t}{2.5} = \frac{15}{2.5}$

$t = 6$

Solution: Kia bought 6 pairs of socks.

B 2 Draw lines to show the correct order of the steps that you could take to solve the equation $\frac{2}{5}\left(x + \frac{5}{2}\right) = 27$.

Step 1	$\frac{2}{5}x = 26$
Step 2	$\frac{2}{5}x \cdot \frac{5}{2} = 26 \cdot \frac{5}{2}$
Step 3	$x = 65$
Step 4	$\frac{2}{5}x + 1 = 27$

M 3 The length of each of the two congruent sides of an isosceles triangle is $3x - 1$. The length of the third side is $2x + 1$. The perimeter is 55 feet. Which equation does NOT represent the perimeter?

A $8x - 1 = 55$

B $6x - 2 + 2x + 1 = 55$

(C) $2(3x - 1 + 2x + 1) = 55$

D $2(3x - 1) + (2x + 1) = 55$

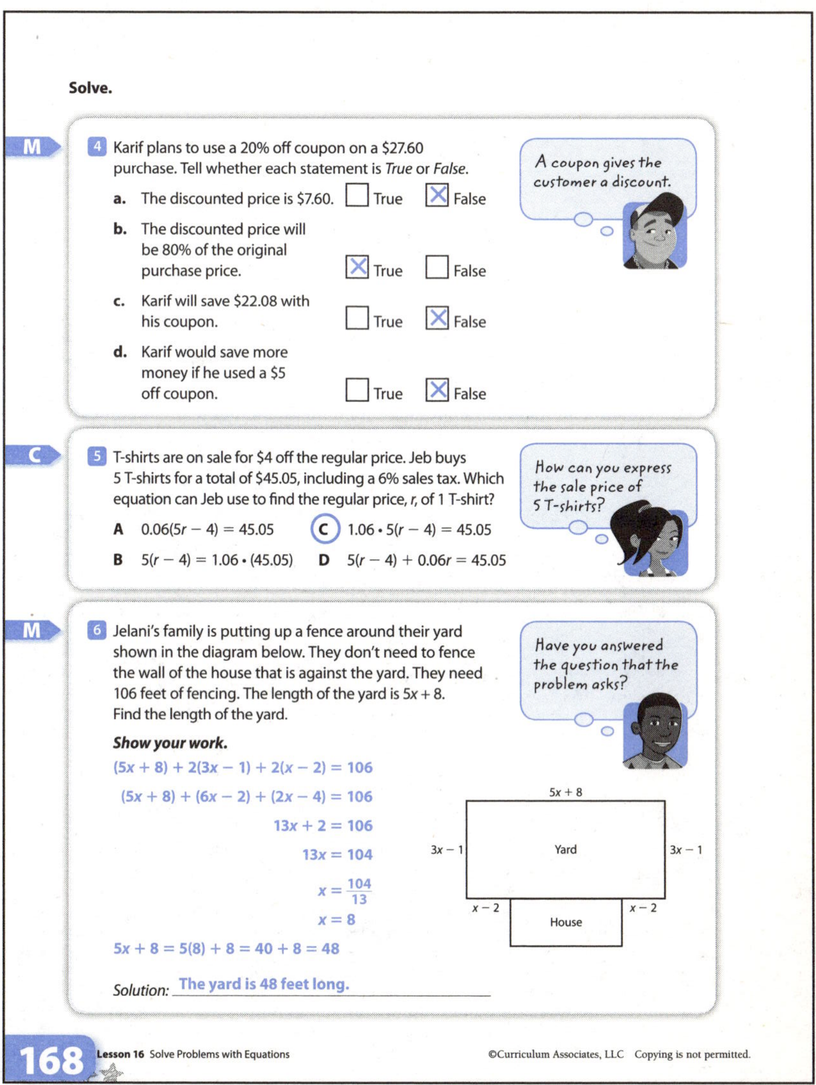

Solve.

M 4 Karif plans to use a 20% off coupon on a $27.60 purchase. Tell whether each statement is *True* or *False*.

	Statement	True	False
a.	The discounted price is $7.60.	☐	☒
b.	The discounted price will be 80% of the original purchase price.	☒	☐
c.	Karif will save $22.08 with his coupon.	☐	☒
d.	Karif would save more money if he used a $5 off coupon.	☐	☒

C 5 T-shirts are on sale for $4 off the regular price. Jeb buys 5 T-shirts for a total of $45.05, including a 6% sales tax. Which equation can Jeb use to find the regular price, r, of 1 T-shirt?

A $0.06(5r - 4) = 45.05$

(C) $1.06 \cdot 5(r - 4) = 45.05$

B $5(r - 4) = 1.06 \cdot (45.05)$

D $5(r - 4) + 0.06r = 45.05$

M 6 Jelani's family is putting up a fence around their yard shown in the diagram below. They don't need to fence the wall of the house that is against the yard. They need 106 feet of fencing. The length of the yard is $5x + 8$. Find the length of the yard.

Show your work.

$(5x + 8) + 2(3x - 1) + 2(x - 2) = 106$

$(5x + 8) + (6x - 2) + (2x - 4) = 106$

$13x + 2 = 106$

$13x = 104$

$x = \frac{104}{13}$

$x = 8$

$5x + 8 = 5(8) + 8 = 40 + 8 = 48$

Solution: The yard is 48 feet long.

Lesson 17

Solve Problems with Inequalities

Name: ____________

Prerequisite: Solve Problems with Equations

Study the example showing how to solve problems with equations. Then solve problems 1–8.

Example

Mrs. Scott brings her car to a service station for repair. Her bill shows a $215 charge for parts and a charge for $3\frac{1}{2}$ hours of labor. The total bill is $495. Write an equation to find the charge x for one hour of labor.

Charge for labor + Charge for parts = Total bill

$3\frac{1}{2}x \quad + \quad 215 \quad = \quad 495$

B 1 Why is $3\frac{1}{2}$ multiplied by x in the equation?

The charge for labor is computed by multiplying the number of hours of labor, $3\frac{1}{2}$, by x, the charge per hour of labor.

B 2 How can you get $3\frac{1}{2}x$ alone on the left side of the equation $3\frac{1}{2}x + 215 = 495$? What is the resulting equation?

Subtract 215 from each side of the equation; $3\frac{1}{2}x = 280$ or $\frac{7}{2}x = 280$.

B 3 Multiply both sides of the simplified equation you wrote in problem 2 by a fraction to get x alone on the left side of the equation. Simplify.

$\frac{7}{2}x \cdot \frac{2}{7} = 280 \cdot \frac{2}{7}$; $x = 80$

B 4 What is the charge for an hour of labor? **$80**

M 5 Explain how to solve the equation $\frac{3}{4}x + 5 = 11$.

Subtract 5 from both sides of the equation to get $\frac{3}{4}x = 6$. Then multiply both sides of the new equation by $\frac{4}{3}$ to get $x = 8$.

Solve.

M 6 Mito bakes biscuits. He uses $\frac{1}{4}$ cup of flour to coat the countertop and the rolling pin. He also uses $2\frac{1}{2}$ cups of flour for each batch of biscuits he bakes. If he uses $7\frac{3}{4}$ cups of flour in all, how many batches of biscuits does he bake? Write and solve an equation.

Show your work.

$2\frac{1}{2}b + \frac{1}{4} = 7\frac{3}{4}$

$2\frac{1}{2}b + \frac{1}{4} - \frac{1}{4} = 7\frac{3}{4} - \frac{1}{4}$

$2\frac{1}{2}b = 7\frac{1}{2}$

$\frac{5}{2}b \times \frac{2}{5} = \frac{15}{2} \times \frac{2}{5}$

$b = 3$

Solution: **Mito bakes 3 batches of biscuits.**

M 7 The formula to convert a temperature C in degrees Celsius to a temperature F in degrees Fahrenheit is $1.8C + 32 = F$. Use this equation to find the Celsius equivalent of 51.8°F.

$1.8C + 32 = 51.8$; $1.8C = 19.8$; $C = 11$; the equivalent is 11°C.

C 8 LeBron mows yards. For each yard, he charges $5.50 for the use of his mower and $3.50 for the use of his trimmer. In addition, LeBron charges $5.00 an hour to mow and $6.50 an hour to trim.

LeBron both mows and trims Mr. Johnson's lawn, using his own mower and trimmer. He takes twice as long to mow as he does to trim. If he earns $25.50 that day, how many hours did he mow?

Show your work.

Possible work: Let x be the number of hours LeBron trimmed.

$(5.00(2x) + 6.50x) + (5.50 + 3.50) = 25.50$

$16.50x + 9.00 = 25.50$

$16.50x = 16.50$

$x = 1$

Solution: **LeBron trimmed for 1 hour, so he mowed for 2 hours.**

Key

B Basic **M** Medium **C** Challenge

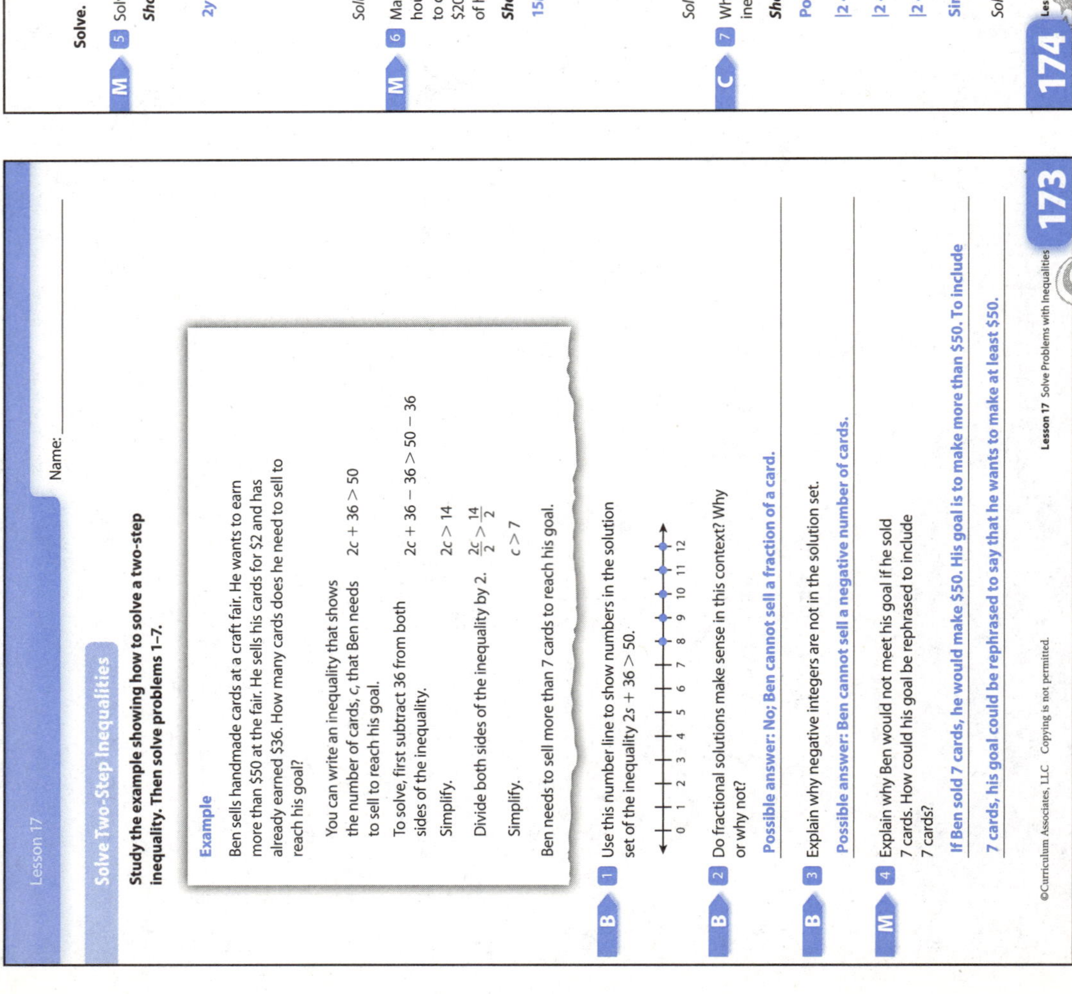

Lesson 17

Name: ____________

Solve Two-Step Inequalities

Study the example showing how to solve a two-step inequality. Then solve problems 1–7.

Example

Ben sells handmade cards at a craft fair. He wants to earn more than \$50 at the fair. He sells his cards for \$2 and has already earned \$36. How many cards does he need to sell to reach his goal?

You can write an inequality that shows the number of cards, *c*, that Ben needs to sell to reach his goal.	$2c + 36 > 50$
To solve, first subtract 36 from both sides of the inequality.	$2c + 36 - 36 > 50 - 36$
Simplify.	$2c > 14$
Divide both sides of the inequality by 2.	$\frac{2c}{2} > \frac{14}{2}$
Simplify.	$c > 7$

Ben needs to sell more than 7 cards to reach his goal.

B 1 Use this number line to show numbers in the solution set of the inequality $2s + 36 > 50$.

B 2 Do fractional solutions make sense in this context? Why or why not?

Possible answer: No; Ben cannot sell a fraction of a card.

B 3 Explain why negative integers are not in the solution set.

Possible answer: Ben cannot sell a negative number of cards.

M 4 Explain why Ben would not meet his goal if he sold 7 cards. How could his goal be rephrased to include 7 cards?

If Ben sold 7 cards, he would make \$50. His goal is to make more than \$50. To include 7 cards, his goal could be rephrased to say that he wants to make at least \$50.

©Curriculum Associates, LLC Copying is not permitted. **Lesson 17** Solve Problems with Inequalities **173**

Solve.

M 5 Solve $2y + 12 < 42$.

Show your work.

$2y + 12 < 42$

$2y + 12 - 12 < 42 - 12$

$2y < 30$

$\frac{2y}{2} < \frac{30}{2}$

$y < 15$

Solution: $y < 15$

M 6 Manuela works as a security guard. She makes \$15 per hour. Her employers deduct \$125 from her weekly check to cover insurance and taxes. If Manuela receives at least \$205 in her weekly paycheck, what is the fewest number of hours she works in a week? Write and solve an inequality.

Show your work.

$15m - 125 \geq 205$

$15m \geq 330$

$m \geq 22$

Solution: **Manuela works at least 22 hours a week.**

C 7 What non-negative integers are solutions of the inequality $|2x - 1| < 3$?

Show your work.

Possible work: I started by substituting 0, 1, and 2 in turn:

$|2 \cdot 0 - 1| = |-1| = 1$, **and** $1 < 3$**; so 0 is a solution.**

$|2 \cdot 1 - 1| = |1| = 1$, **and** $1 < 3$**; so 1 is a solution.**

$|2 \cdot 2 - 1| = |3| = 3$, **and** $3 = 3$**; so 2 is not a solution.**

Similarly, integers greater than 2 are not solutions.

Solution: **The integers 0 and 1 are the only non-negative integer solutions.**

174 **Lesson 17** Solve Problems with Inequalities ©Curriculum Associates, LLC Copying is not permitted.

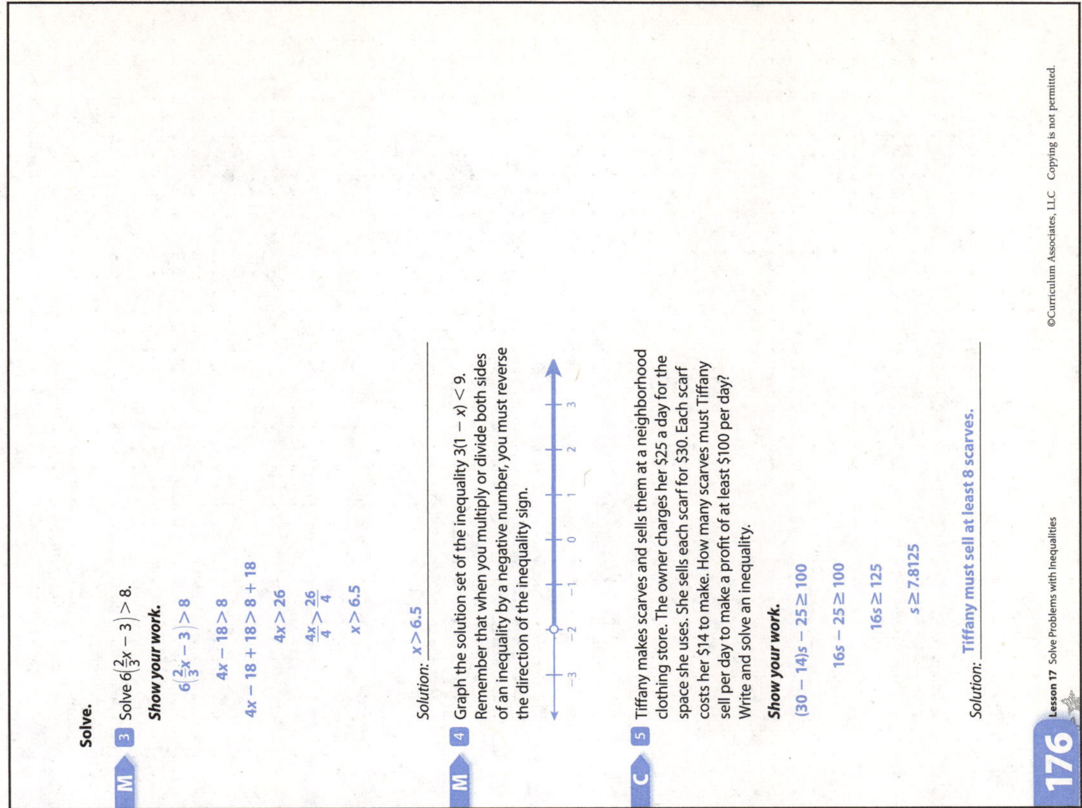

Solve.

M 3 Solve $6\left(\frac{2}{3}x - 3\right) > 8$.

Show your work.

$6\left(\frac{2}{3}x - 3\right) > 8$

$4x - 18 > 8$

$4x - 18 + 18 > 8 + 18$

$4x > 26$

$\frac{4x}{4} > \frac{26}{4}$

$x > 6.5$

Solution: $x > 6.5$

M 4 Graph the solution set of the inequality $3(1 - x) < 9$.
Remember that when you multiply or divide both sides of an inequality by a negative number, you must reverse the direction of the inequality sign.

C 5 Tiffany makes scarves and sells them at a neighborhood clothing store. The owner charges her $25 a day for the space she uses. She sells each scarf for $30. Each scarf costs her $14 to make. How many scarves must Tiffany sell per day to make a profit of at least $100 per day? Write and solve an inequality.

Show your work.

$(30 - 14)s - 25 \geq 100$

$16s - 25 \geq 100$

$16s \geq 125$

$s \geq 7.8125$

Solution: Tiffany must sell at least 8 scarves.

176 Lesson 17 Solve Problems with Inequalities

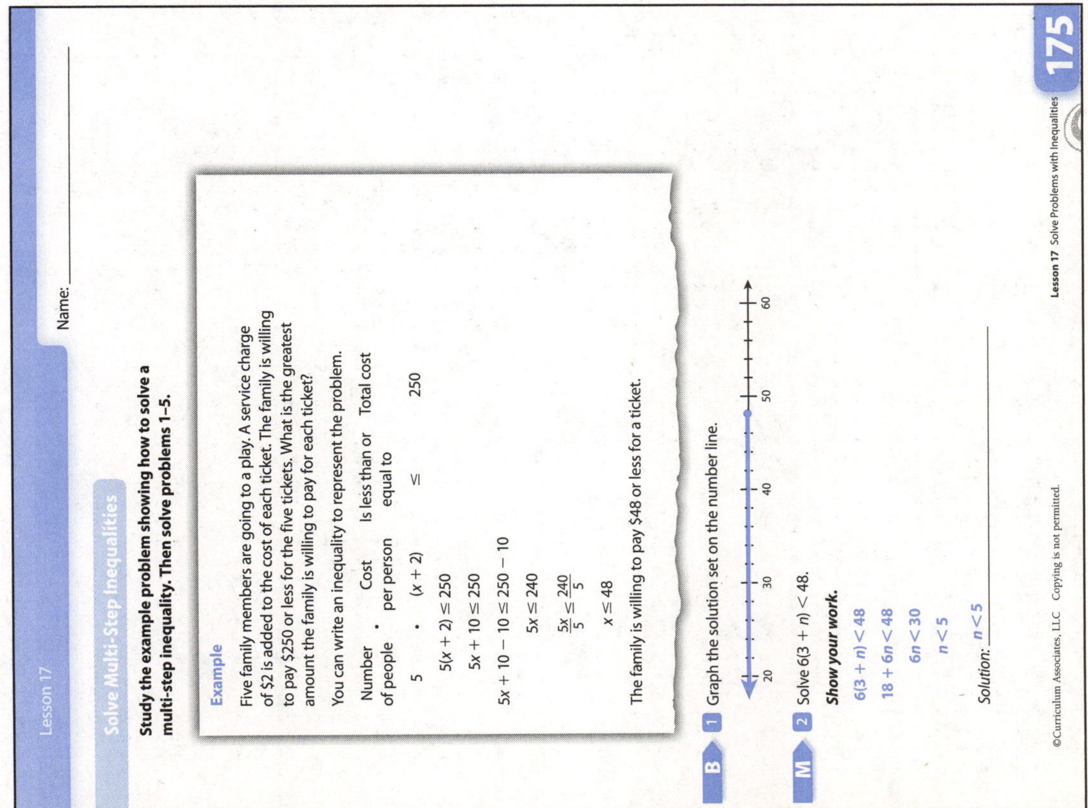

Lesson 17

Name: ____________

Solve Multi-Step Inequalities

Study the example problem showing how to solve a multi-step inequality. Then solve problems 1–5.

Example

Five family members are going to a play. A service charge of $2 is added to the cost of each ticket. The family is willing to pay $250 or less for the five tickets. What is the greatest amount the family is willing to pay for each ticket?

You can write an inequality to represent the problem.

Number of people	•	Cost per person	Is less than or equal to	Total cost
5	•	$(x + 2)$	$\leq$	250

$5(x + 2) \leq 250$

$5x + 10 \leq 250$

$5x + 10 - 10 \leq 250 - 10$

$5x \leq 240$

$\frac{5x}{5} \leq \frac{240}{5}$

$x \leq 48$

The family is willing to pay $48 or less for a ticket.

B 1 Graph the solution set on the number line.

M 2 Solve $6(3 + n) < 48$.

Show your work.

$6(3 + n) < 48$

$18 + 6n < 48$

$6n < 30$

$n < 5$

Solution: $n < 5$

Lesson 17 Solve Problems with Inequalities 175

Practice Lesson 17 Solve Problems with Inequalities

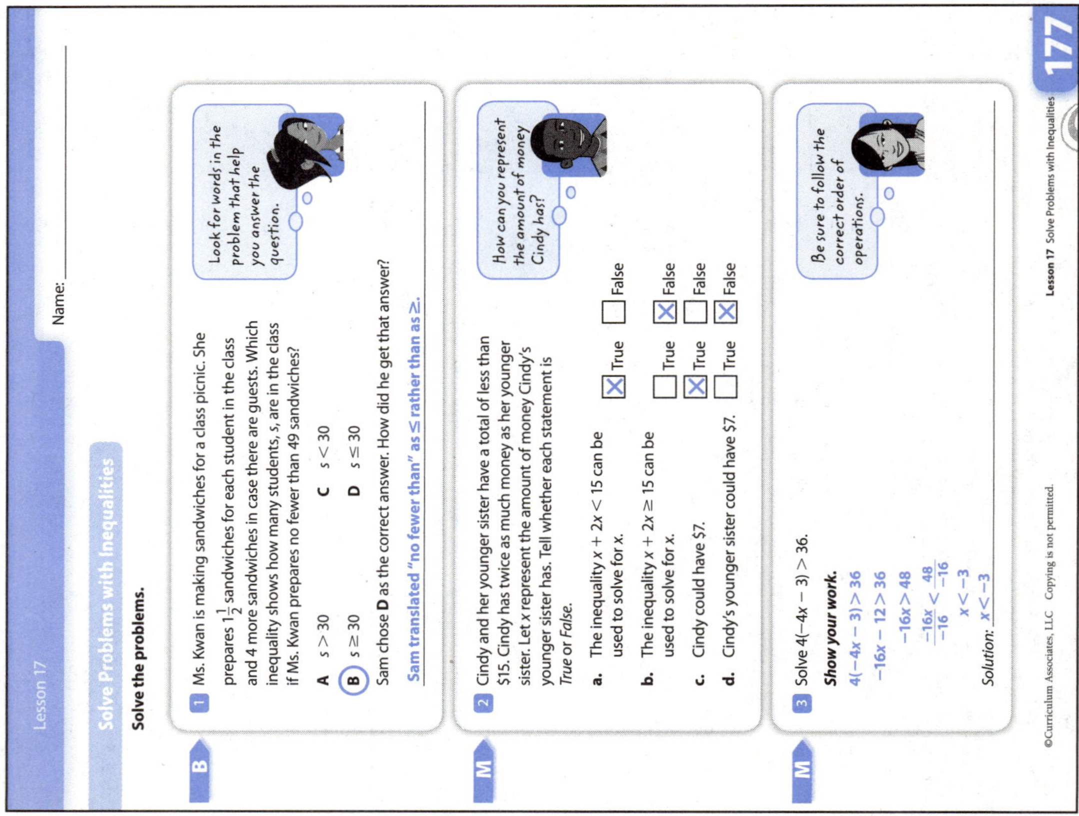

Name: ____________

Solve Problems with Inequalities

Solve the problems.

B

1 Ms. Kwan is making sandwiches for a class picnic. She prepares $1\frac{1}{2}$ sandwiches for each student in the class and 4 more sandwiches in case there are guests. Which inequality shows how many students, s, are in the class if Ms. Kwan prepares no fewer than 49 sandwiches?

- **A** $s > 30$
- **(B)** $s \geq 30$
- **C** $s < 30$
- **D** $s \leq 30$

Sam chose **D** as the correct answer. How did he get that answer?

Sam translated "no fewer than" as ≤ rather than as ≥.

M

2 Cindy and her younger sister have a total of less than $15. Cindy has twice as much money as her younger sister. Let x represent the amount of money Cindy's younger sister has. Tell whether each statement is *True* or *False*.

		True	False
a.	The inequality $x + 2x < 15$ can be used to solve for x.	☒	☐
b.	The inequality $x + 2x \geq 15$ can be used to solve for x.	☐	☒
c.	Cindy could have $7.	☒	☐
d.	Cindy's younger sister could have $7.	☐	☒

M

3 Solve $4(-4x - 3) > 36$.

Show your work.

$4(-4x - 3) > 36$

$-16x - 12 > 36$

$-16x > 48$

$\frac{-16x}{-16} < \frac{48}{-16}$

$x < -3$

Solution: $x < -3$

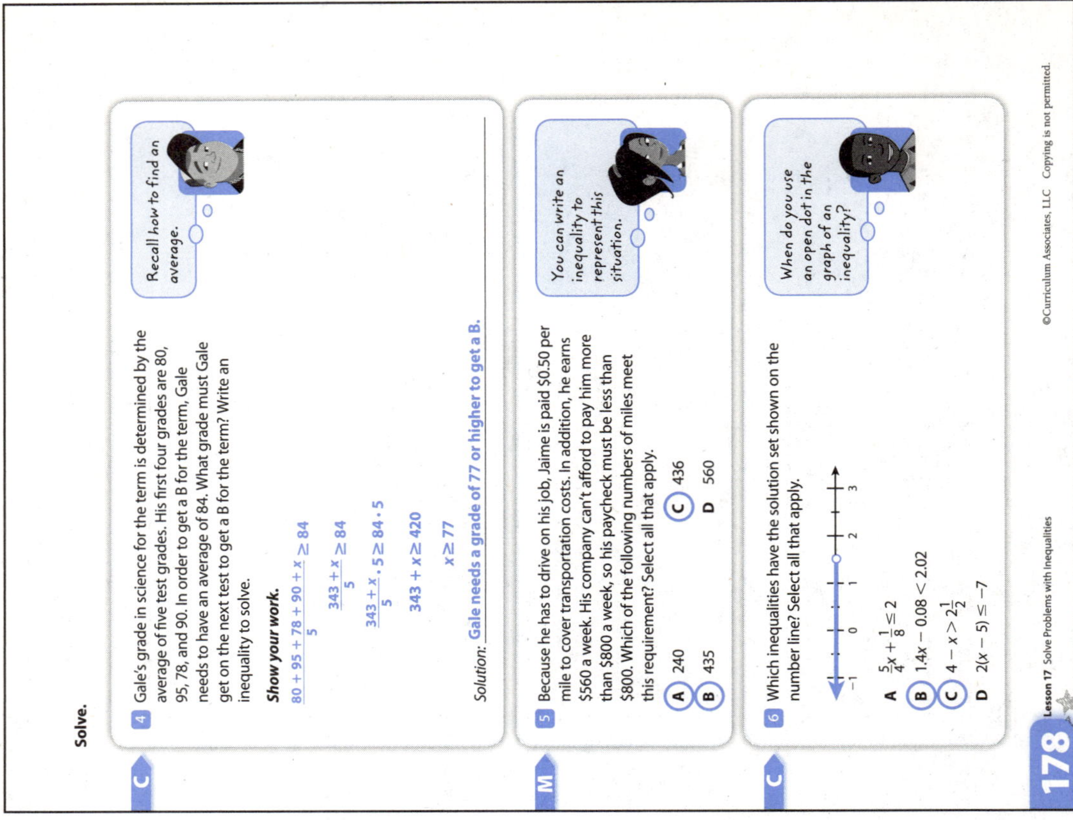

Solve.

C

4 Gale's grade in science for the term is determined by the average of five test grades. His first four grades are 80, 95, 78, and 90. In order to get a B for the term, Gale needs to have an average of 84. What grade must Gale get on the next test to get a B for the term? Write an inequality to solve.

Show your work.

$\frac{80 + 95 + 78 + 90 + x}{5} \geq 84$

$\frac{343 + x}{5} \geq 84$

$\frac{343 + x}{5} \cdot 5 \geq 84 \cdot 5$

$343 + x \geq 420$

$x \geq 77$

Solution: **Gale needs a grade of 77 or higher to get a B.**

M

5 Because he has to drive on his job, Jaime is paid $0.50 per mile to cover transportation costs. In addition, he earns $560 a week. His company can't afford to pay him more than $800 a week, so his paycheck must be less than $800. Which of the following numbers of miles meet this requirement? Select all that apply.

- **(A)** 240
- **(B)** 435
- **(C)** 436
- **D** 560

C

6 Which inequalities have the solution set shown on the number line? Select all that apply.

- **A** $\frac{5}{4}x + \frac{1}{8} \leq 2$
- **(B)** $1.4x - 0.08 < 2.02$
- **(C)** $4 - x > 2\frac{1}{2}$
- **D** $2(x - 5) \leq -7$

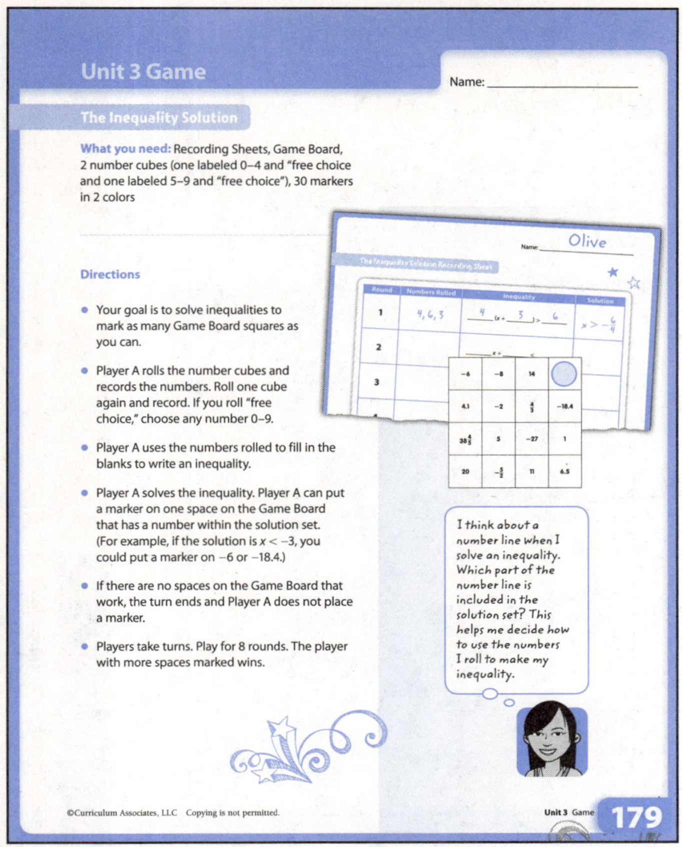

Unit 3 Game

Name: ____________

The Inequality Solution

What you need: Recording Sheets, Game Board, 2 number cubes (one labeled 0–4 and "free choice" and one labeled 5–9 and "free choice"), 30 markers in 2 colors

Directions

- Your goal is to solve inequalities to mark as many Game Board squares as you can.
- Player A rolls the number cubes and records the numbers. Roll one cube again and record. If you roll "free choice," choose any number 0–9.
- Player A uses the numbers rolled to fill in the blanks to write an inequality.
- Player A solves the inequality. Player A can put a marker on one space on the Game Board that has a number within the solution set. (For example, if the solution is $x < -3$, you could put a marker on −6 or −18.4.)
- If there are no spaces on the Game Board that work, the turn ends and Player A does not place a marker.
- Players take turns. Play for 8 rounds. The player with more spaces marked wins.

©Curriculum Associates, LLC Copying is not permitted. Unit 3 Game 179

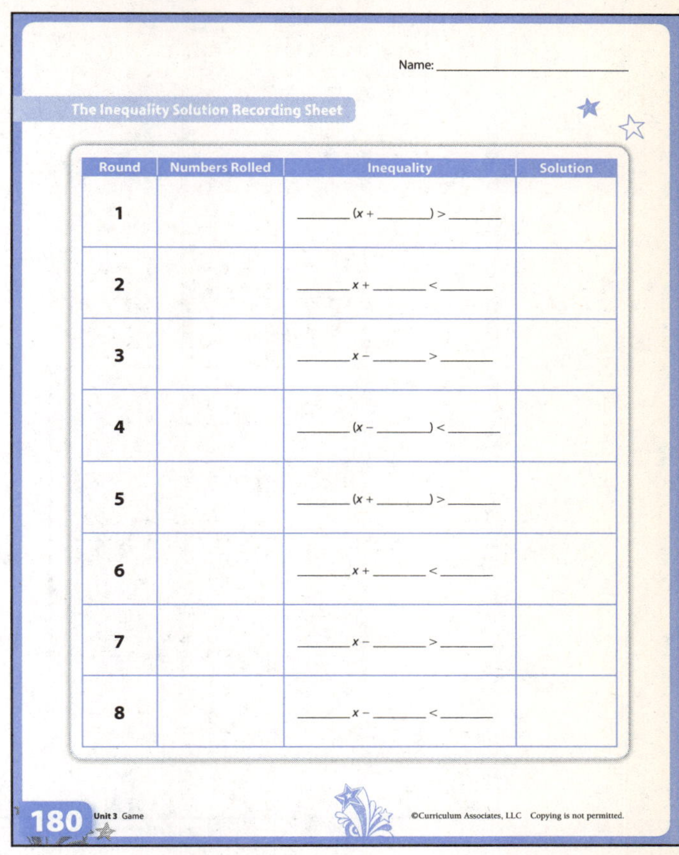

Name: ____________

The Inequality Solution Recording Sheet

Round	Numbers Rolled	Inequality	Solution
1		___(x + ___) > ___	
2		___x + ___ < ___	
3		___x − ___ > ___	
4		___(x − ___) < ___	
5		___(x + ___) > ___	
6		___x + ___ < ___	
7		___x − ___ > ___	
8		___x − ___ < ___	

180 Unit 3 Game ©Curriculum Associates, LLC Copying is not permitted.

STEP BY STEP

CCSS Focus - 7.EE.B.4b *Embedded SMPs* - 1, 5, 6, 8 **Objective** • Solve algebraic inequalities involving rational numbers.	**Materials** For each pair: Recording Sheets (1 for each player) (TR 3), Game Board (TR 4), 2 number cubes (one labeled 0–4 and "free choice and one labeled 5–9 and "free choice"), 30 markers in 2 colors (15 of 1 color for each player)

- Your goal is to solve inequalities to mark as many Game Board squares as you can.
- Player A rolls the number cubes and record the numbers. Roll one cube again and record. If you roll "free choice," choose any number 0–9.
- Player A uses the numbers rolled to fill in the blanks to write an inequality.
- Player A solves the inequality. Player A can put a marker on one space on the Game Board that has a number within the solution set. (For example, if the solution is $x < -3$, you could put a marker on -6 or -18.4.)
- If there are no spaces on the Game Board that work, the turn ends and Player A does not place a marker.
- Players take turns. Play for 8 rounds. The player with more spaces marked wins.
- Model one turn for students before they play. Have students experiment to find ways to get particular solutions, such as negative or positive ranges or ranges that include numbers close to zero, etc.

Vary the Game Roll each number cube twice. Fill one blank with a decimal (tenths) or a fraction formed by two of the numbers.

Challenge Have each player write a word problem scenario for their inequality on an index card and describe what the solution means in this context. Save the problem cards for future use.

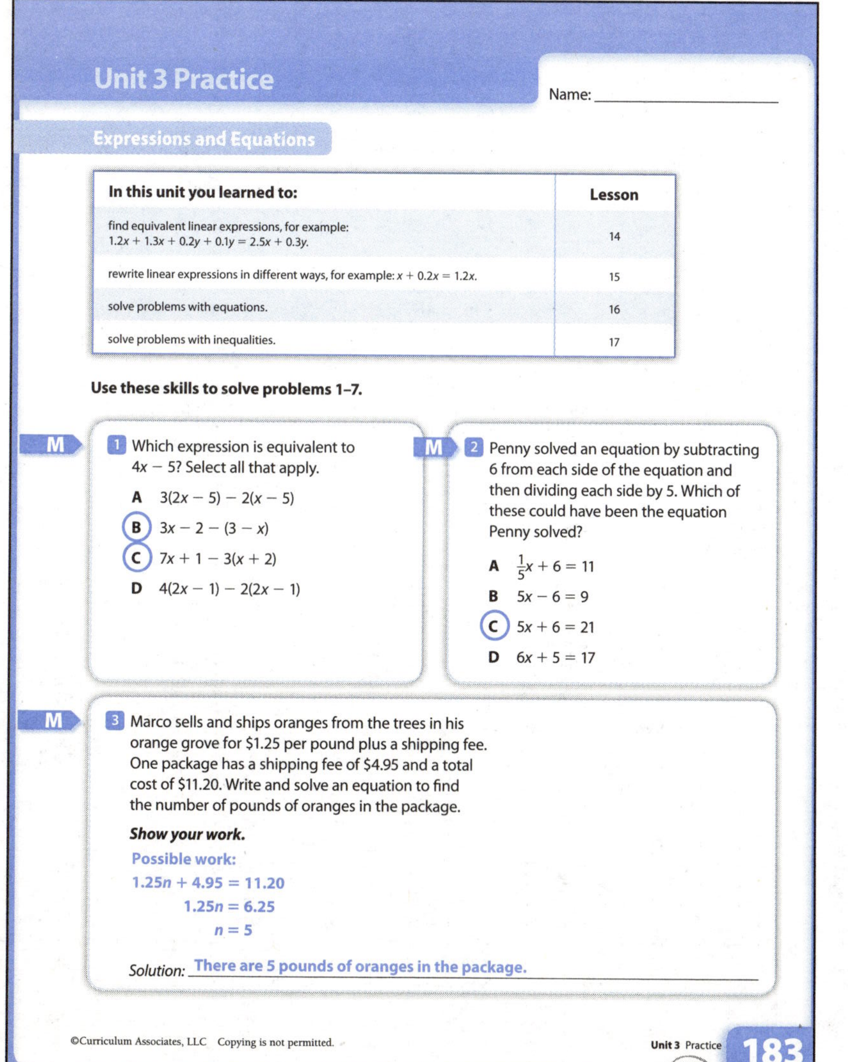

Unit 3 Practice

Expressions and Equations

Name: ______________

In this unit you learned to:	Lesson
find equivalent linear expressions, for example: $1.2x + 1.3x + 0.2y + 0.1y = 2.5x + 0.3y$.	14
rewrite linear expressions in different ways, for example: $x + 0.2x = 1.2x$.	15
solve problems with equations.	16
solve problems with inequalities.	17

Use these skills to solve problems 1–7.

M **1** Which expression is equivalent to $4x - 5$? Select all that apply.

A $3(2x - 5) - 2(x - 5)$

(B) $3x - 2 - (3 - x)$

(C) $7x + 1 - 3(x + 2)$

D $4(2x - 1) - 2(2x - 1)$

M **2** Penny solved an equation by subtracting 6 from each side of the equation and then dividing each side by 5. Which of these could have been the equation Penny solved?

A $\frac{1}{5}x + 6 = 11$

B $5x - 6 = 9$

(C) $5x + 6 = 21$

D $6x + 5 = 17$

M **3** Marco sells and ships oranges from the trees in his orange grove for $1.25 per pound plus a shipping fee. One package has a shipping fee of $4.95 and a total cost of $11.20. Write and solve an equation to find the number of pounds of oranges in the package.

Show your work.

Possible work:

$1.25n + 4.95 = 11.20$

$1.25n = 6.25$

$n = 5$

Solution: **There are 5 pounds of oranges in the package.**

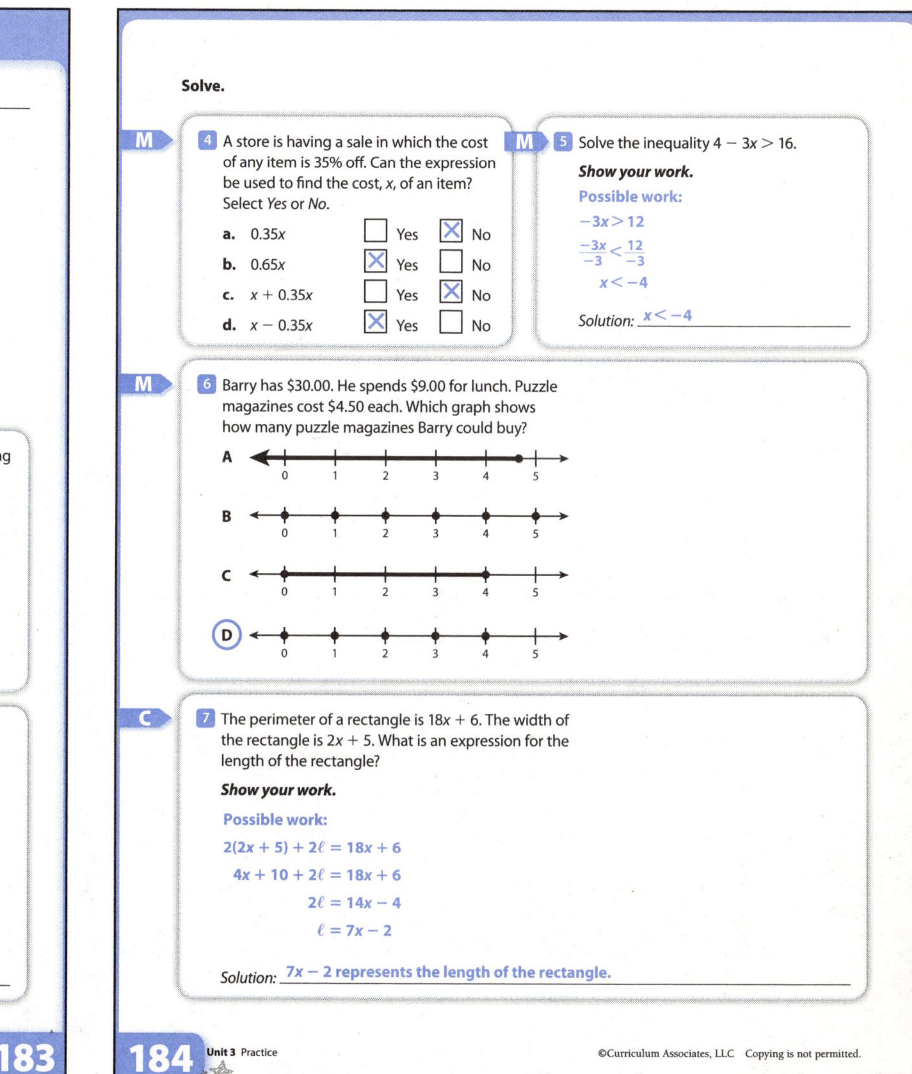

Solve.

M **4** A store is having a sale in which the cost of any item is 35% off. Can the expression be used to find the cost, x, of an item?

Select *Yes* or *No*.

		Yes	No
a.	$0.35x$	☐	☒
b.	$0.65x$	☒	☐
c.	$x + 0.35x$	☐	☒
d.	$x - 0.35x$	☒	☐

M **5** Solve the inequality $4 - 3x > 16$.

Show your work.

Possible work:

$-3x > 12$

$\frac{-3x}{-3} < \frac{12}{-3}$

$x < -4$

Solution: $x < -4$

M **6** Barry has $30.00. He spends $9.00 for lunch. Puzzle magazines cost $4.50 each. Which graph shows how many puzzle magazines Barry could buy?

A (number line 0 to 5)

B (number line 0 to 5)

C (number line 0 to 5)

(D) (number line 0 to 5)

C **7** The perimeter of a rectangle is $18x + 6$. The width of the rectangle is $2x + 5$. What is an expression for the length of the rectangle?

Show your work.

Possible work:

$2(2x + 5) + 2\ell = 18x + 6$

$4x + 10 + 2\ell = 18x + 6$

$2\ell = 14x - 4$

$\ell = 7x - 2$

Solution: **$7x - 2$ represents the length of the rectangle.**

Key

B Basic **M** Medium **C** Challenge

TEACHER NOTES

Common Core Standards: 7.EE.A.2, 7.EE.B.3, 7.EE.B.4a
Standards for Mathematical Practice: 1, 2, 3, 4, 5, 6, 7, 8
DOK: 3
Materials: None

About the Task

To complete this task, students solve a multi-step problem that involves writing an equation using two variables to model a situation and solving the equation. The task requires that they set prices for selling calendars, determine how much money would be made, and find how many calendars must be sold to cover the printing costs.

Getting Started

Read the problem out loud with students and go over the checklist. Have them identify the goal. Have students list what is known and what they need to find out. Encourage students to brainstorm ideas for how to approach the problem. ***(SMP 1)***

Completing the Task

Some students will begin by setting a price. Others may start with the equation. Either approach is fine.

To write the equation, prompt students to describe the money that the shelter will make from selling one calendar at a given price (p). [For example, the amount the shelter makes is p for selling 1 calendar.] Then help students generalize the statement using m for the amount of money and c for the number of calendars. [For example, m is p for every c.] They can then translate the statement to an equation. [$m = pc$] ***(SMP 2, 4)***

Students should use the given information to set pricing. The price will determine the rest of the results. Students choose tools to help them show how much the shelter will make by selling each number of calendars. ***(SMP 2, 5, 6)***

Have students present their results and explain how they determined the number of calendars that must be sold to pay for the cost of printing. ***(SMP 3, 8)***

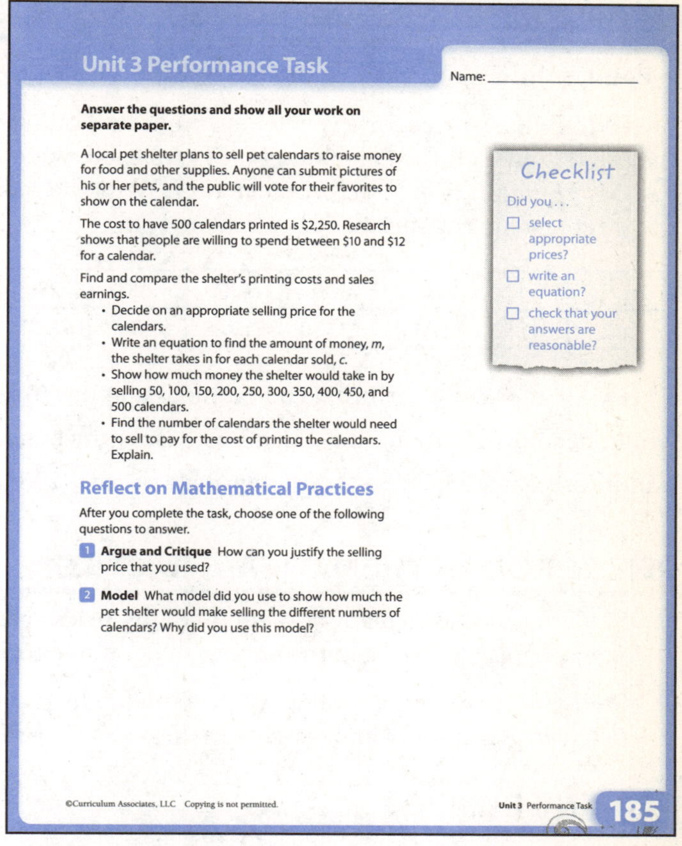
Unit 3 Performance Task

Name: ____________

Answer the questions and show all your work on separate paper.

A local pet shelter plans to sell pet calendars to raise money for food and other supplies. Anyone can submit pictures of his or her pets, and the public will vote for their favorites to show on the calendar.

The cost to have 500 calendars printed is $2,250. Research shows that people are willing to spend between $10 and $12 for a calendar.

Find and compare the shelter's printing costs and sales earnings.

- Decide on an appropriate selling price for the calendars.
- Write an equation to find the amount of money, m, the shelter takes in for each calendar sold, c.
- Show how much money the shelter would take in by selling 50, 100, 150, 200, 250, 300, 350, 400, 450, and 500 calendars.
- Find the number of calendars the shelter would need to sell to pay for the cost of printing the calendars. Explain.

Checklist
Did you . . .
- ☐ select appropriate prices?
- ☐ write an equation?
- ☐ check that your answers are reasonable?

Reflect on Mathematical Practices

After you complete the task, choose one of the following questions to answer.

1 **Argue and Critique** How can you justify the selling price that you used?

2 **Model** What model did you use to show how much the pet shelter would make selling the different numbers of calendars? Why did you use this model?

©Curriculum Associates, LLC Copying is not permitted. Unit 3 Performance Task 185

Extension

If students have more time to spend on this problem, you can have them solve this extension:

Start with the expression pc to represent the money that the shelter gets from selling c calendars at price p. Write a similar expression to represent the money they will get if they increase the price by $0.50. Apply the distributive property to rewrite that expression as a sum. Then compare the two expressions and tell how much more money the shelter would take in if they sold 200 calendars for 50 cents more than the price you chose.

SAMPLE RESPONSE AND RUBRIC

4-Point Solution

I need to name a price for the calendars and find out how much money the shelter can make depending on how many they sell. I will sell the calendars for $11.50 each, which is close to but less than the top price people are willing to pay. My equation is $m = pc$, where m represents the money the shelter makes, p represents the price of 1 calendar, and c represents the number of calendars sold.

c	1	50	100	150	200	250	300	350	400	450	500
m	$11.50	$575	$1,150	$1,725	$2,300	$2,875	$3,450	$4,025	$4,600	$5,175	$5,750

To pay for the cost of printing the calendars, m has to be at least $2,250. Looking at my chart, I know the shelter would need to sell about 200 calendars. Using my equation, $\$2,250 = \$11.50c$, so $\frac{2,250}{11.50} = c$ and to the nearest hundredth $c = 195.65$. So the shelter needs to sell 196 calendars.

REFLECT ON MATHEMATICAL PRACTICES

1. Students should explain how their selling prices are within the range of what customers are willing to pay and how the prices will help the shelter make money. ***(SMP 3)***
2. Students should explain how their model helped them see the patterns involved and what made the model useful to them. Accept any answer that makes sense for the model used. ***(SMP 4)***

SCORING RUBRIC

4 points All parts of the problem are complete and correct. The calendar price is appropriate. The equation and all calculations are correct. Students show all work and correctly explain the number of calendar sales needed to cover the cost of printing.

3 points The student has completed all parts of the problem, with one or two errors. Possible errors might include inappropriate pricing, an incorrect equation, incorrect use of the equation, missing a calculation, or an unclear explanation.

2 points The student has attempted all parts of the problem, with a number of errors. The price may be incorrect. The equation may be incorrect or solved incorrectly. The number of calendar sales needed may be incorrect and/or poorly explained.

1 point Much of the problem is incomplete, with several errors. Pricing, equations, and calculations are incorrect and/or incomplete. The number of calendar sales needed and the explanation are missing, incorrect, or incomplete.

SOLUTION TO THE EXTENSION

Possible Solution

The expression pc represents the amount of money the shelter gets from selling c calendars at price p. If the price goes up by $0.50, I would replace p with $p + 0.50$ to get the expression $(p + 0.50)c$. Apply the distributive property: $(p + 0.50)c = pc + 0.50c$ or $pc + 0.5c$. If I compare the expressions pc and $pc + 0.5c$, the difference is $0.5c$. If the shelter sells 200 calendars at $12.00 each instead of $11.50 this will make 0.5(200) or $100 extra.

Lesson 18

Problem Solving with Angles

Name: ______________________

Prerequisite: Find Unknown Angle Measures

Study the example problem showing how to use subtraction to find unknown angle measures. Then solve problems 1–6.

Example

In most desk chairs, people sit at a 90° angle. The angle that is best for your back is 135°. What is the difference in degrees of these two sitting angles?

You can use a diagram to help you better understand the problem.

90° sitting position — 135° sitting position — difference between angles

The equation $135° - 90° = a°$ represents this situation.

The difference $135° - 90°$ is 45°, so $45° = a°$.

B 1 You can also use a protractor to help you. Start at 0° on the inside scale of the protractor. Count to 90° on the protractor. How many more degrees do you need to count to get to 135°?

45°

B 2 Some desk chairs have as small as a 75° sitting position. What is the difference in degrees between sitting in this chair on its smallest setting and sitting at 135°?

Show your work.

$135° - 75° = 60°$

Solution: The difference is 60°.

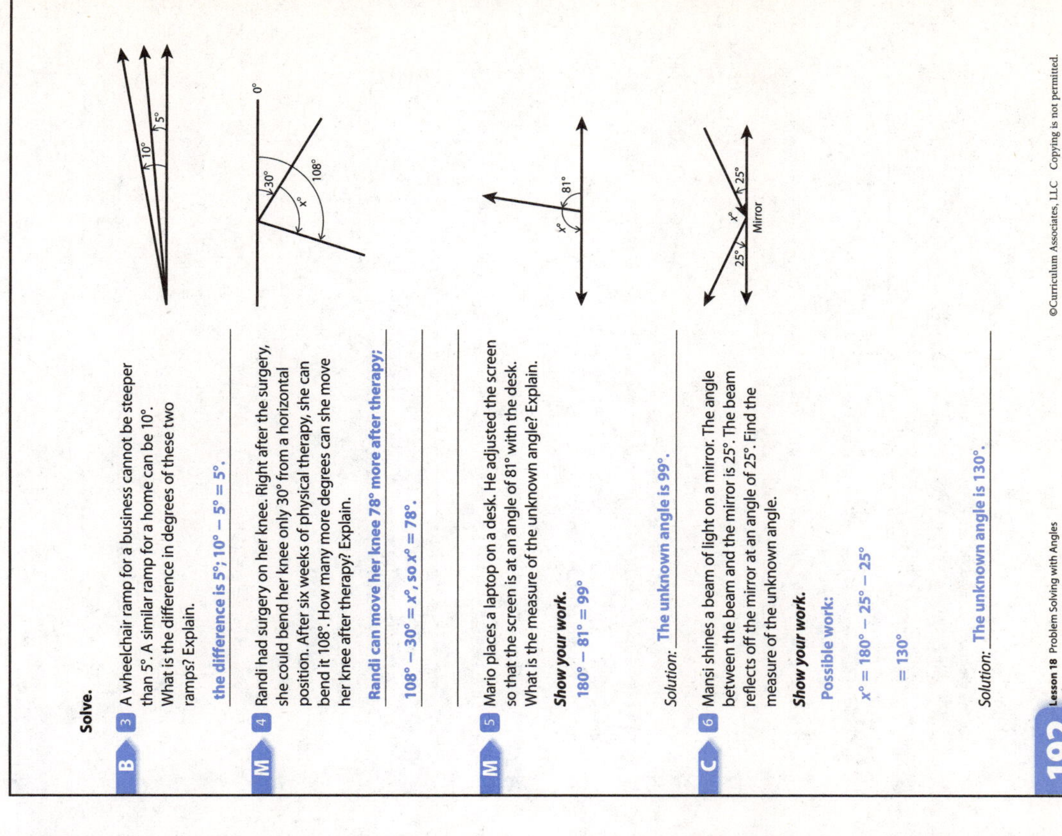

Solve.

B 3 A wheelchair ramp for a business cannot be steeper than 5°. A similar ramp for a home can be 10°. What is the difference in degrees of these two ramps? Explain.

the difference is 5°; $10° - 5° = 5°$.

M 4 Randi had surgery on her knee. Right after the surgery, she could bend her knee only 30° from a horizontal position. After six weeks of physical therapy, she can bend it 108°. How many more degrees can she move her knee after therapy? Explain.

Randi can move her knee 78° more after therapy;

$108° - 30° = x°$, so $x° = 78°$.

M 5 Mario places a laptop on a desk. He adjusted the screen so that the screen is at an angle of 81° with the desk. What is the measure of the unknown angle? Explain.

Show your work.

$180° - 81° = 99°$

Solution: The unknown angle is 99°.

C 6 Mansi shines a beam of light on a mirror. The angle between the beam and the mirror is 25°. The beam reflects off the mirror at an angle of 25°. Find the measure of the unknown angle.

Show your work.

Possible work:

$x° = 180° - 25° - 25°$

$= 130°$

Solution: The unknown angle is 130°.

Key

B Basic **M** Medium **C** Challenge

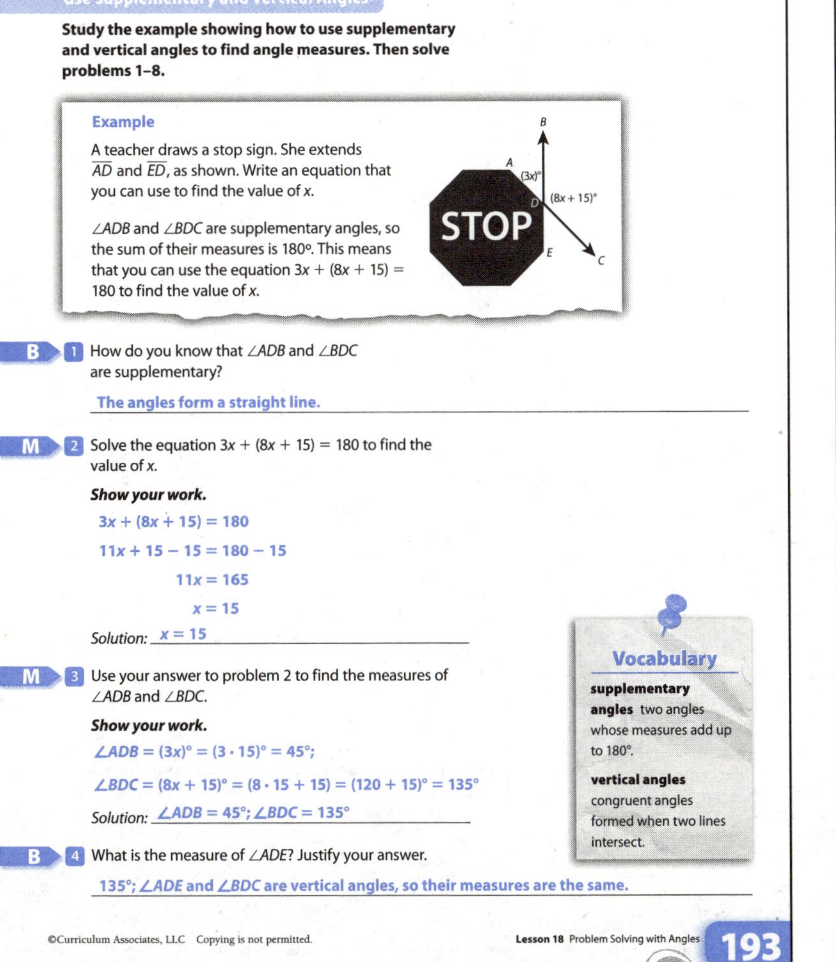

Lesson 18

Name: ____________________

Use Supplementary and Vertical Angles

Study the example showing how to use supplementary and vertical angles to find angle measures. Then solve problems 1–8.

Example

A teacher draws a stop sign. She extends $\overline{AD}$ and $\overline{ED}$, as shown. Write an equation that you can use to find the value of x.

$\angle ADB$ and $\angle BDC$ are supplementary angles, so the sum of their measures is 180°. This means that you can use the equation $3x + (8x + 15) =$ 180 to find the value of x.

B **1** How do you know that $\angle ADB$ and $\angle BDC$ are supplementary?

The angles form a straight line.

M **2** Solve the equation $3x + (8x + 15) = 180$ to find the value of x.

Show your work.

$3x + (8x + 15) = 180$

$11x + 15 - 15 = 180 - 15$

$11x = 165$

$x = 15$

Solution: $x = 15$

M **3** Use your answer to problem 2 to find the measures of $\angle ADB$ and $\angle BDC$.

Show your work.

$\angle ADB = (3x)° = (3 \cdot 15)° = 45°$;

$\angle BDC = (8x + 15)° = (8 \cdot 15 + 15) = (120 + 15)° = 135°$

Solution: $\angle ADB = 45°$; $\angle BDC = 135°$

B **4** What is the measure of $\angle ADE$? Justify your answer.

135°; $\angle ADE$ and $\angle BDC$ are vertical angles, so their measures are the same.

Vocabulary

supplementary angles two angles whose measures add up to 180°.

vertical angles congruent angles formed when two lines intersect.

©Curriculum Associates, LLC Copying is not permitted. **Lesson 18** Problem Solving with Angles **193**

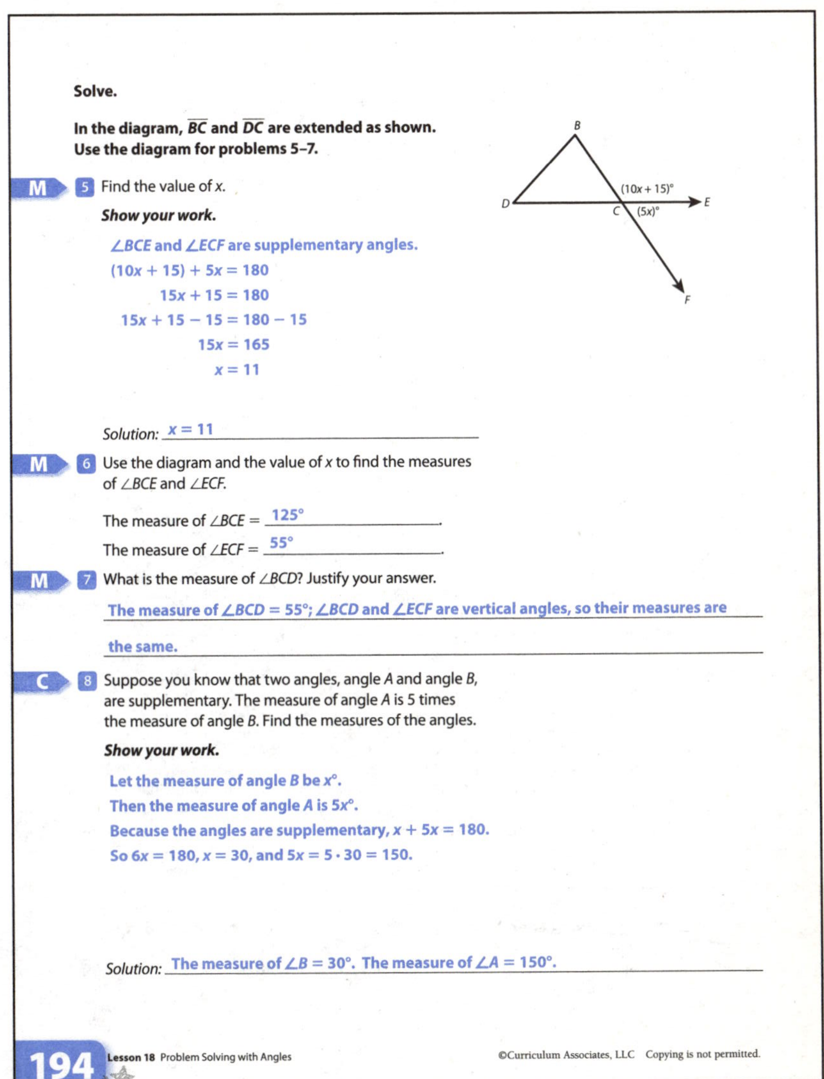

Solve.

In the diagram, $\overline{BC}$ and $\overline{DC}$ are extended as shown. Use the diagram for problems 5–7.

M **5** Find the value of x.

Show your work.

$\angle BCE$ and $\angle ECF$ are supplementary angles.

$(10x + 15) + 5x = 180$

$15x + 15 = 180$

$15x + 15 - 15 = 180 - 15$

$15x = 165$

$x = 11$

Solution: $x = 11$

M **6** Use the diagram and the value of x to find the measures of $\angle BCE$ and $\angle ECF$.

The measure of $\angle BCE =$ 125°.

The measure of $\angle ECF =$ 55°.

M **7** What is the measure of $\angle BCD$? Justify your answer.

The measure of $\angle BCD = 55°$; $\angle BCD$ and $\angle ECF$ are vertical angles, so their measures are the same.

C **8** Suppose you know that two angles, angle A and angle B, are supplementary. The measure of angle A is 5 times the measure of angle B. Find the measures of the angles.

Show your work.

Let the measure of angle B be $x°$.

Then the measure of angle A is $5x°$.

Because the angles are supplementary, $x + 5x = 180$.

So $6x = 180$, $x = 30$, and $5x = 5 \cdot 30 = 150$.

Solution: The measure of $\angle B = 30°$. The measure of $\angle A = 150°$.

194 **Lesson 18** Problem Solving with Angles ©Curriculum Associates, LLC Copying is not permitted.

Practice Lesson 18 Problem Solving with Angles

Unit 4

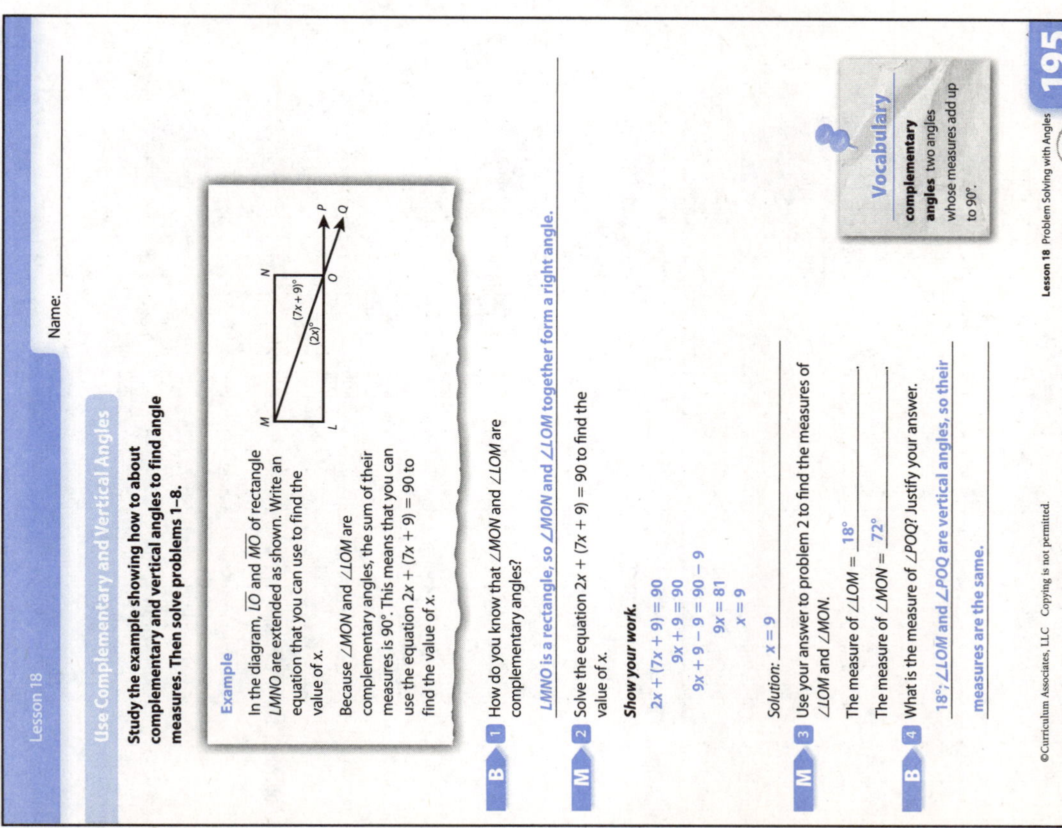

Lesson 18

Name: ____________

Use Complementary and Vertical Angles

Study the example showing how to about complementary and vertical angles to find angle measures. Then solve problems 1–8.

Example

In the diagram, $\overline{LO}$ and $\overline{MO}$ of rectangle *LMNO* are extended as shown. Write an equation that you can use to find the value of *x*.

Because ∠*MON* and ∠*LOM* are complementary angles, the sum of their measures is 90°. This means that you can use the equation $2x + (7x + 9) = 90$ to find the value of *x*.

B 1 How do you know that ∠*MON* and ∠*LOM* are complementary angles?

LMNO is a rectangle, so ∠*MON* and ∠*LOM* together form a right angle.

M 2 Solve the equation $2x + (7x + 9) = 90$ to find the value of *x*.

Show your work.

$2x + (7x + 9) = 90$
$9x + 9 = 90$
$9x + 9 - 9 = 90 - 9$
$9x = 81$
$x = 9$

Solution: $x = 9$

M 3 Use your answer to problem 2 to find the measures of ∠*LOM* and ∠*MON*.

The measure of ∠*LOM* = 18°.

The measure of ∠*MON* = 72°.

B 4 What is the measure of ∠*POQ*? Justify your answer.

18°; ∠*LOM* and ∠*POQ* are vertical angles, so their measures are the same.

Vocabulary

complementary angles two angles whose measures add up to 90°.

©Curriculum Associates, LLC Copying is not permitted. **Lesson 18** Problem Solving with Angles 195

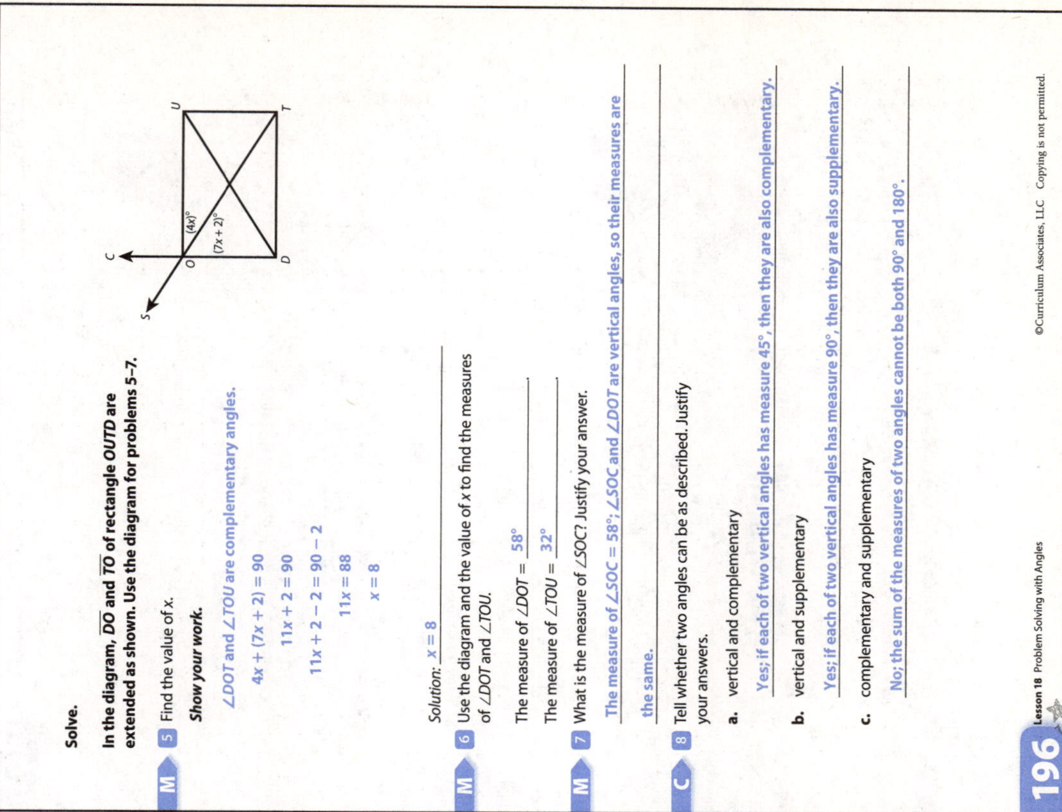

Solve.

In the diagram, $\overline{DO}$ and $\overline{TO}$ of rectangle *OUTD* are extended as shown. Use the diagram for problems 5–7.

M 5 Find the value of *x*.

Show your work.

∠*DOT* and ∠*TOU* are complementary angles.

$4x + (7x + 2) = 90$
$11x + 2 = 90$
$11x + 2 - 2 = 90 - 2$
$11x = 88$
$x = 8$

Solution: $x = 8$

M 6 Use the diagram and the value of *x* to find the measures of ∠*DOT* and ∠*TOU*.

The measure of ∠*DOT* = 58°.

The measure of ∠*TOU* = 32°.

M 7 What is the measure of ∠*SOC*? Justify your answer.

The measure of ∠*SOC* = 58°; ∠*SOC* and ∠*DOT* are vertical angles, so their measures are the same.

C 8 Tell whether two angles can be as described. Justify your answers.

a. vertical and complementary

Yes; if each of two vertical angles has measure 45°, then they are also complementary.

b. vertical and supplementary

Yes; if each of two vertical angles has measure 90°, then they are also supplementary.

c. complementary and supplementary

No; the sum of the measures of two angles cannot be both 90° and 180°.

196 **Lesson 18** Problem Solving with Angles ©Curriculum Associates, LLC Copying is not permitted.

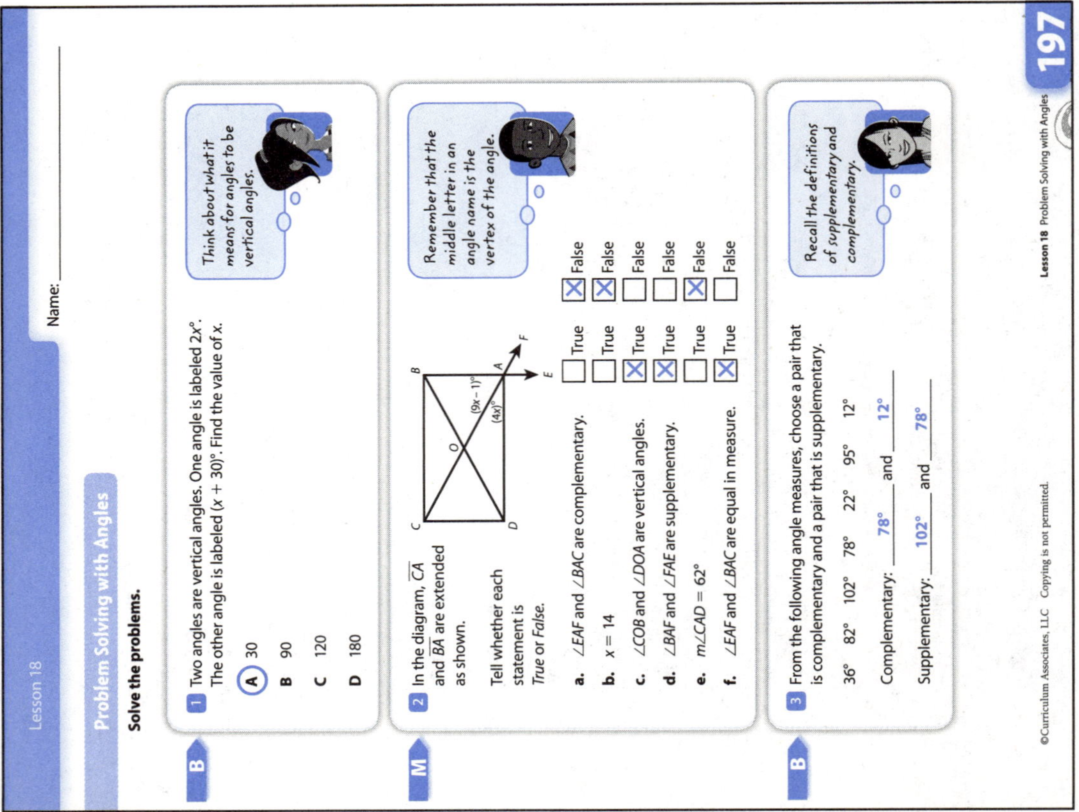

Lesson 18

Name: ______________________

Problem Solving with Angles

Solve the problems.

B

1 Two angles are vertical angles. One angle is labeled $2x°$. The other angle is labeled $(x + 30)°$. Find the value of x.

(A) 30

B 90

C 120

D 180

M

2 In the diagram, $\overline{CA}$ and $\overline{BA}$ are extended as shown.

Tell whether each statement is *True* or *False*.

a.	$\angle EAF$ and $\angle BAC$ are complementary.	☐ True	☒ False
b.	$x = 14$	☐ True	☒ False
c.	$\angle COB$ and $\angle DOA$ are vertical angles.	☒ True	☐ False
d.	$\angle BAF$ and $\angle FAE$ are supplementary.	☒ True	☐ False
e.	$m\angle CAD = 62°$	☐ True	☒ False
f.	$\angle EAF$ and $\angle BAC$ are equal in measure.	☒ True	☐ False

B

3 From the following angle measures, choose a pair that is complementary and a pair that is supplementary.

36° 82° 102° 78° 22° 95° 12°

Complementary: 78° and 12°

Supplementary: 102° and 78°

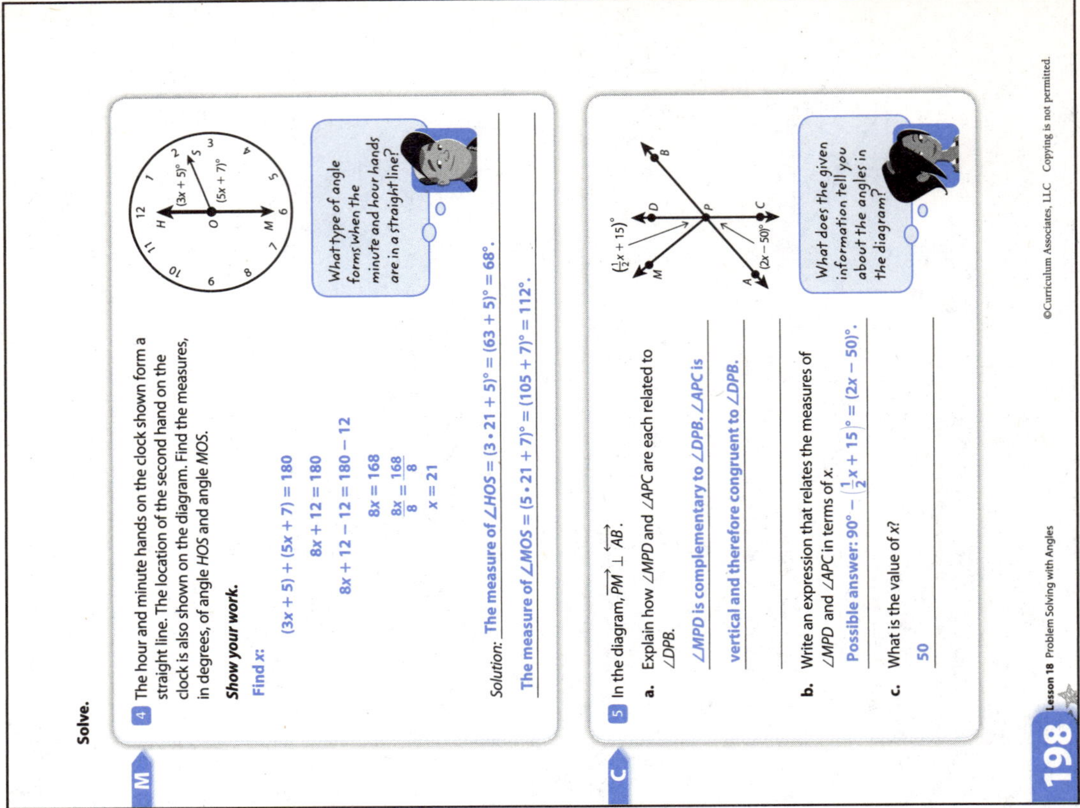

Solve.

M

4 The hour and minute hands on the clock shown form a straight line. The location of the second hand on the clock is also shown on the diagram. Find the measures, in degrees, of angle *HOS* and angle *MOS*.

Show your work.

Find x:

$$(3x + 5) + (5x + 7) = 180$$
$$8x + 12 = 180$$
$$8x + 12 - 12 = 180 - 12$$
$$8x = 168$$
$$\frac{8x}{8} = \frac{168}{8}$$
$$x = 21$$

Solution: The measure of $\angle HOS = (3 \cdot 21 + 5)° = (63 + 5)° = 68°$.

The measure of $\angle MOS = (5 \cdot 21 + 7)° = (105 + 7)° = 112°$.

C

5 In the diagram, $\overrightarrow{PM} \perp \overleftrightarrow{AB}$.

a. Explain how $\angle MPD$ and $\angle APC$ are each related to $\angle DPB$.

$\angle MPD$ is complementary to $\angle DPB$. $\angle APC$ is vertical and therefore congruent to $\angle DPB$.

b. Write an expression that relates the measures of $\angle MPD$ and $\angle APC$ in terms of x.

Possible answer: $90° - \left(\frac{1}{2}x + 15\right)° = (2x - 50)°$.

c. What is the value of x?

50

Lesson 19

Understand Conditions for Drawing Triangles

Name: ____________

Prerequisite: How can you use the coordinate plane to help you analyze polygons?

Study the example showing how to find missing dimensions of a polygon on the coordinate plane. Then solve problems 1–7.

Example

The Parks Department plans to put a triangular flower garden in a corner of a park. The coordinates of the endpoints of the longest side are (−2, −3) and (6, 3). What are the coordinates of the third vertex of the garden?

You can graph the information that is given and sketch the triangle. Draw a horizontal line through (−2, −3) and a vertical line through (6, 3).

B 1 What are the coordinates of the point *P*?

(6, −3)

B 2 Do the three segments form a right triangle? Explain.

Yes; The grid lines are perpendicular and two of the sides of the triangle are along grid lines, so they form a right angle.

B 3 How long is the side through (−2, −3) and point *P*? What are two ways that you can find this length?

8 units; I can count the squares between the points or I can find |6| + |−2|.

B 4 How long is the side through (6, 3) and point *P*? What are two ways that you can find this length?

6 units; I can count the squares between the points or I can find |3| + |−3|.

M 5 The perimeter of the garden is 24 units. What is the distance, *d*, from (−2, −3) to (6, 3)? Justify your answer.

10 units; perimeter = 8 + 6 + *d* = 24. So, *d* = 24 − 14 = 10.

Vocabulary

polygon a closed plane figure whose sides are line segments that intersect only at their endpoints.

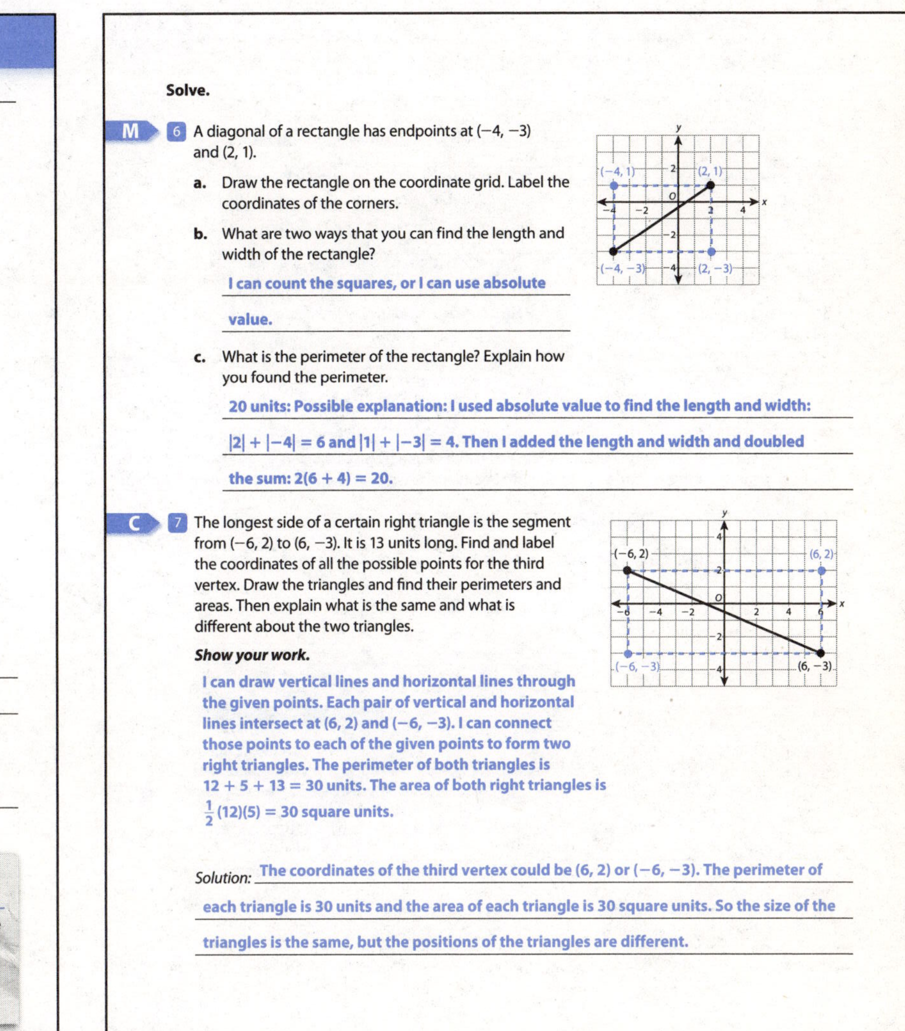

Solve.

M 6 A diagonal of a rectangle has endpoints at (−4, −3) and (2, 1).

a. Draw the rectangle on the coordinate grid. Label the coordinates of the corners.

b. What are two ways that you can find the length and width of the rectangle?

I can count the squares, or I can use absolute value.

c. What is the perimeter of the rectangle? Explain how you found the perimeter.

20 units: Possible explanation: I used absolute value to find the length and width: |2| + |−4| = 6 and |1| + |−3| = 4. Then I added the length and width and doubled the sum: 2(6 + 4) = 20.

C 7 The longest side of a certain right triangle is the segment from (−6, 2) to (6, −3). It is 13 units long. Find and label the coordinates of all the possible points for the third vertex. Draw the triangles and find their perimeters and areas. Then explain what is the same and what is different about the two triangles.

Show your work.

I can draw vertical lines and horizontal lines through the given points. Each pair of vertical and horizontal lines intersect at (6, 2) and (−6, −3). I can connect those points to each of the given points to form two right triangles. The perimeter of both triangles is 12 + 5 + 13 = 30 units. The area of both right triangles is $\frac{1}{2}(12)(5) = 30$ square units.

Solution: The coordinates of the third vertex could be (6, 2) or (−6, −3). The perimeter of each triangle is 30 units and the area of each triangle is 30 square units. So the size of the triangles is the same, but the positions of the triangles are different.

Key

B Basic **M** Medium **C** Challenge

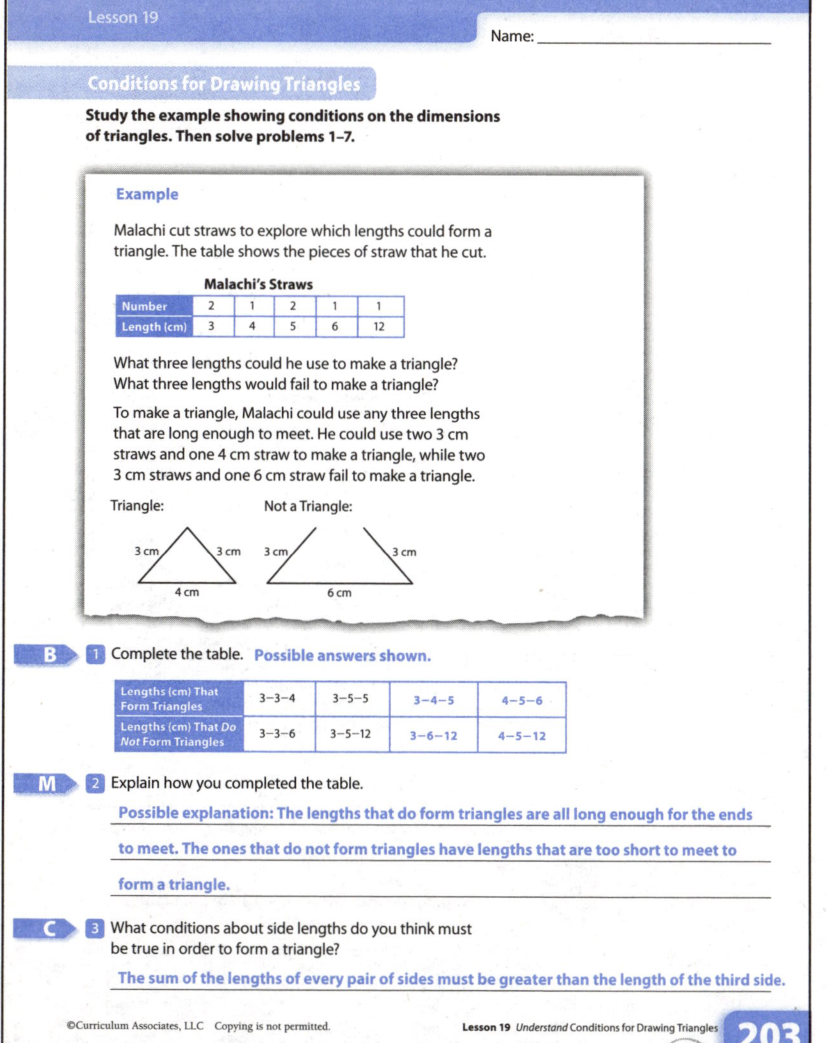

Lesson 19

Conditions for Drawing Triangles

Name: ____________________

Study the example showing conditions on the dimensions of triangles. Then solve problems 1–7.

Example

Malachi cut straws to explore which lengths could form a triangle. The table shows the pieces of straw that he cut.

Malachi's Straws

Number	2	1	2	1	1
Length (cm)	3	4	5	6	12

What three lengths could he use to make a triangle? What three lengths would fail to make a triangle?

To make a triangle, Malachi could use any three lengths that are long enough to meet. He could use two 3 cm straws and one 4 cm straw to make a triangle, while two 3 cm straws and one 6 cm straw fail to make a triangle.

Triangle: Not a Triangle:

B 1 Complete the table. Possible answers shown.

Lengths (cm) That Form Triangles	3–3–4	3–5–5	3–4–5	4–5–6
Lengths (cm) That *Do Not* Form Triangles	3–3–6	3–5–12	3–6–12	4–5–12

M 2 Explain how you completed the table.

Possible explanation: The lengths that do form triangles are all long enough for the ends to meet. The ones that do not form triangles have lengths that are too short to meet to form a triangle.

C 3 What conditions about side lengths do you think must be true in order to form a triangle?

The sum of the lengths of every pair of sides must be greater than the length of the third side.

©Curriculum Associates, LLC Copying is not permitted. Lesson 19 *Understand* Conditions for Drawing Triangles 203

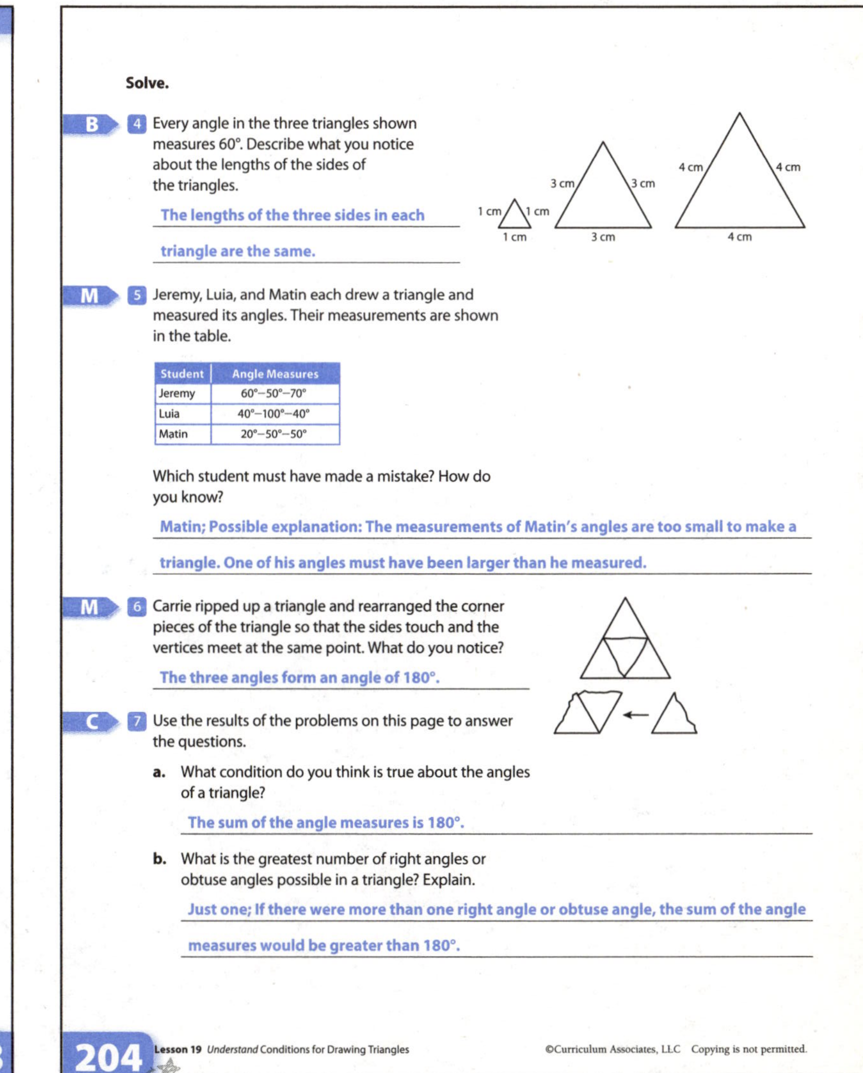

Solve.

B 4 Every angle in the three triangles shown measures 60°. Describe what you notice about the lengths of the sides of the triangles.

The lengths of the three sides in each triangle are the same.

M 5 Jeremy, Luia, and Matin each drew a triangle and measured its angles. Their measurements are shown in the table.

Student	Angle Measures
Jeremy	60°–50°–70°
Luia	40°–100°–40°
Matin	20°–50°–50°

Which student must have made a mistake? How do you know?

Matin; Possible explanation: The measurements of Matin's angles are too small to make a triangle. One of his angles must have been larger than he measured.

M 6 Carrie ripped up a triangle and rearranged the corner pieces of the triangle so that the sides touch and the vertices meet at the same point. What do you notice?

The three angles form an angle of 180°.

C 7 Use the results of the problems on this page to answer the questions.

a. What condition do you think is true about the angles of a triangle?

The sum of the angle measures is 180°.

b. What is the greatest number of right angles or obtuse angles possible in a triangle? Explain.

Just one; If there were more than one right angle or obtuse angle, the sum of the angle measures would be greater than 180°.

204 Lesson 19 *Understand* Conditions for Drawing Triangles ©Curriculum Associates, LLC Copying is not permitted.

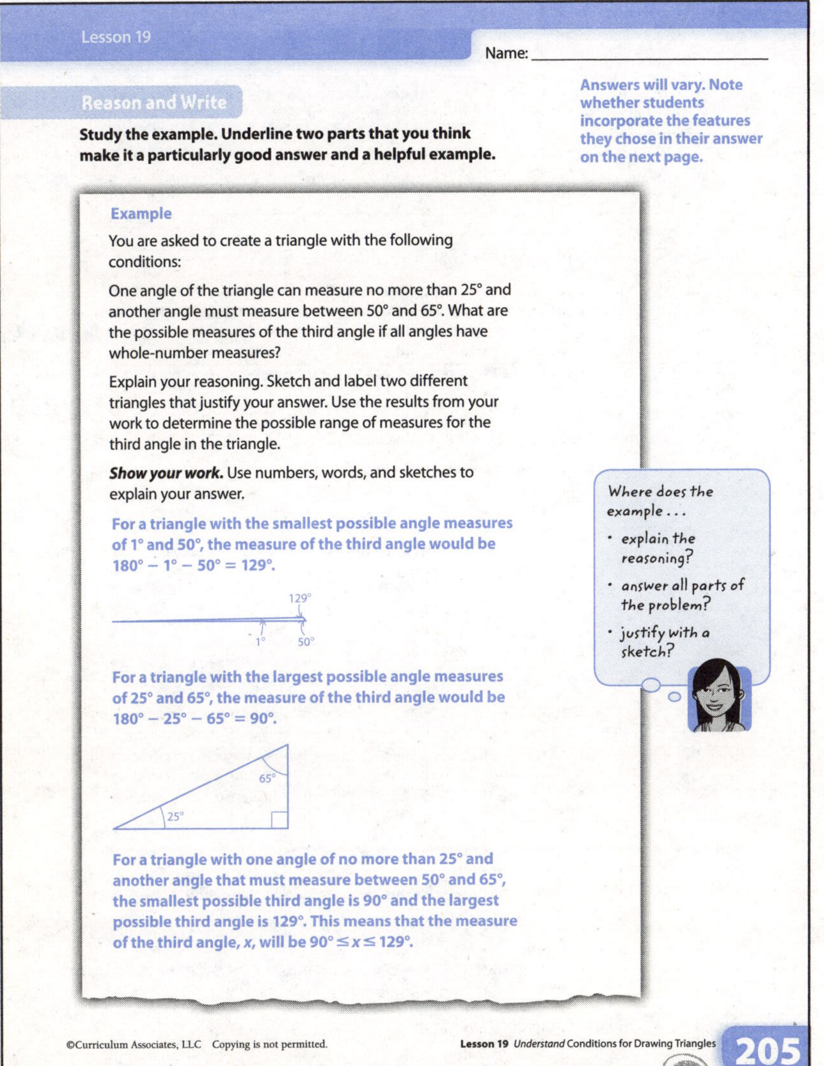

Lesson 19

Name: ________

Reason and Write

Study the example. Underline two parts that you think make it a particularly good answer and a helpful example.

Answers will vary. Note whether students incorporate the features they chose in their answer on the next page.

Example

You are asked to create a triangle with the following conditions:

One angle of the triangle can measure no more than 25° and another angle must measure between 50° and 65°. What are the possible measures of the third angle if all angles have whole-number measures?

Explain your reasoning. Sketch and label two different triangles that justify your answer. Use the results from your work to determine the possible range of measures for the third angle in the triangle.

Show your work. Use numbers, words, and sketches to explain your answer.

For a triangle with the smallest possible angle measures of 1° and 50°, the measure of the third angle would be $180° - 1° - 50° = 129°$.

For a triangle with the largest possible angle measures of 25° and 65°, the measure of the third angle would be $180° - 25° - 65° = 90°$.

For a triangle with one angle of no more than 25° and another angle that must measure between 50° and 65°, the smallest possible third angle is 90° and the largest possible third angle is 129°. This means that the measure of the third angle, x, will be $90° \le x \le 129°$.

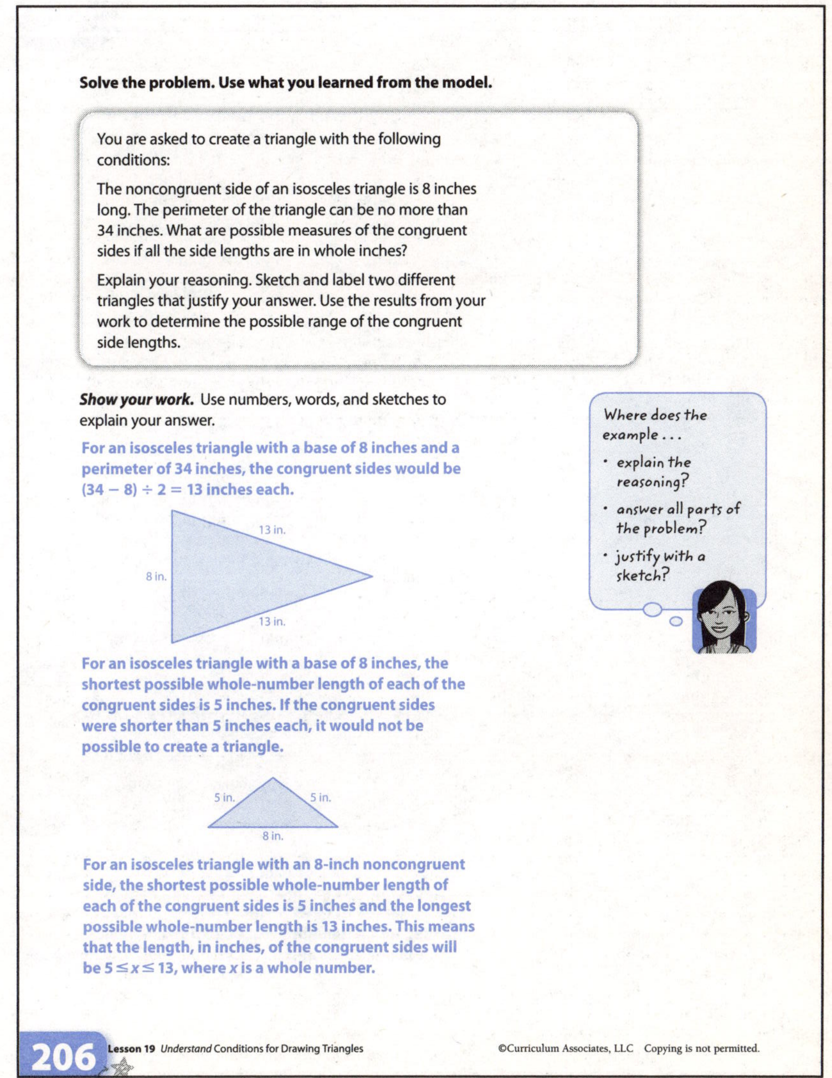

Solve the problem. Use what you learned from the model.

You are asked to create a triangle with the following conditions:

The noncongruent side of an isosceles triangle is 8 inches long. The perimeter of the triangle can be no more than 34 inches. What are possible measures of the congruent sides if all the side lengths are in whole inches?

Explain your reasoning. Sketch and label two different triangles that justify your answer. Use the results from your work to determine the possible range of the congruent side lengths.

Show your work. Use numbers, words, and sketches to explain your answer.

For an isosceles triangle with a base of 8 inches and a perimeter of 34 inches, the congruent sides would be $(34 - 8) \div 2 = 13$ inches each.

For an isosceles triangle with a base of 8 inches, the shortest possible whole-number length of each of the congruent sides is 5 inches. If the congruent sides were shorter than 5 inches each, it would not be possible to create a triangle.

For an isosceles triangle with an 8-inch noncongruent side, the shortest possible whole-number length of each of the congruent sides is 5 inches and the longest possible whole-number length is 13 inches. This means that the length, in inches, of the congruent sides will be $5 \le x \le 13$, where x is a whole number.

Lesson 20

Area of Composed Figures

Name: ______________________

Prerequisite: Separating a Figure to Find the Area

Study the example showing how to decompose a shape to find its area. Then solve problems 1–7.

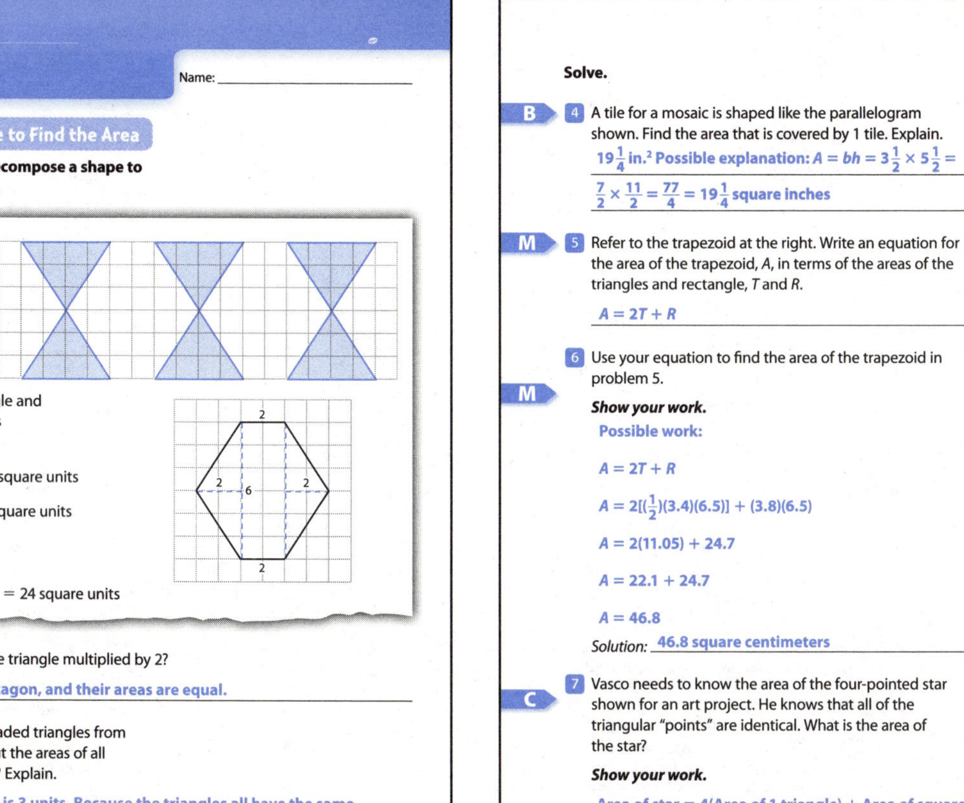

Example

Bev creates the pattern shown. Bev's pattern is made up of 6 triangles, 2 whole hexagons, and 2 half hexagons. She wants to find the area of one of the hexagons.

To find the area of one hexagon, Bev divides a hexagon into 1 rectangle and 2 congruent triangles. Then she finds the area of each shape.

Area of triangle $= \frac{1}{2}bh = \frac{1}{2}(6)(2) = 6$ square units

Area of rectangle $= bh = 2(6) = 12$ square units

Area of hexagon $= 2\left(\text{Area of triangle}\right) + \text{Area of rectangle}$

$= 2(6) + 12 = 24$ square units

B **1** In the example, why is the area of one triangle multiplied by 2?

There are two triangles in the hexagon, and their areas are equal.

B **2** Find the dimensions of one of the shaded triangles from Bev's pattern. What can you say about the areas of all the shaded triangles in Bev's pattern? Explain.

The base is 4 units and the height is 3 units. Because the triangles all have the same dimensions, the areas will be equal.

M **3** What is the total area of the 6 shaded triangles?

Show your work.

Area of 1 triangle $= \frac{1}{2}bh = \frac{1}{2}(4)(3) = 6$ square units

Area of 6 triangles $= 6 \cdot 6 = 36$ square units

Solution: 36 square units

Solve.

B **4** A tile for a mosaic is shaped like the parallelogram shown. Find the area that is covered by 1 tile. Explain.

$19\frac{1}{4}$ in.² Possible explanation: $A = bh = 3\frac{1}{2} \times 5\frac{1}{2} = \frac{7}{2} \times \frac{11}{2} = \frac{77}{4} = 19\frac{1}{4}$ square inches

M **5** Refer to the trapezoid at the right. Write an equation for the area of the trapezoid, A, in terms of the areas of the triangles and rectangle, T and R.

$A = 2T + R$

M **6** Use your equation to find the area of the trapezoid in problem 5.

Show your work.

Possible work:

$A = 2T + R$

$A = 2[(\frac{1}{2})(3.4)(6.5)] + (3.8)(6.5)$

$A = 2(11.05) + 24.7$

$A = 22.1 + 24.7$

$A = 46.8$

Solution: 46.8 square centimeters

C **7** Vasco needs to know the area of the four-pointed star shown for an art project. He knows that all of the triangular "points" are identical. What is the area of the star?

Show your work.

Area of star = 4(Area of 1 triangle) + Area of square

Area of 1 triangle $= \frac{1}{2}bh = \frac{1}{2}(1.5)(2.4) = 1.8$

Area of square $= s \cdot s = (1.5)(1.5) = 2.25$

Area of star $= 4(1.8) + 2.25 = 9.45$

Solution: 9.45 square centimeters

Key

B Basic **M** Medium **C** Challenge

Practice Lesson 20 Area of Composed Figures

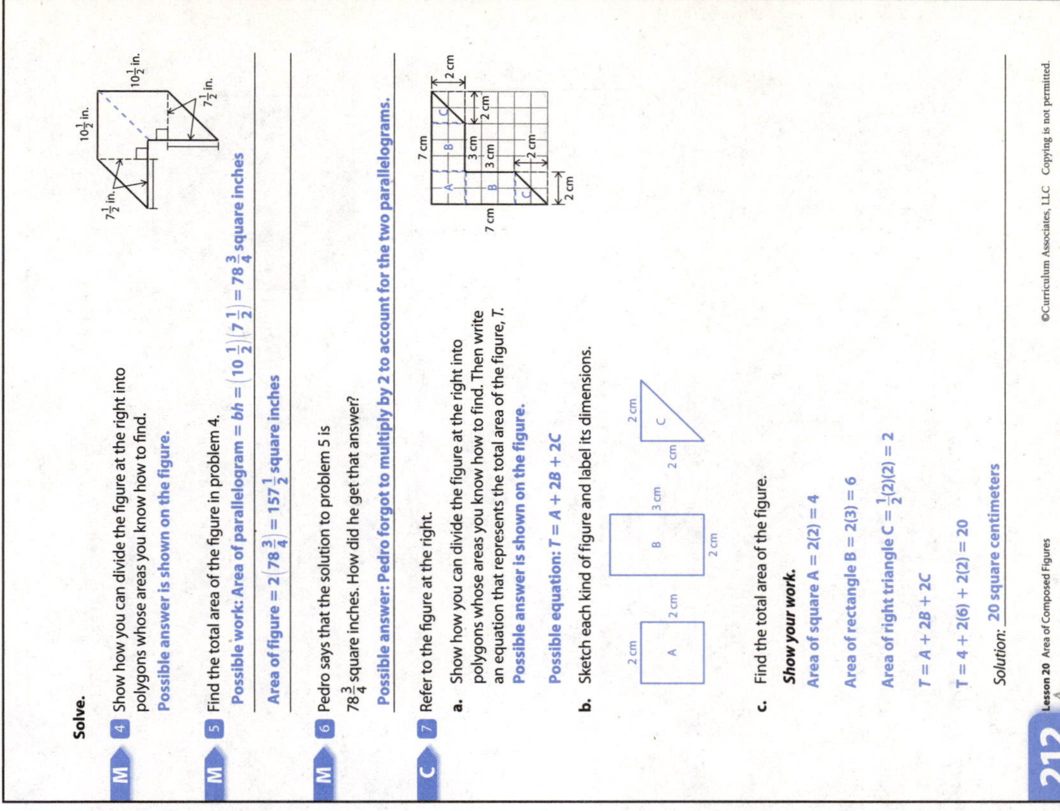
Solve.

M 4 Show how you can divide the figure at the right into polygons whose areas you know how to find.

Possible answer is shown on the figure.

M 5 Find the total area of the figure in problem 4.

Possible work: Area of parallelogram = $bh = \left(10\frac{1}{2}\right)\left(7\frac{1}{2}\right) = 78\frac{3}{4}$ square inches

Area of figure = $2\left(78\frac{3}{4}\right) = 157\frac{1}{2}$ square inches

M 6 Pedro says that the solution to problem 5 is $78\frac{3}{4}$ square inches. How did he get that answer?

Possible answer: Pedro forgot to multiply by 2 to account for the two parallelograms.

C 7 Refer to the figure at the right.

a. Show how you can divide the figure at the right into polygons whose areas you know how to find. Then write an equation that represents the total area of the figure, *T*.

Possible answer is shown on the figure.

Possible equation: $T = A + 2B + 2C$

b. Sketch each kind of figure and label its dimensions.

c. Find the total area of the figure.

Show your work.

Area of square A = 2(2) = 4

Area of rectangle B = 2(3) = 6

Area of right triangle C = $\frac{1}{2}(2)(2) = 2$

$T = A + 2B + 2C$

$T = 4 + 2(6) + 2(2) = 20$

Solution: **20 square centimeters**

212 **Lesson 20** Area of Composed Figures

©Curriculum Associates, LLC Copying is not permitted.

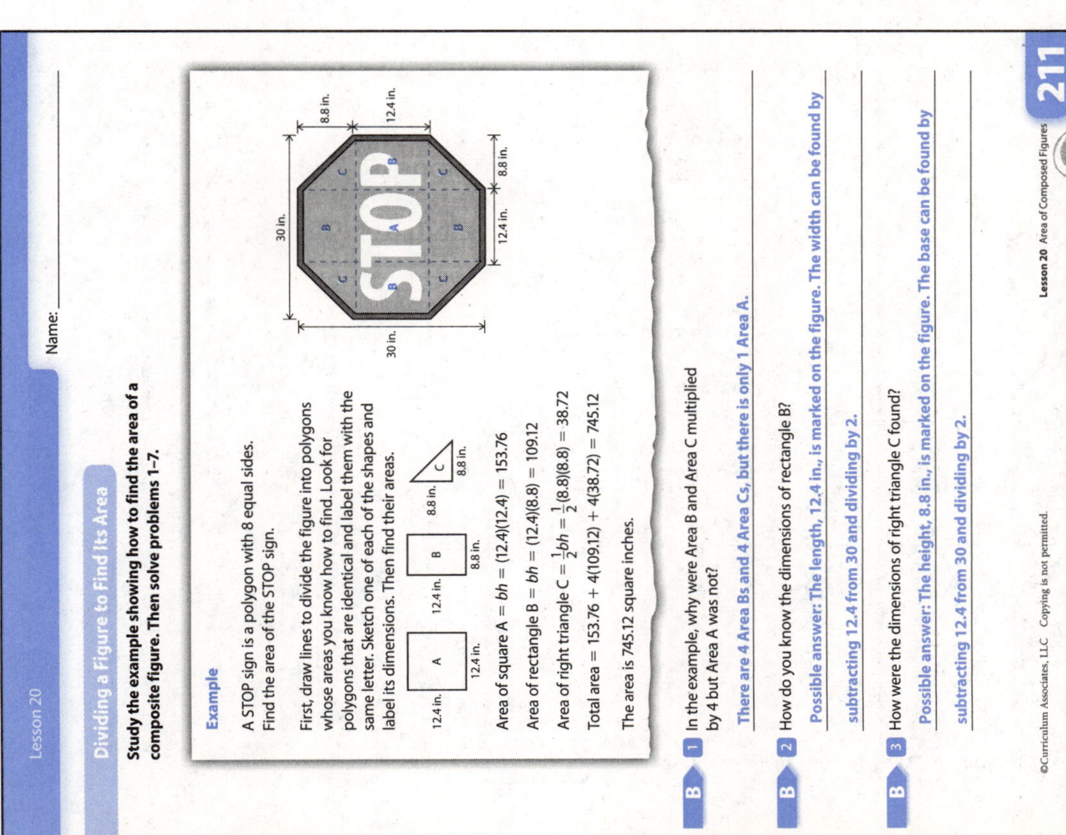
Lesson 20

Name: ____________

Dividing a Figure to Find Its Area

Study the example showing how to find the area of a composite figure. Then solve problems 1–7.

Example

A STOP sign is a polygon with 8 equal sides. Find the area of the STOP sign.

First, draw lines to divide the figure into polygons whose areas you know how to find. Look for polygons that are identical and label them with the same letter. Sketch one of each of the shapes and label its dimensions. Then find their areas.

Area of square A = bh = (12.4)(12.4) = 153.76

Area of rectangle B = bh = (12.4)(8.8) = 109.12

Area of right triangle C = $\frac{1}{2}bh = \frac{1}{2}(8.8)(8.8) = 38.72$

Total area = 153.76 + 4(109.12) + 4(38.72) = 745.12

The area is 745.12 square inches.

B 1 In the example, why were Area B and Area C multiplied by 4 but Area A was not?

There are 4 Area Bs and 4 Area Cs, but there is only 1 Area A.

B 2 How do you know the dimensions of rectangle B?

Possible answer: The length, 12.4 in., is marked on the figure. The width can be found by subtracting 12.4 from 30 and dividing by 2.

B 3 How were the dimensions of right triangle C found?

Possible answer: The height, 8.8 in., is marked on the figure. The base can be found by subtracting 12.4 from 30 and dividing by 2.

©Curriculum Associates, LLC Copying is not permitted.

Lesson 20 Area of Composed Figures 211

Name: ______________________

Solving Problems Related to Area

Study the example showing how to use what you have learned to solve problems related to area. Then solve problems 1–7.

Example

Ben is paving a parking lot with the shape shown. How can he find the area of the parking lot?

One way is to complete a rectangle around the parking lot and then subtract those areas that are *not* part of the parking lot. This is what Ben decides to do.

Area of parking lot = Area of large rectangle − 2(Area A) − Area B

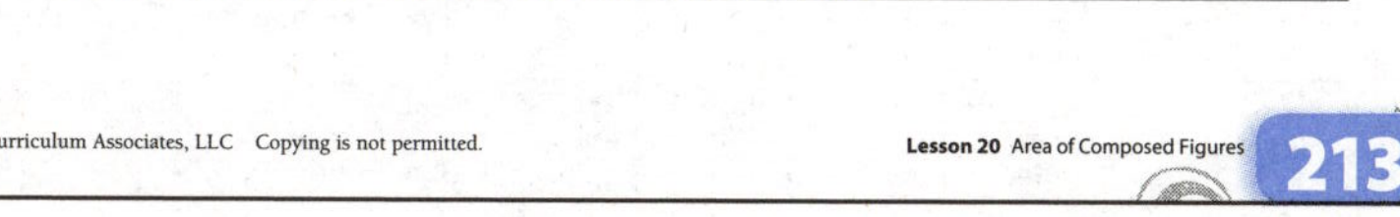

B **1** What is the area of the large rectangle? Show your work.

11,250 square yards; $A = \ell w = (150)(75) = 11{,}250$

B **2** Find the dimensions of rectangle A. Then find the area of rectangle A. Show your work.

The length is 40.5 yards and the width is $\frac{1}{2}(75 - 25) = 25$, or 25 yards. $A = \ell w = (40.5)(25) =$ 1,012.5; 1,012.5 square yards

B **3** Explain how you can find the dimensions of triangle B. Then find the area of triangle B.

The base is $150 - 100 - 40.5 = 9.5$, or 9.5 yards; the height is $75 - 2(25) = 25$ yards.

$A = \frac{1}{2}bh = \frac{1}{2}(9.5)(25) = 118.75$; 118.75 square yards

B **4** Find the area of the parking lot. Explain your calculation.

Area of parking lot = 11,250 − 2(Area A) − (Area B)

= 11,250 − 2(1,012.5) − 118.75 = 9,106.25 square yards

I subtracted 2 times Area A because there are 2 identical rectangles labeled A, as well as the area of triangle B from the area of the large rectangle.

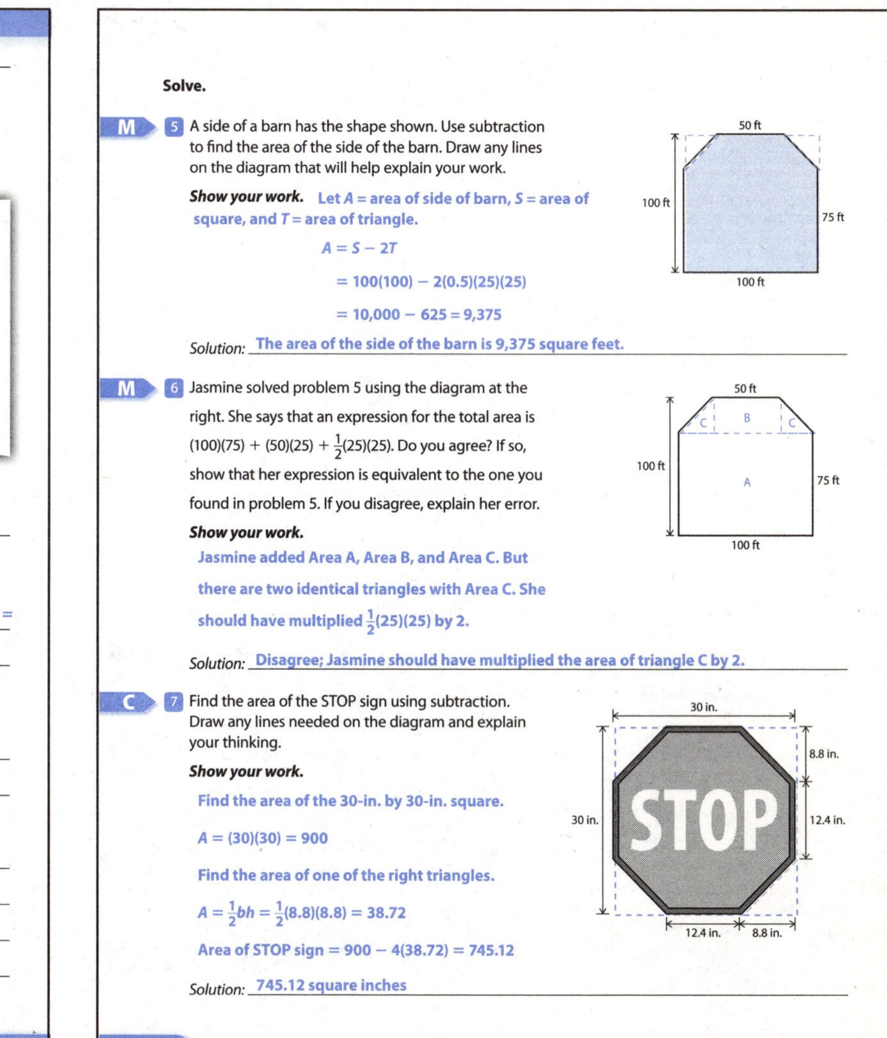

Solve.

M **5** A side of a barn has the shape shown. Use subtraction to find the area of the side of the barn. Draw any lines on the diagram that will help explain your work.

Show your work. Let A = area of side of barn, S = area of square, and T = area of triangle.

$A = S - 2T$

$= 100(100) - 2(0.5)(25)(25)$

$= 10{,}000 - 625 = 9{,}375$

Solution: The area of the side of the barn is 9,375 square feet.

M **6** Jasmine solved problem 5 using the diagram at the right. She says that an expression for the total area is $(100)(75) + (50)(25) + \frac{1}{2}(25)(25)$. Do you agree? If so, show that her expression is equivalent to the one you found in problem 5. If you disagree, explain her error.

Show your work.

Jasmine added Area A, Area B, and Area C. But there are two identical triangles with Area C. She should have multiplied $\frac{1}{2}(25)(25)$ by 2.

Solution: Disagree; Jasmine should have multiplied the area of triangle C by 2.

C **7** Find the area of the STOP sign using subtraction. Draw any lines needed on the diagram and explain your thinking.

Show your work.

Find the area of the 30-in. by 30-in. square.

$A = (30)(30) = 900$

Find the area of one of the right triangles.

$A = \frac{1}{2}bh = \frac{1}{2}(8.8)(8.8) = 38.72$

Area of STOP sign $= 900 - 4(38.72) = 745.12$

Solution: 745.12 square inches

Practice Lesson 20 Area of Composed Figures

Unit 4

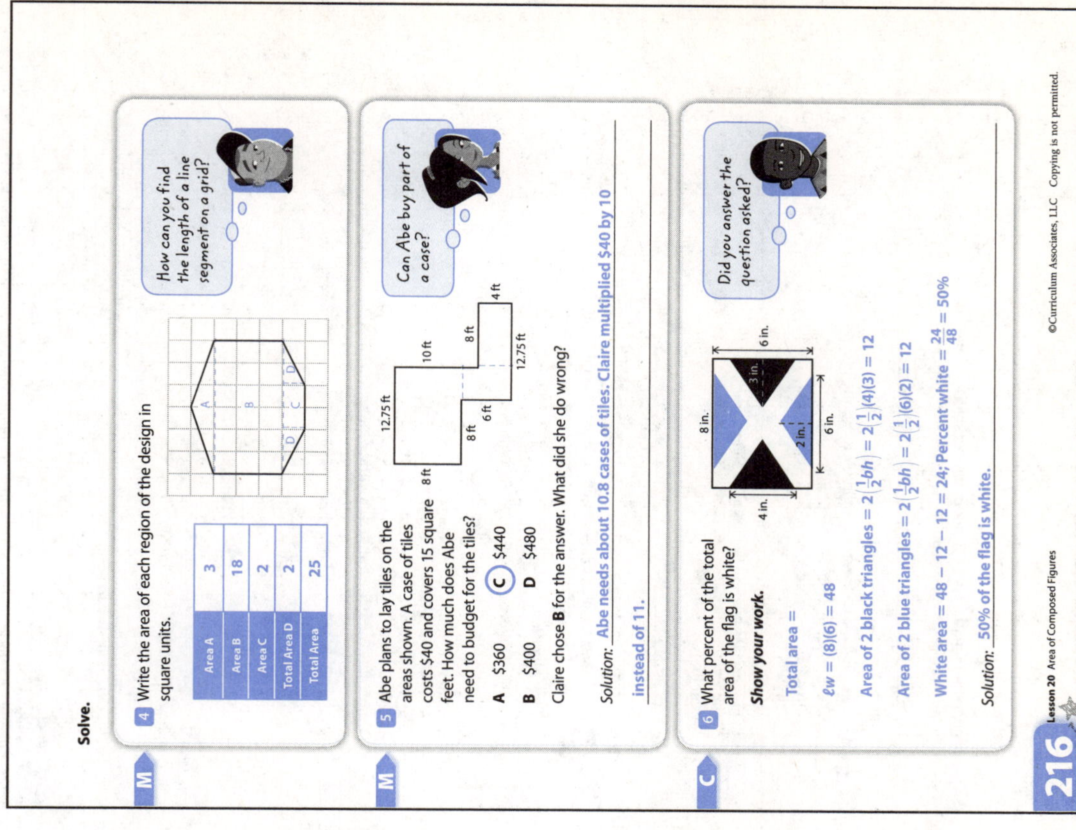

Solve.

M **4** Write the area of each region of the design in square units.

Area A	3
Area B	18
Area C	2
Total Area D	2
Total Area	25

M **5** Abe plans to lay tiles on the areas shown. A case of tiles costs $40 and covers 15 square feet. How much does Abe need to budget for the tiles?

A $360   (C) $440

B $400   D $480

Claire chose **B** for the answer. What did she do wrong?

Solution: Abe needs about 10.8 cases of tiles. Claire multiplied $40 by 10 instead of 11.

C **6** What percent of the total area of the flag is white?

Show your work.

Total area =

$\ell w = (8)(6) = 48$

Area of 2 black triangles $= 2\left(\frac{1}{2}bh\right) = 2\left(\frac{1}{2}\right)(4)(3) = 12$

Area of 2 blue triangles $= 2\left(\frac{1}{2}bh\right) = 2\left(\frac{1}{2}\right)(6)(2) = 12$

White area $= 48 - 12 - 12 = 24$; Percent white $= \frac{24}{48} = 50\%$

Solution: 50% of the flag is white.

216 Lesson 20 Area of Composed Figures ©Curriculum Associates, LLC Copying is not permitted.

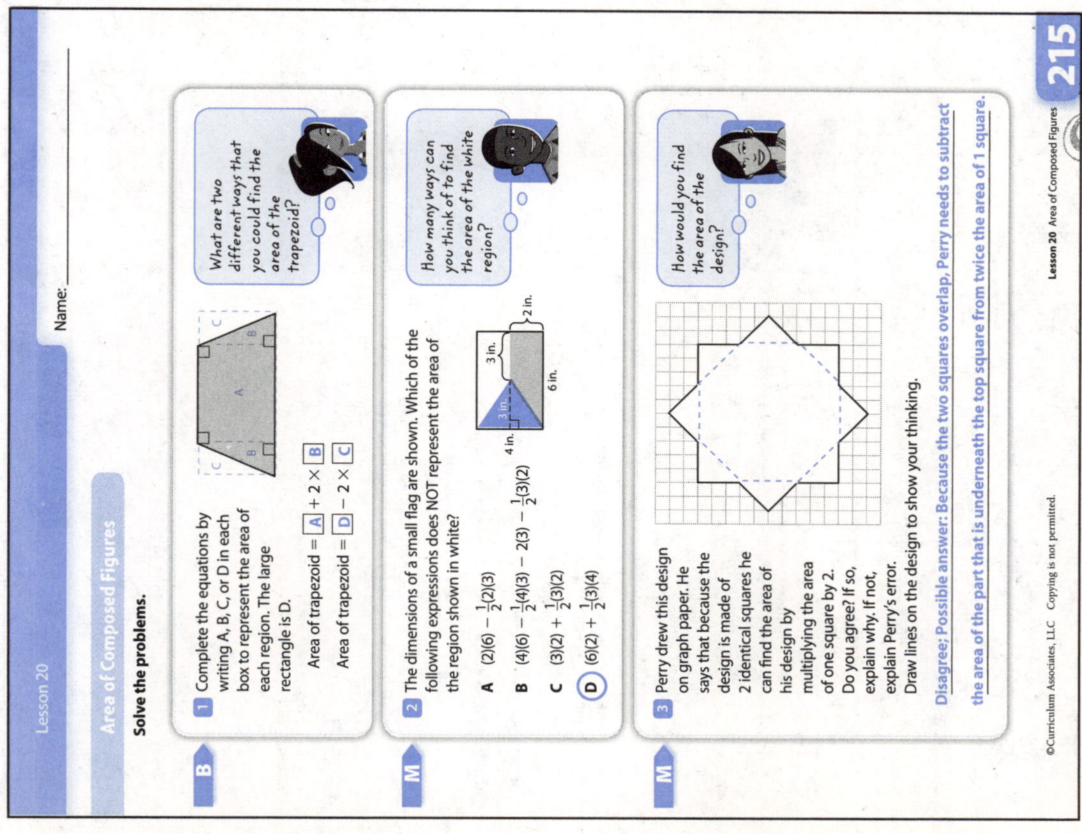

Lesson 20

Area of Composed Figures

Name: ____________

Solve the problems.

B **1** Complete the equations by writing A, B, C, or D in each box to represent the area of each region. The large rectangle is D.

Area of trapezoid = A + 2 × B

Area of trapezoid = D − 2 × C

M **2** The dimensions of a small flag are shown. Which of the following expressions does NOT represent the area of the region shown in white?

A $(2)(6) - \frac{1}{2}(2)(3)$

B $(4)(6) - \frac{1}{2}(4)(3) - 2(3) - \frac{1}{2}(3)(2)$

C $(3)(2) + \frac{1}{2}(3)(2)$

(D) $(6)(2) + \frac{1}{2}(3)(4)$

M **3** Perry drew this design on graph paper. He says that because the design is made of 2 identical squares he can find the area of his design by multiplying the area of one square by 2. Do you agree? If so, explain why. If not, explain Perry's error. Draw lines on the design to show your thinking.

Disagree; Possible answer: Because the two squares overlap, Perry needs to subtract the area of the part that is underneath the top square from twice the area of 1 square.

©Curriculum Associates, LLC Copying is not permitted. Lesson 20 Area of Composed Figures 215

Area and Circumference of a Circle

Name: ____________

Prerequisite: Finding Areas of Polygons

Study the example showing how to find the area of a polygon. Then solve problems 1–9.

Example

A concrete company makes blocks for parking lots. A construction worker who is installing the blocks needs to find the area of the trapezoid at the end of the block.

To find the area, the worker measures the trapezoid and draws this diagram showing the measurements.

6 in.
6 in.
10 in.

He knows how to find the area of a square and the area of a triangle. He plans to divide the trapezoid into a square and two triangles to find the area.

B 1 Label the dimensions in the diagram at the right.

6 in.
6 in.
2 in. 6 in. 2 in.

B 2 Find the area of the square in the diagram.

Area $= s \cdot s = 6 \cdot 6 = 36$ square inches

B 3 Find the area of one of the triangles in the diagram.

Area $= \frac{1}{2}bh = \frac{1}{2} \times 2 \times 6 = 6$ square inches

B 4 Write and solve an equation to find the area of the trapezoid.

Show your work. Possible work:

$A = S + 2T$

$A = 36 + 2 \times 6$

$A = 36 + 12$

$A = 48$

Solution: The total area of the trapezoid is 48 square inches.

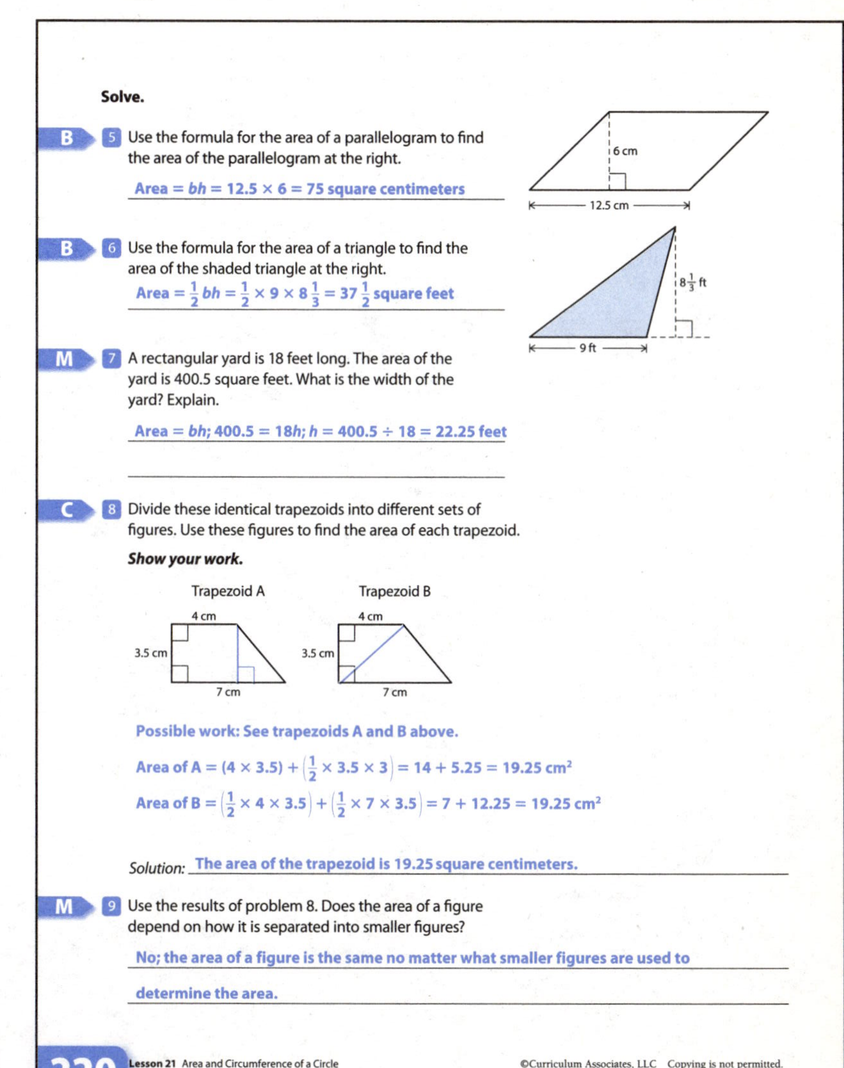

Solve.

B 5 Use the formula for the area of a parallelogram to find the area of the parallelogram at the right.

Area $= bh = 12.5 \times 6 = 75$ square centimeters

B 6 Use the formula for the area of a triangle to find the area of the shaded triangle at the right.

Area $= \frac{1}{2}bh = \frac{1}{2} \times 9 \times 8\frac{1}{3} = 37\frac{1}{2}$ square feet

M 7 A rectangular yard is 18 feet long. The area of the yard is 400.5 square feet. What is the width of the yard? Explain.

Area $= bh$; $400.5 = 18h$; $h = 400.5 \div 18 = 22.25$ feet

C 8 Divide these identical trapezoids into different sets of figures. Use these figures to find the area of each trapezoid.

Show your work.

Possible work: See trapezoids A and B above.

Area of A $= (4 \times 3.5) + \left(\frac{1}{2} \times 3.5 \times 3\right) = 14 + 5.25 = 19.25$ cm^2

Area of B $= \left(\frac{1}{2} \times 4 \times 3.5\right) + \left(\frac{1}{2} \times 7 \times 3.5\right) = 7 + 12.25 = 19.25$ cm^2

Solution: The area of the trapezoid is 19.25 square centimeters.

M 9 Use the results of problem 8. Does the area of a figure depend on how it is separated into smaller figures?

No; the area of a figure is the same no matter what smaller figures are used to determine the area.

Key

B Basic	**M** Medium	**C** Challenge

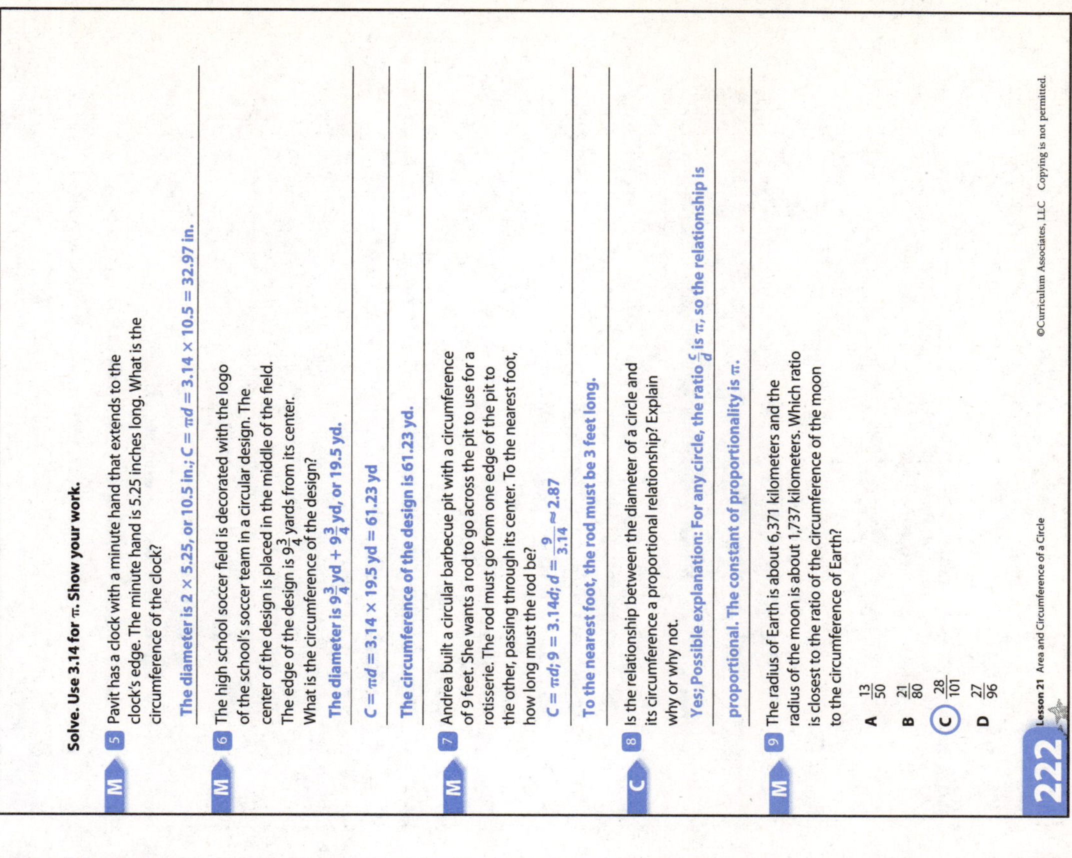

Solve. Use 3.14 for π. Show your work.

M 5 Pavit has a clock with a minute hand that extends to the clock's edge. The minute hand is 5.25 inches long. What is the circumference of the clock?

The diameter is 2×5.25, or 10.5 in.; $C = \pi d = 3.14 \times 10.5 = 32.97$ in.

M 6 The high school soccer field is decorated with the logo of the school's soccer team in a circular design. The center of the design is placed in the middle of the field. The edge of the design is $9\frac{3}{4}$ yards from its center. What is the circumference of the design?

The diameter is $9\frac{3}{4}$ yd + $9\frac{3}{4}$ yd, or 19.5 yd.

$C = \pi d = 3.14 \times 19.5$ yd $= 61.23$ yd

The circumference of the design is 61.23 yd.

M 7 Andrea built a circular barbecue pit with a circumference of 9 feet. She wants a rod to go across the pit to use for a rotisserie. The rod must go from one edge of the pit to the other, passing through its center. To the nearest foot, how long must the rod be?

$C = \pi d$; $9 = 3.14d$; $d = \frac{9}{3.14} \approx 2.87$

To the nearest foot, the rod must be 3 feet long.

C 8 Is the relationship between the diameter of a circle and its circumference a proportional relationship? Explain why or why not.

Yes; Possible explanation: For any circle, the ratio $\frac{C}{d}$ is π, so the relationship is proportional. The constant of proportionality is π.

M 9 The radius of Earth is about 6,371 kilometers and the radius of the moon is about 1,737 kilometers. Which ratio is closest to the ratio of the circumference of the moon to the circumference of Earth?

A $\frac{13}{50}$

B $\frac{21}{80}$

(C) $\frac{28}{101}$

D $\frac{27}{96}$

222 Lesson 21 Area and Circumference of a Circle

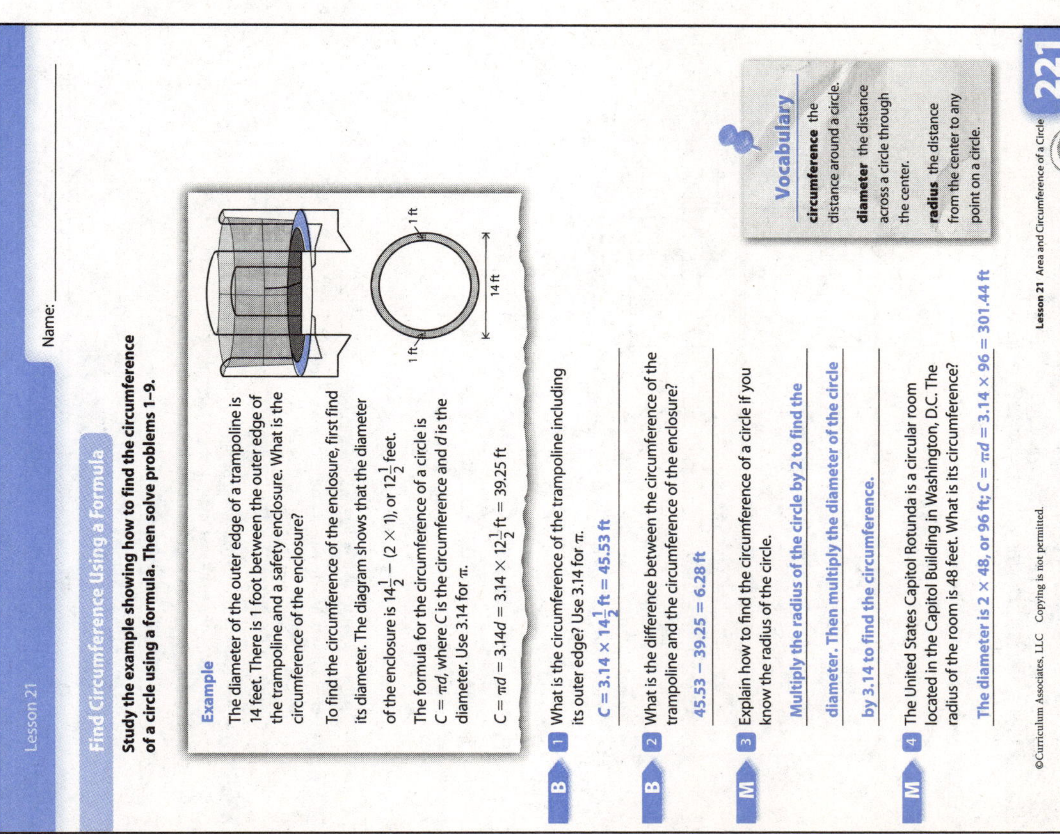

Lesson 21

Name: ____________________

Find Circumference Using a Formula

Study the example showing how to find the circumference of a circle using a formula. Then solve problems 1–9.

Example

The diameter of the outer edge of a trampoline is 14 feet. There is 1 foot between the outer edge of the trampoline and a safety enclosure. What is the circumference of the enclosure?

To find the circumference of the enclosure, first find its diameter. The diagram shows that the diameter of the enclosure is $14\frac{1}{2} - (2 \times 1)$, or $12\frac{1}{2}$ feet.

The formula for the circumference of a circle is $C = \pi d$, where C is the circumference and d is the diameter. Use 3.14 for π.

$C = \pi d = 3.14d = 3.14 \times 12\frac{1}{2}$ ft $= 39.25$ ft

B 1 What is the circumference of the trampoline including its outer edge? Use 3.14 for π.

$C = 3.14 \times 14\frac{1}{2}$ ft $= 45.53$ ft

B 2 What is the difference between the circumference of the trampoline and the circumference of the enclosure?

$45.53 - 39.25 = 6.28$ ft

M 3 Explain how to find the circumference of a circle if you know the radius of the circle.

Multiply the radius of the circle by 2 to find the diameter. Then multiply the diameter of the circle by 3.14 to find the circumference.

M 4 The United States Capitol Rotunda is a circular room located in the Capitol Building in Washington, D.C. The radius of the room is 48 feet. What is its circumference?

The diameter is 2×48, or 96 ft; $C = \pi d = 3.14 \times 96 = 301.44$ ft

Vocabulary

circumference the distance around a circle.

diameter the distance across a circle through the center.

radius the distance from the center to any point on a circle.

Lesson 21 Area and Circumference of a Circle 221

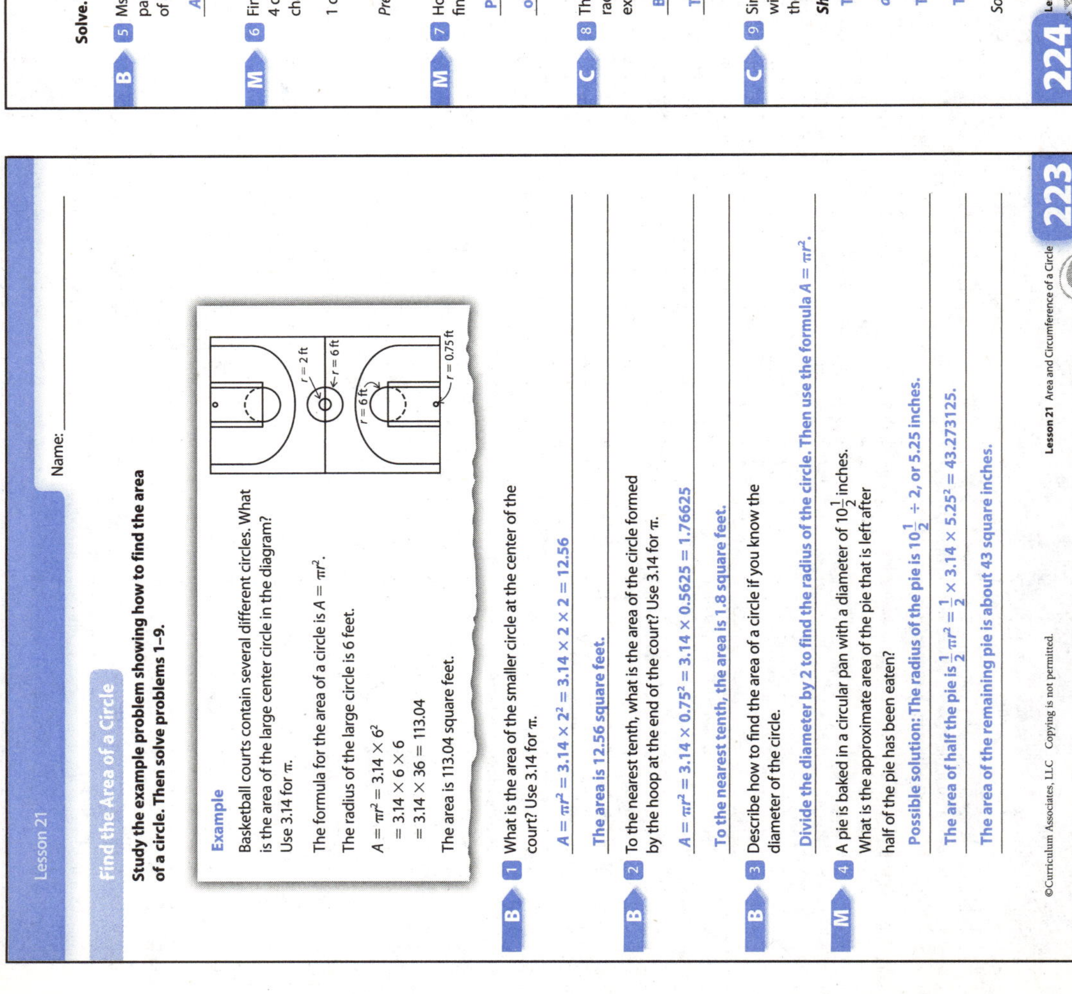

Lesson 21

Name: ______________________

Find the Area of a Circle

Study the example problem showing how to find the area of a circle. Then solve problems 1–9.

Example

Basketball courts contain several different circles. What is the area of the large center circle in the diagram? Use 3.14 for π.

The formula for the area of a circle is $A = \pi r^2$.

The radius of the large circle is 6 feet.

$A = \pi r^2 = 3.14 \times 6^2$
$= 3.14 \times 6 \times 6$
$= 3.14 \times 36 = 113.04$

The area is 113.04 square feet.

B **1** What is the area of the smaller circle at the center of the court? Use 3.14 for π.

$A = \pi r^2 = 3.14 \times 2^2 = 3.14 \times 2 \times 2 = 12.56$

The area is 12.56 square feet.

B **2** To the nearest tenth, what is the area of the circle formed by the hoop at the end of the court? Use 3.14 for π.

$A = \pi r^2 = 3.14 \times 0.75^2 = 3.14 \times 0.5625 = 1.76625$

To the nearest tenth, the area is 1.8 square feet.

B **3** Describe how to find the area of a circle if you know the diameter of the circle.

Divide the diameter by 2 to find the radius of the circle. Then use the formula $A = \pi r^2$.

M **4** A pie is baked in a circular pan with a diameter of $10\frac{1}{2}$ inches. What is the approximate area of the pie that is left after half of the pie has been eaten?

Possible solution: The radius of the pie is $10\frac{1}{2} \div 2$, or 5.25 inches.

The area of half the pie is $\frac{1}{2}\pi r^2 = \frac{1}{2} \times 3.14 \times 5.25^2 = 43.273125$.

The area of the remaining pie is about 43 square inches.

©Curriculum Associates, LLC Copying is not permitted. **Lesson 21** Area and Circumference of a Circle 223

Solve. Use 3.14 for π.

B **5** Ms. Kwan's class is playing games using a circular parachute during recess. The parachute has a radius of 8 feet. What is the area of the parachute?

$A = \pi r^2 = 3.14 \times 8^2 = 3.14 \times 64 = 200.96$ square feet

M **6** Find the areas of circles with radii of 1, 2, and 4 centimeters. Then predict how the area of a circle changes when the radius is doubled.

1 cm: $3.14\ cm^2$ 2 cm: $12.56\ cm^2$ 4 cm: $50.24\ cm^2$

Prediction: When the radius is doubled, the area is multiplied by 4.

M **7** How is finding the area of a circle with a given radius like finding the circumference of the circle?

Possible answer: Both involve the product of r and π. The circumference is the product of 2, π, and r, while the area is the product of r, π, and r.

C **8** The exact area of a circle is 81π square inches. What are the radius and diameter of the circle? Show your equation and explain your answers.

Because $\pi r^2 = 81\pi$, $r^2 = 81$. I know that $9 \times 9 = 81$, so $r = 9$.

Therefore, the radius is 9 inches and the diameter is $2 \times 9 = 18$ inches.

C **9** Simon has 18.5 feet of fencing. He makes a circular garden with the fencing. What is the area of Simon's garden to the nearest square foot?

Show your work.

The circumference of the garden is 18 ft, so $3.14d = 18.5$.

$d = 18.5 \div 3.14$, or about 5.89 feet.

The radius is about $5.89 \div 2$, or about 2.95 feet.

The area of the garden is about 3.14×2.95^2, or about 27.33 square feet.

Solution: To the nearest square foot, the area of the garden is 27 square feet.

224 **Lesson 21** Area and Circumference of a Circle ©Curriculum Associates, LLC Copying is not permitted.

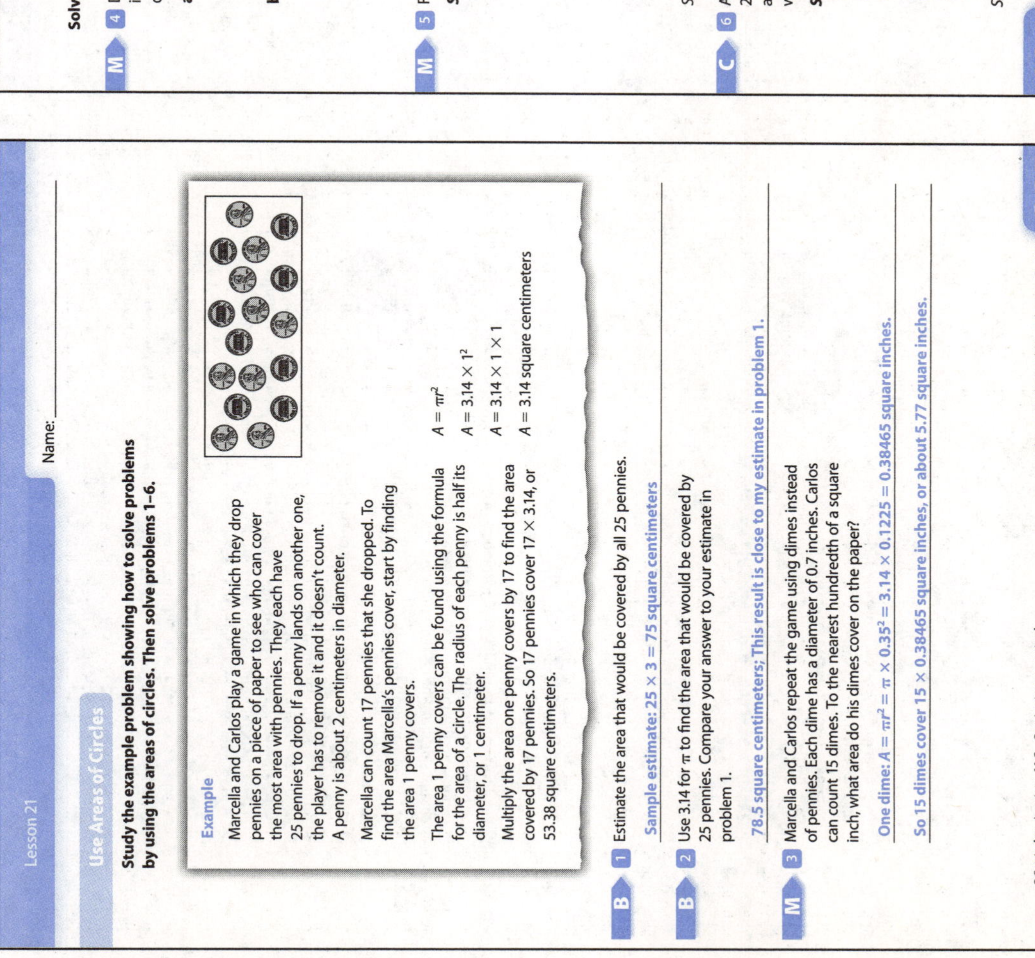

Lesson 21

Name: ______________________

Use Areas of Circles

Study the example problem showing how to solve problems by using the areas of circles. Then solve problems 1–6.

Example

Marcella and Carlos play a game in which they drop pennies on a piece of paper to see who can cover the most area with pennies. They each have 25 pennies to drop. If a penny lands on another one, the player has to remove it and it doesn't count. A penny is about 2 centimeters in diameter.

Marcella can count 17 pennies that she dropped. To find the area Marcella's pennies cover, start by finding the area 1 penny covers.

The area 1 penny covers can be found using the formula for the area of a circle. The radius of each penny is half its diameter, or 1 centimeter.

$A = \pi r^2$

$A = 3.14 \times 1^2$

$A = 3.14 \times 1 \times 1$

$A = 3.14$ square centimeters

Multiply the area one penny covers by 17 to find the area covered by 17 pennies. So 17 pennies cover 17×3.14, or 53.38 square centimeters.

B 1 Estimate the area that would be covered by all 25 pennies.

Sample estimate: $25 \times 3 = 75$ square centimeters

B 2 Use 3.14 for π to find the area that would be covered by 25 pennies. Compare your answer to your estimate in problem 1.

78.5 square centimeters; This result is close to my estimate in problem 1.

M 3 Marcella and Carlos repeat the game using dimes instead of pennies. Each dime has a diameter of 0.7 inches. Carlos can count 15 dimes. To the nearest hundredth of a square inch, what area do his dimes cover on the paper?

One dime: $A = \pi r^2 = \pi \times 0.35^2 = 3.14 \times 0.1225 = 0.38465$ square inches.

So 15 dimes cover 15×0.38465 square inches, or about 5.77 square inches.

©Curriculum Associates, LLC Copying is not permitted. Lesson 21 Area and Circumference of a Circle 225

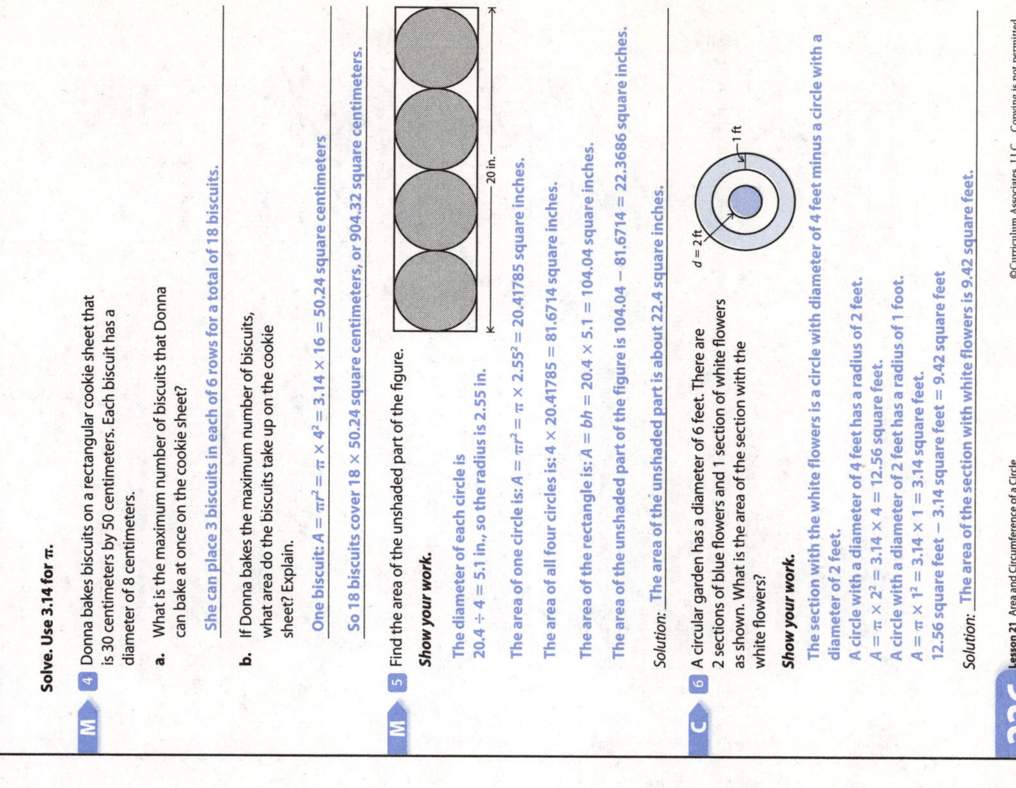

Solve. Use 3.14 for π.

M 4 Donna bakes biscuits on a rectangular cookie sheet that is 30 centimeters by 50 centimeters. Each biscuit has a diameter of 8 centimeters.

a. What is the maximum number of biscuits that Donna can bake at once on the cookie sheet?

She can place 3 biscuits in each of 6 rows for a total of 18 biscuits.

b. If Donna bakes the maximum number of biscuits, what area do the biscuits take up on the cookie sheet? Explain.

One biscuit: $A = \pi r^2 = \pi \times 4^2 = 3.14 \times 16 = 50.24$ square centimeters

So 18 biscuits cover 18×50.24 square centimeters, or 904.32 square centimeters.

M 5 Find the area of the unshaded part of the figure.

Show your work.

The diameter of each circle is $20.4 \div 4 = 5.1$ in., so the radius is 2.55 in.

The area of one circle is: $A = \pi r^2 = \pi \times 2.55^2 = 20.41785$ square inches.

The area of all four circles is: $4 \times 20.41785 = 81.6714$ square inches.

The area of the rectangle is: $A = bh = 20.4 \times 5.1 = 104.04$ square inches.

The area of the unshaded part of the figure is $104.04 - 81.6714 = 22.3686$ square inches.

Solution: The area of the unshaded part is about 22.4 square inches.

C 6 A circular garden has a diameter of 6 feet. There are 2 sections of blue flowers and 1 section of white flowers as shown. What is the area of the section with the white flowers?

Show your work.

The section with the white flowers is a circle with diameter of 4 feet minus a circle with a diameter of 2 feet.

A circle with a diameter of 4 feet has a radius of 2 feet.

$A = \pi \times 2^2 = 3.14 \times 4 = 12.56$ square feet.

A circle with a diameter of 2 feet has a radius of 1 foot.

$A = \pi \times 1^2 = 3.14 \times 1 = 3.14$ square feet.

12.56 square feet − 3.14 square feet = 9.42 square feet

Solution: The area of the section with white flowers is 9.42 square feet.

226 Lesson 21 Area and Circumference of a Circle ©Curriculum Associates, LLC Copying is not permitted.

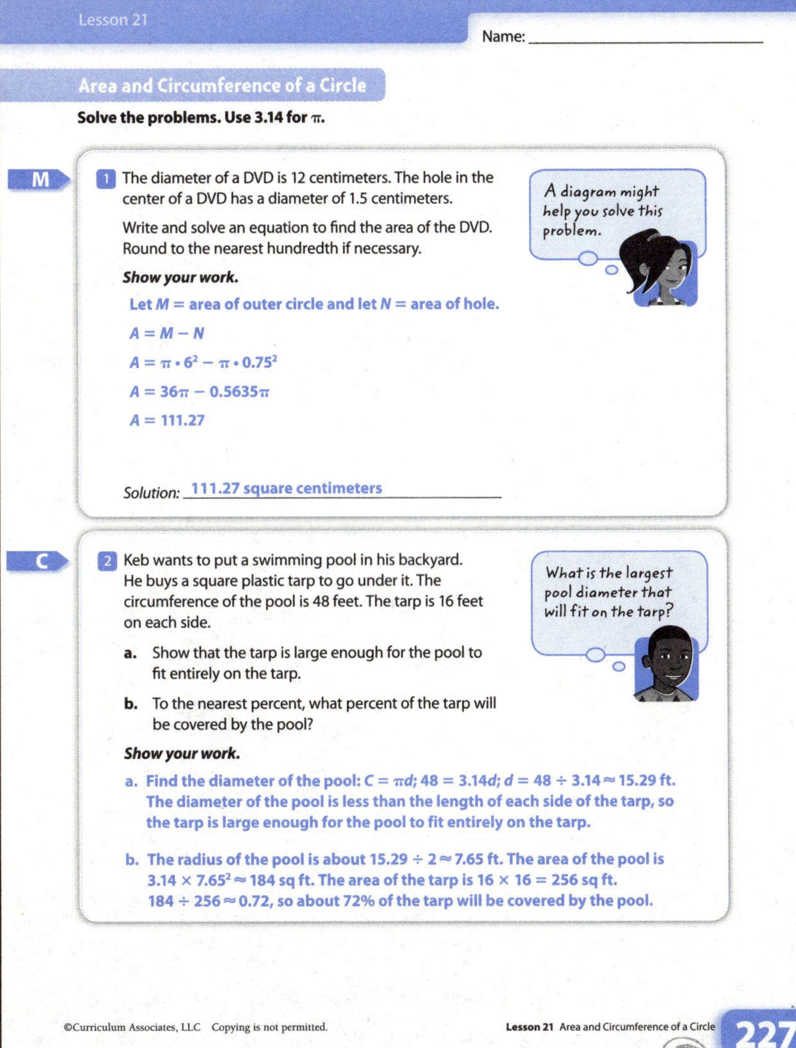
Lesson 21

Area and Circumference of a Circle

Name: ____________________

Solve the problems. Use 3.14 for π.

M

1 The diameter of a DVD is 12 centimeters. The hole in the center of a DVD has a diameter of 1.5 centimeters.

Write and solve an equation to find the area of the DVD. Round to the nearest hundredth if necessary.

Show your work.

Let M = area of outer circle and let N = area of hole.

$A = M - N$

$A = \pi \cdot 6^2 - \pi \cdot 0.75^2$

$A = 36\pi - 0.5635\pi$

$A = 111.27$

Solution: **111.27 square centimeters**

C

2 Keb wants to put a swimming pool in his backyard. He buys a square plastic tarp to go under it. The circumference of the pool is 48 feet. The tarp is 16 feet on each side.

a. Show that the tarp is large enough for the pool to fit entirely on the tarp.

b. To the nearest percent, what percent of the tarp will be covered by the pool?

Show your work.

a. Find the diameter of the pool: $C = \pi d$; $48 = 3.14d$; $d = 48 \div 3.14 \approx 15.29$ ft. The diameter of the pool is less than the length of each side of the tarp, so the tarp is large enough for the pool to fit entirely on the tarp.

b. The radius of the pool is about $15.29 \div 2 \approx 7.65$ ft. The area of the pool is $3.14 \times 7.65^2 \approx 184$ sq ft. The area of the tarp is $16 \times 16 = 256$ sq ft. $184 \div 256 \approx 0.72$, so about 72% of the tarp will be covered by the pool.

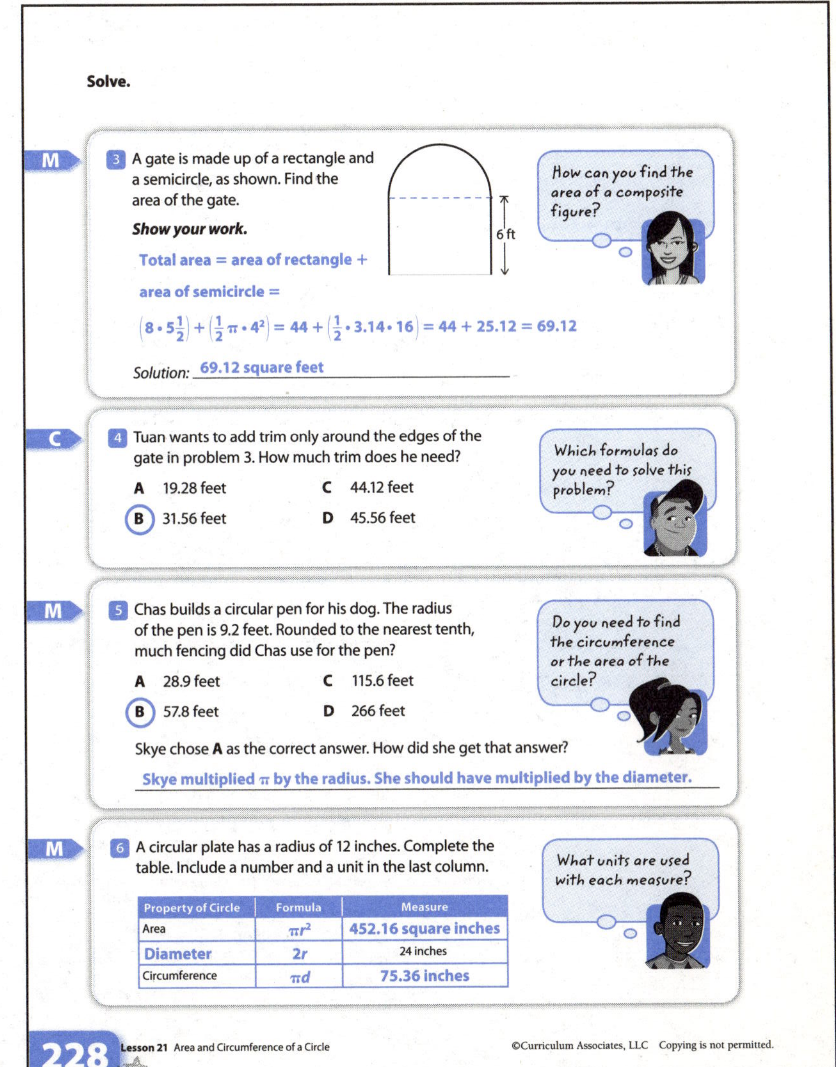
Solve.

M

3 A gate is made up of a rectangle and a semicircle, as shown. Find the area of the gate.

Show your work.

Total area = area of rectangle + area of semicircle =

$\left(8 \cdot 5\frac{1}{2}\right) + \left(\frac{1}{2}\pi \cdot 4^2\right) = 44 + \left(\frac{1}{2} \cdot 3.14 \cdot 16\right) = 44 + 25.12 = 69.12$

Solution: **69.12 square feet**

C

4 Tuan wants to add trim only around the edges of the gate in problem 3. How much trim does he need?

A 19.28 feet
(B) 31.56 feet
C 44.12 feet
D 45.56 feet

M

5 Chas builds a circular pen for his dog. The radius of the pen is 9.2 feet. Rounded to the nearest tenth, much fencing did Chas use for the pen?

A 28.9 feet
(B) 57.8 feet
C 115.6 feet
D 266 feet

Skye chose **A** as the correct answer. How did she get that answer?

Skye multiplied π by the radius. She should have multiplied by the diameter.

M

6 A circular plate has a radius of 12 inches. Complete the table. Include a number and a unit in the last column.

Property of Circle	Formula	Measure
Area	πr^2	**452.16 square inches**
Diameter	**$2r$**	24 inches
Circumference	πd	**75.36 inches**

Scale Drawings

Name: ______________________

Prerequisite: Find Equivalent Ratios

Study the example problem showing how to find equivalent ratios. Then solve problems 1–8.

Example

An art teacher needs to buy 5 boxes of markers to complete a project with a class of 20 students. How many boxes of markers will he need to buy for a class of 28 students?

You can draw a diagram to represent this relationship.

From the diagram, you can see that for every 4 students the teacher needs one box of markers.

B 1 Use the diagram to write a ratio that represents the number of students per box of markers. 4 : 1

B 2 How can you use the ratio you wrote in problem 1 to find the number of boxes of markers needed for a class of 28 students? How many boxes of markers will the teacher need to buy for a class of 28 students?

I can find an equivalent ratio. 4 : 1 is equivalent to 28 : 7, so the teacher will need 7 boxes of markers.

B 3 You can also use a table to relate the number of students to the boxes of markers needed. Complete the table.

Number of Students	4	20	28	36	40
Boxes of Markers	1	5	7	9	10

M 4 How many boxes of markers should the teacher buy for a class of 30 students? Explain your answer.

8; The ratio 30 : 7.5 is equivalent to 4 : 1. But the teacher can't buy half of a box of markers, so he must buy 8 boxes.

Vocabulary

equivalent ratios two or more ratios that are equal to one another.

rate a comparison of the first quantity in a ratio to only one of the second quantity.

Solve.

M 5 Don buys 6 kiwis for $3. What would a customer pay for 9 kiwis? Explain.

$4.50; Possible explanation: The rate is 2 kiwis for $1, or 2 : 1. I can multiply both values in the ratio by 4.50 to get the equivalent ratio 9 : 4.50, so a customer would pay $4.50 for 9 kiwis.

M 6 Aya and Jenny are playing a game in which each correct answer is worth a certain number of points. Jenny got 4 correct answers for a total of 24 points, and then it was Aya's turn. Aya scored 36 points during her turn. How many correct answers did Aya get? Explain.

6; Possible explanation: Jenny scored 24 points for 4 correct answers, which means that each correct answer is worth 6 points, a ratio of 6 : 1. The ratio 6 : 1 is equivalent to 36 : 6, so Aya must have answered 6 questions correctly.

M 7 A school has a pep band, a sports band, a marching band, and a concert band. In each band, there are 2 trombones for every 5 trumpets. Complete the table for the bands.

Band	Trombones	Trumpets
Pep	2	5
Sports	4	10
Marching	8	20
Concert	6	15

C 8 At the Stop and Save grocery store, an 18-ounce box of Crunchy Oats costs $4.59, and a 15-ounce box costs $3.99.

a. Which box is the better buy? Explain.

The cost per ounce for the larger box is $4.59 ÷ 18, or 25.5 cents. The cost per ounce for the smaller box is $3.99 ÷ 15, or 26.6 cents. Because 25.5 < 26.6, the larger box is the better buy.

b. How much money would you save if you bought 90 ounces of cereal in the larger boxes rather than 90 ounces of cereal in the smaller boxes? Explain.

$0.99; Possible explanation: The cost for 90 ounces in the larger boxes is 90($0.255) = $22.95. The cost for 90 ounces in the smaller boxes is 90($0.266) = $23.94. $23.94 − $22.95 = $0.99.

Key

B Basic **M** Medium **C** Challenge

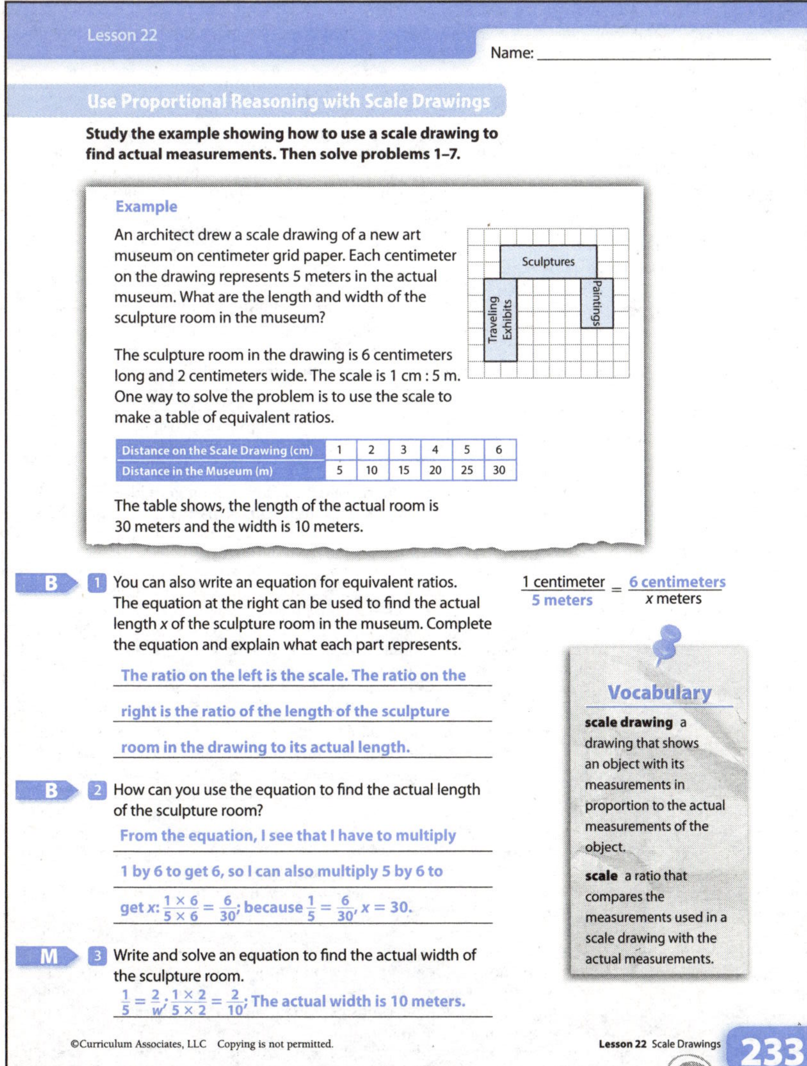

Name: ____________________

Use Proportional Reasoning with Scale Drawings

Study the example showing how to use a scale drawing to find actual measurements. Then solve problems 1–7.

Example

An architect drew a scale drawing of a new art museum on centimeter grid paper. Each centimeter on the drawing represents 5 meters in the actual museum. What are the length and width of the sculpture room in the museum?

The sculpture room in the drawing is 6 centimeters long and 2 centimeters wide. The scale is 1 cm : 5 m. One way to solve the problem is to use the scale to make a table of equivalent ratios.

Distance on the Scale Drawing (cm)	1	2	3	4	5	6
Distance in the Museum (m)	5	10	15	20	25	30

The table shows, the length of the actual room is 30 meters and the width is 10 meters.

B **1** You can also write an equation for equivalent ratios. The equation at the right can be used to find the actual length x of the sculpture room in the museum. Complete the equation and explain what each part represents.

$$\frac{1 \text{ centimeter}}{5 \text{ meters}} = \frac{6 \text{ centimeters}}{x \text{ meters}}$$

The ratio on the left is the scale. The ratio on the right is the ratio of the length of the sculpture room in the drawing to its actual length.

B **2** How can you use the equation to find the actual length of the sculpture room?

From the equation, I see that I have to multiply 1 by 6 to get 6, so I can also multiply 5 by 6 to get x: $\frac{1 \times 6}{5 \times 6} = \frac{6}{30}$; because $\frac{1}{5} = \frac{6}{30}$, $x = 30$.

M **3** Write and solve an equation to find the actual width of the sculpture room.

$\frac{1}{5} = \frac{2}{w}$; $\frac{1 \times 2}{5 \times 2} = \frac{2}{10}$; The actual width is 10 meters.

Vocabulary

scale drawing a drawing that shows an object with its measurements in proportion to the actual measurements of the object.

scale a ratio that compares the measurements used in a scale drawing with the actual measurements.

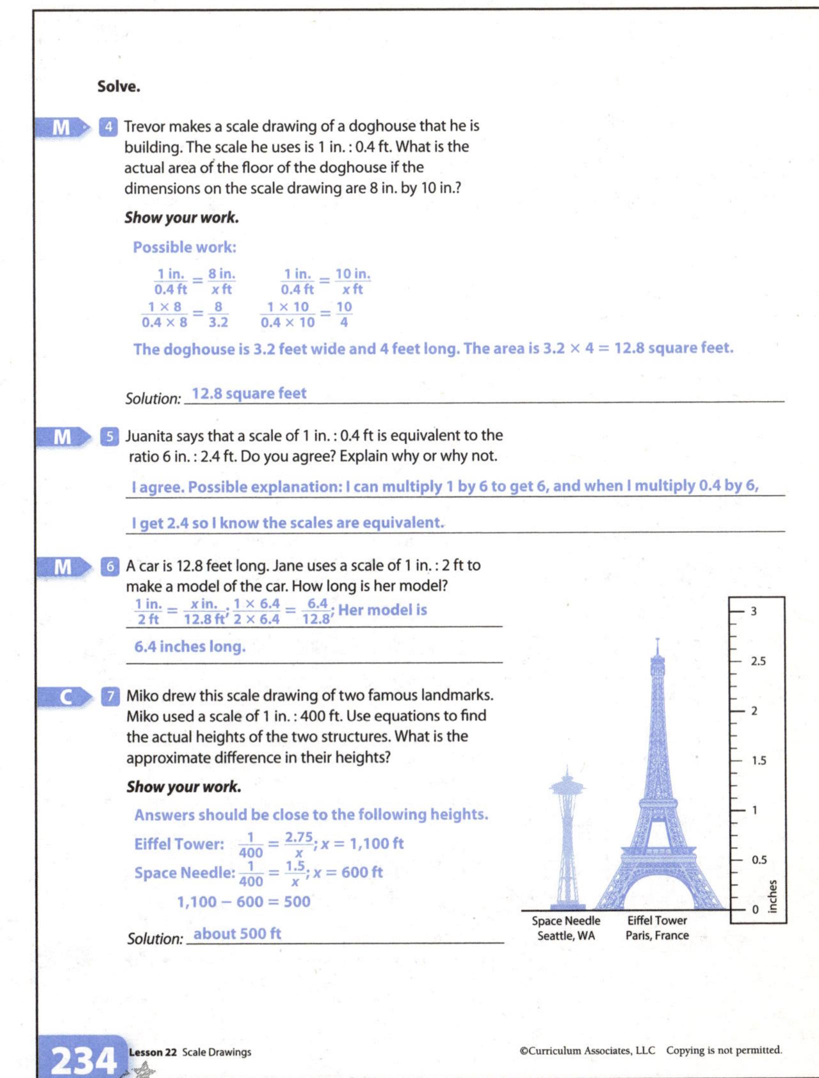

Solve.

M **4** Trevor makes a scale drawing of a doghouse that he is building. The scale he uses is 1 in. : 0.4 ft. What is the actual area of the floor of the doghouse if the dimensions on the scale drawing are 8 in. by 10 in.?

Show your work.

Possible work:

$\frac{1 \text{ in.}}{0.4 \text{ ft}} = \frac{8 \text{ in.}}{x \text{ ft}}$ $\qquad$ $\frac{1 \text{ in.}}{0.4 \text{ ft}} = \frac{10 \text{ in.}}{x \text{ ft}}$

$\frac{1 \times 8}{0.4 \times 8} = \frac{8}{3.2}$ $\qquad$ $\frac{1 \times 10}{0.4 \times 10} = \frac{10}{4}$

The doghouse is 3.2 feet wide and 4 feet long. The area is $3.2 \times 4 = 12.8$ square feet.

Solution: 12.8 square feet

M **5** Juanita says that a scale of 1 in. : 0.4 ft is equivalent to the ratio 6 in. : 2.4 ft. Do you agree? Explain why or why not.

I agree. Possible explanation: I can multiply 1 by 6 to get 6, and when I multiply 0.4 by 6, I get 2.4 so I know the scales are equivalent.

M **6** A car is 12.8 feet long. Jane uses a scale of 1 in. : 2 ft to make a model of the car. How long is her model?

$\frac{1 \text{ in.}}{2 \text{ ft}} = \frac{x \text{ in.}}{12.8 \text{ ft}}$; $\frac{1 \times 6.4}{2 \times 6.4} = \frac{6.4}{12.8}$; Her model is 6.4 inches long.

C **7** Miko drew this scale drawing of two famous landmarks. Miko used a scale of 1 in. : 400 ft. Use equations to find the actual heights of the two structures. What is the approximate difference in their heights?

Show your work.

Answers should be close to the following heights.

Eiffel Tower: $\frac{1}{400} = \frac{2.75}{x}$; $x = 1{,}100$ ft

Space Needle: $\frac{1}{400} = \frac{1.5}{x}$; $x = 600$ ft

$1{,}100 - 600 = 500$

Solution: about 500 ft

Name: ____________

Redraw a Scale

Study the example showing how to redraw a scale drawing using a different scale. Then solve problems 1–9.

Example

Heather uses centimeter grid paper to draw a scale diagram of her garden. Her real garden is 32 meters by 48 meters and Heather uses a scale of 1 cm : 8 m.

Heather needs a smaller scale drawing, so she changes the scale to 1 cm : 16 m. Now each centimeter represents 16 meters, not 8 meters.

B 1 Calculate the dimensions of the garden using the scale 1 cm : 16 m. Are the dimensions the same as they were using the scale 1 cm : 8 m?

3 cm represents 48 m and 2 cm represents 32 m, so the dimensions are the same.

M 2 How do the side lengths of Heather's new scale drawing compare to the side lengths of the original scale drawing? How can you compare the scales she used to explain this relationship?

The lengths in the new drawing are half the lengths in the original drawing because the new scale represents a distance that is twice as long as in the old scale.

B 3 You can also change the scale on a scale drawing to make the representation larger. Draw Heather's garden using a scale of 1 cm : 4 m.

M 4 Would a scale drawing of a door with a scale of 1 in. : 3 ft be longer or shorter than a scale drawing of the same door with a scale of 1 in. : 6 ft? Why?

Longer because the new scale represents a distance that is half as long as in the old scale.

Solve.

M 5 Diagrams A and B are scale drawings of the same field. Each square is 1 centimeter long. If the scale of diagram A is 1 cm : 24 ft, what is the scale of diagram B? 1 cm : 72 ft

A B

M 6 What is the area of the actual field represented in problem 5? How did you find your answer?

41,472 square feet; Possible explanation: I used scale drawing B to find that the length is 288 ft and the width is 144 ft, so the area is 288(144), or 41,472 square feet.

M 7 Jermaine draws a scale drawing of a porch on a grid with 1-centimeter squares. His drawing is a rectangle that is 6 cm by 9 cm, and he used the scale 1 cm : 4 ft. On this grid, redraw the scale drawing using a scale of 1 cm : 6 ft. Then find the actual area of the porch.

The porch is 36 ft long and 24 ft wide;

(36)(24) = 864 square feet.

C 8 Anna designs model planes. Her latest scale drawing has a scale of 1 in. : 24 in. In this drawing, the wing of a plane is 4 inches long. For an advertisement, Anna has to make a larger drawing. In this drawing, the wing of the plane is 10 inches long.

a. What is the actual length of the wing in feet? Explain.

8 ft; Possible explanation: $\frac{1}{24} = \frac{4}{x}$; $x = 96$ in., or 8 ft

b. What scale did Anna use on the advertisement drawing?

Possible answer: $\frac{1}{x} = \frac{10}{96}$; $x = 9.6$, so the scale is 1 in. : 9.6 in.

M 9 Arty says that if you change a scale so that a unit represents a longer distance than in an original scale, then the lengths in the new scale drawing will be longer. Do you agree? Give an example of a scale and some measurements to support your answer.

No; Possible answer: If a scale changes from 1 in. : 4 ft to 1 in. : 8 ft, then the measurements in the new scale drawing will be half as long. A length of 2 inches in the original scale drawing will be a length of 1 inch in the new scale drawing.

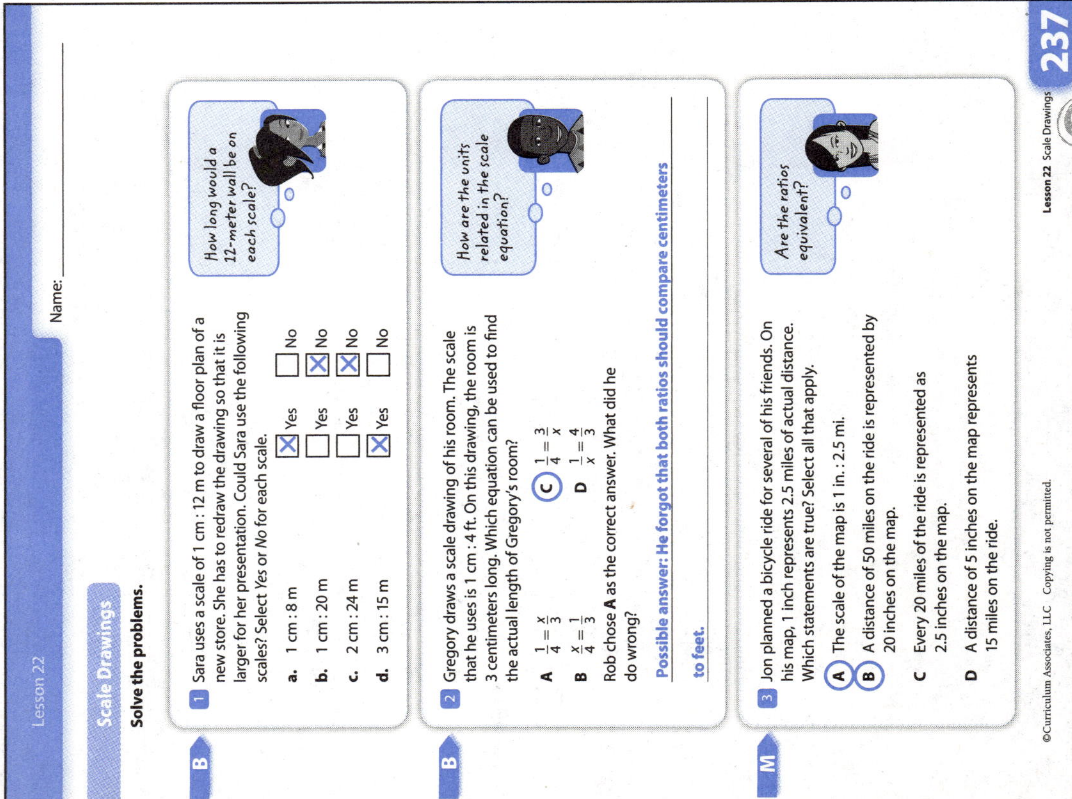

Name: ____________

Scale Drawings

Solve the problems.

B

1 Sara uses a scale of 1 cm : 12 m to draw a floor plan of a new store. She has to redraw the drawing so that it is larger for her presentation. Could Sara use the following scales? Select *Yes* or *No* for each scale.

a.	1 cm : 8 m	☒ Yes	☐ No
b.	1 cm : 20 m	☐ Yes	☒ No
c.	2 cm : 24 m	☐ Yes	☒ No
d.	3 cm : 15 m	☒ Yes	☐ No

B

2 Gregory draws a scale drawing of his room. The scale that he uses is 1 cm : 4 ft. On this drawing, the room is 3 centimeters long. Which equation can be used to find the actual length of Gregory's room?

A $\frac{1}{4} = \frac{x}{3}$ **(C)** $\frac{1}{4} = \frac{3}{x}$

B $\frac{x}{4} = \frac{1}{3}$ **D** $\frac{1}{x} = \frac{4}{3}$

Rob chose **A** as the correct answer. What did he do wrong?

Possible answer: He forgot that both ratios should compare centimeters to feet.

M

3 Jon planned a bicycle ride for several of his friends. On his map, 1 inch represents 2.5 miles of actual distance. Which statements are true? Select all that apply.

(A) The scale of the map is 1 in. : 2.5 mi.

(B) A distance of 50 miles on the ride is represented by 20 inches on the map.

C Every 20 miles of the ride is represented as 2.5 inches on the map.

D A distance of 5 inches on the map represents 15 miles on the ride.

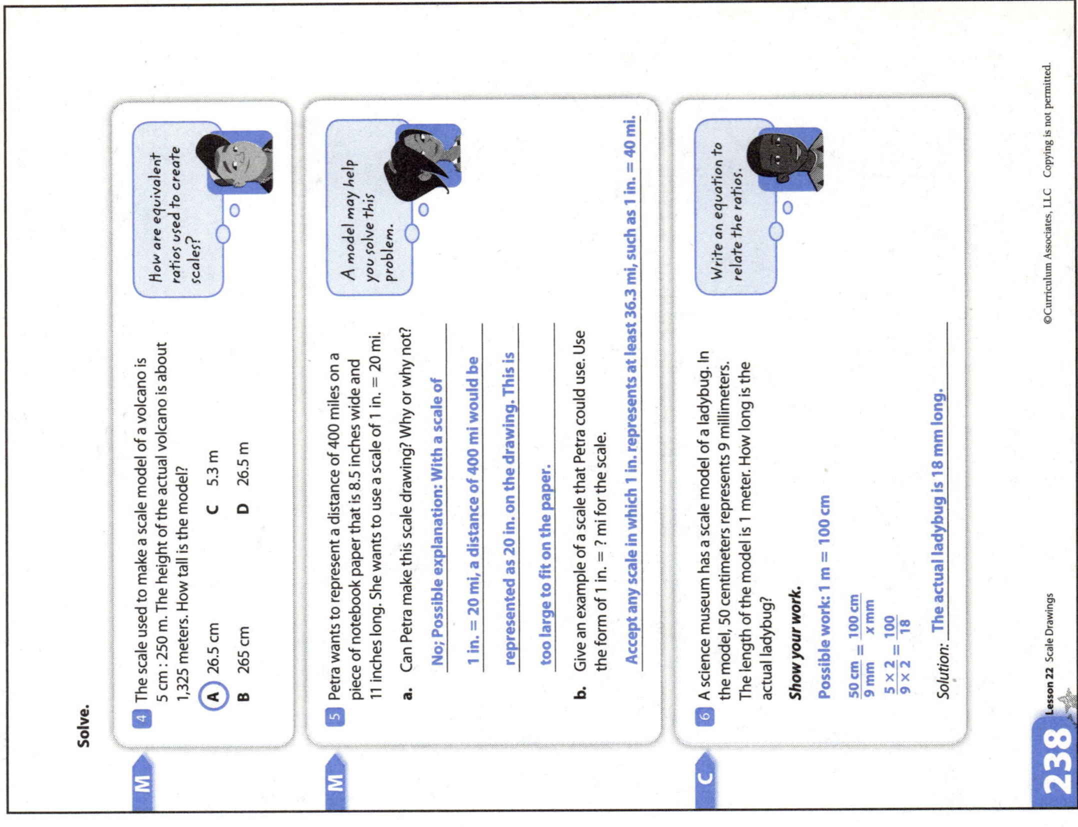

Solve.

M

4 The scale used to make a scale model of a volcano is 5 cm : 250 m. The height of the actual volcano is about 1,325 meters. How tall is the model?

(A) 26.5 cm **C** 5.3 m

B 265 cm **D** 26.5 m

M

5 Petra wants to represent a distance of 400 miles on a piece of notebook paper that is 8.5 inches wide and 11 inches long. She wants to use a scale of 1 in. = 20 mi.

a. Can Petra make this scale drawing? Why or why not?

No; Possible explanation: With a scale of 1 in. = 20 mi, a distance of 400 mi would be represented as 20 in. on the drawing. This is too large to fit on the paper.

b. Give an example of a scale that Petra could use. Use the form of 1 in. = ? mi for the scale.

Accept any scale in which 1 in. represents at least 36.3 mi, such as 1 in. = 40 mi.

C

6 A science museum has a scale model of a ladybug. In the model, 50 centimeters represents 9 millimeters. The length of the model is 1 meter. How long is the actual ladybug?

Show your work.

Possible work: 1 m = 100 cm

$\frac{50 \text{ cm}}{9 \text{ mm}} = \frac{100 \text{ cm}}{x \text{ mm}}$

$\frac{5 \times 2}{9 \times 2} = \frac{100}{18}$

Solution: **The actual ladybug is 18 mm long.**

Lesson 23

Volume of Solids

Name: ______________

Prerequisite: Volume of Rectangular Prisms

Study the example showing how to find the volume of a rectangular prism. Then solve problems 1–7.

Example

Alex is constructing a box in which to grow vegetables on his patio. The box will be 6 feet long, 2 feet wide, and $3\frac{1}{2}$ feet deep. What is the volume of soil needed to fill the box?

You can model the volume using 1-foot unit cubes. Notice that the first three layers are whole cubes, and the top layer is made up of half-cubes.

Cubes in one of the bottom 3 layers: $6 \cdot 2 = 12$

Total cubes in the bottom 3 layers: $3 \cdot 12 = 36$

Cubes in the top layer: $\frac{1}{2}(6 \cdot 2) = 6$

Total cubes needed to fill the box: $36 + 6 = 42$

Alex needs 42 cubic feet of soil to fill the box.

B **1** Why do you multiply 12 by 3 to find the total number of cubes in the bottom 3 layers?

There are 12 cubes in each layer, and there are 3 bottom layers.

B **2** Why do you multiply $(6 \cdot 2)$ by $\frac{1}{2}$ to find the number of cubes in the top layer?

Each cube in the top layer is 1 foot long, 1 foot wide, but only $\frac{1}{2}$ foot tall. This means that the top layer is 6 feet long, 2 feet wide, and $\frac{1}{2}$ foot tall.

B **3** Use the formula $V = lwh$ to find the volume of the box. Compare the volume found using the formula with the volume computed above.

$V = lwh = 6 \cdot 2 \cdot 3\frac{1}{2} = 6 \cdot 2 \cdot \frac{7}{2} = 42$ cubic feet; the volume is the same.

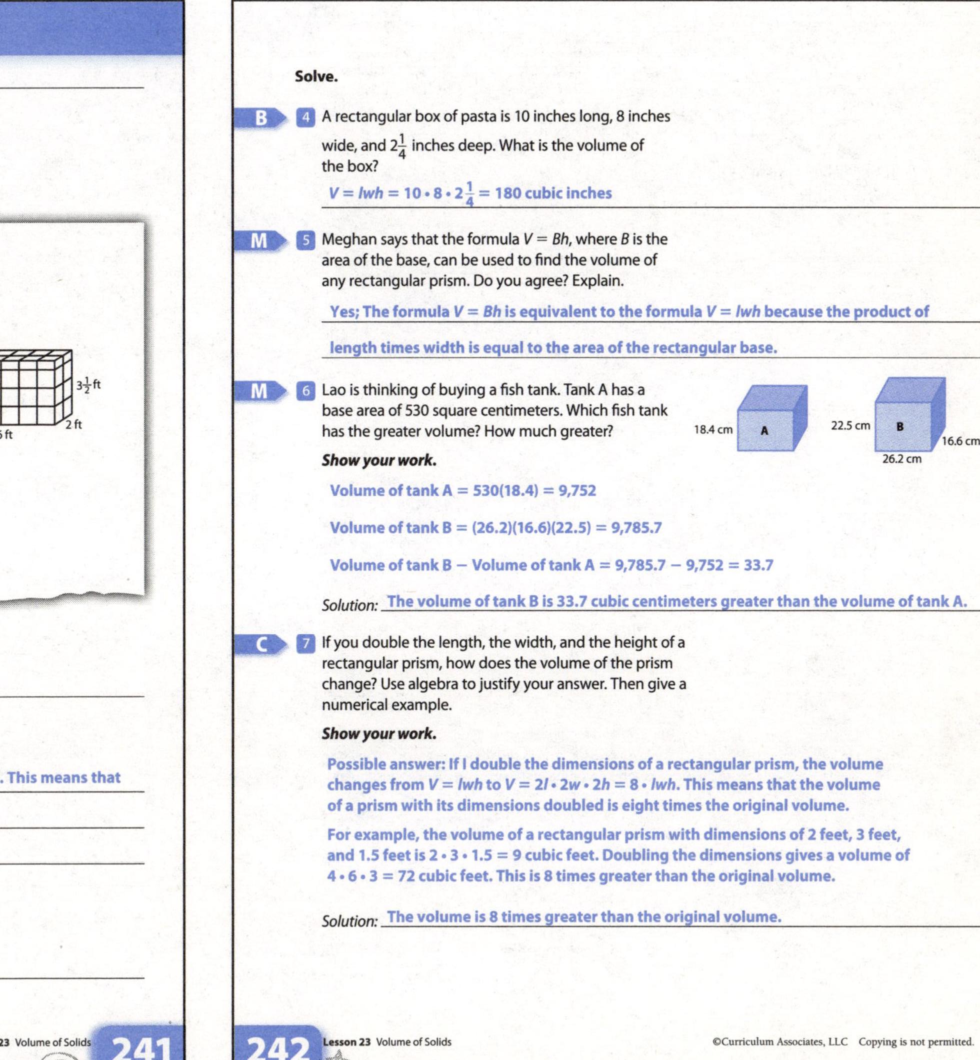

Solve.

B **4** A rectangular box of pasta is 10 inches long, 8 inches wide, and $2\frac{1}{4}$ inches deep. What is the volume of the box?

$V = lwh = 10 \cdot 8 \cdot 2\frac{1}{4} = 180$ cubic inches

M **5** Meghan says that the formula $V = Bh$, where B is the area of the base, can be used to find the volume of any rectangular prism. Do you agree? Explain.

Yes; The formula $V = Bh$ is equivalent to the formula $V = lwh$ because the product of length times width is equal to the area of the rectangular base.

M **6** Lao is thinking of buying a fish tank. Tank A has a base area of 530 square centimeters. Which fish tank has the greater volume? How much greater?

Show your work.

Volume of tank A = 530(18.4) = 9,752

Volume of tank B = (26.2)(16.6)(22.5) = 9,785.7

Volume of tank B − Volume of tank A = 9,785.7 − 9,752 = 33.7

Solution: The volume of tank B is 33.7 cubic centimeters greater than the volume of tank A.

C **7** If you double the length, the width, and the height of a rectangular prism, how does the volume of the prism change? Use algebra to justify your answer. Then give a numerical example.

Show your work.

Possible answer: If I double the dimensions of a rectangular prism, the volume changes from $V = lwh$ to $V = 2l \cdot 2w \cdot 2h = 8 \cdot lwh$. This means that the volume of a prism with its dimensions doubled is eight times the original volume.

For example, the volume of a rectangular prism with dimensions of 2 feet, 3 feet, and 1.5 feet is $2 \cdot 3 \cdot 1.5 = 9$ cubic feet. Doubling the dimensions gives a volume of $4 \cdot 6 \cdot 3 = 72$ cubic feet. This is 8 times greater than the original volume.

Solution: The volume is 8 times greater than the original volume.

Key

B Basic **M** Medium **C** Challenge

Lesson 23

Name: ____________

Volume of Prisms

Study the example problem showing how to find the volume of a prism. Then solve problems 1–7.

Example

A triangular prism is shown at the right. What is the volume of the prism?

The bases of this prism are the right triangles at either end of the prism. So, first find the area of one of the bases.

$\frac{1}{2}bh = \frac{1}{2}(6)(8) = 24$

The area of a triangular base is 24 square inches.

Next, use the formula $V = Bh$, where B is 24 and h is $22\frac{1}{4}$.

$V = Bh = 24(22\frac{1}{4}) = 534$

The volume of the prism is 534 cubic inches.

B 1 How do you know that the right triangles are the bases of the prism?

The bases of a prism are the same size and shape, and they are parallel.

B 2 Describe the faces of the prism that are not bases. How are they alike? How are they different?

The other faces are alike because they are all rectangles. They are different because they have different dimensions.

M 3 A second prism has dimensions that are $\frac{1}{2}$ of the dimensions of the prism in the example. Kathy says that the volume of the smaller prism is $\frac{1}{2}$ of the volume of the prism in the example. Do you agree? Explain.

Show your work.

Possible answer: The dimensions of the second prism are 3 inches, 4 inches, and $11\frac{1}{8}$ inches. The area of its base is $\frac{1}{2}(3)(4)$, or 6 square inches. Its volume is $V = Bh = 6(11\frac{1}{8})$, or $66\frac{3}{4}$ cubic inches, so the volume of the second prism is not $\frac{1}{2}$ of the volume of the prism in the example. It's actually $\frac{1}{8}$ of the volume.

Solution: No, the volume of the second prism is $\frac{1}{8}$ of the volume of the first prism.

Solve.

M 4 What is the volume of the prism shown?

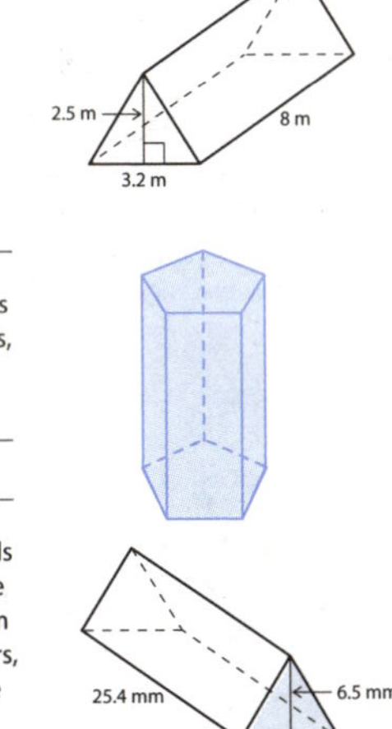

Show your work.

$B = \frac{1}{2}(2.5)(3.2) = 4$

$V = Bh = 4(8) = 32$

Solution: 32 cubic meters

M 5 A pentagonal prism is shown. The volume of the prism is 91.8 cubic inches. If the height of the prism is 10.8 inches, what is the area of each base? Explain.

$V = Bh$; $91.8 = B \cdot 10.8$; $B = 91.8 \div 10.8 = 8.5$

The area of each base is 8.5 square inches.

C 6 A store sells two types of tiny crystals. One of the crystals is a triangular prism whose dimensions are shown at the right. The other crystal is shaped like a rectangular prism with a length of 26 millimeters, a width of 8.5 millimeters, and a height of 7 millimeters. Alice says that the volume of the rectangular crystal is greater than two times the volume of the triangular crystal. Find the volumes to prove whether or not Alice is correct.

Show your work.

Volume of rectangular crystal $= lwh = 26(8.5)(7) = 1{,}547$

Area of base of triangular crystal: $B = \frac{1}{2}(8)(6.5) = 26$

Volume of triangular crystal $= Bh = 26 \cdot 25.4 = 660.4$

Because $660.4(2) = 1{,}320.8$, the volume of the rectangular crystal is greater than two times the volume of the triangular crystal.

Solution: Alice is correct.

C 7 Use the diagram at the right to write a formula in terms of b, h, and l for the volume of a triangular prism.

Show your work.

Area of triangular base: $\frac{1}{2}bh$

Volume of prism: $V = Bh = \frac{1}{2}bh \cdot l$

Solution: $V = \frac{1}{2}bhl$

Practice Lesson 23 Volume of Solids

Unit 4

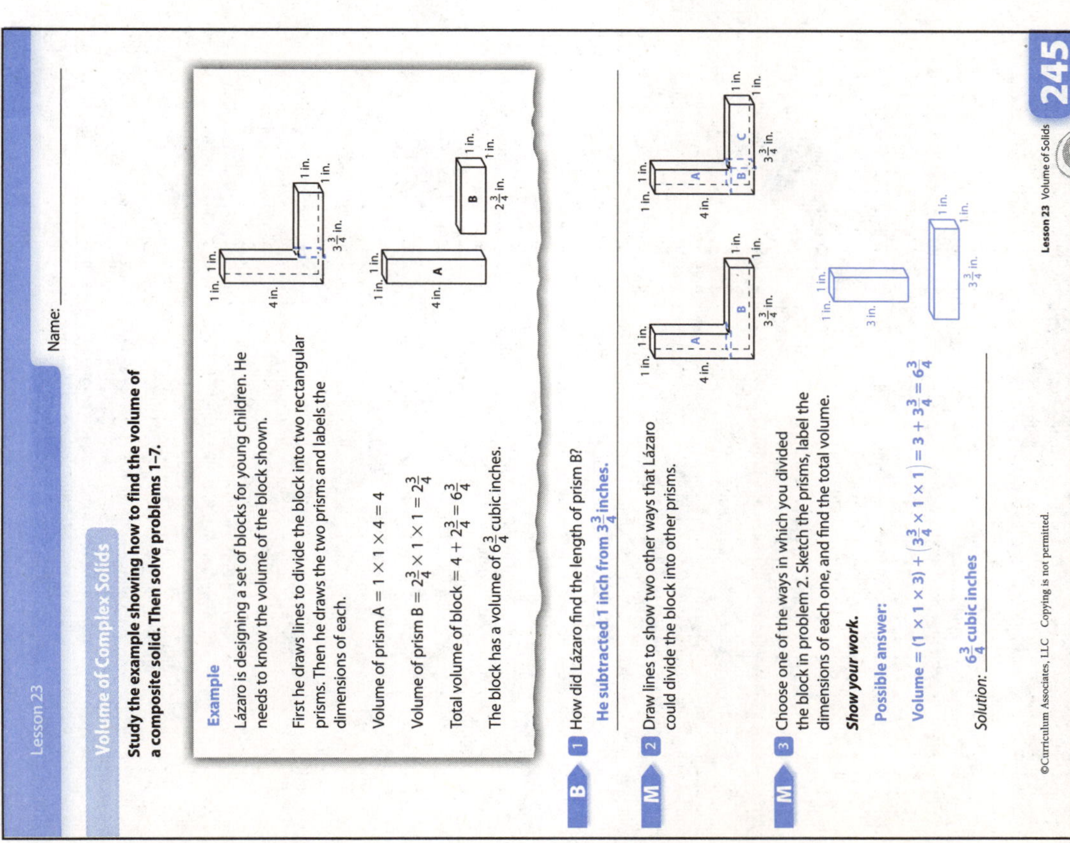

Lesson 23

Name: ______

Volume of Complex Solids

Study the example showing how to find the volume of a composite solid. Then solve problems 1–7.

Example

Lázaro is designing a set of blocks for young children. He needs to know the volume of the block shown.

First he draws lines to divide the block into two rectangular prisms. Then he draws the two prisms and labels the dimensions of each.

Volume of prism A = $1 \times 1 \times 4 = 4$

Volume of prism B = $2\frac{3}{4} \times 1 \times 1 = 2\frac{3}{4}$

Total volume of block = $4 + 2\frac{3}{4} = 6\frac{3}{4}$

The block has a volume of $6\frac{3}{4}$ cubic inches.

B **1** How did Lázaro find the length of prism B?

He subtracted 1 inch from $3\frac{3}{4}$ inches.

M **2** Draw lines to show two other ways that Lázaro could divide the block into other prisms.

M **3** Choose one of the ways in which you divided the block in problem 2. Sketch the prisms, label the dimensions of each one, and find the total volume.

Show your work.

Possible answer:

Volume = $(1 \times 1 \times 3) + \left(3\frac{3}{4} \times 1 \times 1\right) = 3 + 3\frac{3}{4} = 6\frac{3}{4}$

Solution: $6\frac{3}{4}$ cubic inches

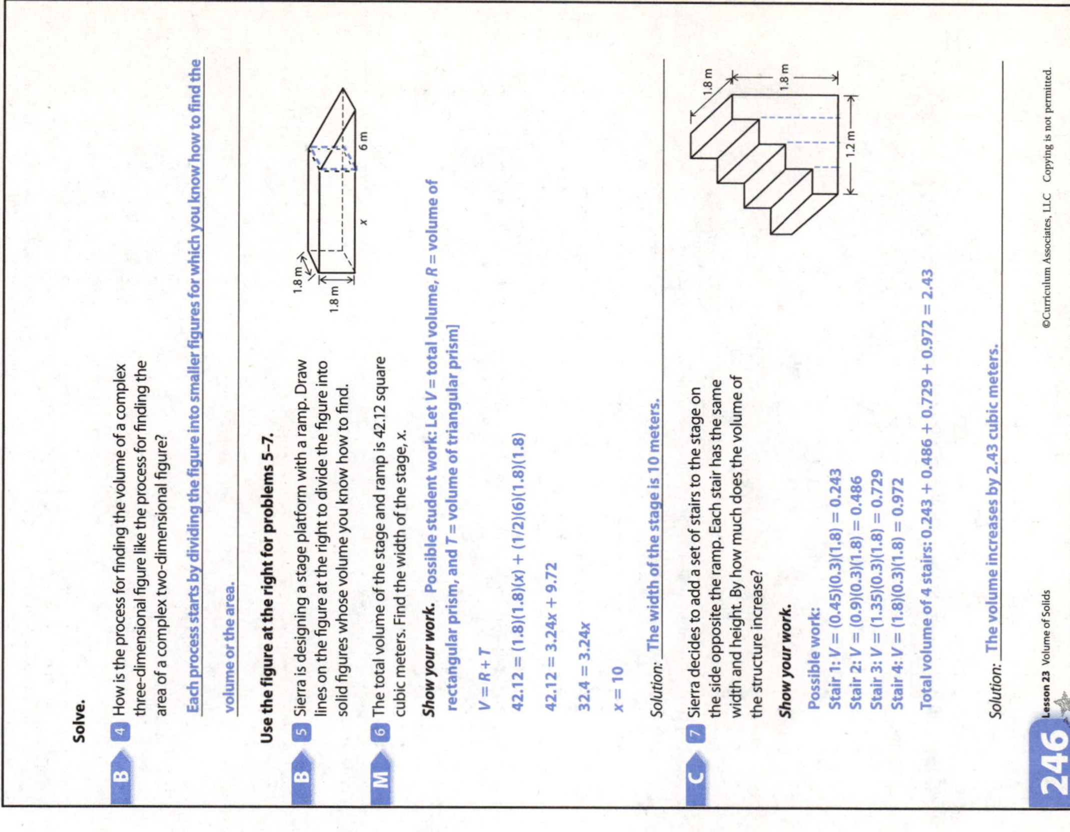

Solve.

B **4** How is the process for finding the volume of a complex three-dimensional figure like the process for finding the area of a complex two-dimensional figure?

Each process starts by dividing the figure into smaller figures for which you know how to find the volume or the area.

Use the figure at the right for problems 5–7.

B **5** Sierra is designing a stage platform with a ramp. Draw lines on the figure at the right to divide the figure into solid figures whose volume you know how to find.

M **6** The total volume of the stage and ramp is 42.12 square cubic meters. Find the width of the stage, x.

Show your work. Possible student work: Let V = total volume, R = volume of rectangular prism, and T = volume of triangular prism]

$V = R + T$

$42.12 = (1.8)(1.8)(x) + (1/2)(6)(1.8)(1.8)$

$42.12 = 3.24x + 9.72$

$32.4 = 3.24x$

$x = 10$

Solution: The width of the stage is 10 meters.

C **7** Sierra decides to add a set of stairs to the stage on the side opposite the ramp. Each stair has the same width and height. By how much does the volume of the structure increase?

Show your work.

Possible work:

Stair 1: $V = (0.45)(0.3)(1.8) = 0.243$

Stair 2: $V = (0.9)(0.3)(1.8) = 0.486$

Stair 3: $V = (1.35)(0.3)(1.8) = 0.729$

Stair 4: $V = (1.8)(0.3)(1.8) = 0.972$

Total volume of 4 stairs: $0.243 + 0.486 + 0.729 + 0.972 = 2.43$

Solution: The volume increases by 2.43 cubic meters.

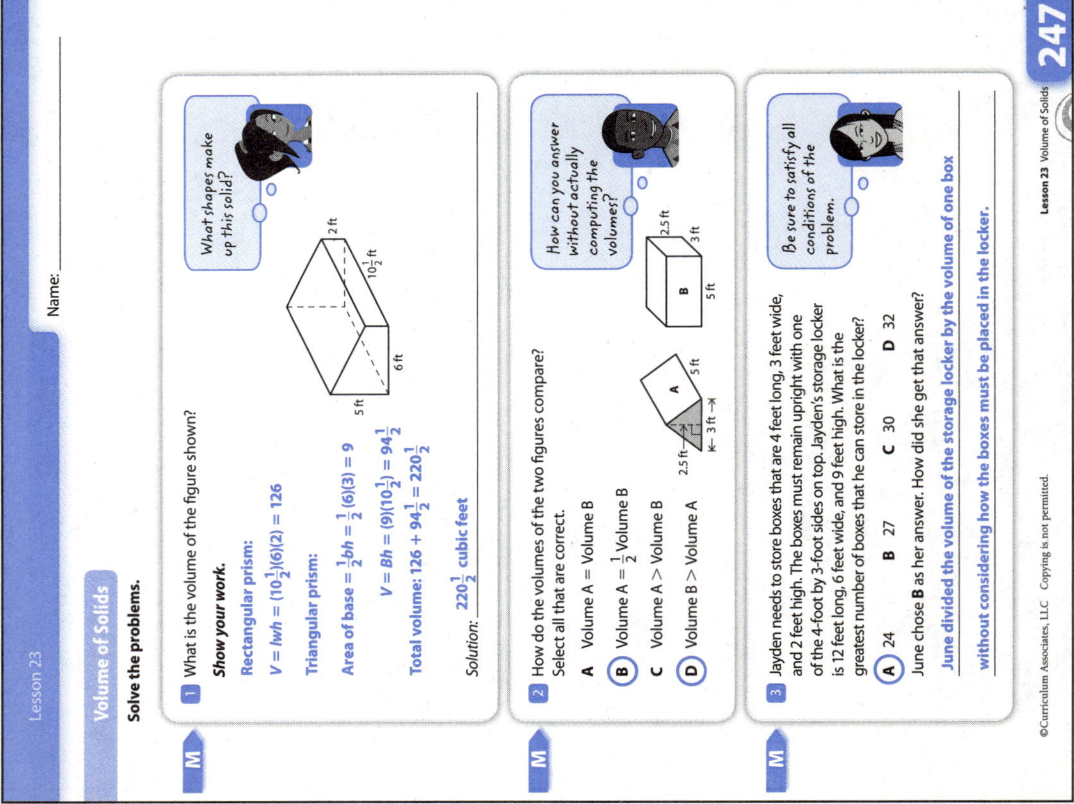

Lesson 23

Name: ______________________

Volume of Solids

Solve the problems.

M

1 What is the volume of the figure shown?

Show your work.

Rectangular prism:

$V = lwh = (10\frac{1}{2})(6)(2) = 126$

Triangular prism:

Area of base $= \frac{1}{2}bh = \frac{1}{2}(6)(3) = 9$

$V = Bh = (9)(10\frac{1}{2}) = 94\frac{1}{2}$

Total volume: $126 + 94\frac{1}{2} = 220\frac{1}{2}$

Solution: **$220\frac{1}{2}$ cubic feet**

M

2 How do the volumes of the two figures compare? Select all that are correct.

A Volume A = Volume B

(B) Volume A = $\frac{1}{2}$ Volume B

C Volume A > Volume B

(D) Volume B > Volume A

M

3 Jayden needs to store boxes that are 4 feet long, 3 feet wide, and 2 feet high. The boxes must remain upright with one of the 4-foot by 3-foot sides on top. Jayden's storage locker is 12 feet long, 6 feet wide, and 9 feet high. What is the greatest number of boxes that he can store in the locker?

(A) 24 B 27 C 30 D 32

June chose **B** as her answer. How did she get that answer?

June divided the volume of the storage locker by the volume of one box without considering how the boxes must be placed in the locker.

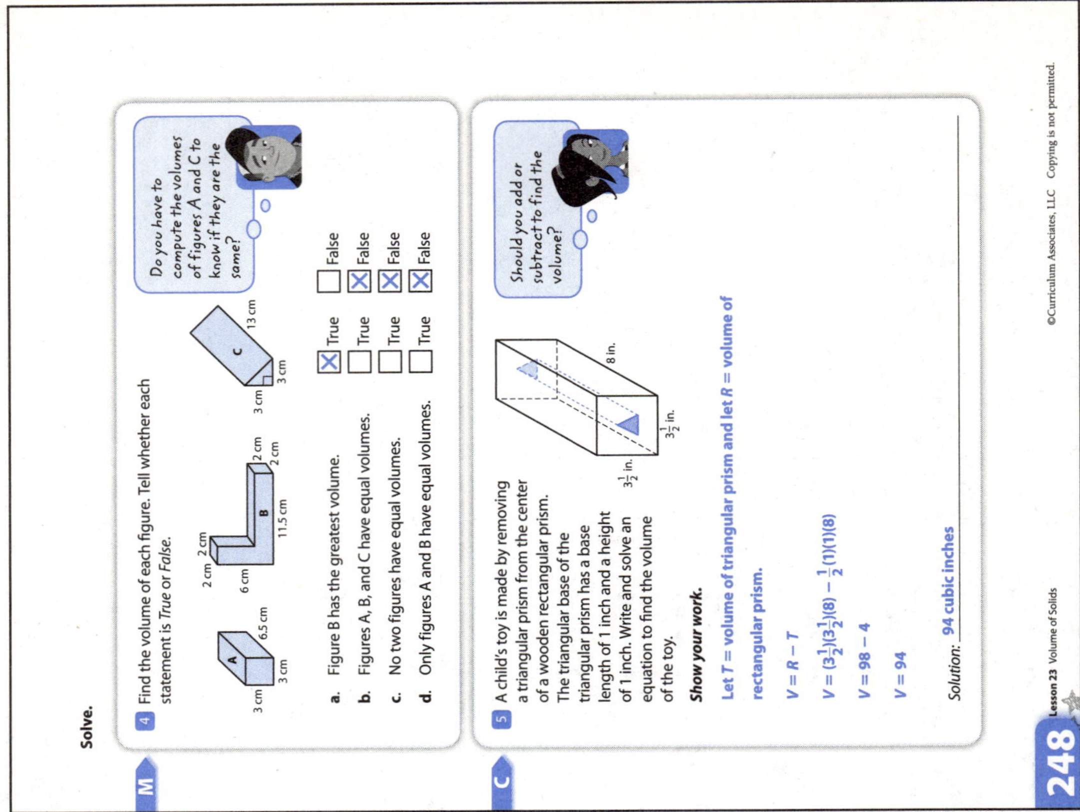

Solve.

M

4 Find the volume of each figure. Tell whether each statement is *True* or *False*.

a.	Figure B has the greatest volume.	☒ True	☐ False
b.	Figures A, B, and C have equal volumes.	☐ True	☒ False
c.	No two figures have equal volumes.	☐ True	☒ False
d.	Only figures A and B have equal volumes.	☐ True	☒ False

C

5 A child's toy is made by removing a triangular prism from the center of a wooden rectangular prism. The triangular base of the triangular prism has a base length of 1 inch and a height of 1 inch. Write and solve an equation to find the volume of the toy.

Show your work.

Let T = volume of triangular prism and let R = volume of rectangular prism.

$V = R - T$

$V = (3\frac{1}{2})(3\frac{1}{2})(8) - \frac{1}{2}(1)(1)(8)$

$V = 98 - 4$

$V = 94$

Solution: **94 cubic inches**

Lesson 24

Surface Area of Solids

Name: ____________________

Prerequisite: Use a Net to Find Surface Area

Study the example showing how to use a net to find the surface area of a prism. Then solve problems 1–7.

Example

Kioshi needs to find the surface area of a triangular prism with the dimensions shown. He begins by drawing a net of the triangular prism and labeling the dimensions of each face. Find the area of each face of the prism.

You can make a table that shows the dimensions and the area of each face of the prism.

Face	Base (in.)	Height (in.)	Area (sq in.)
Triangle	12	16	96
Triangle	12	16	96
Rectangle	10	12	120
Rectangle	10	16	160
Rectangle	10	20	200

B 1 Why do the two triangles have the same base length and height? How did you find the area of each triangle?

The bases of a triangular prism are congruent. I used the formula $A = \frac{1}{2}bh = \frac{1}{2}(12)(16) = 96$.

B 2 Do all the rectangles have equal areas? Explain.

No; The base lengths of the three rectangles are equal, but the heights are different because they touch different sides of the triangles.

B 3 What is the surface area of the prism? Explain how you found the surface area.

672 square inches; I added the areas of all of the faces.

Vocabulary

net a flat representation of a solid when it is "unfolded."

surface area the sum of the areas of all of the faces of a three-dimensional figure.

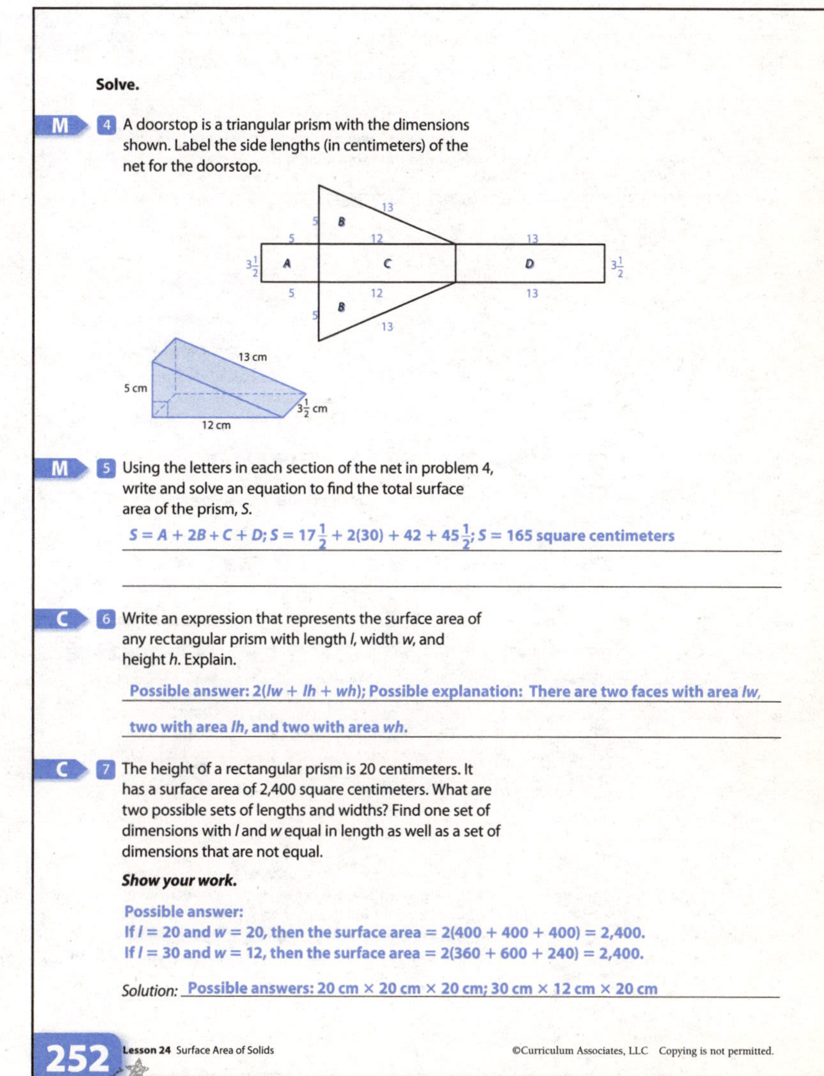

Solve.

M 4 A doorstop is a triangular prism with the dimensions shown. Label the side lengths (in centimeters) of the net for the doorstop.

M 5 Using the letters in each section of the net in problem 4, write and solve an equation to find the total surface area of the prism, *S*.

$S = A + 2B + C + D$; $S = 17\frac{1}{2} + 2(30) + 42 + 45\frac{1}{2}$; $S = 165$ square centimeters

C 6 Write an expression that represents the surface area of any rectangular prism with length *l*, width *w*, and height *h*. Explain.

Possible answer: $2(lw + lh + wh)$; Possible explanation: There are two faces with area *lw*, two with area *lh*, and two with area *wh*.

C 7 The height of a rectangular prism is 20 centimeters. It has a surface area of 2,400 square centimeters. What are two possible sets of lengths and widths? Find one set of dimensions with *l* and *w* equal in length as well as a set of dimensions that are not equal.

Show your work.

Possible answer:
If $l = 20$ and $w = 20$, then the surface area $= 2(400 + 400 + 400) = 2{,}400$.
If $l = 30$ and $w = 12$, then the surface area $= 2(360 + 600 + 240) = 2{,}400$.

Solution: Possible answers: 20 cm × 20 cm × 20 cm; 30 cm × 12 cm × 20 cm

Key

B Basic **M** Medium **C** Challenge

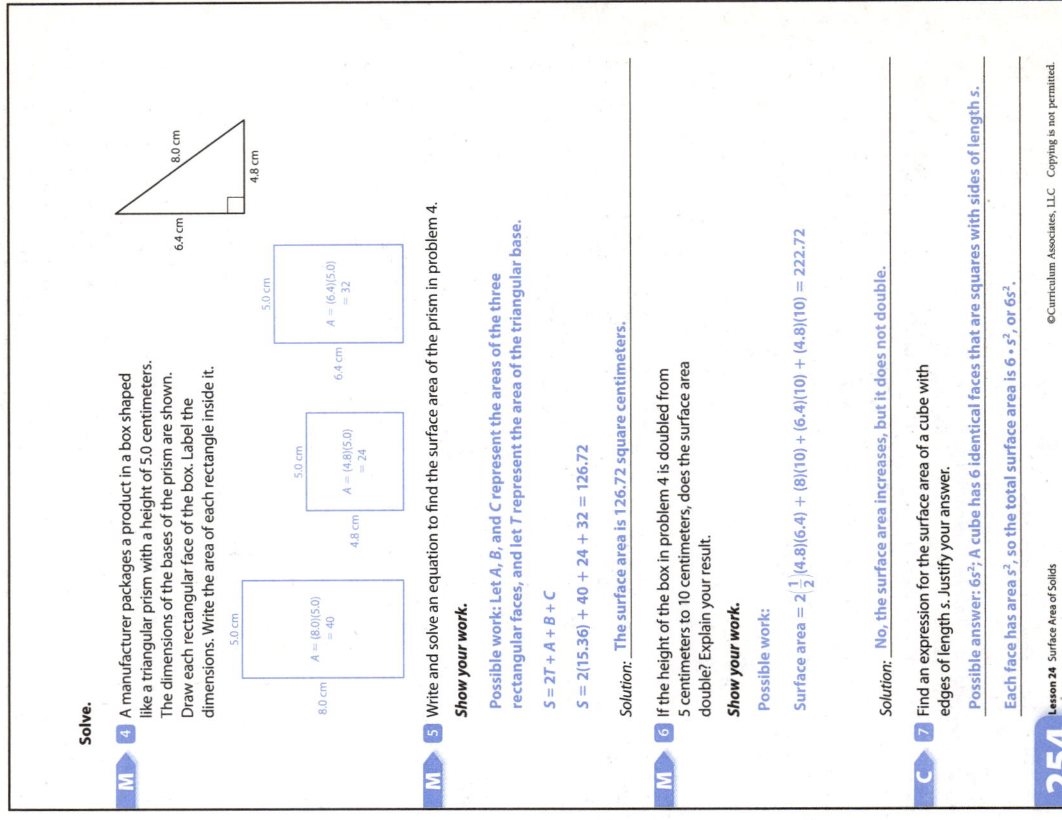

Solve.

M 4 A manufacturer packages a product in a box shaped like a triangular prism with a height of 5.0 centimeters. The dimensions of the bases of the prism are shown. Draw each rectangular face of the box. Label the dimensions. Write the area of each rectangle inside it.

M 5 Write and solve an equation to find the surface area of the prism in problem 4.

Show your work.

Possible work: Let *A*, *B*, and *C* represent the areas of the three rectangular faces, and let *T* represent the area of the triangular base.

$S = 2T + A + B + C$

$S = 2(15.36) + 40 + 24 + 32 = 126.72$

Solution: The surface area is 126.72 square centimeters.

M 6 If the height of the box in problem 4 is doubled from 5 centimeters to 10 centimeters, does the surface area double? Explain your result.

Show your work.

Possible work:

Surface area $= 2\left(\frac{1}{2}\right)(4.8)(6.4) + (8)(10) + (6.4)(10) + (4.8)(10) = 222.72$

Solution: No, the surface area increases, but it does not double.

C 7 Find an expression for the surface area of a cube with edges of length *s*. Justify your answer.

Possible answer: $6s^2$; A cube has 6 identical faces that are squares with sides of length *s*. Each face has area s^2, so the total surface area is $6 \cdot s^2$, or $6s^2$.

254 Lesson 24 Surface Area of Solids ©Curriculum Associates, LLC Copying is not permitted.

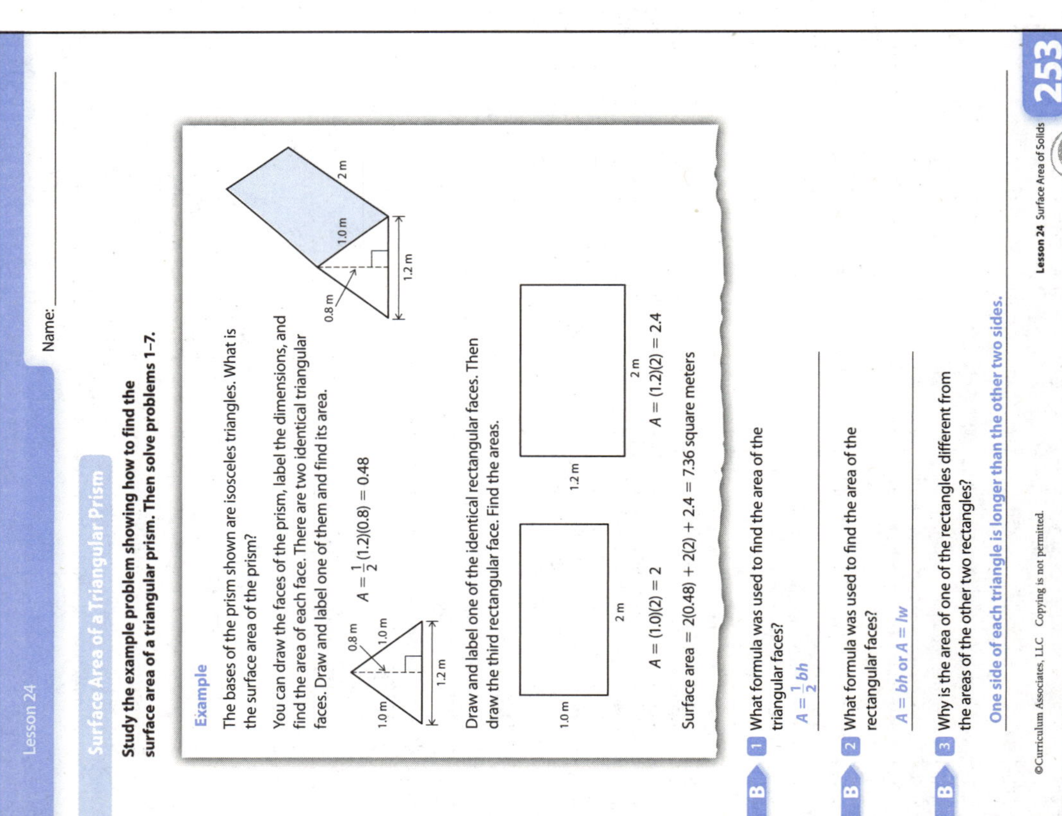

Lesson 24

Name: ____________

Surface Area of a Triangular Prism

Study the example problem showing how to find the surface area of a triangular prism. Then solve problems 1–7.

Example

The bases of the prism shown are isosceles triangles. What is the surface area of the prism?

You can draw the faces of the prism, label the dimensions, and find the area of each face. There are two identical triangular faces. Draw and label one of them and find its area.

$A = \frac{1}{2}(1.2)(0.8) = 0.48$

Draw and label one of the identical rectangular faces. Then draw the third rectangular face. Find the areas.

$A = (1.0)(2) = 2$ $A = (1.2)(2) = 2.4$

Surface area $= 2(0.48) + 2(2) + 2.4 = 7.36$ square meters

B 1 What formula was used to find the area of the triangular faces?

$A = \frac{1}{2}bh$

B 2 What formula was used to find the area of the rectangular faces?

$A = bh$ or $A = lw$

B 3 Why is the area of one of the rectangles different from the areas of the other two rectangles?

One side of each triangle is longer than the other two sides.

©Curriculum Associates, LLC Copying is not permitted. Lesson 24 Surface Area of Solids 253

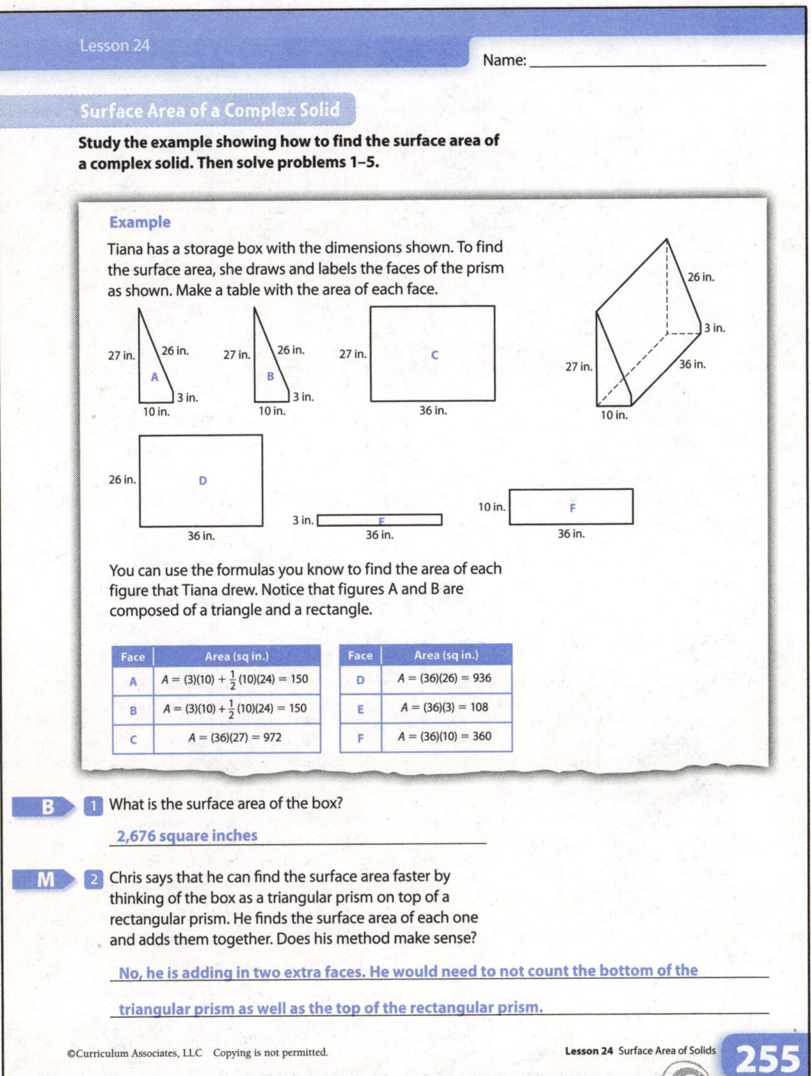

Lesson 24

Name: ____________

Surface Area of a Complex Solid

Study the example showing how to find the surface area of a complex solid. Then solve problems 1–5.

Example

Tiana has a storage box with the dimensions shown. To find the surface area, she draws and labels the faces of the prism as shown. Make a table with the area of each face.

You can use the formulas you know to find the area of each figure that Tiana drew. Notice that figures A and B are composed of a triangle and a rectangle.

Face	Area (sq in.)
A	$A = (3)(10) + \frac{1}{2}(10)(24) = 150$
B	$A = (3)(10) + \frac{1}{2}(10)(24) = 150$
C	$A = (36)(27) = 972$
D	$A = (36)(26) = 936$
E	$A = (36)(3) = 108$
F	$A = (36)(10) = 360$

B **1** What is the surface area of the box?

2,676 square inches

M **2** Chris says that he can find the surface area faster by thinking of the box as a triangular prism on top of a rectangular prism. He finds the surface area of each one and adds them together. Does his method make sense?

No, he is adding in two extra faces. He would need to not count the bottom of the triangular prism as well as the top of the rectangular prism.

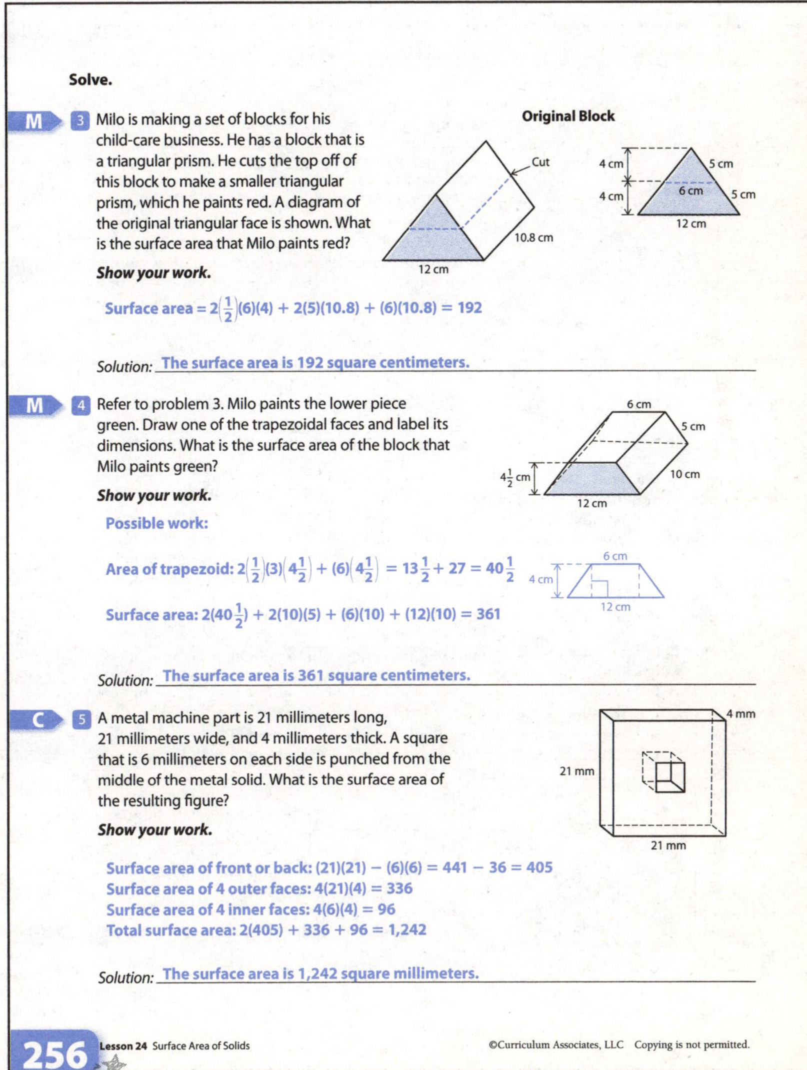

Solve.

M **3** Milo is making a set of blocks for his child-care business. He has a block that is a triangular prism. He cuts the top off of this block to make a smaller triangular prism, which he paints red. A diagram of the original triangular face is shown. What is the surface area that Milo paints red?

Original Block

Show your work.

Surface area $= 2\left(\frac{1}{2}\right)(6)(4) + 2(5)(10.8) + (6)(10.8) = 192$

Solution: The surface area is 192 square centimeters.

M **4** Refer to problem 3. Milo paints the lower piece green. Draw one of the trapezoidal faces and label its dimensions. What is the surface area of the block that Milo paints green?

Show your work.

Possible work:

Area of trapezoid: $2\left(\frac{1}{2}\right)(3)\left(4\frac{1}{2}\right) + (6)\left(4\frac{1}{2}\right) = 13\frac{1}{2} + 27 = 40\frac{1}{2}$

Surface area: $2\left(40\frac{1}{2}\right) + 2(10)(5) + (6)(10) + (12)(10) = 361$

Solution: The surface area is 361 square centimeters.

C **5** A metal machine part is 21 millimeters long, 21 millimeters wide, and 4 millimeters thick. A square that is 6 millimeters on each side is punched from the middle of the metal solid. What is the surface area of the resulting figure?

Show your work.

Surface area of front or back: $(21)(21) - (6)(6) = 441 - 36 = 405$

Surface area of 4 outer faces: $4(21)(4) = 336$

Surface area of 4 inner faces: $4(6)(4) = 96$

Total surface area: $2(405) + 336 + 96 = 1{,}242$

Solution: The surface area is 1,242 square millimeters.

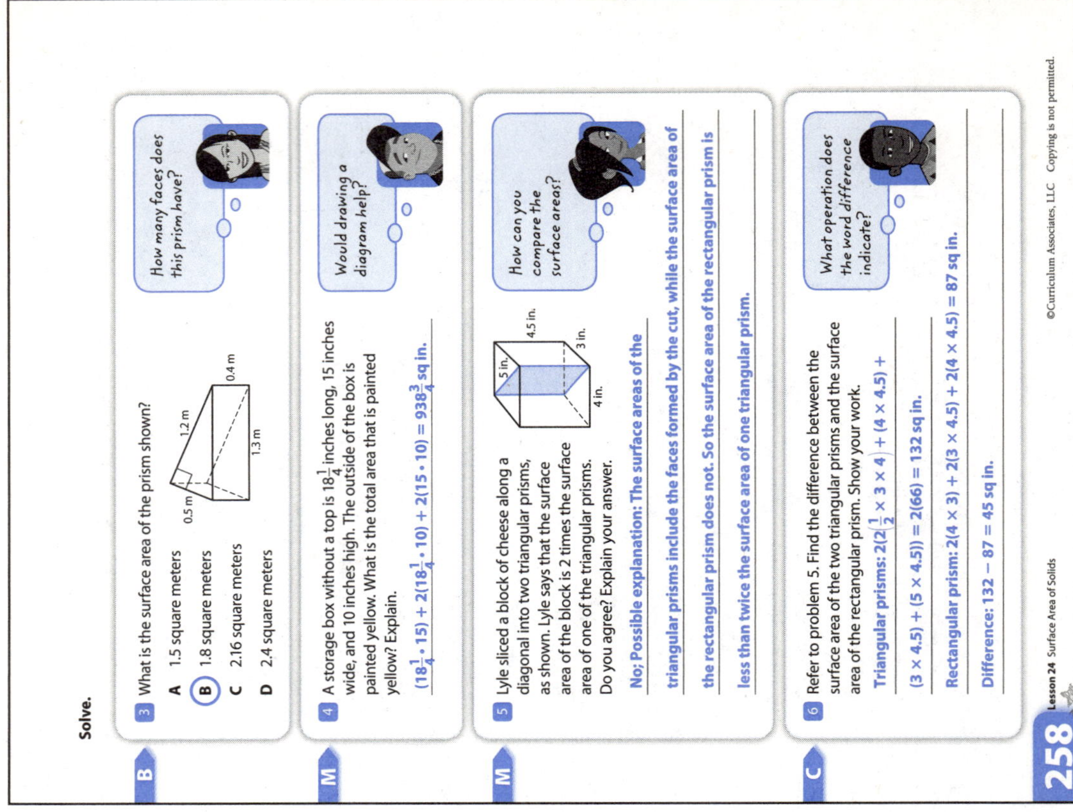

Solve.

B

3 What is the surface area of the prism shown?

A 1.5 square meters

(B) 1.8 square meters

C 2.16 square meters

D 2.4 square meters

M

4 A storage box without a top is $18\frac{1}{4}$ inches long, 15 inches wide, and 10 inches high. The outside of the box is painted yellow. What is the total area that is painted yellow? Explain.

$(18\frac{1}{4} \cdot 15) + 2(18\frac{1}{4} \cdot 10) + 2(15 \cdot 10) = 938\frac{3}{4}$ sq in.

M

5 Lyle sliced a block of cheese along a diagonal into two triangular prisms, as shown. Lyle says that the surface area of the block is 2 times the surface area of one of the triangular prisms. Do you agree? Explain your answer.

No; Possible explanation: The surface areas of the triangular prisms include the faces formed by the cut, while the surface area of the rectangular prism does not. So the surface area of the rectangular prism is less than twice the surface area of one triangular prism.

C

6 Refer to problem 5. Find the difference between the surface area of the two triangular prisms and the surface area of the rectangular prism. Show your work.

Triangular prisms: $2(2(\frac{1}{2} \times 3 \times 4) + (4 \times 4.5) + (3 \times 4.5) + (5 \times 4.5)) = 2(66) = 132$ sq in.

Rectangular prism: $2(4 \times 3) + 2(3 \times 4.5) + 2(4 \times 4.5) = 87$ sq in.

Difference: $132 - 87 = 45$ sq in.

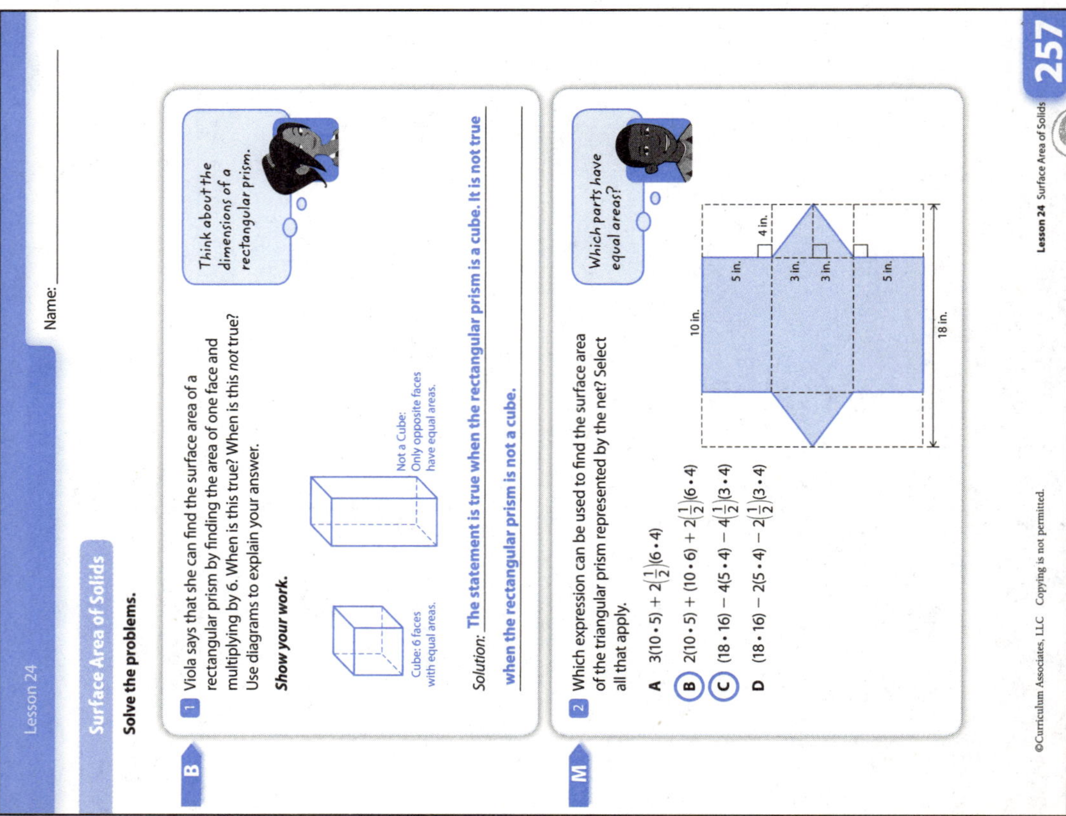

Lesson 24

Name: ____________________

Surface Area of Solids

Solve the problems.

B

1 Viola says that she can find the surface area of a rectangular prism by finding the area of one face and multiplying by 6. When is this true? When is this *not* true? Use diagrams to explain your answer.

Show your work.

Solution: **The statement is true when the rectangular prism is a cube. It is not true when the rectangular prism is not a cube.**

M

2 Which expression can be used to find the surface area of the triangular prism represented by the net? Select all that apply.

A $3(10 \cdot 5) + 2(\frac{1}{2})(6 \cdot 4)$

(B) $2(10 \cdot 5) + (10 \cdot 6) + 2(\frac{1}{2})(6 \cdot 4)$

(C) $(18 \cdot 16) - 4(5 \cdot 4) - 4(\frac{1}{2})(3 \cdot 4)$

D $(18 \cdot 16) - 2(5 \cdot 4) - 2(\frac{1}{2})(3 \cdot 4)$

Lesson 25

Understand Plane Sections of Prisms and Pyramids

Name: ____________________

Prerequisite: How do you identify shapes according to their properties?

Study the example showing how to identify shapes by using their properties. Then solve problems 1–8.

Example

The Venn diagram at the right shows the relationship between plane figures, polygons, triangles, quadrilaterals, and pentagons.

The most general category is plane figures, which include any closed two-dimensional shapes. This category includes polygons because polygons are closed plane figures with straight sides. Polygons include figures such as triangles, quadrilaterals, and pentagons because each of these figures is a closed plane figure with straight sides.

Plane Figures
Polygons
Triangles
Quadrilaterals
Pentagons

B 1 Fill in the blanks using the categories in the Venn diagram.

Quadrilaterals are both **polygons** and **plane figures**.

B 2 An oval is a plane figure.

a. Is an oval a polygon? Explain your answer.

No; it does not have straight sides.

b. Does an oval belong in the Venn diagram hierarchy shown above? Explain.

Yes; it is a plane figure, but it is not a polygon. So ovals belong within the Plane Figures section, but completely outside of the group of Polygons section.

B 3 Where would you include rectangles in the Venn diagram?

Rectangles are special quadrilaterals, so rectangles belong inside the section labeled Quadrilaterals.

Vocabulary

hierarchy a ranking of categories based on properties.

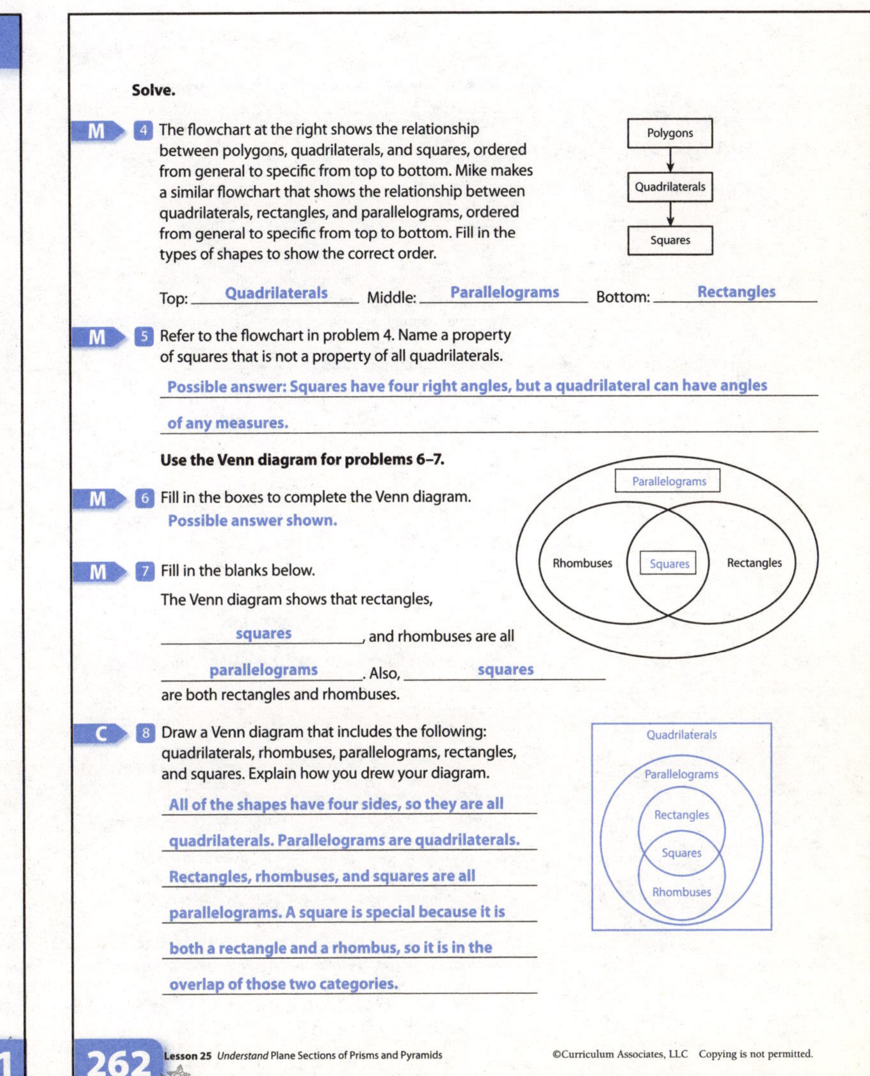

Solve.

M 4 The flowchart at the right shows the relationship between polygons, quadrilaterals, and squares, ordered from general to specific from top to bottom. Mike makes a similar flowchart that shows the relationship between quadrilaterals, rectangles, and parallelograms, ordered from general to specific from top to bottom. Fill in the types of shapes to show the correct order.

Polygons → Quadrilaterals → Squares

Top: **Quadrilaterals** Middle: **Parallelograms** Bottom: **Rectangles**

M 5 Refer to the flowchart in problem 4. Name a property of squares that is not a property of all quadrilaterals.

Possible answer: Squares have four right angles, but a quadrilateral can have angles of any measures.

Use the Venn diagram for problems 6–7.

M 6 Fill in the boxes to complete the Venn diagram.
Possible answer shown.

Parallelograms
Rhombuses
Squares
Rectangles

M 7 Fill in the blanks below.

The Venn diagram shows that rectangles, **squares**, and rhombuses are all **parallelograms**. Also, **squares** are both rectangles and rhombuses.

C 8 Draw a Venn diagram that includes the following: quadrilaterals, rhombuses, parallelograms, rectangles, and squares. Explain how you drew your diagram.

All of the shapes have four sides, so they are all quadrilaterals. Parallelograms are quadrilaterals. Rectangles, rhombuses, and squares are all parallelograms. A square is special because it is both a rectangle and a rhombus, so it is in the overlap of those two categories.

Quadrilaterals
Parallelograms
Rectangles
Squares
Rhombuses

Key

B Basic **M** Medium **C** Challenge

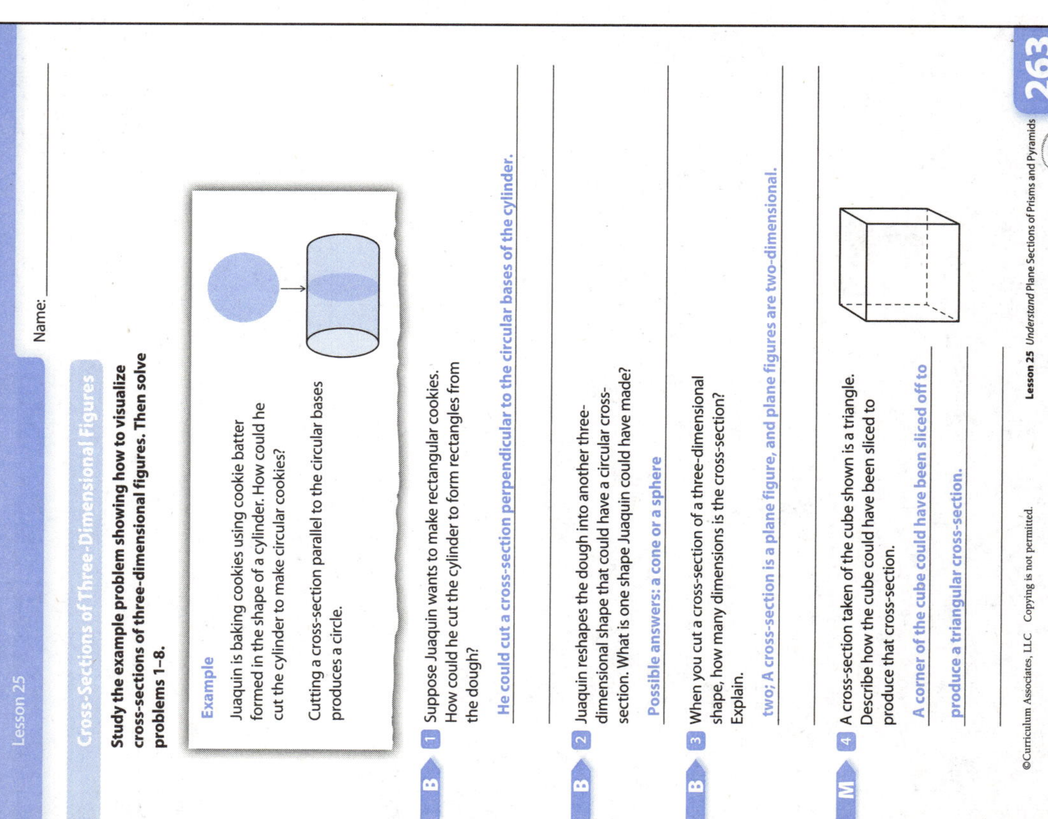

Lesson 25

Name: ____________

Cross-Sections of Three-Dimensional Figures

Study the example problem showing how to visualize cross-sections of three-dimensional figures. Then solve problems 1–8.

Example

Juaquin is baking cookies using cookie batter formed in the shape of a cylinder. How could he cut the cylinder to make circular cookies?

Cutting a cross-section parallel to the circular bases produces a circle.

B 1 Suppose Juaquin wants to make rectangular cookies. How could he cut the cylinder to form rectangles from the dough?

He could cut a cross-section perpendicular to the circular bases of the cylinder.

B 2 Juaquin reshapes the dough into another three-dimensional shape that could have a circular cross-section. What is one shape Juaquin could have made?

Possible answers: a cone or a sphere

B 3 When you cut a cross-section of a three-dimensional shape, how many dimensions is the cross-section? Explain.

two; A cross-section is a plane figure, and plane figures are two-dimensional.

M 4 A cross-section taken of the cube shown is a triangle. Describe how the cube could have been sliced to produce that cross-section.

A corner of the cube could have been sliced off to produce a triangular cross-section.

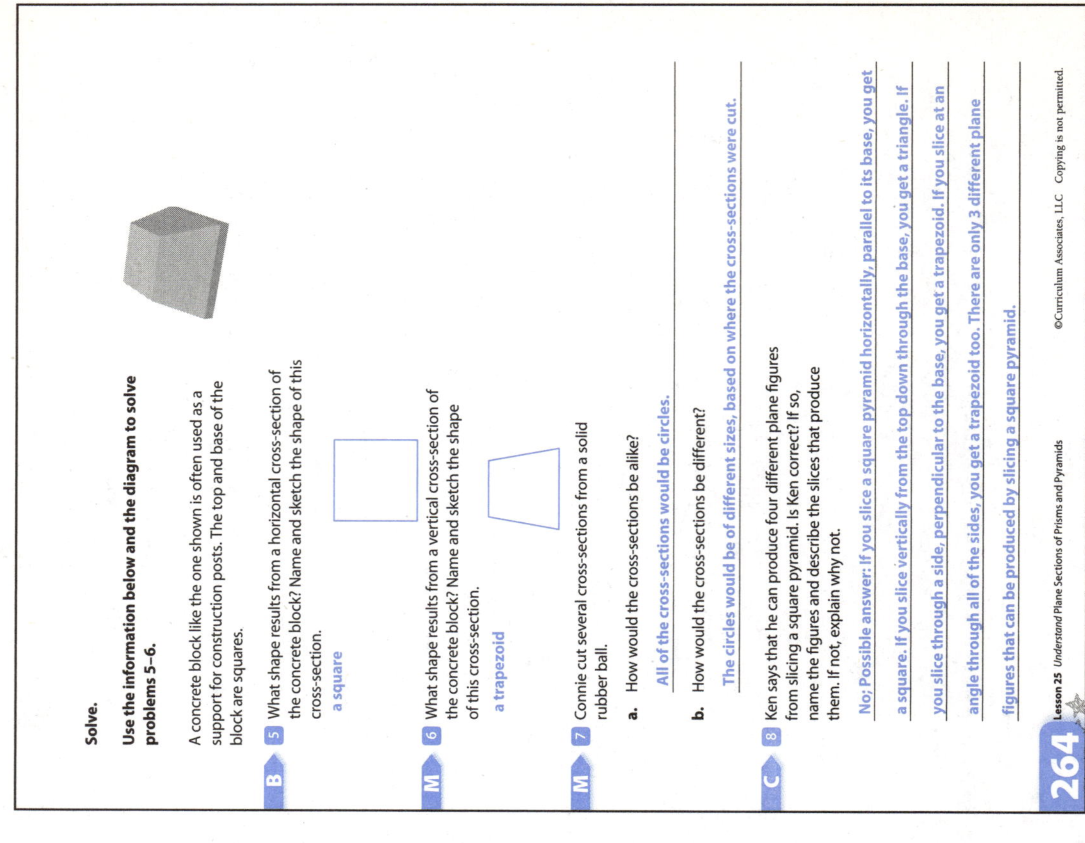

Solve.

Use the information below and the diagram to solve problems 5–6.

A concrete block like the one shown is often used as a support for construction posts. The top and base of the block are squares.

B 5 What shape results from a horizontal cross-section of the concrete block? Name and sketch the shape of this cross-section.

a square

M 6 What shape results from a vertical cross-section of the concrete block? Name and sketch the shape of this cross-section.

a trapezoid

M 7 Connie cut several cross-sections from a solid rubber ball.

a. How would the cross-sections be alike?

All of the cross-sections would be circles.

b. How would the cross-sections be different?

The circles would be of different sizes, based on where the cross-sections were cut.

C 8 Ken says that he can produce four different plane figures from slicing a square pyramid. Is Ken correct? If so, name the figures and describe the slices that produce them. If not, explain why not.

No; Possible answer: If you slice a square pyramid horizontally, parallel to its base, you get a square. If you slice vertically from the top down through the base, you get a triangle. If you slice through a side, perpendicular to the base, you get a trapezoid. If you slice at an angle through all of the sides, you get a trapezoid too. There are only 3 different plane figures that can be produced by slicing a square pyramid.

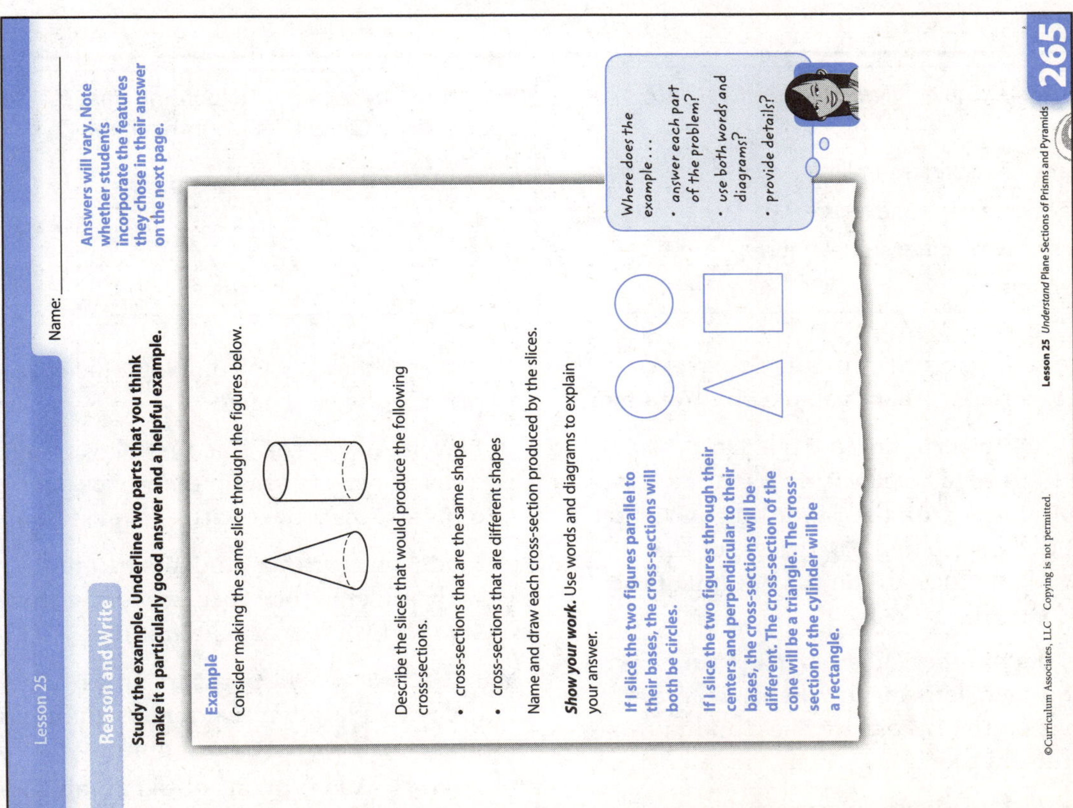

Name: ____________

Reason and Write

Study the example. Underline two parts that you think make it a particularly good answer and a helpful example.

Answers will vary. Note whether students incorporate the features they chose in their answer on the next page.

Example

Consider making the same slice through the figures below.

Describe the slices that would produce the following cross-sections.

- cross-sections that are the same shape
- cross-sections that are different shapes

Name and draw each cross-section produced by the slices.

Show your work. Use words and diagrams to explain your answer.

If I slice the two figures parallel to their bases, the cross-sections will both be circles.

If I slice the two figures through their centers and perpendicular to their bases, the cross-sections will be different. The cross-section of the cone will be a triangle. The cross-section of the cylinder will be a rectangle.

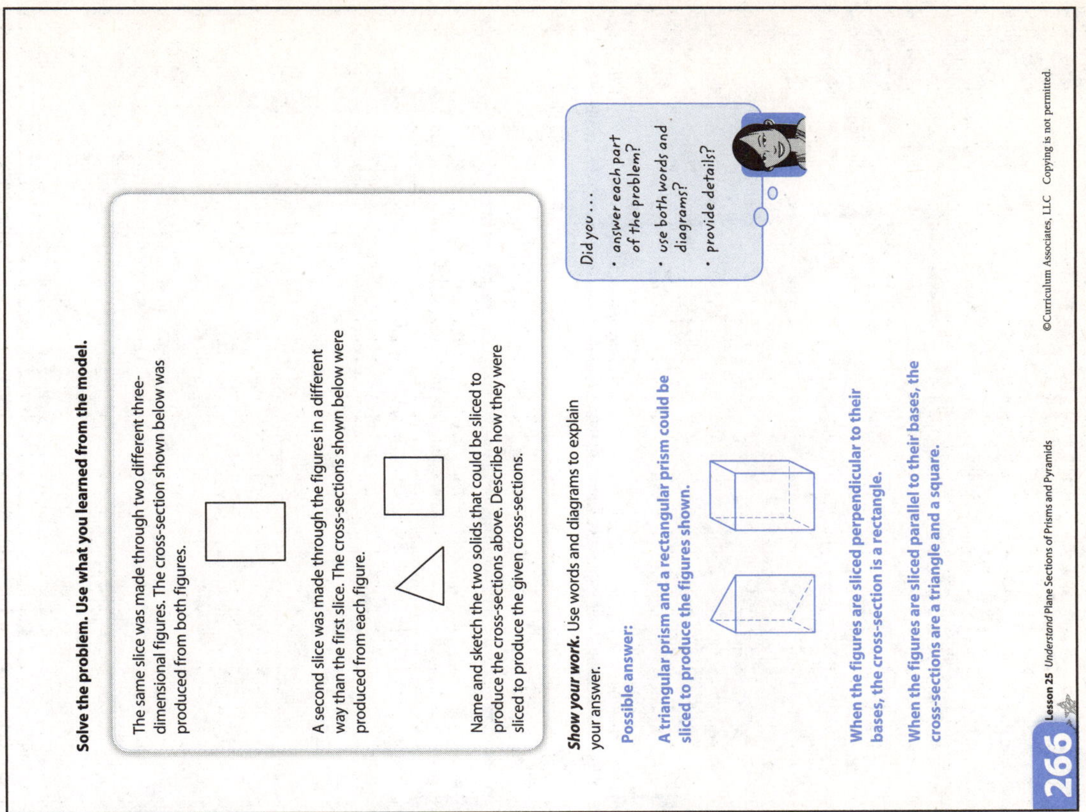

Solve the problem. Use what you learned from the model.

The same slice was made through two different three-dimensional figures. The cross-section shown below was produced from both figures.

A second slice was made through the figures in a different way than the first slice. The cross-sections shown below were produced from each figure.

Name and sketch the two solids that could be sliced to produce the cross-sections above. Describe how they were sliced to produce the given cross-sections.

Show your work. Use words and diagrams to explain your answer.

Possible answer:

A triangular prism and a rectangular prism could be sliced to produce the figures shown.

When the figures are sliced perpendicular to their bases, the cross-section is a rectangle.

When the figures are sliced parallel to their bases, the cross-sections are a triangle and a square.

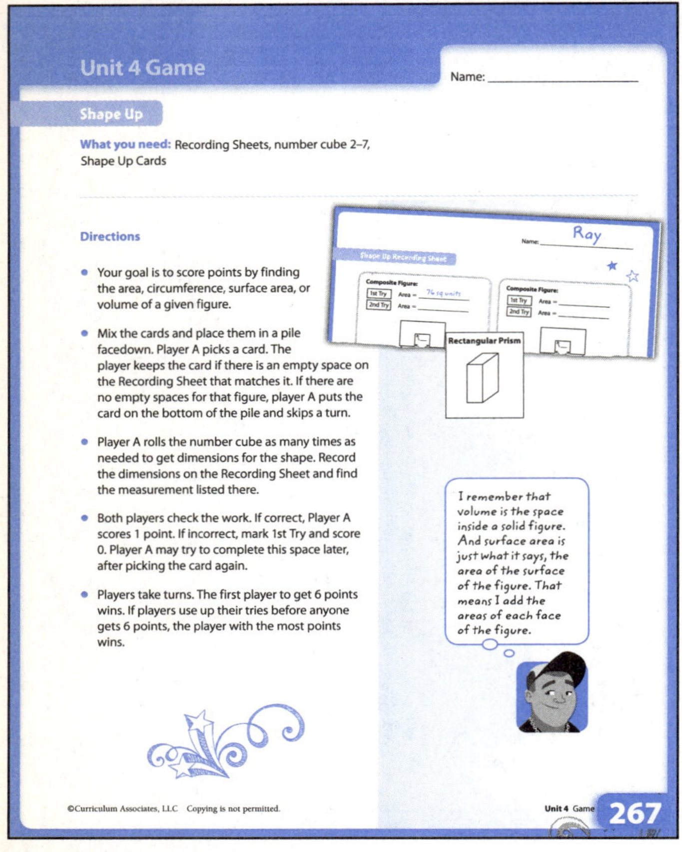
Unit 4 Game

Name: ____________________

Shape Up

What you need: Recording Sheets, number cube 2–7, Shape Up Cards

Directions

- Your goal is to score points by finding the area, circumference, surface area, or volume of a given figure.
- Mix the cards and place them in a pile facedown. Player A picks a card. The player keeps the card if there is an empty space on the Recording Sheet that matches it. If there are no empty spaces for that figure, player A puts the card on the bottom of the pile and skips a turn.
- Player A rolls the number cube as many times as needed to get dimensions for the shape. Record the dimensions on the Recording Sheet and find the measurement listed there.
- Both players check the work. If correct, Player A scores 1 point. If incorrect, mark 1st Try and score 0. Player A may try to complete this space later, after picking the card again.
- Players take turns. The first player to get 6 points wins. If players use up their tries before anyone gets 6 points, the player with the most points wins.

©Curriculum Associates, LLC Copying is not permitted. Unit 4 Game 267

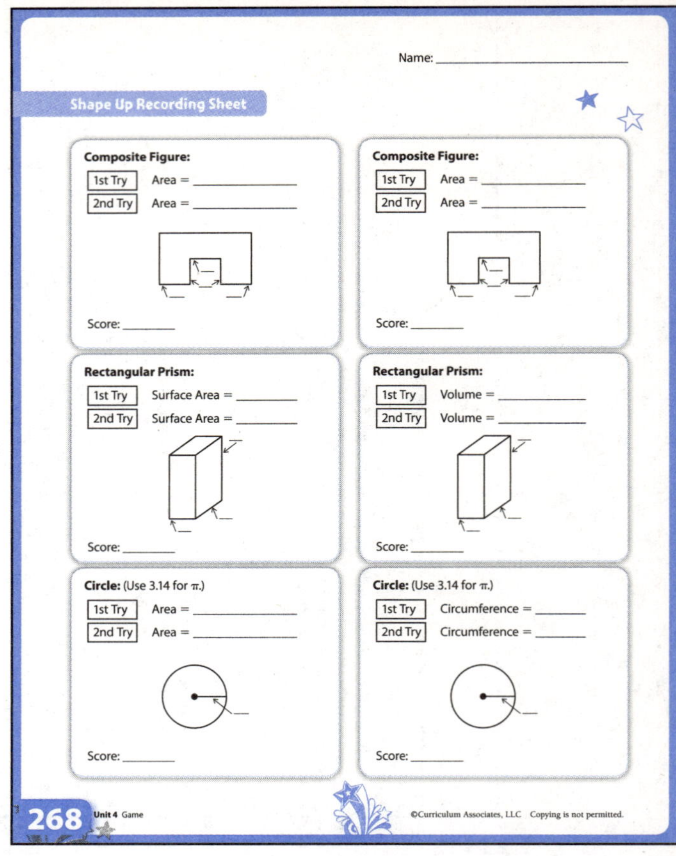
Name: ____________________

Shape Up Recording Sheet

Composite Figure:	Composite Figure:
1st Try Area = ________	1st Try Area = ________
2nd Try Area = ________	2nd Try Area = ________
Score: ______	Score: ______

Rectangular Prism:	Rectangular Prism:
1st Try Surface Area = ______	1st Try Volume = ______
2nd Try Surface Area = ______	2nd Try Volume = ______
Score: ______	Score: ______

Circle: (Use 3.14 for π.)	Circle: (Use 3.14 for π.)
1st Try Area = ________	1st Try Circumference = ______
2nd Try Area = ________	2nd Try Circumference = ______
Score: ______	Score: ______

268 Unit 4 Game ©Curriculum Associates, LLC Copying is not permitted.

STEP BY STEP

CCSS Focus - 7.G.B.4, 7.G.B.6 *Embedded SMPs* - 1, 4, 6, 7, 8 **Objectives** • Find the volume of a solid figure. • Find the surface area of a solid figure. • Find the area of a two-dimensional figure. • Find the circumference of a circle.	**Materials** For each pair: Recording Sheets (1 for each player) (TR 5), Shape Cards (TR 6), number cube (2–7)

- Your goal is to score points by finding the area, circumference, surface area, or volume of a given figure.
- Mix the cards and place them in a pile facedown. Player A picks a card. The player keeps the card if there is an empty space on the Recording Sheet that matches it. If there are no empty spaces for that figure, player A puts the card on the bottom of the pile and skips a turn.
- Player A rolls the number cubes as many times as needed to get dimensions for the shape. Record the dimensions on the Recording Sheet and find the measurement listed there.
- Both players check the work. If correct, Player A scores 1 point. If incorrect, mark 1st Try and score 0. Player A may try to complete this space later, after picking the card again.
- Players take turns. The first player to get 6 points wins. If players use up their tries before anyone gets 6 points, the player with the most points wins.
- Model one turn for students before they play. Review with students the processes for finding the surface area and volume of solid figures.

Vary the Game Players score an extra point for each figure with a larger measurement than the opponent's measurement for the same figure.

Challenge Add $\frac{1}{2}$ to one of the numbers rolled and use the sum as a dimension.

Unit 4 Practice

Name: ____________________

Geometry

In this unit you learned to:	Lesson
solve problems with angles.	18
draw triangles to meet given conditions.	19
find the area of composed figures and circles.	20, 21
solve problems with scale drawings.	22
find the surface area and volume of solid figures.	23, 24
describe plane sections of prisms and pyramids.	25

Use these skills to solve problems 1–6.

B **1** The measure of $\angle ABC$ is 40°.

Part A: What is the measure of the supplement of $\angle ABC$?

140°

Part B: What is the measure of the complement of $\angle ABC$?

50°

C **2** What is the ratio of the area of the circle to the area of the quadrilateral? Write your answer in terms of π.

$\frac{\pi r^2}{2r^2} = \frac{\pi}{2}$

M **3** Kamilah has a cone. She slices it in several different ways. Which of these *cannot* be the shape of one of the cross-sections?

- **A** circle
- **B** triangle
- **C** oval
- **(D)** rectangle

B **4** From which measures can a triangle be drawn? Select all that apply.

- **(A)** angles 40°, 40°, and 100°
- **B** angles 50°, 75°, and 95°
- **C** sides 4 cm, 4 cm, 10 cm
- **(D)** sides 6 cm, 8 cm, 10 cm

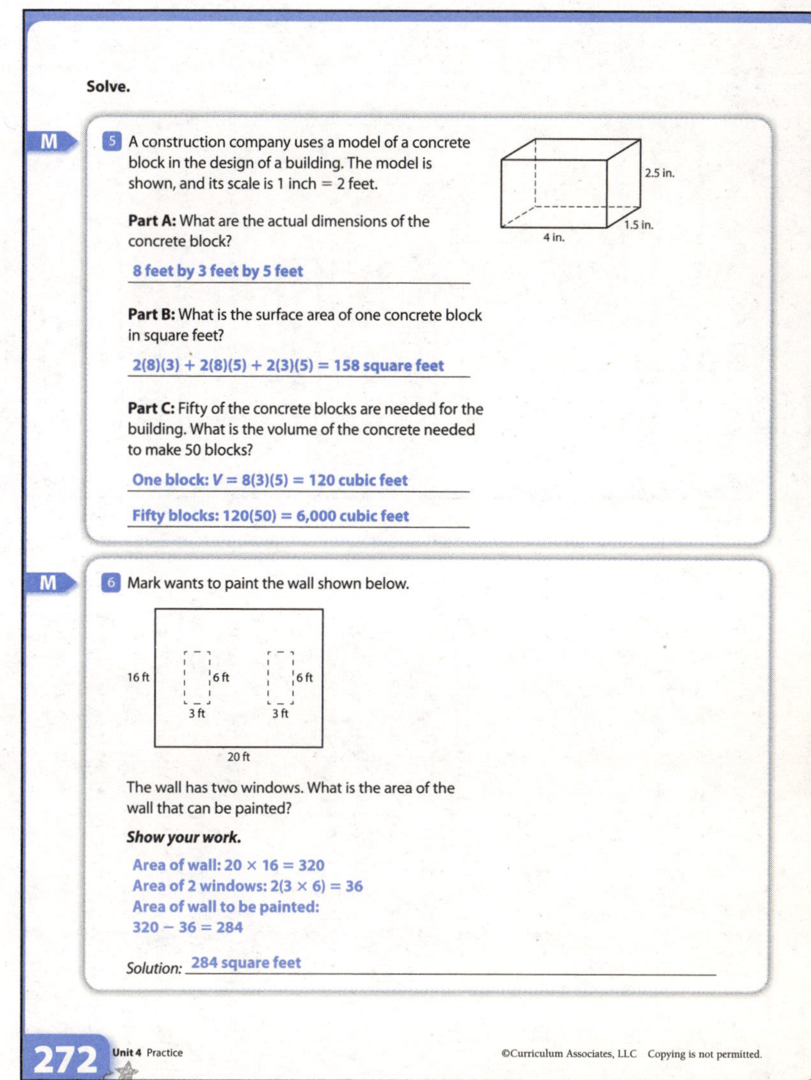

Solve.

M **5** A construction company uses a model of a concrete block in the design of a building. The model is shown, and its scale is 1 inch = 2 feet.

Part A: What are the actual dimensions of the concrete block?

8 feet by 3 feet by 5 feet

Part B: What is the surface area of one concrete block in square feet?

$2(8)(3) + 2(8)(5) + 2(3)(5) = 158$ square feet

Part C: Fifty of the concrete blocks are needed for the building. What is the volume of the concrete needed to make 50 blocks?

One block: $V = 8(3)(5) = 120$ cubic feet

Fifty blocks: $120(50) = 6{,}000$ cubic feet

M **6** Mark wants to paint the wall shown below.

The wall has two windows. What is the area of the wall that can be painted?

Show your work.

Area of wall: $20 \times 16 = 320$
Area of 2 windows: $2(3 \times 6) = 36$
Area of wall to be painted:
$320 - 36 = 284$

Solution: 284 square feet

Key

B Basic **M** Medium **C** Challenge

TEACHER NOTES

Common Core Standards: 7.G.A.1, 7.G.B.4, 7.G.B.6, 7.RP.A.1
Standards for Mathematical Practice: 1, 2, 3, 4, 5, 6, 7, 8
DOK: 3
Materials: None

About the Task

To complete this task, students solve a multi-step problem that involves computing the area of two-dimensional composite figures. The task requires them to set lengths of parts of the figures, compute areas, and ensure that the shapes can fit in the given space.

Getting Started

Read the problem out loud with students and go over the checklist. Have students examine the diagrams and identify the information they must supply in order to calculate the areas of the figures. Point out the scale of the field and ask students why this is important. [It tells them the actual boundaries that they must work within, to fit the shapes.] ***(SMP 1, 2, 4)***

Completing the Task

In this problem, students must place the composite shapes appropriately and—at the same time—determine dimensions that will fit within the space. Some students may solve this dilemma easily while others may need to try several configurations before arriving at one that meets all criteria. Encourage them to use a grid and to pay attention to precision in both drawing and calculations. ***(SMP 5, 6)***

Once they find dimensions that meet the criteria and place the shapes in the field, students find the area of each shape. They break each shape into component shapes: half-circles, rectangles, and triangles. They find the areas of the component shapes and the total area. ***(SMP 7, 8)***

Invite students to present their solutions and discuss how they chose and answered a Reflect on Mathematical Practices question. Encourage them to explain how their solution is like other students' solutions and how their solution is different. ***(SMP 3)***

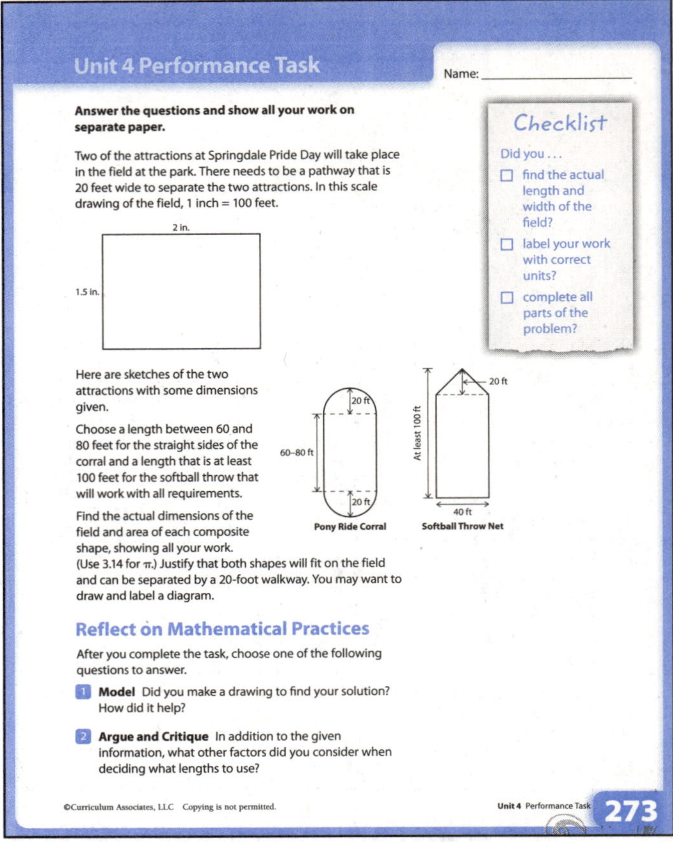
Unit 4 Performance Task

Name: ____________

Answer the questions and show all your work on separate paper.

Two of the attractions at Springdale Pride Day will take place in the field at the park. There needs to be a pathway that is 20 feet wide to separate the two attractions. In this scale drawing of the field, 1 inch = 100 feet.

Checklist
Did you . . .
- ☐ find the actual length and width of the field?
- ☐ label your work with correct units?
- ☐ complete all parts of the problem?

Here are sketches of the two attractions with some dimensions given.

Choose a length between 60 and 80 feet for the straight sides of the corral and a length that is at least 100 feet for the softball throw that will work with all requirements.

Find the actual dimensions of the field and area of each composite shape, showing all your work. (Use 3.14 for π.) Justify that both shapes will fit on the field and can be separated by a 20-foot walkway. You may want to draw and label a diagram.

Reflect on Mathematical Practices

After you complete the task, choose one of the following questions to answer.

1. **Model** Did you make a drawing to find your solution? How did it help?
2. **Argue and Critique** In addition to the given information, what other factors did you consider when deciding what lengths to use?

Extension

If students have more time to spend on this problem, you can have them solve this extension:

Using the same scale of 1 inch = 100 feet, find the overall length and width of the two attractions as they would be drawn on paper.

SAMPLE RESPONSE AND RUBRIC

4-Point Solution

In the scale drawing of the field, 1 inch = 100 feet.

Dimensions of the field: 1.5 × 100 = 150 ft and 2 × 100 = 200 ft

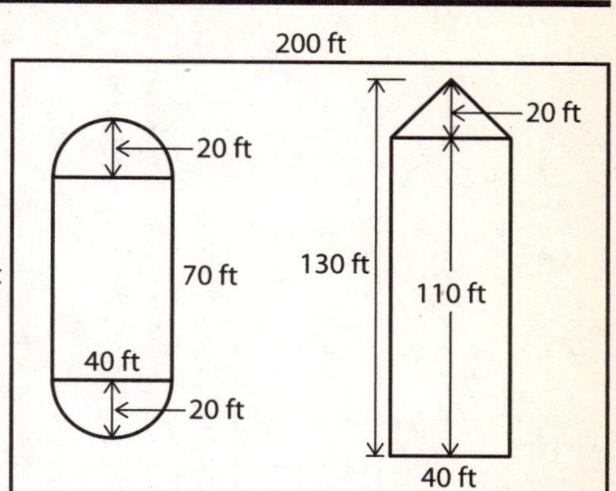

Pony Ride Corral

The width of the corral is the diameter of the circle, or 40 ft. I used 70 ft for the length of the rectangular part. The total length is 110 ft.

Combined area of the half-circles:

$\pi \times (20)^2$

3.14 × 400 = about 1,256 sq ft

Area of rectangle:

70 × 40 = 2,800 sq ft

Total area:

2,800 + 1,256 = 4,056 sq ft

Softball Throw

I used a total length of 130 ft.

Area of triangular section:

$\frac{1}{2}(40)(20) = 400$ sq ft

Area of rectangular section:

130 − 20 = 110 ft and 40 × 110 = 4,400 sq ft

Total area:

4,400 + 400 = 4,800 sq ft

The total length of each attraction (110 ft and 130 ft) is less than the width of the field (150 ft). The field is 200 feet long, and the attractions are each 40 ft wide. 40 + 40 = 80 and 200 − 80 = 120, so there is more than enough room for the pathway.

REFLECT ON MATHEMATICAL PRACTICES

1. Students should explain how their drawing models the situation and how it helped them to accurately understand the relationships between the various dimensions and to find areas. ***(SMP 4)***
2. Students might consider the amount of space needed in a corral for ponies to move around and how far someone might throw a softball. ***(SMP 3)***

SCORING RUBRIC

4 points All parts of the problem are complete and correct. The shapes fit and all calculations are correct. The diagram accurately represents the situation and units are labeled. Students justify decisions.

3 points The student has completed all parts of the problem, with one or two errors. Possible errors might include one incorrect dimension, not labeling all units, or a minor calculation error.

2 points The student has attempted all parts of the problem, with a number of errors. Dimensions may be incorrect and not all calculations are correct. The diagram is incomplete.

1 point Much of the problem is incomplete, with several errors. Dimensions, calculations, and the diagram contain serious errors. Shapes may not fit. The justification is incorrect or missing.

SOLUTION TO THE EXTENSION

Divide the actual lengths and widths by 100 to find the scale drawing length.

Pony Corral actual width: 40 ft, scale drawing width: 0.4 in; actual length 110 ft, scale drawing length 1.1 in.

Softball Throw actual width: 40 ft, scale drawing width: 0.4 in; actual length 130 ft, scale drawing length 1.3 in.

Lesson 26
Understand
Random Samples

Name: ____________

Prerequisite: What are statistical questions?

Study the example showing the difference between a statistical question and a non-statistical question. Then solve problems 1–6.

Example

Statistical question:
You ask the students in your class: "What is your height?"

When you ask a statistical question, you expect to get a variety of answers. The answers have variability. The question above is statistical because you expect to get different answers.

Non-statistical question:
You ask the students in your class: "What is the height of the tallest student in the seventh grade?"

When you ask a non-statistical question, there is only one correct answer and you expect the same answer from everyone you ask.

Vocabulary

statistical question a question that is expected to have variability in the data related to it.

variability the extent to which data are different from each other.

B 1 You ask the students in your class two questions. Which question is statistical and which is non-statistical? Explain.

- What time does the first period begin?
- What time do you leave home to go to school?

The second question is statistical because you expect variability in the times that students leave home to go to school. The first question is non-statistical because first period begins at an exact time.

M 2 Write both a statistical question and a non-statistical question you could ask some classmates to gather information about playing video games.

Possible answers: Statistical: About how many hours do you play video games each day?

Non-statistical: Which classmate owns the most video games?

Solve.

B 3 Silvie asked students in the cafeteria: "How many miles do you live from school?" Determine whether Silvie's question is *statistical* or *non-statistical*. Explain your answer.

The question is statistical because you expect different answers from different people.

M 4 If you ask your classmates, "How many problems were on the math quiz?", you are not asking a statistical question. What is a statistical question you might ask about the quiz? Explain.

Possible answer: "What did you score on the math quiz?"; The question would be statistical because you would expect different answers from different students.

M 5 Look at problem 4. Explain why the non-statistical question does not have variability.

The question does not have variability because the math quiz has a specific number of problems and there is only one correct answer to the question.

C 6 Evan surveyed his classmates to make a prediction about seventh-grade students. Look at his results in the table.

Hours	3	4	5	6	7
Number of Students	2	4	6	5	3

Write two statistical questions that Evan could have asked to get his results. Then explain why Evan could not have asked a non-statistical question to get his results.

Possible answers: "How many hours did you work on your science project?" and "How many hours do you exercise each week?"; Evan could not have used a non-statistical question because the results show that there were different answers, not the same answer, from everyone.

Key

B Basic **M** Medium **C** Challenge

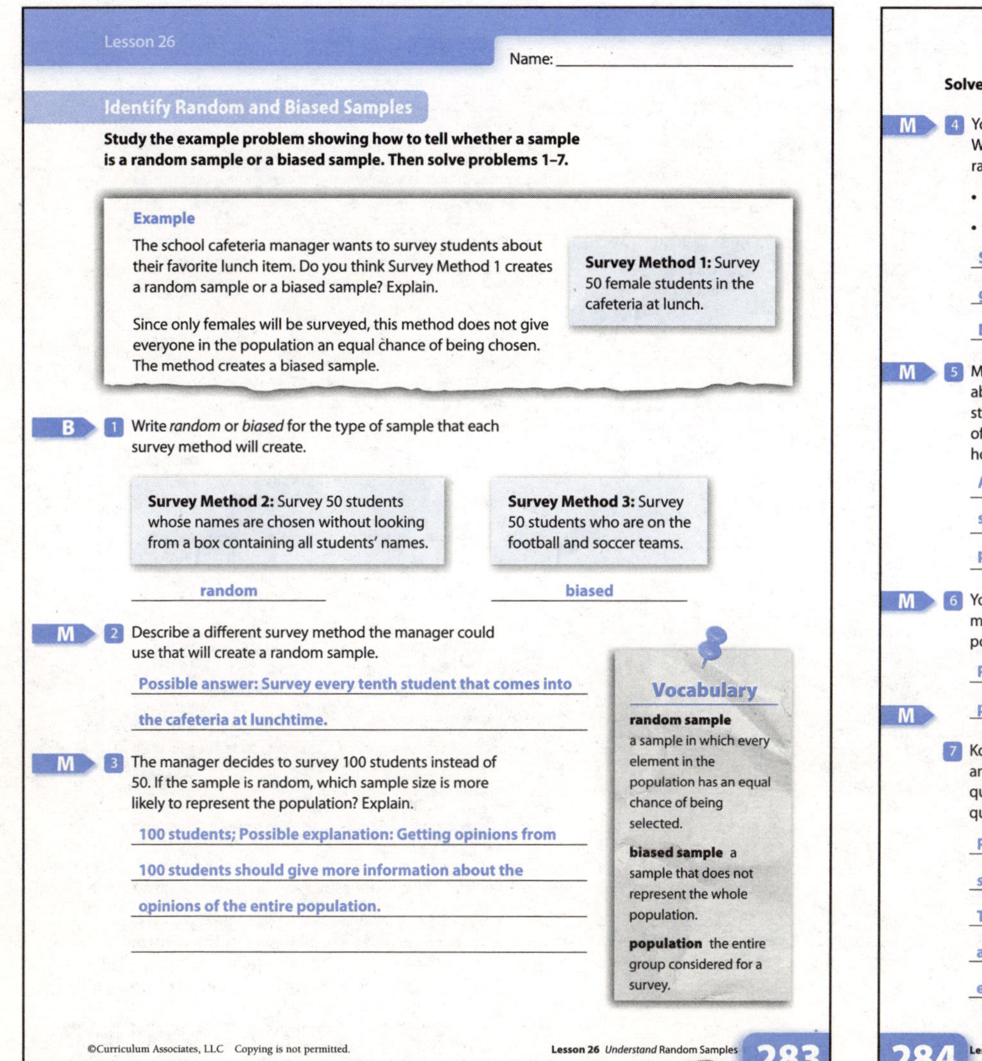

Lesson 26

Name: ____________________

Identify Random and Biased Samples

Study the example problem showing how to tell whether a sample is a random sample or a biased sample. Then solve problems 1–7.

Example

The school cafeteria manager wants to survey students about their favorite lunch item. Do you think Survey Method 1 creates a random sample or a biased sample? Explain.

Survey Method 1: Survey 50 female students in the cafeteria at lunch.

Since only females will be surveyed, this method does not give everyone in the population an equal chance of being chosen. The method creates a biased sample.

B 1 Write *random* or *biased* for the type of sample that each survey method will create.

Survey Method 2: Survey 50 students whose names are chosen without looking from a box containing all students' names.

Survey Method 3: Survey 50 students who are on the football and soccer teams.

random — biased

M 2 Describe a different survey method the manager could use that will create a random sample.

Possible answer: Survey every tenth student that comes into the cafeteria at lunchtime.

M 3 The manager decides to survey 100 students instead of 50. If the sample is random, which sample size is more likely to represent the population? Explain.

100 students; Possible explanation: Getting opinions from 100 students should give more information about the opinions of the entire population.

Vocabulary

random sample a sample in which every element in the population has an equal chance of being selected.

biased sample a sample that does not represent the whole population.

population the entire group considered for a survey.

Solve.

M 4 You want to find out which music store in town is the most popular. Which survey method is more likely to create a representative random sample? Explain.

- You survey customers coming out of Best Sounds music store.
- You survey people at several different shopping areas in town.

Surveying people at several different shopping areas; Possible explanation: You would get a variety of opinions from people at the shopping areas. The people coming out of Best Sounds probably prefer Best Sounds.

M 5 Mr. Lee wants to survey 20 of the 210 students in the seventh grade about the hours they sleep each night. He finds that 2 of the 20 students surveyed sleep for 9 hours each night. About how many of the 210 seventh graders sleep for 9 hours each night? Explain how you found your answer.

About 21 students; Possible answer:The ratio of students who sleep 9 hour per night should be about the same in the sample as in the entire population. I solved the proportion $\frac{2}{20} = \frac{x}{210}$.

M 6 You want to know the favorite band of the 25 students in your math class. Should you survey the whole class, which is the entire population, or a sample of students from the class? Explain.

Possible answer: The whole class is a small enough group to be surveyed. Surveying the population, the class, will be more representative than surveying a sample of students.

M 7 Koby visits one randomly selected science class from each grade and surveys the first ten students who leave the room. What question could he ask so that this group is a random sample? What question could he ask so that this group is a biased sample? Explain.

Possible answer: The group is a random sample for the question "How do you get to school in the morning?" because the group is representative of the school population. The group would be a biased sample for "What is the favorite sport of eighth grade boys at this school?" because the group is not representative of the entire population of the eighth grade boys at this school.

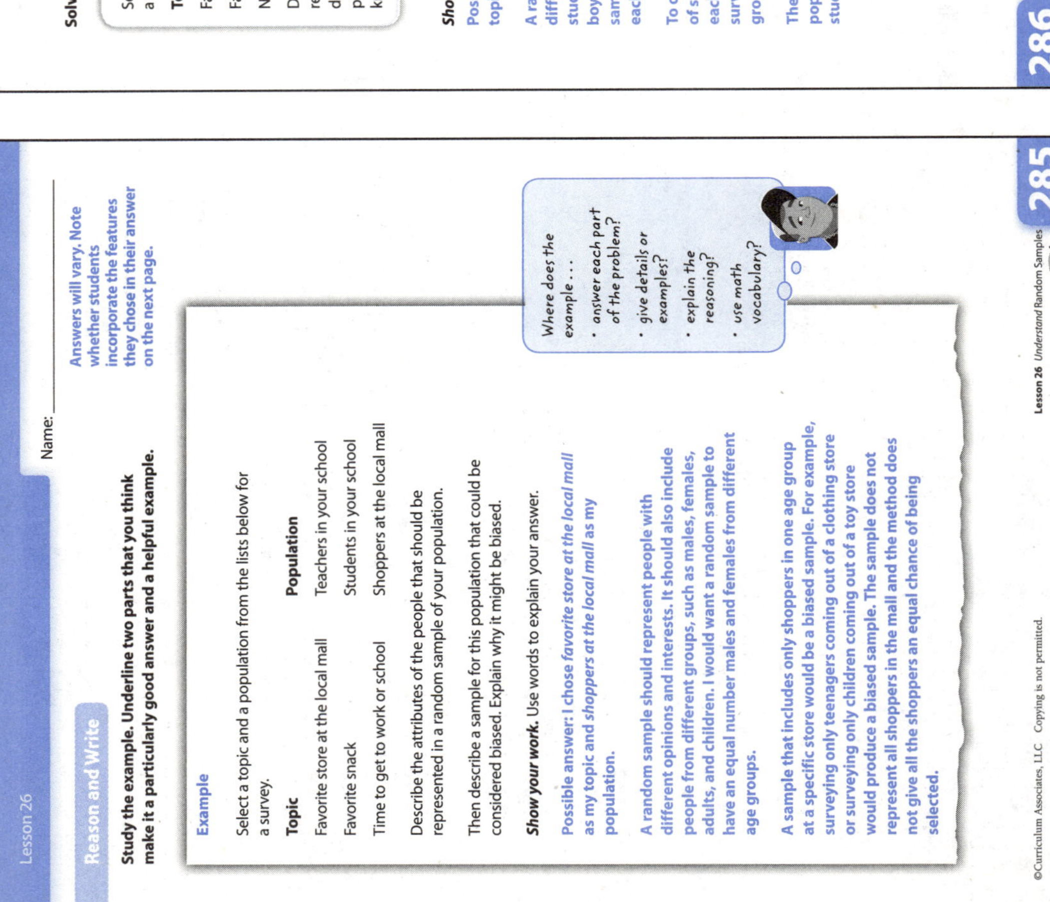

Lesson 26

Reason and Write

Name: ______________________

Answers will vary. Note whether students incorporate the features they chose in their answer on the next page.

Study the example. Underline two parts that you think make it a particularly good answer and a helpful example.

Example

Select a topic and a population from the lists below for a survey.

Topic	Population
Favorite store at the local mall	Teachers in your school
Favorite snack	Students in your school
Time to get to work or school	Shoppers at the local mall

Describe the attributes of the people that should be represented in a random sample of your population.

Then describe a sample for this population that could be considered biased. Explain why it might be biased.

Show your work. Use words to explain your answer.

Possible answer: I chose *favorite store at the local mall* as my topic and *shoppers at the local mall* as my population.

A random sample should represent people with different opinions and interests. It should also include people from different groups, such as males, females, adults, and children. I would want a random sample to have an equal number males and females from different age groups.

A sample that includes only shoppers in one age group at a specific store would be a biased sample. For example, surveying only teenagers coming out of a clothing store or surveying only children coming out of a toy store would produce a biased sample. The sample does not represent all shoppers in the mall and the method does not give all the shoppers an equal chance of being selected.

Solve the problem. Use what you learned from the model.

Select a topic and a population from the lists below for a survey.

Topic	Population
Favorite color	Students in your school
Favorite sports team	Students in your grade
Number of pets	Store customers

Describe the attributes of the people that should be represented in a random sample of your population. Then describe how you would create a random sample of the population to participate in the survey. Explain how you know that the sample is representative of the population.

Show your work. Use words to explain your answer.

Possible answer: I chose *favorite sports team* for my topic and *students in my school* as my population.

A random sample should represent students with different opinions and interests. It should also include students from different groups, such as grade levels, boys, girls, athletes, and musicians. I would want the sample to have an equal number of boys and girls from each grade level.

To create a random sample, I would sort the school list of students into boys and girls, and then I would sort each of those lists into Grades 6, 7, and 8. Then I would survey a random sample from each of the six, sorted groups by selecting every fifth person on each list.

The resulting sample would be representative of the population, students in my school, because all the students have an equal chance of being selected.

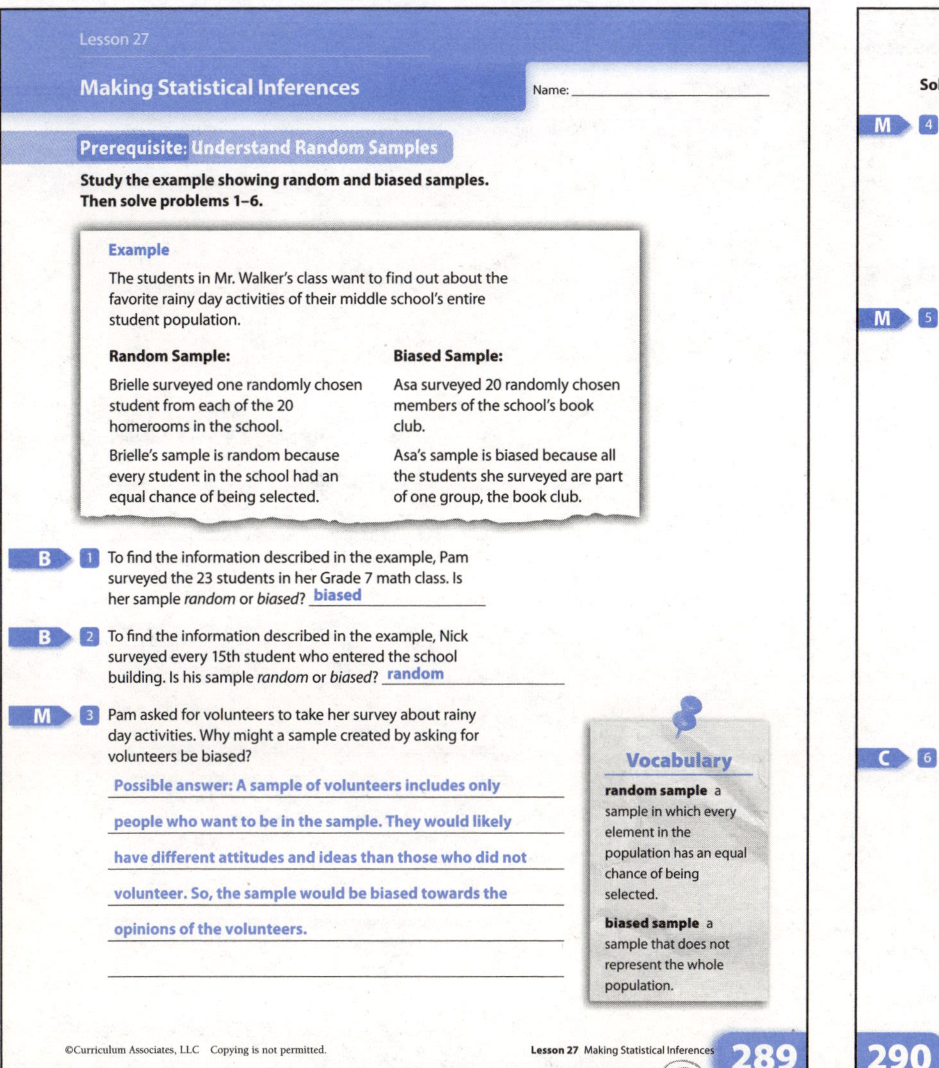

Making Statistical Inferences

Name: ____________

Prerequisite: Understand Random Samples

Study the example showing random and biased samples. Then solve problems 1–6.

Example

The students in Mr. Walker's class want to find out about the favorite rainy day activities of their middle school's entire student population.

Random Sample:

Brielle surveyed one randomly chosen student from each of the 20 homerooms in the school.

Brielle's sample is random because every student in the school had an equal chance of being selected.

Biased Sample:

Asa surveyed 20 randomly chosen members of the school's book club.

Asa's sample is biased because all the students she surveyed are part of one group, the book club.

B 1 To find the information described in the example, Pam surveyed the 23 students in her Grade 7 math class. Is her sample *random* or *biased*? biased

B 2 To find the information described in the example, Nick surveyed every 15th student who entered the school building. Is his sample *random* or *biased*? random

M 3 Pam asked for volunteers to take her survey about rainy day activities. Why might a sample created by asking for volunteers be biased?

Possible answer: A sample of volunteers includes only people who want to be in the sample. They would likely have different attitudes and ideas than those who did not volunteer. So, the sample would be biased towards the opinions of the volunteers.

Vocabulary

random sample a sample in which every element in the population has an equal chance of being selected.

biased sample a sample that does not represent the whole population.

Solve.

M 4 Vivek plans to survey 10 randomly chosen residents out of the 280 people that live in his community about plans for a new neighborhood dog park. Describe one way he can make the sample more likely to represent the population of residents.

Possible answer: He can increase the size of the sample.

M 5 Three park rangers had to report about the ways visitors use their facilities. Each ranger surveyed a sample of park visitors. Compare the methods. Do you think all three rangers' samples are equally representative of their parks' visitors? Explain.

- Ranger Li surveyed 30 randomly chosen visitors to her park's information center.
- Ranger Simpson divided his park into 30 same-sized zones and surveyed one randomly chosen visitor encountered in each zone.
- Ranger Patel surveyed 30 randomly chosen people who posted reviews of the park on a fishing website.

No; Possible answer: No. Ranger Simpson's method is most representative because the parks' visitors are all equally likely to be chosen. Rangers Li's sample may be biased because it includes only visitors at the center. Ranger Patel's sample may be biased toward a particular activity because all visitors in the sample are interested in fishing.

C 6 Jackson uses a random number generator to choose 20 students from each grade and asks how long they spend on homework. Niko says that Jackson's sample is biased. Do you agree? Explain. If it is biased, identify a different 60-student sample that can be chosen to better represent the school population.

Jackson's School

Grade	Students
6	300
7	150
8	150

I agree. There are twice as many Grade 6 students as Grade 7 or Grade 8 students. So the sample should contain twice as many Grade 6 students as Grade 7 or Grade 8. He could use the number generator to randomly choose 30 students from Grade 6, 15 from Grade 7, and 15 from Grade 8.

Key

B Basic **M** Medium **C** Challenge

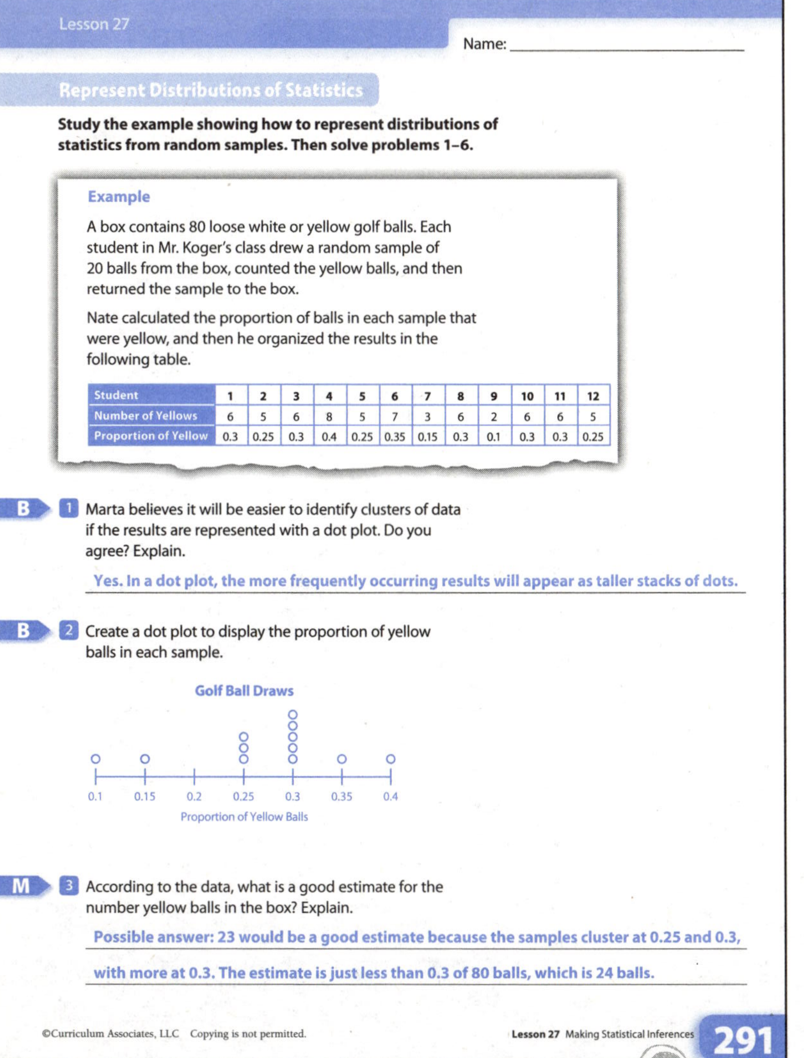

Lesson 27

Name: ____________________

Represent Distributions of Statistics

Study the example showing how to represent distributions of statistics from random samples. Then solve problems 1–6.

Example

A box contains 80 loose white or yellow golf balls. Each student in Mr. Koger's class drew a random sample of 20 balls from the box, counted the yellow balls, and then returned the sample to the box.

Nate calculated the proportion of balls in each sample that were yellow, and then he organized the results in the following table.

Student	1	2	3	4	5	6	7	8	9	10	11	12
Number of Yellows	6	5	6	8	5	7	3	6	2	6	6	5
Proportion of Yellow	0.3	0.25	0.3	0.4	0.25	0.35	0.15	0.3	0.1	0.3	0.3	0.25

B 1 Marta believes it will be easier to identify clusters of data if the results are represented with a dot plot. Do you agree? Explain.

Yes. In a dot plot, the more frequently occurring results will appear as taller stacks of dots.

B 2 Create a dot plot to display the proportion of yellow balls in each sample.

M 3 According to the data, what is a good estimate for the number yellow balls in the box? Explain.

Possible answer: 23 would be a good estimate because the samples cluster at 0.25 and 0.3, with more at 0.3. The estimate is just less than 0.3 of 80 balls, which is 24 balls.

©Curriculum Associates, LLC Copying is not permitted. Lesson 27 Making Statistical Inferences 291

Solve. Use the following situation for problems 4–6.

A box in Ms. Booth's class contains 200 loose white or yellow golf balls. The table below represents the results when 11 students each drew a random sample of the same number of balls, counted the number of yellows, and then returned the sample to the box.

Student	1	2	3	4	5	6	7	8	9	10	11
Proportion of Yellow	0.6	0.7	0.3	0.7	0.5	0.9	0.8	0.8	0.7	0.7	0.9

M 4 Which graphic representation of the data (a table, a dot plot, or a box plot) would best help estimate the number of yellow balls in the box?

Possible answers: A dot plot is best because it lets you see where the data cluster together. A box plot is best because it shows the median, which is a good estimate of the number of yellow balls.

M 5 Construct a box plot to display the data from Ms. Booth's class.

Golf Ball Draws by Ms. Booth's Class

0 0.2 0.4 0.6 0.8 1

Proportion of Yellow Balls

C 6 Lana believes a good estimate of the number of yellow balls in the box is 70 balls. Do you agree? Explain how she may have arrived at that answer.

I disagree; Possible explanation: A good estimate of the proportion of the golf balls that are yellow is 0.7, which is the median, and 0.7 of 200 is 140 yellow balls. Lana probably found 0.7 of 100 is 70, which is the percent of balls that are yellow instead of the number of balls in the box.

292 Lesson 27 Making Statistical Inferences ©Curriculum Associates, LLC Copying is not permitted.

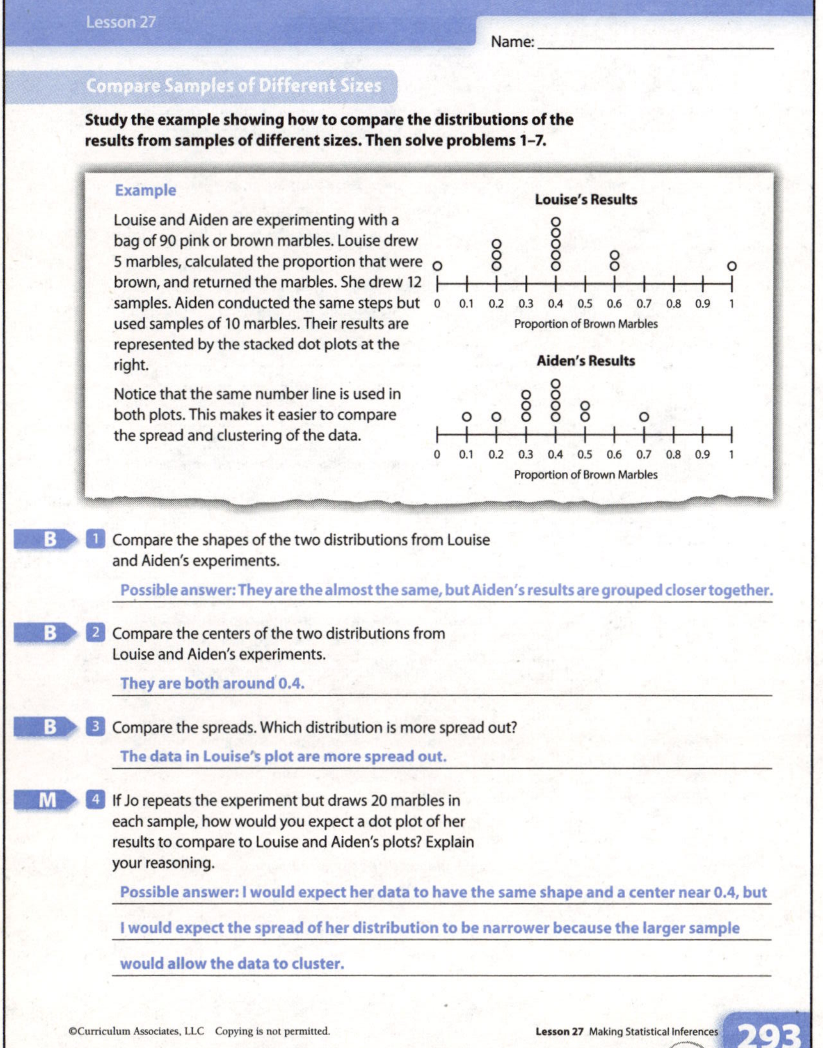

Lesson 27

Name: ______________________

Compare Samples of Different Sizes

Study the example showing how to compare the distributions of the results from samples of different sizes. Then solve problems 1–7.

Example

Louise and Aiden are experimenting with a bag of 90 pink or brown marbles. Louise drew 5 marbles, calculated the proportion that were brown, and returned the marbles. She drew 12 samples. Aiden conducted the same steps but used samples of 10 marbles. Their results are represented by the stacked dot plots at the right.

Notice that the same number line is used in both plots. This makes it easier to compare the spread and clustering of the data.

Louise's Results

0 0.1 0.2 0.3 0.4 0.5 0.6 0.7 0.8 0.9 1

Proportion of Brown Marbles

Aiden's Results

0 0.1 0.2 0.3 0.4 0.5 0.6 0.7 0.8 0.9 1

Proportion of Brown Marbles

B 1 Compare the shapes of the two distributions from Louise and Aiden's experiments.

Possible answer: They are the almost the same, but Aiden's results are grouped closer together.

B 2 Compare the centers of the two distributions from Louise and Aiden's experiments.

They are both around 0.4.

B 3 Compare the spreads. Which distribution is more spread out?

The data in Louise's plot are more spread out.

M 4 If Jo repeats the experiment but draws 20 marbles in each sample, how would you expect a dot plot of her results to compare to Louise and Aiden's plots? Explain your reasoning.

Possible answer: I would expect her data to have the same shape and a center near 0.4, but I would expect the spread of her distribution to be narrower because the larger sample would allow the data to cluster.

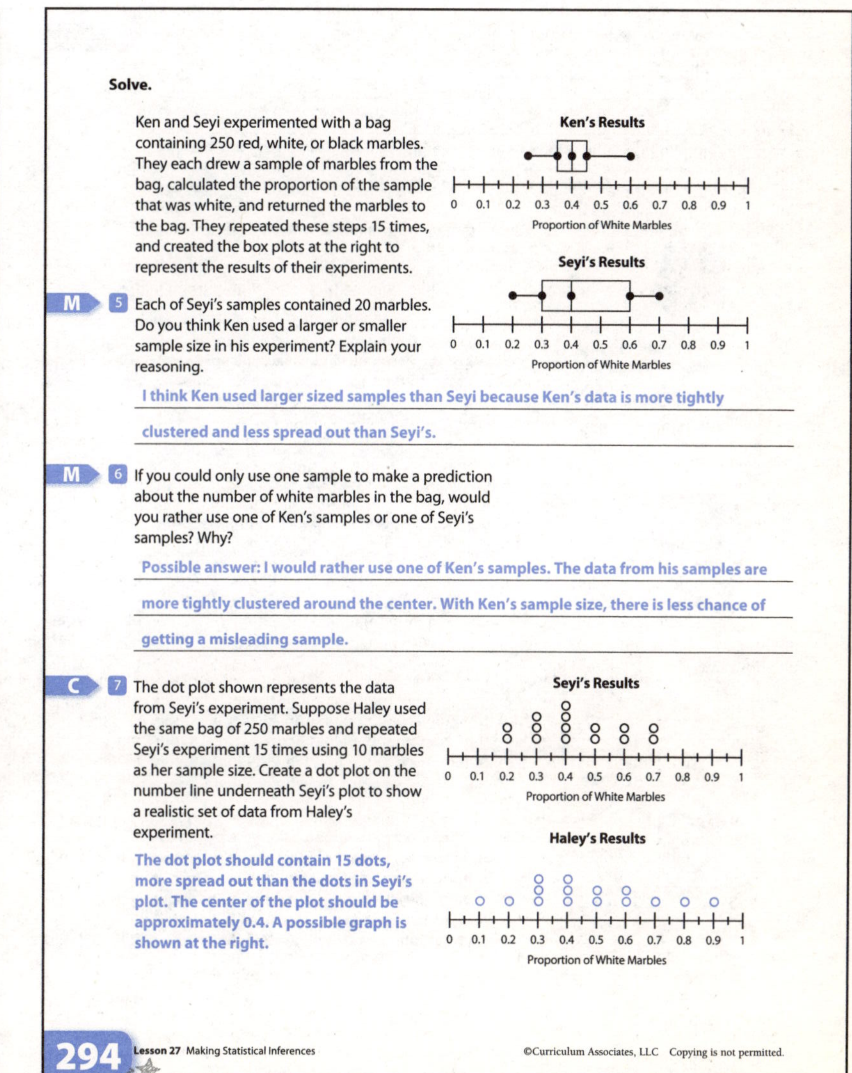

Solve.

Ken and Seyi experimented with a bag containing 250 red, white, or black marbles. They each drew a sample of marbles from the bag, calculated the proportion of the sample that was white, and returned the marbles to the bag. They repeated these steps 15 times, and created the box plots at the right to represent the results of their experiments.

Ken's Results

0 0.1 0.2 0.3 0.4 0.5 0.6 0.7 0.8 0.9 1

Proportion of White Marbles

Seyi's Results

0 0.1 0.2 0.3 0.4 0.5 0.6 0.7 0.8 0.9 1

Proportion of White Marbles

M 5 Each of Seyi's samples contained 20 marbles. Do you think Ken used a larger or smaller sample size in his experiment? Explain your reasoning.

I think Ken used larger sized samples than Seyi because Ken's data is more tightly clustered and less spread out than Seyi's.

M 6 If you could only use one sample to make a prediction about the number of white marbles in the bag, would you rather use one of Ken's samples or one of Seyi's samples? Why?

Possible answer: I would rather use one of Ken's samples. The data from his samples are more tightly clustered around the center. With Ken's sample size, there is less chance of getting a misleading sample.

C 7 The dot plot shown represents the data from Seyi's experiment. Suppose Haley used the same bag of 250 marbles and repeated Seyi's experiment 15 times using 10 marbles as her sample size. Create a dot plot on the number line underneath Seyi's plot to show a realistic set of data from Haley's experiment.

The dot plot should contain 15 dots, more spread out than the dots in Seyi's plot. The center of the plot should be approximately 0.4. A possible graph is shown at the right.

Seyi's Results

0 0.1 0.2 0.3 0.4 0.5 0.6 0.7 0.8 0.9 1

Proportion of White Marbles

Haley's Results

0 0.1 0.2 0.3 0.4 0.5 0.6 0.7 0.8 0.9 1

Proportion of White Marbles

Name: ____________________

Making Statistical Inferences

Solve the problems.

B

1 Gianna wanted to estimate the mean number of words per page in the 180-page book she is reading. Which of these sampling methods gives the best estimate of the mean word count per page in the book?

- **A** Count the words on one randomly chosen page.
- **B** Calculate the mean word count for a sample consisting of the 30 pages with photographs.
- **(C)** Calculate the mean word count for a sample of 20 pages selected by choosing every 9th page.
- **D** Calculate the mean word count for a sample consisting of the 10 pages that appear to have the most words.

What makes a sample biased?

M

2 A representative sample of 80 customers in a clothing store was surveyed about how they paid for their purchases. The table shows the responses.

Payment Method	Number of Customers
Cash	20
Check	12
Credit Card	24
Debit Card	16
Gift Card	8

How can you write the data in the table as proportions?

Based on the survey results, choose *True* or *False* for each statement.

- **a.** Tomorrow, 8 out of the first 80 customers will pay with a gift card. ☐ True ☒ False
- **b.** In a group of 40 customers, it is expected that about 10 will pay with cash. ☒ True ☐ False
- **c.** About 0.3 of all the store's customers will pay with a credit card. ☒ True ☐ False
- **d.** A sample of 100 customers would provide less reliable results. ☐ True ☒ False

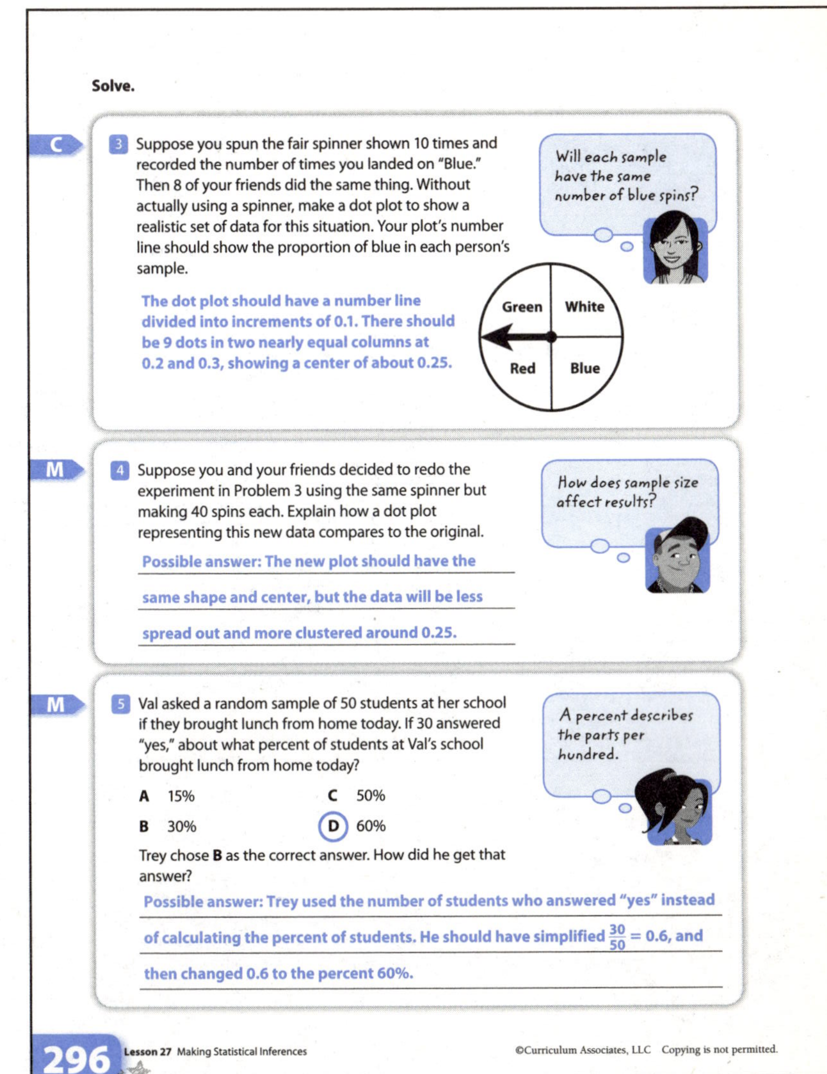

Solve.

C

3 Suppose you spun the fair spinner shown 10 times and recorded the number of times you landed on "Blue." Then 8 of your friends did the same thing. Without actually using a spinner, make a dot plot to show a realistic set of data for this situation. Your plot's number line should show the proportion of blue in each person's sample.

The dot plot should have a number line divided into increments of 0.1. There should be 9 dots in two nearly equal columns at 0.2 and 0.3, showing a center of about 0.25.

Will each sample have the same number of blue spins?

M

4 Suppose you and your friends decided to redo the experiment in Problem 3 using the same spinner but making 40 spins each. Explain how a dot plot representing this new data compares to the original.

Possible answer: The new plot should have the same shape and center, but the data will be less spread out and more clustered around 0.25.

How does sample size affect results?

M

5 Val asked a random sample of 50 students at her school if they brought lunch from home today. If 30 answered "yes," about what percent of students at Val's school brought lunch from home today?

- **A** 15%
- **B** 30%
- **C** 50%
- **(D)** 60%

Trey chose **B** as the correct answer. How did he get that answer?

Possible answer: Trey used the number of students who answered "yes" instead of calculating the percent of students. He should have simplified $\frac{30}{50} = 0.6$, and then changed 0.6 to the percent 60%.

A percent describes the parts per hundred.

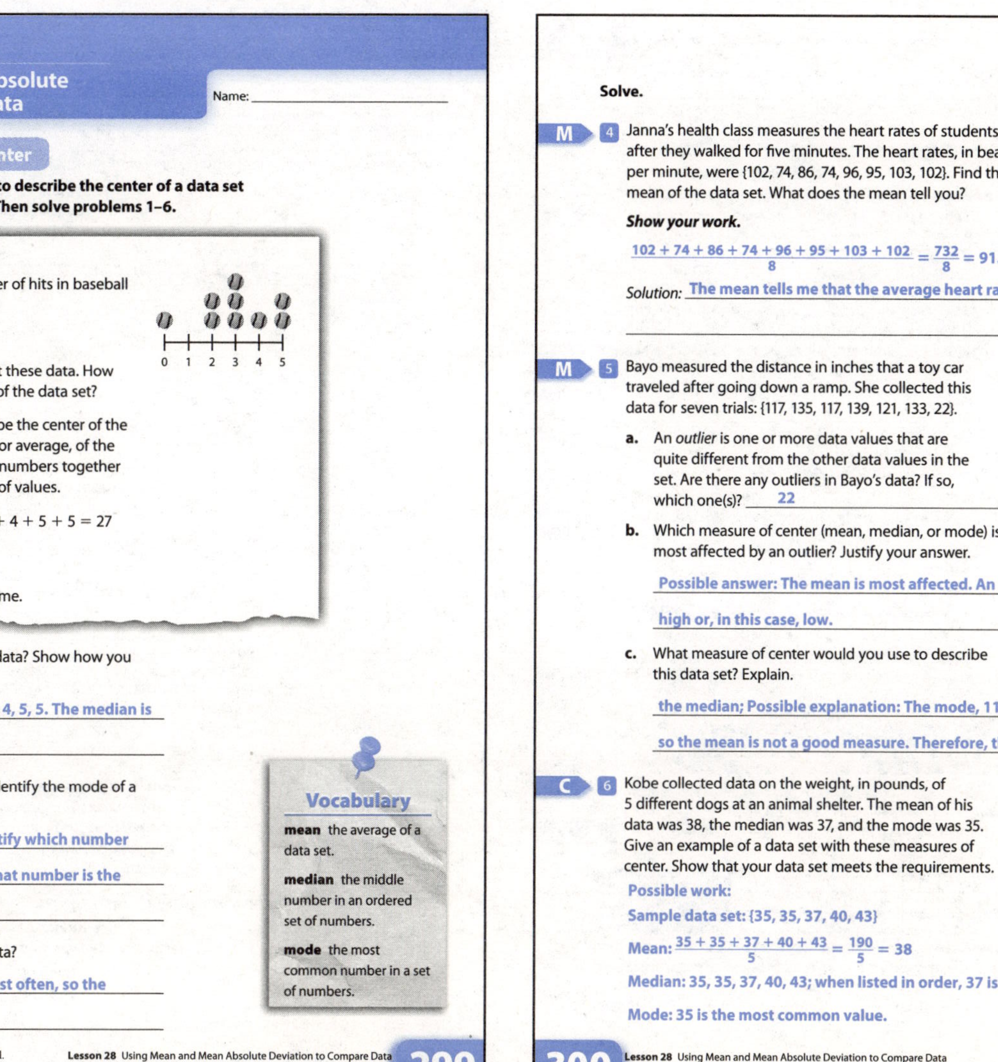

Lesson 28

Using Mean and Mean Absolute Deviation to Compare Data

Name: ______________________

Prerequisite: Measures of Center

Study the example showing how to describe the center of a data set using mean, median, and mode. Then solve problems 1–6.

Example

Miguel keeps track of his number of hits in baseball games this year. His data set is:

{3, 2, 5, 3, 0, 2, 3, 5, 4}

He draws a dot plot to represent these data. How can Miguel describe the center of the data set?

One way that Miguel can describe the center of the data set is by finding the *mean,* or average, of the data. To find the mean, add the numbers together and divide by the total number of values.

Sum = 0 + 2 + 2 + 3 + 3 + 3 + 4 + 5 + 5 = 27

Mean = $\frac{27}{9}$ = 3

Miguel's average is 3 hits per game.

B 1 What is the median of Miguel's data? Show how you found your answer.

Order the data: 0, 2, 2, 3, 3, 3, 4, 5, 5. The median is the middle number, 3.

B 2 How can you use a dot plot to identify the mode of a data set?

Look at the dot plot and identify which number has the most dots above it. That number is the mode of the data set.

B 3 What is the mode of Miguel's data?

In this data set, 3 appears most often, so the mode is 3.

Vocabulary

mean the average of a data set.

median the middle number in an ordered set of numbers.

mode the most common number in a set of numbers.

Solve.

M 4 Janna's health class measures the heart rates of students after they walked for five minutes. The heart rates, in beats per minute, were {102, 74, 86, 74, 96, 95, 103, 102}. Find the mean of the data set. What does the mean tell you?

Show your work.

$\frac{102 + 74 + 86 + 74 + 96 + 95 + 103 + 102}{8} = \frac{732}{8} = 91.5$

Solution: The mean tells me that the average heart rate was 91.5 beats per minute.

M 5 Bayo measured the distance in inches that a toy car traveled after going down a ramp. She collected this data for seven trials: {117, 135, 117, 139, 121, 133, 22}.

a. An *outlier* is one or more data values that are quite different from the other data values in the set. Are there any outliers in Bayo's data? If so, which one(s)? 22

b. Which measure of center (mean, median, or mode) is most affected by an outlier? Justify your answer.

Possible answer: The mean is most affected. An outlier will make the mean artificially high or, in this case, low.

c. What measure of center would you use to describe this data set? Explain.

the median; Possible explanation: The mode, 117, seems too low. There is an outlier, so the mean is not a good measure. Therefore, the median, 121, is the best measure.

C 6 Kobe collected data on the weight, in pounds, of 5 different dogs at an animal shelter. The mean of his data was 38, the median was 37, and the mode was 35. Give an example of a data set with these measures of center. Show that your data set meets the requirements.

Possible work:

Sample data set: {35, 35, 37, 40, 43}

Mean: $\frac{35 + 35 + 37 + 40 + 43}{5} = \frac{190}{5} = 38$

Median: 35, 35, 37, 40, 43; when listed in order, 37 is the middle value.

Mode: 35 is the most common value.

Key

B Basic **M** Medium **C** Challenge

Lesson 28

Name: ______________________

Comparing Variabilities and Centers

Study the example showing how to compare data sets that have similar variabilities. Then solve problems 1–9.

Example

Mr. Markum is ordering sneakers for the boys' baseball team. The sizes ordered and the number of pairs of each size are shown in the table. To the nearest tenth, the mean size of the sneakers for the baseball team is 10.6. What is the mean absolute deviation (MAD)?

Sneaker Size	8.5	9	9.5	10	10.5	11	11.5	12
Number	1	2	0	2	3	4	1	3
Difference from Mean Size	2.1	1.6	0	0.6	0.1	−0.4	−0.9	−1.4

To find the MAD of the sneaker sizes, subtract each data value from the mean. Then average the absolute values of these numbers and round to the nearest tenth.

$$\frac{2.1 + (2 \times 1.6) + (2 \times 0.6) + (3 \times 0.1) + (4 \times 0.4) + 0.9 + (3 \times 1.4)}{16} = \frac{13.5}{16} \approx 0.8$$

B 1 Mr. Markum also orders sneakers for the girls' softball team. He makes the table below. The mean size of the sneakers to the nearest tenth is 8.2. Complete the table.

Sneaker Size	7	7.5	8	8.5	9	9.5	10
Number	2	3	5	1	3	1	1
Difference from Mean Size	1.2	0.7	0.2	−0.3	−0.8	−1.3	−1.8

B 2 Calculate the MAD of the softball sneaker sizes to the nearest tenth.

[(2 × 1.2) + (3 × 0.7) + (5 × 0.2) + 0.3 + (3 × 0.8) + 1.3 + 1.8] ÷ 16 = 11.3 ÷ 16 ≈ 0.7

M 3 What is the difference in the mean sizes of the two types of sneakers? What is the difference in their MADs? Interpret the differences in the means and MADs.

Difference in means: 10.6 − 8.2 = 2.4; Difference in MADs: 0.8 − 0.7 = 0.1. Both the means and the MADs are relatively close to each other, so the data values are not the same but overlap quite a bit.

Solve.

The table gives average speeds of eight horses in a horse race and eight cars in a car race. Use the table to solve problems 4–9.

Number	1	2	3	4	5	6	7	8
Speed of Horse (mph)	29	30	27	25	27	26	27	23
Speed of Car (mph)	233	228	229	234	231	228	232	226

M 4 Calculate the mean of the horses' speeds to the nearest tenth. Then calculate the mean of the cars' speeds to the nearest tenth.

Horses: $\frac{29 + 30 + 27 + 25 + 27 + 26 + 27 + 23}{8} = \frac{214}{8} \approx 26.8$ **mph**

Cars: $\frac{233 + 228 + 229 + 234 + 231 + 228 + 232 + 226}{8} = \frac{1{,}841}{8} \approx 230.1$ **mph**

M 5 Calculate the MAD of the horses' speeds to the nearest tenth. Calculate the MAD of the cars' speeds to the nearest tenth.

Horses: $\frac{2.2 + 3.2 + 0.2 + 1.8 + 0.2 + 0.8 + 0.2 + 3.8}{8} = \frac{12.4}{8} \approx 1.6$ **mph**

Cars: $\frac{2.9 + 2.1 + 1.1 + 3.9 + 0.9 + 2.1 + 1.9 + 4.1}{8} = \frac{19.0}{8} \approx 2.4$ **mph**

M 6 Were the horses' speeds or the cars' speeds closer to their mean? Explain.

The horses' speeds because the MAD for the horses' speeds is less than the MAD for the cars' speeds.

B 7 What is the difference in the means? **230.1 − 26.8 = 203.3**

M 8 By what number would you have to multiply the MAD of the cars' speeds to get the difference between the means that you found in problem 7? Round your answer to the nearest tenth.

203.3 ÷ 2.4 = 84.7

C 9 What do your answers to problems 4, 5, and 8 tell you about the two data sets? Your answers should refer to the means and the MADs of the data sets.

Possible answer: The MADs are fairly close, so the spread of the two data sets is similar. Because the difference of the means is more than 80 times the mean absolute deviation, there is probably no overlap in the data values.

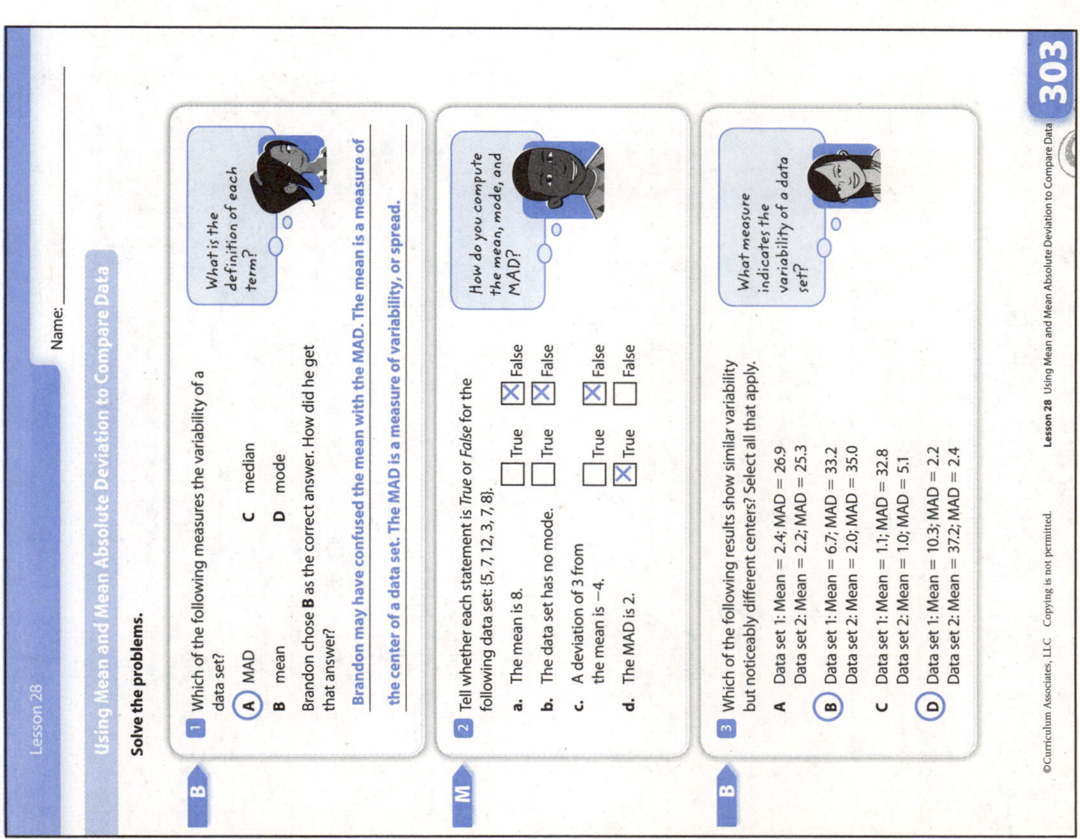

Lesson 28

Name: ______________________

Using Mean and Mean Absolute Deviation to Compare Data

Solve the problems.

B

1 Which of the following measures the variability of a data set?

(A) MAD C median

B mean D mode

Brandon chose **B** as the correct answer. How did he get that answer?

Brandon may have confused the mean with the MAD. The mean is a measure of the center of a data set. The MAD is a measure of variability, or spread.

M

2 Tell whether each statement is *True* or *False* for the following data set: {5, 7, 12, 3, 7, 8}.

a. The mean is 8. ☐ True ☒ False

b. The data set has no mode. ☐ True ☒ False

c. A deviation of 3 from the mean is −4. ☐ True ☒ False

d. The MAD is 2. ☒ True ☐ False

B

3 Which of the following results show similar variability but noticeably different centers? Select all that apply.

A Data set 1: Mean = 2.4; MAD = 26.9
Data set 2: Mean = 2.2; MAD = 25.3

(**B**) Data set 1: Mean = 6.7; MAD = 33.2
Data set 2: Mean = 2.0; MAD = 35.0

C Data set 1: Mean = 1.1; MAD = 32.8
Data set 2: Mean = 1.0; MAD = 5.1

(**D**) Data set 1: Mean = 10.3; MAD = 2.2
Data set 2: Mean = 37.2; MAD = 2.4

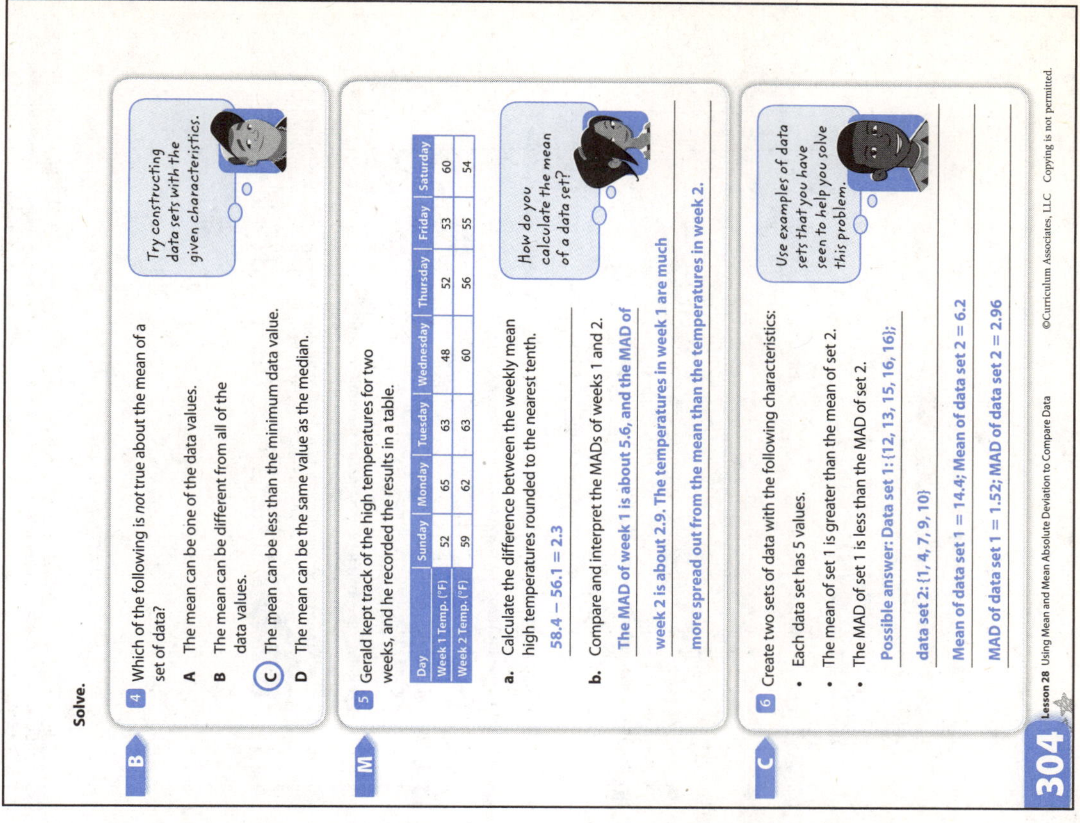

Solve.

B

4 Which of the following is *not* true about the mean of a set of data?

A The mean can be one of the data values.

B The mean can be different from all of the data values.

(**C**) The mean can be less than the minimum data value.

D The mean can be the same value as the median.

M

5 Gerald kept track of the high temperatures for two weeks, and he recorded the results in a table.

Day	Sunday	Monday	Tuesday	Wednesday	Thursday	Friday	Saturday
Week 1 Temp. (°F)	52	65	63	48	52	53	60
Week 2 Temp. (°F)	59	62	63	60	56	55	54

a. Calculate the difference between the weekly mean high temperatures rounded to the nearest tenth.

58.4 − 56.1 = 2.3

b. Compare and interpret the MADs of weeks 1 and 2.

The MAD of week 1 is about 5.6, and the MAD of week 2 is about 2.9. The temperatures in week 1 are much more spread out from the mean than the temperatures in week 2.

C

6 Create two sets of data with the following characteristics:

- Each data set has 5 values.
- The mean of set 1 is greater than the mean of set 2.
- The MAD of set 1 is less than the MAD of set 2.

Possible answer: Data set 1: {12, 13, 15, 16, 16}; data set 2: {1, 4, 7, 9, 10}

Mean of data set 1 = 14.4; Mean of data set 2 = 6.2

MAD of data set 1 = 1.52; MAD of data set 2 = 2.96

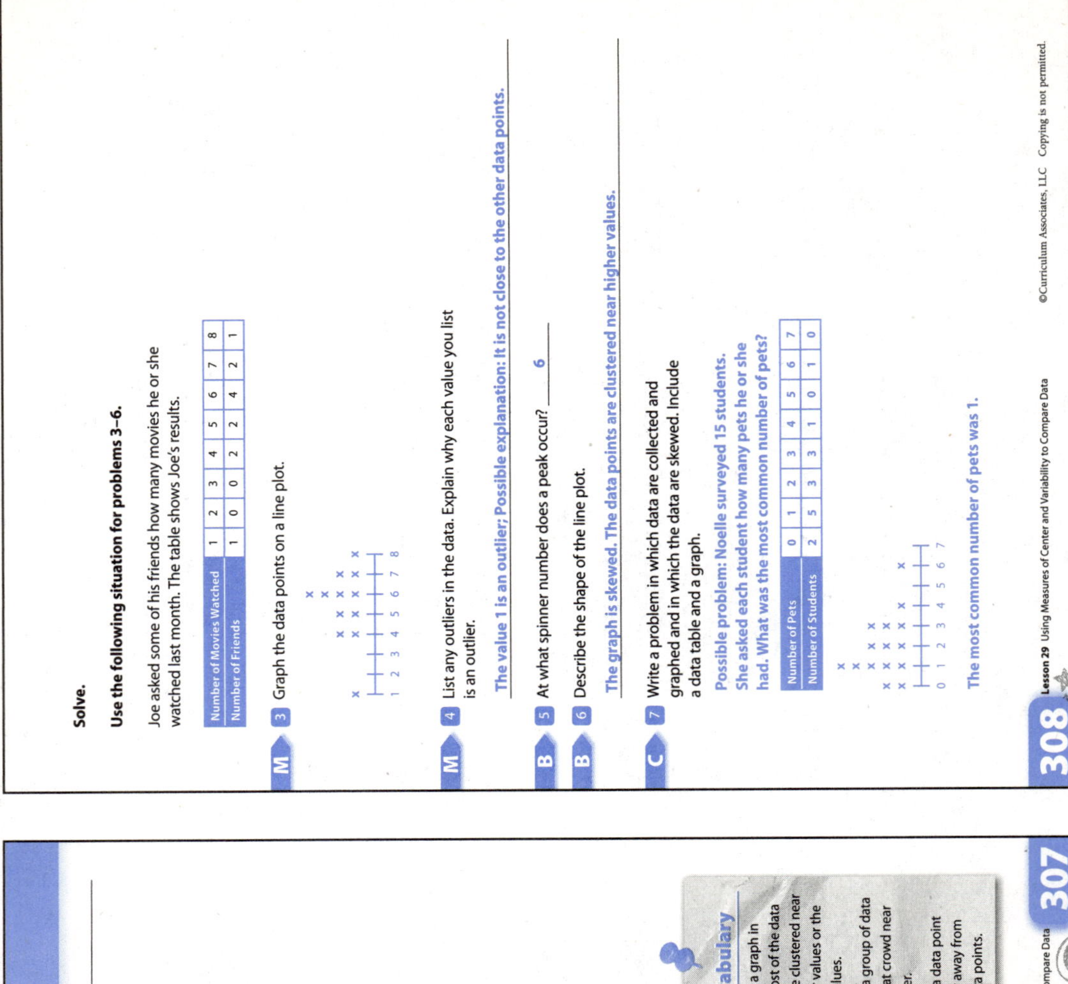

Lesson 29

Using Measures of Center and Variability to Compare Data

Name: ____________

Prerequisite: Shape of Data Points on a Graph

Study the example showing how to describe the shape of a graph. Then solve problems 1–7.

Example

Twelve students in each of three different seventh-grade classes sell flowers to raise money for a class trip. The line plots for each class are shown. Each student is represented by one X. Describe the shape of the graph for Ms. Marcum's class.

The graph for Ms. Marcum's class is *symmetrical* because the same number of data points fall above and below the *peak* at 4.

B 1 Describe the shapes of the graphs for Mr. Wright's class and Mr. Chu's class.

Both graphs are skewed. The data in the graph for Mr. Wright's class are clustered near the lower values. The data in the graph for Mr. Chu's class are clustered near the higher values.

B 2 Which graph does *not* include an outlier? Explain.

The graph for Ms. Marcum's class; Possible explanation: There is no gap in the data values.

Vocabulary

skewed a graph in which most of the data points are clustered near the lower values or the higher values.

cluster a group of data points that crowd near each other.

outlier a data point that is far away from other data points.

©Curriculum Associates, LLC Copying is not permitted. **Lesson 29** Using Measures of Center and Variability to Compare Data 307

Solve.

Use the following situation for problems 3–6.

Joe asked some of his friends how many movies he or she watched last month. The table shows Joe's results.

Number of Movies Watched	1	2	3	4	5	6	7	8
Number of Friends	1	0	0	2	2	4	2	1

M 3 Graph the data points on a line plot.

M 4 List any outliers in the data. Explain why each value you list is an outlier.

The value 1 is an outlier; Possible explanation: It is not close to the other data points.

B 5 At what spinner number does a peak occur? 6

B 6 Describe the shape of the line plot.

The graph is skewed. The data points are clustered near higher values.

C 7 Write a problem in which data are collected and graphed and in which the data are skewed. Include a data table and a graph.

Possible problem: Noelle surveyed 15 students. She asked each student how many pets he or she had. What was the most common number of pets?

Number of Pets	0	1	2	3	4	5	6	7
Number of Students	2	5	3	3	1	0	1	0

The most common number of pets was 1.

308 **Lesson 29** Using Measures of Center and Variability to Compare Data ©Curriculum Associates, LLC Copying is not permitted.

Key

B Basic **M** Medium **C** Challenge

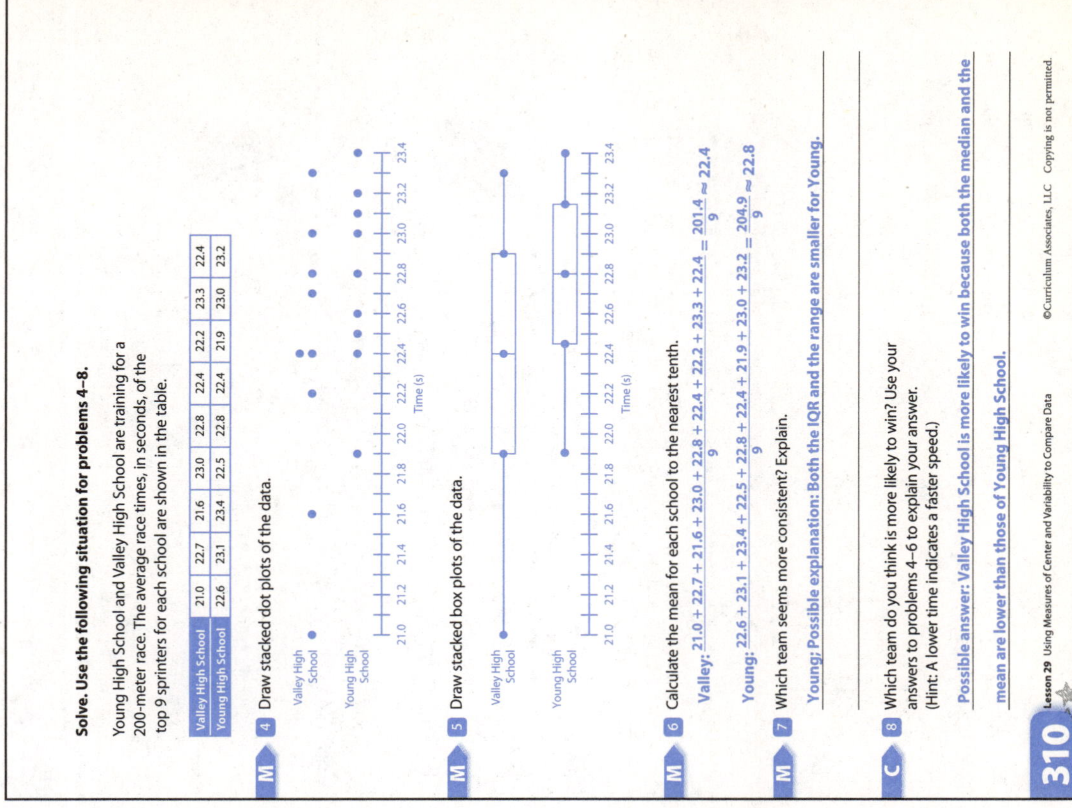

Solve. Use the following situation for problems 4–8.

Young High School and Valley High School are training for a 200-meter race. The average race times, in seconds, of the top 9 sprinters for each school are shown in the table.

Valley High School	21.0	22.7	21.6	23.0	22.8	22.4	22.2	23.3	22.4
Young High School	22.6	23.1	23.4	22.5	22.8	22.4	21.9	23.0	23.2

M 4 Draw stacked dot plots of the data.

M 5 Draw stacked box plots of the data.

M 6 Calculate the mean for each school to the nearest tenth.

Valley: $\frac{21.0 + 22.7 + 21.6 + 23.0 + 22.8 + 22.4 + 22.2 + 23.3 + 22.4}{9} = \frac{201.4}{9} \approx 22.4$

Young: $\frac{22.6 + 23.1 + 23.4 + 22.5 + 22.8 + 22.4 + 21.9 + 23.0 + 23.2}{9} = \frac{204.9}{9} \approx 22.8$

M 7 Which team seems more consistent? Explain.

Young; Possible explanation: Both the IQR and the range are smaller for Young.

C 8 Which team do you think is more likely to win? Use your answers to problems 4–6 to explain your answer. (Hint: A lower time indicates a faster speed.)

Possible answer: Valley High School is more likely to win because both the median and the mean are lower than those of Young High School.

310 Lesson 29 Using Measures of Center and Variability to Compare Data ©Curriculum Associates, LLC Copying is not permitted.

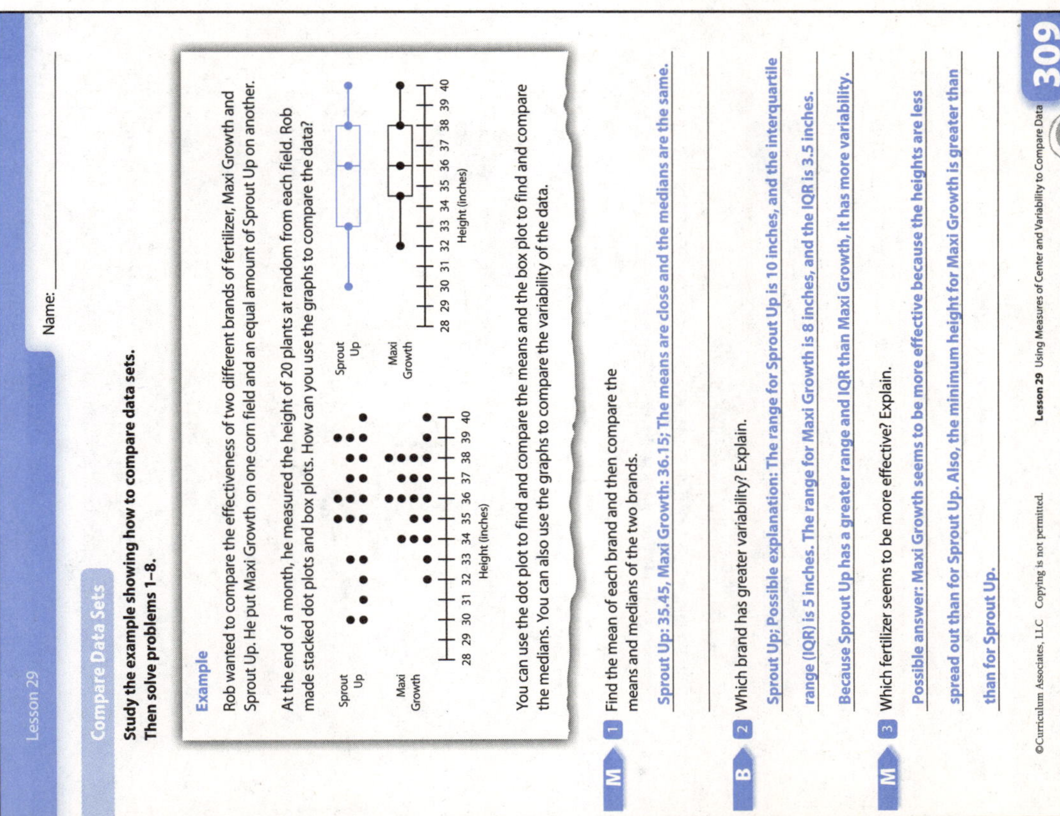

Lesson 29

Name: ____________

Compare Data Sets

Study the example showing how to compare data sets. Then solve problems 1–8.

Example

Rob wanted to compare the effectiveness of two different brands of fertilizer, Maxi Growth and Sprout Up. He put Maxi Growth on one corn field and an equal amount of Sprout Up on another.

At the end of a month, he measured the height of 20 plants at random from each field. Rob made stacked dot plots and box plots. How can you use the graphs to compare the data?

You can use the dot plot to find and compare the means and the box plot to find and compare the medians. You can also use the graphs to compare the variability of the data.

M 1 Find the mean of each brand and then compare the means and medians of the two brands.

Sprout Up: 35.45, Maxi Growth: 36.15; The means are close and the medians are the same.

B 2 Which brand has greater variability? Explain.

Sprout Up; Possible explanation: The range for Sprout Up is 10 inches, and the interquartile range (IQR) is 5 inches. The range for Maxi Growth is 8 inches, and the IQR is 3.5 inches. Because Sprout Up has a greater range and IQR than Maxi Growth, it has more variability.

M 3 Which fertilizer seems to be more effective? Explain.

Possible answer: Maxi Growth seems to be more effective because the heights are less spread out than for Sprout Up. Also, the minimum height for Maxi Growth is greater than than for Sprout Up.

©Curriculum Associates, LLC Copying is not permitted. Lesson 29 Using Measures of Center and Variability to Compare Data 309

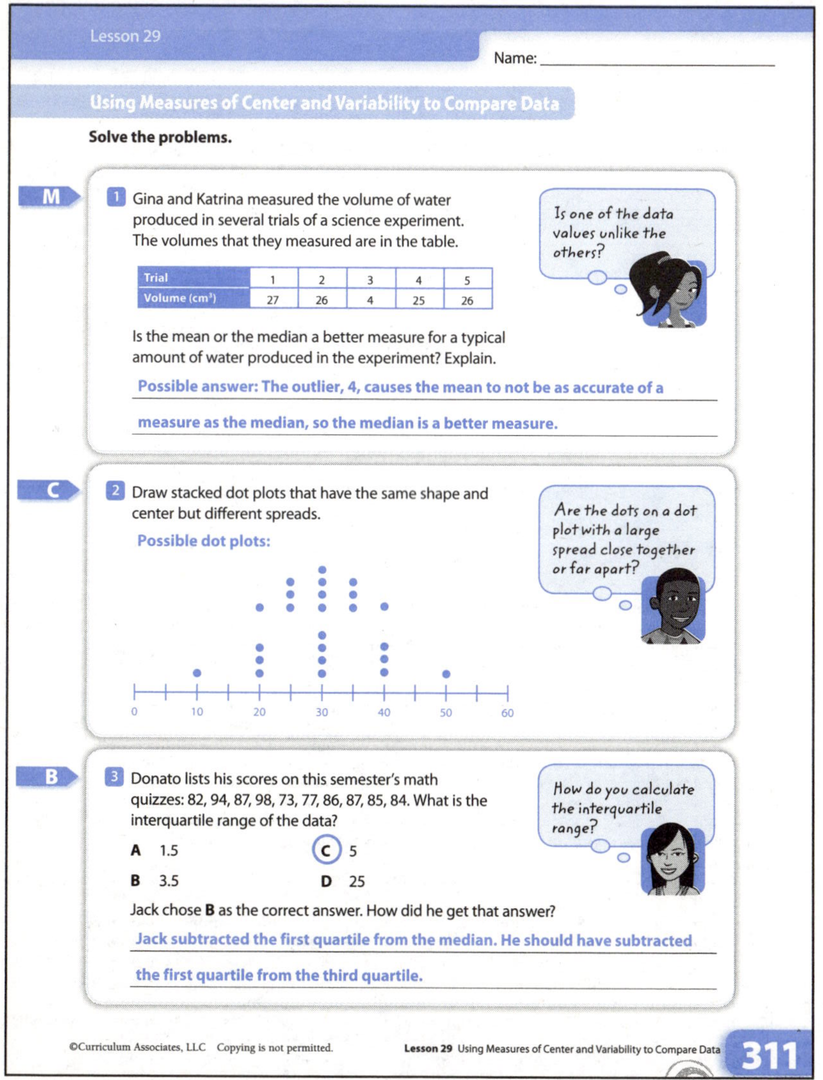

Lesson 29

Name: ____________

Using Measures of Center and Variability to Compare Data

Solve the problems.

M **1** Gina and Katrina measured the volume of water produced in several trials of a science experiment. The volumes that they measured are in the table.

Trial	1	2	3	4	5
Volume (cm³)	27	26	4	25	26

Is the mean or the median a better measure for a typical amount of water produced in the experiment? Explain.

Possible answer: The outlier, 4, causes the mean to not be as accurate of a measure as the median, so the median is a better measure.

C **2** Draw stacked dot plots that have the same shape and center but different spreads.

Possible dot plots:

B **3** Donato lists his scores on this semester's math quizzes: 82, 94, 87, 98, 73, 77, 86, 87, 85, 84. What is the interquartile range of the data?

A 1.5

B 3.5

Ⓒ 5

D 25

Jack chose **B** as the correct answer. How did he get that answer?

Jack subtracted the first quartile from the median. He should have subtracted the first quartile from the third quartile.

©Curriculum Associates, LLC Copying is not permitted. **Lesson 29** Using Measures of Center and Variability to Compare Data 311

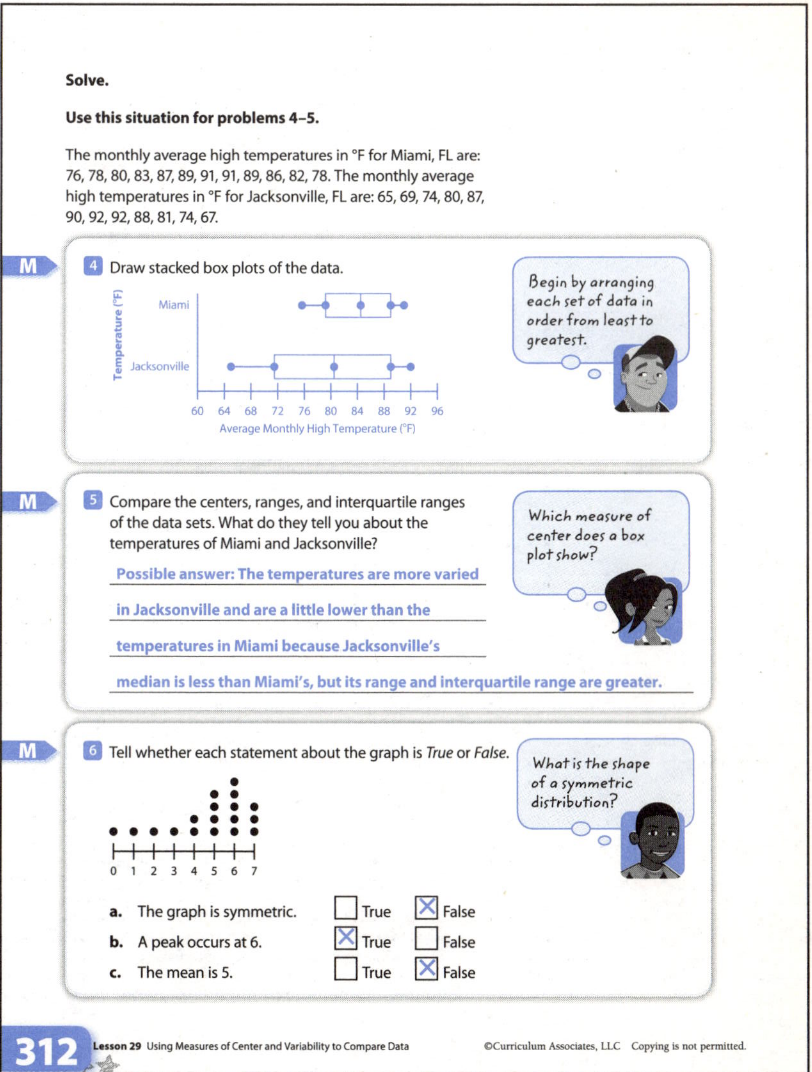

Solve.

Use this situation for problems 4–5.

The monthly average high temperatures in °F for Miami, FL are: 76, 78, 80, 83, 87, 89, 91, 91, 89, 86, 82, 78. The monthly average high temperatures in °F for Jacksonville, FL are: 65, 69, 74, 80, 87, 90, 92, 92, 88, 81, 74, 67.

M **4** Draw stacked box plots of the data.

M **5** Compare the centers, ranges, and interquartile ranges of the data sets. What do they tell you about the temperatures of Miami and Jacksonville?

Possible answer: The temperatures are more varied in Jacksonville and are a little lower than the temperatures in Miami because Jacksonville's median is less than Miami's, but its range and interquartile range are greater.

M **6** Tell whether each statement about the graph is *True* or *False*.

a. The graph is symmetric. ☐ True ☒ False

b. A peak occurs at 6. ☒ True ☐ False

c. The mean is 5. ☐ True ☒ False

312 **Lesson 29** Using Measures of Center and Variability to Compare Data ©Curriculum Associates, LLC Copying is not permitted.

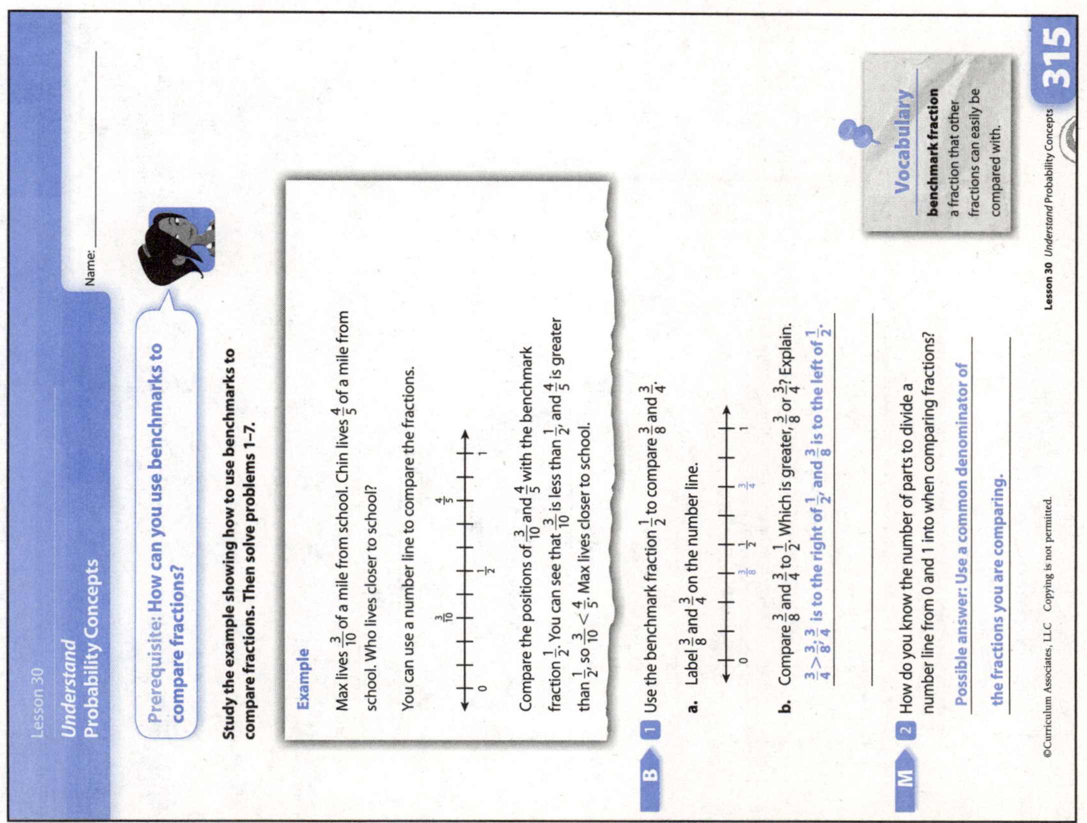

Lesson 30

Understand
Probability Concepts

Name: ____________

Prerequisite: How can you use benchmarks to compare fractions?

Study the example showing how to use benchmarks to compare fractions. Then solve problems 1–7.

Example

Max lives $\frac{3}{10}$ of a mile from school. Chin lives $\frac{4}{5}$ of a mile from school. Who lives closer to school?

You can use a number line to compare the fractions.

Compare the positions of $\frac{3}{10}$ and $\frac{4}{5}$ with the benchmark fraction $\frac{1}{2}$. You can see that $\frac{3}{10}$ is less than $\frac{1}{2}$, and $\frac{4}{5}$ is greater than $\frac{1}{2}$, so $\frac{3}{10} < \frac{4}{5}$. Max lives closer to school.

B 1 Use the benchmark fraction $\frac{1}{2}$ to compare $\frac{3}{8}$ and $\frac{3}{4}$.

a. Label $\frac{3}{8}$ and $\frac{3}{4}$ on the number line.

b. Compare $\frac{3}{8}$ and $\frac{3}{4}$ to $\frac{1}{2}$. Which is greater, $\frac{3}{8}$ or $\frac{3}{4}$? Explain.

$\frac{3}{4} > \frac{3}{8}$; $\frac{3}{4}$ is to the right of $\frac{1}{2}$, and $\frac{3}{8}$ is to the left of $\frac{1}{2}$.

M 2 How do you know the number of parts to divide a number line from 0 and 1 into when comparing fractions?

Possible answer: Use a common denominator of the fractions you are comparing.

Vocabulary

benchmark fraction a fraction that other fractions can easily be compared with.

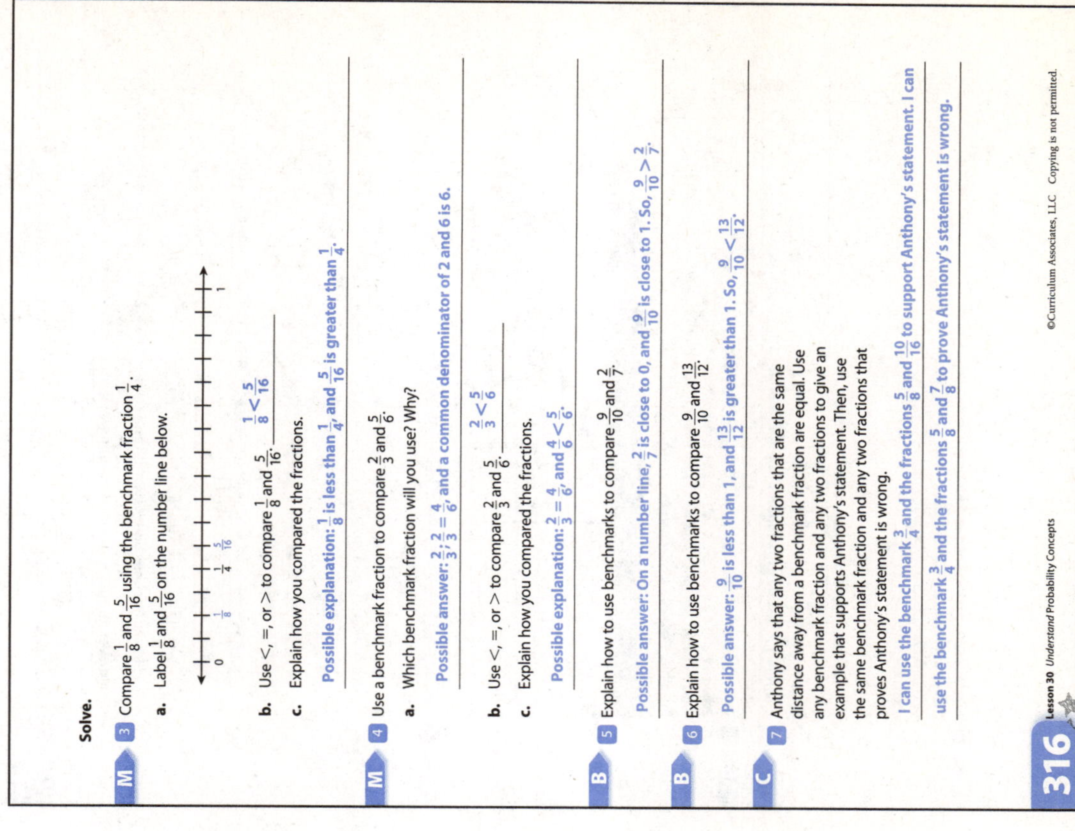

Solve.

M 3 Compare $\frac{1}{8}$ and $\frac{5}{16}$ using the benchmark fraction $\frac{1}{4}$.

a. Label $\frac{1}{8}$ and $\frac{5}{16}$ on the number line below.

b. Use <, =, or > to compare $\frac{1}{8}$ and $\frac{5}{16}$. $\frac{1}{8} < \frac{5}{16}$

c. Explain how you compared the fractions.

Possible explanation: $\frac{1}{8}$ is less than $\frac{1}{4}$, and $\frac{5}{16}$ is greater than $\frac{1}{4}$.

M 4 Use a benchmark fraction to compare $\frac{2}{3}$ and $\frac{5}{6}$.

a. Which benchmark fraction will you use? Why?

Possible answer: $\frac{2}{3}$; $\frac{2}{3} = \frac{4}{6}$, and a common denominator of 2 and 6 is 6.

b. Use <, =, or > to compare $\frac{2}{3}$ and $\frac{5}{6}$. $\frac{2}{3} < \frac{5}{6}$

c. Explain how you compared the fractions.

Possible explanation: $\frac{2}{3} = \frac{4}{6}$, and $\frac{4}{6} < \frac{5}{6}$.

B 5 Explain how to use benchmarks to compare $\frac{9}{10}$ and $\frac{2}{7}$.

Possible answer: On a number line, $\frac{2}{7}$ is close to 0, and $\frac{9}{10}$ is close to 1. So, $\frac{9}{10} > \frac{2}{7}$.

B 6 Explain how to use benchmarks to compare $\frac{9}{10}$ and $\frac{13}{12}$.

Possible answer: $\frac{9}{10}$ is less than 1, and $\frac{13}{12}$ is greater than 1. So, $\frac{9}{10} < \frac{13}{12}$.

C 7 Anthony says that any two fractions that are the same distance away from a benchmark fraction are equal. Use any benchmark fraction and any two fractions to give an example that supports Anthony's statement. Then, use the same benchmark fraction and any two fractions that proves Anthony's statement is wrong.

I can use the benchmark $\frac{3}{4}$ and the fractions $\frac{5}{8}$ and $\frac{10}{16}$ to support Anthony's statement. I can use the benchmark $\frac{3}{4}$ and the fractions $\frac{5}{8}$ and $\frac{7}{8}$ to prove Anthony's statement is wrong.

Key

B Basic **M** Medium **C** Challenge

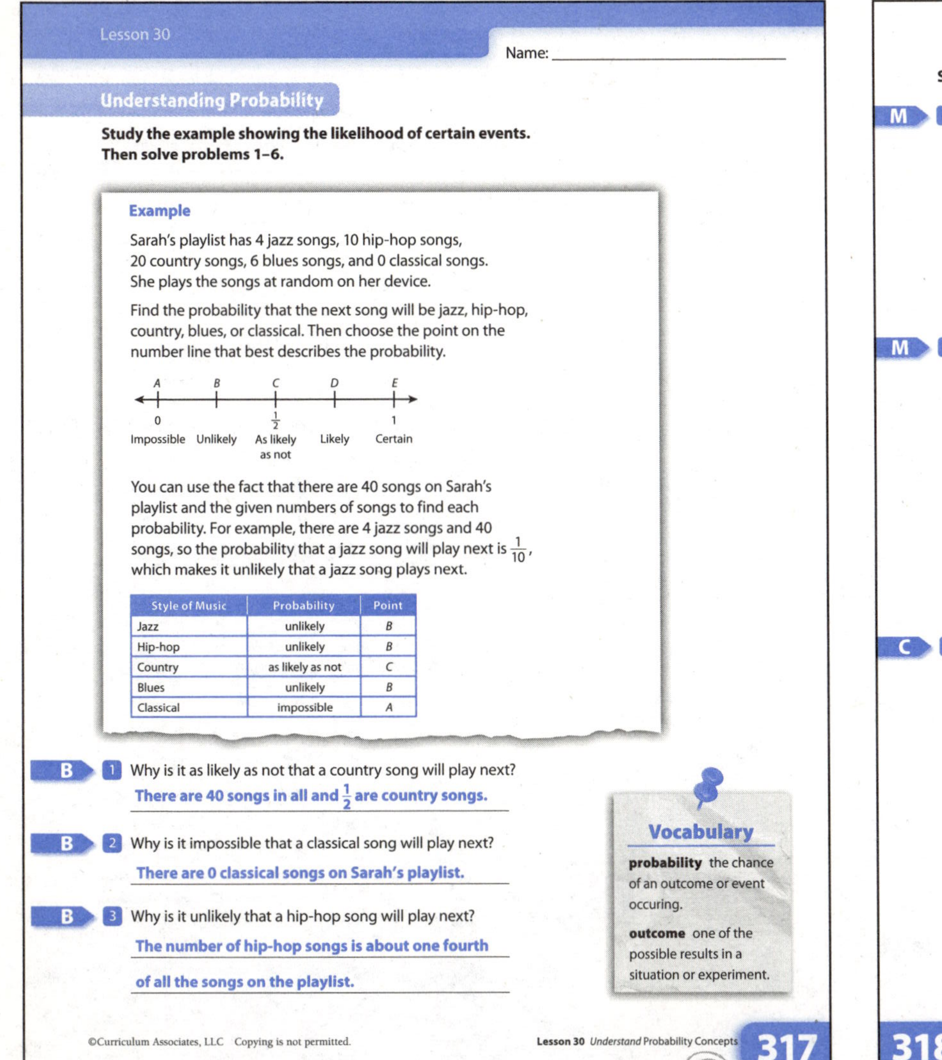

Lesson 30

Name: ____________________

Understanding Probability

Study the example showing the likelihood of certain events. Then solve problems 1–6.

Example

Sarah's playlist has 4 jazz songs, 10 hip-hop songs, 20 country songs, 6 blues songs, and 0 classical songs. She plays the songs at random on her device.

Find the probability that the next song will be jazz, hip-hop, country, blues, or classical. Then choose the point on the number line that best describes the probability.

You can use the fact that there are 40 songs on Sarah's playlist and the given numbers of songs to find each probability. For example, there are 4 jazz songs and 40 songs, so the probability that a jazz song will play next is $\frac{1}{10}$, which makes it unlikely that a jazz song plays next.

Style of Music	Probability	Point
Jazz	unlikely	*B*
Hip-hop	unlikely	*B*
Country	as likely as not	*C*
Blues	unlikely	*B*
Classical	impossible	*A*

B 1 Why is it as likely as not that a country song will play next?

There are 40 songs in all and $\frac{1}{2}$ are country songs.

B 2 Why is it impossible that a classical song will play next?

There are 0 classical songs on Sarah's playlist.

B 3 Why is it unlikely that a hip-hop song will play next?

The number of hip-hop songs is about one fourth of all the songs on the playlist.

Vocabulary

probability the chance of an outcome or event occuring.

outcome one of the possible results in a situation or experiment.

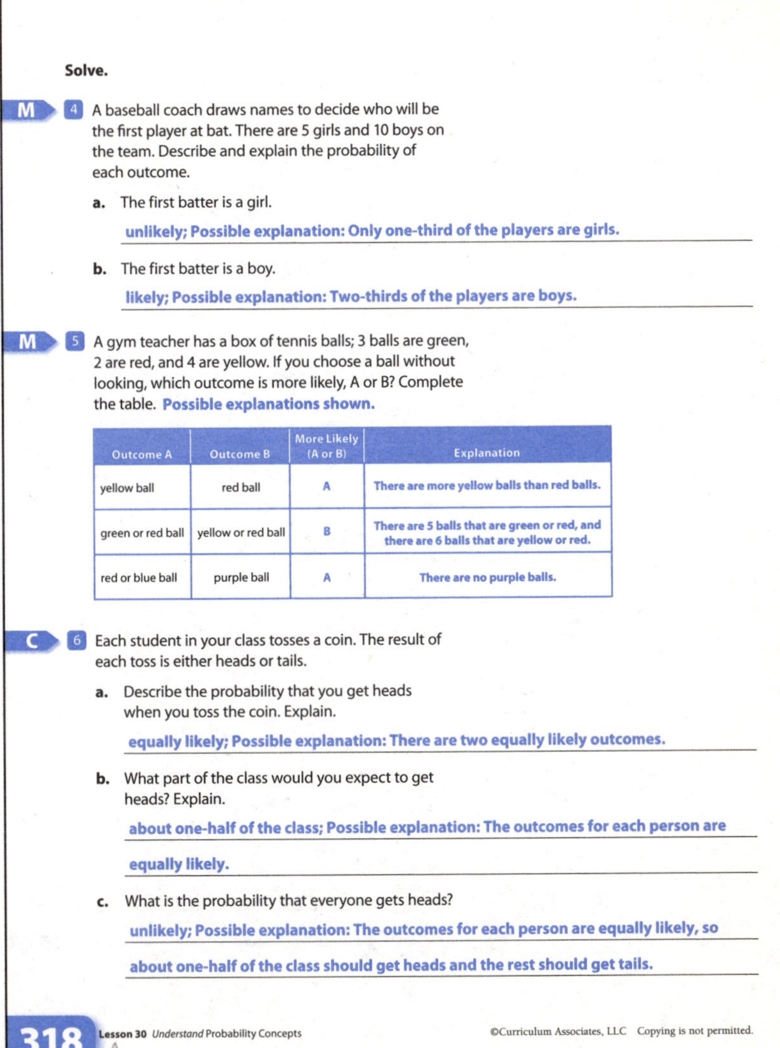

Solve.

M 4 A baseball coach draws names to decide who will be the first player at bat. There are 5 girls and 10 boys on the team. Describe and explain the probability of each outcome.

a. The first batter is a girl.

unlikely; Possible explanation: Only one-third of the players are girls.

b. The first batter is a boy.

likely; Possible explanation: Two-thirds of the players are boys.

M 5 A gym teacher has a box of tennis balls; 3 balls are green, 2 are red, and 4 are yellow. If you choose a ball without looking, which outcome is more likely, A or B? Complete the table. **Possible explanations shown.**

Outcome A	Outcome B	More Likely (A or B)	Explanation
yellow ball	red ball	**A**	**There are more yellow balls than red balls.**
green or red ball	yellow or red ball	**B**	**There are 5 balls that are green or red, and there are 6 balls that are yellow or red.**
red or blue ball	purple ball	**A**	**There are no purple balls.**

C 6 Each student in your class tosses a coin. The result of each toss is either heads or tails.

a. Describe the probability that you get heads when you toss the coin. Explain.

equally likely; Possible explanation: There are two equally likely outcomes.

b. What part of the class would you expect to get heads? Explain.

about one-half of the class; Possible explanation: The outcomes for each person are equally likely.

c. What is the probability that everyone gets heads?

unlikely; Possible explanation: The outcomes for each person are equally likely, so about one-half of the class should get heads and the rest should get tails.

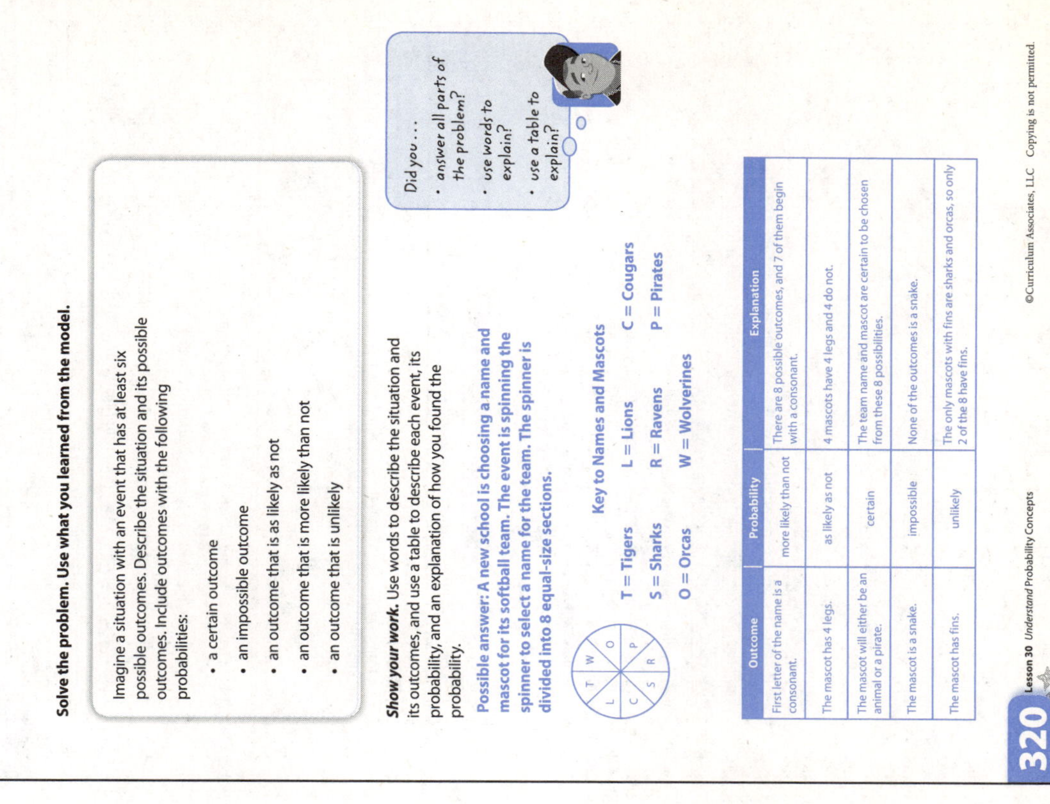

Solve the problem. Use what you learned from the model.

Imagine a situation with an event that has at least six possible outcomes. Describe the situation and its possible outcomes. Include outcomes with the following probabilities:

- a certain outcome
- an impossible outcome
- an outcome that is as likely as not
- an outcome that is more likely than not
- an outcome that is unlikely

Show your work. Use words to describe the situation and its outcomes, and use a table to describe each event, its probability, and an explanation of how you found the probability.

Possible answer: A new school is choosing a name and mascot for its softball team. The event is spinning the spinner to select a name for the team. The spinner is divided into 8 equal-size sections.

Key to Names and Mascots

T = Tigers L = Lions C = Cougars
S = Sharks R = Ravens P = Pirates
O = Orcas W = Wolverines

Outcome	Probability	Explanation
First letter of the name is a consonant.	more likely than not	There are 8 possible outcomes, and 7 of them begin with a consonant.
The mascot has 4 legs.	as likely as not	4 mascots have 4 legs and 4 do not.
The mascot will either be an animal or a pirate.	certain	The team name and mascot are certain to be chosen from these 8 possibilities.
The mascot is a snake.	impossible	None of the outcomes is a snake.
The mascot has fins.	unlikely	The only mascots with fins are sharks and orcas, so only 2 of the 8 have fins.

Did you . . .
- answer all parts of the problem?
- use words to explain?
- use a table to explain?

320 Lesson 30 *Understand* Probability Concepts ©Curriculum Associates, LLC Copying is not permitted.

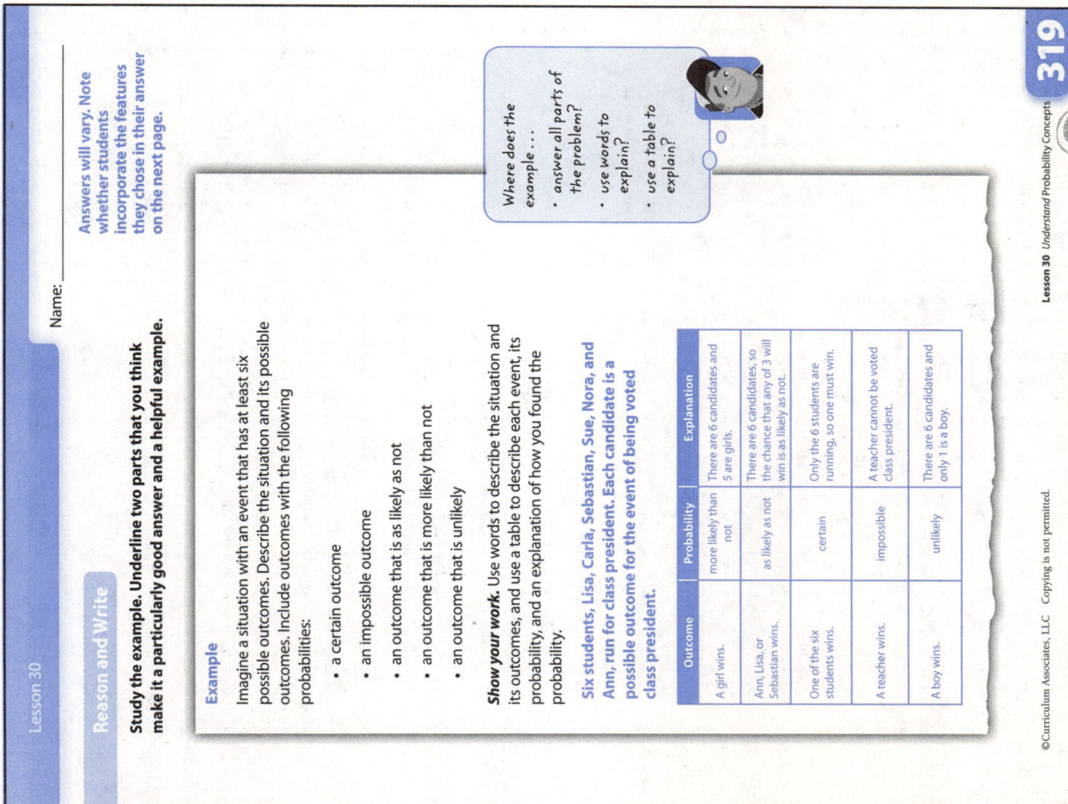

Lesson 30

Name: ______________

Reason and Write

Study the example. Underline two parts that you think make it a particularly good answer and a helpful example.

Answers will vary. Note whether students incorporate the features they chose in their answer on the next page.

Example

Imagine a situation with an event that has at least six possible outcomes. Describe the situation and its possible outcomes. Include outcomes with the following probabilities:

- a certain outcome
- an impossible outcome
- an outcome that is as likely as not
- an outcome that is more likely than not
- an outcome that is unlikely

Show your work. Use words to describe the situation and its outcomes, and use a table to describe each event, its probability, and an explanation of how you found the probability.

Six students, Lisa, Carla, Sebastian, Sue, Nora, and Ann, run for class president. Each candidate is a possible outcome for the event of being voted class president.

Outcome	Probability	Explanation
A girl wins.	more likely than not	There are 6 candidates and 5 are girls.
Ann, Lisa, or Sebastian wins.	as likely as not	There are 6 candidates, so the chance that any of 3 will win is as likely as not.
One of the six students wins.	certain	Only the 6 students are running, so one must win.
A teacher wins.	impossible	A teacher cannot be voted class president.
A boy wins.	unlikely	There are 6 candidates and only 1 is a boy.

Where does the example . . .
- answer all parts of the problem?
- use words to explain?
- use a table to explain?

©Curriculum Associates, LLC Copying is not permitted. Lesson 30 *Understand* Probability Concepts 319

Lesson 31

Experimental Probability

Name: ____________

Prerequisite: Describe the Probability of an Outcome

Study the example showing how to describe the probability of an event. Then solve problems 1–11.

Example

Twelve tiles with the even numbers from 2 through 24 are placed in a bag. You draw a tile without looking.

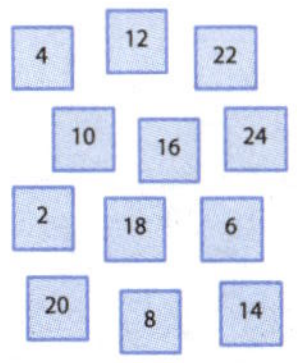

You can describe the probability of various outcomes using words:

- Drawing an odd number is an impossible outcome.
- Drawing a numbered tile is a certain outcome.
- Drawing a prime number is unlikely.
- Drawing a number greater than 12 is as likely as not.
- Drawing a number greater than 6 is likely.

B 1 Why is drawing a number greater than 6 likely?

There are 9 numbers greater than 6 and only 3 that are less than or equal to 6.

M 2 Why is drawing a prime number unlikely?

The only prime number in the set of tiles is the tile numbered 2. It is unlikely that this tile will be drawn out of the 12 possible tiles.

Use the tiles from the example to classify each event as *impossible, unlikely, as likely as not, likely, or certain.*

B 3 Drawing a 4 or an 8. unlikely

B 4 Drawing a number less than 20. likely

B 5 Drawing a number less than 2. impossible

B 6 Drawing a multiple of 2. certain

M 7 Drawing a number that is a factor of 24.

as likely as not

Vocabulary

outcome one of the possible results in a situation or experiment.

event one or more possible outcomes.

probability the chance of an outcome or event occurring.

Solve.

M 8 Suppose you are playing a game using the spinner shown.

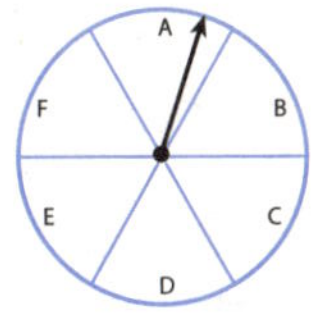

a. Name an outcome that is impossible.

Possible answer: Spinning a G.

b. Name an outcome that is certain.

Possible answer: Spinning one of the first 6 letters of the alphabet.

c. Name an outcome that is as likely as not.

Possible answer: Spinning an A, B, or C.

d. Name an outcome that is likely.

Possible answer: Spinning a consonant.

B 9 At a pep rally, 95% of the fans are students and $\frac{1}{20}$ of the fans are teachers. The name of one fan is drawn at random. Whose name is more likely to be drawn, a teacher or a student? Use the number line to explain your answer.

a student; The probability of drawing a student's name is 95%, or $\frac{19}{20}$, which is greater than $\frac{1}{20}$. An outcome with a probability that is closer to 1 is the more likely outcome.

M 10 The numbers shown describe the probabilities of various outcomes of an event. Show the probabilities on the number line and describe each probability in words.

$\frac{8}{9}$ $\frac{1}{2}$ $\frac{3}{5}$ $\frac{1}{10}$

$\frac{8}{9}$ is likely, $\frac{1}{2}$ is as likely as not, $\frac{3}{5}$ is likely, and $\frac{1}{10}$ is unlikely.

C 11 Each face of a number cube has a different number from 1 to 6 on it. Dmitri rolls the number cube 5 times. Each time he rolls, the number 1 is on top. Dmitri says that if he rolls the cube again, he will most likely get a 1. Do you think that he is correct? Explain your answer.

No; Possible answer: There are 5 other numbers that Dmitri could roll and only one 1, so it is unlikely that he will roll a 1.

Key

B Basic	M Medium	C Challenge

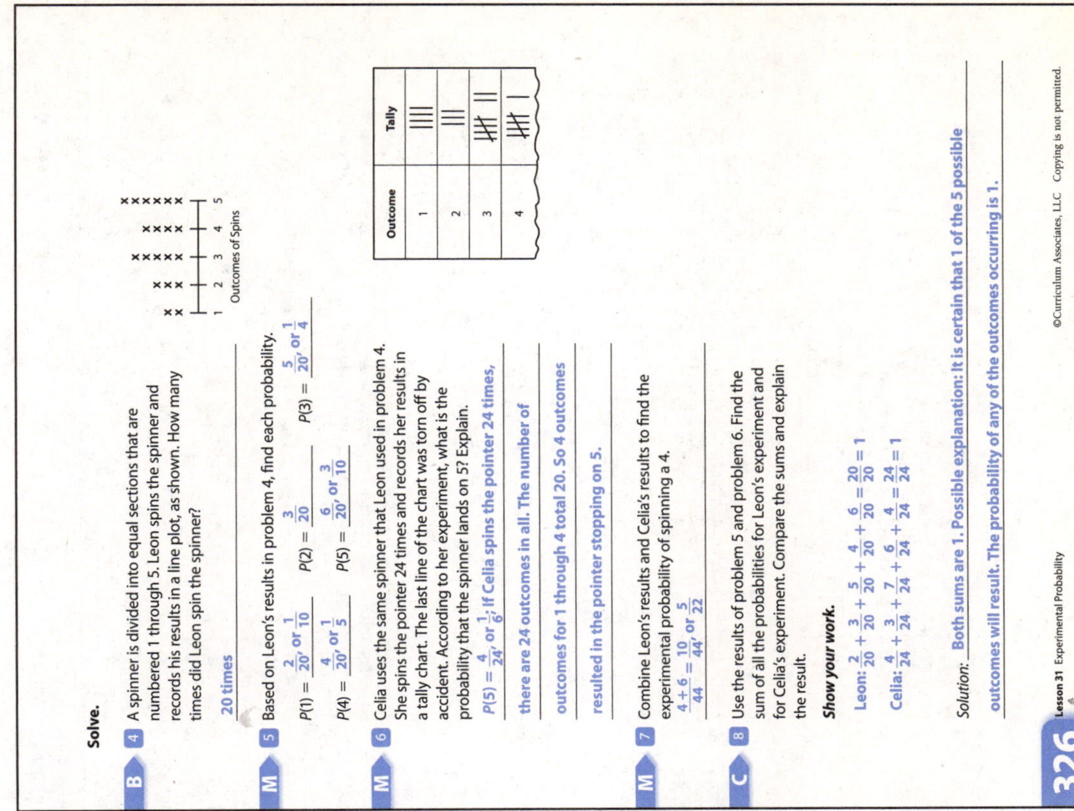

Solve.

B 4 A spinner is divided into equal sections that are numbered 1 through 5. Leon spins the spinner and records his results in a line plot, as shown. How many times did Leon spin the spinner?

20 times

M 5 Based on Leon's results in problem 4, find each probability.

$P(1) = \frac{2}{20}$, or $\frac{1}{10}$ $P(2) = \frac{3}{20}$ $P(3) = \frac{5}{20}$, or $\frac{1}{4}$

$P(4) = \frac{4}{20}$, or $\frac{1}{5}$ $P(5) = \frac{6}{20}$, or $\frac{3}{10}$

M 6 Celia uses the same spinner that Leon used in problem 4. She spins the pointer 24 times and records her results in a tally chart. The last line of the chart was torn off by accident. According to her experiment, what is the probability that the spinner lands on 5? Explain.

<table>
<tr><th>Outcome</th><th>Tally</th></tr>
<tr><td>1</td><td>||||</td></tr>
<tr><td>2</td><td>|||</td></tr>
<tr><td>3</td><td>卌 ||</td></tr>
<tr><td>4</td><td>卌 |</td></tr>
</table>

$P(5) = \frac{4}{24}$, or $\frac{1}{6}$; If Celia spins the pointer 24 times, there are 24 outcomes in all. The number of outcomes for 1 through 4 total 20. So 4 outcomes resulted in the pointer stopping on 5.

M 7 Combine Leon's results and Celia's results to find the experimental probability of spinning a 4.

$\frac{4+6}{44} = \frac{10}{44}$, or $\frac{5}{22}$

C 8 Use the results of problem 5 and problem 6. Find the sum of all the probabilities for Leon's experiment and for Celia's experiment. Compare the sums and explain the result.

Show your work.

Leon: $\frac{2}{20} + \frac{3}{20} + \frac{5}{20} + \frac{4}{20} + \frac{6}{20} = \frac{20}{20} = 1$

Celia: $\frac{4}{24} + \frac{3}{24} + \frac{7}{24} + \frac{6}{24} + \frac{4}{24} = \frac{24}{24} = 1$

Solution: Both sums are 1. Possible explanation: It is certain that 1 of the 5 possible outcomes will result. The probability of any of the outcomes occurring is 1.

326 Lesson 31 Experimental Probability ©Curriculum Associates, LLC Copying is not permitted.

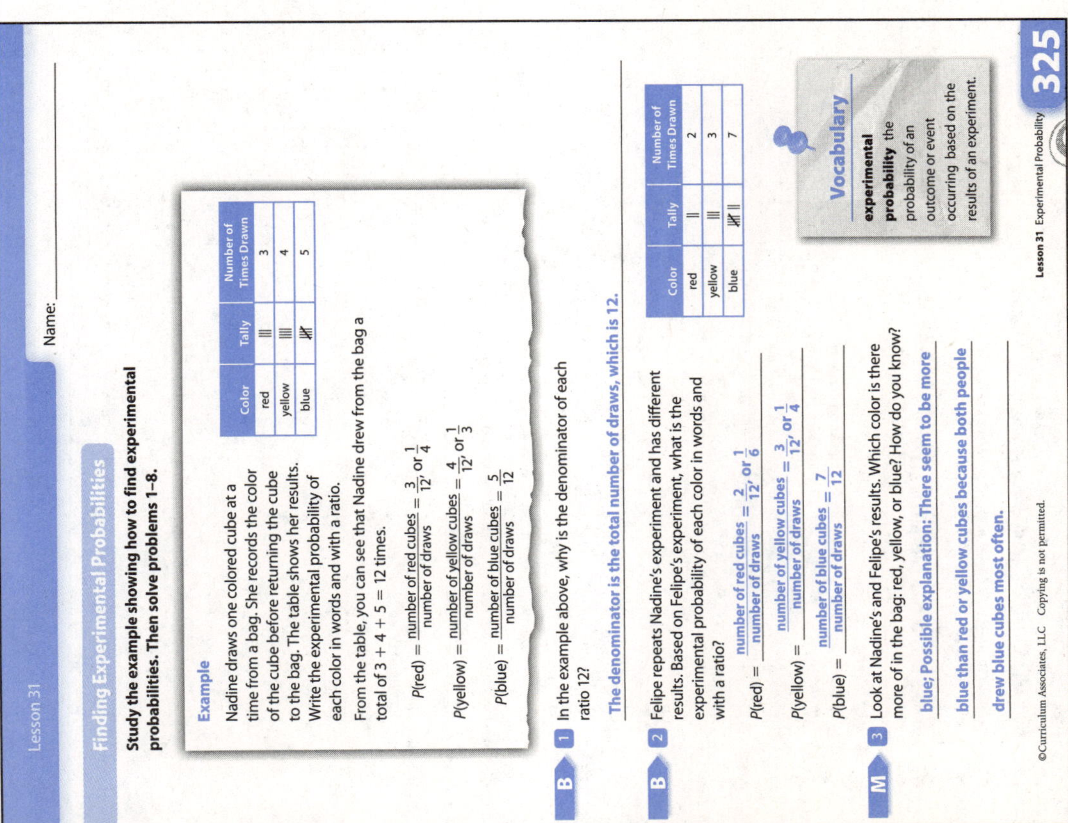

Lesson 31 Name: ____________

Finding Experimental Probabilities

Study the example showing how to find experimental probabilities. Then solve problems 1–8.

Example

Nadine draws one colored cube at a time from a bag. She records the color of the cube before returning the cube to the bag. The table shows her results. Write the experimental probability of each color in words and with a ratio.

<table>
<tr><th>Color</th><th>Tally</th><th>Number of Times Drawn</th></tr>
<tr><td>red</td><td>|||</td><td>3</td></tr>
<tr><td>yellow</td><td>||||</td><td>4</td></tr>
<tr><td>blue</td><td>卌</td><td>5</td></tr>
</table>

From the table, you can see that Nadine drew from the bag a total of 3 + 4 + 5 = 12 times.

$P(\text{red}) = \frac{\text{number of red cubes}}{\text{number of draws}} = \frac{3}{12}$, or $\frac{1}{4}$

$P(\text{yellow}) = \frac{\text{number of yellow cubes}}{\text{number of draws}} = \frac{4}{12}$, or $\frac{1}{3}$

$P(\text{blue}) = \frac{\text{number of blue cubes}}{\text{number of draws}} = \frac{5}{12}$

B 1 In the example above, why is the denominator of each ratio 12?

The denominator is the total number of draws, which is 12.

B 2 Felipe repeats Nadine's experiment and has different results. Based on Felipe's experiment, what is the experimental probability of each color in words and with a ratio?

<table>
<tr><th>Color</th><th>Tally</th><th>Number of Times Drawn</th></tr>
<tr><td>red</td><td>||</td><td>2</td></tr>
<tr><td>yellow</td><td>|||</td><td>3</td></tr>
<tr><td>blue</td><td>卌 ||</td><td>7</td></tr>
</table>

$P(\text{red}) = \frac{\text{number of red cubes}}{\text{number of draws}} = \frac{2}{12}$, or $\frac{1}{6}$

$P(\text{yellow}) = \frac{\text{number of yellow cubes}}{\text{number of draws}} = \frac{3}{12}$, or $\frac{1}{4}$

$P(\text{blue}) = \frac{\text{number of blue cubes}}{\text{number of draws}} = \frac{7}{12}$

M 3 Look at Nadine's and Felipe's results. Which color is there more of in the bag: red, yellow, or blue? How do you know?

blue; Possible explanation: There seem to be more blue than red or yellow cubes because both people drew blue cubes most often.

Vocabulary

experimental probability the probability of an outcome or event occurring based on the results of an experiment.

©Curriculum Associates, LLC Copying is not permitted. Lesson 31 Experimental Probability 325

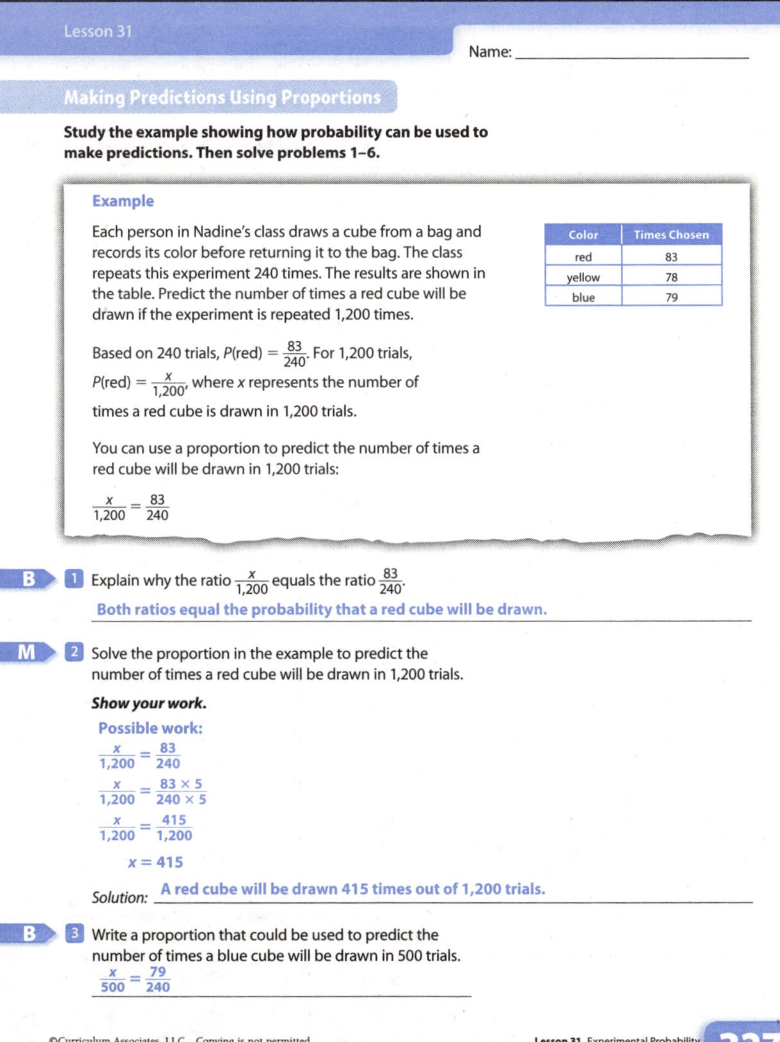

Lesson 31

Name: ______________

Making Predictions Using Proportions

Study the example showing how probability can be used to make predictions. Then solve problems 1–6.

Example

Each person in Nadine's class draws a cube from a bag and records its color before returning it to the bag. The class repeats this experiment 240 times. The results are shown in the table. Predict the number of times a red cube will be drawn if the experiment is repeated 1,200 times.

Color	Times Chosen
red	83
yellow	78
blue	79

Based on 240 trials, $P(\text{red}) = \frac{83}{240}$. For 1,200 trials, $P(\text{red}) = \frac{x}{1{,}200}$, where x represents the number of times a red cube is drawn in 1,200 trials.

You can use a proportion to predict the number of times a red cube will be drawn in 1,200 trials:

$$\frac{x}{1{,}200} = \frac{83}{240}$$

B 1 Explain why the ratio $\frac{x}{1{,}200}$ equals the ratio $\frac{83}{240}$.

Both ratios equal the probability that a red cube will be drawn.

M 2 Solve the proportion in the example to predict the number of times a red cube will be drawn in 1,200 trials.

Show your work.

Possible work:

$\frac{x}{1{,}200} = \frac{83}{240}$

$\frac{x}{1{,}200} = \frac{83 \times 5}{240 \times 5}$

$\frac{x}{1{,}200} = \frac{415}{1{,}200}$

$x = 415$

Solution: A red cube will be drawn 415 times out of 1,200 trials.

B 3 Write a proportion that could be used to predict the number of times a blue cube will be drawn in 500 trials.

$\frac{x}{500} = \frac{79}{240}$

Solve.

B 4 Devi conducts a poll about the election for mayor in her town. The current mayor is running against other candidates. She asks voters whether they plan to vote for the current mayor, against the current mayor, or if they are undecided. Her results are shown in the table. What is the experimental probability of each outcome?

Vote	Number of Voters
for	25
against	12
undecided	3

a. $P(\text{for}) = \frac{25}{40}$, or $\frac{5}{8}$

b. $P(\text{against}) = \frac{12}{40}$, or $\frac{3}{10}$

c. $P(\text{undecided}) = \frac{3}{40}$

M 5 Use the data in problem 4 to write and solve a proportion to predict the number of voters out of 1,000 that will have each response.

Show your work.

For: $\frac{f}{1{,}000} = \frac{25}{40}$

$\frac{f}{1{,}000} = \frac{25 \times 25}{40 \times 25}$

$\frac{f}{1{,}000} = \frac{625}{1{,}000}$

$f = 625$

Against: $\frac{a}{1{,}000} = \frac{12}{40}$

$\frac{a}{1{,}000} = \frac{12 \times 25}{40 \times 25}$

$\frac{a}{1{,}000} = \frac{300}{1{,}000}$

$a = 300$

Undecided: $\frac{u}{1{,}000} = \frac{3}{40}$

$\frac{u}{1{,}000} = \frac{3 \times 25}{40 \times 25}$

$\frac{u}{1{,}000} = \frac{75}{1{,}000}$

$u = 75$

Solution: There will be about 625 for, 300 against, and 75 undecided out of 1,000 voters.

C 6 Alonso spins a spinner and gets a red outcome 12 times. He predicts that if he repeats the experiment 1,000 times, the pointer will stop on red 240 times. How many times did Alonso spin the spinner?

Show your work.

Possible work:

$\frac{12}{x} = \frac{240}{1{,}000}$

$\frac{12}{x} = \frac{240 \div 20}{1{,}000 \div 20}$

$\frac{12}{x} = \frac{12}{50}$

$50 = x$

Solution: Alonso spun the spinner 50 times.

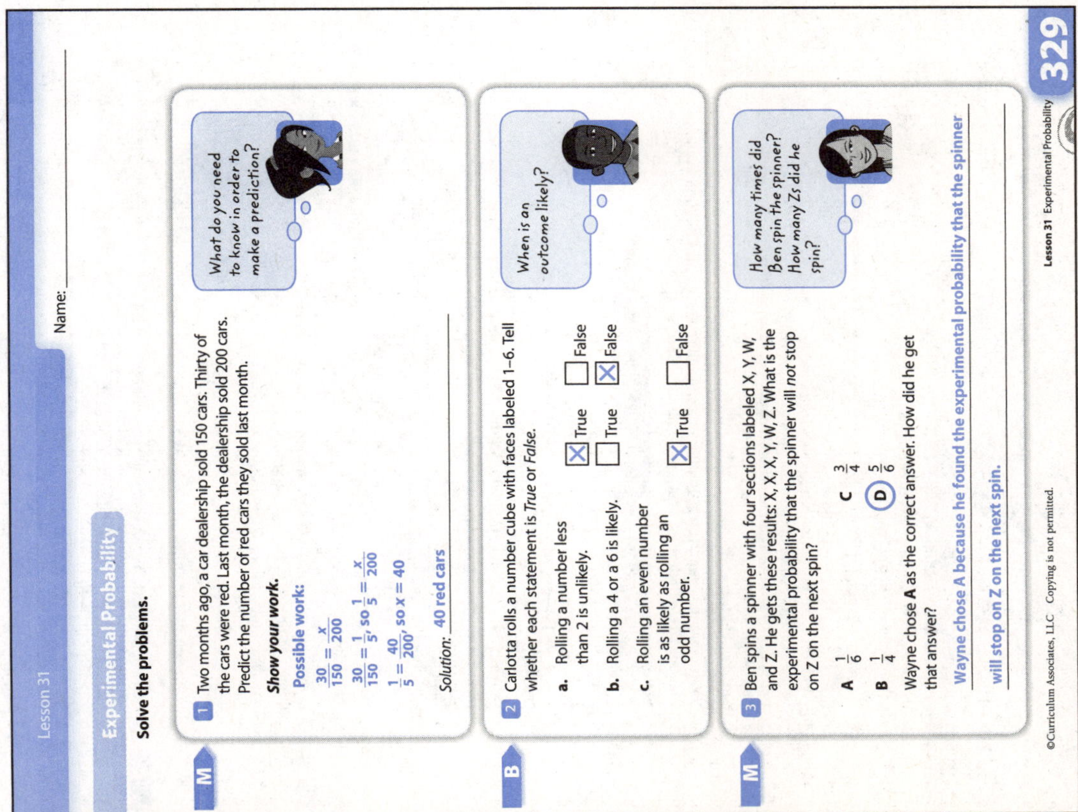

Lesson 31

Name: ______________________

Experimental Probability

Solve the problems.

M

1 Two months ago, a car dealership sold 150 cars. Thirty of the cars were red. Last month, the dealership sold 200 cars. Predict the number of red cars they sold last month.

Show your work.

Possible work:

$\frac{30}{150} = \frac{x}{200}$

$\frac{30}{150} = \frac{1}{5}$, so $\frac{1}{5} = \frac{x}{200}$

$\frac{1}{5} = \frac{40}{200}$, so $x = 40$

Solution: 40 red cars

B

2 Carlotta rolls a number cube with faces labeled 1–6. Tell whether each statement is *True* or *False*.

		True	False
a.	Rolling a number less than 2 is unlikely.	☒	☐
b.	Rolling a 4 or a 6 is likely.	☐	☒
c.	Rolling an even number is as likely as rolling an odd number.	☒	☐

M

3 Ben spins a spinner with four sections labeled X, Y, W, and Z. He gets these results: X, X, X, Y, W, Z. What is the experimental probability that the spinner will *not* stop on Z on the next spin?

A $\frac{1}{6}$

B $\frac{1}{4}$

C $\frac{3}{4}$

(D) $\frac{5}{6}$

Wayne chose **A** as the correct answer. How did he get that answer?

Wayne chose A because he found the experimental probability that the spinner will stop on Z on the next spin.

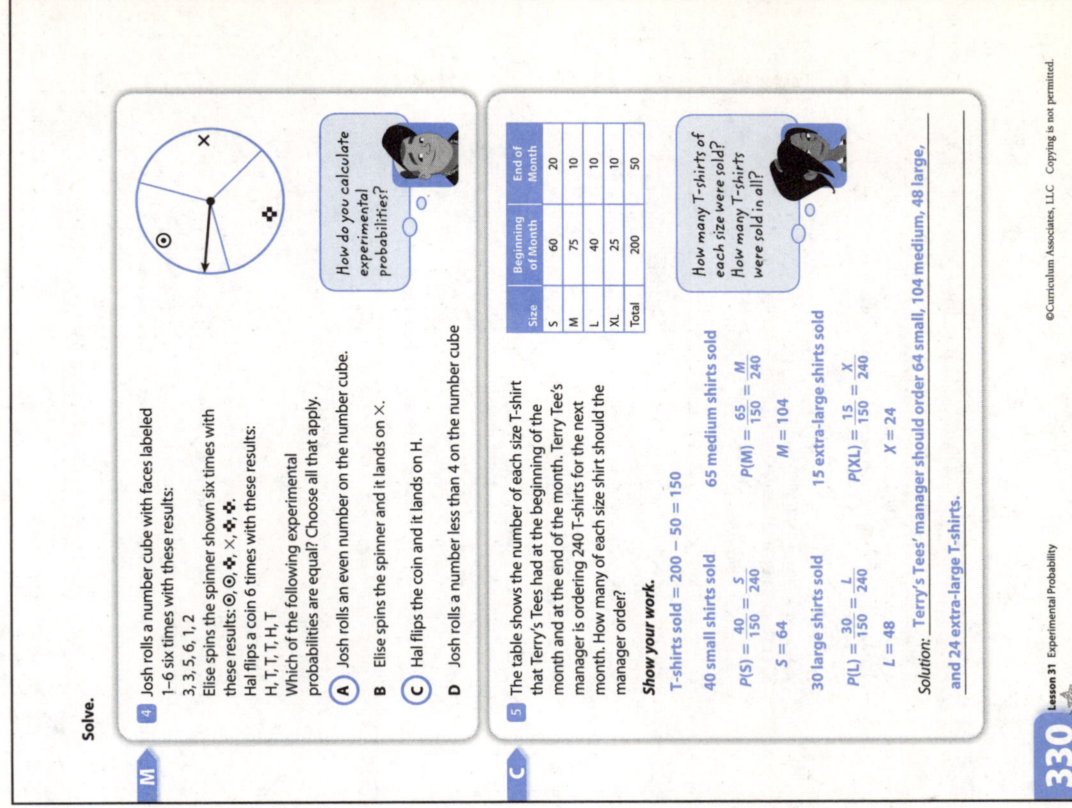

Solve.

M

4 Josh rolls a number cube with faces labeled 1–6 six times with these results:
3, 3, 5, 6, 1, 2
Elise spins the spinner shown six times with these results: ⊙, ⊙, ✤, ×, ✤, ✤.
Hal flips a coin 6 times with these results:
H, T, T, T, H, T
Which of the following experimental probabilities are equal? Choose all that apply.

(A) Josh rolls an even number on the number cube.

B Elise spins the spinner and it lands on ×.

(C) Hal flips the coin and it lands on H.

D Josh rolls a number less than 4 on the number cube

C

5 The table shows the number of each size T-shirt that Terry's Tees had at the beginning of the month and at the end of the month. Terry Tee's manager is ordering 240 T-shirts for the next month. How many of each size shirt should the manager order?

Size	Beginning of Month	End of Month
S	60	20
M	75	10
L	40	10
XL	25	10
Total	200	50

Show your work.

T-shirts sold = 200 − 50 = 150

40 small shirts sold

$P(S) = \frac{40}{150} = \frac{S}{240}$

$S = 64$

65 medium shirts sold

$P(M) = \frac{65}{150} = \frac{M}{240}$

$M = 104$

30 large shirts sold

$P(L) = \frac{30}{150} = \frac{L}{240}$

$L = 48$

15 extra-large shirts sold

$P(XL) = \frac{15}{150} = \frac{X}{240}$

$X = 24$

Solution: Terry's Tees' manager should order 64 small, 104 medium, 48 large, and 24 extra-large T-shirts.

Lesson 32

Probability Models

Name: ____________________

Prerequisite: Predict an Outcome

Study the example showing how to use proportions to make predictions. Then solve problems 1–5.

Example

A class collected data on the types of vehicles parked in various parking lots near their school. They collected data on 250 vehicles. Use this data to predict how many of each type of vehicle there would be if they had collected data on 1,000 vehicles.

You can make a table and use proportions to predict the number of each type of vehicle there would be out of 1,000 vehicles.

Vehicle Type	Number	Probability Based on Data	Proportion	Prediction for 1,000 Vehicles
2-door cars	50	$\frac{50}{250}$	$\frac{50}{250} = \frac{x}{1,000}$	200
4-door cars	60	$\frac{60}{250}$	$\frac{60}{250} = \frac{x}{1,000}$	240
minivans	80	$\frac{80}{250}$	$\frac{80}{250} = \frac{x}{1,000}$	320
SUVs	32	$\frac{32}{250}$	$\frac{32}{250} = \frac{x}{1,000}$	128
trucks	28	$\frac{28}{250}$	$\frac{28}{250} = \frac{x}{1,000}$	112
Total	**250**			1,000

If the students had collected data on 1,000 vehicles, there would be 200 2-door cars, 240 4-door cars, 320 minivans, 128 SUVs, and 112 trucks.

Vocabulary

experimental probability the probability of an outcome or event occurring based on the results of an experiment.

trial one of several identical experiments.

prediction a forecast of an outcome based on experimental results.

B 1 Describe a method that may have been used to solve the proportions in the table.

Possible answer: 1,000 is 4 times the denominator, 250, of each probability ratio. So you can multiply the numerator of each probability by 4.

M 2 How can you check that your predictions are correct?

Possible answer: Find the total to see whether the sum is 1,000.

Solve.

B 3 A dog show has 6 small dogs, 12 medium-sized dogs, and 6 large dogs.

a. What is the probability that a dog chosen at random is a small dog? Explain your reasoning.

$P(\text{small}) = \frac{6}{24}$, or $\frac{1}{4}$; There are 6 small dogs and 24 dogs in all.

b. What is the probability that a dog chosen at random is *not* a large dog? Explain your reasoning.

$P(\text{not large}) = \frac{18}{24}$, or $\frac{3}{4}$; There are 18 dogs that are not large and 24 dogs in all.

M 4 Sam spins a spinner 24 times and gets the results shown in the table. If he were to spin the spinner 1,200 times, predict the number of times he would spin each color.

Color	Frequency
red	10
yellow	6
green	8

Show your work.

$P(\text{red})$: $\frac{10}{24} = \frac{r}{1,200}$; $\frac{10 \times 50}{24 \times 50} = \frac{500}{1,200}$; $r = 500$

$P(\text{yellow})$: $\frac{6}{24} = \frac{y}{1,200}$; $\frac{6 \times 50}{24 \times 50} = \frac{300}{1,200}$; $y = 300$

$P(\text{green})$: $\frac{8}{24} = \frac{g}{1,200}$; $\frac{8 \times 50}{24 \times 50} = \frac{400}{1,200}$; $g = 400$

Solution: **He will spin red 500 times, yellow 300 times, and green 400 times.**

C 5 Esperanza rolls a number cube and gets a six 8 times. Based on this experiment, she predicts that if she rolls the cube 1,600 times, she would get a six 640 times. How many times did she roll the number cube in her experiment? Explain your reasoning.

Show your work.

Possible explanation: According to the prediction, $P(6) = \frac{640}{1,600}$; according to the experiment, $P(6) = \frac{8}{x}$, where x is the number of times Esperanza rolled the number cube. So $\frac{640}{1,600} = \frac{8}{x}$. The numerator of the predicted probability is 80 times the numerator in the experimental probability. So $80x = 1,600$, which means $x = 20$.

Solution: **Esperanza rolled the number cube 20 times in her experiment.**

Key

B Basic **M** Medium **C** Challenge

Name: ______________________

Using a Probability Model

Study the example showing how a probability model can be used to predict an outcome. Then solve problems 1–7.

Example

Dave, Rachel, and Kira are going to be chosen at random in a drawing. A spinner with three equal sections, one for each student, is used to predict who will be chosen. The results of the experiment are shown in the table. Use the result to predict who will be chosen.

Outcome	Frequency
Dave	8
Kira	9
Rachel	7

The spinner in the experiment was spun 24 times. The experimental probabilities for each person are:

$P(\text{Dave}) = \frac{8}{24}$ $P(\text{Kira}) = \frac{9}{24}$ $P(\text{Rachel}) = \frac{7}{24}$

The individual with the greatest experimental probability is Kira, so you can predict that Kira will be chosen.

B 1 What is the sample space of this experiment?

{Dave, Kira, Rachel}

B 2 In this model, why is it important that the three sections of the spinner be the same size?

Because the outcomes of the drawing are equally likely and the probability of any outcome using the model must be the same as the situation it is modeling.

B 3 What is the theoretical probability that Kira will be chosen? Is it equal to the experimental probability?

$\frac{1}{3}$; no

B 4 Will the theoretical probability always be different from the experimental probability? Explain.

no; They may be the same, but experimental probability depends on the results of an experiment. So the probabilities are often different.

Solve.

M 5 A computer game has two equally likely paths that a player can take. Path A has a favorable result, and Path B has an unfavorable result. You toss a coin to model the possible paths a player can take. Heads represents Path A and tails represents Path B. The results are shown in the tally chart.

Outcome	Tally
Heads (Path A)	卌 卌 IIII
Tails (Path B)	卌 卌

a. What is the experimental probability that the path taken is Path A?

$P(\text{Path A}) = \frac{14}{24}$, or $\frac{7}{12}$

b. What is the theoretical probability that the path taken is Path A?

$P(\text{Path A}) = \frac{1}{2}$

c. Why is the experimental probability different from the theoretical probability?

Possible answer: The experimental probability is based on chance; the theoretical probability is based on logic.

M 6 Refer to problem 5. Suppose the number of coin flips were increased to 200. How would this affect the experimental probability that the path taken is Path A?

Possible answer: As the number of trials increases, the experimental probability gets closer to the theoretical probability.

C 7 A survey shows that at a certain intersection 50% of the traffic goes straight, 25% turns left, and 25% turns right. Describe a model for finding the probability that a randomly chosen car approaching that intersection continues straight ahead. Explain why you think your model is a good predictor for the outcomes at the intersection.

Possible answer: I could place four different-colored marbles in a bag and let two colors represent going straight, one color going left, and one color going right. Each trial would consist of drawing a marble out of the bag without looking, noting its color on a table, and replacing the marble. This model is a good predictor for the outcomes because there are 4 equally likely outcomes, and 2 of them represent 50% of the outcomes.

Lesson 32

Name: ____________

Experimental and Theoretical Probabilities

Study the example showing how to compare probabilities. Then solve problems 1–6.

Example

Kimi places 1 red, 1 blue, 1 black, and 1 green cube in a bag. She draws a cube without looking, records the outcome, and puts the cube back in the bag. Her results are shown in the table. Find and compare the experimental probability and the theoretical probability that the next cube Kimi draws will be red.

Kimi's Results

Outcome	Frequency
red	8
blue	4
black	7
green	5

The sample space is the same for both probabilities. The equally possible outcomes are red, blue, black, and green.

Theoretical probability: $P(\text{red}) = \frac{\text{number of favorable outcomes}}{\text{number of possible outcomes}} = \frac{1}{4}$

Experimental probability: $P(\text{red}) = \frac{\text{number of red cubes drawn}}{\text{total number of trials}} = \frac{8}{24}$

Because $\frac{1}{4} = \frac{6}{24}$ and $\frac{6}{24} < \frac{8}{24}$, the theoretical probability is less than the experimental probability.

B **1** The other students in Kimi's class conduct the same experiment. Their results are shown in the table. Do you expect the experimental probability of the class results to be closer to the theoretical probability than Kimi's results? Why?

Class Results

Outcome	Frequency
red	116
blue	121
black	124
green	119

Yes, the class results should be closer to the theoretical probability because there are more trials.

B **2** Compare the experimental probability from the class results with the theoretical probability. Are the class results closer to the theoretical probability than Kimi's results? Explain.

The class's experimental probability is $P(\text{red}) = \frac{116}{480}$, which is less than $\frac{1}{4}$ because $\frac{1}{4} = \frac{120}{480}$, and $\frac{116}{480} < \frac{120}{480}$. The class results are closer to the theoretical probability than Kimi's results because $\frac{116}{480}$ is closer to $\frac{1}{4}$ than $\frac{8}{24}$, or $\frac{160}{480}$.

Solve.

M **3** Heidi spins the spinner shown. She records her results in the line plot.

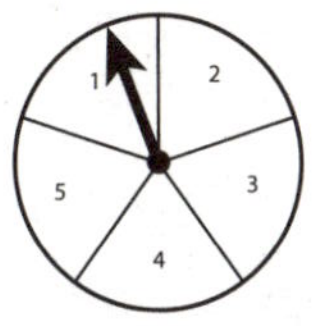

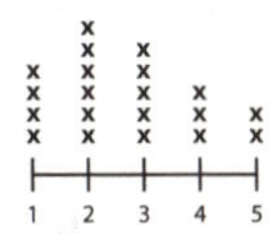

a. What is the theoretical probability of each outcome?

The theoretical probability for each outcome is $\frac{1}{5}$.

b. What is the experimental probability of each outcome?

$P(1) = \frac{4}{20}$; $P(2) = \frac{6}{20}$; $P(3) = \frac{5}{20}$; $P(4) = \frac{3}{20}$; $P(5) = \frac{2}{20}$

M **4** Heidi's class conducts the same experiment and combines the results. Find the experimental probability based on the class results shown in the table. Record the probabilities in the table.

Outcome	Frequency	Experimental Probability
1	85	$\frac{85}{400}$
2	80	$\frac{80}{400}$
3	90	$\frac{90}{400}$
4	75	$\frac{75}{400}$
5	70	$\frac{70}{400}$

M **5** Compare the experimental probabilities from the class data to those from Heidi's data.

Possible answer: The probabilities based on the class data are closer to one another and to the theoretical probability.

C **6** Describe an event involving a number cube for which the experimental probability and the theoretical probability are both equal to $\frac{1}{3}$.

Possible answer: You roll a number cube 30 times and you roll a 5 or a 6 on 10 out of the 30 rolls. The experimental probability of rolling a 5 or a 6 is $\frac{10}{30}$, or $\frac{1}{3}$. The theoretical probability is $\frac{\text{number of favorable outcomes}}{\text{number of possible outcomes}} = \frac{2}{6}$, or $\frac{1}{3}$.

Name: ______________

Solve Problems with Experimental Probability

Study the example showing how to find experimental probabilities. Then solve problems 1–6.

Example

A floor is covered with black tiles and white tiles that alternate. Chau rolls marbles on the floor. Some stop on a white tile, some on a black tile, and some on a line between the tiles. Chau's results are shown in the table. What is the experimental probability of each outcome?

Outcome	Frequency
black tile	30
white tile	35
line between tiles	55

The experimental probabilities are:

$P(\text{black}) = \frac{30}{120}$ $P(\text{white}) = \frac{35}{120}$ $P(\text{line}) = \frac{55}{120}$

B 1 Do the outcomes appear to be equally likely? Explain.

No, the outcomes do not appear to be equally likely because the probability of a marble landing on a line is much higher than landing on one particular color of tile.

B 2 What is the probability that a marble lands on a tile? Explain.

$P(\text{tile}) = \frac{65}{120}$ or $\frac{13}{24}$; a marble lands on a tile 30 + 35 = 65 times.

M 3 Another 120 marbles are rolled on the floor. The combined results are shown in the table. Find the experimental probability of each outcome. Predict the outcome if another marble is rolled on the floor. Explain.

Outcome	Frequency
black tile	72
white tile	64
line between tiles	104

$P(\text{black}) = \frac{72}{240}$; $P(\text{white}) = \frac{64}{240}$; $P(\text{line}) = \frac{104}{240}$

The marble is most likely to stop on a line because the probability of a marble stopping on a line is greater than the probability that it stops on one particular color of tile.

B 4 Can you tell from the experiments how many tiles there are? Could you find the theoretical probabilities of landing on each color for this situation? Explain.

No; no; you cannot tell how many tiles of each color there are, so you do not have enough information to find the theoretical probabilities.

Solve.

M 5 Chloe tracks the number of phone calls that she receives each day for one month.

Outcome (Number of Calls)	Frequency (Number of Days)
0	||
1	卌 |
2	卌 卌 ||
3	卌
4	|||
5	||

a. Do the outcomes appear to be equally likely? Explain.

No; the frequencies vary quite a bit.

b. What is the experimental probability of each outcome?

$P(0) = \frac{2}{30}$; $P(1) = \frac{6}{30}$; $P(2) = \frac{12}{30}$; $P(3) = \frac{5}{30}$;

$P(4) = \frac{3}{30}$; $P(5) = \frac{2}{30}$

c. Is it possible to find the theoretical probability using this data? Explain.

No; there is insufficient information.

d. Predict the number of phone calls that Chloe might expect to receive on the first day of the month following her experiment. Explain.

It is most likely that Chloe will receive 2 phone calls because the probability of receiving 2 phone calls is much greater than any other probability.

C 6 Suppose you want to design a spinner with outcomes that have the same probabilities as those in problem 5. What should be the measure of the angle for each section? Recall that there are 360° around the center of a circle. Number the sections of the spinner 0 through 5.

Show your work.

$P(0)$: $\frac{2}{30} = \frac{x}{360}$ $x = 24$	$P(1)$: $\frac{6}{30} = \frac{x}{360}$ $x = 72$	$P(2)$: $\frac{12}{30} = \frac{x}{360}$ $x = 144$
$P(3)$: $\frac{5}{30} = \frac{x}{360}$ $x = 60$	$P(4)$: $\frac{3}{30} = \frac{x}{360}$ $x = 36$	$P(5)$: $\frac{2}{30} = \frac{x}{360}$ $x = 24$

Solution: Section 0: 24°; Section 1: 72°; Section 2: 144°; Section 3: 60°; Section 4: 36°; Section 5: 24°

Lesson 32

Name: ____________

Probability Models

Solve the problems.

M **1** A tollbooth collector estimates that 85% of the vehicles that go through her tollbooth are cars and the other vehicles are not cars. She uses sixty random numbers from 00 to 99 to simulate the next sixty cars that will drive through her tollbooth.

Which numbers could she have used to represent the two types of vehicles? What is the experimental probability that the next vehicle is not a car? Explain your answer.

89	03	86	75	55	41	96	97	38	33	79	91	22	20	24	39	75	08	48	29
96	09	89	19	69	77	24	70	06	34	12	91	73	94	57	21	10	72	23	57
97	50	04	39	49	58	12	19	02	10	76	44	51	15	98	71	03	75	26	47

Possible answer: The numbers 00 through 84 could represent cars and 85 through 99 could represent other vehicles. 11 out of the 60 numbers are between 85 and 99, so the experimental probability that the next vehicle is not a car is $\frac{11}{60}$.

B **2** You spin a spinner with 4 equal sections labeled A, A, B, C. Which statements are true? Select all that apply.

(A) The theoretical probability that you land on an A is twice the theoretical probability that you land on C.

(B) The theoretical probability that you land on B is $\frac{1}{4}$.

C The theoretical probability that you land on A is $\frac{1}{4}$.

D Every time you perform an experiment in which you spin the spinner 20 times, you will land on C exactly 5 times.

©Curriculum Associates, LLC Copying is not permitted. Lesson 32 Probability Models 341

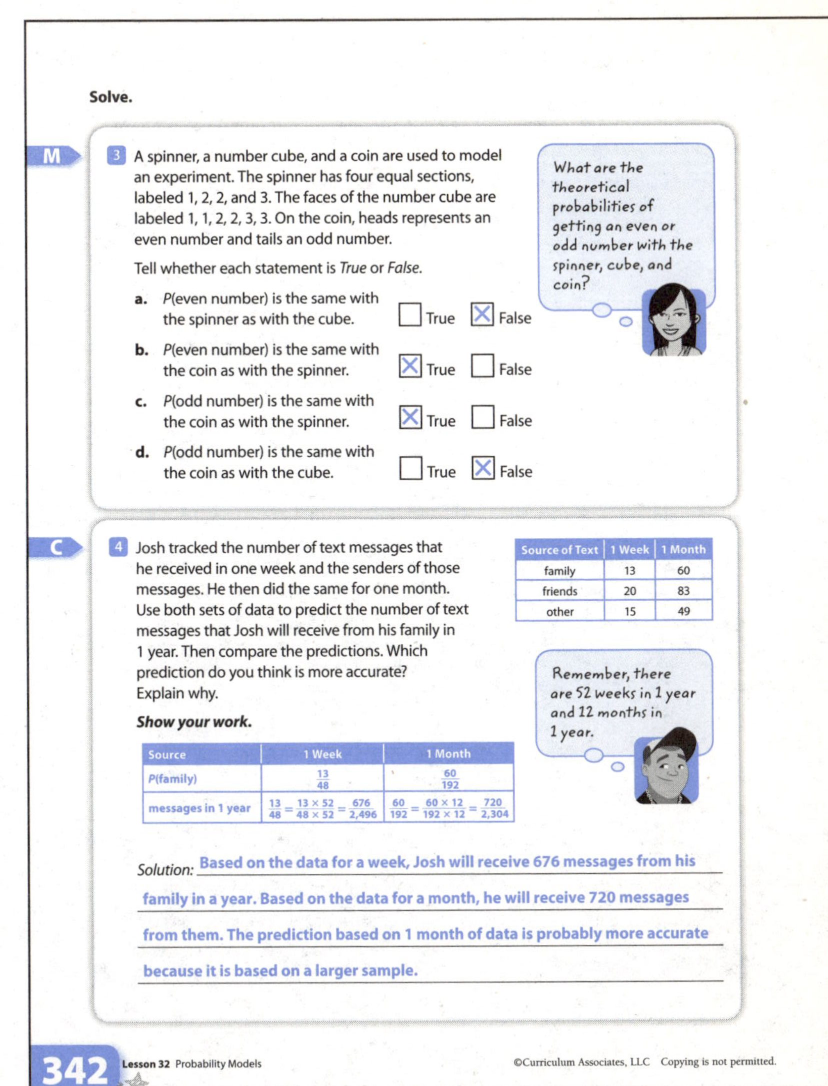

Solve.

M **3** A spinner, a number cube, and a coin are used to model an experiment. The spinner has four equal sections, labeled 1, 2, 2, and 3. The faces of the number cube are labeled 1, 1, 2, 2, 3, 3. On the coin, heads represents an even number and tails an odd number.

Tell whether each statement is *True* or *False*.

a. *P*(even number) is the same with the spinner as with the cube. ☐ True ☒ False

b. *P*(even number) is the same with the coin as with the spinner. ☒ True ☐ False

c. *P*(odd number) is the same with the coin as with the spinner. ☒ True ☐ False

d. *P*(odd number) is the same with the coin as with the cube. ☐ True ☒ False

C **4** Josh tracked the number of text messages that he received in one week and the senders of those messages. He then did the same for one month. Use both sets of data to predict the number of text messages that Josh will receive from his family in 1 year. Then compare the predictions. Which prediction do you think is more accurate? Explain why.

Source of Text	1 Week	1 Month
family	13	60
friends	20	83
other	15	49

Show your work.

Source	1 Week	1 Month
P(family)	$\frac{13}{48}$	$\frac{60}{192}$
messages in 1 year	$\frac{13}{48} = \frac{13 \times 52}{48 \times 52} = \frac{676}{2{,}496}$	$\frac{60}{192} = \frac{60 \times 12}{192 \times 12} = \frac{720}{2{,}304}$

Solution: Based on the data for a week, Josh will receive 676 messages from his family in a year. Based on the data for a month, he will receive 720 messages from them. The prediction based on 1 month of data is probably more accurate because it is based on a larger sample.

342 Lesson 32 Probability Models ©Curriculum Associates, LLC Copying is not permitted.

Lesson 33

Probability of Compound Events

Name: ____________

Prerequisite: Describe Sample Space

Study the example showing how to describe the sample space for an experiment. Then solve problems 1–8.

Example

Marcus and Bea play a game that involves rolling a number cube. Each face of the cube displays a different number from 1 through 6. Describe the sample space for this situation. What is the probability that the next roll of the cube results in an even number?

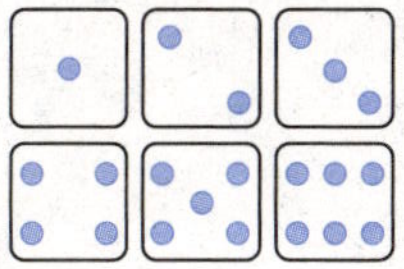

The sample space is the set of all possible outcomes. In this case, the sample space is {1, 2, 3, 4, 5, 6}. When all of the outcomes are equally likely, the theoretical probability of an event is the ratio of the number of favorable outcomes to the total number of outcomes.

There are 3 favorable outcomes for an even number: 2, 4, and 6. There are 6 possible outcomes.

$P(\text{even}) = \frac{\text{number of favorable outcomes}}{\text{total number of outcomes}} = \frac{3}{6} = \frac{1}{2}$

B **1** What is the theoretical probability of rolling a multiple of 3 in the example? Explain.

$\frac{1}{3}$; There are 2 favorable outcomes, 3 and 6, so $P(\text{multiple of 3}) = \frac{2}{6} = \frac{1}{3}$.

M **2** What is the theoretical probability of rolling an 8 in the example? Explain.

0; There is no 8, so $P(8) = \frac{0}{6} = 0$.

M **3** Describe two events that have the same probability using the sample space in the example.

Possible answer: rolling a 1 and rolling a 3.

B **4** What is the sample space when you flip a coin? What is the theoretical probability of landing on heads?

{heads, tails}; $\frac{1}{2}$

Vocabulary

sample space the set of possible outcomes for a situation or experiment.

theoretical probability the probability of an event or outcome occurring based on the possible outcomes in a same space.

Solve.

M **5** Trevon has 12 socks in a drawer. There are equal numbers of blue, black, and white socks. What is the sample space? Find the theoretical probability that a sock drawn at random out of the drawer is blue. Explain.

{blue, black, white}; $P(\text{blue}) = \frac{\text{number of favorable outcomes}}{\text{total number of outcomes}} = \frac{4}{12}$, or $\frac{1}{3}$

M **6** A bag contains 3 red marbles, 4 blue marbles, 5 purple marbles, and 6 white marbles.

a. Find the theoretical probability of drawing a marble of each color.

$P(\text{red}) = \frac{3}{18}$, or $\frac{1}{6}$; $P(\text{blue}) = \frac{4}{18}$, or $\frac{2}{9}$; $P(\text{purple}) = \frac{5}{18}$; $P(\text{white}) = \frac{6}{18}$, or $\frac{1}{3}$

b. Jack performs an experiment and finds that the probability of drawing a purple marble is $\frac{1}{4}$. He concludes that the theoretical probability is incorrect. What is wrong with Jack's conclusion?

Theoretical and experimental probabilities are often different, so the experimental probability can be something other than $\frac{5}{18}$.

C **7** You toss a nickel and a dime. One outcome is heads for the nickel and tails for the dime: HT. What is the sample space for this experiment? What is the theoretical probability of getting at least 1 head? Explain.

{HH, HT, TH, TT}; There are 3 favorable outcomes: HH, HT, and TH, so $P(\text{at least 1 head}) = \frac{3}{4}$.

C **8** Describe an experiment that has 12 possible outcomes. Then describe an event for that experiment that has a theoretical probability of $\frac{1}{4}$.

Possible answer: You choose a month at random from the 12 months of the year. There are 3 months that begin with the letter J: January, June, and July. So the theoretical probability that you choose a month that begins with the letter J is $\frac{3}{12}$, or $\frac{1}{4}$.

Key

B Basic **M** Medium **C** Challenge

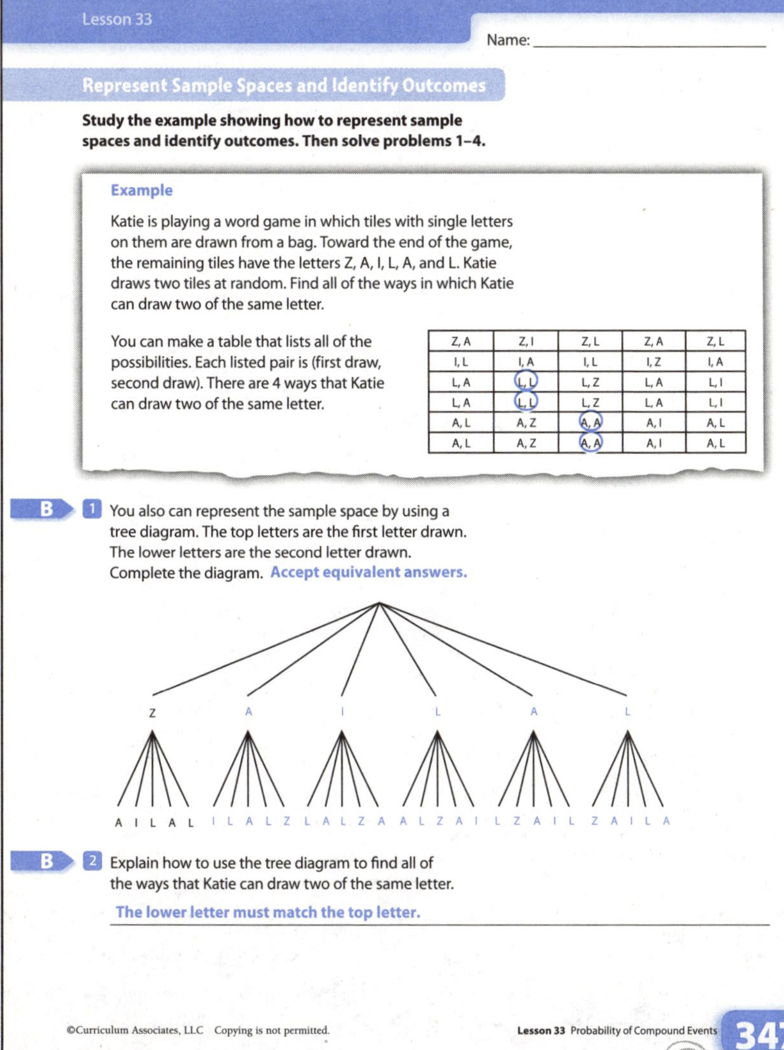

Lesson 33

Name: ______________________

Represent Sample Spaces and Identify Outcomes

Study the example showing how to represent sample spaces and identify outcomes. Then solve problems 1–4.

Example

Katie is playing a word game in which tiles with single letters on them are drawn from a bag. Toward the end of the game, the remaining tiles have the letters Z, A, I, L, A, and L. Katie draws two tiles at random. Find all of the ways in which Katie can draw two of the same letter.

You can make a table that lists all of the possibilities. Each listed pair is (first draw, second draw). There are 4 ways that Katie can draw two of the same letter.

Z, A	Z, I	Z, L	Z, A	Z, L
I, L	I, A	I, L	I, Z	I, A
L, A	L, L	L, Z	L, A	L, I
L, A	L, L	L, Z	L, A	L, I
A, L	A, Z	A, A	A, I	A, L
A, L	A, Z	A, A	A, I	A, L

B 1 You also can represent the sample space by using a tree diagram. The top letters are the first letter drawn. The lower letters are the second letter drawn. Complete the diagram. Accept equivalent answers.

B 2 Explain how to use the tree diagram to find all of the ways that Katie can draw two of the same letter.

The lower letter must match the top letter.

©Curriculum Associates, LLC Copying is not permitted. **Lesson 33** Probability of Compound Events **347**

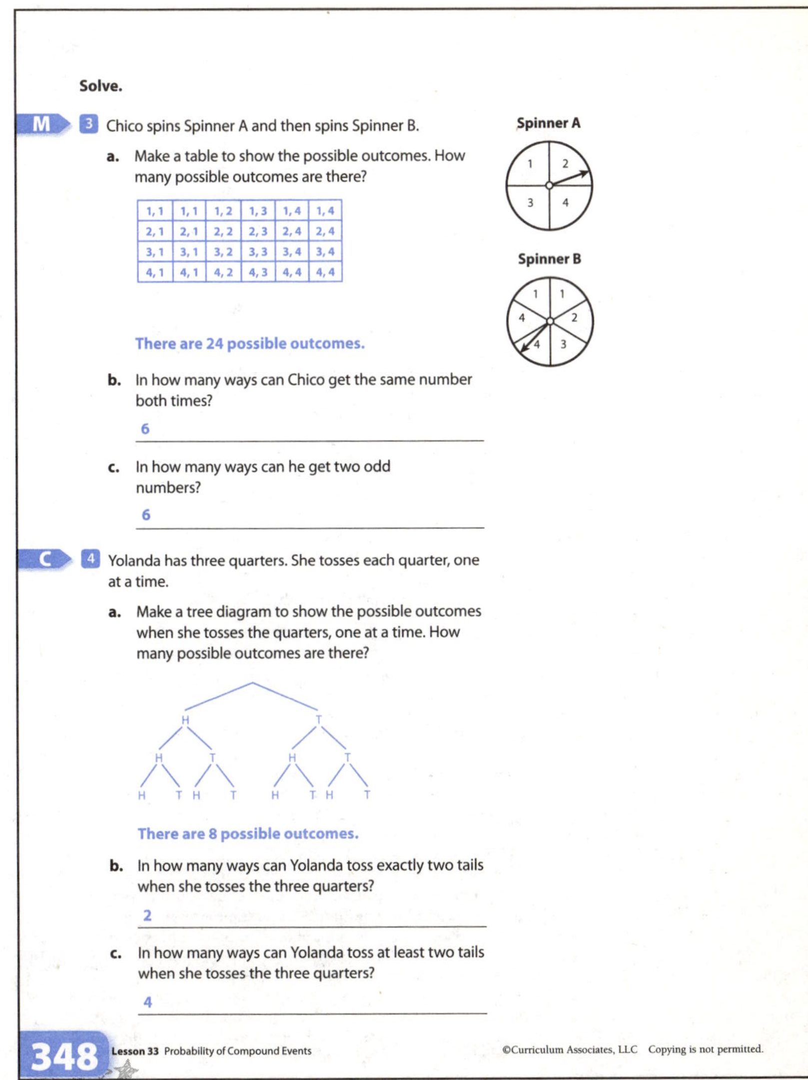

Solve.

M 3 Chico spins Spinner A and then spins Spinner B.

a. Make a table to show the possible outcomes. How many possible outcomes are there?

1, 1	1, 1	1, 2	1, 3	1, 4	1, 4
2, 1	2, 1	2, 2	2, 3	2, 4	2, 4
3, 1	3, 1	3, 2	3, 3	3, 4	3, 4
4, 1	4, 1	4, 2	4, 3	4, 4	4, 4

There are 24 possible outcomes.

b. In how many ways can Chico get the same number both times?

6

c. In how many ways can he get two odd numbers?

6

C 4 Yolanda has three quarters. She tosses each quarter, one at a time.

a. Make a tree diagram to show the possible outcomes when she tosses the quarters, one at a time. How many possible outcomes are there?

There are 8 possible outcomes.

b. In how many ways can Yolanda toss exactly two tails when she tosses the three quarters?

2

c. In how many ways can Yolanda toss at least two tails when she tosses the three quarters?

4

348 **Lesson 33** Probability of Compound Events ©Curriculum Associates, LLC Copying is not permitted.

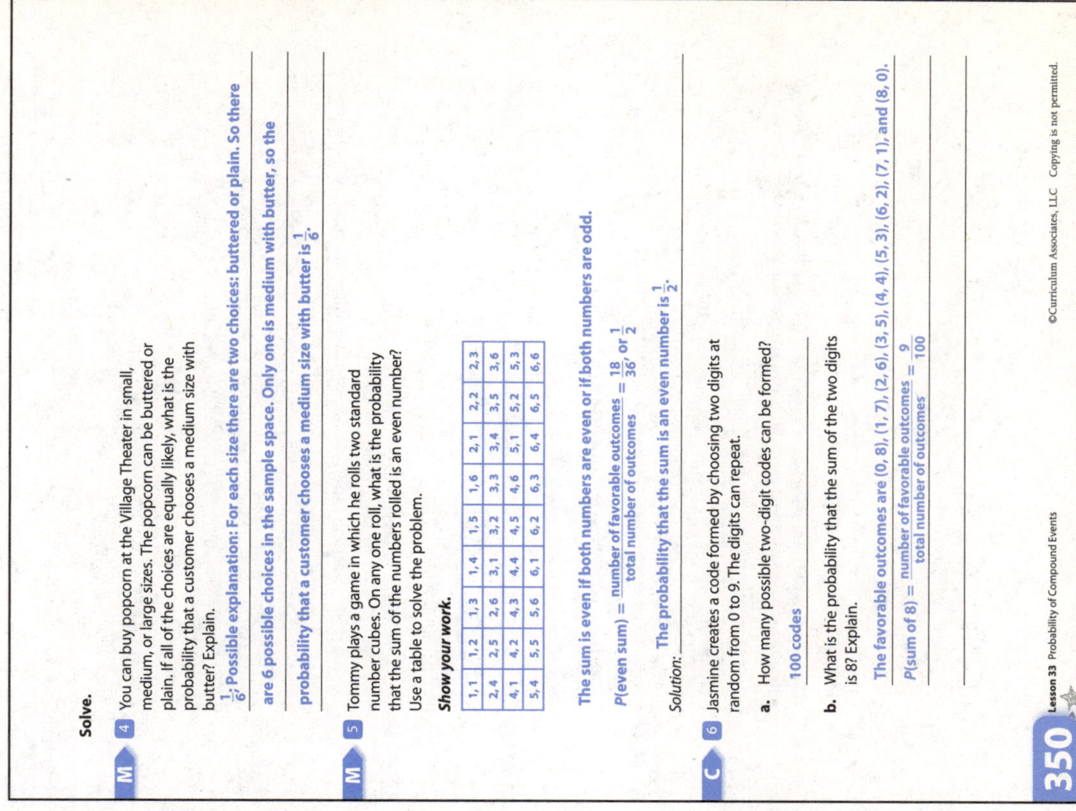

Lesson 33

Name: ____________________

Probabilities of Compound Events

Study the example showing how to find probabilities of compound events. Then solve problems 1–6.

Example

Jeanne is playing a game with this spinner. She spins the pointer twice. What is the probability that the spinner lands on X exactly once?

You can draw a tree diagram to understand the problem.

There are 16 possible outcome. List the outcomes where the spinner landed on X exactly once: WX, XW, XY, XZ, YX, ZX. There are 6 favorable outcomes. The probability that the spinner will land on X exactly once is $\frac{6}{16}$, or $\frac{3}{8}$.

B 1 List the outcomes in which the spinner lands on X at least once. WX, XW, XX, XY, XZ, YX, ZX

B 2 What is the probability that the spinner lands on X at least once? Explain.

$P(\text{X at least once}) = \frac{\text{number of favorable outcomes}}{\text{total number of outcomes}} = \frac{7}{16}$

M 3 You can also use a table to help you. Complete the table. Use the table to find the probability that the spinner lands on Y exactly once. Explain.

	W	X	Y	Z
W	WW	WX	WY	WZ
X	XW	XX	XY	XZ
Y	YW	YX	YY	YZ
Z	ZW	ZX	ZY	ZZ

$P(\text{Y exactly once}) = \frac{\text{number of favorable outcomes}}{\text{total number of outcomes}} = \frac{6}{16}$, or $\frac{3}{8}$

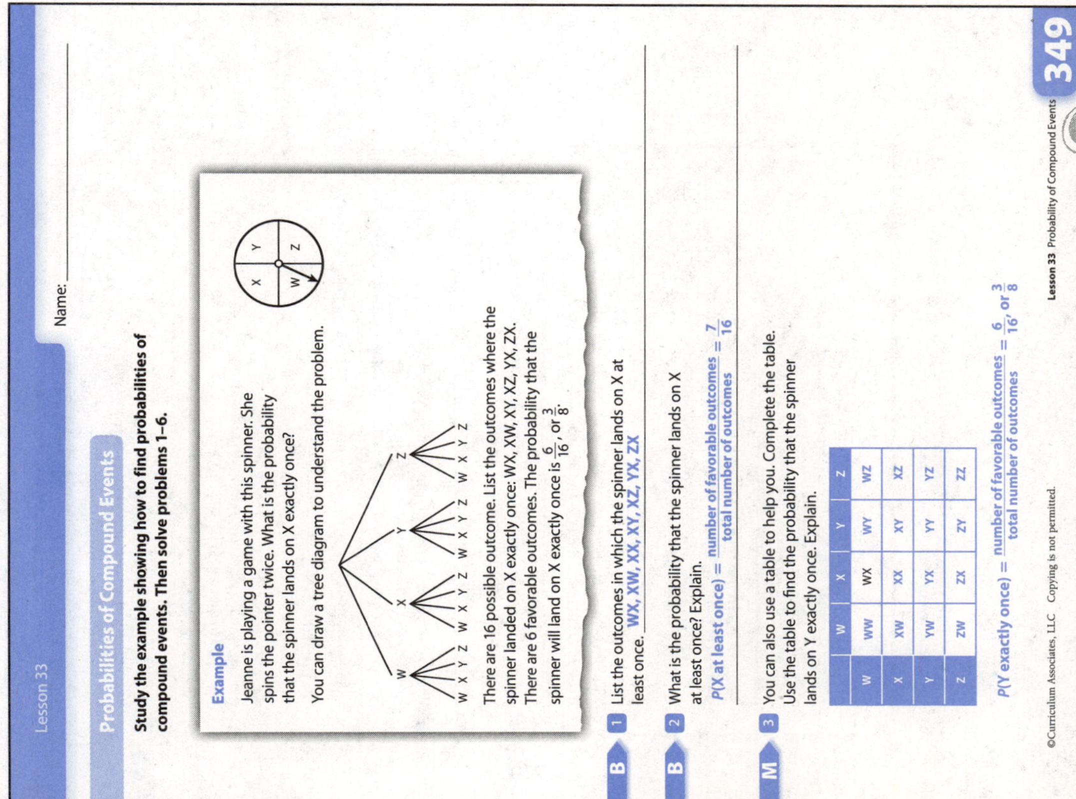

Solve.

M 4 You can buy popcorn at the Village Theater in small, medium, or large sizes. The popcorn can be buttered or plain. If all of the choices are equally likely, what is the probability that a customer chooses a medium size with butter? Explain.

$\frac{1}{6}$; Possible explanation: For each size there are two choices: buttered or plain. So there are 6 possible choices in the sample space. Only one is medium with butter, so the probability that a customer chooses a medium size with butter is $\frac{1}{6}$.

M 5 Tommy plays a game in which he rolls two standard number cubes. On any one roll, what is the probability that the sum of the numbers rolled is an even number? Use a table to solve the problem.

Show your work.

1, 1	1, 2	1, 3	1, 4	1, 5	1, 6	2, 1	2, 2	2, 3
2, 4	2, 5	2, 6	3, 1	3, 2	3, 3	3, 4	3, 5	3, 6
4, 1	4, 2	4, 3	4, 4	4, 5	4, 6	5, 1	5, 2	5, 3
5, 4	5, 5	5, 6	6, 1	6, 2	6, 3	6, 4	6, 5	6, 6

The sum is even if both numbers are even or if both numbers are odd.

$P(\text{even sum}) = \frac{\text{number of favorable outcomes}}{\text{total number of outcomes}} = \frac{18}{36}$, or $\frac{1}{2}$

Solution: The probability that the sum is an even number is $\frac{1}{2}$.

C 6 Jasmine creates a code formed by choosing two digits at random from 0 to 9. The digits can repeat.

a. How many possible two-digit codes can be formed?

100 codes

b. What is the probability that the sum of the two digits is 8? Explain.

The favorable outcomes are (0, 8), (1, 7), (2, 6), (3, 5), (4, 4), (5, 3), (6, 2), (7, 1), and (8, 0).

$P(\text{sum of 8}) = \frac{\text{number of favorable outcomes}}{\text{total number of outcomes}} = \frac{9}{100}$

Lesson 33

Name: ____________________

Find Compound Probability

Study the example showing how to find the probability of a compound event. Then solve problems 1–9.

Example

At the gift wrap counter of a store, a customer can choose white or silver gift wrap; a red, blue, or green bow; and a plain or decorated gift tag. If all of the possible choices are equally likely, what is the probability that a customer orders a gift with a red bow and a decorated gift tag?

You can use an organized table to identify the possible choices. Let W and S represent white and silver paper. Let R, B, and G represent red, blue, and green bows. Let P and D represent plain and decorated tags.

WRP	WBP	WGP
WRD	WBD	WGD
SRP	SBP	SGP
SRD	SBD	SGD

There are 12 possible outcomes. List the outcomes where a customer chooses a red bow and a decorated tag: WRD and SRD. There are 2 favorable outcomes. The probability that the a customer chooses a red bow and a decorated tag is $\frac{2}{12}$, or $\frac{1}{6}$.

B 1 Did you have to take the paper color into account when you found the probability in the example?

No, only the bow color and the type of tag mattered.

M 2 What is the probability that a customer does NOT choose a red bow and a decorated tag? Explain.

Possible answer: 2 of the the 12 possible outcomes represent a red bow and a decorated tag, so the other 10 outcomes represent not choosing a red bow and a decorated tag. So the probability is $\frac{10}{12}$, or $\frac{5}{6}$.

B 3 List the favorable outcomes if you want to find the probability that a customer chooses white wrapping paper and a plain tag.

WRP, WBP, WGP

B 4 What is the probability that a customer chooses white wrapping paper and a plain gift tag? Show how you found your answer.

$P(\text{white and plain}) = \frac{\text{number of favorable outcomes}}{\text{total number of outcomes}} = \frac{3}{12}$, or $\frac{1}{4}$

Solve.

Use this situation for problems 5–8.

Daren sells sweatshirts in small, medium, and large sizes. The sweatshirts are sold both with and without hoods, and they are available in gray, red, and yellow.

M 5 Draw a tree diagram or make a table to represent the sample space. How many outcomes are possible?

There are 18 possible outcomes. Possible table: Let S be small, M be medium, L be large, H be with hoods, W be without hoods, G be gray, R be red, and Y be yellow.

SHG	SHR	SHY	SWG	SWR	SWY
MHG	MHR	MHY	MWG	MWR	MWY
LHG	LHR	LHY	LWG	LWR	LWY

M 6 How many of the possible sweatshirts are medium sweatshirts with hoods? Use your answer to find the probability that a randomly chosen sweatshirt is a medium with a hood.

3; $P(\text{medium with hood}) = \frac{3}{18}$, or $\frac{1}{6}$.

M 7 How many outcomes are sweatshirts with hoods? Use your answer to find the probability that a randomly chosen sweatshirt has a hood.

9; $P(\text{hood}) = \frac{9}{18}$, or $\frac{1}{2}$.

C 8 Suppose you select a sweatshirt at random. What are two compound events that have a probability of $\frac{1}{9}$?

Possible answer: Selecting a small, red sweatshirt and selecting a large, yellow sweatshirt.

M 9 You spin the spinner shown three times. How many possible outcomes are there? What is the probability that the pointer stops on the letter A exactly two times? Explain.

C A B

There are 27 possible outcomes. The favorable outcomes are AAB, AAC, ABA, ACA, BAA, and CAA. So $P(\text{A exactly 2 times}) = \frac{6}{27}$, or $\frac{2}{9}$.

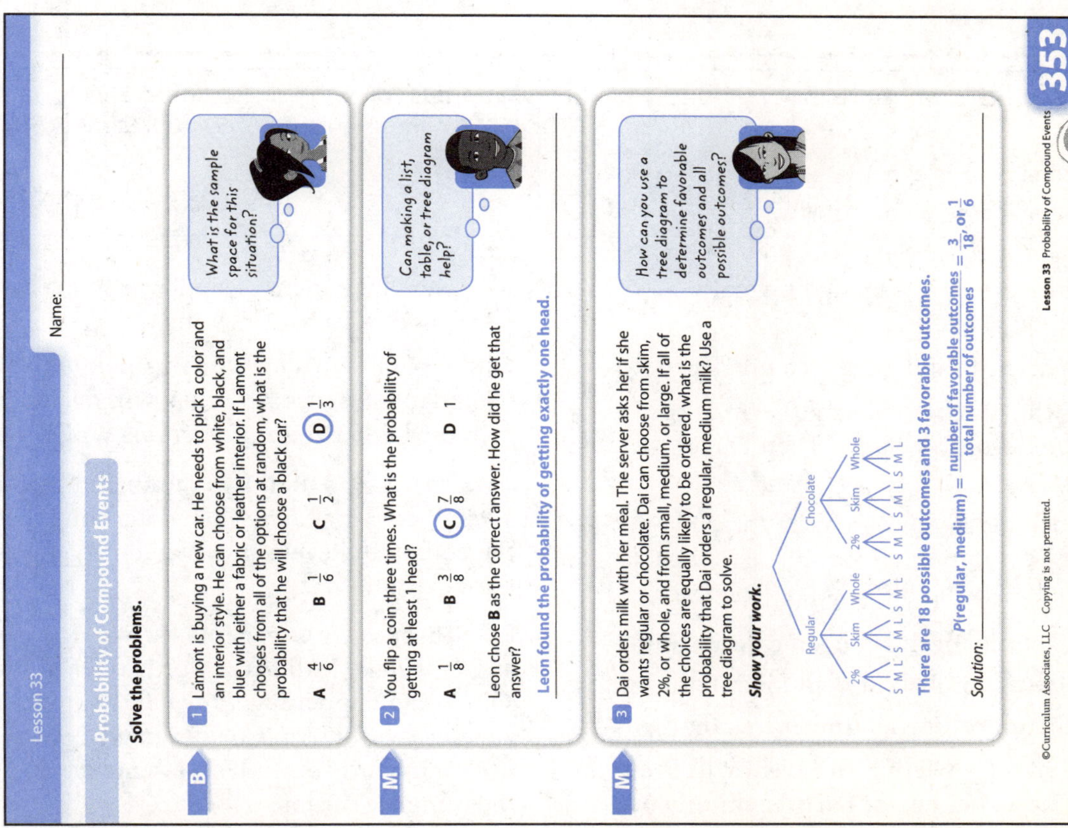

Name: ______________________

Probability of Compound Events

Solve the problems.

B **1** Lamont is buying a new car. He needs to pick a color and an interior style. He can choose from white, black, and blue with either a fabric or leather interior. If Lamont chooses from all of the options at random, what is the probability that he will choose a black car?

A $\frac{4}{6}$ B $\frac{1}{6}$ C $\frac{1}{2}$ **(D)** $\frac{1}{3}$

M **2** You flip a coin three times. What is the probability of getting at least 1 head?

A $\frac{1}{8}$ B $\frac{3}{8}$ **(C)** $\frac{7}{8}$ D 1

Leon chose **B** as the correct answer. How did he get that answer?

Leon found the probability of getting exactly one head.

M **3** Dai orders milk with her meal. The server asks her if she wants regular or chocolate. Dai can choose from skim, 2%, or whole, and from small, medium, or large. If all of the choices are equally likely to be ordered, what is the probability that Dai orders a regular, medium milk? Use a tree diagram to solve.

Show your work.

There are 18 possible outcomes and 3 favorable outcomes.

Solution: $P(\text{regular, medium}) = \frac{\text{number of favorable outcomes}}{\text{total number of outcomes}} = \frac{3}{18}$, or $\frac{1}{6}$

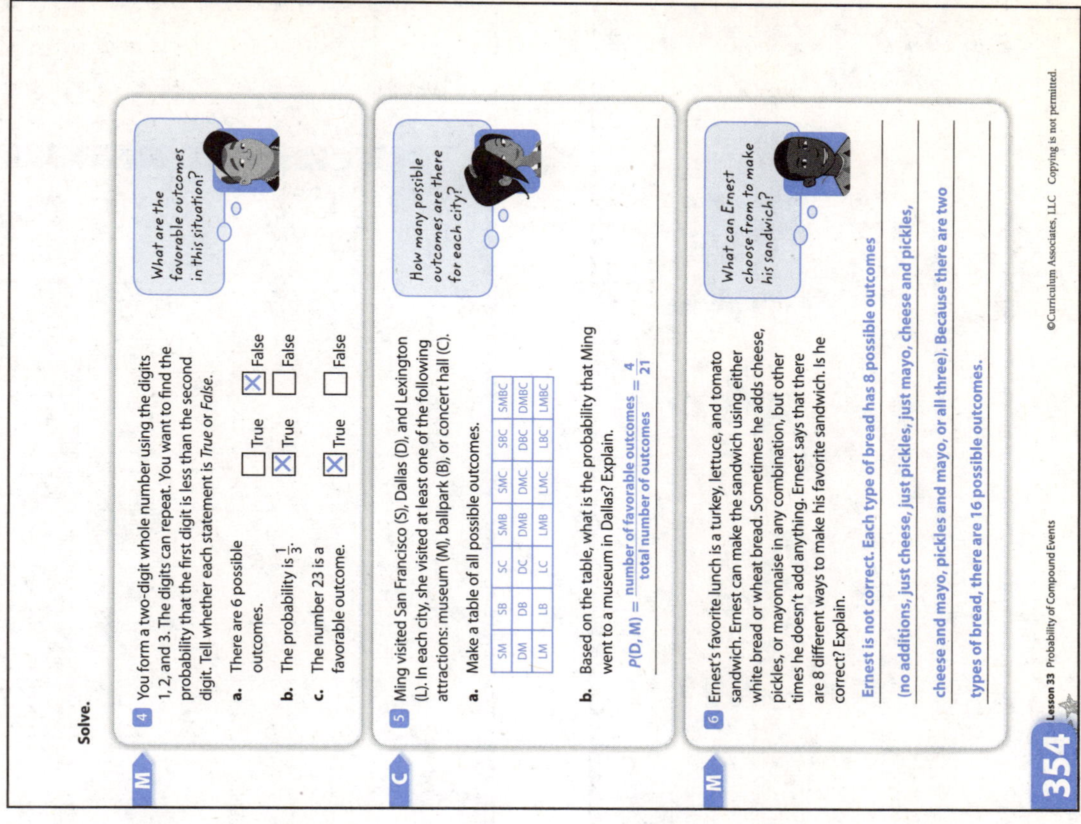

Solve.

M **4** You form a two-digit whole number using the digits 1, 2, and 3. The digits can repeat. You want to find the probability that the first digit is less than the second digit. Tell whether each statement is *True* or *False*.

a. There are 6 possible outcomes. ☐ True ☒ False

b. The probability is $\frac{1}{3}$. ☒ True ☐ False

c. The number 23 is a favorable outcome. ☒ True ☐ False

C **5** Ming visited San Francisco (S), Dallas (D), and Lexington (L). In each city, she visited at least one of the following attractions: museum (M), ballpark (B), or concert hall (C).

a. Make a table of all possible outcomes.

SM	SB	SC	SMB	SMC	SBC	SMBC
DM	DB	DC	DMB	DMC	DBC	DMBC
LM	LB	LC	LMB	LMC	LBC	LMBC

b. Based on the table, what is the probability that Ming went to a museum in Dallas? Explain.

$P(D, M) = \frac{\text{number of favorable outcomes}}{\text{total number of outcomes}} = \frac{4}{21}$

M **6** Ernest's favorite lunch is a turkey, lettuce, and tomato sandwich. Ernest can make the sandwich using either white bread or wheat bread. Sometimes he adds cheese, pickles, or mayonnaise in any combination, but other times he doesn't add anything. Ernest says that there are 8 different ways to make his favorite sandwich. Is he correct? Explain.

Ernest is not correct. Each type of bread has 8 possible outcomes (no additions, just cheese, just pickles, just mayo, cheese and pickles, cheese and mayo, pickles and mayo, or all three). Because there are two types of bread, there are 16 possible outcomes.

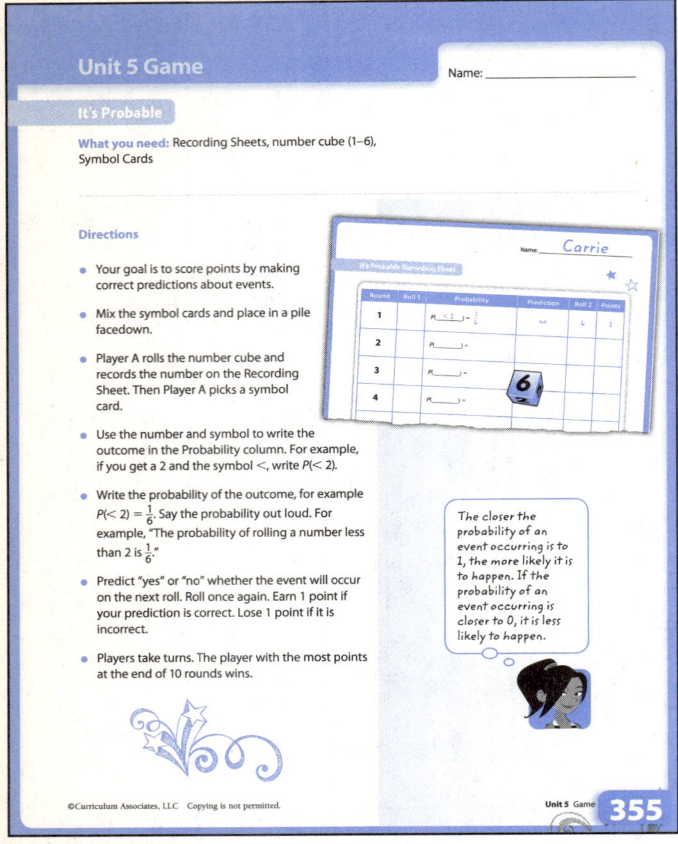
Unit 5 Game

Name: ______________________

It's Probable

What you need: Recording Sheets, number cube (1–6), Symbol Cards

Directions

- Your goal is to score points by making correct predictions about events.
- Mix the symbol cards and place in a pile facedown.
- Player A rolls the number cube and records the number on the Recording Sheet. Then Player A picks a symbol card.
- Use the number and symbol to write the outcome in the Probability column. For example, if you get a 2 and the symbol <, write $P(< 2)$.
- Write the probability of the outcome, for example $P(< 2) = \frac{1}{6}$. Say the probability out loud. For example, "The probability of rolling a number less than 2 is $\frac{1}{6}$."
- Predict "yes" or "no" whether the event will occur on the next roll. Roll once again. Earn 1 point if your prediction is correct. Lose 1 point if it is incorrect.
- Players take turns. The player with the most points at the end of 10 rounds wins.

©Curriculum Associates, LLC Copying is not permitted. Unit 5 Game 355

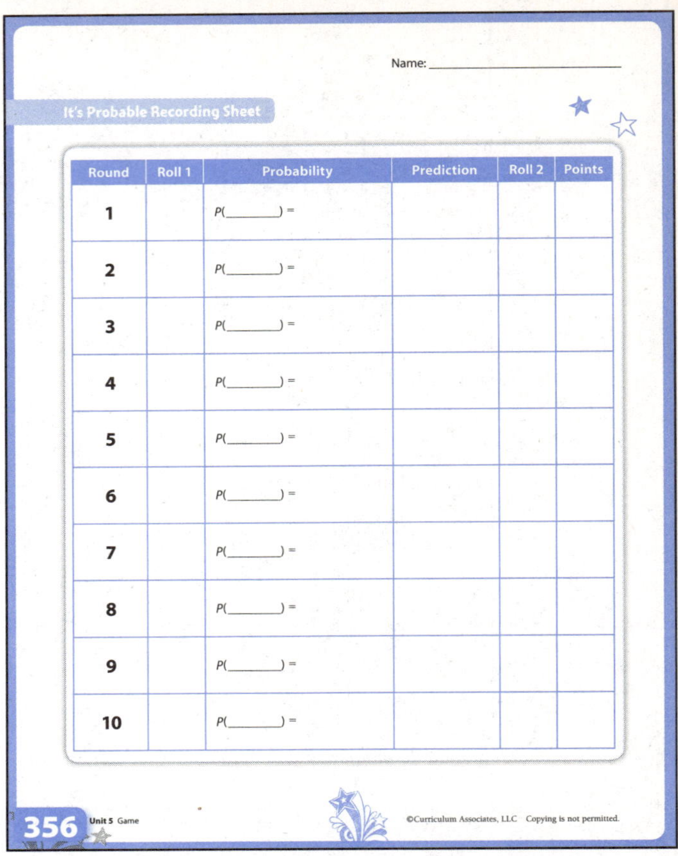
Name: ______________________

It's Probable Recording Sheet

Round	Roll 1	Probability	Prediction	Roll 2	Points
1		P(_______) =			
2		P(_______) =			
3		P(_______) =			
4		P(_______) =			
5		P(_______) =			
6		P(_______) =			
7		P(_______) =			
8		P(_______) =			
9		P(_______) =			
10		P(_______) =			

356 Unit 5 Game ©Curriculum Associates, LLC Copying is not permitted.

STEP BY STEP

CCSS Focus - 7.SP.C.5, 7.SP.C.7a *Embedded SMPs* - 1, 2, 3, 4, 5, 7 **Objectives** • Find the probability of an event. • Make a prediction based on probability.	**Materials** For each pair: Recording Sheets (1 for each player) (TR 7), number cube (1–6), Symbol Cards (TR 8)

- Your goal is to score points by making correct predictions about events.
- Mix the symbol cards and place in a pile facedown.
- Player A rolls the number cube and records the number on the Recording Sheet. Then Player A picks a symbol card.
- Use the number and symbol to write the outcome in the Probability column. For example, if you get a 2 and the symbol <, write $P(< 2)$.
- Write the probability of this outcome, for example $P(< 2) = \frac{1}{6}$. Say the probability out loud. For example, "The probability of rolling a number less than 2 is $\frac{1}{6}$."
- Predict "yes" or "no" whether the event will occur on the next roll. Roll once again. Earn 1 point if your prediction is correct. Lose 1 point if it is incorrect.
- Players take turns. The player with the most points at the end of 10 rounds wins.
- Model one turn for students before they play. Have students discuss how they will decide what to predict and whether their predictions will always come true.

Vary the Game Roll two number cubes (1–6). Pick a symbol card for each. Then determine the probability of the compound event in which both outcomes occur on the next roll.

ELL Discuss with students the words *probable, probably,* and *probability.* All three words refer to the likelihood of something happening. *Probability* is a noun, *probable* is an adjective, and *probably* is an adverb. Have students use each word correctly in a sentence and describe what the sentence means.

Unit 5 Practice

Name: ____________

Statistics and Probability

In this unit you learned to:	Lesson
identify random samples.	26
make statistical inferences from random samples.	27
compare data with measures of center and variability.	28, 29
find probabilities of single and compound events.	30, 31, 32, 33
compare theoretical and experimental probabilities.	31, 32

Use these skills to solve problems 1–6.

B **1** Which number best represents the probability that an outcome is unlikely to occur?

A 0
(B) $\frac{1}{10}$
C $\frac{1}{2}$
D $\frac{7}{8}$

B **2** A standard number cube is rolled and a coin is tossed. What is the probability of getting tails and an odd number?

A $\frac{1}{6}$
(B) $\frac{1}{4}$
C $\frac{1}{3}$
D $\frac{1}{2}$

B **3** Which sampling method or methods will produce a random sample of the students in your school? Select all that apply.

(A) Select every fifth student who enters the school.
B Choose the students on the boys' and girls' basketball teams.
C Ask for volunteers to take a survey.
(D) Assign each student a number and then select numbers at random.

M **4** There are 45 students on a field trip. Six students are chosen at random, five different times. The results are given.

2 boys and 4 girls
1 boy and 5 girls
2 boys and 4 girls
1 boy and 5 girls
3 boys and 3 girls

How many boys and girls do you think are on the field trip? Explain your answer.

Possible answer: 15 boys and 30 girls; the combined results are 9 boys and 21 girls, which is close to $\frac{1}{3}$ boys and $\frac{2}{3}$ girls.

Solve.

C **5** In baseball, a good hitter will get a hit 3 times out of every 10 times at bat. Vince ran an experiment in which a computer generated a random number from 00 to 99. He assigned the numbers 00 to 29 to represent a hit.

Part A: Is the experiment valid? Explain.

Yes; 00 to 29 is 30 numbers, and 30 out of 100 is equivalent to 3 out of 10.

Part B: After generating 200 random numbers, Vince counted 48 numbers from 00 to 29. Is this batter likely to be a good hitter? Explain.

No; Possible explanation: To get 3 hits for every 10 times at bat, a hitter would need 60 hits in 200 times at bat. This hitter had only 48.

M **6** The box plots show the results for two different classes on the same test. Select whether each statement is *True* or *False*.

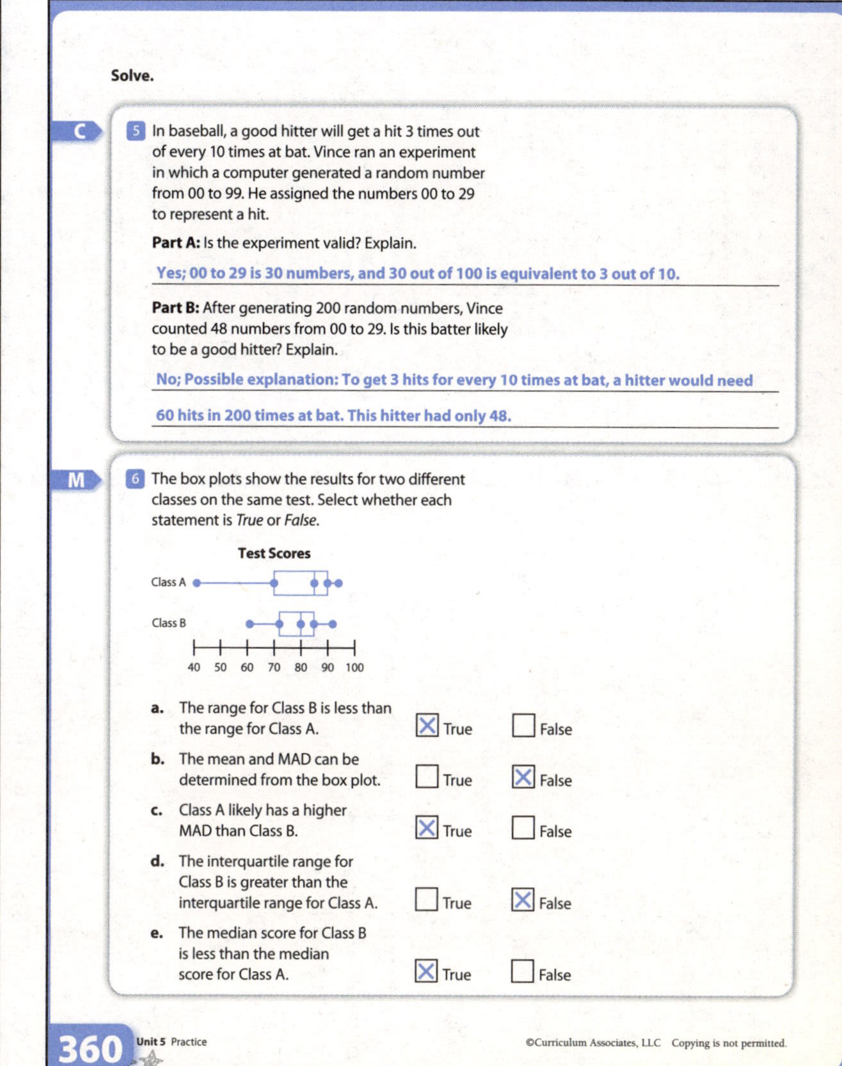

		True	False
a.	The range for Class B is less than the range for Class A.	☒	☐
b.	The mean and MAD can be determined from the box plot.	☐	☒
c.	Class A likely has a higher MAD than Class B.	☒	☐
d.	The interquartile range for Class B is greater than the interquartile range for Class A.	☐	☒
e.	The median score for Class B is less than the median score for Class A.	☒	☐

Key

B Basic **M** Medium **C** Challenge

TEACHER NOTES

Common Core Standards: 7.SP.C.6, 7.SP.C.7a, 7.SP.C.7b
Standards for Mathematical Practice: 1, 2, 3, 4, 5, 6, 7, 8
DOK: 3
Materials: Slips of paper, a paper bag

About the Task

To complete this task, students find theoretical and experimental probabilities. The task requires them to determine the theoretical probabilities of two separate events, conduct a probability experiment, and record the data. Then students discuss how the experimental results compare to the theoretical probabilities that they determined.

Getting Started

Read the problem out loud with students and go over the checklist. Have them describe what Mr. Alvarez wants to find out [how likely he is to pick a boy, or pick a girl, in the first week of class]. Ensure that students recognize that this is not a compound event. Mr. Alvarez is choosing one student, not trying to choose a boy and a girl. Discuss the experiment. Ask, *Why do you put the paper back in the box?* [Because you want to repeat the exact same experiment 50 times.] ***(SMP 1, 3)***

Completing the Task

Students begin by describing the sample space. The possible outcomes are picking a boy and picking a girl. They then use the methods that they have learned to determine the theoretical probability. As you circulate, ensure that students understand the difference between theoretical and experimental probability. ***(SMP 2, 5)***

As students move into the experimental part of the task, remind them to record their data in a precise and organized way. ***(SMP 4, 6)***

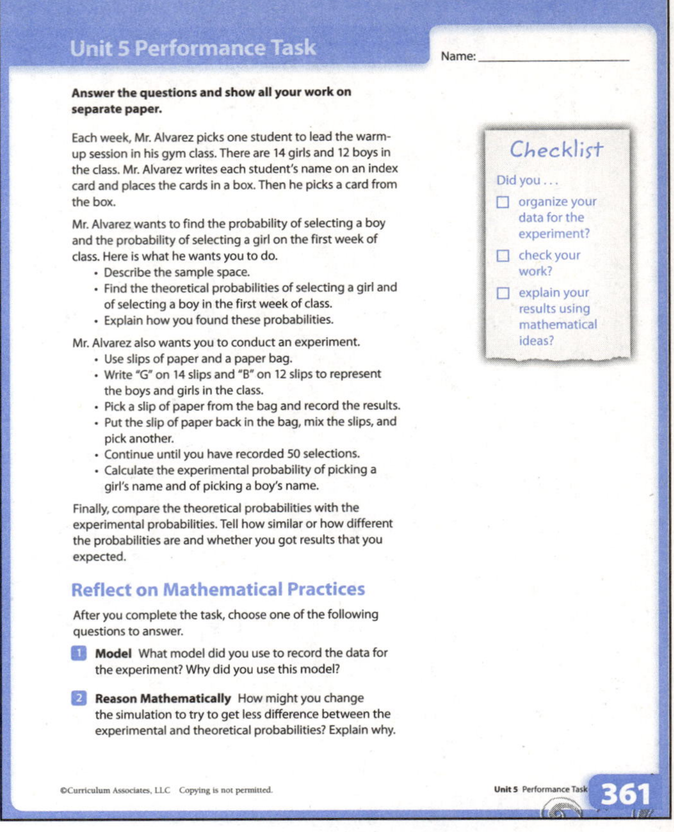
Unit 5 Performance Task

Name: ______________

Answer the questions and show all your work on separate paper.

Each week, Mr. Alvarez picks one student to lead the warm-up session in his gym class. There are 14 girls and 12 boys in the class. Mr. Alvarez writes each student's name on an index card and places the cards in a box. Then he picks a card from the box.

Mr. Alvarez wants to find the probability of selecting a boy and the probability of selecting a girl on the first week of class. Here is what he wants you to do.

- Describe the sample space.
- Find the theoretical probabilities of selecting a girl and of selecting a boy in the first week of class.
- Explain how you found these probabilities.

Mr. Alvarez also wants you to conduct an experiment.

- Use slips of paper and a paper bag.
- Write "G" on 14 slips and "B" on 12 slips to represent the boys and girls in the class.
- Pick a slip of paper from the bag and record the results.
- Put the slip of paper back in the bag, mix the slips, and pick another.
- Continue until you have recorded 50 selections.
- Calculate the experimental probability of picking a girl's name and of picking a boy's name.

Finally, compare the theoretical probabilities with the experimental probabilities. Tell how similar or how different the probabilities are and whether you got results that you expected.

Checklist
Did you . . .
- ☐ organize your data for the experiment?
- ☐ check your work?
- ☐ explain your results using mathematical ideas?

Reflect on Mathematical Practices

After you complete the task, choose one of the following questions to answer.

1. **Model** What model did you use to record the data for the experiment? Why did you use this model?
2. **Reason Mathematically** How might you change the simulation to try to get less difference between the experimental and theoretical probabilities? Explain why.

©Curriculum Associates, LLC Copying is not permitted. Unit 5 Performance Task 361

It is important that students analyze their results and think critically about how the theoretical and experimental probabilities relate to each other. Discuss results as a class, focusing on any surprising results and possible reasons why the experimental results were close to or far from the predicted (theoretical) results. ***(SMP 3, 7, 8)***

Extension

If students have more time to spend on this problem, you can have them solve this extension:

Mr. Alvarez picked a girl the first week. He does not put her name back in the box. What is the probability that he picks a girl the second week? What is the probability that he picks a boy the second week? How do you know?

SAMPLE RESPONSE AND RUBRIC

4-Point Solution

The sample space for this problem includes picking a boy and picking a girl. Of 26 students, there are 14 girls and 12 boys. So the theoretical probability of picking a girl is $\frac{14}{26}$. For picking a boy, the theoretical probability is $\frac{12}{26}$.

Results of My Experiment	
Event	**Tally**
Pick a girl	卌 卌 卌 卌 卌 卌 ||
Pick a boy	卌 卌 卌 |||

Comparison of Theoretical and Experimental Probabilities		
Event	**Theoretical Probability**	**Experimental Probability**
Pick a girl	$\frac{14}{26}$, or about 54%	$\frac{32}{50}$, or 64%
Pick a boy	$\frac{12}{26}$, or about 46%	$\frac{18}{50}$, or 36%

My experimental probability for picking a boy was a lot less than the theoretical probability, and my experimental probability for picking a girl was lot greater than the theoretical probability. This surprised me. I thought the theoretical and experimental probabilities would be closer.

REFLECT ON MATHEMATICAL PRACTICES

1. Responses should address the usefulness and efficiency of the recording model. ***(SMP 4)***
2. Students' ideas may include running a greater number of trials. Look for plausible explanations as to why their suggestions will improve the results. ***(SMP 3)***

SCORING RUBRIC

4 points All parts of the problem are complete and correct. Students show all work for both parts of the problem and provide clear mathematical explanations containing correct statements about the probabilities. The comparison is correct and the explanation makes sense.

3 points The student has completed all parts of the problem, with one or two errors. He or she might set up the probability correctly but calculate incorrectly. Other possible errors might include more or fewer than 50 trials, or a correct comparison with an incomplete explanation.

2 points The student has attempted all parts of the problem, with a number of errors. Calculations may contain errors. The probabilities may not reflect the number of trials or the correct sample space. Not all work is shown and explanations may be unclear or incomplete.

1 point Much of the problem is incomplete, with several errors. Calculations are incorrect and may not reflect the parameters of the problem. Parts of the problem are missing. The comparison is missing or incorrect. Explanations are missing or incorrect.

SOLUTION TO THE EXTENSION

Possible Solution

The first week, Mr. Alvarez picked a girl. He takes her name out of the box. So for the second week, there are 13 girls' names and 12 boys' names in the box. The probability of picking a girl is now $\frac{13}{25}$, or 52%, which is a little more than $\frac{1}{2}$ and a little less than it was before. The probability of picking a boy is now $\frac{12}{25}$, or 48%, which is a little less than $\frac{1}{2}$ and a little greater than it was before.

Addition and Subtraction with Rational Numbers—Skills Practice

Name: ____________

Add integers. **Form A**

1. $-5 + (-3) =$ __−8__
2. $14 + (-4) + 6 + (-16) =$ __0__
3. $9 + (-4) =$ __5__
4. $15 + (-7) + (-3) =$ __5__
5. $-17 + 16 =$ __−1__
6. $-18 + (-17) =$ __−35__
7. $14 + (-16) =$ __−2__
8. $-16 + (-7) + (-4) =$ __−27__
9. $-19 + 36 =$ __17__
10. $19 + 13 + (-9) =$ __23__
11. $-17 + 14 + 7 + 10 =$ __14__
12. $-12 + (-7) =$ __−19__
13. $-8 + 14 + (-2) + 6 =$ __10__
14. $-17 + (-19) =$ __−36__
15. $79 + (-24) =$ __55__
16. $23 + 14 + (-3) =$ __34__
17. $-8 + 11 =$ __3__
18. $-9 + 43 + (-11) =$ __23__
19. $-6 + 12 + (-12) + 6 =$ __0__
20. $16 + (-26) =$ __−10__
21. $45 + (-33) =$ __12__
22. $18 + 19 + (-8) + (-19) + 7 =$ __17__
23. $15 + (-3) + (-2) + 11 + 9 =$ __30__
24. $7 + (-14) + (-6) + 13 + 4 =$ __4__

Addition and Subtraction with Rational Numbers—Skills Practice

Name: ____________

Add integers. **Form B**

1. $-6 + (-4) =$ __−10__
2. $16 + (-8) + (-2) =$ __6__
3. $17 + (-13) =$ __4__
4. $13 + (-3) + 7 + (-17) =$ __0__
5. $-13 + (-16) =$ __−29__
6. $-18 + 17 =$ __−1__
7. $15 + (-18) =$ __−3__
8. $-18 + (-9) + (-2) =$ __−29__
9. $-14 + 32 =$ __18__
10. $18 + 16 + (-8) =$ __26__
11. $-14 + 18 + 4 + 10 =$ __18__
12. $-13 + (-4) =$ __−17__
13. $-16 + (-12) =$ __−28__
14. $-5 + 13 + (-5) + 7 =$ __10__
15. $86 + (-12) =$ __74__
16. $26 + 17 + (-6) =$ __37__
17. $-4 + 12 =$ __8__
18. $-2 + 64 + (-18) =$ __44__
19. $-8 + (-2) =$ __−10__
20. $4 + (-5) + (-9) + 10 =$ __0__
21. $-13 + (-13) =$ __−26__
22. $14 + 7 + (-4) + (-7) + 8 =$ __18__
23. $16 + (-4) + (-2) + 17 + 13 =$ __40__
24. $7 + (-14) + (-10) + 17 + 15 =$ __15__

Addition and Subtraction with Rational Numbers—Skills Practice

Name: ____________

Subtract integers. **Form A**

1. $-8 - (-14) =$ 6
2. $-8 - 4 - (-8) =$ −4
3. $17 - (-8) =$ 25
4. $6 - (-7) - (-3) - 16 =$ 0
5. $-12 - 4 =$ −16
6. $-13 - (-7) =$ −6
7. $6 - (-3) =$ 9
8. $-5 - (-17) - (-5) =$ 17
9. $-62 - (-11) =$ −51
10. $-4 - 8 - 16 =$ −28
11. $-8 - 15 =$ −23
12. $4 - 17 - (-6) - 3 =$ −10
13. $11 - (-15) =$ 26
14. $-46 - 21 =$ −67
15. $41 - (-13) - 21 =$ 33
16. $14 - (-17) =$ 31
17. $55 - (-29) - (-45) =$ 129
18. $8 - (-14) - (-2) - 4 =$ 20
19. $6 - 7 - (-4) - 3 =$ 0
20. $-25 - 25 =$ −50
21. $30 - (-15) - 40 =$ 5
22. $-7 - (-14) - 4 - (-27) - 5 =$ 25
23. $-12 - (-7) - (-19) - (-13) - (-2) =$ 29
24. $-11 - (-5) - 9 - (-13) - (-5) =$ 3
25. $8 - (-3) - 10 - (-12) - (-7) =$ 20

372 Fluency Practice

Addition and Subtraction with Rational Numbers—Skills Practice

Name: ____________

Subtract integers. **Form B**

1. $-4 - (-19) =$ 15
2. $-7 - 9 - (-7) =$ −9
3. $18 - (-9) =$ 27
4. $-13 - 11 =$ −24
5. $8 - (-6) - (-4) - 18 =$ 0
6. $-16 - (-8) =$ −8
7. $2 - (-5) =$ 7
8. $-4 - (-18) - (-4) =$ 18
9. $-73 - (-11) =$ −62
10. $-3 - 6 - 17 =$ −26
11. $-7 - 14 =$ −21
12. $12 - (-13) =$ 25
13. $8 - 19 - (-2) - 1 =$ −10
14. $-41 - 38 =$ −79
15. $56 - (-17) - 46 =$ 27
16. $13 - (-19) =$ 32
17. $35 - (-31) - (-65) =$ 131
18. $18 - 3 - (-2) - 7 =$ 10
19. $12 - (-6) =$ 18
20. $-15 - 10 =$ −25
21. $14 - (-11) - 21 =$ 4
22. $-8 - (-16) - 6 - (-38) - 5 =$ 35
23. $-17 - (-19) - (-18) - (-1) - (-7) =$ 28
24. $-13 - (-12) - 15 - (-8) - 3 =$ −11
25. $-4 - (-8) - 4 - (-12) - 8 =$ 4

Fluency Practice 373

Addition and Subtraction with Rational Numbers—Skills Practice

Name: ____________

Form A

Add rational numbers.

1. $-7.25 + 8.67 =$ 1.42
2. $-\frac{5}{6} + 7 + \left(-\frac{1}{6}\right) =$ 6
3. $-5 + \frac{1}{4} =$ $-4\frac{3}{4}$
4. $9 + (-10.2) =$ −1.2
5. $-\frac{1}{8} + \left(-\frac{7}{8}\right) =$ −1
6. $-\frac{5}{8} + \left(-\frac{1}{8}\right) + \frac{3}{4} =$ 0
7. $15.4 + (-16) =$ −0.6
8. $-1\frac{2}{5} + \frac{4}{5} =$ $-\frac{3}{5}$
9. $-8 + \left(-3\frac{1}{2}\right) =$ $-11\frac{1}{2}$
10. $-18.04 + 7.9 =$ −10.14
11. $-11 + (-4.25) =$ −15.25
12. $-\frac{5}{6} + \left(-\frac{5}{6}\right) =$ $-1\frac{2}{3}$
13. $\frac{2}{3} + \left(-\frac{1}{3}\right) =$ $\frac{1}{3}$
14. $5.3 + (-16.4) =$ −11.1
15. $1\frac{3}{4} + \left(-\frac{1}{2}\right) + \left(-\frac{1}{4}\right) =$ 1
16. $-5.75 + 10 =$ 4.25
17. $-8.9 + (-7.2) + 18.9 =$ 2.8
18. $-4.2 + (-3.7) =$ −7.9
19. $3.5 + (-13.5) + (-5.6) =$ −15.6
20. $-3\frac{1}{6} + (-8) =$ $-11\frac{1}{6}$

Addition and Subtraction with Rational Numbers—Skills Practice

Name: ____________

Form B

Add rational numbers.

1. $-5.25 + 9.76 =$ 4.51
2. $-\frac{5}{8} + 11 + \left(-\frac{3}{8}\right) =$ 10
3. $-6 + \frac{3}{4} =$ $-5\frac{1}{4}$
4. $6 + (-8.2) =$ −2.2
5. $-1\frac{3}{8} + \frac{5}{8} =$ $-\frac{3}{4}$
6. $-2\frac{1}{5} + \frac{3}{5} =$ $-1\frac{3}{5}$
7. $14.9 + (-17) =$ −2.1
8. $-\frac{1}{3} + \left(-\frac{5}{6}\right) + 1\frac{1}{6} =$ 0
9. $-9 + \left(-1\frac{1}{2}\right) =$ $-10\frac{1}{2}$
10. $-16.08 + 5.2 =$ −10.88
11. $-12 + (-6.75) =$ −18.75
12. $-\frac{3}{4} + \left(-\frac{3}{4}\right) =$ $-1\frac{1}{2}$
13. $\frac{4}{5} + \left(-\frac{3}{5}\right) =$ $\frac{1}{5}$
14. $3.6 + (-18.8) =$ −15.2
15. $2\frac{1}{2} + \left(-\frac{1}{8}\right) + \left(-\frac{3}{8}\right) =$ 2
16. $-4.25 + 10 =$ 5.75
17. $-9.1 + (-4.3) + 19.1 =$ 5.7
18. $-4.1 + (-2.8) =$ −6.9
19. $4.5 + (-8.2) + (-14.5) =$ −18.2
20. $-4\frac{1}{3} + (-7) =$ $-11\frac{1}{3}$

Addition and Subtraction with Rational Numbers—Skills Practice

Name: ____________

Add and subtract rational numbers. **Form A**

1. $4\frac{3}{4} - \left(-2\frac{1}{4}\right) =$ **7**
2. $-16.5 - 11 =$ **−27.5**
3. $\frac{1}{5} - \left(-\frac{4}{5}\right) =$ **1**
4. $7.75 - 14.25 =$ **−6.5**
5. $-8\frac{1}{3} - (-4) =$ **$-4\frac{1}{3}$**
6. $-15.7 - (-16.2) =$ **0.5**
7. $8.7 - (-5.2) =$ **13.9**
8. $6\frac{5}{6} - 9\frac{1}{6} =$ **$-2\frac{1}{3}$ or $-\frac{7}{3}$**
9. $6.2 - (-6.8) =$ **13**
10. $11.92 - 4.5 =$ **7.42**
11. $2\frac{1}{4} - 8\frac{1}{2} + 7\frac{3}{4} =$ **$1\frac{1}{2}$**
12. $4.2 - 17.6 + 5.8 =$ **−7.6**
13. $-12.6 + 4.2 - (-2.6) =$ **−5.8**
14. $-5\frac{2}{5} - 8\frac{4}{5} + 15\frac{2}{5} =$ **$1\frac{1}{5}$**
15. $-6.5 + 11 - (-6.5) =$ **11**
16. $\frac{1}{6} - (-7) + 3 - \left(-\frac{5}{6}\right) =$ **11**
17. $\frac{1}{4} - 1\frac{3}{4} + 2\frac{3}{4} - \left(-2\frac{3}{4}\right) =$ **4**
18. $-6.1 - 6 - (-6.1) + 16 =$ **10**
19. $1.25 - 2.75 - (-3.75) + (-7.25) =$ **−5**
20. $8\frac{1}{5} - \frac{3}{5} + \left(-\frac{4}{5}\right) - \left(-1\frac{2}{5}\right) =$ **$8\frac{1}{5}$**

376 Fluency Practice

Addition and Subtraction with Rational Numbers—Skills Practice

Name: ____________

Add and subtract rational numbers. **Form B**

1. $5\frac{5}{8} - \left(-3\frac{3}{8}\right) =$ **9**
2. $-14.5 - 8 =$ **−22.5**
3. $9.75 - 16.25 =$ **−6.5**
4. $\frac{1}{6} - \left(-\frac{5}{6}\right) =$ **1**
5. $-6\frac{1}{4} - (-2) =$ **$-4\frac{1}{4}$**
6. $-14.3 - (-17.1) =$ **2.8**
7. $9.2 - (-8.6) =$ **17.8**
8. $4\frac{2}{5} - 7\frac{1}{5} =$ **$-2\frac{4}{5}$**
9. $4.7 - (-9.3) =$ **14**
10. $9.84 - 8.5 =$ **1.34**
11. $3\frac{5}{6} - 2\frac{1}{3} + 6\frac{1}{6} =$ **$7\frac{2}{3}$**
12. $6.7 - 19.2 + 3.3 =$ **−9.2**
13. $-13.4 + 3.9 - (-3.4) =$ **−6.1**
14. $-6\frac{1}{2} - 7\frac{1}{2} + 16\frac{1}{2} =$ **$2\frac{1}{2}$**
15. $-4.5 + 13 - (-4.5) =$ **13**
16. $-4.1 - 8 - (-4.1) + 18 =$ **10**
17. $\frac{2}{5} - 1\frac{3}{5} + 3\frac{3}{5} - \left(-3\frac{3}{5}\right) =$ **6**
18. $\frac{1}{3} - (-8) + 2 - \left(-\frac{2}{3}\right) =$ **11**
19. $9\frac{3}{8} - \frac{5}{8} + \left(-\frac{5}{8}\right) - \left(-1\frac{1}{4}\right) =$ **$9\frac{3}{8}$**
20. $4.25 - 16.75 - (-0.75) + (-3.25) =$ **−15**

Fluency Practice 377

Addition and Subtraction with Rational Numbers—Repeated Reasoning

Name: ____________

Find patterns in adding integers.

Set A

1. $-6 + (-48) + 6 =$ **−48**
2. $-6 + (-148) + 6 =$ **−148**
3. $-16 + (-48) + 16 =$ **−48**
4. $-16 + (-148) + 16 =$ **−148**
5. $-26 + (-48) + 26 =$ **−48**
6. $-26 + (-148) + 26 =$ **−148**
7. $-36 + (-48) + 36 =$ **−48**
8. $-36 + (-148) + 36 =$ **−148**

Set B

1. $-6 + (-48) + 16 =$ **−38**
2. $-16 + (-48) + 26 =$ **−38**
3. $-26 + (-48) + 36 =$ **−38**
4. $-6 + (-148) + 16 =$ **−138**
5. $-16 + (-148) + 26 =$ **−138**
6. $-26 + (-148) + 36 =$ **−138**
7. $-16 + (-48) + 6 =$ **−58**
8. $-26 + (-48) + 16 =$ **−58**
9. $-36 + (-48) + 26 =$ **−58**
10. $-16 + (-148) + 6 =$ **−158**
11. $-26 + (-148) + 16 =$ **−158**
12. $-36 + (-148) + 26 =$ **−158**

Describe a pattern you see in one of the sets of problems above.

Answers will vary. Students may see in Set A that they can pair numbers by combining the same positive number with the same negative number to get zero. The sum is the other addend in the equation.

Addition and Subtraction with Rational Numbers—Repeated Reasoning

Name: ____________

Find patterns in subtracting integers.

Set A

1. $-9 - 37 - (-9) =$ **−37**
2. $-9 - 137 - (-9) =$ **−137**
3. $-19 - 37 - (-19) =$ **−37**
4. $-19 - 137 - (-19) =$ **−137**
5. $-29 - 37 - (-29) =$ **−37**
6. $-29 - 137 - (-29) =$ **−137**
7. $-39 - 37 - (-39) =$ **−37**
8. $-39 - 137 - (-39) =$ **−137**

Set B

1. $-9 - 37 - (-19) =$ **−27**
2. $-19 - 37 - (-29) =$ **−27**
3. $-29 - 37 - (-39) =$ **−27**
4. $-9 - 137 - (-19) =$ **−127**
5. $-19 - 137 - (-29) =$ **−127**
6. $-29 - 137 - (-39) =$ **−127**
7. $-19 - 37 - (-9) =$ **−47**
8. $-29 - 37 - (-19) =$ **−47**
9. $-39 - 37 - (-29) =$ **−47**
10. $-19 - 137 - (-9) =$ **−147**
11. $-29 - 137 - (-19) =$ **−147**
12. $-39 - 137 - (-29) =$ **−147**

Describe a pattern you see in one of the sets of problems above.

Answers will vary. Students may see in Set A that they can pair numbers by subtracting a negative number from the same negative number to get zero. The difference is the third term on that side of the equation.

Addition and Subtraction with Rational Numbers—Repeated Reasoning

Name: ____________

Find patterns in adding rational numbers.

Set A

1. −0.9 + 4.9 + (−4.0) = 0
2. −0.8 + 4.9 + (−4.0) = 0.1
3. −0.7 + 4.9 + (−4.0) = 0.2
4. −0.6 + 4.9 + (−4.0) = 0.3
5. −0.5 + 4.9 + (−4.0) = 0.4
6. −0.4 + 4.9 + (−4.0) = 0.5
7. −0.3 + 4.9 + (−4.0) = 0.6
8. −0.2 + 4.9 + (−4.0) = 0.7
9. −0.1 + 4.9 + (−4.0) = 0.8

Set B

1. −0.9 + 5.9 + (−5.0) = 0
2. −0.9 + 5.8 + (−5.0) = −0.1
3. −0.9 + 5.7 + (−5.0) = −0.2
4. −0.9 + 5.6 + (−5.0) = −0.3
5. −0.9 + 5.5 + (−5.0) = −0.4
6. −0.9 + 5.4 + (−5.0) = −0.5
7. −0.9 + 5.3 + (−5.0) = −0.6
8. −0.9 + 5.2 + (−5.0) = −0.7
9. −0.9 + 5.1 + (−5.0) = −0.8

Describe a pattern you see in one of the sets of problems above.

Answers will vary. In Set B, students may see that as they decrease the positive addend by 0.1, the sum decreases by 0.1.

Addition and Subtraction with Rational Numbers—Repeated Reasoning

Name: ____________

Find patterns in subtracting rational numbers.

Set A

1. 4 − 2 = 2
2. 2 − 4 = −2
3. 6 − 5 = 1
4. 5 − 6 = −1
5. 8 − 3 = 5
6. 3 − 8 = −5
7. 5 − 1.5 = 3.5
8. 1.5 − 5 = −3.5
9. 7 − 2.5 = 4.5
10. 2.5 − 7 = −4.5
11. 12 − 3.5 = 8.5
12. 3.5 − 12 = −8.5

Set B

1. −3 − 4 = −7
2. −2 − 4 = −6
3. −1 − 4 = −5
4. −4 − 3 = −7
5. −4 − 2 = −6
6. −4 − 1 = −5
7. −13 − 0.5 = −12.5
8. −12 − 0.5 = −11.5
9. −11 − 0.5 = −10.5
10. 0.5 − 13 = −12.5
11. 0.5 − 12 = −11.5
12. 0.5 − 11 = −10.5

Describe a pattern you see in one of the sets of problems above.

Answers will vary. Students may see in Set A that the difference of $a - b$ is the opposite of the difference of $b - a$. For example, 4 − 2 = 2 and 2 − 4 = −2.

Multiplication and Division with Rational Numbers—Skills Practice

Name: ________________

Multiply rational numbers.

Form A

1. $-\frac{3}{5} \times \left(-\frac{5}{8}\right) =$ $\frac{15}{40}$ or $\frac{3}{8}$
2. $2 \times (-5) \times 3 \times (-4) =$ 120
3. $-0.2 \times (-0.4) =$ 0.08
4. $-\frac{1}{6} \times \frac{5}{6} =$ $-\frac{5}{36}$
5. $-9 \times (-4) =$ 36
6. $-8 \times 7 =$ −56
7. $0.2 \times (-0.05) \times 0.3 =$ −0.003
8. $-0.6 \times 0.03 =$ −0.018
9. $6 \times (-6) =$ −36
10. $-\frac{1}{5} \times \frac{3}{5} \times \frac{4}{5} =$ $-\frac{12}{125}$
11. $-\frac{1}{4} \times \left(-\frac{3}{4}\right) =$ $\frac{3}{16}$
12. $-0.5 \times 0.4 \times 0.3 =$ −0.06
13. $0.5 \times (-0.7) =$ −0.35
14. $-7 \times (-3) \times (-4) =$ −84
15. $-7 \times (-4) =$ 28
16. $\frac{1}{3} \times \left(-\frac{2}{3}\right) =$ $-\frac{2}{9}$
17. $5 \times (-8) =$ −40
18. $-2 \times -6 \times -3 =$ −36
19. $-10 \times 14 =$ −140
20. $-\frac{5}{8} \times \frac{2}{5} \times \left(-\frac{1}{4}\right) =$ $\frac{10}{160}$ or $\frac{1}{16}$
21. $100 \times (-9) =$ −900
22. $-\frac{1}{4} \times \frac{3}{2} \times \frac{1}{2} =$ $-\frac{3}{16}$
23. $-0.5 \times 0.1 \times (-0.2) \times (-0.4) =$ −0.004
24. $-\frac{1}{2} \times \frac{3}{2} \times \frac{5}{2} \times \left(-\frac{1}{2}\right) =$ $\frac{15}{16}$

382 Fluency Practice

Multiplication and Division with Rational Numbers—Skills Practice

Name: ________________

Multiply rational numbers.

Form B

1. $\frac{1}{4} \times \left(-\frac{3}{4}\right) =$ $-\frac{3}{16}$
2. $5 \times (-2) \times 6 \times (-3) =$ 180
3. $-0.3 \times (-0.2) =$ 0.06
4. $-\frac{1}{3} \times \frac{2}{3} =$ $-\frac{2}{9}$
5. $-3 \times (-8) =$ 24
6. $-9 \times 6 =$ −54
7. $0.3 \times (-0.05) \times 0.6 =$ −0.009
8. $-0.4 \times 0.04 =$ −0.016
9. $9 \times (-9) =$ −81
10. $-\frac{2}{5} \times \frac{1}{5} \times \frac{3}{5} =$ $-\frac{6}{125}$
11. $-\frac{7}{8} \times \left(-\frac{3}{8}\right) =$ $\frac{21}{64}$
12. $-0.2 \times 0.4 \times 0.6 =$ −0.048
13. $0.9 \times (-0.5) =$ −0.45
14. $-2 \times (-4) \times (-8) =$ −64
15. $-7 \times (-3) =$ 21
16. $-16 \times 10 =$ −160
17. $-\frac{5}{6} \times \frac{2}{5} \times \left(-\frac{1}{8}\right) =$ $\frac{10}{240}$ or $\frac{1}{24}$
18. $100 \times (-7) =$ −700
19. $-5 \times (-7) =$ 35
20. $9 \times (-8) =$ −72
21. $-\frac{1}{5} \times \left(-\frac{1}{2}\right) =$ $\frac{1}{10}$
22. $-0.4 \times 0.1 \times (-0.3) \times (-0.5) =$ −0.006
23. $-\frac{1}{2} \times \frac{3}{2} \times \left(-\frac{3}{2}\right) \times \left(-\frac{1}{2}\right) =$ $-\frac{9}{16}$
24. $0.5 \times -0.2 \times (-2) \times 5 =$ 1

 Fluency Practice 383

Multiplication and Division with Rational Numbers—Skills Practice

Name: ____________________

Form A

Divide rational numbers.

1. $-\frac{1}{3} \div \left(-\frac{1}{6}\right) =$ $\frac{6}{3}$ or 2
2. $56 \div (-8) =$ -7
3. $-3.6 \div 0.1 =$ -36
4. $-\frac{1}{2} \div \frac{1}{8} =$ $-\frac{8}{2}$ or -4
5. $-44 \div (-4) =$ 11
6. $-9.8 \div (-1) =$ 9.8
7. $\frac{1}{6} \div \left(-\frac{1}{6}\right) =$ $-\frac{6}{6}$ or -1
8. $6.4 \div (-2) =$ -3.2
9. $35 \div (-5) =$ -7
10. $-\frac{3}{4} \div \left(-\frac{1}{2}\right) =$ $\frac{6}{4}$ or $\frac{3}{2}$ or $1\frac{1}{2}$
11. $-90 \div 9 =$ -10
12. $\frac{2}{5} \div \left(-\frac{2}{3}\right) =$ $-\frac{6}{10}$ or $-\frac{3}{5}$
13. $-8.9 \div 10 =$ -0.89
14. $-36 \div (-3) =$ 12
15. $-24 \div (-0.2) =$ 120
16. $-\frac{5}{3} \div \frac{5}{6} =$ -2
17. $-100 \div (-50) =$ 2
18. $5.5 \div (-0.5) =$ -11
19. $\frac{1}{8} \div \left(-\frac{1}{5}\right) =$ $-\frac{5}{8}$
20. $-7.5 \div (-2.5) =$ 3
21. $-32 \div 4 =$ -8
22. $-3.6 \div 1.2 =$ -3
23. $-42 \div (-6) =$ 7
24. $-\frac{1}{3} \div \left(-\frac{1}{3}\right) =$ 1

384 Fluency Practice

Multiplication and Division with Rational Numbers—Skills Practice

Name: ____________________

Form B

Divide rational numbers.

1. $-32 \div 8 =$ -4
2. $-\frac{1}{4} \div \left(-\frac{1}{8}\right) =$ $\frac{8}{4}$ or 2
3. $-4.8 \div 0.1 =$ -48
4. $-\frac{1}{2} \div \frac{1}{6} =$ -3
5. $\frac{1}{5} \div \left(-\frac{1}{5}\right) =$ -1
6. $-7.6 \div (-1) =$ 7.6
7. $-66 \div (-6) =$ 11
8. $8.2 \div (-2) =$ -4.1
9. $56 \div (-7) =$ -8
10. $-\frac{5}{6} \div \left(-\frac{1}{2}\right) =$ $\frac{5}{3}$ or $1\frac{2}{3}$
11. $-48 \div (-4) =$ 12
12. $\frac{3}{8} \div \left(-\frac{3}{5}\right) =$ $-\frac{5}{8}$
13. $-5.4 \div 10 =$ -0.54
14. $-70 \div 7 =$ -10
15. $7.5 \div (-2.5) =$ -3
16. $-\frac{5}{2} \div \frac{5}{8} =$ $-\frac{40}{10}$ or -4
17. $-100 \div (-25) =$ 4
18. $2.5 \div (-0.5) =$ -5
19. $\frac{1}{5} \div \left(-\frac{1}{3}\right) =$ $-\frac{3}{5}$
20. $-39 \div (-0.3) =$ 130
21. $30 \div (-5) =$ -6
22. $3.2 \div (-8) =$ -0.4
23. $-4.8 \div 1.2 =$ -4
24. $\frac{1}{4} \div \left(-\frac{1}{5}\right) =$ $-\frac{5}{4}$ or $-1\frac{1}{4}$

Fluency Practice 385

Expressing Rational Numbers as Decimals—Skills Practice

Name: ____________

Write fractions as decimals.

Form A

1 $-\frac{4}{5} = -0.8$	**2** $-\frac{1}{2} = -0.5$	**3** $-\frac{5}{9} = -0.\overline{5}$
4 $-\frac{2}{3} = -0.\overline{6}$	**5** $-\frac{2}{9} = -0.\overline{2}$	**6** $\frac{2}{5} = 0.4$
7 $\frac{9}{2} = 4.5$	**8** $\frac{5}{3} = 1.\overline{6}$	**9** $-\frac{7}{5} = -1.4$
10 $-\frac{1}{4} = -0.25$	**11** $-\frac{10}{9} = -1.\overline{1}$	**12** $\frac{3}{2} = 1.5$
13 $\frac{7}{2} = 3.5$	**14** $-\frac{8}{5} = -1.6$	**15** $\frac{5}{6} = 0.8\overline{3}$
16 $-\frac{11}{4} = -2.75$	**17** $\frac{5}{12} = 0.41\overline{6}$	**18** $\frac{7}{6} = 1.1\overline{6}$
19 $-\frac{5}{8} = -0.625$	**20** $\frac{5}{4} = 1.25$	**21** $\frac{9}{8} = 1.125$

386 Fluency Practice

Expressing Rational Numbers as Decimals—Skills Practice

Name: ____________

Write fractions as decimals.

Form B

1 $-\frac{1}{2} = -0.5$	**2** $\frac{3}{5} = 0.6$	**3** $-\frac{7}{9} = -0.\overline{7}$
4 $-\frac{1}{5} = -0.2$	**5** $-\frac{1}{3} = -0.\overline{3}$	**6** $\frac{2}{9} = 0.\overline{2}$
7 $\frac{7}{3} = 2.\overline{3}$	**8** $-\frac{9}{5} = -1.8$	**9** $-\frac{3}{4} = -0.75$
10 $-\frac{9}{2} = -4.5$	**11** $-\frac{6}{5} = -1.2$	**12** $-\frac{7}{2} = -3.5$
13 $-\frac{3}{2} = -1.5$	**14** $\frac{1}{6} = 0.1\overline{6}$	**15** $\frac{11}{9} = 1.\overline{2}$
16 $\frac{11}{6} = 1.8\overline{3}$	**17** $-\frac{9}{4} = -2.25$	**18** $-\frac{3}{8} = -0.375$
19 $-\frac{9}{8} = -1.125$	**20** $\frac{7}{12} = 0.58\overline{3}$	**21** $\frac{7}{4} = 1.75$

Fluency Practice 387

Expressing Rational Numbers as Decimals—Repeated Reasoning

Name: ____________

Find patterns with repeating decimals. Write each fraction or fraction sum as a repeating decimal.

Set A

1. $\frac{1}{3} = 0.\overline{3}$
2. $\frac{2}{3} = 0.\overline{6}$
3. $\frac{4}{3} = 1.\overline{3}$
4. $\frac{5}{3} = 1.\overline{6}$
5. $\frac{7}{3} = 2.\overline{3}$
6. $\frac{8}{3} = 2.\overline{6}$
7. $\frac{10}{3} = 3.\overline{3}$
8. $\frac{11}{3} = 3.\overline{6}$
9. $\frac{13}{3} = 4.\overline{3}$
10. $\frac{14}{3} = 4.\overline{6}$

Set B

1. $\frac{1}{6} = 0.1\overline{6}$
2. $\frac{2}{6} = 0.\overline{3}$
3. $\frac{3}{6} = 0.5$
4. $\frac{1}{6} + \frac{3}{6} = 0.\overline{6}$
5. $\frac{2}{6} + \frac{2}{6} = 0.\overline{6}$
6. $\frac{4}{6} = 0.\overline{6}$
7. $\frac{2}{6} + \frac{3}{6} = 0.8\overline{3}$
8. $\frac{1}{6} + \frac{4}{6} = 0.8\overline{3}$
9. $\frac{5}{6} = 0.8\overline{3}$

Describe a pattern you see in one of the sets of problems above.

Answers will vary. Students may see in Set A that when increasing the fraction by $\frac{3}{3}$ or 1 whole, the decimal equivalent of the fraction also increases by 1 whole.

Expressing Rational Numbers as Decimals—Repeated Reasoning

Name: ____________

Find more patterns with repeating decimals. Write each fraction as a decimal.

Set A

1. $\frac{1}{9} = 0.\overline{1}$
2. $\frac{2}{9} = 0.\overline{2}$
3. $\frac{3}{9} = 0.\overline{3}$
4. $\frac{4}{9} = 0.\overline{4}$
5. $\frac{5}{9} = 0.\overline{5}$
6. $\frac{6}{9} = 0.\overline{6}$
7. $\frac{10}{9} = 1.\overline{1}$
8. $\frac{11}{9} = 1.\overline{2}$
9. $\frac{12}{9} = 1.\overline{3}$

Set B

1. $\frac{1}{11} = 0.\overline{09}$
2. $\frac{2}{11} = 0.\overline{18}$
3. $\frac{3}{11} = 0.\overline{27}$
4. $\frac{4}{11} = 0.\overline{36}$
5. $\frac{5}{11} = 0.\overline{45}$
6. $\frac{6}{11} = 0.\overline{54}$
7. $\frac{7}{11} = 0.\overline{63}$
8. $\frac{8}{11} = 0.\overline{72}$
9. $\frac{9}{11} = 0.\overline{81}$

Describe a pattern you see in one of the sets of problems above.

Answers will vary. Students may see that in Set B, when a fraction has 11 as the denominator and the numerator is not evenly divisible by 11, the quotient is a repeating decimal. The repeating decimal is the numerator multiplied by 0.09.

Using Properties of Operations—Skills Practice

Name: ____________

Write an equivalent expression without parentheses, and combine terms if possible. **Form A**

1. $5x + 6x =$ **11x**
2. $6n - 3(2n - 5) =$ **15**
3. $0.5(-12p - 4) =$ **$-6p - 2$**
4. $\frac{1}{4}y + \frac{3}{4}(y - 8) =$ **$y - 6$**
5. $4(x - 6) + 30 =$ **$4x + 6$**
6. $-8\left(m + \frac{1}{4}\right) =$ **$-8m - 2$**
7. $-8x - 4x + 3x + 2 =$ **$-9x + 2$**
8. $4.5a + 7 + 3.5a + 2 =$ **$8a + 9$**
9. $-4 + 7y - 3y - 5 =$ **$4y - 9$**
10. $\frac{1}{6}(12n + 36) =$ **$2n + 6$**
11. $3(y + 7) - 5y =$ **$-2y + 21$**
12. $9y - 4x + 3y + 4x =$ **$12y$**
13. $8(6a + 7) =$ **$48a + 56$**
14. $\frac{1}{6}y + 6 - \frac{7}{6}y - 4 =$ **$-y + 2$**
15. $\frac{3}{2}x - \frac{1}{2}(x + 4) =$ **$x - 2$**
16. $6 + 2x + 4(x + 5) =$ **$6x + 26$**
17. $-8(x + 3) =$ **$-8x - 24$**
18. $3y + 3(y - 2.5) =$ **$6y - 7.5$**
19. $9\left(-\frac{1}{3}m + 4\right) - 6m =$ **$-9m + 36$**
20. $6.25m + 9 + 3.75m - 12 =$ **$10m - 3$**

Using Properties of Operations—Skills Practice

Name: ____________

Write an equivalent expression without parentheses, and combine terms if possible. **Form B**

1. $7x + 6x =$ **$13x$**
2. $10n - 5(2n - 5) =$ **25**
3. $\frac{5}{4}x - \frac{1}{4}(x + 12) =$ **$x - 3$**
4. $4 + 2x + 7(x + 2) =$ **$9x + 18$**
5. $6(x - 7) + 50 =$ **$6x + 8$**
6. $-6\left(m + \frac{1}{2}\right) =$ **$-6m - 3$**
7. $-3 + 8y - 6y - 4 =$ **$2y - 7$**
8. $\frac{1}{4}y + 9 - \frac{5}{4}y - 2 =$ **$-y + 7$**
9. $9(3a + 8) =$ **$27a + 72$**
10. $\frac{1}{8}(16n + 24) =$ **$2n + 3$**
11. $-7(x + 4) =$ **$-7x - 28$**
12. $2y + 3(y - 1.5) =$ **$5y - 4.5$**
13. $-9x - 5x + 6x + 3 =$ **$-8x + 3$**
14. $2.5a + 5 + 4.5a + 3 =$ **$7a + 8$**
15. $15\left(-\frac{1}{5}m + 2\right) - 4m =$ **$-7m + 30$**
16. $4.25m + 7 + 6.75m - 11 =$ **$11m - 4$**
17. $7(y + 7) - 11y =$ **$-4y + 49$**
18. $8x - 2 - 5x + 2 =$ **$3x$**
19. $0.5(-16p - 6) =$ **$-8p - 3$**
20. $\frac{1}{5}y + \frac{4}{5}(y - 10) =$ **$y - 8$**

Using Properties of Operations—Skills Practice

Name: ______________

Use the distributive property to write the expression as a product. **Form A**
Problems may have more than one answer.

1. $7x + 7 =$ $7(x + 1)$
2. $6y + 14 - 8y =$ $2(7 - y)$
3. $25x - 5 =$ $5(5x - 1)$
4. $16y + (-4) =$ $4(4y - 1)$
5. $4 - 8y =$ $4(1 - 2y)$
6. $-8x - 16 =$ $-8(x + 2)$
7. $-11x - 44 =$ $-11(x + 4)$
8. $10 + 70x =$ $10(1 + 7x)$
9. $10 - (-4y) =$ $2(5 + 2y)$
10. $-2x + 12 - 4x =$ $6(2 - x)$
11. $-25y + (-55) =$ $-5(5y + 11)$
12. $20y - (-5) =$ $5(4y + 1)$
13. $-21x + 14 =$ $7(-3x + 2)$
14. $18x - 33 =$ $3(6x - 11)$
15. $4y + 22 + 7y =$ $11(y + 2)$
16. $-7 + (-21x) =$ $-7(1 + 3x)$
17. $6 + (-12y) =$ $6(1 - 2y)$
18. $-5x + 33 + 16x =$ $11(x + 3)$
19. $15y - 35 =$ $5(3y - 7)$
20. $-40y + 100 =$ $20(-2y + 5)$

Using Properties of Operations—Skills Practice

Name: ______________

Use the distributive property to write the expression as a product. **Form B**
Problems may have more than one answer.

1. $8x + 8 =$ $8(x + 1)$
2. $8y + 20 - 12y =$ $4(5 - y)$
3. $5y + 33 + 6y =$ $11(y + 3)$
4. $-5x + 18 - 4x =$ $9(2 - x)$
5. $6 - 18y =$ $6(1 - 3y)$
6. $-9x - 18 =$ $-9(x + 2)$
7. $-9 + (-27x) =$ $-9(1 + 3x)$
8. $20 - (-6y) =$ $2(10 + 3y)$
9. $-24x + 18 =$ $6(-4x + 3)$
10. $16x - 44 =$ $4(4x - 11)$
11. $4 + (-16y) =$ $4(1 - 4y)$
12. $3 + 39x =$ $3(1 + 13x)$
13. $-4x + 28 + 11x =$ $7(x + 4)$
14. $30y - (-6) =$ $6(5y + 1)$
15. $-11x - 66 =$ $-11(x + 6)$
16. $20 + 80x =$ $20(1 + 4x)$
17. $25y - 45 =$ $5(5y - 9)$
18. $36x - 6 =$ $6(6x - 1)$
19. $-60y + 90 =$ $30(-2y + 3)$
20. $24y + (-3) =$ $3(8y - 1)$

Two-Step Equations—Skills Practice

Name: ____________________

Solve equations of form $px + q = r$ with integers. **Form A**

1. $6x + 6 = 0$ — $x = -1$
2. $-3x + 9 = 6$ — $x = 1$
3. $5x + 4 = -6$ — $x = -2$
4. $-275 = 25x - 50$ — $x = -9$
5. $90 = 20x - 10$ — $x = 5$
6. $46 = 3x + 19$ — $x = 9$
7. $-15x - 45 = -45$ — $x = 0$
8. $12x - 14 = -38$ — $x = -2$
9. $97 = 10x + 27$ — $x = 7$
10. $-6x - 13 = 35$ — $x = -8$
11. $-127 = -50x + 23$ — $x = 3$
12. $8x + 5 = -3$ — $x = -1$
13. $7x + 4 = -38$ — $x = -6$
14. $-4x - 52 = -152$ — $x = 25$
15. $-8 = -6x - 2$ — $x = 1$
16. $-25 = 10x - 25$ — $x = 0$

394 Fluency Practice

Two-Step Equations—Skills Practice

Name: ____________________

Solve equations of form $px + q = r$ with integers. **Form B**

1. $-4x + 12 = 8$ — $x = 1$
2. $8x + 8 = 0$ — $x = -1$
3. $5x + 6 = -14$ — $x = -4$
4. $-250 = 25x - 75$ — $x = -7$
5. $30 = 20x - 10$ — $x = 2$
6. $38 = 3x + 17$ — $x = 7$
7. $11x - 16 = -49$ — $x = -3$
8. $-18x - 36 = -36$ — $x = 0$
9. $86 = 10x + 26$ — $x = 6$
10. $-8x - 11 = 45$ — $x = -7$
11. $-164 = -50x + 36$ — $x = 4$
12. $0 = 12x - 12$ — $x = 1$
13. $-12 = -9x - 3$ — $x = 1$
14. $9x + 7 = -2$ — $x = -1$
15. $-8x + 23 = 103$ — $x = -10$
16. $-6x + 53 = 5$ — $x = 8$

Fluency Practice 395

Two-Step Equations—Skills Practice

Name: ____________

Solve equations of form $px + q = r$ with rational numbers. **Form A**

1. $-3x + 6 = 9.9$
   $x = -1.3$
2. $8\frac{3}{5} = -4x + 5\frac{3}{5}$
   $x = -\frac{3}{4}$
3. $1.2x + 5.3 = 0.5$
   $x = -4$
4. $-\frac{1}{4}x + 6 = 10$
   $x = -16$
5. $7 = 11 - 0.2x$
   $x = 20$
6. $0.4x + 15 = 39.8$
   $x = 62$
7. $1\frac{3}{8} = \frac{1}{4}x + 1$
   $x = \frac{3}{2}$ or $1\frac{1}{2}$
8. $\frac{2}{3}x - 4 = 36$
   $x = 60$
9. $\frac{1}{5} = \frac{7}{5} - \frac{1}{10}x$
   $x = 12$
10. $-8.2 = -7.1 + 11x$
    $x = -0.1$
11. $-13\frac{3}{4} = -\frac{7}{10}x + \frac{1}{4}$
    $x = 20$
12. $\frac{1}{8}x + \frac{3}{4} = \frac{1}{4}$
    $x = -4$
13. $-5.6x + 8.8 = 3.2$
    $x = 1$
14. $8x - 4\frac{2}{3} = 19\frac{1}{3}$
    $x = 3$

396 Fluency Practice

Two-Step Equations—Skills Practice

Name: ____________

Solve equations of form $px + q = r$ with rational numbers. **Form B**

1. $-4x + 8 = 12.8$
   $x = -1.2$
2. $3\frac{1}{6} = -5x + 1\frac{1}{6}$
   $x = -\frac{2}{5}$
3. $-35\frac{1}{4} = -\frac{9}{10}x + \frac{3}{4}$
   $x = 40$
4. $9 = 18 - 0.3x$
   $x = 30$
5. $-4.2x + 9.5 = 5.3$
   $x = 1$
6. $6x - 12\frac{1}{3} = 23\frac{2}{3}$
   $x = 6$
7. $-9.4 = -8.6 + 8x$
   $x = -0.1$
8. $\frac{1}{4}x + \frac{7}{8} = \frac{3}{8}$
   $x = -2$
9. $-0.25x - 8.5 = 2.5$
   $x = -44$
10. $-14.5 = 0.5x - 14.5$
    $x = 0$
11. $1\frac{5}{6} = \frac{1}{2}x + 1$
    $x = \frac{5}{3}$ or $1\frac{2}{3}$
12. $\frac{3}{4}x - 6 = 54$
    $x = 80$
13. $0.2x + 21 = 49.6$
    $x = 143$
14. $0.1x + 4.75 = -1.5$
    $x = -62.5$

Fluency Practice 397

Two-Step Equations—Skills Practice

Name: ____________

Solve equations of form $p(x + q) = r$ with integers. **Form A**

1. $6(x + 4) = 36$
   $x = 2$
2. $21 = 7(x + 3)$
   $x = 0$
3. $56 = -8(x + 9)$
   $x = -16$
4. $2(x - 6) = -26$
   $x = -7$
5. $-4(x - 5) = -44$
   $x = 16$
6. $5(x + 4) = 35$
   $x = 3$
7. $-6(x - 12) = 48$
   $x = 4$
8. $-9 = -9(x + 4)$
   $x = -3$
9. $10(x - 15) = -70$
   $x = 8$
10. $-2(x - 13) = 18$
    $x = 4$
11. $-36 = 12(x + 7)$
    $x = -10$
12. $-7(x + 7) = 49$
    $x = -14$
13. $3(x - 6) = 24$
    $x = 14$
14. $-24 = 4(x - 6)$
    $x = 0$
15. $-11(x + 2) = -66$
    $x = 4$
16. $8(x - 14) = 64$
    $x = 22$

398 Fluency Practice

Two-Step Equations—Skills Practice

Name: ____________

Solve equations of form $p(x + q) = r$ with integers. **Form B**

1. $8(x + 4) = 32$
   $x = 0$
2. $24 = 4(x + 7)$
   $x = -1$
3. $-9(x + 5) = 54$
   $x = -11$
4. $-5(x - 6) = -15$
   $x = 9$
5. $-12 = -3(x - 7)$
   $x = 11$
6. $10(x + 15) = 40$
   $x = -11$
7. $2(x - 4) = 22$
   $x = 15$
8. $-7(x + 8) = -7$
   $x = -7$
9. $-11(x - 12) = -77$
   $x = 19$
10. $5(x - 16) = 45$
    $x = 25$
11. $25(x - 14) = -75$
    $x = 11$
12. $42 = -6(x + 9)$
    $x = -16$
13. $9(x + 8) = 63$
    $x = -1$
14. $-8(x + 8) = -48$
    $x = -2$
15. $-12 = 3(x - 4)$
    $x = 0$
16. $-2(x + 12) = 24$
    $x = -24$

Fluency Practice 399

Two-Step Equations—Skills Practice

Name: ____________

Solve equations of form $p(x + q) = r$ with rational numbers.

Form A

1. $-\frac{1}{8}(x + 6) = \frac{1}{8}$
   $x = -7$
2. $0.25(p + 8) = 2$
   $p = 0$
3. $-0.2(w - 6) = -4$
   $w = 26$
4. $\frac{2}{5}(y + 5) = \frac{4}{5}$
   $y = -3$
5. $-6.9 = 3(x + 4.6)$
   $x = -6.9$
6. $-25(p - 7) = -2.5$
   $p = 7.1$
7. $\frac{1}{3} = \frac{1}{6}(m - 9)$
   $m = 11$
8. $4.5 = 5(x + 3)$
   $x = -2.1$
9. $10(x - 24.2) = 50$
   $x = 29.2$
10. $\frac{1}{4}(n + 2) = -\frac{5}{2}$
    $n = -12$
11. $11(x - 0.4) = 44$
    $x = 4.4$
12. $20 = \frac{5}{6}(m + 8)$
    $m = 16$
13. $-\frac{1}{5}(y + 2) = 4$
    $y = -22$
14. $7.6 = 2(n + 5.7)$
    $n = -1.9$

400 Fluency Practice

Two-Step Equations—Skills Practice

Name: ____________

Solve equations of form $p(x + q) = r$ with rational numbers.

Form B

1. $-\frac{1}{4}(x + 7) = \frac{1}{4}$
   $x = -8$
2. $-0.2(p - 4) = -2$
   $p = 14$
3. $0.5(w + 10) = 5$
   $w = 0$
4. $\frac{3}{8}(y + 9) = \frac{3}{4}$
   $y = -7$
5. $-8.4 = 4(x + 6.3)$
   $x = -8.4$
6. $-75(p - 6) = -7.5$
   $p = 6.1$
7. $\frac{1}{4} = \frac{1}{8}(m - 7)$
   $m = 9$
8. $3.5 = 5(x + 4)$
   $x = -3.3$
9. $10(x - 31.4) = 40$
   $x = 35.4$
10. $\frac{1}{6}(n + 5) = -\frac{4}{3}$
    $n = -13$
11. $11(x - 0.6) = 66$
    $x = 6.6$
12. $15 = \frac{3}{5}(m + 6)$
    $m = 19$
13. $-\frac{1}{4}(y + 5) = 3$
    $y = -17$
14. $9.4 = 2(n + 6.5)$
    $n = -1.8$

Fluency Practice 401

Two-Step Equations—Repeated Reasoning

Name: ____________________

Find patterns in two-step equations of form $px + q = r$. Solve each equation.

Set A

1. $2x + 3 = 19$; $x =$ 8
2. $2x + 3 = 20$; $x =$ $\frac{17}{2}$ or $8\frac{1}{2}$
3. $2x + 3 = 21$; $x =$ 9
4. $4x + 3 = 19$; $x =$ 4
5. $4x + 3 = 20$; $x =$ $\frac{17}{4}$ or $4\frac{1}{4}$
6. $4x + 3 = 21$; $x =$ $\frac{9}{2}$ or $4\frac{1}{2}$
7. $8x + 3 = 19$; $x =$ 2
8. $8x + 3 = 20$; $x =$ $\frac{17}{8}$ or $2\frac{1}{8}$
9. $8x + 3 = 21$; $x =$ $\frac{9}{4}$ or $2\frac{1}{4}$

Set B

1. $0.25x - 3 = 2$; $x =$ 20
2. $0.25x - 4 = 2$; $x =$ 24
3. $0.25x - 5 = 2$; $x =$ 28
4. $0.5x - 3 = 2$; $x =$ 10
5. $0.5x - 4 = 2$; $x =$ 12
6. $0.5x - 5 = 2$; $x =$ 14
7. $x - 3 = 2$; $x =$ 5
8. $x - 4 = 2$; $x =$ 6
9. $x - 5 = 2$; $x =$ 7

Describe a pattern you see in one of the sets of problems above.

Answers will vary. Students may see in Set B that as the number subtracted increases by 1, the answer changes by 1 ÷ (coefficient of *x*). For example, in Set B in problems 4, 5, and 6, each answer increases by 1 ÷ (0.5) = 2.

Two-Step Equations—Repeated Reasoning

Name: ____________________

Find patterns in two-step equations of form $p(x + q) = r$. Solve each equation.

Set A

1. $3(x + 3) = 30$; $x =$ 7
2. $3(x + 4) = 30$; $x =$ 6
3. $3(x + 5) = 30$; $x =$ 5
4. $3(x + 6) = 30$; $x =$ 4
5. $3(x + 7) = 30$; $x =$ 3
6. $3(x + 8) = 30$; $x =$ 2
7. $3(x + 9) = 30$; $x =$ 1
8. $3(x + 10) = 30$; $x =$ 0
9. $3(x + 11) = 30$; $x =$ −1

Set B

1. $3(x - 2) = 18$; $x =$ 8
2. $3(x - 3) = 18$; $x =$ 9
3. $3(x - 4) = 18$; $x =$ 10
4. $3(x - 5) = 18$; $x =$ 11
5. $3(x - 6) = 18$; $x =$ 12
6. $3(x - 7) = 18$; $x =$ 13
7. $3(x - 8) = 18$; $x =$ 14
8. $3(x - 9) = 18$; $x =$ 15
9. $3(x - 10) = 18$; $x =$ 16

Describe a pattern you see in one of the sets of problems above.

Answers will vary. Students may see that, in both sets, they can divide both sides by the same factor and then solve for *x* by adding or subtracting. As the number that is added to *x* increases by 1, the solution decreases by 1. As the number that is subtracted increases by 1, the solution increases by 1.

Two-Step Inequalities—Skills Practice

Name: ___________________

Solve inequalities with integers.

Form A

1. $3(m - 4) < 27$ $m < 13$
2. $-13 < 4x + 7$ $x > -5$
3. $-2x + 7 < 19$ $x > -6$
4. $-45 < 5(p - 2)$ $p > -7$
5. $21 < -7(x - 2)$ $x < -1$
6. $-9x + 10 > -8$ $x < 2$
7. $42 > 6(m + 10)$ $m < -3$
8. $10(n - 11) > -60$ $n > 5$
9. $-97 < -11x - 9$ $x < 8$
10. $25x - 9 < -109$ $x < -4$
11. $36 < 12(w + 1)$ $w > 2$
12. $-130 > 50x + 20$ $x < -3$
13. $-8(x - 3) < -40$ $x > 8$
14. $2x - 22 > -8$ $x > 7$
15. $-35 < -5(x + 9)$ $x < -2$

Two-Step Inequalities—Skills Practice

Name: ___________________

Solve inequalities with integers.

Form B

1. $12(w - 3) > 60$ $w > 8$
2. $-5x + 15 > -30$ $x < 9$
3. $-22 < 11x - 77$ $x > 5$
4. $-75 > 25(m - 1)$ $m < -2$
5. $-32 > -8(x - 7)$ $x > 11$
6. $10x - 4 < -84$ $x < -8$
7. $40 < 4(n + 14)$ $n > -4$
8. $-7x - 3 < -45$ $x > 6$
9. $9(y - 16) < -63$ $y < 9$
10. $8 < -2(x - 3)$ $x < -1$
11. $50x + 6 > -94$ $x > -2$
12. $33 > 3(p + 7)$ $p < 4$
13. $6 > 8x + 30$ $x < -3$
14. $-11(x + 7) < -88$ $x > 1$
15. $5x - 18 < 17$ $x < 7$

Two-Step Inequalities—Skills Practice

Name: ____________

Form A

Solve inequalities with rational numbers.

1. $0.5x + 0.3 < -0.7$
   $x < -2$
2. $\frac{1}{4}(m + 8) > \frac{1}{2}$
   $m > -6$
3. $4 < -0.2x + 7$
   $x < 15$
4. $-9 < -0.1(y - 5)$
   $y < 95$
5. $-\frac{5}{8}x + 6 < 5$
   $x > \frac{8}{5}$ or $> 1\frac{3}{5}$
6. $-\frac{1}{6}(x - 24) < 4$
   $x > 0$
7. $1.2m + 6.3 < 1.5$
   $m < -4$
8. $0.5 < 0.25(p + 8)$
   $p > -6$
9. $2.5n - 4.5 < 0.5$
   $n < 2$
10. $-2\left(y - \frac{1}{4}\right) > -\frac{1}{2}$
    $y < \frac{1}{2}$
11. $-\frac{1}{4}x + 2\frac{1}{4} < 2$
    $x > 1$
12. $0.8x + 0.6 < 0.6$
    $x < 0$
13. $-\frac{3}{4} > \frac{1}{8}(n + 24)$
    $n < -30$
14. $4 > -\frac{1}{2}x - 5$
    $x > -18$

Two-Step Inequalities—Skills Practice

Name: ____________

Form B

Solve inequalities with rational numbers.

1. $0.2x + 0.4 < -0.6$
   $x < -5$
2. $\frac{1}{8}(m + 16) > \frac{1}{2}$
   $m > -12$
3. $-\frac{1}{10}(x - 20) > 2$
   $x < 0$
4. $-\frac{2}{3} > \frac{1}{6}(n + 12)$
   $n < -16$
5. $0.9x + 0.7 > 0.7$
   $x > 0$
6. $-\frac{3}{4}x + 7 < 6$
   $x > \frac{4}{3}$ or $> 1\frac{1}{3}$
7. $8 > -\frac{1}{2}x - 3$
   $x > -22$
8. $2.5n - 5.5 < 2$
   $n < 3$
9. $-4\left(y - \frac{1}{8}\right) > -\frac{1}{2}$
   $y < \frac{1}{4}$
10. $\frac{5}{6}x + 7 < 12$
    $x < 6$
11. $-4.9x + 2.7 < 7.6$
    $x > -1$
12. $-\frac{1}{5}x + 3\frac{1}{5} > 3$
    $x < 1$
13. $9.4 < 8x + 3.8$
    $x > 0.7$
14. $1.1m + 5.1 < 2.9$
    $m < -2$

Two-Step Inequalities—Repeated Reasoning

Name: ____________

Find patterns in two-step inequalities. Solve each inequality.

Set A

1. $3(x + 1) > 6$; x > 1
2. $-3(x + 1) > -6$; x < 1
3. $3(x + 1) > 3$; x > 0
4. $-3(x + 1) > -3$; x < 0
5. $3(x + 1) > 0$; x > -1
6. $-3(x + 1) > 0$; x < -1

Set B

1. $4(x + 2) > 12$; x > 1
2. $-4(x + 2) > -12$; x < 1
3. $4(x + 3) > 12$; x > 0
4. $-4(x + 3) > -12$; x < 0
5. $4(x + 4) > 12$; x > -1
6. $-4(x + 4) > -12$; x < -1

Describe a pattern you see in one of the sets of problems above.

Answers will vary. Students may see in Set A that as the factor that distributes over the sum in the parentheses and the term on the other side of the inequality change from positive to negative, the inequality sign reverses but the number remains the same. For example, the solution changes from $x > -1$ to $x < -1$.

Two-Step Inequalities—Repeated Reasoning

Name: ____________

Find more patterns in two-step inequalities. Solve each inequality.

Set A

1. $2x + 2 > -4$; x > -3
2. $-2x + 2 > -4$; x < 3
3. $3x + 2 > -4$; x > -2
4. $-3x + 2 > -4$; x < 2
5. $4x + 2 > -4$; x $> -\frac{3}{2}$ (or $> -1\frac{1}{2}$)
6. $-4x + 2 > -4$; x $< \frac{3}{2}$ (or $< 1\frac{1}{2}$)

Set B

1. $0.5x - 2 > -3$; x > -2
2. $-0.5x - 2 > -3$; x < 2
3. $0.5x - 3 > -3$; x > 0
4. $-0.5x - 3 > -3$; x < 0
5. $0.5x - 4 > -3$; x > 2
6. $-0.5x - 4 > -3$; x < -2

Describe a pattern you see in one of the sets of problems above.

Answers will vary. Students may see in Set B that as the coefficient of x changes from positive to negative, the inequality sign in the solution reverses and the value of x changes from positive to negative.

Unit Game Teacher Resource Table of Contents

Name: ______________________________

Operation: Integers Recording Sheet

Target Numbers: + or – _____ and + or – _____			
Round	**Numbers**	**Addition or Subtraction Equation**	**Sum or Difference**
1	0, _____		
2	_____, _____		
3	_____, _____		
4	_____, _____		
5	_____, _____		
6	_____, _____		
7	_____, _____		
8	_____, _____		
9	_____, _____		
10	_____, _____		

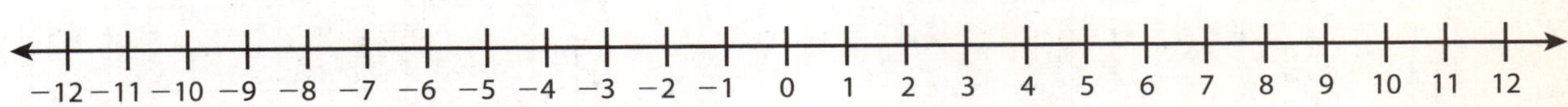

Score: ______________________________ = __________
Tally marks Total

Name: ______________________________

Rolling Ratios Recording Sheet

Equation: ______________________________

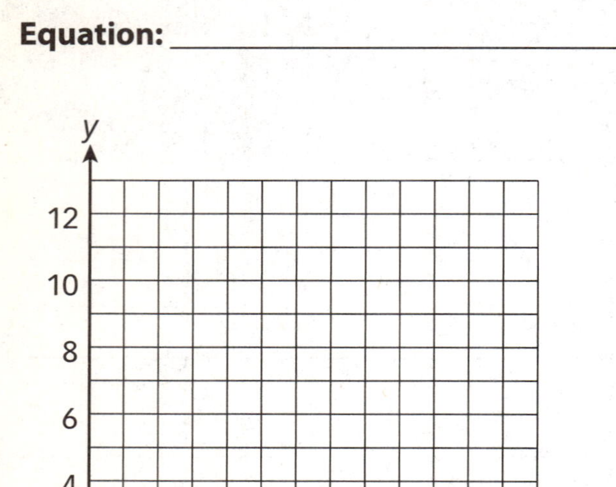

Equation: ______________________________

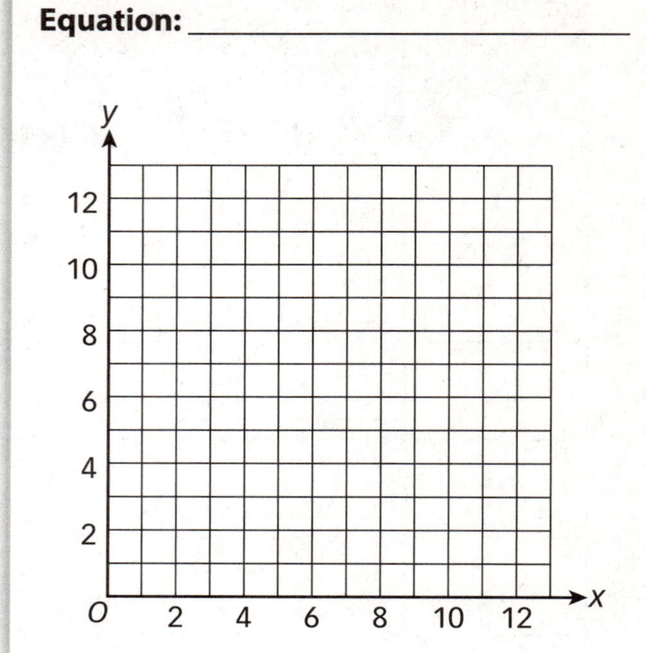

Equation: ______________________________

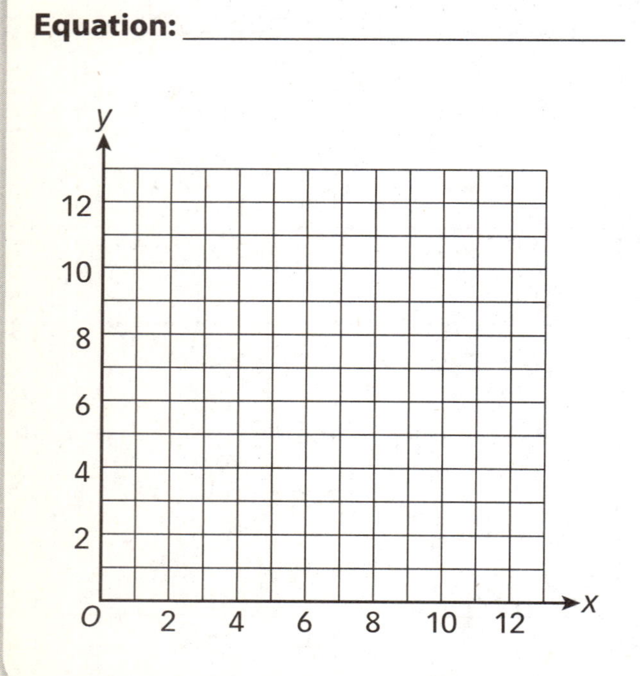

Equation: ______________________________

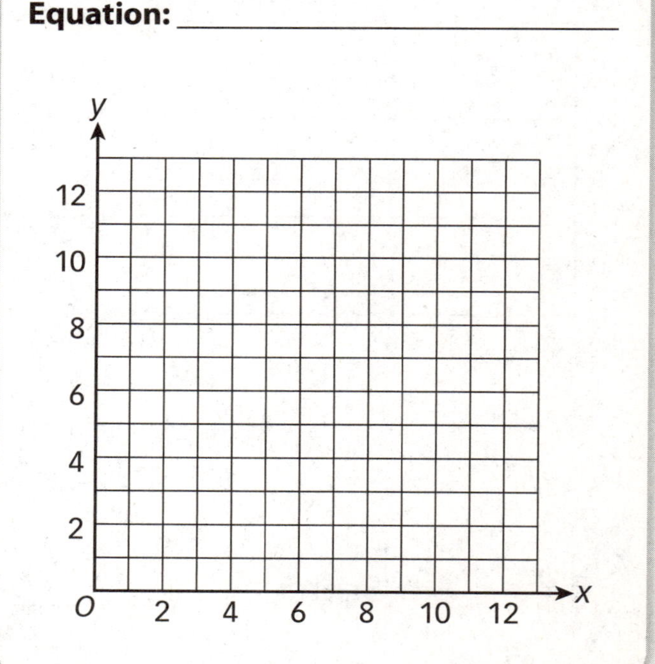

Name: ______________________

TR 3

The Inequality Solution Recording Sheet

Round	Numbers Rolled	Inequality	Solution
1		______ $(x +$ ______$) >$ ______	
2		______ $x +$ ______ $<$ ______	
3		______ $x -$ ______ $>$ ______	
4		______ $(x -$ ______$) <$ ______	
5		______ $(x +$ ______$) >$ ______	
6		______ $x +$ ______ $<$ ______	
7		______ $x -$ ______ $>$ ______	
8		______ $x -$ ______ $<$ ______	

Name: ____________________

TR 4

The Inequality Solution Game Board

-6	-8	14	$\frac{1}{2}$
4.1	-2	$\frac{4}{3}$	-18.4
$38\frac{4}{5}$	5	-27	1
20	$-\frac{5}{2}$	11	6.5

Name: ____________________

Shape Up Recording Sheet

Composite Figure:

1st Try Area = ____________

2nd Try Area = ____________

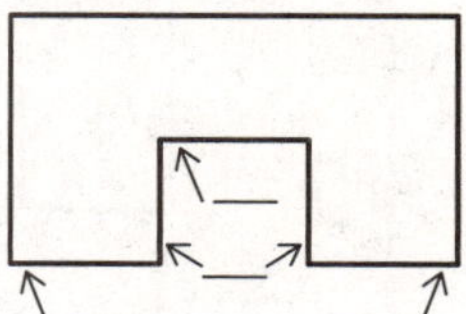

Score: ________

Composite Figure:

1st Try Area = ____________

2nd Try Area = ____________

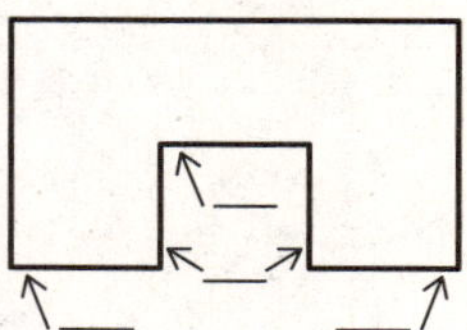

Score: ________

Rectangular Prism:

1st Try Surface Area = ________

2nd Try Surface Area = ________

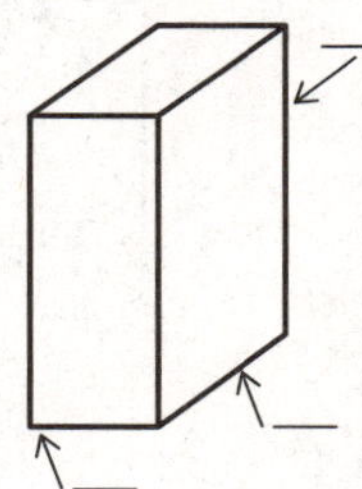

Score: ________

Rectangular Prism:

1st Try Volume = ____________

2nd Try Volume = ____________

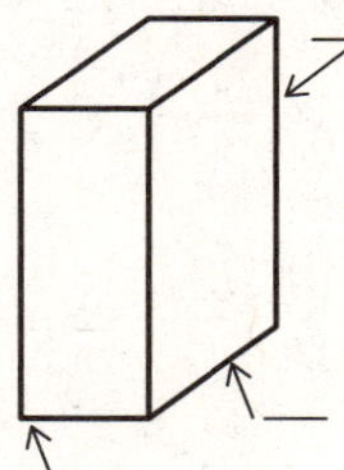

Score: ________

Circle: (Use 3.14 for π.)

1st Try Area = ____________

2nd Try Area = ____________

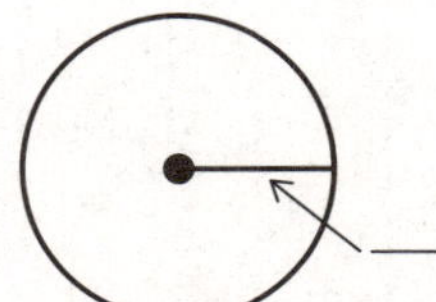

Score: ________

Circle: (Use 3.14 for π.)

1st Try Circumference = ________

2nd Try Circumference = ________

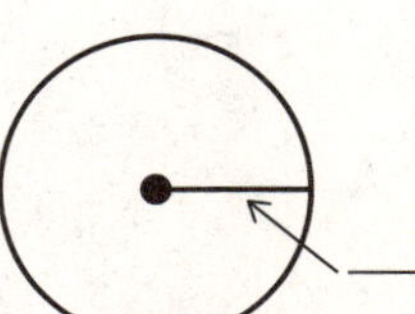

Score: ________

Name: ____________________

TR 6

Shape Up Game Cards

Circle

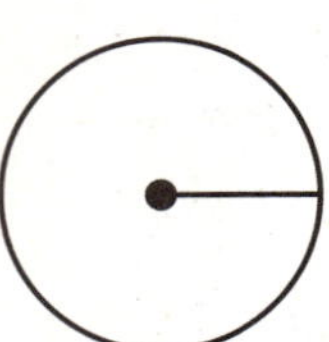

Rectangular Prism

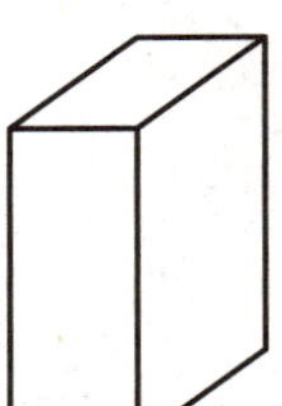

2-Dimensional Composite Figure

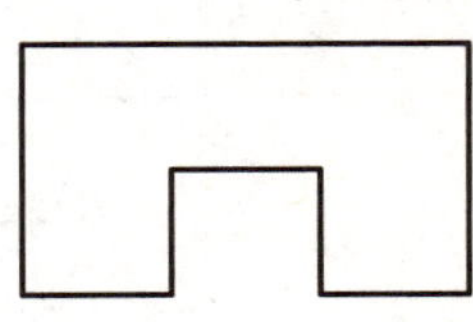

Circle

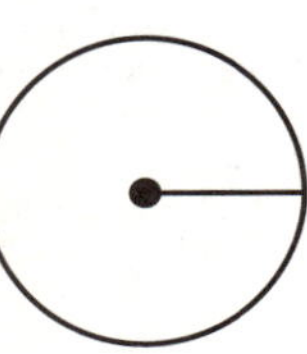

Rectangular Prism

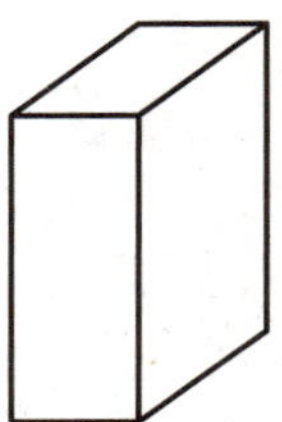

2-Dimensional Composite Figure

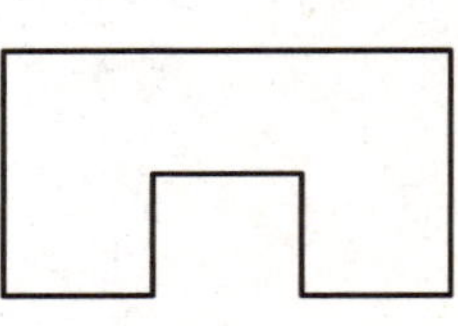

Circle

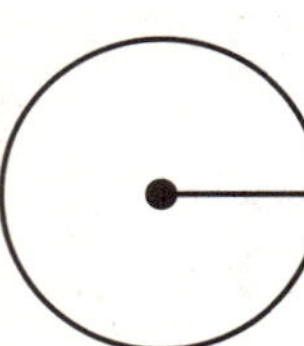

Rectangular Prism

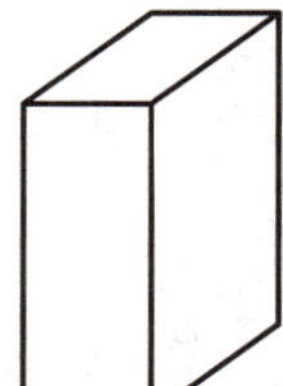

2-Dimensional Composite Figure

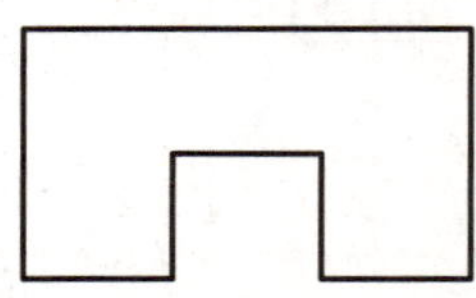

Name: ______________________

TR 7

It's Probable Recording Sheet

Round	Roll 1	Probability	Prediction	Roll 2	Points
1		P(________) =			
2		P(________) =			
3		P(________) =			
4		P(________) =			
5		P(________) =			
6		P(________) =			
7		P(________) =			
8		P(________) =			
9		P(________) =			
10		P(________) =			

Name: ______________________

TR 8

It's Probable Game Cards

Symbol Cards

$<$	$>$	$=$
$<$	$>$	$=$
$<$	$>$	$=$
$<$	$>$	$=$